Harvard Historical Studies

Published under the direction of
the Department of History
from the income of the
Henry Warren Torrey Fund
and the Paul Revere Frothingham Bequest

Volume LXXXVIII

Constantinople and the Latins

*The Foreign Policy of Andronicus II
1282–1328*

Angeliki E. Laiou

Harvard University Press
Cambridge, Massachusetts
1972

To my parents and to my grandmother,
Anna Apostolidou

Acknowledgments

This book was written over a period of six years, during which it has been changed very considerably from its original form. Several of my friends and teachers have helped me to collect the material and to organize my thoughts. Professor D. A. Zakythinos, my teacher at the University of Athens, was the first to show me the delights of Byzantine history and to introduce me to some important aspects of the discipline. I am grateful for his help then and subsequently.

When I began research, Professor Charles H. Taylor of Harvard University and Professor Charles T. Wood of Dartmouth College brought to my attention the information contained in the French National Archives. In fact, part of the book derives from work done in a seminar directed by Mr. Taylor. Later, the director of the French National Archives gave kind and valuable help in locating material from often faulty references. I am also grateful to the Vatican Library for permission to publish the letters of Athanasios I which appear in Appendix I.

A grant from the Canaday Fund, in the summer of 1967, allowed me to spend three uninterrupted months working on the manuscript.

The book was read by several people at various stages. Professor Giles Constable read it when it was still a dissertation, and made important suggestions. Professor H. J. Hanham was very helpful with ideas which cleared up significant portions of the book. I should also like to thank Professor Donald Fleming and Mr. and Mrs. S. D. Warren for giving the manuscript their attention and comments.

Professor R. L. Wolff, my teacher, advisor, and colleague, directed my Ph.D. dissertation and has since read the manuscript almost as many times as I have, offering unstinting help and advice at every point. Always ready to discuss questions of conceptualization and detail, presenting an example of scholarly excellence, he has been the perfect teacher and advisor. Without his direction, this book would have been impossible.

A. E. L.

March 1972
Paris

Contents

Maps

Constantinople and the Latins

Abbreviations Used in the Notes

AFP	*Archivum Fratrum Praedicatorum*
BEC	*Bibliothèque de l'École des Chartes*
BZ	*Byzantinische Zeitschrift*
ΕΕΒΣ	Ἐπετηρὶς Ἑταιρείας Βυζαντινῶν Σπουδῶν
HF	*Recueil des historiens des Gaules et de la France*
MGH Ss	*Monumenta Germaniae Historica. Scriptores*
OCP	*Orientalia Christiana Periodica*
PG	Migne, *Patrologia Graeca*
REB	*Revue des Études byzantines*
RIS	Muratori, *Rerum Italicarum Scriptores*
Viz. Vrem.	*Vizantiiskii Vremennik*

Introduction

Andronicus II Ducas Angelus Comnenus Palaeologus, pious Emperor of the Romans, became sole ruler of Byzantium in his twenty-second year, on the death of his father, Michael VIII, December 11, 1282.[1] For forty-six years he ruled a state which he and all his contemporaries still called an empire, although it was smaller than most European kingdoms and weaker at sea than either of the two great Italian maritime republics, Venice and Genoa. For forty-six years he tried to preserve his patrimony against Turks, Bulgars, Serbs, Venetians, Catalans, and Tartars, finally to be deposed in 1328 at the age of sixty-eight by his young grandson, Andronicus III.

Michael VIII had been a dashing, imposing figure. A good general, a brilliant and subtle diplomat, he had left his mark on the Europe of his day. He had entered Constantinople on August 15, 1261, hailed as the liberator who had ended the hated Latin occupation of fifty-seven years. Michael's contemporaries could forgive him much because of that one glorious victory. He has come down through history as the last successful Byzantine emperor, a soldier who began the reconquest of the old territories of the empire, a diplomat who formed alliances with Aragonese, and Mongols, and Egyptians to serve his own ends, a statesman who managed to foil the most ambitious and able ruler of his times, Charles of Anjou, the brother of Louis IX of France.[2]

Viewed against the brilliant exploits of his father, Andronicus seems by contrast a pale, colorless man. He had to pay the bills for Michael's expensive policies, and his reign was a long story of frustrations and disasters. Any man would have suffered by comparison with Michael VIII. Andronicus, young,

1. Andronicus had been crowned co-emperor in 1272: A. Th. Papadopulos, *Versuch einer Genealogie der Palaiologen, 1259–1453*, diss., Munich (Speyer, 1938), no. 58. On the extensive prerogatives granted to him on that occasion, see Franz Dölger, *Regesten der Kaiserurkunden des Oströmischen Reiches*, III (Munich, 1932), no. 1994.; August Heisenberg, *Aus der Geschichte und Literatur der Palaiologenzeit*, Sitzungsberichte der Bay. Akad., Philol.—Philos.—Hist. Klasse (Munich, 1920), pp. 37–81; Franz Dölger, "Die dynastische Familienpolitik des Kaisers Michael Palaiologos," *E. Eichmann Festschrift* (Paderborn, 1940), pp. 183ff. Both Michael VIII and Andronicus II adopted the traditional Byzantine imperial title when writing in Greek: Ἀνδρόνικος, ἐν Χριστῷ τῷ Θεῷ πιστὸς βασιλεὺς καὶ αὐτοκράτωρ Ῥωμαίων Δούκας, Ἄγγελος, Κομνηνὸς ὁ Παλαιολόγος. In some of their Latin documents, though, they adopted the title "Andronicus [or Michael] in Christo Deo fidelis Imperator et moderator Romeorum, Ducas, Angelus, Comninus, Paleologus, semper Augustus". The words "et moderator" seem to have been added in imitation of the similar title adopted by the Latin emperors of Constantinople. Michael VIII at times also added the words "novus Constantinus," to celebrate his recovery of Constantinople from the Latins. See G. L. Tafel and G. M. Thomas, *Urkunden zur älteren Handels-und Staats- geschichte der Republik Venedig*, III (1857), 134; Franz Dölger, *Facsimiles Byzantinishcher Kaiserur- kunden* (Munich, 1931), p. 14.

2. On Michael VIII's reign, see Conrad Chapman, *Michel Paléologue, restaurateur de l'Empire byzantin (1261–1282)* (Paris, 1926); D. J. Geanakoplos, *The Emperor Michael Palaeologus and the West, 1258–1282* (Cambridge, Mass., 1959).

1

inexperienced, and pious, inherited almost insoluble problems. Posterity has dealt unkindly with him, losing sight of his few successes and not evaluating properly the great burdens bequeathed to him. Critics have blamed him for his failure to stop the Turkish conquest of Anatolia. The accusation is easy to make: it is more difficult, and more important, to discover why Andronicus failed. Here opinions differ. One modern historian has argued that Andronicus neglected Asia Minor and left it open to the Turks because he was so pre-occupied by his relations with western Europe.[3] But a European contemporary —Marino Sanudo Torsello—maintained that Andronicus' stubborn refusal to cooperate with the West, on the West's terms, undermined the defense both of Europe and of Andronicus' own empire against the Turks, and the same judgment has been passed by V. Laurent.[4]

A superficial glance at the events of his long reign lends support to the adverse judgment of history. By 1328, when his reign ended, almost all of Asia Minor had been lost to the Turks. Only a few cities, of which the most important was Nicaea, were left to the Byzantines. Westerners—the Genoese of Phocaea, the Hospitalers of Rhodes, the Venetians of Crete and Nigroponte (Euboea)—had taken over the defense of much of the Aegean. Andronicus had invited a Catalan army to help him fight the Turks, but instead of obtaining the victory he had expected, had become involved in hostilities with these mercenaries. Other dangers were not well parried. It was as if Michael VIII's masterly diplomacy had been reversed. Venice and Genoa were no longer balanced against one another. Instead, they fought a bloody war in imperial waters and dragged the empire into a conflict that could bring it no profit. Charles of Valois at one point seemed about to take over the moribund empire, whose neighbors, Serbs, Bulgars, and Turks, had already started to overrun it. Byzantium was diplomatically isolated and, after repeated devaluations of the coinage, poor.[5] During the years of Andronicus' reign, the empire seemed to be shut in upon itself. Deeply concerned with the preservation of orthodoxy, relinquishing its centralized form of government and losing its cohesion, troubled by civil wars, the empire fought a deadly and mostly lonely war against the Turks. Its failures during the reign of Andronicus II forecast the eventual collapse of 1453.

On the whole, historians have been satisfied with passing judgment, without undertaking a careful study of Andronicus II's reign, which, after all, encompasses forty-six of the most formative years of the restored Byzantine Empire. To place Andronicus II's reign in the proper perspective is neither an easy nor an engaging task, but it is a necessary one, if one is to understand not

---

3. George Georgiades-Arnakes, Οἱ πρῶτοι Ὀθωμανοί (Athens, 1947), p. 109.

4. F. Kunstmann, "Studien über Marino Sanudo Torsello den Aelteren," *Abh. der Bayer. Akademie der Wissenschaften*, 7 (1853), 802, 803, 804; Vitalien Laurent, "Grégoire X et son projet de ligue antiturque," *Echos d'Orient*, 37 (1938), 272–273.

5. D. A. Zakythinos, *Crise monétaire et crise économique à Byzance du XIIe au XVe siècle* (Athens, 1948), p. 18–19; G. I. Brătianu, "L'hyperpère byzantin et la monaie d'or des républiques italiennes au XIIIe siècle," *Mélanges Charles Diehl*, I (Paris, 1930), 37–48, and as well in *Études byzantines d'histoire économique et sociale* (Paris, 1938), 221–239.

only Byzantine policy during the period of Andronicus II, but also the predicament of the Byzantine state during the remaining years of its existence. This book is not a comprehensive history of the reign of Andronicus II, but a study of his foreign policy, and particularly of his relations with western Europe. The recovery of Constantinople by the Byzantines gave the West an incentive to attack Byzantium in an effort to restore a Latin dynasty to the throne. Thus, both Michael VIII and Andronicus II had to face the hostility of western powers—Venice, the Angevins of Naples, the papacy, the French royal house—and had to make considerable efforts to forestall a western attack. This had far-reaching implications for their domestic policy, as well as for their policy toward other powers. As long as the West was hostile, neither Michael VIII nor Andronicus II could use their full resources to defend the imperial territories in Asia Minor and the Balkans. Andronicus II made a continued and strenuous effort to clarify the Byzantine position with regard to western Europe, while trying to save the eastern part of his empire.

The empire inherited by Andronicus II from his father was only part of the Byzantine Empire which had been lost to the crusaders in 1204. In Europe, the empire now included Thrace, south of Mesembreia, Macedonia with the frontier stretching south of Philippopolis, Strumica, Prošek, and Prilep, all of which were garrison towns; much of Epirus was still in the hands of a Greek splinter state—the Despotate of Epirus—until parts of it reverted to the Byzantine Empire in 1314–1319. Thessaly, too, was an independent state, although the northern region reverted to the empire in 1318. To the south were the numerous feudal states set up after the conquest of 1204; of these, the Principality of Achaia in the Peloponnesus was the most important, and it was here that the most productive Byzantine effort took place to recover their heritage from the Franks. In the islands of the Aegean, too, Byzantines and westerners clashed; Nigroponte (Euboea) was the most serious point of conflict, while on Crete the Byzantines maintained agents to stir up opposition against the Venetians. Andronicus II saw it as his task to continue his father's policy of consolidating Byzantine power by recovering the "lost territories" in Greece and the Morea.

In terms of revenue, the empire of Andronicus II was very poor. The monies available to the emperor consisted of private and public revenues. His personal income was obtained from his estates, and he also had crown treasures: jewels, and gold and silver plate. Occasionally, the emperor made use of these personal funds, and during the Catalan adventure he melted down some of his treasures. In terms of state revenues proper, the picture is somewhat confused. The peasantry paid a land tax, which was the basis of state revenues. But although these taxes were collected with zeal, and with some abuses, it was necessary to levy extraordinary taxes to meet particular expenses. Several extraordinary taxes, affecting the large landowner and the small cultivator, as well as urban dwellers, will be mentioned in context. The state still collected some money in the form of duties on shipbuilding, navigation, and commerce, but commercial duties affected domestic merchants, since western ones were granted privileges. Occasionally, domestic merchants, too, were exempted from duties: Michael

VIII and Andronicus II granted to the inhabitants of Monembasia privileges which allowed them to engage in virtually untaxed trade.

The fiscal system was also undermined by the spread of the *pronoia*, whose holders were exempted from most taxes, except when an emergency arose. As an institutional term, a pronoia grant designates the grant of a source of revenue to soldiers, as a reward for past services or, in this period, as a guarantee of future participation in the army. Most often, the grant consisted of land. The pronoia had appeared in the Byzantine Empire in the late eleventh century, but it was Michael VIII who, after his accession to the throne, rewarded his several followers with such grants, and also changed the, until then, personal character of the pronoia: upon petition to the emperor, the pronoia-holder could now convert his holding to a hereditary one, although he could still not sell it. It is difficult to reach firm conclusions about the pronoia system at any particular point in this period, since its spread was sporadic, and not the result of a unified policy. Andronicus II made many pronoia grants, and *in general* the pronoia may be seen as the equivalent of a western fief rather than as that of a Byzantine peasant-military holding of the tenth century. That is, the pronoia was a larger grant than the earlier military holding, and with different social implications: it was given not to simple soldiers but to members of an elite, who collected rents and tithes from peasants on the estates granted, and who thus differed substantially from the peasant-soldier of the tenth century.[6] While this situation obtained in general, the period of Andronicus II was still very fluid; in the sources, the word pronoia was occasionally used to denote small military holdings. Also, although Andronicus made several grants of large pronoiai, he also tried, for a few years in the late thirteenth and early fourteenth century, to reverse the trend and create small military holdings in the place of the large, concentrated ones. But in this he failed.

The Byzantine army in this period was a complicated and inefficient institution. There were army units stationed in Asia Minor, Macedonia, Thrace, and the Morea. The commanders were appointed from Constantinople, but the army itself consisted of both local pronoia-holders and soldiers from different parts of the empire (some were refugees), who apparently were paid in cash. There were also foreign mercenaries—Tartars, Alans, Catalans, Turks, and Serbs. All too often, armies were created on the spot, for particular campaigns, and, as will become obvious, they lacked both discipline and training.

Such was the state which Andronicus II tried to preserve, reform, and extend. To this state also he had to give form and direction. The Byzantine Empire was then at a critical point: was it going to become a European state, involved and closely connected with the affairs of Europe, as had seemed possible under the reign of Michael VIII? Or would it remain an eastern power, Orthodox, concerned with Asia Minor and the Balkans, but aloof from developments in western Europe? The issue was fundamental and urgent, and it was decided during Andronicus II's reign.

6. The basic work on the *pronoia* is George Ostrogorsky, *Pour l'histoire de la féodalité byzantine*, Corpus Bruxellense Historiae Byzantinae, Subsidia I (Brussels, 1954).

Foreign policy in this period was still made by the senior emperor and his close advisers. Even the co-emperors, Andronicus' son Michael IX, and his grandson Andronicus III, were not involved in policy-making which affected foreign relations. For this reason, the personality of the emperor and of his confidants is an important part of this study. However, a fundamental question arises which must be answered before the personality of the emperor can be considered. The Byzantine Empire of Andronicus II's period was a relatively decentralized state, and one may well wonder to what extent decisions taken at Constantinople affected the state as a whole. It is a well-attested fact, for example, that imperial officials often acted in ways opposed to state policy: there were officials who did not follow the directives of Constantinople concerning the commercial privileges of Venetian and Genoese merchants, thus giving rise to strained relations between Byzantium, Genoa, and Venice. In the more remote areas—Asia Minor, the Morea, the reconquered parts of Thessaly and Epirus, Greece, even on occasion Macedonia—the control of Constantinople was not very tight insofar as domestic affairs were concerned. Throughout this period privileges granted to walled towns made them resemble communes of the western type: towns with a charter, with a certain amount of self-government, with specific administrative, judicial, and commercial privileges. To some degree this development will be followed, but its effects lie outside our scope, except for one thing: they point up the progressive decentralization of the Byzantine state, and so present the possibility of a discrepancy between expectations and realities—the expectation of Constantinople that its foreign policy decisions would be followed throughout the realm, and the reality that parts of the empire were becoming semi-independent. Foreign policy was taking place at the state level, while the state was degenerating.

To what extent, then, is a study of Byzantine foreign policy—as made in Constantinople—justified and possible? First, one has to remember that the process of the collapse of the Palaeologan state was still at an early stage. By the late fourteenth and early fifteenth century, successive civil wars and enemy invasions had so disrupted the Byzantine state that the emperor's authority was limited to Constantinople and parts of Thrace, while individual towns, or individual great landlords, or regional governors such as the despot of the Morea occasionally made their own foreign policy decisions. In Andronicus II's time a different situation obtained. Imperial decisions might be very weakened by the time they filtered down to the outlying provinces, but there was still *one* level of policymaking, and no one but the emperor took it on himself to make decisions on foreign policy. There were a few exceptions to this rule— the emperor's wife, Irene, was one—but they were infrequent. Furthermore, no private individual or imperial official had the military or financial power which would enable him to take and enforce independent decisions. Andronicus III did have considerable power during the civil war of the 1320's, but he lacked interest in foreign policy. In Asia Minor, of course, as imperial control virtually disappeared after 1302, the governors of cities might decide to surrender to the Turks—as happened in Brusa in 1326—but such action can hardly be considered foreign policy. In any event, Asia Minor was a special case, because the Turkish threat was still considered a domestic problem, although by its great importance it affected foreign policy.

The foreign policy of Andronicus II is a subject capable of study because Constantinople was recognized in this period as the place where responsible foreign policy was made. The popes, the kings of France, the kings of Naples, the Holy Roman Emperor, Venice, Genoa, Aragon, Sicily, treated with the emperor; only he made and implemented treaties; only he could be held responsible in the last instance if these treaties were broken. The problems surrounding the union of the churches, or alliances with western European powers, or the grant of commercial privileges to western merchants could be resolved only by the emperor. In the eyes of westerners, no one else had the authority to discuss these matters to their conclusion, and this was still a correct interpretation of matters as they stood in the Byzantine Empire. So, in foreign policy, although not necessarily in domestic policy, the center of the Byzantine Empire was still Constantinople, the palace, the emperor.

The emperor's personality was of particular importance. Andronicus II was not skillful at analyzing political and diplomatic issues, and he often allowed emotional reactions to dictate his policy. Indeed, the differences in the policies of Michael VIII and Andronicus II may be explained in part by the different personal characteristics of the two men.

Michael VIII was an aggressive soldier and diplomat; Andronicus was neither. He was a gentle, contemplative man. He went on a campaign only once, and that was during his father's lifetime, in 1280, when he went to southern Asia Minor to fight the Turks. Yet even on that occasion he was more interested in rebuilding the ancient city of Tralleis than in fighting. At a time when soldiers were needed, Andronicus' lack of the martial virtues no doubt contributed to the contempt with which he was viewed by many of his contemporaries. It is strange that he was of so peaceful a disposition, since his immediate family could boast of a number of men who were brave, if often ineffectual, soldiers; his father, his eldest son Michael IX, his grandson Andronicus III were all more interested than he in warfare, while his relatives, the Tarchaneiotes and the Philanthropenoi, were excellent generals.

Michael VIII was fully aware of the contrast between his own temperament and that of Andronicus. It is said that he had much preferred Andronicus' younger brother, Constantine, who from infancy had been the favorite. Constantine the Porphyrogenitus—born in the purple—had all the virtues an emperor was expected to have, and to those he added a pleasant disposition and a sense of humor. Gregoras wrote that Michael would have liked to bequeath the empire to Constantine, but could not do so because Andronicus was older. Had Michael VIII been a legitimate emperor, he might perhaps have changed the line of succession; he was certainly unscrupulous enough to have done so. But he himself had usurped the throne, and it seems almost certain that the one thing which kept him from making Constantine his heir was the fear of undermining yet further the legitimacy of the dynasty. As it was, he did his best to make Constantine independent of Andronicus: he tried to find a good, rich Latin princess for the boy, and apparently contemplated giving him Macedonia, including Thessalonica, as a semi-independent appanage.[7] Along with the burdens of government the young Andronicus thus inherited the emotional burden of knowing that his father did not really want him as an heir. He must have harbored resentments against his father, and it is not accidental that as soon as he became sole emperor he proceeded to reverse many of his father's policies, and even to clear the administration of the men who had been closest to Michael. Andronicus' early lack of interest in western European affairs, his passionate concern with Asia Minor, his tolerance for religious and political groups which had opposed Michael must all be seen in the context of his uneasy relations with his domineering father. Only late in his life was Andronicus able to overcome this emotional impediment, and he then embarked upon policies which closely resembled those of his father.

There were further differences in temperament between Andronicus II and Michael VIII. Unlike his father, Andronicus was a profoundly pious man, and his piety was to have unfortunate diplomatic results. Where Michael VIII had subordinated the religious feelings of his orthodox subjects to his own desire for a political and religious union with the West, Andronicus II reversed his father's policy, bowed to the sentiments of monks, clerics, and people, and dissolved the union of the churches. As a result, there was now no restraint on the ambitions and plans of the various western pretenders to the Byzantine throne whom the union of the churches had held in check. On at least two occasions, in 1311 and in 1324–1327, Andronicus recognized the dangers of his policy, and allowed political realities to overcome his piety; he then suggested a new union of the Byzantine and Latin churches. But none of these negotiations came to a conclusion. In his later years, piety was reinforced by superstition, a sad combination, but understandable in a sad, disappointed, and harassed man.

Andronicus had many attractive personal characteristics. He was intelligent, very honorable, and had a high concept of family loyalty. Yet this was a dangerous period, which demanded that in a ruler intelligence be tempered with tough realism, honesty with diplomatic agility, family feelings with a degree of harshness. Only rarely did Andronicus behave in accordance with the demands of his times. He surrounded himself with a number of intellectuals, such as Nicephorus Choumnos, Theodore Metochites, and Nicephorus Gregoras, all of whom made important contributions to Byzantine letters and scientific thought. But he should not have permitted Metochites—neither very able, nor very honest—to influence domestic and foreign policy. Metochites, in fact, was a greedy opportunist whose only saving grace was that he used some of the wealth he acquired to rebuild and decorate the monastery of the Chora

---

7. The story of Michael's preference for Constantine comes from Nicephori Gregorae, *Byzantina Historia*, ed. L. Schopen (Bonn, 1829), I, 187, and is there reported as part of the accusations and calumnies hurled against Constantine by his enemies in 1290. Andronicus, who was noted for his strong family feelings, believed these accusations, and certainly it seems reasonable that Michael should feel uneasy about the great difference in temperament between himself and his heir. Georgius Pachymeres, (*De Andronico Palaeologo*, [Bonn, 1835], II, 154–162), does not mention Michael's predilection for Constantine, but he does say that by 1290 Constantine had great pronoiai, cattle, warehouses, minted and unminted gold, silver and cloth—all in all, substantial wealth.

(Khariye Djami), whose beautiful frescoes and mosaics are now once again restored.[8] Andronicus II's entourage, including as it did a large number of intellectuals, reflected the emperor's love for erudite discussion. It is, of course, not possible to assess how much time, which might profitably have been allotted to policy matters, was diverted to the perusal of theological or philosophical matters. Yet a glance at Pachymeres and Gregoras, the main Byzantine sources for this period, indicates that the emperor spent a considerable part of his time in such discussions. Byzantium had an intellectual emperor at a time when it could ill afford him; and the strange phenomenon of rapid deterioration of the state on the one hand, and the flourishing of cultural life on the other, a phenomenon typical of the Byzantine Empire in the last century of its existence, began during the reign of Andronicus II.

In his relations with his family, Andronicus showed a curious mixture of passionate attachment and violent withdrawal when he thought his relatives had betrayed him. One of the most crushing blows of his life came in 1295 when a nephew whom he loved and trusted rebelled against him; it was a blow that he could not respond to rationally. His love for his second wife, Yolanda-Irene of Montferrat, at times led him to give way to her whims, to the discomfiture of his friends. His piety apparently did not restrain his sexual ardor; he was so persistent a husband, that his wife accused him of satyriasis when she was angry with him. Yet much as he loved her, when she tried to persuade him to parcel out the empire among her sons, he refused, and continued to refuse even though she left his palace and Constantinople itself, and retired to Thessalonica.[9]

The two basic traits of Andronicus' character were his sense of honor and his high regard for the office of emperor. Those who advised actions that flagrantly reflected on his honor or dignity did so at their peril. He himself voiced his lofty conception of the duties and responsibilities of his office:

> [The emperor] must examine the lists of his armies, and must make ready with arms, and he must be able to raise many and great forces for [his] struggles against the enemies . . . For there is a time of peace and a time of war, and the things pertaining to each are clearly separated, and the emperor must be able to meet both in a worthy manner . . . I say that he who reigns by the grace of God must no less think it his duty to provide for the souls [of his subjects], that they may turn toward heaven and that they may choose to live according to divine precepts.[10]

Certainly these are worthy sentiments. That he failed to live up to them was the result partly of his own inability to assess developments correctly as they

---

8. J. Verpeaux, *Nicéphore Choumnos, homme d'état et humaniste byzantin, ca. 1250/1255–1327* (Paris, 1959); Ihor Ševčenko, *Études sur la polémique entre Théodore Métochite et Nicéphore Choumnos,* Corpus Bruxellense Historiae Byzantinae, Subsidia III (Brussels, 1954); Hans-Georg Beck, *Theodoros Metochites: Die Krise des byzantinischen Weltbildes im 14. Jahrhundert* (Munich, 1952); P. J. Underwood, *The Kariye Djami*, 3 vols. (New York, 1966).

9. He also had two illegitimate daughters, Maria and Irene. There may have been another illegitimate daughter, the mysterious Byzantine wife of Uzbek, khan of the Golden Horde: Steven Runciman, "The Ladies of the Mongols," Εἰς Μνήμην K. Ἀμάντου (Athens, 1960), pp. 46–53.

10. F. Miklosich and J. Müller, *Acta et Diplomata Graeca medii aevi*, V (Vienna, 1887), 264–265, the preface to the chrysobull to the monasteries of Galesiou and Hagias Anastaseos.

arose, partly of factors beyond his control, and partly of the fact that he was a weak man, easily swayed by others and unable to pursue his aims long enough and persistently enough to accomplish them. During much of his life he was under the influence of his father, his second wife, his eldest son, Michael, Theodore Metochites, and the patriarch Athanasios I, all of them people of very forceful character. Even so, he surprised them all at times by going against their advice.

The most striking example of this was his conflict with the patriarch Athanasios, who normally had his way with the emperor. In the winter of 1306–1307, the population of Constantinople was under the double threat of famine and conquest by the Catalans, who were in control of Thrace. Andronicus conceived the difficult and dangerous plan of starving the Catalans out of Thrace before they could attack the city. He forbade his subjects to cultivate the fields of Thrace, so that the Catalans would be forced by hunger to leave. The obvious danger was that the inhabitants of Constantinople would starve before the Catalans did; and the patriarch, in his role as protector of the poor, implored, advised, and requested the emperor to retract his orders. Andronicus, for once, stood firm, and in doing so saved his empire from a threat that was only too real.[11] Unfortunately, his convictions were rarely strong enough to enable him to override the advice of others.

In general, Andronicus was a good, pious, honorable, and generous man. One should not allow the flamboyant successes of Michael VIII to obscure the real problems he left to his son, or pass too harsh a judgment on a man who had to contend with more dangerous situations and take more important and difficult decisions than fall to the lot of most statesmen. Andronicus II cuts a sad figure when contrasted with his father and with the young, chivalrous, handsome grandson who succeeded him. Perhaps he reigned too long and was too tired by the end of his reign.[12] But he did prevent Constantinople from becoming the capital of a second Latin empire, where the Catalans, the

11. Angeliki Laiou, "The Provisioning of Constantinople during the Winter of 1306–1307," *Byzantion*, 37 (1967), 91–113.

12. U. V. Bosch, *Andronikos III Palaiologos* (Amsterdam, 1965), pp. 7–13, makes much of the distinction between Andronicus II, the intellectual who lived in an ivory tower, and his martial, brilliant, charming young grandson, Andronicus III. Andronicus II certainly was a difficult subject for his panegyrists, who had only two ways to praise his virtue: either they attributed to him the successes of Michael VIII, or they praised his uncontested achievements as a philosopher and a scientist. See Theodore Metochites, βασιλικὸς β′, Cod. Vindob. Philol. Gr. 95, fols. 148vo–149ro; Cod. Par. Gr. 2077 fol. 278ro (Μονῳδία Γρηγορᾶ εἰς ᾿Ανδρόνικον Β′); Manuel Philes, Στῖχοι μονῳδικοὶ εἰς τόν... ᾿Ανδρόνικον τὸν Παλαιολόγον, τὸν μετωνομασθέντα ᾿Αντώνιον, Cod. Par. Coisl. 192, fols. 98ro–100ro, vv. 16–23; cf. Beck, *Krise*, p. 87. There are some extant portraits of Andronicus II, but being in the traditional manner they do not tell us much about the physiognomy of the man. The most beautiful portrait is a miniature, appended to a chrysobull of 1301, and published by Sp. Lambros, Λεύκωμα Βυζαντινῶν Αὐτοκρατόρων (Athens, 1930), pl. 79. Lambros has also published other miniatures (pl. 77, 78, 80), of which the most interesting is the fourteenth-century portrait of pl. 77. Apparently, there is a fresco of Andronicus and his whole family in the chapel of the Virgin near Berat, which he restored, and one in the monastery of Pójani, in Albania: A. Alexoudes, Σύντομος ἱστορικὴ περιγραφὴ τῆς ἱερᾶς Μητροπόλεως Βελεγράδων (Corfu, 1868), p. 76; A. Alexoudes, «Δύο σημειώματα ἐκ χειρογράφων,» Δελτίον τῆς ῾Ιστορικῆς καὶ ᾿Εθνολογικῆς ῾Εταιρείας τῆς ῾Ελλάδος, 4 (1892), 279ff; K. Jireček, "Valona im Mittelalter," in L. Thalloczy, *Illyrische-Albanische Forschungen*, I (Munich-Leipzig, 1916), 174; P. J. Alexander, "A Chrysobull of the Emperor Andronicus II Palaeologus in Favor of the See of Kanina in Albania," *Byzantion*, 15 (1940–1941), 167ff.

Venetians, and Charles of Valois would have reenacted the miseries of the first Latin Empire. This was no mean feat, and he accomplished it alone. For the rest, the reader will have to keep an open mind, and temper his criticism with a certain amount of compassion for this man who had grandiose ideas without the means to fulfill them, great learning but little political wisdom, and on whom it fell to be the impotent witness of the visible beginnings of the long decline of the empire restored by his father.

This study of Andronicus II's relations with western Europe is not a diplomatic history of the traditional type. The trend in modern historiography is to see diplomatic relations as much more than the sum of dispatches, negotiations and treaties, and this is a healthy trend. For such things are only the end result of complex issues which transcend the diplomatic game or form its background. When we move from the level of description to that of interpretation and explanation, the end result is no longer sufficient. The same argument applies a fortiori to discussions of foreign policy. One can describe the foreign policy of Andronicus II by looking at his treaties with western states, by following his negotiations, successful or not, and the effect of these on his subsequent policy.[13] But such an enterprise would explain very little. Foreign policy does not take place at a rarified sphere, where nothing intrudes upon statesmen except their relations to each other. On the contrary, domestic issues inform foreign policy as much as international ones, and are perhaps more important in explaining it. Andronicus II's relations with western Europe cannot be explained without an adequate understanding of the Byzantine attitude to the question of the union of the Greek and Latin churches, without discussion of the internal pressures on both Andronicus II and his western counterparts, above all, without a discussion of the means through which foreign policy becomes effective: the army, the navy, finances. It is a truism today that diplomatic arrangements are only as effective as the relative strength of the states which have undertaken them. That was not less so in the Middle Ages. Therefore, a substantial part of this work has been devoted to domestic issues. Without these sections, this book would have been a different one: more concise but more arid, and much less useful as an aid to understanding Byzantine foreign policy in the reign of Andronicus II.

13. One book describes Byzantine-western European relations during part of our period. That is E. Dade's *Versuche zur Wiedererrichtung der lateinischen Herrschaft in Konstantinopel im Rahmen der abendländischen Politik (1261 bis etwa 1310)* (Jena, 1938). Dade's monograph is not an analytical essay, nor is it directly concerned with Byzantine policy. It was written before the publication of some important sources, such as the *Diplomatari de l'Orient Català 1302–1409*, published in 1947 by Antonio Rubió y Lluch.

I

The Sins of the Fathers

Michael VIII was the last emperor whose orientation was primarily European. Although Andronicus II, in his later years, would also turn to Europe, and although other Palaeologan rulers would also forge more or less strong connections with the West, their policy was different from Michael's. He was of a European stature; his gravest concerns during most of his reign had been with Europe, and there he had won his most brilliant diplomatic victories. By destroying the Latin empire of Constantinople, Michael had only solved half a problem; he was quite aware of the probability that the West would launch an attack to retrieve the empire it had lost to the schismatic Greeks. The danger could come from many quarters: the dispossessed Latin emperor, Baldwin II, went to the West and tried to interest in his cause the pope, Urban IV, the king of France, Louis IX, the kings of Castile and Aragon, and Manfred of Hohenstaufen, Frederick II's heir. Venice, too, was furious at the Greek recovery of Constantinople, which had been preceded by an alliance between Michael and Genoa, the most hated rival of Venice (Treaty of Nymphaeum, March 13, 1261). Venice now saw herself excluded from the Black Sea and the Byzantine Empire, where for fifty-seven years she had held a commercial monopoly.

A combination of the forces of the disaffected could have proved disastrous for the Byzantines. But Michael was helped by the unwillingness of most western rulers to launch a crusade, and most important, by the struggle in Italy between the Hohenstaufen and the papacy, which held in check the Byzantine ambitions of both rivals. Making full use of the existing animosities between Europeans, Michael set about his double aim, the preservation of his throne and the restoration of the Byzantine Empire as it had been before the first crusade. He courted the papacy, promising to unite the Byzantine and Roman churches, and, in 1268, following a period of uneasy relations with Genoa, he made a treaty with Venice in an effort to establish friendly relations.[1]

Michael's careful diplomacy was disrupted by the appearance in Italy of Charles of Anjou, the brother of Louis IX of France, and a most ambitious man who "aspired to the monarchy of the world," and dreamed of creating a kingdom which would include southern Italy and Sicily, and perhaps North

---

1. On Michael VIII's reign see Chapman, *Michel Paléologue*. Geanakoplos, *Michael Palaeologus*, p. 138, mentions the two aims of Michael's policy, and see also pp. 139–154, 175–185, 206–209. Also P. Wirth, "Die Begründung der Kaisermacht Michaels VIII. Palaiologos," *Jahrbuch der österreichischen byzantinischen Gesellschaft*, 10 (1961), 85–91. On western plans for the reconquest of Constantinople, see Dade, *Versuche*, pp. 3–4, 27–28, 53–59, 67–157; also R. L. Wolff, "Mortgage and Redemption of an Emperor's Son: Castile and the Latin Empire of Constantinople," *Speculum*, 29 (1954), 45–84.

Africa, Jerusalem, and the Byzantine Empire.[2] Charles of Anjou had been invited into Italy by Pope Urban IV, to lead a "crusade" against Manfred of Sicily. In 1266, at the battle of Benevento, the Angevin forces defeated the Hohenstaufen, and Manfred perished in the battle. Charles became king of Sicily, and in 1267 he signed the treaties of Viterbo with Baldwin II of Constantinople and William of Villehardouin, ruling prince of Achaia. A marriage between William's heiress, Isabella, and Charles' son Philip was to ensure to the Angevins the suzerainty over the Principality of Achaia. The second treaty of Viterbo provided for the restoration of Baldwin II to his throne at Constantinople and the marriage of Baldwin's son and heir, Peter of Courtenay, to Béatrix, Charles' daughter, which took place in 1273.[3]

In an effort to eliminate the danger presented by the treaties of Viterbo, Michael VIII sought the support of the papacy. He tried to prevent a new anti-Byzantine crusade, led by Charles of Anjou and blessed by the pope. Instead, he suggested or supported the idea of a joint Christian crusade against the infidel; he tried to substitute Jerusalem for Constantinople. No pope, however, could assent to this without the union of the Greek and Latin churches, and Michael VIII realized and accepted this fact. After protracted but not always zealous negotiations, his ambassadors to the council of Lyons celebrated the union of the churches, on July 6, 1274.[4] Michael VIII was not necessarily persuaded by the religious aspects of the union, but he was convinced that as a political expedient the act was necessary, and once the formal union had been proclaimed, he did his best to enforce it in his empire. By this single but important act, Michael brought the papacy to his side and ensured that no war of Charles of Anjou against his empire could be proclaimed a crusade.

Michael VIII immediately launched an offensive against Latin territories in western Greece and the Morea. Charles of Anjou had become king of Albania in 1272, and had sent a representative to Durazzo. Now, in 1274, Michael attacked and captured Berat and the port of Butrinto, and besieged Durazzo and Avlona. Charles, unable to attack Constantinople, decided instead to concentrate his own efforts in Albania and Epirus with a view toward marching on to Thessalonica. In Albania, in March 1281, the Byzantines won their greatest victory against the Angevin armies. At the battle of Berat, the army of Charles of Anjou was defeated, and his vicar-general, Hugo le Rousseau de Sully, taken prisoner. The Angevin offensive in Albania collapsed, and the Byzantine army proceeded to reconquer the towns held by the Angevins. At

---

2. Georgii Pachymeres, I (*De Michaele Palaeologo*, Bonn, 1835), 317; Gregoras, I, 123–124: "he [Charles of Anjou] dreamed of restoring the whole Empire of Julius Caesar and Augustus if he should take Constantinople." Cf. Marino Sanudo Torsello, *Istoria del Regno di Romania*, in Karl Hopf, ed. *Chroniques Gréco-romanes* (Berlin, 1873), p. 138. Cf. Geanakoplos, *Michael Palaeologus*, pp. 196–200, 216, 222. See also E. Jordan, *Les origines de la domination angevine en Italie* (Paris, 1909), *passim*.

3. Geanakoplos, *Michael Palaeologus*, pp. 197–200.

4. W. Norden, *Das Papsttum und Byzanz* (Berlin, 1903, reprinted in New York, 1958), pp. 520–524; Geanakoplos, *Michael Palaeologus*, pp. 258–263; Chapman, *Michel Paléologue*, pp. 111–120.

an unspecified date, they took Kanina and the city of Durazzo, which they managed to hold until 1296.[5]

But the effects of the union of the churches did not last for very long. By July 1281, Charles of Anjou had formed with Venice an alliance directed against Constantinople. The combined forces, it was agreed, would leave for Constantinople by April 1283. It may be that Charles was already certain that the pope would bless such an offensive: in February 1281, he had managed to secure the election to the papal throne of Martin IV, a Frenchman and an instrument of Angevin policy. On October 18, 1281, Martin IV excommunicated Michael VIII, the "supporter of the ancient Greek schismatics and therefore heretics." Michael VIII, on hearing the news of his excommunication, suspended the mention of the pope in the Orthodox liturgy.[6] The way was now open for Charles of Anjou and the Venetians to declare a crusade against Byzantium. There was very little Michael could do, except to seek alliances with the other enemies of Charles of Anjou. To counteract Charles' system of alliances, which involved Venice, the papacy, the Greek state of Thessaly, the Serbs, the Bulgars, and the Hungarians, Michael formed his own coalitions. Genoa, afraid of possible Venetian expansion in the East, had remained faithful to Michael to the extent of sending some ships to his aid (1280).[7] The Ghibelline city of Pisa had been willing to join the anti-Angevin camp, but was prevented from doing so by the combined pressure of Charles of Anjou and Pope Martin IV.[8] The marquis of Montferrat and his ally, King Alfonso X of Castile, were willing to maintain friendly relations with the Byzantines, at least so long as Byzantium followed Michael's unionist policy.[9]

Michael VIII's most useful ally turned out to be the king of Aragon, Peter III, who was married to Constance, daughter of Manfred of Sicily and a sworn enemy of the man who had killed her father. To her, Charles of Anjou was a usurper, and she was the legitimate queen of Sicily. Sometime in 1281 or early 1282, Michael VIII and Peter of Aragon formed an alliance, and Peter began

5. Geanakoplos, *Michael Palaeologus*, pp. 229–235, 279–280, 329–334; Alexander, "A Chrysobull of the Emperor Andronicus II," pp. 195–196. The date of the capture of the two cities is uncertain. Durazzo was still in Angevin hands in 1284, while Kanina was taken by the Byzantine general Michael Tarchaneiotes Glabas at some point between 1281 and 1294.

6. Odoricus Raynaldus, *Annales Ecclesiastici denuo excusi . . . ab A. Theiner* (Barri-Ducis, 1870), 1281, §25; on the date, see G. La Mantia, "Studi sulla rivoluzione siciliana del 1282," *Archivio storico Siciliano*, 6 (1940), 99–100. Cf. Geanakoplos, *Michael Palaeologus*, pp. 335–344; Pachymeres, I, 506; Tafel and Thomas, *Urkunden*, III, 287–295.

7. Geanakoplos, *Michael Palaeologus*, pp. 232–235, 358; W. Heyd, *Histoire du commerce du Levant au moyen-âge* (Leipzig, 1923), I, 444; Camillo Minieri-Riccio, "Il regno di Carlo I d'Angiò dal 2 Gennaio 1273 al 31 Dicembre 1283," *Archivio storico Italiano*, 4th ser., 3 (1879), 165.

8. F. Kern, *Acta Imperii Angliae et Franciae* (Tübingen, 1911), nos. 25, 27, 28; D. Winter, *Die Politik Pisas während die Jahre 1268–1282* (Halle, 1906), pp. 67–70; S. Borsari, "I rapporti tra Pisa e gli stati di Romania nel duecento," *Rivista di storia Italiana*, 67 (1955), 486–488.

9. O. Cartellieri, *Peter von Aragon und die Sizilianische Vesper* (Heidelberg, 1904), p. 65; A. Bozzola, "Un capitano di guerra e signore subalpino," *Miscellanea di storia Italiana*, R. Dep. di storia patria per le antiche provincie, 3rd ser., 19 (Turin, 1922) 386ff; H. Wieruszowski, "La corte di Pietro d'Aragona e i precedenti dell'impresa Siciliana," *Archivio storico Italiano*, 96 (1938), 141–162, 200–217; H. Wieruszowski, "Conjuraciones y alianzas políticas del rey Pedro de Aragón contra Carlos de Anjou antes de las Vísperas Sicilianas," *Boletín de la Acad. de Historia*, 107 (1935), 547–602; Wolff, "Mortgage and Redemption," 45–84.

to plan an invasion of Sicily. Michael, meanwhile, had been sending money both to Peter and to anti-Angevin cardinals at the Roman court. Both men helped the Sicilian refugees who had fled the rule of Charles of Anjou. Discontent against the Angevins and their heavy taxation mounted in Sicily, no doubt aided by the certain knowledge that Aragon and Byzantium would support a rebellion. The discontent erupted on March 30, 1282, in the uprising of the Sicilian Vespers. Soon after the revolt of the native population, Peter of Aragon disembarked in Sicily to lead the struggle against Charles of Anjou.[10]

The revolt of the Sicilians quickly developed into a war in Italy and Sicily which kept the Angevins occupied until 1302. The war of the Sicilian Vespers involved all the Italian powers, and to some extent also the royal houses of Aragon, Castile, and France. In Italy, it was partly a fight that pitted the Ghibellines, led by the marquis of Montferrat, against the Guelphs, who favored Charles of Anjou. The colonial rivalries of Pisa, Genoa, and Venice also played an important part in the war. Occupied as they were with this struggle, western powers could not find the time or the resources to attack Byzantium. Soon after the Sicilian Vespers, Venice found it in her interest to begin negotiations with Byzantium, and these resulted in a truce, signed in 1285.[11]

To the extent that Michael VIII's policy had helped the Sicilian uprising and the subsequent Aragonese-Angevin war, he left a most precious gift to his son. In other areas, however, Michael VIII's heritage was less welcome. At the time of his death the financial situation was deplorable, the empire was in grave religious turmoil, and Asia Minor was not adequately defended. Andronicus faced grave domestic problems which curtailed his opportunity of pursuing an independent and successful foreign policy.

The financial situation was, perhaps, the gravest if not the most immediate problem. The best of diplomats would have needed a great amount of money in order to deal with the many enemies Andronicus faced in the West, in Asia Minor, and in the Balkans. Andronicus, who was not the best of diplomats, also inherited an appallingly poor state from his father.

Michael VIII's resources, although not comparable to those of emperors in the years of Byzantium's prosperity, were greater than his son's would be. Under Michael VIII the imperial domain was larger, including the area around the Maeander River, which was later lost to the Turks, as well as parts of Thessaly, Lemnos, and other lands. Moreover, Michael had revenues from land taxes, from state monopolies such as salt, and from customs, although the latter were much reduced by the commercial privileges he granted to Venice and Genoa. He also had extraordinary revenues, from treasure-trove, from the

---

10. Bartolomeo of Neocastro, *Historia Sicula*, ed. G. Paladino, in L. A. Muratori, ed., *RIS.*, XIII, pt. 3 (1921), 42. On the Sicilian Vespers, see M. Amari, *La guerra del Vespro Siciliano* 9th ed. (Milan, 1886); Steven Runciman, *The Sicilian Vespers* (Cambridge, Eng., 1958); O. Cartellieri, *Peter von Aragon*; Geanakoplos, *Michael Palaeologus*, pp. 344–351 and appendix A.

11. Dade, *Versuche*, p. 65.

savings of his predecessors, and from the confiscation of property belonging to his political opponents.[12] His expenses were enormous. Apart from gifts and bribes abroad, he had to pay his army, part of which consisted of foreign mercenaries or of Byzantines paid in cash rather than in land. Even before 1261, Michael VIII had found his resources unequal to his expenses. In order to meet his obligations to his Italian mercenaries, Michael used a time-honored expedient, the adulteration of the coinage.[13]

After the reconquest of Constantinople, he minted new coins, with the city on the reverse, and reduced the gold content of the *hyperpyron*. Under the Nicene emperors, and until 1259, the hyperpyron contained 16 carats of gold and 8 of alloy in one ounce. Sometime after 1261, the gold content was reduced to 15 carats, while the alloy was 9 carats.[14]. This was a quick but unhealthy way of obtaining money. Andronicus II, following his father's example, further reduced the proportion of gold to alloy, first to 14 : 10 and then to 12 : 12.[15] As the amount of gold was reduced, the value of the hyperpyron relative to other currency declined. Creditors might refuse to accept the debased coinage, as Venice did in 1310, or they might accept it only for use within the empire, as did the Catalans in 1304.[16] In the second case, the burden fell on the Byzantines who traded with the Catalans and who were forced to accept devalued currency at its nominal value. The Byzantine coinage rapidly lost its prestige. Pegolotti makes it clear that around 1335 the Genoese of Pera accepted the hyperpyron (then at 11 carats of gold to 6 of silver and 7 of copper) by weight

12. Zakythinos, *Crise*, pp. 80–81; G. Rouillard, *La vie rurale dans l'empire byzantin* (Paris, 1953), p. 306; Miklosich and Müller, *Acta et Diplomata*, V, 257; Ioannis Cantacuzeni, Eximperatoris, *Historiarum libri IV*, I (Bonn, 1828), 117–118; II (Bonn, 1831), 89; and Pachymeres, I, 209–210, 222–223.

13. Pachymeres, II, 493–494. On the salaried Byzantine soldiers, see the prostagma of Michael VIII (November 8, 1272), allowing Andronicus to raise their salaries to twenty-four nomismata a year: Heisenberg, *Aus der Geschichte*, pp. 40ff. Cf. Ostrogorsky, *La féodalité byzantine*, pp. 96–97, and p. 96, note 1; P. Charanis, "On the Social Structure and Economic Organization of the Byzantine Empire in the 13th Century and Later," *BS* 12 (1951), 133 and n. 181. Nicephorus Botaneiates (1078–1081) had been the first to devaluate the Byzantine coinage, until then perhaps the most stable in the world. Alexius I (1081–1118), in great need of money, continued the devaluation, to the detriment of both the taxpayer and, eventually, the treasury itself, and earned the title of the first great Byzantine "faux-monnayeur." Michael VIII also reduced the gold content of the *hyperpyron*: F. Dölger, *Beiträge zur Geschichte der byzantinischen Finanzverwaltung* (Leipzig and Berlin, 1927), p. 75; G. Ostrogorsky, *Histoire de l'état byzantin* (Paris, 1956), pp. 371, 390–391; F. Chalandon, *Essai sur le règne d'Aléxis Ier Comnène* (Paris, 1900), pp. 320ff; W. Wroth, *Catalogue of the Imperial Byzantine Coins in the British Museum* (London, 1908), I, lxi; II, 540ff.

14. Pachymeres, II, 493–494; Zakythinos, *Crise*, p. 9; Brătianu, "L'hypérpère," pp. 229ff; Wroth, *Catalogue*, II, 614–618, and 618, n.1.

15. Pachymeres, II, 493–494. For an interpretation of this passage, see Zakythinos, *Crise*, pp. 8–10.

16. G. M. Thomas and R. Predelli, *Diplomatarium Veneto-Levantinum sive acta et diplomata res Venetas Graecas atque Levantis Illustrantia a. 1300 [1453]* (Venice, 1880), I, 84; G. I. Brătianu, *Recherches sur Vičina et Četatea Alba* (Bucharest, 1935), p. 152; fifty-one hyperpyra of 1281 were taken to be equivalent to forty-seven of old mintage; G. Giomo, "Le Rubriche dei Libri misti del Senato perdutti," *Archivio Veneto*, 18 (1879), books II, III: Venice complains of receiving hyperpyra of the wrong alloy. The Catalans' acceptance of the coinage for use in the empire only is the meaning of a passage by Ramon Muntaner, *The Chronicle of Muntaner*, trans. Lady Goodenough, (London, 1920, 1921), chap. ccxi; cf. Zakythinos, *Crise*, p. 19.

and not by number.[17] Byzantine commerce and Byzantine prestige suffered. Money was either diverted to uneconomic uses like hoarding—since every new issue increased the value of the old—or it was exported to pay off creditors.[18]

It is not known exactly what money was available to Andronicus II when he came to the throne, but in 1283 he was forced to revert to extraordinary measures in order to raise money to finance an expedition against Thessaly. From that point onward, almost every time money was needed he either introduced a new tax, or debased the coinage, or stopped paying his palace officials. Clearly, his treasury was chronically empty. Moreover, there was a shortage of money in the empire as a whole. To meet his payments to the Catalans, Andronicus II had to levy a tax in kind—this was partly done in order to take advantage of the inflated grain prices. By 1305 the amount of gold bullion available to the emperor was so far reduced that Andronicus II was obliged to offer the Genoese unminted gold, presumably from the imperial jewels. The monetary system was thrown toward silver, which, at this period, had an unstable market.[19]

Michael VIII's devaluation of the coinage, unaccompanied by any economic measures that might mitigate its results, undermined confidence in the Byzantine currency, both in the empire and elsewhere. Even the devalued coins were scarce, and their circulation limited. There is also some evidence that the cost of living rose during his reign and continued to rise during the reign of his son. Unfortunately, the evidence is limited, and its real significance is in dispute. In Michael's two treaties with Venice (1265 and 1277), there was a clause regulating the export of wheat grown in the empire. Wheat could not be exported until its price in the empire had fallen below a certain point. Presumably, wheat prices in Constantinople were taken as the measure of prices in the empire. Even though at this period both Thrace and the Black Sea, the two sources of grain, were open, the provisioning of Constantinople was a problem, and high prices could be expected. In the treaty of 1265 Michael VIII forbade the export of wheat when its price was over 50 hyperpyra per centenarium. In the treaty of 1277, it was stipulated that prices must fall below 100 hyperpyra before wheat could be exported.[20] This change, which, according to some historians, benefited the exporter, was retained in Andronicus' treaties with Venice.[21]

The significance of the change in the treaty of 1277 is a matter of debate. One can argue either that the price of wheat doubled between 1266 and 1277,

17. Francesco Balducci Pegolotti, *La pratica della mercatura*, ed. Allan Evans (Cambridge, Mass., 1936), p. 40.

18. Zakythinos, *Crise*, pp. 111–112. Michael VIII forbade the export of unminted gold and silver: *Liber Jurium reipublicae Genuensis*, ed. H. Riccotius, in *Monumenta Historiae Patriae* (Turin, 1872), I, col. 1355.

19. Zakythinos, *Crise*, pp. 41–43.

20. Tafel and Thomas, *Urkunden*, III, 85, 144; Miklosich and Müller, *Acta et Diplomata*, III, 81, 91. On the normal price of wheat, see St. Novaković, "Le prix normal du blé à Constantinople pendant le moyen âge et le Code de St. Dushan," *Archiv für slavische Philologie*, 27 (1905), 173–174. The change to one-hundred hyperpyra first appeared in 1277, not in 1285, as Bratianu claimed. On the provisioning of the city, see G. I. Brătianu, "Études sur l'approvisionnement de Constantinople et le monopole du blé à l'époque byzantine et ottomane," *Études byzantines d'histoire économique et sociale* (Paris, 1938); Laiou, "Provisioning," pp. 92–95.

21. G. Ostrogorsky, "Löhne und Preise in Byzanz," *BZ* 30 (1932), 293–333.

or that the purchasing power of the Byzantine hyperpyron fell to one half its pre-1265 level, pushing up correspondingly the price of primary commodities.[22] One can also argue, with Ostrogorsky, that the original quoted price of 50 hyperpyra per centenarium was far below the normal price of wheat; in that case, the clause was modified simply to take account of realities, and did not necessarily imply any major change either in the value of the coinage or in the price of wheat. Although it is difficult to decide which theory is correct, it is certain that the price of wheat was high during the reign of Michael VIII. In 1278 a Venetian merchant complained that Michael forced him to sell his wheat at 1 hyperpyron per $1\frac{1}{4}$ *modium*, while its current price in Constantinople was 1 hyperpyron per $\frac{3}{4}$ modium.[23] Thus, at that time the price of wheat had reached 133 hyperpyra per centenarium. Even if there were a temporary shortage of wheat, this is still far above the 50 hyperpyra of 1265 or even the 100 hyperpyra of 1277. A rise in the price of wheat does not necessarily imply a commensurate rise in the cost of living. There is even evidence that the price of land was relatively stable during Michael's reign.[24] But given the large number of refugees and other destitute people who inundated Constantinople and Thrace in the late thirteenth and early fourteenth centuries, it is reasonable to assume that for many people food was by far the largest item of expenditure, and a rise in its price was important. In the early fourteenth century, of course, there was both a shortage of bread and very high prices, due to special circumstances which will be mentioned in context.

Despite Michael VIII's high taxes and his efforts to find money, the treasury was empty at the time of his death, the coinage devalued, and the empire seemed to be moving towards an economy of kind.[25] As soon as his father died, Andronicus began a policy of retrenchment which included the dismantling of the navy and the reduction of the army. Lack of money seemed to make these measures necessary, but, given the many enemies of the empire, the policy of cutting the costs of defense was self-defeating in the long run.

Along with an empty treasury, Andronicus II also inherited a potentially explosive rift in the Byzantine church. Michael VIII had been, first and foremost, a politician and a diplomat. When he found his personal ambitions or political designs opposed, he did not hesitate to use diplomacy or even force to make his opinion prevail. In the long run, his high-handed attitude disrupted the unity of the Byzantine church and even brought danger to his dynasty.

22. A. Andréadès, "De la monnaie et de la puissance d'achat des métaux précieux dans l'Empire byzantin", *Byzantion*, 1 (1924), 100ff; G. I. Brătianu," L'hypérpère"; Franz Dölger, book review in *BZ* 49 (1956), 426–429; Ostrogorsky, "Löhne und Preise." Brătianu and Dölger accept the theory that the value of the Byzantine currency was halved between 1265 and 1277.
23. Tafel and Thomas, *Urkunden*, III, 171–172.
24. Andréadès, "De la monnaie," claims that wheat was much too expensive a commodity to be a valid index of the cost of living; cf. Ostrogorsky, "Löhne und Preise."
25. Pachymeres, I, 222. Among other works on Byzantine finance, see I. N. Sboronos, «Βυζαντιακὰ νομισματικὰ ζητήματα,» *Journal international d'archéologie numismatique*, 2 (1899), 358–361; A. Diomedes, «Τὰ αἴτια τῆς οἰκονομικῆς παρακμῆς τοῦ Βυζαντίου,» Ἐπιθεώρησις Κοινωνικῆς καὶ Δημοσίας Οἰκονομικῆς, 6 (1937), 139–155; G. I. Brătianu, *Recherches sur le commerce dans la mer noire au XIIIe siècle* (Paris, 1929); G. I. Brătianu, *Actes des notaires génois de Péra et de Caffa de la fin du XIIIe siècle*, Académie Roumaine, *Études et Recherches* II (Bucharest, 1927); A. Andréadès, "Byzance, paradis du monopole et du privilège," *Byzantion*, 9 (1934), 171–181.

SERBIA

BULGARIA

Danube *River*

Curzola

ZETA

ADRIATIC
SEA

Varna

Sliven •
• Yamboli
Philippopolis •
Stenimachus

Mesembreia
Anchialos
Sozopolis

Skopje •

Strymon R.

Adrianople •

Debar •
Durazzo
Ochrid
• Prilep
• Stip
• Strumica
• Prosek

Nestos (Mesta) R.

Didymoteichon

Viz
Tzurru

ITALY

• Berat
Avlona
Kanina

Serres •
• Christopolis

Vardar R.

Rodosto
Heracle
Sea

Mat R.

Veroia •

Aliakmon R.

Thessalonica •

Aenos •

Sel

Butrinto •

Corfu

• Janina
(Ioannina)

EPIRUS
Arta

THESSALY

• Larisa

Demetrias •
Domokos •

Thasos

Athos •
Lemnos

Gallipoli •
Madytos•

Abydos •

Cyzic

Cassandra

AEGEAN

Adramyttio

• Vonitza
Neopatras
Angelokastro
Lepanto   Loidoriki

• Lamia

*Gulf of
Halmyros*

SEA

Pergamu

Cephallonia

Galaxeidi

Thebes •
Athens •

*Euboea
(Nigroponte)*

Lesbos

Phocaea •

Magne

Chios

Smyr

Patras

Salamis

PRINCIPALITY

OF ACHAIA

Modon
(V)

• Mistra

Coron (V)

Monembasia •

Seriphos

Andros
Tenos *Ikaria*

Keos

Siphnos

Mykonos

Naxos
(V)

Santorini

Samos

Ephesus

Trai

Am

Mil

Kalymnos

Amorgos

Kos
Astypalaia

Rhoa

*Cerigo
(Kythera)*

MEDITERRANEAN

Canea •

CRETE
(V)

Karpathos

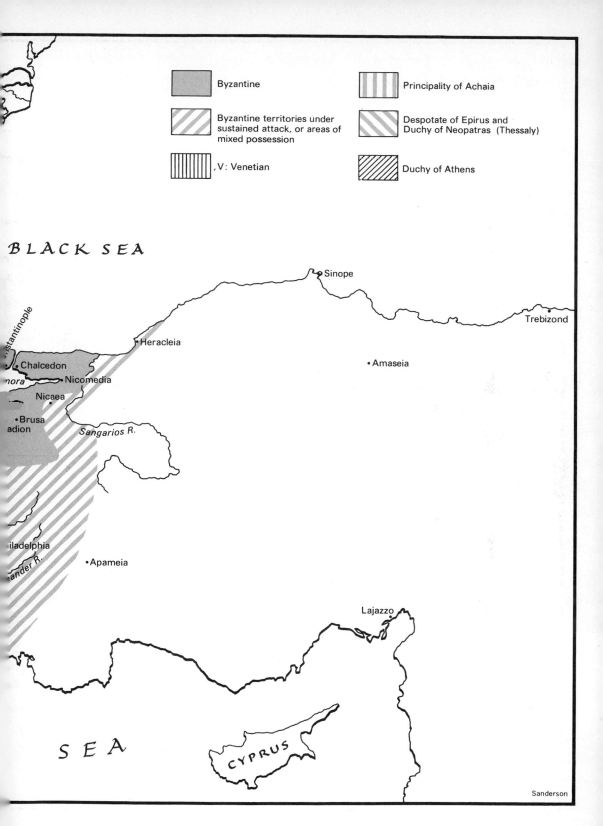

Legend

- **Byzantine**
- **Byzantine territories under sustained attack, or areas of mixed possession**
- **V: Venetian**
- **Principality of Achaia**
- **Despotate of Epirus and Duchy of Neopatras (Thessaly)**
- **Duchy of Athens**

BLACK SEA

Sinope

Trebizond

Constantinople

Heracleia

Chalcedon

Amaseia

Nicomedia

nora

Nicaea

Brusa

adion

Sangarios R.

iladelphia

ander R.

Apameia

Lajazzo

SEA

CYPRUS

Sanderson

The Byzantine Empire, 1282

Michael Palaeologus had secured his position on the Byzantine throne through an act of treason. The legitimate emperor was John IV Lascaris, a young boy and Michael's ward. Michael was crowned co-emperor on December 25, 1258. After the reconquest of Constantinople, he had the young boy blinded, and became sole emperor of Byzantium. The patriarch Arsenius (1255–1259, 1261–1265), rebelling against this act of cruelty, excommunicated Michael. The emperor had to wait for almost four years before taking his revenge; in May 1265, an ecclesiastical synod deposed Arsenius and replaced him with Joseph I (1266–1275, 1282–1283) who promised to raise the excommunication of Michael.[26]

The followers of Arsenius continued to oppose the Palaeologan dynasty and the church hierarchy as it had developed after the patriarch's deposition. The Arsenites supported Lascarid legitimacy, and the church union with Rome, which Michael VIII's church hierarchy eventually brought about. The political aspect of the Arsenite schism stood out with perfect clarity in Asia Minor. Here the deposed Lascarids had been known and loved, whereas Constantinople had not known the Lascarids, and had accepted Michael VIII as its savior from the rule of the Latins. While the pro-Lascarid faction and the Arsenite faction were not identical, both were strong in Asia Minor. The Arsenite faction was the more vocal of the two, perhaps because it could operate more openly, since it attacked the Palaeologan dynasty only implicitly: its explicit attack was on the new ecclesiastical hierarchy.

The Arsenite party in Asia Minor was difficult to conciliate.[27] In later years, when Andronicus II was trying to reorganize the defense of Asia Minor, he found it necessary to use men who had strong connections with the Arsenites. An Arsenite party existed in Constantinople itself, and probably in other parts of the empire as well. It had good leaders, some of them members of the imperial family, but its aims were somewhat diffuse, and the number of its members slowly dwindled. In the early fourteenth century, most of them became reconciled to the Palaeologan establishment, but not before they had challenged Andronicus' authority in a dangerous rebellion.[28]

The greatest ecclesiastical problem of Michael's reign, however, was not that presented by the Arsenites, but that presented by the policy of religious union with the West. Michael's pursuit and acceptance of the church union had been motivated by purely political factors, as he himself made clear in two speeches to the Byzantine clergy.[29] But his subjects did not share his system of values. For them, or at least for most of them, the church union was anathema. Michael VIII had to face the opposition of most of the Arsenites, most of the

---

26. Pachymeres, I, 79–81, 190–192; Gregoras, I, 92; Chapman, *Michel Paléologue*, pp. 36–38, 49–50, 100–103.

27. Pachymeres, I, 337–342, 483–491, 502–503; II, 88–89; Gregoras, I, 127; Georgiades-Arnakes, Οἱ πρῶτοι Ὀθωμανοί, p. 43; M. Gedeon, Ὁ Ἄθως (Constantinople, 1885), p. 140; V. Laurent, "Les grandes crises religieuses à Byzance: La fin du schisme arsénite," *Académie Roumaine, Bulletin de la section historique*, 26 (1945), 225–238. Laurent's study is the best work on the Arsenite schism. On the same subject see also J. Sykoutres, «Περὶ τὸ σχίσμα τῶν Ἀρσενιατῶν,» Ἑλληνικά, 2 (1929), 267–332.

28. D. J. Geanakoplos, "Michael VIII Paleologos and the Union of Lyons," *Harvard Theological Review*, 46 (1953), 79ff; and below, Chapter III.

29. Pachymeres, I, 386–388, 457–459.

prelates, and most of the clergy. The monks were particularly intransigent, as so often in the past, and they carried the people with them.

It has sometimes been maintained that social factors underlay the struggle between unionists and anti-unionists.[30] The first were, it is argued, rich land-owners, concerned with the preservation of their property in Asia Minor and favorable to the spread of feudalism which western influence would entail. The anti-unionists were the depressed part of the population—monks, peasants, and small property owners. This interpretation is false. Michael VIII's unionist policy was opposed by a large and diversified section of the population, including his own sister, for political, emotional, and religious reasons.

During his father's lifetime, Andronicus II had embraced the union and taken an oath of obedience to the pope.[31] He was motivated partly by regard for his father and partly by the hope that the pope would launch a crusade against the Turks. To Pope John XXI he wrote in 1277: "Therefore I was rushing to rise up in arms, to raise armies for war and to insist strongly on the defense of the Christian people . . . to fight for this fatherland ['pro patria'], which, alas! is being continuously defied by the insults [of the Turks] and to stop the Turkish impetus . . . And to totally defeat these same [Turks] with God's help, and to throw them out of their lands."[32] But he was not a sincere believer in the union, nor could he afford to overlook the sentiments of his people. His first action after the death of his father was to dissociate himself from Michael VIII's religious policy; such an action meant great upheavals in the church hierarchy and among the laity, and also entailed the danger of precipitating a western attack.

Michael VIII concentrated most of his attention on western Europe and the western part of his empire. His reasons for so doing were no doubt good, but this policy was detrimental to Asia Minor, where a grave danger had appeared. Michael did not totally neglect the area. But Asia Minor, which for so long had enriched the empire with men and money, which indeed for almost sixty years *had been* the empire, now occupied a decidedly secondary place in Michael's political aims. Contemporaries wrote that he did not much care about this province, since he considered its defense to be an easy matter once he had found time to undertake it.[33] Andronicus II had to contend with the

30. Pachymeres, I, 491–492, 482ff; Sanudo, *Istoria*, p. 135; H. Evert-Kapessowa, "Une page de l'histoire des relations byzantino-latines," *BS* 17, (1956), 1–18.

31. Raynaldus, *Annales Eccl.*, 1280, §19–22; Geanakoplos, *Michael Palaeologus*, pp. 262, 306–307, 320, and n.58; V. Grumel, "Les ambassades pontificales à Byzance après le IIme concile de Lyon," *Échos d'Orient*, 23 (1924), 442, 447; J. Gay, *Les registres de Nicolas III* (Paris, 1898), p. 84; A. Theiner and F. Miklosich, *Monumenta spectantia ad unionem ecclesiarum Graecae et Romanae* (Vienna, 1872), pp. 15–21.

32. Raynaldus, *Annales Eccl.*, 1277, §XXXI. The text reads: *Tamen ferebar ad arma consurgere, turmas belli instruere, ac . . . pro defensione Christiani generis . . . potenter insistere, pugnare pro patria, quae, pro, dolor! continuis insultibus ab ipsis lacessitur, et ad reprimendum Turcorum impetum . . . ac ipsos Dei praesidio in propria expugnare, ac de eorum confiniis eiicere . . .*

33. Pachymeres, I, 223, 310; Georgius Sphrantzes, ed. I. B. Papadopulos, (Leipzig, 1935), p. 28; Gregoras, I, 138–140; G. G. Arnakis, "Byzantium's Anatolian Provinces During the Reign of Michael Palaeologus," *Actes du XIIe Congrès International d'études byzantines*, II (Belgrade, 1964), 37–44, discusses the disaffection of the pro-Lascarid and Arsenite factions in Asia Minor, and Michael VIII's unwise policy regarding Anatolia.

feeling of alienation that Michael's policy had created among the people of Asia Minor. His own policy reversed his father's: he broke away from the West, and focused his resources and his efforts on Asia Minor. This concern for Asia Minor was the single greatest difference between Michael VIII and his son, and it must be seen as the backbone of Andronicus' foreign policy. His interest in Asia Minor became apparent even before Michael VIII's death.

Appeasing the hostility of the population of Asia Minor would have been a difficult task, even if Michael VIII had had the best possible intentions. But Michael's usurpation of the Lascarid throne could not easily be forgiven. When he blinded the young emperor, John IV, the people of Tricoccia, near Nicaea, rose in arms (1262). It was thought that the patriarch Arsenius encouraged the rebellion, and although he denied any active involvement it is significant that the first anti-Palaeologan uprising should have been connected with the patriarch's name.[34] Given the basic antagonism of Asia Minor to the Palaeologan coup d'état, Michael VIII's subsequent policy was designed to punish, rather than to reconcile, those who opposed him. He taxed Asia Minor very heavily indeed, and although he was undeniably in need of money, his taxation was a punitive measure rather than simply an effort to fill the treasury. In attempting to cripple Asia Minor financially, he hoped to weaken its power of opposition to the government. Michael had questionable success in this enterprise. The inhabitants of the province found it very difficult to pay their taxes, for even when crops were good there was an acute shortage of gold and silver. In the former *themes* of Paphlagonia, Maryandinon, and Bucellarion, some men were driven by Michael's financial exactions to join the Turks.[35] In this way, the defense of Asia Minor was weakened at a time when the Turkish threat was becoming acute.

The Turks were under pressure from the Mongols of Persia, whose advances had the combined effect of furthering the disintegration of the Seljuk states and driving various Turkish tribes north and west into Anatolia. In southern Asia Minor, the enemy advanced along the Maeander River; Caria and the area around Miletus were in grave danger. The situation deteriorated after the death in 1274 of the despot John (Michael's brother) who had been defending the area.[36] In northern Asia Minor, the Sangarius front was threatened, and by 1280 even Bithynia was not safe. The frontiers were not adequately defended, and for this Michael must be held responsible: he had withdrawn some of his eastern forces to fight his western wars, and the soldiers of the frontier garrisons who had not received their salaries abandoned their posts.[37]

34. Pachymeres, I, 193–201; Arsenius, *Testament*, ed. J. P. Migne, *PG*, CXL (Paris, 1865 and 1887), col. 956a.

35. Pachymeres, I, 18, 201, 221–223; Migne, *PG*, CXL, col. 956a; Georgiades-Arnakes, Οἱ πρῶτοι Ὀθωμανοί, p. 49.

36. Pachymeres, I, 468; Papadopulos, *Genealogie*, p. 5, no. 23; S. Lambros, «Ἐνθυμήσεων ἤτοι χρονικῶν σημειωμάτων συλλογή πρώτη,» Νέος Ἑλληνομνήμων, 7 (1910), 136, no. 35. On Turkish Asia Minor, and the effect of the Mongol invasions on the Seljuks and Turcomans of Anatolia, see C. Cahen, *Pre-Ottoman Turkey* (London, 1968), and Barbara Flemming, "Landschaftsgeschichte von Pamphylien, Pisidien und Lykien im Spätmittelalter," *Abhandlungen für die Kunde des Morgenlandes*, 35, (Wiesbaden, 1964), 1–76.

37. Pachymeres, I, 243–244; Gregoras, I, 137–138.

Only at the end of his reign did Michael VIII awaken to the seriousness of the situation, and he then took belated steps to save his eastern provinces. Between 1280 and 1282, he went twice to the northern part of Asia Minor, and he dispatched another army to the south. His first expedition (June–September 1280) was undertaken with a small army, and had a purely defensive aim, that of securing the Sangarius front. Michael returned to the same area the following year, because he was told that the situation was becoming dangerous. Observing the devastation of a once-prosperous region, he admitted to shock and sorrow, and recalled with longing the days of his regency, before Asia Minor had been abandoned to its fate. He did not blame himself for the decline; rather, he put the blame on the religious fanatics and those who had chosen to fight against him. Once again the Arsenite group and the anti-Palaeologan group are accused of opposition to the government and to Michael's dynastic and religious policy.[38]

The expedition of 1281 was not really successful; Michael VIII advanced and the Turks retreated, but only to regroup further inland. No pitched battle took place, no Turk was thrown out of Anatolia. All Michael actually did was to build and restore forts along the Sangarius and to plant forests along the river to impede any Turkish advances. Preparing his subjects in this way for a lifelong siege, he returned to Brusa to meet his ambassadors, who had just come from the court of Martin IV bearing the news that the new pope, at the behest of Charles of Anjou, had excommunicated Michael VIII. This was at the end of 1281, and he left Asia Minor for Constantinople at the end of the summer of 1282.[39] Both his expeditions were doomed from the start. By their nature, the Turkish incursions could not be stopped by short campaigns, even by victorious short campaigns.

Asia Minor, once a rich and important province, needed a careful imperial policy of reconciliation. It was depopulated and lay in ruins. Some wise people

---

38. Pachymeres, I, 493–496, 502–504. The chronology of Michael VIII's two eastern expeditions and of Andronicus' reconstruction of Tralleis during the first expedition is disputed. This is, briefly, my reconstruction of the events: Gregoras (I, 142–144) says that Andronicus was twenty-one years old at the time of the reconstruction of Tralleis. So this would have taken place in 1280 or 1281 (see Papadopulos, *Genealogie*, no. 58). We know (Pachymeres, I, 468–497), that Michael VIII and Andronicus II were in the East for approximately the same length of time, from June to September. We also know that Andronicus' wife, the Empress Anne, died in the East some time before June of the following year (Pachymeres, I, 499–501). After her death, Michael returned to the East, visited the Sangarius front, and came back to Brusa to receive the news of his excommunication by Martin IV. The excommunication did not take place until October 1281. Therefore, Anne died in the late spring of 1281, and the first expedition of Michael VIII and the reconstruction of Tralleis took place in the summer of 1280. P. Lemerle, *L'Émirat d'Aydin, Byzance et l'Occident* (Paris, 1957), pp. 14–15, 255, places the expedition of Andronicus II in 1278, while admitting the possibility of 1280. P. Wittek, *Das Fürstentum Mentesche* (Istanbul, 1934), p. 26, also adopts 1278, without discussing his choice of date.

39. Pachymeres, I, 504–505, 524; Dölger, *Regesten*, III, no. 2049; R. Souarn, "Tentatives d'union avec Rome: un patriarche grec catholique au XIIIe siècle," *Échos d'Orient*, 3 (1899), 356. The embassy was sent before August 1280 (death of Nicholas III). The ambassadors were Leo of Heracleia and Theophilus of Nicaea. The bishop of Nicaea, on his return, informed Michael of his excommunication by Martin IV (the bishop of Heracleia had died meanwhile). It would seem that after fortifying the Sangarius and perhaps after the episode in Brusa, Michael fortified Achyraous and Lopadion, in Bithynia, to the west of Brusa (Pachymeres, I, 523–524).

urged that it be rebuilt and people encouraged to return.[40] The native population had lost faith in the emperor of Constantinople, and the courage instilled in them by the Lascarids was beginning to fail. The problem of Anatolia was more complicated than the Turkish advance; it was a political and social problem of the local population. These men would have to be coaxed back to a desire to defend themselves, perhaps by a change in the religious policy of the government, certainly by a show of interest from Constantinople.[41] The army, too, had been virtually dismantled, and contemporaries realized the importance of local recruitment and good leadership.

Andronicus II understood this, and his policy until 1302 was to reorganize Anatolia as well as defend it. His first expedition in the East (1280) was conceived along the same lines. Although it has not, until now, been carefully examined, this campaign was highly illustrative of the young emperor's character, of his political concerns, and of the policies he would later pursue.

Pachymeres, the major Byzantine source, argued that Andronicus, still overshadowed by his father, was merely executing Michael VIII's order in 1280. Andronicus' panegyrists, on the other hand, attributed the initiative to the young co-emperor; but, of course, their aim was to glorify him, and they often attributed to him policies for which he was clearly not responsible.[42]

Andronicus certainly went to the East under orders, but his subsequent behavior apparently owed more to him than it did to his father. It bore the stamp of his later policies: great concern for Asia Minor, high ideas about the nature of the empire, and hopes for the restoration of its ancient glory. His attitude in 1280 was approximately the same as it would be in 1293 when his aims were threefold: to restore the people's morale by his protracted presence in the East; to bring armies and money into the area; and to make the area safe by rebuilding forts, towns, and villages along the frontiers.[43]

In 1280 his efforts were concentrated on the Maeander River. On his way, he came across the ancient city of Tralleis, now depopulated and ruined. Andronicus stayed in the vicinity for a while, and was seized with the idea of restoring the city to its past glory. It was to be renamed Andronikopolis or Palaiologopolis, both rather ungainly names. He was in a hurry; an old omen found amongst the ruins seemed to justify both his plans and his haste. Unfortunately, he did not think of examining the terrain carefully. Since the only source of water was the Maeander, a fair distance away, the city could survive only so long as the surrounding territory was in safe hands. Tralleis was duly rebuilt, and repopulated with 20,000 or 36,000 people who were to live under

---

40. Pachymeres, I, 502–503; Theodore Metochites, βασιλικὸς α´ (oration in praise of Andronicus II), Cod. Vindob. Philol. Gr. 95, fol. 87ro.

41. Metochites, βασιλικὸς α´ Cod. Vindob. Philol. Gr. 95, fol. 87ro.

42. Pachymeres, I, 468; cf. Gregoras, I, 142; Metochites, βασιλικὸς α´ Cod. Vindob. Philol. Gr. 95, fols. 87vo, 88ro; Nicephorus Choumnos, in J. fr. Boissonade, ed., *Anecdota Graeca e codicibus regiis* (Paris, 1830), II, 1–56.

43. Metochites, βασιλικὸς α´ fol. 87ro; βασιλικὸς β´ (second oration to Andronicus II), Cod. Vindob. Philol. Gr. 95, fols. 149ro, 150ro, 151ro.

Andronicus' special protection.[44] Michael VIII, in his autobiography, boasted that "if we did not exterminate all those we conquered near Caria, the sources of the Maeander, and that part of Phrygia which lies nearby, we only spared those whom we decided to make our slaves."[45] Nothing so dramatic happened. Although defended by valiant generals, Tralleis fell after four years to the Turkish emirate of Menteshe, whose ruler cut off its water supply.[46] In September 1280 Andronicus rejoined his father in Nymphaeum, while the Turks, emboldened by the departure of the emperor, continued with their depredations.

Andronicus II's first enterprise in Asia Minor was far from spectacular, and yet it represented the beginning of a change of policy. Michael VIII had been virtually indifferent to the problems of the region; Andronicus would give Asia Minor a primary role in his policy. He took a personal interest in the troubled province, which he visited again in 1290–1293. He sent his best generals, and spent a very considerable part of his limited resources in an effort to save Asia Minor. His task was very difficult, for the Byzantines had lost much of Asia Minor before Michael VIII's death. An intelligent observer, Marino Sanudo, later wrote that after his excommunication by Martin IV, Michael, "as though in despair, abandoned the custody of one of his provinces, the best and most powerful, which was called Paphlagonia, and which was taken by the Turks . . . [This province] is great and full of beautiful rivers, streams and lakes and fields and is well cultivated." The whole province, he wrote, was lost, except for the area around Heracleia on the Black Sea, "and this loss brought immense damage."[47] This was an exaggerated account; writing in the 1330's, Sanudo obviously confused the situation of his own day with that of the reign of Michael VIII. Yet, despite the confusion, Sanudo was right in linking the abandonment of Asia Minor to Michael VIII's western policy, and placing the blame on Michael rather than on Andronicus.

Michael VIII was not completely unconcerned about the fate of Asia Minor—had he been, he would have been a unique Byzantine emperor. He thought of solving the problems of Asia Minor within the context of his western policy, and seriously considered using western crusaders to recover his eastern provinces. For this purpose he sent ambassadors to Pope Gregory X in 1275, shortly after the celebration of the union of the churches in Lyons. The pope,

---

44. On the Tralleis episode, see ibid., fols. 87vo–88ro; Pachymeres, I, 468–474; Gregoras, I, 142; Georgius Cyprius in Migne, *PG*, CXLII (Paris, 1865), col. 405; Metochites, Cod. Vindob. Philol. Gr. 95, fol. 88ro. Pachymeres says there were 36,000 people; Gregoras gives the figure as "no less than 20,000."

45. I. E. Troitskii, ed., *Imperatoris Michaelis Palaeologi de vita sua opusculum* (St. Petersburg, 1885), pp. 7–8.

46. Pachymeres, I, 472–474; Lemerle, *L'Émirat d' Aydin*, pp. 14–15; Wittek, *Mentesche*, pp. 29–30. Georgius Cyprius, in Migne, *PG*, CXLII, col. 405, also says that Tralleis flourished for four years and protected the whole of Ionia against the Turks.

47. Sanudo, *Istoria*, p. 144: "come disperato lassiò la custodia d'una sua Provincia ottima e Potente, che si chiama Paphlagonia, tolta da' Turchi . . . laqual è grande e piena di belle Riviere, Fiumi e Laghi e Erbazo e ben coltivata . . . della qual perdita se ne ebbe immenso danno."

too, was convinced that Anatolia, with a rich Christian heritage, should revert to its ancient masters, the Byzantines, now in full communion with Rome. He agreed to a crusade, which was to take place at the end of 1276 or the spring of 1277.[48] Andronicus II expressed full agreement with his father's policies in a letter to Pope John XXI (April 1277).[49] The text of the young man's letter was almost identical with that of his father's, but his subsequent attitudes indicated that the unionist policy had been forced upon him.

Had Michael VIII's plan materialized, he might well have been called the savior of Asia Minor—just as Alexius I Comnenus was so called after the first crusade. Of course, this new crusade might also have brought the emperor problems similar to those that Alexius I had to face, once the first crusade was upon him. Still, Michael VIII's policy was not intrinsically wrong. So long as Byzantium was unable to defeat the Turks on its own, the logical course would have been to fight them in cooperation with Venice, the papacy, the West. Had Michael VIII lived longer, he might possibly have had the time and the ability to achieve such cooperation. The fate of Byzantium might then have been quite different.

Since Andronicus II abandoned his father's European policy for his own Balkan and eastern policy, the possibility of common action with the West was delayed for so long that when it came it proved illusory.[50] Michael VIII's death opened the doors to the forces of antiwestern reaction which had been active even during his lifetime. Andronicus repudiated the union with Rome, and Rome was bent on church union before political alliance, at least until the 1330's. Thus Michael VIII's plans for Asia Minor were never realized. After 1282, Asia Minor was in a deplorable state, although the damage was not yet irreparable.

While Michael VIII left Asia Minor to its fate, he considered Greece and the Balkans an important area, and here he exhibited considerable military and diplomatic activity. The second aim of his policy, after the preservation of his throne, was to restore the Byzantine Empire to its pre-1204 frontiers. Thus, he wanted to expand into Epirus, Thessaly, and Greece, defeating the splinter Greek and Latin states which had sprung up after the fourth crusade. He also wanted to create a Byzantine sphere of influence in the Balkans, and tried to accomplish this as much by war as by a system of alliances. In his foreign alliances, Michael VIII tried the tactic of making friends with states which

48. J. Guiraud, *Les registres de Grégoire X* (Paris, 1892–1906), X, 314, 315; V. Laurent, "Grégoire X et son projet de ligue anti-turque," *Échos d'Orient*, 37 (1938), 257ff; V. Laurent, "Le rapport de Georges le Métochite, apocrisiaire de Michel VIII Paléologue auprès du Pape Grégoire X," *Revue historique du sud-est Européen*, 23 (1946), 233ff; M.-H. Laurent, *Le bienheureux Innocent V et son temps* (Vatican, 1947), appendix 4, "Le récit d'une mission diplomatique de Georges le Métochite, 1275–1276," 435–440; V. Laurent, "La croisade et la question d'Orient sous le pontificat de Grégoire X," *Revue historique du sud-est Européen*, 22 (1945), 105ff; M.-H. Laurent, "Georges le Métochite ambassadeur de Michel VIII Paléologue auprès du bienheureux Innocent V," *Miscellanea Giovanni Mercati*, III; Norden, *Papsttum und Byzanz*, 484–528; Joh. Müller, "Die Legationen unter Papst Gregor X," *Röm. Quartalschrift*, 37 (1929), 57–135; V. Grumel, "Les ambassades pontificales à Byzance," 446.

49. Raynaldus, *Annales Eccl.*, 1277, §XXXI.

50. On this, see my article, "Marino Sanudo Torsello, Byzantium and the Turks: The Background to the Anti-Turkish League of 1332–1334," in *Speculum*, 45 (1970), 374–392.

bordered those of his enemies. Marriage negotiations were a useful instrument of this policy, as was the expenditure of vast sums of money. Marriage negotiations had another aim: that of conciliating the friends of the deposed Lascarids, and thus legitimizing Michael's own accession to the throne.

Andronicus II, his heir presumptive, was the trump card of Michael's matrimonial policy. By 1271 Andronicus "had become a man," and was being prepared for the succession. It was necessary to find him the right wife.[51] Possibly some thought was given to marrying him to a daughter of Alfonso X of Castile. Indeed, the initiative came from Alfonso, who wanted to include Byzantium in his system of alliances: "he wanted to give his other daughter to the son of Palaeologos, the Emperor of the Greeks, and enemy of King Charles because . . . the said King Charles wanted to occupy the said Empire of the Greeks."[52] The expression "the son of Palaeologos" would seem to indicate that the eldest surviving son was being considered. Besides, these negotiations, if such they may be called, took place in 1271, when Andronicus was the only eligible Byzantine prince. Of his surviving brothers, Theodore was, at this time, no more than eight years old, and at approximately the same time, Michael was trying to marry his second surviving son, Constantine, to a daughter of Stephen Uroš I of Serbia.[53] Michael's negotiations with Castile were not pursued very far. The reason may perhaps be ascribed to the difficulty of exchanging embassies through hostile territory.[54] In any case, given the diplomatic situation, Michael preferred to seek for his heir a marriage that would improve his position in the Balkans.

To the north of the empire, the two most dangerous powers were Hungary and Serbia. In 1269 Bela IV of Hungary concluded a marriage alliance with Charles of Anjou. The terms of the alliance included a defensive clause and an offensive one, against all enemies of the Catholic church.[55] Michael VIII managed to counteract this by arranging a marriage between Andronicus and Anne of Hungary, a granddaughter of Theodore Lascaris. The marriage took place in the late summer of 1272. It had a double aim, to help improve relations with Hungary and to provide further legitimacy for the Palaeologan dynasty, through a matrimonial link with a descendant of the Lascarids.[56]

51. Pachymeres, I, 317–320.

52. *Annales Placentini Ghibellini*, in G. H. Pertz, ed., *Monumenta Germaniae Historica. Scriptores*, XVIII (Hanover, 1863), 553 (hereafter cited as *MGH Ss*).

53. Papadopulos, *Genealogie*, no. 43; Geanakoplos, *Michael Palaeologus*, p. 223; Camillo Minieri-Riccio, *Saggio di codice diplomatico*, I (Naples, 1878), 114, no. 133; Pachymeres, I, 350; V. Makušev, *The Italian Archives and the Material They Contain on the History of the Slavs*, II (St. Petersburg, 1871), 67–88. The projected marriage of Constantine did not take place. Before his death, Michael VIII also tried to marry Constantine to a rich Latin princess (Gregoras, I, 187).

54. Pachymeres, I, 317.

55. Camillo Minieri-Riccio, *Alcuni fatti riguardanti Carlo I di Angiò dal 6 di Agosto 1252 al 30 di Dicembre 1270* (Naples, 1874), pp. 55, 68, 69, 71.

56. There is some confusion in the sources as to the date of the marriage and its connection with Andronicus' coronation. The coronation took place on November 8, 1272 (Dölger, *Regesten*, III, 60, 76; Papadopulos, *Genealogie*, no. 58); Gregoras claims that the marriage took place simultaneously, while Pachymeres places it in the previous year (Gregoras, I, 109; Pachymeres, I, 317–320). Modern historians also differ. Papadopulos places the coronation in 1272 and the marriage in 1273, while Geanakoplos prefers November, 1272 as the date of both (*Michael Palaeologus*, p. 233). In this case, I see no reason to dispute Pachymeres' authority, as

Michael's diplomacy was less successful in the Balkan states of Serbia and Bulgaria, both of which were troublesome neighbors. Serbia had become an important power. The position of the country enabled the Serbs to intercept communications between Constantinople and Michael's Italian allies. Moreover, they had a close connection with the king of Hungary, one of whose daughters had married Stephen Dragutin, eldest son of Stephen Uroš I, King of Serbia. As one Byzantine was to observe later, the Serbians could not be trusted to keep their promises unless they were bound by the bonds of marriage.[57] Michael VIII tried to arrange a marriage between his daughter Anne and Stephen Milyutin, the Serbian king's second son. He sent the patriarch of Constantinople, Joseph I, and John Beccos to Serbia to discuss this marriage (1271–1272). The young princess was also sent along, possibly for the purpose of inspection. They went to Ochrid via Verroia, and sent representatives to the Serbs. As Theodore Metochites was to confirm at the end of the century, the Serbs were unused to pomp and luxury—they were even contemptuous of it. While the Byzantines seemed to them effeminate and pompous, the Serbs gave the Byzantines the impression of living by hunting and thieving, which they are said to have practiced even on the ambassadors. Frightened and rather disgusted, the envoys returned to Constantinople by way of Thessalonica.[58] Stephen Milyutin would have been a valuable ally, for there were already hopes of his becoming king of Serbia: his elder brother, Stephen Dragutin, had broken his leg and was in great danger of losing his life. The failure of the Byzantine embassy, therefore, was all the more significant.

Michael VIII's decision to revive the old Patriarchate of Ochrid with jurisdiction over Serbia and Bulgaria (August 1272)[59] and his attack on Thessaly and Albania led the Serbs to entertain increasingly friendly relations with Charles of Anjou. These culminated in an alliance and a Serbian attack against Byzantium (1282). Even after the failure of Charles of Anjou's plans and Michael VIII's death, the Serbs continued their guerrilla-type attacks on the Byzantine possessions in Macedonia. In fact, relations between the empire

Papadopulos does—without explaining why. Moreover, Pachymeres is quite clear that the marriage and the coronation took place in two different years. The Byzantine year began on September 1. Pachymeres' text indicates that in fact the two events took place quite close together. After he has finished discussing the marriage, he continues: "and soon [thereafter?], on November 8 of the following year, the patriarch and the emperor crowned them." Gregoras' confusion too may indicate that the two events took place so close together that he telescoped them into a single one. Therefore, I think that the marriage took place in the late summer of 1272 (before September 1), that is, in the Byzantine year 6780. The coronation took place on November 8, 1272, that is in the Byzantine year 6781. Andronicus II received extraordinary privileges on his coronation, because Michael VIII was trying to secure the succession against the ambitions of his brother, the despot John. On the marriage, see also Olgierd Górka, *Anonymi Descriptio Europae orientalis* (Cracow, 1916), p. 53. See also R.-J. Loenertz, O.P., "La chronique brève de 1352, texte, traduction et commentaire," *Orientalia Christiana Periodica*, 29 (1963), 333, no. 7, and p. 334 (hereafter cited as *OCP*). This short chronicle supports my argument.

57. Pachymeres, I, 350–355; Pachymeres, II, 272.

58. Pachymeres, I, 350–355; Souarn, "Tentatives," pp. 231–232. Stephen Uroš II Milyutin became king of Serbia in 1282: C. Jireček, *Geschichte der Serben* (Gotha, 1911).

59. H. Gelzer, "Ungedruckte und wenig bekannte Bistümerverzeichnisse der orientalischen Kirche," *BZ*, 2 (1893), 42–46.

and the Serbs did not improve until the end of the century, when Andronicus II, under the double threat of the Turks and the Venetians, was forced to give his five-year-old daughter Simonis as wife to the middle-aged Milyutin.[60]

Michael VIII's relations with Bulgaria were conditioned by two factors, strategic and political. Bulgaria's political situation was in flux, giving Byzantium the opportunity to play off one claimant to the Bulgarian throne against the other. Byzantium could not afford a strong Bulgaria, which might threaten it from the north, or make alliances with the enemies of the empire. On the other hand, Bulgaria should be strong enough to form an efficient buffer state between the empire and the Tartars of the north. The aim of Byzantine diplomacy was to keep Bulgaria relatively strong and friendly by placing and supporting a pro-Byzantine candidate on the Bulgarian throne.

Michael VIII hoped that in Bulgaria as in Hungary he might attach himself to those connected by marriage to the deposed Lascarids. Constantine Tiš Asên, king of the Bulgarians since 1257, had been married to Irene, a daughter of Theodore Lascaris. Michael VIII in 1270 or 1272, arranged a marriage between Maria, the daughter of his own sister Irene, and Constantine of Bulgaria, and promised in the new marriage settlement to surrender Mesembreia and Anchialos to the Bulgarians.[61] In 1277 Constantine Tiš was killed in battle against the Bulgarian rebel Lachanas (a former swineherd), who secured Maria as part of the spoils. To oppose Lachanas, Michael started negotiations with a certain Mytzes, Lord of Trnvo, who was also related to the Lascarids by marriage. In order to cement the alliance, Mytzes' son, John Asên III, was married to Irene, Michael's daughter (1278).[62] He fought against Lachanas and became king of Bulgaria for one year (1279–1280).

If Asên was acceptable to the Byzantines, he was unwelcome in Bulgaria, where the native boyars preferred a man of their own, George I Terter. In his one year of rule, Asên tried to secure Terter's loyalty and even forced him to divorce his wife and marry Asên's sister. But Terter rebelled, deposed Asên, and, "the Bulgarians also willing," was proclaimed king in 1280. He promptly concluded an alliance against Byzantium with Charles of Anjou and the sebastrokrator of Thessaly, John I (1280–1282).[63] After Michael's death, Andronicus did not have a large enough army to fight the Bulgarians. In 1283 he recognized Terter as king of Bulgaria, while John Asên became a despot in the empire. The Bulgarians remained hostile to Byzantium until the

---

60. Francesco Carabellese, *Carlo d'Angiò nei rapporti politici e commerciali con Venezia e l'oriente* (Bari, 1911), pp. 39–40; *Archivio storico Italiano*, 4th ser., 4, 10; Jireček, *Geschichte der Serben*, 280, 333ff. Cf. below, Chapter IV.

61. Pachymeres, I, 342–349; Gregoras, I, 130–133; Papadopulos, *Genealogie*, no. 33 (1270); Geanakoplos, *Michael Palaeologus*, p. 232 (1272).

62. Pachymeres, I, 349, 439–440; Gregoras, I, 132–133. Cf. I. Dujčev, "Una poesia di Manuele Filè dedicata a Irene Paleologina Asenina," *Mélanges Georges Ostrogorsky*, II (Belgrade, 1964), 91–99.

63. Pachymeres, I, 447; *Archivio storico Italiano*, 4th ser., 4, 12 (July 9, 1281). Charles of Anjou orders the vice-justiciar of Sicily "di somministrare tutti i mezzi di trasporto agli ambasciadori spediteglii dall'imperadore di Aragoras [Zagora], appena giungeranno nella città di Napoli, affinchè senza ritardo siano alla sua presenza." On George Terter, see Pachymeres, I, 447–448; II, 265; C. Jireček, *Geschichte der Bulgaren* (Prague, 1876), pp. 280ff.

end of the century, but the danger they presented was not very grave until Theodore Svetoslav came to the throne in 1300. Only then was Andronicus forced to change his father's policy toward Bulgaria.[64]

The most immediate military problem Andronicus had to face was the result of Michael VIII's expansionist policies in Greece and of his own inability to pursue them. The Despotate of Epirus, born during the early years of the Latin conquest of the empire, continued its independent existence during the reign of Michael VIII. In 1271, Michael II of Epirus died, leaving Thessaly to his illegitimate son, John I Angelos (1271–1289). Michael VIII wanted to reunite the provinces of Epirus and Thessaly to the empire, while these splinter Greek states preferred to retain their independence. In 1282, John I of Thessaly joined the Angevin camp and attacked Macedonia in conjunction with the king of Serbia.

Michael VIII requested the help of his ally and son-in-law, the Tartar Nogai, a general of the Golden Horde who had rebelled against the legitimate khan and controlled the area north of Bulgaria. Four thousand men arrived in Constantinople in November 1282, but Michael died before he could make use of them. Michael himself was not certain of the loyalty of these mercenaries. Andronicus found them not merely useless, but positively dangerous. Other urgent problems dictated the postponement of hostilities against John I, and the Tartars were unwilling to leave without payment or a chance to plunder. Andronicus was neither able nor willing to buy them off with the little money he had inherited. He decided to send them out of of Byzantine territory as quickly as possible. Taking a decision not unworthy of his father, he sent them off against Serbia, under the command of Michael Glabas. The Tartars collected some booty in Serbia and then returned to their lands across the Danube.[65] As for John of Thessaly, Andronicus launched his own expedition against him in 1283. It failed, and the problem of Epirus and Thessaly remained unsolved until 1318.

By great diplomatic ability and good luck, Michael VIII had been able to save the empire from recovery by the Latins. But the state he left to his son was burdened with many and difficult problems. The West had only postponed, not abandoned, its plans of conquest. The situation in the Balkans was unstable. Asia Minor was undefended. The state of Byzantine finances was very poor. But the most pressing difficulties, and certainly the most emotional ones, concerned the restoration of orthodoxy. So hated was Michael for his unionist policies that when he died his son "did not give his father an imperial funeral, nay, not even a funeral worthy of lowly men . . . During the night, he ordered a few men to take the body away from the camp, and cover it with earth,

64. Pachymeres, II, 57; Dölger, *Regesten*, no. 2094. There was a peace treaty in the spring of 1284: Dölger, *Regesten*, no. 2099; cf. below, Chapter VI.

65. I. Sokolov, "Kroupnye i melkie vlasteli v Fessalii," *Vizantiiskii Vremennik*, 24 (1925–1926), 35ff (hereafter referred to as *Viz. Vrem.*); A. Soloviev, "Fessalijskie arkhonti v XIV v.," *BS* 4 (1932), 159ff. Pachymeres, I, 524–525; Gregoras, I, 149–150, 158–159; Geanakoplos, *Michael Palaeologus*, pp. 369–370.

taking care only that no wild beasts should mutilate the imperial body . . .
And the reason for this was the emperor's deviation from orthodox doctrine."
Michael VIII did receive extreme unction; but he was buried in Selyvria,
without religious rites and without ceremony.[66]

66. Gregoras, I, 153, 159; Pachymeres, I, 530–532; II, 107–108. Michael died in Thrace,
on his way to fight the Thessalians.

II

Diplomatic Realignments, 1282–1296

During his first years as sole ruler of Byzantium, Andronicus II continued to some extent his father's foreign policy.[1] He could do this in continental Greece and the Morea, where he pursued Michael VIII's expansionist policy for a time. He might have wanted to do the same in the Balkans, but there he was forced, for lack of money, to reduce his activities. But in the most important areas, in Asia Minor and western Europe, Andronicus' policy inevitably diverged from that of Michael VIII.

Like his father, Andronicus II wanted to secure Byzantium against western aggression, but he realized that because of the Sicilian Vespers Byzantium was, for the moment, safe from western invasions. Andronicus was therefore free to change his father's ecclesiastical policy, and to enter a period of sustained diplomatic activity, whose purpose was to establish friendly, or at least correct, relations with Venice and Genoa, and to gather into Byzantine hands all claims to the imperial throne or to parts of the empire. But Andronicus' reversal of Michael's ecclesiastical policy would gradually change the tenor of his western policy to one of disengagement from the West. The purpose of this disengagement was to concentrate his resources on Asia Minor, which now assumed a central role in his plans. In domestic and foreign policy, Andronicus' repudiation of the union of the churches was his first important action.

Religious Policy

Michael VIII's death allowed those who had, openly or secretly, opposed his religious policy, to prevail. Andronicus, acting in accord with the wishes of the majority of his subjects, provided for the reestablishment of Orthodoxy; this was virtually the first action he took as sole ruler, in December 1282. It would be an idle exercise to enquire into the new emperor's motives, or to try to discover whether the initiative was his own, or whether he was merely following the lead of others. As soon as Michael died, the young emperor was besieged by those who, like his Aunt Eulogia and the grand logothete (first minister), Mouzalon, desired to restore the independence of the Byzantine church. But

---

1. Michael, Andronicus' eldest son, was proclaimed heir to the throne in 1281, to allay Andronicus' fear of being circumvented by his own brother, Constantine; he was not, however, crowned emperor until May 21, 1294. Pachymeres, II, 195; Gregoras, I, 193; Franz Dölger, "Die dynastische Familienpolitik des Kaisers Michael Palaiologos," *E. Eichmann Festschrift*, (Paderborn, 1940), pp. 179–190; H. Constantinidi-Bibikou, "Yolande de Montferrat Impératrice de Byzance," *L'Hellénisme Contemporain*, 4 (1950), 428; Dölger, *Regesten*, III, no. 2061; Papadopulos, *Genealogie*, p. 36. R. Verpeaux, "Notes chronologiques sur les livres II et III du *De Andronico Paleologo* de Georges Pachymère," *Revue des études byzantines* 17 (1959), 171, (hereafter *REB*); B. T. Gorjanov, "Anonymous Byzantine Chronicle of the 14th Century" (in Russian), *Viz. Vrem.* n. s., 2 (1949), 282.

Andronicus himself was certainly predisposed in the same direction. His interest in the Byzantine church and in religion was much deeper than that of his father, and he clearly felt unable to justify the union of the churches on political grounds, as Michael had done. The fact that Charles of Anjou was involved in a time-consuming revolt and thus had been rendered relatively harmless no doubt made a break with Rome less dangerous. Finally, it is perfectly clear from the sources that Andronicus wanted to restore peace to his church and to heal the schism created by Michael's unionist policy. The disruption in the church was disturbing to Andronicus, both because he was a pious man and because, as emperor, he needed a quiet and orderly clergy.[2]

Two weeks after Michael VIII's death, on December 26, 1282, the unionist patriarch, John Beccos, sensing the trouble ahead, quietly abdicated.[3] Joseph I, who in 1273 had sworn never to embrace the union and had subsequently lost his office, once more ascended the patriarchal throne on the last day of 1282. At the same time, imperial heralds proclaimed the return to the orthodox faith and the restoration of those opponents of the union who had been exiled or ill-treated under Michael. Meanwhile, the clergy decided that those clerics who had taken the oath to the pope should abstain from the performance of their duties for three months.[4]

These measures, far from bringing peace to the church, were only the beginning of long struggles and disagreements. Those members of the clergy who had suffered through their refusal to accept the union thought that the time had at last arrived when they could take revenge on the "renegades" and appropriate the highest and most lucrative honors and positions. Apparently, many of these people were monks who, in the words of the historian Gregoras, who disliked them, were rude and common plebeians; they had never even seen an emperor before, Gregoras wrote, yet now they found themselves in a position of power. This they wanted to use to their advantage, and they urged the deposition of all those members of the clergy who had supported Michael.[5]

A certain amount of disruption while the church was adjusting to new conditions was perhaps to be expected. It was quite natural, and certainly within the Byzantine tradition, for those who had suffered because of their beliefs to wish to supplant the ecclesiastical hierarchy which they had opposed. Similar problems had faced the Byzantine church and the state after the two restorations of the icons, in 787 and 843. Now, however, there was a complicating and dangerous new factor.

2. Pachymeres, II, 12–15, 14ff; Gregoras, I, 160ff; Salimbene Parmensis, *Chronicon ab a. 1167–1287*, ed. O. Holder-Egger, in *MGH Ss*, XXXII (Hanover, 1905–1913), 510; Souarn, "Tentatives"; H. Evert-Kapessowa, "Une page de l'histoire des relations byzantino-latines," *BS*, 17 (1956), 1–18; anonymous Greek chronicle in J.A.C. Buchon, *Recherches historiques sur la principauté française de Morée et ses hautes baronies* (Paris, 1845), II, verses 710ff.

3. Pachymeres, II, 15–19; Evert-Kapessowa, "Une page de l'histoire des relations byzantino-latines." On John Beccos see also V. Laurent, "Les signataires du 2me synode de Blachernes," *Échos d'Orient*, 26 (1927), 129–149; V. Laurent, "La date de la mort de Jean Beccos," *Échos d'Orient*, 25 (1926), 316–319.

4. Pachymeres, I, 382; II, 20–21; Gregoras, I, 160; J. Mansi, *Sacrorum conciliorum nova et amplissima collectio* vol. XXIV (Venice, 1770), cols. 74ff.

5. Gregoras, I, 162–171.

The patriarch, Joseph I, could not be accused of having supported the union with Rome. But a group among the extremist members of the clergy—among the Zealots, as they were then called—bitterly resented Joseph I. Their quarrel with the patriarch went back to the deposition of Patriarch Arsenius, in 1265. They claimed that, because Arsenius had been illegally deposed, Joseph, who succeeded him, was a usurper. The Arsenite faction held to Arsenius' excommunication of Joseph, and would not accept the authority of the new patriarch. The Josephites, on the other hand, thought Joseph's election legitimate, and Arsenius' excommunication of Joseph invalid.[6] Clearly such a split was damaging to the church, but it was equally dangerous to Andronicus personally. To the Arsenites, the Palaeologans were usurpers. And the Arsenites had the power, perhaps from this very opposition to the dynasty, to carry with them many members of the clergy and many of the populace.[7]

Andronicus was particularly grieved by the lack of unity in the church. In addition to its raising a problem of public peace, the disunity of the clergy endangered the spiritual welfare of his subjects.[8] The people of Constantinople were ever eager to join in riots, and they might be aroused by the sight of so many monks and unruly members of the clergy who had gathered in the capital, ready for trouble. And certainly, the authority of the church often depends on a lack of vindictiveness toward those of its members who have gone astray.

The emperor tried to persuade the warring factions to make peace. He would not take harsh measures: "Being mild by nature, and not desiring to grieve one party or the other . . . he preferred to take a middle course."[9] His caution was deplored by all the fanatics. He even allowed Greek and "Italian" (western) clergy and laity to celebrate Epiphany in the same church, which to some of the Greeks was almost blasphemous. As one would expect, he took the part of the Josephites, yet did not at first adopt strong measures against the Arsenites. After Joseph I's death (March 13, 1283), Andronicus appointed Gregory III Kyprios (1283–1289) to be patriarch. Gregory, he thought, would appeal to both factions. Both factions opposed him.[10]

In an effort to put an end to the quarrel between Josephites and Arsenites, Andronicus invited all the prelates and the clergy to come to Adramyttion, in

---

6. Pachymeres, II, 36ff; Gregoras, I, 161–162. See also J. Sykoutres, «Περὶ τὸ σχίσμα τῶν Ἀρσενιατῶν,» pp. 267–332.

7. Pachymeres, II, 58: ἡ γὰρ τῶν Ἀρσενιατῶν ἐπισύστασις πολλή τις οὖσα καὶ καθ' ἑκάστην πληθυομένη, ἠρεμεῖν οὐκ εἴα. Pachymeres, II, 51. The Arsenites were able to exercise this power for quite a long time. In September 1304 Andronicus complained that they were inciting the people to trouble: ἀξίωσιν ἀπενέγκας καὶ δεσποτικὴν παρακέλευσιν μᾶλλον, τόν . . . λαὸν οὐδὲν ἐπιταράττειν ἐχόμενα τρίβου τιθέντος σκάνδαλα. Pachymeres, II, 479. On this subject see also V. Laurent, "La fin du schisme arsénite," Académie Roumaine, *Bulletin de la section historique*, 26 (1945), 239–245.

8. Pachymeres, II, 23.

9. Gregoras, I, 162: φύσει πρᾷος ὢν καὶ μήτε τούτους ἐθέλων λυπεῖν μήτ' ἐκείνους . . . τὴν μέσην ἔγνω βαδίζειν.

10. Pachymeres, II, 22–23, 42–45; Gregoras, I, 163, 164–165; Laurent, "La fin du schisme arsénite," p. 245. They claimed that since he had lived in Cyprus until his twentieth year, he had become accustomed to Latin customs and therefore could not be trusted. Gregory could not be consecrated on the patriarchal throne, for no bishop who had accepted the union could carry out the ceremony. Fortunately, there were in Constantinople a bishop from Epirus (which had remained Orthodox) and one from Macedonia. They consecrated a member of the clergy as bishop of Heracleia; then he, following the tradition, consecrated Gregory.

Asia Minor, sometime around Easter 1284. There he subjected two volumes, each containing the beliefs of each faction, to an ordeal by fire. The party whose teachings escaped the fire, would be vindicated. Of course both volumes burned, and both parties temporarily subjected themselves to Gregory's authority. Some Arsenites did return to the body of the church. They then asked Andronicus to allow them to move Arsenius' body from Proikonnesos and rebury it in Constantinople. This they did. Somewhat later, Andronicus took another step to placate the Arsenites. He visited the blind former emperor, John Lascaris, in his place of exile in Bithynia and tried to ease the conditions under which he lived.[11]

Their quarrel somewhat appeased by the decision of Adramyttion, the zealots of both parties returned to Constantinople. There they persuaded Andronicus to agree to the deposition of all members of the clergy who had supported the union of the churches. They caused the unionists to assemble in Sancta Sophia and there behaved in a shameful manner, taunting and assaulting the deposed clerics.[12]

The supporters of the restoration of orthodoxy had not yet given a doctrinal justification of their position. A full discussion of doctrine was urged by the leader of the unionist party, the former patriarch John Beccos, early in 1285. From his exile in Brusa, he accused Andronicus and the Byzantine prelates of injustice to himself. Looking for a confrontation, he expressed surprise that he, a Roman (Greek), properly brought up as a Roman, should be calumniated while the patriarch Gregory, a Cypriot brought up among the Latins, who followed Latin customs, should be in a place of honor. It seems that several people were quick to embrace Beccos' cause and spread the rumor of injustice. Gregoras does not say whether the pro-Beccos sentiment was strong in Constantinople or in the provinces. It is possible that Beccos found his supporters in Asia Minor, where the strength of anti-Palaeologan feelings might for the moment make people forget about the unionist tendencies of the former patriarch. In any case, Beccos provoked a doctrinal debate, and the clergy in Constantinople eagerly seized this opportunity to refute Beccos' writings and his whole unionist policy. Andronicus recalled Beccos to Constantinople, to appear before an assembly of prelates, clergy, and the high nobility. Beccos' chief opponents in the debate were the Patriarch Gregory III and the Grand Logothete, Mouzalon. The case of the Orthodox was proved, at least to their own satisfaction, and Beccos was exiled to Bithynia along with two other unrepentent unionists, George Metochites and Theodoros Meliteiniotes.[13]

11. Pachymeres, II, 83; Gregoras, I, 166–167, 173–174; V. Laurent, "Les signataires," p. 132; Laurent, "La fin du schisme arsénite," pp. 245–246.

12. Gregoras, I, 171–172.

13. Pachymeres, II, 27, 34, 88–89ff; Gregoras, I, 168–171. The discussion took place at the second synod of Blachernae, in the early part of 1285: Laurent, "Les signataires," pp. 132, 133. The case of the unionists against Gregory III has been preserved in the writings of George Metochites, Λόγος ἀντιρρητικὸς ἐπὶ τῷ τοῦ Κυπρίου τόμῳ in A. Mai, ed., *Patrum Novae Bibliothecae,* VIII, pt. 2 (Rome, 1871), 179–227. Andronicus, ever mild, later received George Metochites' son Theodore in his court, (ca. 1290), and bestowed great favors upon him. Ševčenko, *Métochite et Choumnos,* 131–134, 270; V. Laurent, "Jean Beccos," p. 317; Max Treu, *Dichtungen des Gross-Logotheten Theodoros Metochites,* Programm des Victoria-Gymnasiums zu Potsdam, Ostern 1895 (Potsdam, 1895), A, verses 450–454.

Thus the church union with Rome was destroyed, and the Byzantine Empire returned, once more, to its traditional faith and rites. Andronicus assumed the mantle of the restorer of orthodoxy, and an inscription in the chapel of the Monastery of the Virgin in Berat celebrates him as "the new Constantine Comnenus-Angelus-Palaeologus, the true lover of Christ and of the monks."[14] The new Constantine, however, had not restored peace to his church. In 1289 Gregory III, whose arrogance had aroused the prelates' opposition, was forced to abdicate.[15] He was succeeded by Athanasios I (1289–1293, 1303–1309), a monk from the Peloponnesus, a man with little learning, but personally just and free from corruption. Athanasios realized that the church would never be pacified so long as the prelates, each fond of intrigue and eager for office, remained in Constantinople.[16] Eventually, he managed to persuade most of them to return to their sees. The problem of absenteeism was very grave, and although Athanasios did his best to solve it, his solution was far from permanent.

Athanasios had no toleration for the worldliness of the monks and clergy, and so was much disliked. He was insulted and ridiculed, opposed by clergy and powerful laymen. He hoped that Andronicus would support him, but the emperor was too weak a man for that. Athanasios abdicated on October 16, 1293, anathematizing the emperor and those prelates who had opposed him when in office.[17] John XII Kosmas, who succeeded Athanasios on January 1, 1294, was a favorite of the monks. During his patriarchate, which ended in 1303, a measure of quiet was restored in the church.

The religious policy of Andronicus II had held two objectives: to restore orthodoxy as quietly and gently as possible, and to bring peace and unity to the church. The attitude of most of the prelates, the clergy, and the monks made it virtually impossible to realize these objectives. Andronicus himself did not have the moral courage to object to the extreme measures demanded by the Zealots. The Arsenites, who were the most coherent opponents of the established church, were not pacified until about 1312. They would cause more trouble for the emperor and the empire in the years 1295–1306.

Andronicus II's repudiation of the church union with Rome was a political action of the first importance, since it changed the basis of his father's policy toward the West. By reinforcing, as it were, Pope Martin IV's dissolution of the union, Andronicus placed orthodoxy and spiritual salvation above any potential benefits that might accrue from cooperation with the West. He chose to stand alone in his fight with the Turks; he had decided to try to save Asia Minor with his own resources, and without help from western crusaders.

14. Anthimos Alexoudes, Metropolitan of Berat, Σύντομος ἱστορικὴ περιγραφὴ τῆς ἱερᾶς Μητροπόλεως Βελεγράδων, (Corfu, 1868), p. 76.

15. Pachymeres, II, 130–133; Gregoras, I, 176–179. The first rebellion of the bishops against Gregory occurred in the spring of 1289: Laurent, "Signataires," p. 133.

16. Gregoras, I, 180–182; Pachymeres, II, 139–152. Also, Athanasios' unpublished correspondence, especially Cod. Vat. Gr. 2219, fols. 8vo–9ro, 9ro–vo,12vo, 13ro–vo, 13vo–14ro, 14ro–vo,14vo, 41ro–vo. Also, below, Appendix I, letters I, II, and Migne, *PG*, CXLII (1885), col. 513.

17. Pachymeres, II, 168–177, 185–186; Gregoras, I, 185–186, 191.

This aroused the ire of Catholics of his day, and even centuries later so able an historian as Father V. Laurent can say

> The over-long reign of Andronicus II was, in effect, one of anti-Roman phobia. Faithful until the end to an oath which, in his improvident youth, he had sworn to a conspiracy of monks, this prince was imprudent enough to wish to defeat the growing peril with Latin aid, but not with that of the Holy See . . . The desire of the fanatics, who said that they preferred the Muslim yoke to the tyranny of the Pope, began to be granted without delay. And this explains why George Metochites, ardent patriot and faithful catholic, on hearing in his prison of the continued advance of the Turks, should wish the Muslim arms to fall upon those narrow heads who, by hatred of the Pope, abandoned the policy of salvation and expansion of which he had been the fortunate negotiator, for a policy of suicide. It is true that during the fourteenth century sincere efforts were made to seek Roman help, but by then the disease was much too advanced, and the power of the Holy See too diminished; above all, the West which, in an upsurge of chivalrous faith, had become impassioned for the deliverance of the Holy Land, was to see without excess emotion the gradual sinking of an empire which could not, or did not know how to retain the interest of the West, or win its sympathy.[18]

This view fails to do justice to Andronicus' policies, and refuses to take into account the climate of opinion Andronicus found in 1282. After the fourth crusade, after Charles of Anjou, after the already tragic abuse of the idea of the crusade by the papacy, Laurent's judgment seems not only unfair but unhistorical.

The Balkans, Greece, and Achaia

The problem of reuniting a divided church and nation, combined with lack of money, necessitated a retrenchment on several fronts. The solution of the immediate military problems in the Balkans was deferred. Michael VIII's projected war against John of Thessaly was postponed in 1282. Also, since the Byzantine army was not large enough to be diverted in a Bulgarian war, the rebel George Terter was recognized in his possession of Bulgaria.

Even this did not bring safety to Thrace. Terter was unable to stop the Tartar incursions into Bulgarian and Byzantine territories. In 1284, 10,000 Tartars left their Danubian abode, ravaged Bulgaria, and were expected to do the same in Thrace and Macedonia. The situation was saved by the local strategos of Mesembreia, Umbertopoulos. Not only did he act quite independently on this occasion, but he seems to have generally exercised an authority of his own in the area. He managed to defeat the Tartars; some of them were drowned in the Marica River, and the rest went home. Andronicus learned all this after the fact, and rewarded Umbertopoulos with horses, gold, gifts, and titles.[19]

18. V. Laurent, "Grégoire X et son projet d'une ligue anti-turque," pp. 272–273.
19. Pachymeres, II, 57, 80, 105–106, 267; Dölger, *Regesten*, nos. 2093, 2099, 2103.

In Greece and in the Morea, Andronicus continued for a time his father's aggressive policy. In part this was a domestic matter: Andronicus considered Epirus and Thessaly as parts of the Byzantine Empire that should return to the empire. But since these two states were independent, Andronicus' attitude toward them was also an issue of foreign policy. This was the more so since in the case of the despotate of Epirus and, a fortiori, in the principality of Achaia, the Byzantines clashed with the interests of the Angevins. Much of what follows has already been ably discussed by others, especially regarding Achaia.[20] The purpose here is to relate these developments to the larger issue of Andronicus' foreign policy.

In Thessaly, the sebastrokrator Michael, son of John I, took advantage of Michael VIII's death to increase his anti-Byzantine activities. Andronicus, although at first reluctant, countered this with a large-scale operation.[21] He sent an army under the command of his first cousin, the protovestiarios Michael Tarchaneiotes, to Demetrias, in the Gulf of Halmyros. A fleet of eighty ships, under the joint command of Tarchaneiotes' brother-in-law, Alexius Raoul, and the stratopedarches Synadenos, was sent to support the Byzantine army besieging the city. At the same time Andronicus began negotiations with his niece, Anne of Epirus, whose lands, bordering on Thessaly, seemed in danger from the ambitions of the Thessalians. Anne was the wife of Nicephorus I, despot of Epirus (1271?–1296?), but she was a strong-minded woman and often followed policies that differed from those of her husband. On this occasion, she promised to capture and deliver Michael of Thessaly to the emperor, and fulfilled her promise. But Andronicus' army was decimated by an epidemic during the siege of Demetrias and, although the city was taken and held, there were no further operations.[22]

Anne's cooperation with Andronicus in 1283 had long-term results. Although her husband soon broke off relations with the Byzantines, she remained on good terms with them, promised to restore the despotate to the emperor and, after her husband's death in 1295, recognized Andronicus as the natural over-lord of Epirus. Thessaly remained safe from the Byzantines until the death of Constantine Angelos, John I's son, who died in 1303, leaving the state in chaos and almost inviting the intervention of Byzantium and Epirus.

The circumstances of the Thessaly campaign of 1283, just a year after the death of Michael VIII, provide a striking insight into imperial finances. Everyone knew that the campaign would be expensive, and advice on how to finance it was divided. The protovestiarios Tarchaneiotes, who was to lead the army, suggested using funds from the imperial treasury. On the other hand,

20. D. A. Zakythinos, *Le despotat grec de Morée*, I (Paris, 1932); W. Miller, *The Latins in the Levant: A History of Frankish Greece (1204–1566)* (London, 1908).

21. Pachymeres, II, 67–73. Cf. K. Hopf, *Griechische Geschichte*, vol. 85 of J. S. Ersch and J. G. Gruber, eds. *Allgemeine Encyklopädie*, LXXXV (Leipzig, 1867), 330.

22. Pachymeres does not mention the conquest of Demetrias in his account of the campaign of 1283. Later, however, talking of Andronicus' negotiations with Thessaly in 1300, he says that Demetrias was taken in 1283, was subsequently promised to one of John I's sons as the dowry of the Armenian princess Theophano (sister of Michael IX's wife Maria) whom the young man was to marry (1294), and then reclaimed by Andronicus because the marriage never took place: Pachymeres, II, 284.

the emperor's council, which probably had better information about the state of the treasury, suggested that the money be collected from a special tax of 10 percent on the revenus of the pronoia-holders. The council's advice prevailed.[23] It seems clear, then, that from the beginning of his reign Andronicus II operated on a very limited budget and was forced to create an ad hoc fund for every important military expedition. The 10 percent tax on the pronoiai imposed on this occasion was not discontinued after the end of the Thessaly campaign. But no large army was sent south of Macedonia for a long time, perhaps because of the failure of the Thessaly campaign. Indeed, with the exception of the army sent against Nicephorus of Epirus in 1292, the next Byzantine expedition into Greece did not occur until 1308–1310, when a force was sent against the Catalans.

For the first seven years of his reign, Andronicus II seems to have continued his father's aggressive policy in the Morea. The *Chronicle of the Morea* tells us that by 1289 continuous warfare had left the region devastated and impoverished. But in September 1289, the situation changed, because Florent of Hainaut became prince of Achaia by his marriage to Isabeau, daughter of William II Villehardouin, widow of Philip of Anjou, and heiress to the principality. When Florent arrived in the Morea as prince of Achaia, he was advised by his barons to make peace with the Greeks so that the country could recover. He sent messengers to the Byzantine governor of the Morea, in Mistra, to begin peace negotiations. At that time, and until 1308, the Byzantine governors of the Morea served for only one year each. The governor's term being nearly over, he could not negotiate effectively, but he wrote to the emperor and recommended peace.[24] Andronicus was happy with the suggestion because "at that time the emperor had a great war in the East against the Turks who were fighting him very bitterly and took his castles and his land; he was also at war with the despot of Arta and the emperor of Zagora [*i.e.* king of the Bulgarians]." Besides, the war in the Morea was too expensive.[25]

In the late fall of 1289, Andronicus sent as his envoy to the Morea a certain Philanthropenos. This was, perhaps, Alexius Philanthropenos, Michael VIII's nephew, who had led a victorious campaign in the Morea in 1270. At the request of Florent, who would not consider a subject's oath assurance enough of a sovereign's faith, two French envoys went to Constantinople with Philanthropenos and there received a chrysobull setting forth the terms of the peace.

23. Pachymeres, II, 68–69.

24. Zakythinos, *Despotat*, I, 52ff; J. Schmitt, ed., *The Chronicle of the Morea* (London, 1904), verses 8666–8673, 8690 (Greek version of the Chronicle); Jean de Longnon, ed., *La chronique de Morée: Livre de la conqueste de la princée de l'Amorée* (Paris, 1911), §597; A. Morel-Fatio, ed., *Libro de los Fechos et Conquistas del Principado de la Morea* (Geneva, 1885), §§454–455 (Aragonese version); Hopf, *Griechische Geschichte*, pp. 315ff, 332ff.

25. "Cellui temps l'Empereur avoit moult grant guerre au Levant à les Turcs qui le guerroioient moult asprement et lui tolloient ses chastiaux et son pays, et auxi avet guerre avec le despote de l'Arte et à l'Empereur de Jaguora." *La chronique de Morée*, §601. Cf. *Chronicle of the Morea*, verse 8767. The "Empereur de Jaguora" is the king of Bulgaria (Zagora). The title is very usual among western writers, and Longnon's identification as the "sultan d'Angora" is wrong (§601, n. 1). Asia Minor was indeed suffering from Turkish invasions, and in 1290 Andronicus himself went on a long trip in the area.

The text of the treaty has not survived, but from the text of the *Chronicle of the Morea* it seems that this was a simple cessation of hostilities and that each party was to keep the areas it possessed. The peace lasted for seven years, and although there were some isolated hostilities, prosperity returned to the country. In 1296, the Byzantines, hoping to extend their acquisitions in the Morea, broke the treaty. Florent of Hainaut died in 1297, and Isabeau became princess of Achaia under the suzerainty of Charles II, king of Naples, the son of Charles of Anjou.[26]

Meanwhile, Andronicus' relations with the Despotate of Epirus had deteriorated and a full-scale war broke out in 1292. According to the French version of the *Chronicle of the Morea*, Nicephorus of Epirus had begun hostilities before 1289, and that was one of the reasons the emperor had been forced to make peace with Achaia.[27] In 1292, "30,000 infantry and 14,000 cavalry" under the command of the megas domestikos (Syrgiannes?) came through Thessaly and besieged Janina (Ioannina).[28] Forty or sixty Genoese ships carrying Byzantine soldiers sailed around the Peloponnesus and arrived near Arta.[29] It would seem from these operations that the real objective of the war was the conquest of the despotate, whose two principal cities were besieged. Nicephorus called to his defense Richard, the count of Cephallonia, and Florent of Hainaut. Florent came, but in order to assure his cooperation, Nicephorus had to send his son Thomas to Achaia as a hostage, and to promise to pay the expenses of the prince and his knights.[30]

The Byzantine commander decided to pursue the siege of Janina even after he heard of Florent's arrival. After the first skirmishes, however, he came to believe that the emperor himself, were he there, would prefer to escape rather than be killed. The Byzantine army retreated in haste and confusion through Thessaly and Macedonia; they were "si cortoys," such good knights, that their

26. Miller, *Latins in the Levant*, p. 178; Dölger, *Regesten*, nos. 2137, 2138; Pachymeres, I, 109; *La chronique de Morée*, §602, n. 2, 603–605, 664–679, 721ff, 801ff; *The Chronicle of the Morea*, verses 8700–8775, 8780; Morel-Fatio, *Libro de los Fechos*, §454ff, 471ff; Zakythinos, *Despotat*, I, 52ff, 65ff.

27. *La chronique de Morée*, §601. Miller, *Latins in the Levant*, pp. 178–182, claims that Nicephorus attacked Andronicus because he was insulted by the emperor's refusal to accept his daughter Thamar as wife for Michael IX. Miller does not mention his source, and I have been unable to find anything—apart from conjecture—that supports his theory.

28. *Chronicle of the Morea*, verse 8990; *La chronique de Morée*, §607; Morel-Fatio, *Libro de los Fechos*, §§456–465. The number of Byzantine soldiers is obviously grossly exaggerated. Andronicus II had nothing like 44,000 soldiers—plus those who must have been on the Genoese ships. As a large number of the soldiers are said to have been mercenaries, the given figure becomes even more unlikely. In any case, part of the Byzantine army was in the East with Andronicus himself. Between two and three thousand seems a more acceptable number. The name of the megas domestikos is not given in the source. The one likely candidate seems to be Syrgiannes, a hellenized Cuman chieftain, who married Andronicus' first cousin, Eugenia, in 1290: Papadopulos, *Genealogie*, no. 34a; cf. S. Binon, "A propos d'un Prostagma inédit d' Andronic III Paléologue," *BZ*, 38 (1938), 144–146.

29. The Greek version of *The Chronicle of the Morea* gives sixty ships; the French version gives forty.

30. Zakythinos, *Despotat*, I, 62, claims that Florent was urged by Charles II of Naples to help Nicephorus. His source is a letter written on July 1, 1295 and published by Minieri-Riccio, *Saggio di codice diplomatico*, supplement 1 (Naples, 1882), no. 92, p. 95. This letter however, refers to a later attack on Epirus, launched by the "duke of Neopatras" (John I of Thessaly).

haste almost killed their horses.[31] If one is to believe the Greek version of the *Chronicle of the Morea*, the inhabitants of Janina had no special love for the emperor and his men, and they hastened to inform Nicephorus of the flight of the Byzantine army. Florent decided to pursue the retreating army, if only in order to loot the lands of the Byzantines. He and his followers raided Byzantine territories (which can only have been in southern Macedonia) for two days, collected much booty and took many prisoners.

While Florent was thus engaged, the Byzantine soldiers disembarked from the Genoese ships, plundered much of the area around Arta, and planned to besiege the city. When they heard that the other half of the operation had collapsed and that Florent and Nicephorus' army were arriving, they went back the way they had come. The campaign was totally unsuccessful, except for minor looting raids on both sides.

The circumstances of the Epirus campaign demonstrate the inability of the Byzantines to operate at sea without the agreement and help of Genoa. The Byzantine army, increasingly relying on mercenaries, was rapidly becoming inefficient. The megas domestikos had an army composed of Turks and Cumans who heeded their own leaders, and he had little control over them. For this reason he was unable to stop their flight and give Florent the battle he requested in the name of chivalry: "If the army I have from the emperor would obey my will, then I would do what they [Florent and his followers] want," that is, he would fight.[32] The Byzantine army was in urgent need of reform. John Tarchaneiotes tried to carry out this reform a short while later and failed.

On the whole, Andronicus' relations with the two independent Greek states and with the principality of Achaia, whether warlike or peaceful, were not as successful as he might have wished. Janina was not recovered until 1318, when it received extraordinary privileges.[33] Worse still, Epirus resumed friendly relations with the Angevins for a time, and after Nicephorus' death it was in danger of becoming an Angevin dependency. This was partly the result of Andronicus' failure to contract a matrimonial alliance with the despotate of Epirus. At some point, Anne of Epirus tried to arrange a marriage between her beautiful daughter Thamar, and Michael, eldest son of Andronicus II and heir to the Byzantine throne. If the date of these negotiations could be established, both the negotiations themselves and the reasons for their failure might be explained. Unfortunately, the information provided by the major source, Pachymeres, is confusing. He wrote that Anne began these negotiations after Nicephorus' death, because she was afraid that John of Thessaly would try to punish her for her earlier help to the Byzantines and avenge the capture of his son. In return for marrying her daughter into the imperial family, Anne promised Andronicus "to return cheerfully the whole land that belonged to her and to her children, and which would revert to her, as her children's guardian,

31. *La chronique de Morée*, §634.
32. *Chronicle of the Morea*, verses 9981–9987: ὅτι, ἐὰν ἦτο ὁ λαὸς τοῦ βασιλέως, ὅπου ἔχω, εἰς ἐδικόν μου θέλημα, νὰ ἔποικα τὸ κελεύουν.
33. February 1319, Chrysobull for Janina: Miklosich and Müller, *Acta et Diplomata*, V, 77–84.

for this land belonged of old to the Romans."[34] Pachymeres claims that the negotiations failed, because Michael and Thamar were related to the sixth degree—surely a mere pretext.[35]

The difficulty with this passage from Pachymeres lies in the fact that Nicephorus' death is usually placed in 1295, by which date both Michael and Thamar were already married. Pachymeres, however, discusses the Epirus marriage plans in a context that would place them, as well as the death of Nicephorus, in 1294, when the two young people were still single.[36] One's first impulse would be to dismiss Pachymeres' date as totally wrong, and place the negotiations before 1288, by which time Andronicus II had begun to entertain other proposals for his son. So long as the question is open, it may be more attractive to believe that Pachymeres dated the discussions correctly (1294), but wrongly thought that Nicephorus was dead at the time they took place. If this is so, Anne acted in direct opposition to her husband's plans. On June 1, 1291, Charles II, king of Naples, informed the prince of Achaia, Florent, that he and his council were discussing a possible marriage between Thamar and one of his own sons, Robert. Charles also wrote that he preferred Thamar to marry not Robert, who was his eldest son, but another of his children, Philip of Taranto. On July 1, 1291, Charles sent to Nicephorus an emissary, Peter de Insula, to continue the discussions.[37] Thamar did marry Philip of Taranto in September 1294, and her dowry then was "not few of the lands and cities [of Epirus]." She received Lepanto, Agrinion (Vrachori), Angelocastro, and Vodonitza. In the marriage settlement, it was stipulated that on Nicephorus' death Thamar's brother Thomas would become a vassal of Philip. If Thomas also died, Philip was to take over the despotate in his own name.[38]

Anne of Epirus may have begun her discussions with Andronicus in 1294, right in the midst of her husband's discussions with the Angevins, in an effort to forestall Thamar's marriage to Philip of Taranto and save the despotate from possibly falling into the hands of the Angevins. This idea is supported by the text of Anne's suggestions to Andronicus, as reported by Pachymeres. She promised to return the despotate to its natural lord, and made no mention of lands which had been alienated or promised to the Angevins. Surely she would have done this after September 1294. In any case, her plans failed for many

---

34. Pachymeres, II, 201–202: καὶ πᾶσαν χώραν καὶ ἑαυτὴν καὶ παῖδα ὡς ἀρχαῖα ἐλλείμματα Ῥωμαῖδος ἐγχειρίζειν χαίρουσαν ὡς εἰ καὶ αὐτὴ ἐπ᾿ ἐκείνοις τόσα λαβεῖν ἔμελλε.

35. R. Guilland, "Les noces plurales à Byzance," *Études byzantines* (Paris, 1959), pp. 259–260.

36. Pachymeres' passage follows his discussion of Michael IX's coronation ceremonies, May 21, 1294, and he seems to place the two events close to each other. The difficulty of establishing a correct date for the negotiations with Anne is compounded by modern historians' incorrect interpretations of Pachymeres. Hopf, for unknown reasons, claims that Pachymeres wrote that Nicephorus died in 1290: Hopf, *Griech. Gesch.*, p. 334.

37. Minieri-Riccio, *Saggio di codice diplomatico*, supplement 1, 56–57, no. 54, p. 65; C. Minieri-Riccio, *Della dominazione Angioina nel reame di Sicilia* (Naples, 1876), pp. 7–8.

38. Pachymeres, II, 202; Hopf, *Chroniques gréco-romanes*, p. 529. J. A. C. Buchon, *Recherches historiques sur la principauté française de Morée*, I, 320–324; *La chronique de Morée*, §658; C. Minieri-Riccio, *Saggio di codice diplomatico*, supplement 1, nos. 60 (February 1294), pp. 69–72, 69 (July 1294); Hopf, *Griech. Gesch.*, pp. 336–337.

reasons. Andronicus' attitude was probably negative. He desired the return of Epirus to obedience to him, but in 1294 he was in the midst of very serious negotiations to marry Michael IX to Catherine of Courtenay, the Latin heiress to the title of emperor of Constantinople.[39] In the context of the Palaeologan matrimonial policies, Catherine was a much more desirable bride than Thamar.

Thamar's marriage to Philip of Taranto created a dangerous diplomatic situation in western Greece. It was the more disquieting because in 1294, shortly before his marriage, Philip of Taranto received from his father all the Angevin claims in Greece, that is, the suzerainty of Achaia, Athens, Albania, Thessaly, and Corfu with its dependencies.[40] This unpleasant situation was somewhat mitigated by Anne's unwillingness to fulfill her husband's treaties. When Nicephorus died (1295), Charles II sent ambassadors to demand either homage from Thomas or the cession of the despotate to Philip. Anne replied that Nicephorus did not have the right to disinherit his own son, treaties notwithstanding. Thomas' natural overlord was the Byzantine emperor. He, Thomas, must hold his lands from Constantinople, and if he paid homage to Philip he would be giving his "oath against his natural seigneur" ("serement contre son naturel seignor"). As a result, Philip of Taranto attacked Epirus.[41]

Anne of Epirus enunciated an interesting concept of the connection between the Greek splinter states and the Byzantine emperor. Admittedly, she was addressing herself to westerners, and thus may have deliberately adopted the use of terms which westerners would best understand. Yet her offer to Andronicus, to return to him her lands "for they belong of old to the Romans" shows that even when she spoke to Byzantines she tended to think in terms of feudal relationships. She and her children regarded themselves as holding their lands from the emperor—presumably, not through any formal feudal investiture but by reason of common nationality and of the original sovereignty of the emperor of Constantinople in these regions. Feudal concepts were even more prevalent in Thessaly, which, on the death of John II Angelos in 1318, reverted to the empire because it was an "old fief" of the emperors. These developments, taking place outside the empire proper, influenced the emperor as well. Andronicus declined to create fiefs when he did not need to do so.[42] In practice, however, he did not insist on governing in person when he could; he often delegated his authority and real sovereignty to feudal lords or to communities.

Western Claims to Byzantium

So long as the western powers were not reconciled to the loss of Constantinople, the Byzantines had much to fear from a counterattack by the West. Traditionally, the Byzantines preferred diplomacy to war. In this case, diplomatic

39. On the negotiations for Michael's marriage to Catherine of Courtenay, which opened in the summer of 1288, see below, "Western Claims to Byzantium," in Chapter II.

40. J. A. C. Buchon, *Nouvelles recherches historiques sur la principauté française de Morée* (Paris, 1843), pp. 407–409; Miller, *Latins in the Levant*, pp. 182–185.

41. *La chronique de Morée*, §974ff; Charles Du Fresne Du Cange, *Histoire de Constantinople sous les empereurs françois*, ed. J. A. C. Buchon, (Paris, 1826), II, 32–34; Górka, *Descriptio*, pp. 16–17.

42. Gregoras, I, 233–235.

action could and did take two forms. One was to prevent or foil any attempts against the empire, whether by winning away one of the allies, as Michael VIII had done at the council of Lyons; or by stirring up opposition to the main enemy, as he had done before the Sicilian Vespers. The other was to absorb all legitimate or semilegitimate claims to the Byzantine throne by uniting the imperial family by marriage to the various pretenders. Andronicus II's marriage to Yolanda-Irene of Montferrat and his effort to marry Michael IX to Catherine of Courtenay, as well as the negotiations for uniting the future Andronicus III to Catherine of Valois all fell within the last category. This dynastic solution to the diplomatic problem was initiated by Michael VIII and practiced by Andronicus II. It is one of the few threads of continuity that ran through the policies of both men.

When Andronicus II's first wife, Anne of Hungary, died in 1281, the young emperor, distressed though he was, became once again an eligible bridegroom and as such a precious instrument of Byzantine diplomacy. Michael VIII used his son's eligibility to strengthen his anti-Angevin alliances. The strongest western opponent of the ambitious Charles of Anjou was King Peter III of Aragon. Aragon, expanding on land and in the seas, had come into conflict with the French royal house in Spain itself. In Sicily, the Aragonese royal house had a strong claim which conflicted with that of the Angevins: Peter III was married to Constance, daughter of Manfred of Sicily, who, after Manfred's death (1266), was the legitimate heiress of Sicily. To this legal claim was added the practical consideration of the advantages of occupying Sicily. The kings of Aragon were overlords of the island of Majorca, and Peter III had established a protectorate over Tunis. In this Aragonese expansion in the western Mediterranean, Sicily, with its unique strategic position, would surely be next. Since the Angevins ruled Sicily, it was good diplomacy and good sense for the Aragonese and the Byzantines to get together.

Some time in 1281, Michael VIII initiated negotiations with Peter of Aragon for the marriage of Peter's daughter to the co-Emperor Andronicus II. Andronicus pursued the negotiations after his father's death. Queen Constance was more eager than her husband to expedite this marriage. She needed money for the completion of a fleet against the Angevins and, on the advice of John of Procida, who was the most important go-between in the Byzantine-Aragonese negotiations, she considered a Byzantine alliance the best way to get funds.[43] On the other hand, Peter III was somewhat reticent: an alliance with the schismatic Byzantines would jeopardize almost irretrievably his relationship with the papacy. He had been excommunicated in 1282 by Pope Martin IV, but excommunications imposed for political reasons could for

43. Runciman, *Sicilian Vespers*, pp. 245–246; F. Cognasso, "Una crisobolla di Michele IX Paleologo per Teodoro I di Monferrato," *Studi Bizantini*, 2 (1927), 39–47; *De rebus regni Siciliae documenti inediti, 1282–1283*, ser. 1 (Palermo, 1882), V, 4–5, 433–436. This marriage was part of the treaty between Michael VIII and Peter of Aragon in 1281: Dölger, *Regesten*, no. 2059. Cf. Wieruszowski, "Conjuraciones." C. Carucci, *La guerra del Vespro Siciliano nella frontiera del principato* (Subiaco, 1934), p. 122; Steven Runciman, "Thessalonica and the Monferrat Inheritance," Γρηγόριος ὁ Παλαμᾶς 42 (1959), 30.

political reasons be lifted. It would be quite another matter if he contracted a marriage alliance with an emperor like Andronicus, a supporter of Orthodoxy, a man who had just made it perfectly clear that he would not be reconciled to the Catholic church.[44] In a letter to John of Procida, Peter wrote: "especially at this time, when the Greeks are in such a position with the church, we will not consent in any way to making with them any family alliance, especially one concerning our daughter."[45] Michael VIII could probably have arranged such an alliance; Andronicus' religious policy made the arrangement impossible.

Andronicus, still following his father's policy, next approached King Alfonso X of Castile, a somewhat less staunch opponent of the Angevins.[46] Alfonso sent to Byzantium not a daughter of his own, but his granddaughter Yolanda of Montferrat, the child of Marquis William VII who was an important member of the anti-Angevin coalition. Since the pope had forbidden marriages between Greeks and Catholics, Alfonso's behavior seemed like an anti-papal move to Byzantine observers.[47] In fact, the alliance between the houses of the Palaeologi and Montferrat was of double advantage to Byzantium. First, Michael VIII had been concerned with strengthening his connections with the powers opposing Charles of Anjou, and Montferrat was such a power. Even after the Sicilian Vespers Michael continued this policy, and his son followed it as long as he could. The proof is that he sent his father-in-law some men to help him in his war against the Angevins (1284). Second, the marquis of Montferrat considered himself the natural heir of the "kingdom of Thessalonica," given to Boniface of Montferrat at the time of the fourth crusade.[48] Yolanda, who was renamed Irene at the time of her marriage, received the kingdom as her dowry because her father "had no useful benefit from the kingdom of Thessalonica

44. Runciman, *Sicilian Vespers*, pp. 245–246; Cartellieri, *Peter von Aragon*; cf. Gregoras, I, 167.

45. *Documenti Siciliae*, p. 434: "nos maxime isto tempore quo Greci sunt taliter cum ecclesia nullo modo consentiremus ad faciendum cum eis de filia nostra precipué aliquam parentelam" (July 29, 1283). In spite of this refusal, Peter did not become actively hostile to the Byzantines for some time. In February 1284, he sent a letter to Andronicus' ambassadors, who had been detained because of poor weather, urging them to come to him in Barcelona, and saying that he longed to hear the emperor's message: I. Carini, *Gli archivi e le biblioteche di Spagna in rapporto alla storia d'Italia in generale e di Sicilia in particolare*, II (Palermo, 1884), 55.

46. In 1281, Alfonso X of Castile revived an earlier effort (1261) to negotiate a marriage between Philip of Courtenay, son of Baldwin II and, since 1275, titular emperor of Constantinople, and Alfonso's daughter, Berenguela. Alfonso's son Sancho was to marry a daughter of Charles of Anjou. This would bring Castile into the Angevin camp. Peter III of Aragon consented, but the marriage did not take place, and Philip died in 1283. See R. L. Wolff, "Mortgage and Redemption," pp. 64–71, 73–74.

47. Gregoras, I, 168; Pachymeres, II, 87–88; Cognasso, "Crisobolla di Michele IX Paleologo," p. 39. On the marriage, see *Annales Veronenses de Romano*, ed. C. Cipolla, in *Antiche Cronache Veronesi*, I (Venice, 1890), 428 (hereafter, *Annales Veronenses*); Salimbene, *Chronicon*, p. 542; *Annales Placentini Ghibellini*, in *M.G.H. Ss*, XVIII (1863), 578; *Memoriale Potestatum Regiensium*, in Muratori, *RIS*, VIII (Milan, 1726), cols. 1164–1165. On William of Montferrat, see Bozzola, "Un capitano di guerra," pp. 386ff; A. Bozzola, "Guglielmo VII di Monferrato e Carlo I," *Archivio Storico per le province napoletane*, 36 (1911), 289–328, 451–474; 37 (1912), 1–28.

48. *Memoriale Pot. Reg.*, cols. 1164–1165; *Annales Veronenses*, p. 428; F. Cognasso, "Partiti politici e lotte dinastiche in Bisanzio," *Mem. R. Acc. Scienze* (Turin, 1912), p. 220; R. L. Wolff, "The Fourth Crusade" in K. M. Setton, R. L. Wolff, H. W. Hazard, eds., *A History of the Crusades*, II, (Philadelphia, 1962), 165.

because of the power of the Greeks."[49] As far as the West was concerned, the rights of the house of Montferrat to Thessalonica were by no means unchallenged. The Latin kings of Thessalonica were vassals of the Latin emperor of Constantinople, who thought he could grant the kingdom to others if he so chose. Thus, after 1266, the deposed Emperor Baldwin II and his son, Philip of Courtenay, conferred the titles to the kingdom of Thessalonica on various westerners who might help them in their efforts to recover Constantinople.[50]

The Byzantines, however, accepted the pretensions of the house of Montferrat and of no one else. Perhaps they did so because these rights had originated with the gift of a Byzantine emperor, Manuel I, who had given Thessalonica in pronoia to Renier of Montferrat, Boniface's brother (ca. 1180).[51] On his marriage to Yolanda (1284), Andronicus now paid the marquis some money "for the revenues which he [Andronicus] and his father had received from the kingdom of Thessalonica which belonged . . . to the Marquis."[52] He also promised to keep in Lombardy, during his father-in-law's lifetime, five hundred soldiers to help William VII in his Italian wars.[53] The fact that only the western sources mention that Andronicus recognized the Montferrat rights to Thessalonica might make this testimony suspect. But the emperor's payment indicates that he attributed some legitimacy to William's claims to the kingdom. Later on, after Irene's death, Andronicus II and Michael IX gave her two surviving sons, Demetrius and Theodore, money and lands which seem to have been the equivalent of part of her dowry of Thessalonica.[54]

Andronicus II's Montferrat marriage and his promise to subsidize his father-in-law's Italian wars may have been used later as an excuse for an attack on his empire. In the summer of 1292, Roger de Lluria, the Sicilian admiral of the Aragonese fleet, attacked with thirty galleys the islands of Lesbos, Lemnos, Santorin, Tenos, Andros, Myconos, and Chios, where he took a number of prisoners and two galley-loads of mastic. On the way back to Sicily he attacked the Morea as well. Plunder was clearly the reason for the expedi-

---

49. "Propter Grecorum dominium de regno Thessalonicae nullam utilitatem haberet,": *Memoriale Pot. Reg.*, col. 1165; cf. Benvenuto di San Giorgio, *Historia Montis Ferrati*, in Muratori, *RIS*, XXIII (Milan, 1733), 576. The terms used here reflect feudal terminology. The meaning, in feudal terms, would be that since the Greeks acquired the *dominium eminens* in Thessalonica, the marquis of Montferrat was deprived of his *dominium utile*.

50. Dom Plancher, *Histoire générale et particulière de Bourgogne*, II (Dijon, 1741), 33; O. Tafrali, *Thessalonique des origines jusqu'au XIVe siècle* (Paris, 1917), pp. 243–246; J. A. C. Buchon, *Recherches et matériaux pour servir à une histoire de la domination française en Grèce* (Paris, 1840), I, 28; Buchon, *Recherches Historiques*, I, 342; A. Meliarakes, Ἱστορία τοῦ Βασιλείου τῆς Νικαίας καὶ τοῦ Δασποτάτου τῆς Ἠπείρου, 1204–1261 (Athens, 1898), p. 523; Du Cange, *Histoire de Constantinople*, pp. 179, 183, and *Chartes*, nos. 21, 22. On Philip of Courtenay, see Wolff, "Mortgage and Redemption."

51. Wolff, "Fourth Crusade," p. 165 and notes 35, 36.

52. *Annales Veronenses*, p. 428. The money involved amounted to 6,000 livres génois. In 1281 one hyperpyron was equivalent to 11.5 sous of the silver Genoese pound (Zakythinos, *Crise*, p. 26).

53. *Memoriale Pot. Reg.*, cols. 1164–1165. Salimbene, *Chronicon*, p. 542, says that Andronicus paid the money he promised and that he sent the men whom William of Montferrat used in his Italian wars.

54. Cognasso, "Crisobolla," pp. 44–47; Gregoras, I, 240; Benvenuto di San Giorgio, *Historia Montis Ferrati*, p. 429; Thomas and Predelli, *Diplomatarium Veneto-Levantinum*, I, 117, 119.

tion.[55] Part of the money he realized from the sale of the mastic—2,000 ounces of gold—was requisitioned by James II, king of Aragon.[56] Andronicus II retaliated by confiscating the merchandise of Catalan merchants who traded in the empire, and James II used some of Lluria's spoils to compensate the victims of the Byzantine retaliation.[57]

Lluria's stated reasons for the attack are interesting, and have been taken to refer to the marriage of Andronicus II to Yolanda. Lluria told Marino Sanudo Torsello the Elder that he had attacked the lands of the emperor "because the emperor had promised to give the king of Aragon 60,000 hyperpyra every year until the end of the war, and because the said king of Aragon claimed that he should have from the said emperor 60,000 ounces of gold for a certain lady of the kingdom of Sicily, who had been married to the emperor who was then reigning."[58] This is a very confused account of events and agreements. The first part refers to one of two agreements, that of Michael VIII with Peter of Aragon,[59] or Andronicus' promise of help to William VII of Montferrat. The second part has been taken by Hopf to refer to the marriage of Andronicus II to Irene of Montferrat, erroneously described as "una certa Madonna del Regno di Sicilia." Unless "Regno di Sicilia" is considered as a faulty reference to the "Regno di Salonica,"[60] the connection is very tenuous. It seems much more likely that Lluria, and Sanudo, were referring to Constance, the illegitimate daughter of Frederick II of Hohenstaufen, and therefore a Sicilian. She had married John III Vatatzes (1222–1254), and in her widowhood had sought refuge at the court of James II of Aragon. In 1306 she transferred to James II her various rights to the Romania (the Byzantine Empire). These consisted of her dowry, jewels, money, and some lands in Asia Minor, with an annual rent of 30,000 hyperpyra.[61]

The interest of Roger de Lluria's statement lies more in its implications than in the statement itself. The emperor's marriage to Yolanda is not expressly mentioned. But the statement that Andronicus had promised the king of Aragon money for the Italian war may go back to Andronicus' promise to

55. *La chronique de Morée*, §§755, 758: "pour gaagnier par aventure"; Morel-Fatio, *Libro de los Fechos*, §§483–505; Muntaner, *Cronica Catalana*, chaps. cxvii, cxxxix.

56. H. Finke, *Acta Aragonensia*, I (Leipzig and Berlin, 1908), no. 6, pp. 10–11. James's letter to the Infante Frederick, incorporated in a note to document no. 6, and dated April, 1293, refers to the mastic "nuper per eum [Roger] in Romanie partibus acquisite." This indicates that the expedition took place in 1292, probably late in the summer or early in the fall (it is unlikely that Roger sailed East in the early spring of 1293).

57. A. Rubió y Lluch, *Diplomatari de l'Orient Català, 1302–1409* (Barcelona, 1947), no. 11, p. 11, n. 2 (documents of May 2, 1293 and February 27, 1294).

58. Sanudo, *Istoria*, p. 133: "perche il . . . Imperatore avea promesso dar al Rè d'Aragona ogn'anno 60 mila Lipperi insino a guerra finita, e perche anco il detto Rè d'Aragona pretendeva aver dal detto Imperatore 60 mila onze d'oro per una certa Madonna del Regno di Sicilia, ch'era stata maritata all'Imperatore, che allora regnava."

59. It is so taken by Geanakoplos, *Michael Palaeologus*, p. 356 and n. 68a.

60. This was suggested to me by Professor R. L. Wolff. Such a faulty reference would not be unique in Sanudo's account. However, since the whole passage is concerned with Aragon and, secondarily, with Sicily, it seems more probable that Sanudo *was* talking about a Sicilian lady. For Hopf's view, see Sanudo, *Istoria*, p. 133, n. 5.

61. See below, Chapter VI, n. 75 for bibliographical note and details.

William VII; if so, Lluria correctly placed Andronicus' marriage to Yolanda within the context of the war against Charles of Anjou.

The second marriage of Andronicus II was a diplomatic triumph, fulfilling the two purposes of Palaeologan matrimonial policy: strengthening the anti-Angevin alliance and reducing the western claims to portions of the Byzantine Empire. The marriage was celebrated in 1284, when Andronicus was twenty-four or twenty-five years old, and Yolanda-Irene only eleven.[62] She was not crowned empress until after she had her first son, in 1288–June 1289.[63] Surprisingly, her marriage at such a tender age did not convert her into a true Byzantine. She had feudal ideas of government, and managed to create endless trouble for her husband later in life. Thessalonica she considered her own city, and in 1303 she repaired there in a huff after a series of disagreements with her husband. She nourished great ambitions for her children and treated poorly their elder half-brother Michael IX. She tried to persuade Andronicus to divide the empire into fiefs for her sons. As Gregoras wrote, "What is worse, she wanted each of her sons to rule the cities and villages of the Romans not by monarchical government, as had been the custom among the Romans from the beginning, but sharing them out in the Latin way . . . [But] the emperor said that it was impossible for him to disrupt the imperial political system, which has been hallowed and confirmed by the passage of many years."[64] At Andronicus' refusal, she turned her energies towards contracting good marriages for her children, often acting contrary to her husband's own political and dynastic plans.

Andronicus' marriage to Yolanda-Irene may in itself indicate a shift in the Byzantine concept of sovereignty. For by accepting the kingdom of Thessalonica from his father-in-law, Andronicus II accepted—no doubt for reasons of political expediency—the principle that sovereignty over the entire Byzantine Empire did not necessarily reside with the emperor at Constantinople. As an isolated example this does not prove much. Taken along with the examples already cited and with the privileges Andronicus granted to parts of his empire, it serves as one more indication of the influence of western ideas on the political practice of the Byzantines. Western concepts, such as that of feudal suzerainty, were used when the Byzantine emperors could not recover what they considered their rightful heritage in any other way.

As part of his larger plan to clarify the diplomatic position of Byzantium in relation to the West, Andronicus II initiated in 1288 negotiations for the possible marriage of his eldest son, Michael, then eleven years old, to the titular

---

62. Salimbene, *Chronicon*, p. 542; *Memoriale Pot. Reg.*, cols. 1164–1165, Miller, *Latins in the Levant*, p. 175; Cognasso, "Crisobolla," p. 40 and n. 7. Gregoras (I, 168), says that Andronicus was twenty-three years old when the marriage took place. This would make the date 1282 or 1283, which seems to contradict the rest of the evidence. J. Strzygowski, *BZ*, 10 (1901), 546–567, has published an epithalamium which may refer to this marriage. (But, see Papademetriou, «Ὁ ἐπιθαλάμιος ᾽Ανδρονίκου Β΄ τοῦ Παλαιολόγου,» *BZ*, 11, (1902), 452, 460.

63. Pachymeres, II, 87; Cognasso, "Crisobolla," p. 41 and n. 10.

64. Gregoras, I, 233–235: τὸ δὲ καινότερον ὅτι οὐ μοναρχίας τρόπῳ κατὰ τὴν ἐπικρατήσασαν ῾Ρωμαίοις ἀρχῆθεν συνήθειαν, ἀλλὰ τρόπον Λατινικὸν διανειμαμένους τὰς ῾Ρωμαίων πόλεις καὶ χώρας ἄρχειν κατὰ μέρη· τοῦ δὲ βασιλέως ἀδύνατον εἶναι λέγοντος παραλύειν τὰ διὰ πολλῶν ἤδη τῶν χρόνων κυρωθέντα τε καὶ βεβαιωθέντα βασιλικὰ νόμιμα.

empress of Constantinople, Catherine of Courtenay. Marriages, if productive of issue, assured the reversion of titles; treaties such as that with Venice, dealt with questions of titles, rights, and possessions. Catherine of Courtenay had inherited the rights to the crown of Constantinople from her father, Philip of Courtenay, who had married Béatrix of Anjou and who had died in 1283. Catherine was certainly the most desirable bride for Michael, and her dowry would have been a great diplomatic success for the Byzantines. But the obstacles to such a marriage were formidable indeed. The Byzantines were not the only ones to see what a useful bride Catherine would make: Aragon and France were soon to compete for her favors, and her dowry. The king of France, Philip IV, and the pope, Nicholas IV, were on friendly terms, and it is difficult to imagine that Catherine could have been married to Michael without the consent of the king of France, which was far from certain. And, of course, Andronicus' renunciation of the union of the churches in itself created almost insuperable difficulties. It is hardly surprising, therefore, that these negotiations failed. Much more surprising is the fact that they took place at all, and that for a while they seemed to have a possibility of success. Strangest of all is that the western powers which most desired the marriage were the Angevins of Naples and the pope, Nicholas IV. This was quite a reversal of the situation at the time of the death of Michael VIII, and it merits some discussion and analysis.

In the summer of 1288 Andronicus II sent an embassy to Robert of Artois, then regent of Naples, to ask for the hand of his great-niece, Catherine of Courtenay.[65] Perhaps the ambassadors were also to meet the pope; in any case, Nicholas IV was told of the negotiations and he instructed Robert not to proceed without asking the advice of Philip IV of France. Nicholas seemed willing to further this marriage, which he took to be the beginning of Andronicus' return to the true faith.[66] Nevertheless, he asked Robert of Artois to proceed very cautiously and, should the king of France prove agreeable, to seek the pope's advice once more before giving the Byzantines any final answer.[67] The Byzantine envoys themselves seem to have made the journey to France. On their return in 1290, Nicholas IV wrote a very friendly letter to Andronicus, apologizing for not having earlier announced his accession and urging that negotiations be further pursued.[68] From the beginning, therefore,

---

65. Dölger, *Regesten*, IV, no. 2129; E. Langlois, *Les registres de Nicholas IV*, I (Paris, 1905), no. 594; Raynaldus, *Annales Eccl.*, 1288, §18; Norden, *Papsttum und Byzanz*, pp. 648ff; Zakythinos, *Despotat*, I, 60ff; C. Marinescu, "Tentatives de mariage de deux fils d'Andronic II Paléologue avec des princesses latines," *Revue historique du sud-est Européen*, 1 (1924), 139–143; G. I. Brătianu, "Notes sur le projet de mariage entre l'empereur Michel IX Paléologue et Catherine de Courtenay," *Revue historique du sud-est Européen*, 1 (1924), 59–63. Dade's discussion of these negotiations is inadequate: *Versuche*, pp. 68–71. According to Pachymeres, (II, 153), one of the most active proponents of the marriage was the queen of Naples, Mary of Hungary, wife of Charles II of Naples (May 29, 1289–1309). Mary was an aunt by marriage of both Michael and Catherine. She was a sister of Michael's mother, the deceased Anne of Hungary; and her husband, Charles II, was the brother of Catherine's mother, Béatrix of Anjou.

66. E. Langlois, *Registres de Nicholas IV*, I, nos. 594, 7242. On Robert of Artois, see R. Caggese, *Roberto d'Angiò e i suoi tempi* 2 vols. (Florence, 1922, 1930). Also, G. M. Monti, *Da Carlo I a Roberto di Angiò: Richerche e documenti* (Trani, 1936).

67. Raynaldus, *Annales Eccl.*, 1288, §18.

68. E. Langlois, *Registres de Nicholas IV*, I, no. 7242 (letter to Andronicus II, January 13, 1290).

the Byzantines had to obtain the consent of the pope, the king of Naples, and the king of France, if the marriage were to take place.

In the summer of 1291 another Byzantine embassy was sent to Robert of Artois with full powers to enter into discussions about the marriage. For the regent of Naples, the purpose of the marriage remained the same as in 1288: to secure between the Angevins and the Byzantines "perpetual peace and friendship."[69] Because he was needed in Calabria, Robert was unable to talk in person to the ambassadors, but he asked Sparano da Bari, the logothete of Sicily, to do so on his behalf. In the same year, Andronicus II received ambassadors who had come from Naples to see Michael and to continue the talks. They professed themselves pleased with the reports of Michael's behavior in Constantinople.[70] The Greek historians claimed that the Italians were the ones to suggest—and even to request—the marriage, although Pachymeres admitted that the "returns" would be very good and worthy of an emperor. Andronicus II and his council were certainly very eager.

Ambassadors were exchanged again in the spring of 1294. The Italian embassy, headed by "Sir Petrus," attended the coronation of young Michael on May 21, 1294.[71] In the spring of the same year, Andronicus had sent to Naples the monk Sophonias to deal with the pope and the king of Naples, Charles II. These embassies are somewhat more interesting than the previous ones. The embassy of Sophonias points up once again the need for the Byzantines to reconcile themselves with the papacy before the marriage negotiations could be concluded. According to Pachymeres, Sophonias was sent as a personal imperial emissary to the pope because Andronicus did not want to write the pope a letter. Writing letters apparently raised an issue of protocol which had best be avoided: "in such letters it would have been necessary to address the pope as 'most Holy,' which would have been the greatest crime in the estimation of those secure in the [Orthodox] faith."[72] The question of ecclesiastical protocol thus was sidestepped through a delicate diplomatic maneuver. Nor is it incidental that Sophonias was a monk, a wise and reasonable one, as Pachymeres characterized him: such a man might more easily than a layman deal with the probable overtures of the papacy.

69. Brătianu, "Notes sur le projet de mariage," appendix, p. 63 (June 12, 1291): "Pacis et amicicie perpetuam firmitatem."

70. Pachymeres, II, 153–154; Gregoras, I, 193. Hopf, *Griechische Geschichte*, p. 334, dates the embassy September 22, 1291, names the ambassadors as Petrus de Surie and Bertrand de Boccamaria, and claims that they stayed in Constantinople for four years. In fact, Hopf confuses two separate embassies: see below, Chapter II.

71. There is some debate on the date of the coronation of Michael IX. Pia Schmidt ("Zur Chronologie von Pachymeres, Andronikos L. II-VII," *BZ* 51 (1958), 83) dates it 1295. Her arguments for this are very tenuous, and Verpeaux has presented a much more convincing case for the date 1294: J. Verpeaux, "Notes chronologiques," *REB.*, 18 (1959), 168–174. Schmidt also claims that this Italian embassy appeared in the spring of 1295. But this is quite unreasonable, for Catherine went to France in the summer of 1294, and negotiations stopped. The Short Chronicle of the Moscow Codex also gives the date 1294: Loenertz, "La chronique brève de 1352," 333, no. 10.

72. Pachymeres, II, 202; Dölger, *Regesten*, IV, no. 2156a. Dade does not mention this embassy, and Pia Schmidt places it at the end of 1294. It is impossible to accept this dating: Pachymeres quite clearly links the embassy to the preparations for the coronation of Michael IX. The embassy, therefore, must have been sent sometime before May 21, 1294, probably in the spring of that year.

Sophonias was unsuccessful, but he lingered on in the West, returning to Constantinople in March 1296, over a year after Michael IX's marriage to Rita-Maria of Armenia. While he was in Italy, Sophonias came into contact with at least one Catholic Greek, Simon Constantinopolitanus, actually a Cretan who had gone to Rome and become a member of the Dominican Order. At some point, after 1304, Simon was sent by the pope to Byzantium to discuss the church union with the Greek clergy. He then wrote a letter to Sophonias, presenting the Latin beliefs on the procession of the Holy Spirit.[73]

The Italian embassy of 1294 gives insight into the reasons for the reversal of Angevin policy, and for the Angevins' desire to contract a marriage alliance with the Byzantines. The "Sir Petrus" who led the embassy has been variously identified. D. A. Zakythinos identified him, probably correctly, with Petrus de Insula who had been sent from Naples to Epirus in 1291 to negotiate the marriage of Thamar to one of the sons of Charles II of Naples.[74] The Angevins, like the Byzantines, were pursuing their eastern aims through diplomacy since war was, at the moment, impossible. The *Chronicle of the Morea* relates that, in 1294, Charles II promised Andronicus to give him "good letters and documents from the pope of Rome and the king of France and from himself, giving him [Andronicus] all the rights and claims which they had or might have in the empire of Constantinople."[75] The *Chronicle* is not the most reliable of sources, but in this case the information seems plausible. The Angevins were still at war with the Aragonese in Sicily and Italy, and it is possible that they desired an accommodation with Byzantium.

The dowry they promised to Michael, then, included not only the inheritance of Catherine of Courtenay—the western titles to Constantinople—but also the solemn promise of all the interested parties to respect this settlement. This is precisely the sort of concession Andronicus II desired, and for a moment his aims coincided with those of the Angevins. Charles II, less warlike than his father, Charles of Anjou, and already beset with the Italian wars, may well have decided to pursue a less intransigent policy in the East. The Angevin embassies of 1291 and 1294 coincided with Angevin efforts to extend their control over Epirus, again through marriage. Both the Epirus and the projected Constantinopolitan marriage may be seen as integral parts of an Angevin policy

73. Hopf, *Griechische Geschichte*, p. 338. The letter began, "I recall that when your great holiness was sent by the most great Emperor . . ." (μέμνημαι ὡς ὅτε ἡ μεγάλη ἁγιωσύνη σου ἀπέσταλτο παρὰ καὶ τρισμεγίστου βασιλέως). This letter has not been published, and so it is impossible to tell whether Simon considered Sophonias as an opponent or a sympathizer of the church union. The only mention of this letter is in Leo Allatius, *De Ecclesiae Occidentalis atque Orientalis perpetua consensione libri tres* (Coloniae Agrippinae, 1648), pp. 774–775. Our Sophonias was probably the same one who produced a rather dull commentary on Aristotle: M. Hayduck, ed., *Commentaria in Aristotelem Graeca*, Accademia Litterarum regia Borussica, XXIII, pt. 1 (Berlin, 1883). On Simon Constantinopolitanus, see also R.-J. Loenertz, O.P., *La Société des Frères Pérégrinants*, I (Institutum Historicum FF. Praedicatorum Romae ad S. Sabinae, Rome, 1937, fasc. VII), pp. 78–79.

74. Zakythinos, *Despotat*, I, 63, n.1. Hopf, *Griechische Geschichte*, p. 334, identifies him as "Petrus de Surie." During the time of Peter's sojourn in Constantinople, Florent of Hainaut sent envoys to protest the seizure of Calamata by the Greeks. Through the mediation of Peter, the city was returned to the Franks. *La chronique de Morée*, §§639–719; Zakythinos, *Despotat*, I, 62–63; Hopf, *Griechische Geschichte*, p. 352.

75. *La chronique de Morée*, §706.

of reconciliation with the empire and expansion in the other parts of Greece. That is not to say that either the Angevins or their greatest source of support, the pope, were once and for all reconciled to the permanence of the Byzantine presence in Constantinople. Even in 1293, in the midst of the marriage negotiations, the pope was considering an invasion of Byzantium. The meaning of the negotiations is rather that the Angevins and the pope were not, at this moment, completely opposed to a settlement with the Byzantines. The fluidity of diplomatic arrangements in the West itself and between Byzantium and various western countries is one of the most important factors of East–West relations in this period.

If the Angevins were to give up their claims to the empire of Constantinople, they doubtless expected some long-term and some immediate benefits. It is not too far-fetched to suggest that in the long run they expected Catherine to influence the policy of her husband: Byzantium would become an ally of the Angevins, and perhaps her charm and her connections might persuade the imperial family to return to the Catholic church. Conversion of the Christians of the East to Catholicism through the persuasion of Catholic wives was a measure which the French crusading propagandist, Pierre Dubois, was to advocate, only a few years afterwards. As for more immediate advantages, the French version of the *Chronicle of the Morea* relates that Andronicus had decided to give Charles II the kingdom of Thessalonica.

Some historians have taken this to mean that Thessalonica was in fact offered to the Angevins in the course of the negotiations.[76] This cannot be correct. To give up Thessalonica, a major and important part of his empire, would nullify for Andronicus the results of his marriage to Yolanda of Montferrat. Beyond that, it would entail abandoning the whole basis of early Palaeologan policy, which was the recovery of all those parts of Asia Minor and the Balkans that had belonged to the empire before 1204. The testimony of the *Chronicle* probably echoes western claims to the kingdom of Thessalonica, and should be rejected as one of the many inaccuracies of the source.

One further inaccuracy of the *Chronicle* should be mentioned here. In describing the marriage negotiations initiated by Andronicus II, the *Chronicle* ascribes to him the following aims: Andronicus feared that Charles II of Naples and Philip IV of France would help Charles of Valois, Philip's brother, to recover his wife's empire; hence Andronicus' eagerness to marry his son to Catherine of Courtenay, and thus forestall the invasion.[77] The inconsistency of this statement is painfully obvious. Charles of Valois married Catherine of Courtenay in 1301, after the Byzantine negotiations had failed; only then did he acquire any claims to his wife's empire. As a piece of factual information, the statement of the *Chronicle* is useless; but it does give the historian occasion to reflect on the attitude of the French royal house toward the marriage negotiations of 1288–1294. Philip IV was very much interested in Catherine's heritage, and eventually managed to acquire it for his family. His opinion must have carried weight at every stage of the negotiations.

76. Ibid., §§710, 718; Dade, *Versuche*, p. 68.
77. *La chronique de Morée*, §709.

The negotiations of 1294 were the last effort to bring about the marriage of Michael IX to Catherine of Courtenay. Their failure has been variously interpreted. Modern historians attribute it to Philip IV and to Boniface VIII. Pachymeres certainly thought that the pope's reluctance to accept the ecclesiastical status quo made further discussions very difficult.[78] But two things seem clear: first, that in principle the avowed, long-term interests of both the papacy and the Angevins were against such an alliance with Byzantium, despite their temporary flirtations with the idea; and second, that the deciding factor in making the alliance impossible was the slow improvement, or hope of improvement, in the relations between the Angevins, the Aragonese, and France.

Catherine of Courtenay had been, since 1293, a pawn in the Sicilian game. In August 1293, James II of Aragon drew up the plan of a treaty to end the war with France which dated back to the "Aragonese crusade" of 1285. In one of the clauses of the proposal, James offered to return Calabria to the kings of Naples, and to return Sicily to the papacy after his death. In exchange, the infante Frederick would marry either the daughter of Charles II of Naples or Catherine of Courtenay. In the second eventuality, he would get the title to Constantinople, plus 50,000 ounces of gold, provided by Charles II, for the recovery of the empire. The pope, the king of Aragon, and Charles II would help Frederick in this enterprise.[79] Thus, less than eleven years after Michael VIII's death, Aragonese policy towards Byzantium suffered a complete reversal. This is the first intimation that the king of Aragon would not oppose, would even condone a western effort to retake Constantinople, so long as it benefited himself or his family. The year 1293 may also be taken as the first appearance of the infante Frederick (later Frederick III of Sicily) as a potential claimant to the Byzantine throne. There would be more dramatic examples of both these developments after the peace of Caltabelotta, which ended the Italian war (1302).

Philip IV of France was eager to get Catherine under his influence, but did not particularly like the settlement offered by James. In the summer of 1294, Catherine went to France, and from then on negotiations for her eventual marriage were handled by Philip IV and not by the Angevins.[80] Philip IV and Pope Boniface VIII disagreed on the matter of Catherine's marriage, as they would on so many other more important issues. Unlike Philip IV, Boniface VIII found James' proposals (repeated in March 1295)[81] quite acceptable. In June 1295 the pope negotiated directly with Frederick, and

---

78. Norden, *Papsttum und Byzanz*, p. 648; Brătianu, "Notes sur le projet de mariage"; Marinescu, "Tentatives de mariage," p. 139.

79. Finke, *Acta Aragonensia*, III, no. 11, pp. 19–20. Cf. Ch.–V Langlois, in Ernest Lavisse, *Histoire de France*, II, pt. 2 (Paris, 1901), 291–292, 113ff. On Frederick, see Antonino de Stefano, *Federico III d'Aragona, Rè di Sicilia, 1296–1337*, (Palermo, 1937); Dade, *Versuche*, pp. 69–70.

80. Norden, *Papsttum und Byzanz*, pp. 648–649. Catherine had promised in May 1294 not to marry without the consent of Charles II: Du Cange and Buchon, *Histoire de Constantinople*, II, 35. On January 14, 1295, Charles II wrote to Andronicus II that he could answer nothing further on the negotiations until Catherine returned under his potestas: Norden, *Papsttum und Byzanz*, p. 649, n. 3.

81. Finke, *Acta Aragonensia*, III, no. 20, pp. 33–42.

increased the inducements. Frederick was now promised 60,000 ounces of gold "and 30,000 ounces per year, for three years, to help conquer the empire of Romania."[82] On June 27, Boniface urged Catherine of Courtenay to consent to this marriage, and on July 13, he asked and advised Philip IV to swear that Catherine would marry the Aragonese prince.[83] His letter to Catherine gives a clear indication of the main preoccupations of the papacy. Boniface VIII wanted the war between Charles II and the Aragonese to end, in part so that the cause of the Holy Lands could be furthered. What better guarantee of such a peace than the marriage of an Angevin princess, Catherine of Courtenay, to an Aragonese prince, Frederick? As a further guarantee of the stability of a settlement of the Italian war, Boniface wanted both the peace treaty and the marriage to be made with the full consent of Philip IV of France. For Catherine, the Aragonese marriage, contracted with French and papal blessing, would provide the best opportunity of recovering her empire and bringing its people back to the Catholic church. The marriage, Boniface said, should take place before September 1, 1295.

Eventually, this plan also failed. Frederick preferred the Sicily he held to the Constantinople he might never see, and another royal house captured the prize of Catherine's dowry. Charles of Valois, brother of Philip IV, had lost his first wife, Margaret, in 1299. In 1301, Philip IV married Charles to Catherine of Courtenay, and the French royal family now inherited the eastern ambitions of the Angevins.[84] One of the papal conditions for allowing the marriage was that Charles of Valois should aid his Angevin relations in the struggle over Sicily; peace had been made between France and Aragon in 1295, but the Italian war continued.[85] Meanwhile, it is not surprising that the Byzantines would look elsewhere for a bride as they did, successfully, in 1294.

Having failed in his effort to marry his heir to the most eligible western princess, Andronicus II tried to find an acceptable bride in the East. The Byzantine historians claim that the initiative came from the kings of Cyprus and Armenia.[86] The two kingdoms were the only remaining Christian states in the East, and were threatened by the expanding power of Egypt. Armenia had been in the gravest danger since 1285. Her main hope lay in her alliance with the Mongols, which was proving increasingly ineffective. Between 1293 and 1298, however, she had a relatively quiet period because the Egyptians were faced with internal problems. In 1294 King Hetoum II married his sister

82. Finke, *Acta Aragonensia*, I, no. 20 (June 8, 1295): "et per III ans per cascun an XXX mil unc. en ayudar de conquere lempero de Romania."

83. A Potthast, *Regesta Pontificum Romanorum*, II (Graz, 1957), nos. 24116, 24117, 24134; Raynaldus, *Annales Eccl.*, 1295, §29; A. Thomas, M. Faucon, and G. Digard, *Les Registres de Boniface VIII* (Paris, 1907), I, no. 874 (text).

84. Du Cange, *Histoire de Constantinople*, (1657), pt. 2, pp. 41–43 (not reproduced in the edition of 1826); J. Delaville le Roulx, *La France en Orient au XIVe siecle*, (Paris, 1886), I, 40–47, 48. Du Cange, *Histoire de Constantinople*, (1657), part I, p. 204, claims that Irene of Montferrat tried to marry her son John to Catherine of Courtenay in 1303. Catherine was already married then. This is omitted in the edition of 1826.

85. Langlois, in Lavisse, *Histoire de France*, II, pt. 2, 292.

86. Pachymeres, II, 202; Gregoras, I, 193.

Isabel to Amalric, the brother of Henry II of Cyprus, presumably to cement the friendship between the two kingdoms.[87]

Fear of Turkish and Egyptian advances, and a vague notion of common action between the Christians of the area may also have been among the reasons Andronicus considered a Cypriot or an Armenian princess for his son. The only condition he seems to have imposed was that no concessions in matters of theology would be made when dealing with Catholic princes. For this reason, he chose his ambassadors rather carefully. The first embassy was headed by the patriarch of Alexandria, Athanasios, who had gained great influence at the court after the abdication in 1293 of Athanasios I of Constantinople. Attacked by pirates, the expedition did not go further than Phocaea.[88]

The second embassy, which left Constantinople in the summer of 1294, included among its members John Glykys and the young Theodore Metochites, both important Byzantine officials.[89] They had been chosen not because of their diplomatic experience, but because they were learned in theology, knew the tenets and doctrines of the Greek faith, and could expound them eloquently and in good Greek. Glykys became patriarch of Constantinople in 1315. The negotiations with Cyprus broke down on just this matter of religion, for the king of Cyprus made papal consent a necessary condition for the marriage.[90]

But the Armenians, although flirting with the Roman church, were not yet members of it. The Byzantine ambassadors returned to Constantinople with both sisters of the Armenian king. Rita, renamed Maria, married Michael IX on January 16, 1295.[91] Theodora, renamed Theophano, was engaged to marry the son of John of Thessaly, but died before she could get to Thessaly. According to Armenian sources, Hetoum himself went to Constantinople for the marriage. It may have been this same marriage that provoked the rebellion in 1296 of his brother Sempad, helped by the Catholicus and Boniface VIII.[92]

---

87. On the Kingdom of Armenia, see Sirarpie der Nersessian, "The Kingdom of Cilician Armenia," in *A History of the Crusades*, ed. Setton, Wolff, and Hazard, II (Philadelphia, 1962), 630–659. On Cyprus, L. de Mas-Latrie, *Histoire de l'île de Chypre sous le règne des princes de la maison de Lusignan*, I (Paris, 1861); Sir G. Hill, *A History of Cyprus*, 4 vols. (Cambridge, Eng., 1940–1952).

88. Pachymeres, II, 203.

89. Dölger, *Regesten*, IV, nos. 2156b, 2157a, reverses the order of the two embassies without apparent reason. Pachymeres is very clear on this point (cf. Verpeaux, "*Notes chronologiques*," p. 173). Pachymeres, II, 203–205; Gregoras, I, 194; Treu, *Dichtungen des Metochites*, A, verses 475ff; 464–465; Ševčenko, *Métochite et Choumnos*, appendix 2; J. Verpeaux, "Le cursus honorum de Théodore Métochite," *REB.*, 18 (1960), 195–198; H. Hunger, "Theodorus Metochites als Vorläufer des Humanismus in Byzanz," *BZ*, 45 (1952), 4ff; R. Guilland, *La correspondance de Nicéphore Grégoras* (Paris, 1927), p. 359. Metochites was then λογοθέτης τῶν ἀγελῶν (logothete of the troops, an honorary title), and Glykys, ἐπὶ τῶν δεήσεων, a judicial office.

90. Pachymeres, II, 205; cf. Gregoras, I, 194.

91. Pachymeres, II, 206; P. Lamma, "Un discorso inedito per l'incoronazione di Michele IX Paleologo," *Aevum*, 29 (1955), 53; J. F. Boissonade, *Anecdota Nova* (Paris, 1844), pp. 14–16. I have adopted Verpeaux's dates both for the embassies and for the marriage: "Notes chronologiques," p. 173. Pia Schmidt ("Chronologie," p. 84), does not make a convincing case for advancing the date of these events by one year.

92. Sirarpie der Nersessian, "Cilician Armenia," p. 657.

Thus ended the long negotiations for the marriage of Michael IX. The original aim of Andronicus' diplomacy, to bring the western claims to Constantinople back into his family and so to legalize his position in western eyes, had failed.

To illustrate the fluidity of the diplomatic situation in the West, another abortive effort at a matrimonial alliance with the Byzantines should be mentioned. This time the initiative certainly came from the West, and was, once more, connected with the continued rivalry of Angevins and Aragonese. On April 3, 1296, Frederick III wrote to his brother James II announcing his coronation as king of Sicily and his intention to hold the island. To get help, he thought of reverting to the traditional Byzantine-Aragonese alliance. He said that there had been talks between himself and Andronicus II on the possibility of marrying his sister Yolanda to Michael IX.[93] Andronicus could not have initiated negotiations since Michael was already married. Since Frederick, on the other hand, had not yet sent an embassy to Constantinople, he must have spoken to some accredited Byzantine who was already in Italy or Sicily. The monk Sophonias, Andronicus' ambassador to Charles II in 1294, was in Italy until the spring of 1296. It is probable that Frederick discussed with him the proposal for a Byzantine-Aragonese marriage. Sophonias' return to Constantinople in March 1296 may well have been connected with these discussions. Frederick also sent to Constantinople Arnald de Ruisacco and one brother Paul to meet Andronicus and continue the negotiations.

Marinescu says that the project failed for unknown reasons, but the reasons are self-evident. For one thing, Frederick's ambassadors left shortly before April 1296, when Michael IX had been married for well over a year. Had he not been married, they might still have failed. At this point Frederick was more of a liability than an asset, and Yolanda could offer nothing to compare with the dowry of Catherine of Courtenay. It does, however, reflect unfavorably on the Byzantine diplomatic services that Robert of Artois knew nothing of Michael's marriage in January 1295,[94] nor Frederick in 1296. This may be partly ascribed to difficult communications; yet if Andronicus was able to send an embassy to Italy in 1294, there is no reason why he could not let the interested parties know when the purpose of the embassy had become obsolete.

---

93. Finke, *Acta Aragonensia*, III, no. 26, pp. 53–55: "verba habita et tractata fuerunt." The Yolanda in question had been mentioned as a possible bride for Andronicus in 1282.

94. Norden, *Papsttum und Byzanz*, p. 649, n.3.

III

Retrenchment and the Turn to Asia Minor, 1282–1296

The Italian Maritime Cities

The European matrimonial negotiations were intended to forestall a European attack on Constantinople by removing the legal pretext for such an attack, and also, to strengthen those forces in Europe that opposed the expansionist policies of the Angevin house. An equally important question was the relations of the empire with the maritime cities of Italy, especially Venice and Genoa. Michael VIII had granted important commercial privileges to both, and Andronicus II had entertained friendly relations with Genoa from the time of his accession to the throne.[1] After the death of Charles of Anjou on January 7, 1285, the only state with which Byzantium was technically at war was Venice. This was formally terminated on Friday, June 15, 1285, when Andronicus II signed at the palace of the Blachernai a ten-year truce with Venice. The treaty was ratified by the doge Giovanni Dandolo in July 1285.[2]

The first mention of efforts to conclude a peace treaty appears on September 16, 1283, and it comes from Venetian sources. Given the fact that official Venetian records for this period are sparse, this date provides only a terminus ante quem; but there is reason to believe that the first mention we find in the sources was, in fact, the first attempt at negotiation. On September 16, 1283, the Venetian Major Council voted on the following proposal: "to see whether we could make . . . a treaty with the Emperor Andronicus." The decision went in favor of the proposal, 166 to 40, with 38 abstentions. On September 18, it was decided to send two ambassadors to Constantinople with a certain commission, which has not been preserved. The ambassadors were to try to make a truce for seven to ten years, whatever seemed possible, and to discuss the question of Venetian prisoners and of reparations for damages done by Byzantines to Venetians. If they had no success in two months, they were to come back. The truce was not to allow either party to make alliances against the other. And, if at all possible, the island of Nigroponte (Euboea) should be included in the cessation of hostilities.[3]

Despite the meager information, the tone of the documents makes it quite certain that the negotiations began on Venetian initiative. This is very im-

---

1. Tafel and Thomas, *Urkunden*, III, no. 368, Treaty with Venice, March 19, 1277 (cf. Miklosich and Müller, *Acta et Diplomata*, III, 84–96); *Liber Jurium*, in *Monumenta Historiae Patriae*, VII (I) (Turin, 1872), document 945; G. Caro, *Genua und die Mächte am Mittelmeer, 1257–1311*, I (Halle, 1895), 196–197, 301–302.

2. Tafel and Thomas, *Urkunden*, III, nos. 378, 379.

3. R. Cessi, *Deliberazioni del maggior consiglio di Venezia*, R. Accademia dei Lincei, Commissione per gli Atti delle Assemblee Costituzionali Italiane, III (Bologna, 1934), 49, nos. 157, 160, 163 (September 23); 50, nos. 164, 165, 167 (September 25); 52, no. 184 (October 14). Summaries of the negotiations are to be found in F. Thiriet, *Délibérations des assemblées vénitiennes concernant la Romanie*, I (Paris, 1966). 45ff. The Venetian treaty of 1277 with Michael VIII had excluded Euboea from the terms of peace (see Tafel and Thomas, *Urkunden*, III, no. 138).

portant, for it argues that the Venetians were losing more than the Byzantines from the continuation of hostilities. It also indicates that hardly eighteen months after the beginning of Charles of Anjou's Italian war, and not even a year after Andronicus II had repudiated the union of the churches, Venice was eager to come to terms with the Byzantines, the great enemies of both Charles of Anjou and the Roman church. The Venetian insistence that neither party should be allowed to make alliances against the other has a strange ring under the circumstances: a similar article had been included in the Venetian treaties of 1265 and 1277 with Michael VIII, and Venice had broken this provision by her alliance with Charles of Anjou.[4] Was she now afraid of an anti-Venetian alliance between Byzantium and Genoa? Was she perhaps already recognizing the decline in Angevin power? On May 18, 1283, the Venetians had written to Charles of Anjou that, given the Sicilian Vespers, and therefore the impossibility of attacking Byzantium, Venice reserved her freedom of action with regard to the empire.[5] Or was Venice, in September 1283, simply trying to give the Byzantines adequate guarantees so that they would agree to sign a truce? As we shall see, the answer lies in the grave inconvenience which Venice incurred because of the hostilities with Byzantium.

Negotiations, once begun, continued slowly. On October 14, 1283, the Venetian ambassadors were still in Venice, were perhaps not yet chosen.[6] The two men who were finally chosen, Andrea Zeno and Marino Morosini, must have reached Constantinople in the spring of 1284: it was still difficult to navigate in wintertime, and the ambassadors probably left Venice in the early spring. By June 17, 1284, there were imperial ambassadors in Venice, discussing the possibility of a truce.[7] The Byzantine ambassadors were not plenipotentiaries. They had come offering Andronicus' terms for peace; if Venice found the terms unacceptable, a further exchange of ambassadors would take place. It seems that the point of disagreement centered on the compensation the Byzantines should pay to Venice and to those Venetian merchants who had suffered damages between 1277 and 1281, and it appears that Venice estimated the compensation at between 67,000 and 100,000 hyperpyra. Andronicus did not wish to pay so much, and a further exchange of ambassadors ensued.

4. Tafel-Thomas, *Urkunden*, III, 94–95 (1265), 147–148 (1277).
5. Cessi, *Deliberazioni del maggior consiglio*, p. 28, nos. 50, 51.
6. Ibid., p. 52, no. 184.
7. Cessi, *Deliberazioni del maggior consiglio*, p. 69, no. 53. The names of the two Venetian ambassadors appear in the text of this decision which reads in part: "capta fuit pars quod debeat mitti nuncius vel nuncii ad . . . Andronicum cum plena commissione firmandi . . . treguam secundum commissionem, que facta fuit nobilibus viris dominis Andree Geno et Marino Mauroceno." Both men were members of important Venetian families, and Morosini was a member of the Consiglio dei Rogati (Senate), at least after 1301: R. Cessi and P. Sambin, *Le deliberazioni del Consiglio dei Rogati (Senato), serie "mixtorum."* I (Venice, 1960), passim. Throughout the late thirteenth and fourteenth centuries, the same names recur in connection with the affairs of the Romania, and in negotiations with Byzantium: Zeno, Morosini, Dolphin, Michiel, Dandolo, Tiepolo, Quirini. These families had strong ties with the Levant, and all had contained members who were Podestàs at Constantinople during the Latin occupation of the city. Virtually all these families had also given doges to Venice. See R. L. Wolff, "A New Document for the Period of the Latin Empire of Constantinople: The Oath of the Venetian Podestà," *Mélanges Henri Grégoire* (Brussels, 1953), especially pp. 559–573.

The second Venetian embassy left sometime soon after July 15, 1284.[8] Two Venetian ambassadors went to Constantinople, taking with them the Byzantine emissaries and two Venetian merchants who wished to argue in person their case for compensation payments. The Venetian government stipulated that none of the people going to Constantinople on this voyage should be allowed to take with them merchandise to sell; nor were they allowed to use their compensation money to buy anything except cereals and other provisions. It was specifically forbidden to them to buy any *mercationes de Levante*, which probably meant spices.[9] The Venetian government was clearly trying to avoid prejudicing the interests of other merchants. Since it was still forbidden to Venetian merchants to sail and trade in Byzantium, the envoys and the other men sailing with them could have made a fortune had they been allowed to engage in trade, and there would have been ill-feeling in the merchant community. Cereals and food products, however, were a state necessity and so could be purchased with the state's blessing.

The second Venetian embassy was not successful. On February 15, 1285, Byzantine emissaries were in Venice once again; and on March 10 of the same year, the Venetian government decided to send a third embassy, which proved to be the last.[10] The terms that the Venetian ambassadors were to present to Andronicus are not known, but they must have been substantially those found in the text of the truce. On one point the Venetians had clearly already given in: the ambassadors would ask for only 24,000 hyperpyra in compensation, and they were instructed to try, if possible, to negotiate some kind of additional money payments to several Venetian merchants who had suffered losses. The injunction to include Nigroponte in the truce seems to have been dropped. Perhaps on this point, too, the Byzantines had already won.

The third Venetian embassy, consisting of Angelo Marcello and Marco Zeno, left for Constantinople in the early spring of 1285, perhaps about March 27.[11] Meanwhile, Venice had received from the Romania disquieting news, whose exact nature remains obscure. The burden of the news was that there might be a revolution in Constantinople, and that Andronicus II might be replaced by someone else. If this were the case, the ambassadors were authorized to negotiate with this unknown new ruler.[12] There is no evidence of the internal turmoil the Venetians considered so serious. The only domestic troubles the Byzantine sources discuss were the difficulties and upheavals in the Byzantine church, which certainly were still very serious. It seems difficult to believe that Pachymeres at least, so close to the court, would be unaware of any major

---

8. The last mention of the embassy as being still in Venice appears on July 15: Cessi, *Deliberazioni del maggior consiglio*, p. 75, nos. 88–89. Document no. 88 refers to the galley "que nuper debet ire Constantinopolim."

9. Ibid., pp. 70, no. 56 (June 18), and no. 59; 71, nos. 60–62 (June 20), 65–66 (June 27); 73, nos. 74, 76 (July 8), 77 (July 9); 74, no. 81 (July 10); 75, nos. 88–89 (July 15).

10. Ibid., pp. 96, no. 214; 98, no. 9; cf. 98–99, nos. 15–19 (March 12).

11. On March 12 it was stipulated that the Venetian ambassadors should leave ten days after the day of their appointment. On March 17, the chancery was instructed to prepare their documents, but the ambassadors were still in Venice on March 22: ibid., pp. 100–101, nos. 26–28 (March 17), 30 (March 20), 33 (March 22).

12. Ibid., pp. 100–101, nos. 30, 33.

plot to unseat the emperor. Perhaps the Venetians had received false information, perhaps they simply exaggerated the probable results of the controversies
within the church. The one specific event that may have given rise to the rumor
was the unrest created by John Beccos at the end of 1284. Beccos had requested
a full discussion of his views and those of his opponents, and, according to
Gregoras, he had a certain popular following, potentially dangerous.[13] Venice
almost certainly had agents in the Byzantine Empire, perhaps even in the
neighborhood of Brusa, where the difficulties with Beccos originated. Did they
report that trouble was coming? Did Venetian agents in Constantinople report
back home the turbulent, dangerous, volatile mood of the population at that
time? Whatever the rumor, one suspects it *was* connected with the problems
arising out of the restoration of orthodoxy. Perhaps Venice even thought that
Beccos might win the argument and—who knows—a unionist, pro-Catholic
emperor might replace Andronicus.

Venetian hopes or misgivings were unfounded; the two ambassadors did in
fact find Andronicus well and reigning, and a truce was concluded on June 15,
1285. The ambassadors must have returned to Venice between July 7, 1285,
and July 22, when the Major Council gave its approbation to the terms of the
treaty. On July 7, the Venetian Republic had been so uncertain that hostilities
would end, that it had authorized the captain of a newly constituted force of
ten galleys to fight the Byzantines unless he received news that a truce had in
fact been concluded.[14]

There were strong incentives both for the Byzantines and for the Venetians
to put an end—however temporary—to hostilities. To the Byzantines, the
alliance between Venice and Charles of Anjou, concluded in 1281, had meant
a most dangerous diplomatic development: the two strongest enemies of the
empire had come together.[15] In 1285, this unfavorable diplomatic situation
came to an end, and Andronicus II achieved a temporary victory. With
Charles of Anjou incapacitated and with Venice at peace, a certain stability,
a degree of security from western attack was restored to his empire. One more
step, the marriage of his son to Catherine of Courtenay, was to be tried, and
then Andronicus would be free to turn his attention to Asia Minor. The
illusion of security is highlighted by the decision, later that year, to dismantle
the navy, so that money could be diverted elsewhere.[16]

For Venice, a restoration of peace with the Byzantine Empire was at least
equally important. The republic was going through a difficult period in its
history: there was a rebellion in Trieste, a war with the patriarch of Aquileia;
famine threatened, and Pope Martin IV had placed Venice under an interdict.[17] If the Byzantine Empire was not to be recovered by the westerners,
Venice could only lose by continuing hostilities and letting Genoa benefit

13. Pachymeres, II, 88ff; Gregoras, I, 189.
14. Cessi, *Deliberazioni del maggior consiglio*, pp. 113, no. 103 (July 7), 115, no. 115 (July 22).
15. Treaty of Orvieto (1281). Tafel and Thomas, *Urkunden*, III, nos. 373, 374.
16. Pachymeres, II, 70–71.
17. S. Romanin, *Storia documentata di Venezia*, 2d ed., II (Venice, 1825); H. Kretschmayr,
Geschichte von Venedig, II (Gotha, 1920), 192; R. Cessi, *Storia della Repubblica di Venezia*, I (Milan
and Messina, 1944), 259.

from the existing order at Constantinople. What she lost is clear from the records. The governmental decrees regulating trade with the East specifically forbade all commerce with the Byzantine Empire. There are several such decrees, dated April 7, 1282; April 10, 1283; March 16, 1284; April 14, 1285. Even while the second embassy to Constantinople was being discussed (June 17, 1284), the Major Council specifically forbade all Venetian merchants to travel to Byzantium.[18] The prohibition was imposed because the state could not guarantee the safety of the merchants. And Venice, at this point, needed desperately to trade with the empire, if only in order to get the wheat of the fertile Black Sea coasts. As soon as the truce was concluded, on July 29, 1285, the Venetian government allowed its merchants to sail to the Byzantine Empire and the Black Sea. When the fall convoy returned, in May 1286, so enormous was the quantity of merchandise it brought from Egypt and the Romania, that the state appointed three inspectors to look over the cargoes and prevent any fraud.[19]

While Venetian commerce suffered from the war with Byzantium, the political losses were also great. Venice was fighting with the Byzantines in Nigroponte, and it is fairly clear that the republic was losing. Venetian records speak of the need to maintain ships and men at Nigroponte: on August 8, 1283, the government of the island was authorized to borrow 5,000 hyperpyra, "occasione defendendi civitatem et insulam Nigropontis, si expedierit, contra exercitum Imperatoris Grecorum."[20] The Venetian insistence on including Nigroponte in the terms of the truce, and the Byzantine refusal to do so, tell the same story.

It is probable, too, that there had been some Byzantine intervention on the island of Crete, a turbulent Venetian possession. There is little concrete evidence of the activities of Byzantine agents in Crete in the years 1283–1285, but that little is clear enough. One of the first articles of the truce of 1285 stipulated that the emperor would not fight, nor let his men fight, the Venetians in Crete, "and that we will remove from this island the men we have there."[21] This was a verbatim repetition of one of the articles in the treaty of 1277 with Michael VIII, a proof that the intervention had started under Michael's reign. It became more important after his death, because it coincided with the first phases of a Cretan rebellion under the Greek noble Kallergis.[22] The fact that this article was not specifically mentioned in the treaties of 1303 and 1310 would indicate either that the Byzantines had fulfilled it, or that after Kallergis' rebellion ended (1299), the Venetians were not so much concerned with the Byzantine agents. Significantly enough, less than a year after the conclusion of the truce of 1285, the Venetian government was able to step up the war against Kallergis: on April 23, 1286, the Major Council voted to send to Crete every

18. Cessi, *Deliberazioni del maggior consiglio*, pp. 25, 62, 103, 69. Thiriet, *Délibérations*, p. 41.
19. Cessi, *Deliberazioni del maggior consiglio*, p. 116, no. 123; p. 144, no. 35 (May 14).
20. Ibid., p. 41, no. 116.
21. Tafel and Thomas, *Urkunden*, III, 325: "et quod homines quos habet Imperium nostrum ad ipsam insulam, extrahet eos inde."
22. Ibid., III, 144, 137; William Miller, *Essays on the Latin Orient*, (Cambridge, 1921); Kretschmayr, *Geschichte von Venedig*, pp. 21–22.

year, for the duration of the war, the large sum of 14,000 hyperpyra to be used against the rebel.[23]

It is established, then, that Venice had most to gain from the temporary stabilization of her relations with the Byzantine Empire. It has also been established that Venice did in fact take the initiative in the negotiations. The text of the treaty illustrates this state of affairs. The Byzantine text spoke in general terms of the desire of both parties for peace and of the exchange of several embassies. On the other hand, the Venetian confirmation began by declaring the intention and desire of the doge and his council "to reconcile ourselves and the entire commune of Venice with the most excellent lord Andronicus . . . emperor and moderator of the Romans [*Romeorum*] . . . forever August." The doge also claimed that he had tried to find ways "by which this love [he was talking of the earlier friendly relations between Venice and Byzantium] could best and most properly result to the honor of the Empire . . . and ours." For the most part, the treaty was a confirmation of the earlier one, negotiated between Michael VIII and Marco Bembo in September 1277. The new additions were not detrimental to the Byzantines. Indeed the last one, promising in effect that Venice would not repeat her offensive alliance with the Angevins, was clearly a guarantee demanded by Byzantium and conceded by the republic.[24]

Andronicus II swore solemnly to keep the terms of the treaty, and did so in the presence of some of the most important men of the empire, including the megas logothetes, Theodore Mouzalon, and the legothetes tou genikou (minister of finance), Constantine Acropolites.[25] The doge took the same oath before the two Byzantine envoys, the metropolitan of Mytilene, Demetrius Eirenikos, and Constantine Physcomallos. The truce called for a cessation of all war activities on land and sea for ten years. This included the Venetian possessions of Crete, Coron, and Modon; in Nigroponte, both sides were free to continue the war. The Venetian-held islands of Naxos, Tenos, and Mykonos, although not subject to the authority of the doge, could benefit from the truce so long as they did not break its provisions and did not offer refuge and help to pirates. The clauses referring to piracy were ineffective. Piracy was becoming increasingly endemic in the Aegean. Both Byzantine and Venetian islands harbored

---

23. Cessi, *Deliberazioni del maggior consiglio*, p. 142, no. 26; Thiriet, *Délibérations*, p. 52.

24. Tafel and Thomas, *Urkunden*, III, no. 378; p. 339: "ad reconciliandum nos et totum comune Venetiarum cum excellentissimo domino Andronico . . . Imperatore et moderatore Romeorum . . . semper Augusto"; and pp. 339–340: "per que ipse amor posset melius et decentius terminari ad honorem Imperii . . . et nostrum." Dade, *Versuche*, p. 65, states that Venice initiated negotiations during the years 1282–1285, but does not produce any further evidence for his statement. Cf. Hopf, *Griechische Geschichte*, p. 327.

25. The title of μέγας λογοθέτης was introduced at the end of the twelfth century, and the official who bore it supplanted the λογοθέτης τῶν σεκρέτων who, under Alexius I Comnenus, controlled all the civil departments of the administration. The title and the office of the λογοθέτης τοῦ γενικοῦ were much older, going back to the reforms of Heracleius. See Codinus Curopalata, *De officialibus palatii Constantinopolitani et de officiis magnae ecclesiae liber*, *Corpus Scriptorum Historiae Byzantinae*, (Bonn, 1839), pp. 34, 36; Ch. Diehl, "Un haut fonctionnaire Byzantin, le logothète τῶν σεκρέτων," *Mélanges N. Iorga* (Paris, 1933), pp. 217ff; Laurent, in *Échos d'Orient*, 38 (1939), 368ff; Dölger, in *BZ* 40 (1940), 520; D. M. Nicol, "Constantine Akropolites, A Prosopographical Note," *Dumbarton Oaks Papers*, 19 (1965), 249–256.

some of the pirates, and the island population sometimes took part in such activities.[26]

The Venetians were given fixed quarters in Thessalonica and Constantinople; in the capital, they simply recovered the quarters granted them by Michael VIII in 1277. As soon as the truce was ratified, on July 29, 1285, Venice decided to appoint a *bailo* of Constantinople, that is, a man who would have the combined function of representing his government to the emperor and of heading the Venetian colony at Constantinople.[27] If the residential areas granted to the Venetians proved inadequate to house merchants who came for a short time, the emperor would allot to them another twenty-five houses, without rent.

The most important article was also a rather vague one: "All Venetians and those who consider themselves and are known as Venetians, from whatever part they may come to our empire, should be safe and secure, free and privileged throughout our empire . . . on land and at sea, with or without all their possessions and their merchandise. And they will be free to go, stay and return, and free to buy and sell without impediment, or damage, or any duty, commercial duty, port duty, . . . or any other duty . . . The Venetians may buy and sell to whomever they wish, whatever they wish, both to Greeks and to Latins, . . . in absolute freedom."[28] At first glance, this article appears clear and not open to misinterpretation. Yet there were some difficulties. For one thing, who was a Venetian? Was it only a man born in Venice, or also a man born elsewhere of one or two Venetian parents? And what about the man who had been granted a charter of citizenship by Venetian officials—for a consideration— simply so that he could take advantage of the privileges of the Venetians? The article also stated that if Venetian ships were carrying merchandise belonging to non-Venetians, the captains should declare all such cargoes to the Byzantine customs officials so that the cargoes could be taxed. Here, too, there was room for misconduct on both sides. The Venetians and the Byzantines both broke virtually all the provisions of this article and readjustments had to be made in 1319, 1320, 1322, and 1324.

The next article almost begged to be disregarded: "because of the franchises [privileges] of the Venetians, which they hold in our empire, we will not impose, or cause to be imposed, or permit anyone to impose on any Greek or Latin or on any other person in any land or part of our empire any duty or burden in

26. Thomas and Predelli, *Diplomatarium*, p. 126; Pachymeres, II, 326; G. Bertolotto, "Nuova serie di documenti sulle relazioni di Genova coll'impero bizantino," *Atti della Società Ligure di storia patria*, 28 fasc. 3 (1898), no. 21, pp. 511–545; below, Chapters V, VI, VII passim.

27. Tafel and Thomas, *Urkunden*, III, 139, 326–327; Miklosich and Müller, *Acta et Diplomata*, III, 88; Cessi, *Deliberazioni del maggior consiglio*, p. 116, no. 124.

28. Tafel and Thomas, *Urkunden*, III, 329–330: "Item habeant libertatem omnes Veneti, et qui pro Venetis se tenent et distringuntur, de quacumque parte venerint ad Imperium nostrum, quod debeant habere et esse salui et securi, liberi et franki per totum nostrum Imperium, . . . cum omnibus rebus et mercationibus eorum et sine, tam in mari, quam in terra. Et quod sit in eorum libertate eundi, standi et redeundi, emendi et uendendi sine aliquo impedimento uel dampno et sine aliquo dacito, theloneo, pedagio, comerclo, scaliatico et onmi alio datio . . . Et quod Veneti possint uendere et emere cuicumque homini uel quibuscumque hominibus, et a quocumque et quibuscumque uoluerint, tam Latinis quam Grecis, . . . libere et absolute." On the commercium, see J. Danstrup, "Indirect Taxation at Byzantium," *Classica et Mediaevalia*, 8 (1946), 139–167.

any way, or by any means, which would be in any way against the franchises of the Venetians."[29] As the Venetians interpreted this statement, it constituted a very heavy curtailment of the sovereignty of the emperor. It meant that he could not levy taxes on goods bought and consumed by his own subjects, if this in any way conflicted with the interests and privileges of the Venetians. Given the freedom of Venetian merchants to buy and sell virtually anything in the empire, the loss of revenue—and of sovereignty—could be heavy indeed for the Byzantines. An argument was bound to arise, and it came over the issue of Black Sea grain. According to the treaty of 1285, Venetians were allowed to buy and export grain grown in the Black Sea area, but there was no specific provision concerning its sale *within* the empire. As it happened, during the early fourteenth century, the Venetians were able to buy Black Sea grain which was probably cheaper than the scarce, homegrown Byzantine product.[30] The Venetians insisted that they were allowed by the treaty to sell this grain freely. But such an undercutting of the native grower could not be tolerated by the Byzantine government, except possibly in times of actual famine. There were long discussions of principle and practice, and the issue was finally resolved in favor of Venice in 1324.[31]

Controversies of a similar nature arose out of the same article as it applied to the hiring of Byzantine manpower—surely, thought the Venetians, a commodity in which they could deal as freely as in any other. The Venetians always—at least, before their fifteenth-century expansion into the Italian hinterland—needed foreign sailors to man their ships. The Byzantine navy had been dismantled at approximately the time of the treaty of 1285, and Andronicus' subsequent efforts to rebuild it did not yield anything like the eighty ships he had had in 1283. Presumably, those Byzantine sailors who did not become pirates, and could not or would not become farmers, were in need of employment.[32] Andronicus saw fit to levy what may be called a trade tax on the Greek sailors in Venetian employ, and the Venetians objected immediately that this infringed on their franchises. These negotiations, too, will be followed in the proper context; it is important, however, that the point be made here that the treaty of 1285 contained provisions that could and did become very controversial. Poor Andronicus, presented with interpretations he had never thought of, could only exclaim that if he abandoned his right to tax his

29. Tafel and Thomas, *Urkunden*, III, 330–331: "occasione frankisie Venetorum, quam habent in Imperio nostro, non imponet, nec imponi faciet, nec permittet Imperium nostrum de cetero dacitam aliquam vel gravamen alicui Greco vel Latino vel alicui persone in aliqua terra vel parte Imperii nostri nullo modo vel ingenio, et quod sit in aliquo contra franchisiam Venetorum."

30. Pegolotti, writing some thirty-five years later, (ca. 1340), said that even the best Black Sea grain, that of Caffa, was at that time cheaper to the wholesaler than the best Byzantine wheat, grown in Rodosto. The grain of Mavrocastro (Četatea Alba) and Anchialos commanded the same price as that of Caffa. The wheat of Varna, Zagora and Sinopolis was cheaper: Francesco Balducci Pegolotti, *La pratica della mercatura*, ed. A. Evans, (Cambridge, Mass., 1936), p. 42. It seems reasonable to assume that a similar state of affairs existed at least as early as 1305, when the Catalan and Bulgarian raids disrupted the agriculture of Thrace. The situation probably did not improve noticeably between 1307 and 1340, since the civil wars would have contributed to the disruption and the consequent rise in prices.

31. Thomas and Predelli, *Diplomatarium*, p. 200.

32. Pachymeres, II, 71; Gregoras, I, 175–176.

own subjects, he would no longer be the lord of his subjects and his vassals.[33]

The Venetian *gasmuloi* would become another center of conflict. The gasmuloi (or gasmouli) were children of mixed descent, born of Greek and Latin parents. Many of them came from the Morea, where relations between the two groups were close, and they were famous for their abilities as sailors. The treaty of 1285 stated that "all Venetian gasmuloi and their heirs, who were subjects of the Venetians when the Venetians held Constantinople [1204–1261], will be free and privileged like Venetians."[34] During the Venetian-Genoese war of 1293–1299, and during the ensuing Greco-Venetian war (1296–1302), many of these men found it convenient to turn Byzantine. Later, some of their sons, those born before their fathers' reversion, wanted to claim Venetian citizenship, and the republic tried to plead their cause.[35]

The commercial privileges of Venetian subjects constituted a large section of the treaty, and were very extensive. The Byzantines, on the other hand, were allowed to trade freely in Venice, although they had to pay the usual duties imposed by the government. However, this was an article suggested by courtesy rather than reality. The Byzantines had virtually abandoned foreign trade, and the number of merchants who were likely to reach Venice was so small as to be negligible. The language of the clause indicates how remote was the possibility: "If any merchants of our empire and our lands should wish to come to Venice to engage in trade, they may sell merchandise in Venice, in any quantity."[36]

The activities of Venetian merchants *were* restricted in one area: grain grown within the empire was subject to special provisions. As in the treaty of 1277, the Venetians could not export Byzantine grain to states unfriendly to the empire. They were not allowed to export this grain at all, unless its price fell below 100 hyperpyra per centenarium. In 1302 the prohibition of export was extended to include salt and mastic.[37]

The last group of articles of interest here deal with political matters, which occupied a more important place in this treaty than in previous ones. Most of these provisions were present in the peace treaty of 1277. Each party agreed not to form an offensive alliance with a third power against the other party.[38] It was stated that the Venetians and the Genoese were not to engage in hostilities in the empire; if they fought against each other in the Hellespont or the Black Sea it was the emperor's responsibility to make the guilty party pay

33. Thomas and Predelli, *Diplomatarium*, p. 145. Andronicus claimed that all these exactions were legal by tradition and that if he abandoned them, as Venice requested, "non erimus domini vassalorum et subiectorum nostorum." The phraseology is interesting, but would be much more illuminating if one had the Greek version of the document.

34. Tafel and Thomas, *Urkunden*, III, 328.

35. Thomas and Predelli, *Diplomatarium*, p. 105 (1317).

36. Tafel and Thomas, *Urkunden*, III, 334: "Item, si aliqui mercatores Imperii nostri et terrarum nostrarum voluerint venire Venecias ad mercandum, possint in Veneciis vendere merces, quascunque voluerint, sine aliquo impedimento, solvendo tamen comercla per Ducem et comune Venecie ordinata."

37. Ibid., p. 335; Thomas and Predelli, *Diplomatarium*, p. 14; Zakythinos, *Crise*, p. 81; Gregoras, I, 301; Cantacuzenus, *Historiarum*, I, 117–118, II, 89.

38. Tafel and Thomas, *Urkunden*, III, 325.

compensation. It would appear that from the beginning this article was not thought to apply in the case of a general Venetian-Genoese war. The words of the treaty were: "and if it happens that some offense or damage should be done within these boundaries of the said land of our Empire . . ."[39] Obviously, this referred to one-sided injury inflicted in time of peace. In fact, the Venetians, although victorious in a war that began against the Genoese and ended against the Byzantines (1293–1302), did not seek to apply this provision to the period of the war.[40]

Measures were taken for freeing Venetian and Byzantine prisoners in the whole empire and in all Venetian possessions, including Modon, Coron, Nigroponte, and Crete. If the Greek prisoners wanted to return to the empire with their families, they were to be allowed to do so.[41] The question of reparations for damages done to Venetians at the time of Michael VIII and Andronicus II was settled. This refers to damages done during times of peace, that is, between 1277 and 1281. The emperor agreed to pay to Venice, without delay, the sum of 24,000 hyperpyra. Here, too, the Byzantines won a point, for originally Venice had asked for heavier payments, and the last embassy to Constantinople had been instructed to try to get some extra money. The agreed sum was paid by December 6, 1286, and on that date the Major Council ordered the mint to convert this money into gold ducats.[42]

According to the treaty the emperor was not allowed to requisition Venetian ships, nor should he suffer anyone to prepare in his empire for an attack on Venice. This last provision was obviously directed toward the Genoese and toward pirates of all nationalities. As in 1265 and in 1277, Venice promised that neither she nor her subjects would attack any part of the Byzantine Empire, or any of its subjects. Neither the commune nor any Venetian would ally with anyone, Christian or pagan, against the empire, or permit anyone to transport the enemies of the empire or hire ships to them.[43] All of these articles had, of course, been violated in 1281, in the Venetian treaty with Philip of Courtenay and Charles of Anjou. For this reason, it was reiterated at the end of the treaty of 1285 that for the ten years of its existence the Venetian government and individuals were not at liberty to make "any conventions or treaties" with anyone against the empire.[44] This sentence was probably added to give more weight to the obligation, after the relevant clauses of the previous treaties had been repeated. It illustrates the circumstances under which the truce of 1285 was negotiated: the Byzantines wanted to annul the Venetian-Angevin alliance, and wanted all the assurances they could get on this point.

Thus was ended, for the first period of Andronicus II's reign, the immediate danger from the Venetian republic. The truce of 1285 had been a diplomatic

39. "Etsi acciderit, fieri aliquam offensam seu dampnum infra hos confines dicte terre Imperii nostri . . ."
40. Tafel and Thomas, *Urkunden*, III, 329, 346–347. Cf. ibid., p. 141.
41. Ibid., III, 333.
42. Ibid., III, 337–338; Cessi, *Deliberazioni del maggior consiglio*, pp. 160–161, no. 147.
43. Tafel and Thomas, *Urkunden*, III, 335–336, 341–342. Cf. ibid., pp. 94–95 (1265); pp. 147–148 (1277).
44. Ibid., III, 336.

victory for the Byzantines. Mighty Venice had been obliged to ask, repeatedly, for a cessation of hostilities, and the Byzantines had been able to impose their own terms on certain points. One should not be misled, however, by temporary success. Venice's humility in 1283–1285 does not indicate that Byzantium was the stronger state. And once the treaty had been signed and confirmed, Venice gained great privileges, and the Byzantines gained nothing in the long term. Peace they had bought—for ten years—but the price was very high. In the last analysis, the treaty was as meaningful as the power of either state. Venice profited from the commercial clauses, to the extent that her ships and her merchants could once again go to the Byzantine Empire and to the Black Sea. She could break the political clauses, and Byzantium would have no power to retaliate politically. Meanwhile, she could demand, successfully for the most part, that the commercial and other clauses be implemented by Byzantium. Andronicus II had merely allowed into his empire a strong power that he knew to be basically hostile. Yet what else could he have done? If he wanted temporary peace, he had to make a truce with Venice; in the circumstances, he secured the most advantageous terms possible. Most of the privileges he conferred on the Venetians had already been granted by his father. But while Michael VIII ruled a state that was still powerful in military and political terms, Andronicus' empire would slowly decline and become unable to oppose the inevitable hostility of Venice.

The Venetian-Byzantine treaty of 1285 made very little impression on the chroniclers of either side. Pachymeres did not discuss it directly, but he did refer vaguely to the peaceful attitude of the Venetians. Marino Sanudo Torsello, far from mentioning the treaty, implied that the Venetian-Byzantine war of 1296–1302 was a continuation of the hostilities of 1282:[45] The behavior of Venice, both during that war and after, at the time of the Catalan expedition and of the alliance with Charles of Valois, indicated that for the republic the treaty of 1285 was merely a temporary measure. The words of Marino Sanudo on the treaty of 1310 apply equally well to the earlier one: "The doge and the commune of Venice forever went from truce to truce with the emperor of the Greeks, without wanting to make peace."[46]

Venetian-Byzantine relations were correct but somewhat uneasy from 1285 until 1294. The Venetian merchants returned to the Byzantine empire, to Constantinople, to the Black Sea. In the spring of every year the government issued the usual decree permitting navigation and commerce in these areas. In January 1292, a special decree permitted Venetian merchants to go freely to the Romania and the Black Sea between April 1 and October 15, and to bring merchandise back to Venice.[47] The Black Sea colonies which Venice had possessed at the time of the Latin empire of Constantinople appear to have been flourishing again: on April 4, 1288, a Venetian consul was sent to the

45. Pachymeres, II, 70–71; and Sanudo, *Istoria*, p. 133.

46. R. L. Wolff, "The So-called Fragmentum of Marino Sanudo," in *Joshua Starr Memorial Volume*, (New York, 1956), p. 153: "Dominus . . . et comune Venetiarum transeunt de treugua in treuguam cum Imperatore Graecorum numquam pacem agere volentes."

47. Cessi, *Deliberazioni del maggior consiglio*, p. 311, no. 129; cf. p. 313, no. 140.

city of Soldaia, in the Crimea. Soldaia now became, as it had been earlier, the main Venetian colony in the Black Sea area, and its consul had authority over all Venetian colonies and merchants in the entire Crimea. On April 8, 1288, the Venetian consul was allowed to spend a substantial amount of money for the freeing of slaves, presumably Venetians held by the Tartars of the Golden Horde.[48] Venice was coming back to the Black Sea area, where the Genoese were, at the same time, trying to create and preserve a commercial monopoly.

Despite the resumption of political and commercial relations with Byzantium, there were tensions between the two states. In 1287 Venice sent ambassadors to Constantinople to discuss the question of damages done to the Venetians by Byzantines.[49] Whatever these damages may have been, the Byzantines were not the only ones to act against the provisions of the treaty of 1285. In 1291 the Venetian citizen Pancratio Malipiero attacked various parts of the empire; the island of Kos was saved only by the insubordination of his fleet. In 1292 Giacopo Tiepolo launched another, more successful, attack.[50] Whether in retaliation or on their own initiative, Byzantines, probably imperial officials, confiscated the property of some Venetians. The senate appointed Andrea Zeno as ambassador to see Andronicus II and complain about this action. The veneer of friendship in the relations between the two states was clearly wearing off. In June 1293 the senate had once again to discuss the difficulties Venice faced in the Byzantine Empire, and on September 5 the bailo of Constantinople, Delphino Dolfin, was entrusted with a mission to the emperor.[51]

In the summer of 1293, however, hostilities had begun between Venice and Genoa in a skirmish off Coron, in the Peloponnesus. The war between Venice and Genoa was on; much of it would be fought in the Aegean, and relations between Venice and Byzantium after 1294 should be considered in the context of the war. A Venetian document of November 28, 1294, illustrates the connection rather nicely. Until then, matters pertaining to Constantinople had been discussed in the senate, which had jurisdiction over all foreign affairs, and in the Major Council. On May 22, 1294, a new body was created, the Council of the Thirty, whose authority extended to all matters having to do with Genoa. A decision of the Venetian Major Council, of November 28, 1294, ordered the Council of the Thirty to examine Dolfin's reports from his embassy to Constantinople.[52] The Byzantine Empire was henceforth to be discussed in connection with Venice's enemy, Genoa; the short period of détente in Venice's relations with Byzantium was ended.

Byzantine relations with Genoa, the other major Italian maritime city, were fairly friendly. Whereas Venice was basically hostile to the presence of a

48. Ibid., p. 201, nos. 14, 16; cf. Thiriet, *Délibérations*, p. 55 and n. 1; Heyd, *Commerce*, II, 168.

49. Cessi, *Deliberazioni del maggior consiglio*, pp. 170, no. 25; 171, no. 28.

50. Andreae Danduli, *Chronica*, in Muratori, *RIS*, XII (Milan, 1728), col. 403 (hereafter, Dandolo). Tiepolo's family had contributed one Venetian podestà of Constantinople, and two doges.

51. Cessi, *Deliberazioni del maggior consiglio*, pp. 320, no. 45; 326, no. 46; 344, no. 69; 348, no. 98.

52. Ibid., pp. 358–359, no. 18; 368, no. 71.

Byzantine imperial family in Constantinople, Genoa was basically committed to the Palaeologi. During the period of the Latin emperors of Constantinople, Genoa had been excluded from the empire and from the Black Sea. On March 13, 1261, the Genoese had signed with Michael VIII the treaty of Nymphaeum, which provided for a joint effort to take Constantinople. Genoa would give Michael VIII naval assistance, and in return the Genoese would receive important privileges, among them the exclusion of all enemies of Genoa (except for Pisa) from the Black Sea. This would mean the end of Venetian preponderance there.[53]

Michael VIII had taken Constantinople before the Genoese could send the help they had promised, and by 1265 the emperor had temporarily quarreled with his allies. He concluded a treaty with Venice which somewhat curtailed the privileges of the Genoese. After prolonged discussions, however, in 1267 and 1272, friendly relations were restored between Byzantium and Genoa, and the Genoese found themselves in a privileged position in the empire. The emperor gave them a special residential area in Pera (Galata), so situated as to minimize the possibility of conflict between Greeks and Genoese; from Pera, the Genoese spread into the Black Sea area and began to colonize it. Caffa became an important commercial station after 1266, and was to be the center of Black Sea trade until it fell to Mohammed II, the conqueror of Constantinople, in 1475. In Asia Minor, Michael VIII gave Phocaea, with its important alum mines, to the Genoese Zaccaria family (1275), who built great fortunes based on alum. For all these reasons, while Venice agreed, in 1281, to attack the Byzantine Empire along with Charles of Anjou, Genoa refused him her help. Indeed, Genoese envoys informed Michael VIII of Charles' plans.[54]

After the Sicilian Vespers, the alignment of forces remained essentially the same. In Italy, Genoa maintained a neutrality favorable to the Aragonese in the conflict between the houses of Anjou and Aragon. Her major part in the conflict was a selfish one; she became engaged in a lengthy war with Pisa, a supporter of the Angevins, but also a long-standing commercial rival of Genoa. The war lasted from 1282 to 1288, but after the great Genoese victory at the naval battle of Meloria in 1284 Pisa was, to all intents and purposes, defeated.[55] This is of some interest here, because the war crushed Pisa as a commercial power of international importance; Pisa would play no role in the relations of

53. C. Manfroni, "Le relazioni fra Genova, l'impero bizantino e i Turchi," *Atti della Società Ligure di storia patria*, 28, fasc. 3 (1898), 791ff; *Liber Jurium*, cols. 1350ff, no. 945; Geanakoplos, *Michael Palaeologus*; R. L. Wolff, "The Latin Empire of Constantinople," in Setton, Wolff, and Hazard, *History of the Crusades*, II, 230.

54. Pachymeres, I, 358, 366; Bertolotto, "Nuova serie," document 19; Caro, *Genua*, I, 196–197, 301–302; Manfroni, "Relazioni," pp. 673–675; G. I. Brătianu, *Recherches sur le commerce génois dans la mer noire au XIIIe siècle* (Paris, 1929), book II, chap. iii; L. Sauli, *Storia della colonia dei Genovesi in Galata* (Torino, 1831), II, 204ff, chap. viii. Brătianu, *Recherches sur le commerce*, pp. 198ff; R. S. Lopez, *Genova marinara nel duecento: Benedetto Zaccaria ammiraglio e mercante* (Messina and Milan, 1933); R. S. Lopez, *Storia delle colonie Genovesi nel Mediterraneo* (Bologna, 1938), p. 218; Jacobi Auriae, *Annales*, vol. 18 of *MGH Ss*, p. 293.

55. Caro, *Genua*, II, 1ff, 45ff; Manfroni, *Storia della marina Italiana dal trattato di Ninfeo alla caduta di Constantinopoli, 1261–1453*, I (Livorno, 1902), 109–138; T. O. de Negri, *Storia di Genova* (Milan, 1968), pp. 413–421.

Italian states and the Byzantine Empire, as she would play no role in the overseas activities of the other Italian naval powers. The great powers operating in the East were reduced to two, Venice and Genoa. Given Genoa's generally unfavorable attitude toward the Angevins, it was to be expected that she would maintain friendly relations with Andronicus II.

In December 1282 and again in 1283, Andronicus II wrote to the podestà and the captains of the people of Genoa to acquaint them with the death of his father and with his own legitimate accession to the throne.[56] In the same letter, he promised to carry his state to new and golden heights, and to preserve a favored place for the Genoese in the empire. Indeed, he insisted that in the future Genoese merchants and citizens would find a more friendly welcome than ever before. His own heart was with the commune, he assured the Genoese, and added that "you can and you should have great confidence and firm hope in the present and the future, that our love for you will increase and your position in . . . our empire will be provided for honorably and decently." In this case, the exaggerations of Byzantine diplomatic language may well be taken at their face value, for Genoa was the empire's one firm friend.

Unfortunately, it is not easy to follow the development of this friendship, because documents are rather sparse. Perhaps this is *because* Genoese-Byzantine relations were friendly, and embassies were usually simple good-will missions. Such an embassy from Genoa appeared in Byzantium in 1284. Andronicus had just strengthened his tie with the anti-Angevin group by negotiating his marriage to Yolanda-Irene of Montferrat. The future empress came to her new home accompanied by three Genoese ships, equipped at the expense of the commune. Two ambassadors came with her, "to honor . . . the lord emperor."[57]

In August 1286, Andronicus II acknowledged another Genoese embassy, led by Jacopo D'Oria.[58] Jacopo D'Oria presented letters from his government and a number of petitions to the emperor. Andronicus expressed his joy at receiving the letters, and promised the Genoese to keep inviolable all the treaties that bound the two states together, and to persevere in the pure friendship and love that he felt for the commune. The nature of the petitions remains unknown, again because the two states were so friendly that few written documents seemed necessary. Andronicus heard the complaints, wished to discuss them, and confided his messages to the Genoese emissary himself. Consider the difference between this informal approach, and the repeated exchanges of formal embassies which preceded the Venetian treaty of 1285.

Andronicus' reply to the Genoese letters indicates that some of the com-

56. L. T. Belgrano, "Cinque documenti Genovesi-Orientali," *Atti della Società Ligure di Storia Patria*, 17 (1885), 239–241. The date from Dölger, *Regesten*, IV, nos. 2077, 2088; cf. Geanakoplos, *Michael Palaeologus*, p. 358, n. 76.

57. Auriae, *Annales*, pp. 310–311; Salimbene, *Chronicon*, p. 312; *Annales Placentini Ghibellini*, ed. G. H. Pertz, in *MGH Ss*, XVIII (1863), 578; *Annales Veronenses*, p. 429; Caro, *Genua*, II, 101ff; Heyd, *Commerce*, I, 144.

58. Bertolotto, "Nuova serie," no. 20 (1285); C. Desimoni, "Sui quartieri dei Genovesi a Constantinopoli nel secolo XII," *Giornale Ligustico di Archeologia*, 1 (1874), 217–274; Caro, *Genua*, II, 227; Brǎtianu, *Recherches sur le commerce*, p. 99. Chronology from Dölger, *Regesten*, IV, no. 2117.

plaints had to do with commerce: it appears that imperial officials had harassed Genoese merchants, probably by making them pay duties. Andronicus promised to give compensation and to punish with the utmost severity any similar future offenses. The whole tone of his letter of reply was one of friendship toward and confidence in Genoa. One cannot escape the feeling that the letter was also meant to be reassuring: this appears to have been the first exchange of messages since the conclusion of the Byzantine treaty with Venice, and Andronicus must have wished to let the Genoese know that their friendship had not diminished.

Throughout the first period of Andronicus' reign, the Genoese merchants in the empire were in a much more privileged situation than were the Venetians. The colony of Pera was thriving, so much so that its boundaries had to be extended in 1303.[59] From Pera Genoese ships sailed regularly to the Black Sea, where their activities far exceeded those of the Venetians. The Genoese commercial station of Caffa, founded sometime in the late 1260's, appears in 1289 as a full-fledged colony with a consul, and exhibits signs of political and economic vitality. Certainly, Caffa was a better established and more prosperous colony than the Venetian outpost of Soldaia.[60] The balance of power in the Black Sea area weighed heavily in favor of the Genoese, and this Venice could not permit without challenge.

After 1291 the importance of the Black Sea ports became even more obvious: when Acre, the last Latin port in Palestine, fell to the Egyptians, commodities from Asia were gradually diverted through the northern trade routes into the northern coasts of the Black Sea. Immediately afterward, in April 1292, Venice tried to conclude an alliance with Nogai, the Tartar general, and thus to extend her power at the expense of the Genoese.[61] But this effort was not successful, and the Black Sea issue would be one of the major causes of the Venetian-Genoese war of 1293–1299.

The Aegean, too, which for almost sixty years had been a *mare nostrum* to the Venetians, was now full of Genoese ships—in Coron, Monembasia, Rhodes, Thessalonica, Lemnos, Chios, Ania, Smyrna, Panormos, Adramyttion, and Thasos. In the Sea of Marmora, Genoese traders are found at Rodosto and Passequia.[62] Sixty (or forty) Genoese ships were able, in 1292, to sail around the Peloponnesus and attack Epirus for Andronicus II. Clearly, the Genoese presence in the Aegean was of some benefit to the Byzantines, and to some extent the Genoese were aware of their obligations to the state which permitted them free play in the area. In 1292, for example, they complained to Frederick

59. Desimoni, "Quartieri," pp. 247ff.

60. G. I. Brătianu, "Contributions à l'histoire de Cetatea-Alba (Akkerman) aux XIIIe et XIVe siècles," *Bulletin de l'Académie Roumaine, Section historique*, 13 (1927), 25–31; Heyd, *Commerce*, II, 165ff; Caro, *Genua*, II, 54ff.

61. Brătianu, *Recherches sur le commerce*, pp. 233–234, 256–261; Cessi, *Storia di Venezia*, p. 263; Cessi, *Deliberazioni del maggior consiglio*, p. 315, nos. 10 (April 10, 1292), 12 (April 17).

62. Manfroni, "Relazioni," pp. 686ff. The Genoese annals mentioned, around the year 1286, that a considerable number of Genoese merchant ships sailed in the Aegean; some brought alum from the Black Sea where they had been granted a monopoly by Michael VIII: *Annales*, pp. 316–317.

of Sicily about the activities of his admiral, Roger de Lluria, who had attacked Byzantine possessions in the Aegean.[63] But here, too, the situation was intolerable to the Venetians, and the first incident in the war of 1293–1299 involved a skirmish between some Venetian ships on their way to Cyprus and some Genoese merchants on their way home from the Black Sea; the two met off Coron.[64]

For a while, the Byzantines condoned the Genoese expansion. So far as is known there was no vocal opposition to the immoderate growth of Genoese power and influence until the end of the century. This does not mean that relations between Genoese merchants and imperial officials or even with the emperor himself were always smooth. The government of Genoa presented a long list of complaints in 1290 and 1294.[65] This and the similar complaints presented by the Venetians a few years later provide interesting information about the way treaties were being implemented by the Byzantine officials, about the extent of foreign trade in Byzantium, and about the extent of piracy in the Aegean.[66] It seems that even in Constantinople itself the emperor did not always control the activities of his officials, who could impose all manner of extortions on foreign merchants. Genoese merchants were often forced by customs officials to pay customs duties, although these had been abolished by the treaties. This happened in the ports of Ani, Smyrna, Panormos, Passequia, and in Nymphaeum (?"Nifo").[67] Much of the Genoese trade was with Asia Minor, and most of the deviations from imperial policy took place in this area, which seems to have been outside the close control of the emperor. On one occasion, in Passequia, a merchant was forced to pay duties even though he had received a special imperial charter relieving him of the obligation.[68]

The fact that the emperor had to issue special charters in spite of the existence of general treaties indicates the decentralization of authority. In Constantinople, the main offender was Cinnamus, the chief customs official ("captain of the port of Constantinople"). Sometimes he prevented Genoese ships from entering the Black Sea unless their owners bribed him. Time and again the Genoese demanded the restitution of money he had taken *sine causa*. In one case he refused to recognize an imperial charter authorizing the export of 1,500 *modii* of grain. In another, he simply kept the charter and refused to return it to its owner. Other officials outside Constantinople were guilty of similar misdemeanors. The governor of Thessalonica was accused of having robbed some Genoese merchants of money and goods. One Johanino Zambono lost a total

63. *Annales*, p. 343.

64. Cessi, *Storia di Venezia*, chap. iv; Manfroni, "Relazioni," pp. 686ff.

65. Bertolotto, "Nuova serie," document 21, pp. 511–545. For the date, see Manfroni, "Relazioni," pp. 683ff.

66. Thomas and Predelli, *Diplomatarium*, nos. 7 (1302), 8 (1303), 46 (1310), 59 (1317), and so on.

67. Passequia was a harbor on the Asiatic coast of the Sea of Marmora. See K. Kretschmer, *Die italienischen Portolane des Mittelalters* (Berlin, 1909), p. 652. I am not certain that "Nifo" should be read "Nymphaeon." Kretschmer (p. 654) refers to Nife, a large city fifteen miles inland.

68. Bertolotto, "Nuova serie," p. 512. On this and the following cf. Brătianu, *Recherches sur le commerce*, pp. 133–150.

of 1,006 hyperpyra to officials in Rhodes and Ani in 1289. When asked to return the money, the duke of Ani referred him to the emperor. A similar offense was committed by the governor of Passequia. Once the emperor himself was responsible for a breach of the treaties. His representative confiscated some grain belonging to a Genoese merchant "because of lack of food in a certain fort of the lord emperor."[69]

The same list of complaints provides valuable information about the nature of Genoese commerce in 1285–1294, and especially about the trade in grain, which has not been adequately studied, at least for this period.[70] For most of this period, for example, the Genoese could and did buy and export Byzantine wheat, mostly from Rodosto and Monembasia. The price at which they bought it seems to have varied. In one case they paid 1 hyperpyron and 14 keratia to the modium. (In the Byzantine treaties with Venice export of imperial wheat was allowed only when its price in the empire fell below 1 hyperpyron.) In another case, a Genoese merchant purchased 2,000 modii of Rodosto grain from the emperor for 4,000 hyperpyra.[71] It is impossible to determine whether the merchant paid too high a price; whether, in other words, the normal price of wheat at this point was closer to two hyperpyra per modium, or to the one hyperpyron mentioned in the Venetian treaty. One can hazard a guess: the merchant would probably not have bought at prices much higher than the market prices, and so wheat that year must have sold at near two hyperpyra. If that be the case, it is significant that a Genoese man was able to buy and export Byzantine wheat selling at such high prices, whereas Venetians, of course, could not.

The question of imperial monopoly of the wheat trade also arises from this document. Although it cannot be stated that such a monopoly existed then, it is at least clear that Andronicus II controlled much of the sale of wheat to foreigners. The Genoese bought grain from Andronicus, from the agents of one of his officials, or from "the Sebastos Palaeologos," son of the sebastokrator and a relative of Andronicus.[72] The text does not indicate whether this was wheat grown on the imperial domain or whether it was merely handled by the imperial officials acting as middlemen between the cultivators and the Genoese merchants. The reference to purchases of Rodosto wheat from the emperor would seem to argue the second case. Other commodities handled by the Genoese included mastic from Chios, carpets from Passequia, vellum, nutmegs, and cattle.[73]

Even when the Genoese were not having trouble with imperial officials, sailing in the Aegean was far from safe. Ever since the twelfth century the sea

69. Bertolotto, "Nuova serie," pp. 511, 512, 513, 515, 517, 520, 521, 524–525, 530, 532, 535, 538–541.

70. On this see Brătianu, *Recherches sur le commerce*, passim.

71. Bertolotto, "Nuova serie," pp. 511, 515–516, 524, 526, 532, 533. One *hyperpyron* had twenty-four *keratia*.

72. Ibid., pp. 524, 515–516 (1285), 526. The sebastos was probably Andronicus Palaeologus, son of the Sebastokrator Constantine, brother of Michael VIII. See Papadopulos, *Genealogie*, nos. 5, 7.

73. Bertolotto, "Nuova serie," pp. 511, 513, 521, 524, 532, 537, 545.

had been infested with pirates of all nationalities. They seem to have parceled out areas of operation among themselves. Monembasia bred intrepid pirates, among them George "de Malvasia" and John Curtese. Curtese operated around Lemnos and Passequia. Ani, Adramyttion, and Lemnos were threatened by John Sclavo and George Matricheri (Makrycheris?), also from Monembasia. The gasmuloi, famous even among the Byzantines for their piratical activities, were active in Rodosto, and even the sea of Marmora was not free of pirates.[74] The Venetians, the Byzantines, and the Genoese all tried, more or less whole-heartedly, to reduce the number of pirates operating in the Aegean. They were unsuccessful, for the instability of the political situation and the lack of effective authority in the area helped the pirates rather than their opponents.[75] In the early fourteenth century, the Venetian-Genoese war, the Turkish invasion of Asia Minor, and the Catalan expedition would create even more favorable conditions for pirates.

Andronicus II has been accused of virtually handing his empire over to the Genoese by his onesided policy of favoring them over their rivals. The accusation holds better for the first period of his reign than for later years, and Byzantium came to depend heavily upon Genoa for its defense, especially at sea. This was partly the result of a shift in the focus of interest. The Byzantine navy was dismantled in order to save money; thus the maritime defenses of the empire were abolished. Andronicus, feeling relatively secure in his relations with the West, turned his attention to his eastern and Balkan frontiers where, in this period, fighting was done on land. Since there was no Byzantine sea-power, the Genoese were expected to do their share for the defense of the empire; but when real dangers appeared Genoa did not perform adequately.

The real error made by Andronicus and his advisers was not that they preferred the Genoese to the Venetians: maintaining a balance between the two powers, each bent on political and commercial domination in an increasingly contracting sphere, would have been impossible, and in the end no less dangerous for Byzantium. The unforgivable error lay in the demolition of the Byzantine fleet, an action which delivered the empire into the hands of any enemy strong enough to attack it from the sea or into the hands of any so-called friend who promised to defend it—in return for ever increasing privileges.

Ironically enough, the Byzantine fleet was demolished as a result of Andronicus' minor successes in his relations with western Europe. In 1285 there was an undisputed détente in Byzantine relations with western Europe. This convinced Andronicus' advisers that maintaining a fleet was expensive and unnecessary.[76] Their arguments were rather fragile. That Charles of Anjou was dead, and that Venice and Genoa were at peace in imperial waters at the time was no guarantee for the future, as even some contemporaries could see. The assurance the advisers gave to Andronicus, that God would guard the

74. Ibid., pp. 522–523, 527, 529, 530 (1294), 531, 544–545; Pachymeres, II, 71; Gregoras, I, 175–176.

75. On piracy in the western Mediterranean in the fourteenth century, see F. L. Cheyette, "The Sovereign and the Pirates, 1332," *Speculum*, 45 (1970), 40–68.

76. Gregoras, I, 174; Pachymeres, II, 69–71.

empire because of his return to Orthodoxy was obviously calculated to persuade the emperor, who was easily swayed by flattering courtiers. Apparently, Andronicus needed persuading, for he was not at first favorable to the idea of dismantling his navy.

There was not much of a navy to demolish. In 1283 the fleet consisted of at least eighty ships, but the exact number is unknown.[77] Even the strength of Michael VIII's fleet cannot be accurately determined. Even so, the decision to scrap these ships was a momentous one. Kekaumenos, who had written in the eleventh century that "the navy is the glory of the Romania," had pointed to one of the basic elements of Byzantine power.[78] During most of its history, the empire included the coasts of the Aegean and the Ionian Sea; the fate of Constantinople itself depended on control of the Black Sea and the Straits. This basic element of Byzantine and, later, Ottoman history sounds like a truism; yet it must be emphasized: the Byzantines simply could not afford to destroy their sea defense. Contemporary observers close to Andronicus made the obvious comment, repeated by later historians, that Constantinople and the islands of the Aegean could not possibly be held without sea power; that dismantling the navy would only increase the already excessive power of the Italians, and that all independent policy would be rendered impossible.[79] It would be crediting Andronicus with stupidity to imagine that he did not realize this; but he nonetheless succumbed. The fleet was not destroyed to the last ship. Yet for all practical purposes it was nonexistent after 1285.

The folly of the Byzantine retreat from the sea became obvious during the war with Venice (1296–1302) and during the troubles with the Catalans; on both occasions, the Byzantines complained bitterly about the impotence to which the lack of a fleet had reduced them, and Andronicus had to make an effort to rebuild the fleet. Even the immediate results of the demolition of the fleet were catastrophic: the unemployed sailors joined the pirate ships which attacked imperial and Italian possessions alike. Others joined the fleets of Genoa and Venice. Others still of the proud, brave race of the gasmuloi who had manned the ships joined the ranks of subsistence-level peasants or personal dependents of the *dynatoi*.[80]

The destruction of the Byzantine fleet illustrates the weakness of Andronicus' character and the short-term considerations which determined his policies and those of his councillors. He was fully aware that the growth, indeed the preservation, of the empire depended on the navy, yet he succumbed to the advice of his councillors. Their main argument was financial. The imperial

77. Pachymeres, II, 69.

78. B. Wassilievsky and V. Jernstedt, *Cecaumeni Strategikon et incerti scriptoris de officii libellus* (Petropolis, 1896), p. 101. Cf. Bănescu, "A propos de Kekaumenos," *Byzantion*, 13 (1938), 129ff., where he proves that the two treatises have a common author.

79. Gregoras, I, 175; Pachymeres, II, 70.

80. Pachymeres, II, 70–71; Gregoras, I, 175–176; Thomas, *Diplomatarium*, p. 175. Not all the ships were demolished; most of them, however, were left to rot in the Golden Horn: Gregoras, I, 176. Maximus Planoudes, in a letter written around 1300, was so afraid of pirates that he wished a certain volume of Boethius, which he had lent to a doctor in Ephesus, to be returned to him by land, not by sea: see *Maximi monachi Planudis epistulae*, ed. M. Treu, *Programm des Königl. Friedrichs-Gymnasiums* (Breslau, 1886), letter 5.

treasury, they claimed, would be richer by the money saved on payments to sailors, while the ships, released for commercial activities, would pay the duties avoided by the Italians.[81] These councillors were accused by contemporaries of considering their private interest before that of the state. But if they benefited from duties paid to the treasury, they must have been imperial officials; and for these, the diminution of the defensive forces of the empire backfired. Their pay was later stopped in a desperate effort to finance Andronicus' dealings with the Catalan mercenaries, and the success of these mercenaries was due in part to the lack of naval power.

Asia Minor

While regulating his relations with the West, Andronicus II tried to secure the Byzantine position in Asia Minor. In 1290–1293, he himself undertook a long journey to the area. It was not a particularly easy time for the empire; Andronicus was engaged in negotiations for the marriage of his son Michael to Catherine of Courtenay, and his western army was fighting Nicephorus of Epirus. On the other hand, there was no immediate threat of an attack from the West, so that his absence from Constantinople was not overly dangerous. He must have thought a trip to Asia Minor essential, for not only did he stay there for three years, but he took with him some of the most important officials of the realm, including the grand logothete and *mesazon*—the equivalent of a prime minister—Theodore Mouzalon. In a sense, Andronicus transported, for the space of three years, the seat of his government from Constantinople to Asia Minor. Surprisingly, there is little information about what he did in Asia Minor, and modern historians have been content to simply mention his journey.[82] But the paucity of information can be explained, and some of his activities in Asia Minor can be described in a general way.

In part, the difficulty of discovering what Andronicus did in Asia Minor is inherent in the nature of the sources. Pachymeres, the usually trustworthy source, is useless on this matter, for he probably stayed behind at Constantinople. He provides accurate information only for the dates of Andronicus' departure and return. The other major source for this topic is a historical sermon on doctrinal quarrels within the Byzantine church, delivered by George Metochites, who had been one of Michael VIII's closest advisers on the affair of union with Rome.[83] If George's account is to be believed, Andronicus' sojourn in Asia Minor was occupied with discussions between Andronicus, Mouzalon, and the imprisoned unionist leaders, chief among whom was the former patriarch John Beccos. No doubt this is true, but it is only a partial truth. Andronicus and Mouzalon were trying to persuade Beccos and his friends to admit their errors, so that one source of discontent within the church and the laity would

---

81. Pachymeres, II, 70; Gregoras, I, 174.

82. Andronicus' journey is mentioned in Laurent, "Jean Beccos," pp. 318–319, and in Ševčenko, *Métochite et Choumnos*, p. 139 and n. 3. In dating the journey I have followed the convincing arguments of Verpeaux, "Notes chronologiques," p. 28. Pia Schmidt, "Chronologie," says that Andronicus returned to Constantinople in 1294, after four years in Asia Minor.

83. Georgius Metochita, *De historia dogmatica, Sermo III* in A. Mai. ed., *Patrum Novae Bibliothecae*, X, pt. 1 (Rome, 1905), 327–330.

disappear. Yet, granted Andronicus' deep piety and concern with peace in the church, did such an effort warrant his long personal presence in the East? It seems rather doubtful, and a further explanation of the imperial journey can be gleaned from the writings of Theodore Metochites.

Theodore Metochites, the son of George Metochites, was probably born in Constantinople in 1269–70. When the family fortunes declined with the death of Michael VIII, Theodore followed his father into exile in Asia Minor, and there he remained at least until 1290. In 1290, in his twentieth year, his life suddenly changed: he was introduced to Andronicus II, and within one year he was made λογοθέτης τῶν ἀγελῶν (logothete of the troops)—an honorary title, to be sure, but even so an unexpected honor for a young man whose main claim to fame was that he was the son of one of the emperor's enemies. Metochites himself, in his later works, expressed surprise at Andronicus' kind treatment.[84] His rise to power after 1290 was meteoric: he went to Armenia to negotiate the marriage of Michael IX to Rita-Maria, and upon his return he was rewarded with the office of λογοθέτης τῶν οἰκειακῶν. His functions are unclear, but were probably those of treasurer of the private imperial purse. He ended his long career as grand logothete, or first minister of the state, a dignity to which he was promoted in 1321.[85]

Where did this man meet Andronicus, and why was he immediately taken into the imperial entourage? One thing known with certainty is that Metochites was with Andronicus at least during part of the emperor's journey in Asia Minor; this is known from Metochites' second *Imperial* oration, which may have been delivered in Nicaea in 1290 or 1291, and which in any case shows first-hand knowledge of Andronicus' journey.[86] It seems probable that Andronicus met the young Theodore in Asia Minor, during the first stages of his sojourn there, and that Metochites' ideas about policy concerning Asia Minor endeared him to the emperor.

Metochites pronounced two *Imperial* orations, probably close together. These are important documents, which deserve publication. In particular, they provide fascinating information about Asia Minor, and it is surprising that they have not been used before in this connection. Both orations discussed Andronicus' feats in Anatolia. This can be interpreted either as an effort by Metochites to flatter the emperor *after* he had been taken into Andronicus' court or, on the contrary, as an expression of Metochites' plans for Asia Minor, which were the cause of the sudden change in his fortunes. The second alternative seems preferable, for his orations sound less like an eulogy and more like the enunciation of a plan on which both Metochites and Andronicus agreed.

84. Ševčenko, *Métochite et Choumnos*, pp. 129–135, 274. Ševčenko conclusively solves the debate as to whether George Metochites was Theodore's father. But he does not explain Andronicus' sudden interest in the young man. Other works on Metochites' family: R. P. T. Kaeppeli, "Deux nouveaux ouvrages de fr. Philippe Incontri de Péra," p. 175, and R.-J. Loenertz, "Théodore Métochite et son père," pp. 184–194 in *Archivum Fratrum Praedicatorum*, 23, (1953).

85. On Metochites' career, see Ševčenko, *Métochite et Choumnos*, passim, and R. Verpeaux, "Le cursus honorum de Théodore Métochite," 196.

86. Ševčenko, *Métochite et Choumnos*, pp. 139–140.

Both orations described conditions in Asia Minor, and praised—indeed overpraised—Andronicus' activities there.[87] The reconstruction of Tralleis in the first oration and the slow progress of the imperial suite through northern Anatolia in the second oration were celebrated in Metochites' extremely learned and tortuous style. He was not blind to the grave dangers threatening Anatolia. Indeed, in his poems as in his orations he deplored the impotence of the Byzantine Empire, and invoked ancient glories to highlight the present decline. He lamented the victories of the barbarians who were ignorant of proper government and justice, but who nevertheless managed to conquer the Romans—or Byzantines—of Asia Minor. He repeatedly wrote of the sad fate of beautiful Ionia, Lydia, Phrygia, Aeolis, all of Asia Minor, places he had loved since his youth and which had now succumbed to the infidel.[88] With equally great sorrow he pondered over the internal sickness of the Byzantine Empire: Asia Minor had been deserted and depopulated before the Turkish conquest, and its people had lost their morale and sense of citizenship because of the attitude of the central government toward them. He recognized and deplored his own inability to stop the deterioration of Byzantine affairs.

Metochites then turned to the Emperor Andronicus, from whom might come the salvation of Anatolia. He saw Andronicus as the man to fit the times, an emperor who had given himself wholeheartedly "to the salvation of your Hellenes."[89] This is one of the earliest uses of the word "Hellene" to mean "Byzantine." Until the mid-thirteenth century, the term "Hellene" had been shunned, because it had connotations of paganism. It would become increasingly common in the fourteenth and fifteenth centuries, until George Gemistos (Plethon) could proclaim with pride: "We whose ruler and emperor Thou art, are Hellenes by race, as both our language and our national culture testify." The word became respectable because of a cultural renaissance that brought the Byzantines closer to their classical Greek heritage; also, as the frontiers of the Palaeologan empire retreated, its population became more homogeneous. And, partly because of Greek opposition to the Latins, a proto-nationalist sentiment evolved. All these factors were already present when Metochites delivered his orations, and made it possible for him to speak of Hellenes.

Metochites declared that Andronicus II had proved his sincere interest in his people by his journey and residence in Anatolia. The emperor, according to the orations, was worried about the Turkish invasions, which had been made possible by the concentration of Byzantine troops in the West during the reign of Michael VIII and during the first years of his own reign. Such had been the neglect of Asia Minor, that the inhabitants of the inland regions "did not dare live in their houses and cultivate their lands," but hid in ravines, living as best they could, like animals.[90] But now Andronicus had taken an interest in them,

87. Cod. Vindob. Philol. Gr. 95. fols. 86v–94r, 145r–158v. *Ibid.*, fol. 154v.: οἳ δίκην οὐ νομίζουσι· πολιτείαν οὐκ ἴσασι . . . ; βασιλικὸς β΄, passim.

88. *Ibid.*, passim.

89. Cod. Vindob. Philol. Gr. 95, fol. 150v: ὑπὲρ τῆς τῶν σῶν Ἑλλήνων σωτηρίας. On the use of the terms "Hellene" and "Hellas" in the Empire of Nicaea, and on the rise of a Hellenic consciousness see A. E. Vacalopoulos, *Origins of the Greek Nation, The Byzantine Period, 1204–1461* (New Brunswick, N.J., 1970), pp. 27–43.

90. Cod. Vindob. Philol. Gr. 95, fols. 149r, 156r–v.

and had sent men and money into Asia Minor, and tried to stimulate the will of its people to defend themselves. Metochites insisted that the way to win the hearts of the inhabitants of Anatolia was through the emperor's personal presence in the province. This is precisely what Andronicus was doing in 1290–1293. Metochites also considered that Andronicus had, and should have, two aims: his immediate objective was to rebuild the fortifications of villages and towns, thus placing a barrier between the barbarians and the Byzantine territories; while his long-term aim was to reinforce the morale of the inhabitants and their will to stay and defend their lands.[91] Whether this was Andronicus' aim or Metochites' plan is in a sense irrelevant: clearly, Metochites was formulating a policy which Andronicus found most acceptable.

With this background Andronicus' activities in Asia Minor in 1290–1293 become more intelligible. He went to Bithynia, inspected the fortifications of the Sangarius River, and then visited Nicaea, Lopadion, and Nymphaeum. He stayed in each city for a long period of time, and he stayed for two years in Nymphaeum. According to George Metochites, he returned to Constantinople only because Mouzalon had fallen gravely ill, and no doctor could cure him— he died at Constantinople in March 1294.[92] There seems no doubt that Andronicus' journey was an effort to woo back the disaffected inhabitants by exhibiting in the most dramatic way possible, by his own presence, the interest of the central government in Asia Minor. Nothing is mentioned about military success—one has to discount as mere rhetoric Metochites' comparison of Andronicus to the ancient Agesilaus[93]—and probably there were no battles with the Turks. Andronicus' journey was a political, not a military, excursion and the discussions with Beccos, as reported by George Metochites, must be viewed as part of the general program of appeasement.

The presence of Andronicus in Asia Minor apparently had no great effect on the sentiments of the population. Perhaps it was too brief, and came too late; but it was also too intellectualized. The people of Asia Minor must have wanted not only emotional reinforcement but also a tangible proof of the government's ability to deliver them from the Turks. The extent of the population's state of panic over the Turkish danger was made clear in a strange, and, to Andronicus, disconcerting episode which took place in 1294. In that year, there appeared near Constantinople a certain Bulgarian who claimed to be Lachanas, the "kitchen-gardener" who had rebelled against Michael VIII and his protégé, Constantin Tiš of Bulgaria, in 1277, and who in fact had been killed years before.[94] It was soon discovered that his identity was false, and the imposter was thrown into jail. There had been many pretenders throughout Byzantine history, but most of them claimed to be people of some importance:

91. βασιλικὸς α´ and βασιλικὸς β´: Cod. Vindob. Philol. Gr. 95, fols. 87ro, 149ro, 150ro, 151ro.
92. Cod. Vindob. Philol. Gr. 95, fols. 155r, 156r–v; Georgius Metochita, *De historia dogmatica*, p. 329; Ševčenko, *Métochite et Choumnos*, pp. 139–140.
93. Cod. Vindob. Philol. Gr. 95, fol. 150r.
94. Pachymeres, II, 188–192. Pseudo-Lachanas' deeds in Asia Minor must have taken place just before March 1294, for Pachymeres discusses them together with the death of Mouzalon, which took place in that month. This date follows from Verpeaux's argument that Andronicus II returned to Constantinople in June 1293; Mouzalon died in the following March. Laurent, "Jean Beccos," pp. 318–319, advances these events by one year.

emperors, or at least successful rebels. The claims of pseudo-Lachanas were modest, indeed so modest that they defy explanation. Why should anyone pretend to be Lachanas, a failed rebel, and an unheroic one? Assuming that the pseudo-Lachanas might want a stake in Bulgaria, what was he doing at Constantinople, where the name of Lachanas aroused no feelings of support but rather memories of trouble? The whole incident is very strange indeed.

By contrast, in Asia Minor, so direly in need of a savior, the name of Lachanas evoked certain hopes. Rumor had it that the Turks had heard oracles say that Lachanas would destroy them, and as a result they were in great fear of the name and the man. Learning that the population of Asia Minor believed in the pretender and in his alleged powers, Andronicus released the pseudo-Lachanas and sent him off to the Sangarius front, in Bithynia. There the pretender collected a motley army of peasants, who in their desperation abandoned their fields and cattle and followed him wherever he went. They had, of course, no knowledge of the art of war, but were willing to fight under the command of the pseudo-Lachanas. Soon their numbers increased, spreading like fire, as Pachymeres put it, and the government at Constantinople began to feel apprehensive. Andronicus could see no happy outcome from this venture, for if the peasants ever met the Turks in battle they would, he feared, all be slaughtered. If, against all expectations, they emerged victorious, he feared a revolution.

So the pretender was recalled to Constantinople and imprisoned, and his peasant army, which had covered the land like a stream (again, Pachymeres' imagery) soon dispersed. Such was the inglorious end of the pseudo-Lachanas, the first hero that Marxist historians can produce in what they consider the struggle of the late-Byzantine peasantry against the combined forces of their government, the landlords, and the Turks.[95] But the pseudo-Lachanas episode proves one thing only: that the population of Asia Minor was so frightened by the Turks that they behaved in an irrational, totally emotional, and suicidal manner. To this extent, of course, the conciliatory policy of the central government had failed.

Andronicus himself had behaved irrationally. He should have known better than to send a Bulgarian adventurer to redeem Asia Minor. Soon afterward, however, he took a step which at first seemed perfectly reasonable, and indeed desirable, but soon proved disastrous. In 1294 or 1295 he sent to Asia Minor a young man, Alexios Philanthropenos, who was given the military title of pincernes.[96] Alexios' commission was to govern Asia Minor, with the exception

95. See E. Francès, "La féodalité byzantine et la conquête turque," *Studia et Acta Orientalia*, 4 (1962), 71.

96. Pachymeres, II, 210ff; Gregoras, I, 195. The date I have ascribed to the expedition is different from that suggested by Pia Schmidt who places the rebellion of Philanthropenos in 1296, connecting it with an abortive trip to Asia Minor attempted by Andronicus. According to her, the rebellion would have taken place in December 1296 (Pachymeres, II, 229) and Andronicus' trip to Asia Minor would have been attempted in May 1296 (Pachymeres, II, 233). Pachymeres, however, makes no connection between Andronicus' trip and Philanthropenos' expedition; he seems to place the trip after the rebellion, which is more logical. Andronicus had much faith in Philanthropenos, at least at first (Pachmeres, II, 212–213), and I can see no reason why he would go to Asia Minor while he had a perfectly able general in the area. On the other hand, after the rebellion, he may have wished to reestablish his authority. Therefore,

of the Ionian coast, and fight the Turks who were raiding the banks of the Meander River. The protovestiarios Livadarios governed the Ionian coast. Philanthropenos was given command of the entire army of the East, and the most important part of his forces consisted of a body of Cretan cavalry under the leadership of a certain Chortatzes. These were Greek refugees from the Venetian-held island of Crete, whom Andronicus had settled in Asia Minor.[97]

Alexios Philanthropenos was the second son of the provestiarios Michael Tarchaneiotes and so a member of an important Byzantine military family, and a nephew of the emperor.[98] He was young, a good soldier, and enjoyed the emperor's full confidence. He was sent to Asia Minor as the one man who could save it; the hopes of the emperor, the administration, and the people of Constantinople accompanied him in his mission. In Asia Minor, Philanthropenos had considerable and immediate success. Not only was he a brave general, he was also a kind, just, and wise conqueror, whose generosity to the enemy was often praised and sometimes deplored at Constantinople. In a short while he had inflicted grave defeats on the Turks; he took Miletus, and went on campaigns on both sides of the Meander River. He sent his spoils back to Constantinople: gold and silver and the skins of sheep and donkeys. The monk Planoudes, writing to Philanthropenos, was so happy to see the spoils of the

---

I would place the rebellion in December 1295. Alexius had been in the East for some time before his formal rebellion, as Pachymeres' narrative makes clear; so it is possible that he was sent sometime in 1294 or in early 1295.

97. On Philanthropenos' rebellion see Pachymeres, II, 210–229; Gregoras, I, 195–202. On Philanthropenos see also Rodolphe Guilland, "Aléxis Philanthropène," *Revue des Lyonnais*, (1922), pp. 47–59. Athenagoras, Metropolitan of Paramythia and Philiates, «Συμβολαὶ εἰς τὴν ἱστορίαν τοῦ Βυζαντινοῦ οἴκου τῶν Φιλανθρωπηνῶν,» Δελτίον τῆς Ἱστορικῆς καὶ Ἐθνολογικῆς Ἑταιρείας τῆς Ἑλλάδος. n.s. I (1929), 61–74.

98. Unfortunately, the genealogy of the important families of the Tarchaneiotes and the Philanthropenoi has not yet been satisfactorily established. Both Papadopulos, *Genealogie*, no. 24, and Guilland ("Fonctions et dignités des eunuques," *Études Byzantines*, III [1945], 194–195), say that Alexios Philanthropenos was the second son of Michael Tarchaneiotes Glabas. Pachymeres, I, 94, I, 206, I, 295, and II, 210, gives the following information: Michael VIII had a sister named Maria (nun Martha), who in 1237 married Nicephorus Tarchaneiotes. She had three sons, Andronicus, Michael, and John, and a daughter named Theodora. Michael Tarchaneiotes received the title of protovestiarios, and married the daughter of Michael VIII's general, Alexios Philanthropenos; their second son was our Alexios. The trouble is that there were two men with the same name: the protovestiarios Michael Tarchaneiotes, and Michael Tarchaneiotes Glabas. Both Papadopulos and Guilland confuse the two men, but they should not, because Michael Tarchaneiotes died in the Thessaly campaign of 1283, while Glabas lived on to achieve great glory and died after 1307. Pachymeres himself seems to distinguish between the two men, for he calls Tarchaneiotes by the title of protovestiarios, and Glabas by his various titles, megas kontostaulos, (grand constable), protostrator (commander of an army). Alexios, then, was the second son of the Michael Tarchaneiotes who died in 1283. This however plays havoc with the genealogy of Michael Tarchaneiotes Glabas, as established by Papadopulos. G. I. Theocharides, ʺΜιχαὴλ Δούκας Γλαβᾶς Ταρχανειώτης (Προσωπογραφικά),ʺ Ἐπιστημονικὴ Ἐπετηρὶς Φιλοσοφικῆς Σχολῆς Πανεπιστημίου Θεσσαλονίκης, 7 (1957) 183–206, makes the distinction, and tries to trace the family of Glabas Tarchaneiotes. P. J. Alexander, "A Chrysobull of the Emperor Andronicus II Palaeologus in favor of the See of Kanina in Albania," *Byzantion*, 15 (1940–1941), 206, n. 115, recognizes the distinction between the two Tarchaneiotes, but does not see what difficulties the distinction creates in the accepted genealogies. Guilland too has been surprisingly careless about the Philanthropenoi. In his article "Études de titulature et de prosopographie byzantines. Le Protostrator," *REB.*, 7 (1949), 164ff, he says that Alexios Philanthropenos became a protostrator in the reign of Andronicus II: he refers the reader to his other article, "Fonctions et dignités des eunuques," pp. 194–195, where he states, correctly, that Alexios never went beyond the title of pincernes.

"Persians," "that I wish you had sent me the skins and heads of the barbarians, had you not been so humane [φιλάνθρωπος]." Philanthropenos took so many prisoners, that the price of a Turkish slave in Asia Minor dropped below that of a sheep![99]

At Constantinople, a spirit of elation and relief reigned. Clearly, the general had come just in the nick of time to save Asia Minor from the barbarians, and to restore the fortunes of the empire. The whole city rejoiced in his triumphs— of which he sent frequent news—and even those who envied him kept their tongues under control. Planoudes took it upon himself to send Philanthropenos words of advice: take the initiative in war, he wrote, and do not make treaties with the barbarians, because they are a notoriously untrustworthy lot. But the time came when the barbarians asked for peace, and Planoudes rejoiced that Philanthropenos granted it, "for there is a time of war and a time of peace, and you have shown yourself brilliant in both."[100]

The Turks were not an all-conquering power yet. In fact, they were rather frightened of the Ilkhanids, the Mongols of Persia, and were quite happy to surrender to Philanthropenos, who treated them honorably. In time, a Turkish contingent formed an important and loyal part of his army.[101]

Then, at the end of 1295, Philanthropenos rebelled against Andronicus. Unlike other rebels of the period he was not motivated by purely selfish reasons; indeed, he was very reluctant to put on the imperial insignia and even pleaded with Andronicus that he be replaced before he was forced into rebellion. The rebellion was really started by his soldiers and encouraged by a large part of the population of Asia Minor. The Cretans were afraid that their leader might suffer the fate of other successful generals, which was disgrace and imprisonment.[102] They tried to secure their position and his before the threat became real. For the population of Asia Minor, Philanthropenos was a hero through whom they could express their feelings of discontent with the central government. Both soldiers and inhabitants were bitter against the lazy, luxury-loving officials of Constantinople who expected the army to receive the brunt of the Turkish attacks while they lived a life of relative comfort and safety in the capital. The peasants also resented the various financial exactions of the central government or of its representatives.[103] All these people supported Philanthropenos; here was a general who, for once, had proved his worth against the enemy, and who had enough power to rebel successfully against a government they despised. Further success came easily, and Philanthropenos took control of the area he had been sent to govern: "From then on, the emperor's name was not mentioned in those parts, except in mockery." Even some monasteries, "many in number and those the greatest," mentioned

---

99. Planoudes, *Epistulae*, letter 78, p. 99: οὐ μόνον προβάτων, ἀλλὰ καὶ βαρβάρων ἠβουλόμην δορὰς καὶ κεφαλὰς δεῦρο πεμπομένας ἰδεῖν, εἰ μὴ τὸ σὸν εἶργε φιλάνθρωπον. Cf. letter 120.

100. Ibid., letters 60, 61, 71–74, 77, 78–80, 84–85, 90, 94, 95, 98, 99, 101–107, 110–112, 118–120.

101. Pachymeres, II, 211–212, 215; Gregoras, I, 196, 361–362; Planoudes, *Epistulae*, letter 112.

102. Pachymeres, II, 212, 213, 221–222; Gregoras, I, 190–191, 197.

103. Pachymeres, II, 214–217.

Philanthropenos' name in the liturgy instead of that of Andronicus.[104] This suggests that Philanthropenos may have enjoyed the favor of the Arsenite faction in Asia Minor. The Arsenites, being a political, anti-Palaeologan movement as much as a religious one, may well have supported this rebellion against the authority of Constantinople. Philanthropenos was particularly suited to arouse the sympathy of the Arsenites, for his paternal uncle was John Tarchaneiotes, one of the leaders of the Arsenite party in Constantinople, who had lately been released from prison.[105]

Philanthropenos, then, had enough local support in Asia Minor to make his rebellion a success. It is unlikely that he would have been able to attack Constantinople successfully—nor did he want to—but he might have tried to govern Asia Minor on his own, perhaps with the nominal assent of the rather frightened Andronicus II. Had he succeeded, the fate of Asia Minor might have been different. But he was hesitant in his rebellion, and this cost him his most effective source of support. The Cretan soldiers were not content with a cautious leader, and changed sides when the opportunity appeared. For Philanthropenos had one implacable enemy in Asia Minor. This was Livadarios, whose position would have made him the first victim of the extension of Philanthropenos' power. The daughter of Livadarios had married Andronicus II's brother, Theodore Palaeologus, whom Philanthropenos had unwisely attacked. Livadarios saw his chance to acquire glory, imperial favor, and vengeance by quashing the rebellion. Andronicus, badly frightened, helped with money. Livadarios bribed the Cretan soldiers, and they captured and blinded Philanthropenos.[106]

Andronicus II's attitude during the rebellion was ambivalent. He helped Livadarios, and prayed to the Virgin for deliverance, yet at the same time he sent ambassadors to the rebel to invite him to return to obedience, and offered him the title of caesar—much debased, to be sure, but still quite high in the hierarchy.[107] Andronicus realized that he could not successfully oppose the rebellion with his own forces. The halfhearted measures he took against Philanthropenos bear a striking resemblance to those employed a few years later, when his Catalan mercenaries rebelled. To them, too, he offered the

---

104. Ibid., II, 219–220.

105. Ibid., II, 206–208, 210.

106. Ibid., II, 221–222; Gregoras, I, 196–197. Livadarios had been the man in charge of Tralleis when it was occupied by the Turks (1284). Pachymeres, II, 180–182, 220. Cf. Papadopulos, *Genealogie*, no. 43. Also, Pachymeres, II, pp. 221–229; Gregoras, I, 198–201. Philanthropenos was restored to favor at the end of 1323, with the intervention of the patriarch Isaias. On that occasion the old soldier was sent to Philadelphia, which was threatened by the Turks. Andronicus could not spare any men or army, but Philanthropenos, we are told, persuaded the Turks to abandon the siege of the city: Gregoras, I, 360–362. At the time of his downfall, it seems that those connected with him also suffered. Constantine Akropolites, the grand logothete, was his father-in-law; it seems that at about the same time he was banished from Constantinople, perhaps to Thessalonica: Nicol, "Constantine Akropolites," p. 250 and n. 10. Constantine's brother, the monk Melchisedek Akropolites, was among those who incited Philanthropenos to rebellion: Pachymeres, II, 214.

107. Pachymeres, II, 229, 230; Gregoras, I, 199, 200. Apparently, Andronicus dedicated the month of August to the Virgin, as thanksgiving for his deliverance from Philanthropenos: V. Grumel, "Le mois de Marie des Byzantins," *Échos d'Orient*, 31 (1932), 257–269.

government of Asia Minor, along with high titles. And yet one wonders whether conciliation was not the best course of action in 1295. Certainly, no emperor can encourage rebellion. But it was clear that Asia Minor wanted new leadership, and who better than Philanthropenos to provide it? A good general, related to the imperial family, who also enjoyed the confidence of the people was more than Andronicus could easily hope to find. Given Philanthropenos' own reluctance to rebel, no doubt some reasonable compromise could have been found. But the interference of Livadarios tipped the balance in Andronicus' mind, and the rebellion was quashed.

Andronicus showed quite unexpected bitterness and disappointment during Philanthropenos' rebellion; his actions both during the rebellion and after it were those of a shattered man. Fear alone cannot have so discomfited Andronicus—the rebellion certainly did not threaten his life. But Philanthropenos' disloyalty offended the emperor's most basic values, his sense of honor and his love of family. Andronicus felt cheated that his own beloved nephew to whom he had given his trust with so little reservation should have broken his word, repudiated the emperor's leadership, in fact betrayed him. The historian Gregoras understood the emperor's pain and his emotional reaction: "After the tumultuous events of Philanthropenos' time, he [Andronicus] said he suspected all the Romans . . . For this reason he dreamt day and night of foreign alliances, which he should not have done. Because of his disapprobation of all the Romans, the affairs of the Romans went badly and came to the worst of dangers."[108]

The results of Philanthropenos' defeat were sad for Asia Minor. The Turks who had feared and respected him were now free once again to resume their raids. The native population that had fought for him and for the homeland had been let down yet again. Gregoras dates from this period the collapse of the Byzantine army in Anatolia and the consequent fatal Turkish invasions. The Turks expanded along the coast, from the Black Sea to Lycia; apparently the fortifications Andronicus had erected along the coasts were ineffective.[109] But the judgment of Gregoras should be somewhat modified. There were further attempts to put things right in Asia Minor. Andronicus tried several times to organize the defense of Anatolia, and the real Byzantine failure there did not occur until 1302. Asia Minor was not irretrievably lost in 1296, and the emperor could still hope for a favorable turn in his fortunes.

---

108. Gregoras, I, 205: Μετὰ γὰρ τὴν τοῦ Φιλανθρωπινοῦ συμβᾶσαν ἐκείνην σύγχυσιν πάντας ἔλεγεν ὑποπτεύειν Ῥωμαίους . . . διὸ καὶ συμμαχίας ὑπερορίους ὠνειροπόλει νυκτὸς καὶ ἡμέρας, ὡς μὴ ὤφελεν. Ἀποδοκιμαζομένων γὰρ ἁπάντων Ῥωμαίων, τὰ Ῥωμαίων ἐνόσητε πράγματα καὶ πρὸς ἐσχατιὰς κατηνέθχη κινδύνων.

The correspondence of Planoudes depicts the atmosphere of confidence which Philanthropenos inspired, and then betrayed. Repeatedly, Planoudes extolled Philanthropenos, and communicated to him Andronicus II's great joy at the victories of the general. How bitter the disappointment must have been! Planoudes, *Epistulae*, letters 78, 98, 105.

109. Gregoras, I, 214ff; Pachymeres, II, 235–236.

IV

The Failure of Retrenchment, 1296–1302

During the early part of the reign of Andronicus II, and until 1311, Byzantine foreign policy suffered a change of direction, and its sphere of activity became restricted. As one Byzantine statesman put it, contemporaries witnessed "the diminution of the affairs of the Romans and a change in their erstwhile great felicity."[1] Whereas Michael VIII had made of Byzantium a European power, his successors for the most part retreated from Europe. Their attitude toward the western powers was defensive, passive. Their sphere of activity became limited to the Balkans, their sphere of interest to Thrace, Macedonia, Greece and Asia Minor, and by this shift of interest Byzantium became a mere Balkan power, and not the strongest one at that. This process began with Andronicus II.

Between 1282 and 1296, Andronicus II was still working within the context of the policies of Michael VIII. His behavior toward the West was governed by two main factors, the Italian wars and his own repudiation of the union of the churches. There was no danger of an immediate western invasion of Byzantium after the Sicilian Vespers, but real rapprochement with the West was made difficult by his religious policy. Thus, the alliance with Aragon was slowly abandoned. In general, during that period Andronicus followed a policy of disengagement from the West. His treaty with Venice was designed to end hostilities, but did little to decrease the tension between the two states. His relations with Genoa were more positive. The Genoese were encouraged in their commercial activities in the empire, and it is almost certain that Andronicus thought he could depend on them to defend him at sea. Meanwhile, the empire's relations with Charles II of Naples slowly improved. There was a conflict of interests in Epirus, but in the Morea a détente lasted until 1296.

On the whole, Andronicus' policy of disengagement from the West was moderately successful until 1296. Certainly, his diplomacy looks heavy-handed after his father's elegantly intricate statesmanship. But Andronicus had no wish to emulate his father, and the relative peace he had achieved in the West allowed him to turn his attention to the area Michael had neglected, Asia Minor. That his efforts there were not even modestly successful is another matter.

Andronicus II and his officials continued their clear and conscious policy of minimum relations with the West after 1296, and concentrated on the Balkans and Asia Minor. Although Andronicus II would later change his attitude and try to form an active European policy, in fact the fate of his state, and particularly of Asia Minor, was sealed during the years 1296–1302.

By 1296 Andronicus must have thought that he could reap the benefits of

1. K. Sathas, Μεσαιωνικὴ Βιβλιοθήκη, I (Venice, 1872), κε΄. From the βασιλικὸς β΄ of Theodore Metochites: Θρηνεῖ ἐπὶ τῇ τῶν Ῥωμαϊκῶν πραγμάτων ἐλαττώσει καὶ μεταβολῇ τῆς μεγάλης ἐκείνων εὐδαιμονίας.

the moderately successful diplomatic activity of the first years of his reign. Now he could concentrate his resources in the East, and from 1296 to 1302 he made constant efforts to save Asia Minor from the Turks; most of his army and his resources were diverted to that area. At the same time, the Serbian challenge was met, not so much by war as by marriage negotiations. In 1299 the northwestern frontiers of the empire seemed safe from the Serbs. But although the imperial government shifted its interest and its activities into the Balkans and Anatolia, it was not allowed to follow its new direction in peace. Though the Byzantines tried to disengage themselves from western Europe, Europe was far from ready to permit them to go their own way. And the great failure of Andronicus II's diplomatic policy became evident in the years 1296–1302, when he was forced to engage in a very expensive European war, a war from which he could gain nothing and which had originally involved only Venice and Genoa.

Since security in the Balkans and Asia Minor was the justification for Andronicus' passive European policy, it is necessary to examine briefly Byzantine activities in these areas. Our judgment of Andronicus' political wisdom is contingent on our evaluation of his aims, his policies, and his success in the Balkans and in Asia Minor.

Asia Minor

Andronicus II was not alone in his determination to shift his center of interest eastward to Asia Minor, the Orthodox, populous but beleaguered province; his most important officials seem to have shared his views. During the years 1296–1302, Theodore Metochites was already an important official, in control of the emperor's private treasury. In Metochites' writings one finds very little mention of Europe as a complex of states with which Byzantium had to deal; his main interest was focused on Asia Minor, which he rightly saw as the most precious Byzantine territory, and the most threatened. Andronicus' measures in Asia Minor after 1296 indicate that the emperor continued his attempts to reform the region along the lines Metochites had suggested.

The rebellion of Philanthropenos had left Asia Minor virtually undefended. It had also proved yet again that the people of the area were disappointed with Constantinople, and that major steps were needed to oppose the Turks and to regain the confidence and the loyalty of the population. Soon after the failure of Philanthropenos' rebellion, Andronicus decided to undertake a third journey to the East, in order to restore his prestige there and to provide for the defense of Asia Minor. He left the capital on May 29, 1296. He had not gone very far when, on June 1, there was a major earthquake. The emperor took this as a proof of divine disapproval of his enterprise. Frightened, he returned to Constantinople, and there tried to regain divine favor by reforming the judiciary and singing litanies.[2] This was his last trip to the East, and his last effort to prove his interest in Asia Minor by residing there, as Metochites had suggested.

2. Pachymeres, II, 233–236. Date: according to Pachymeres this event occurred shortly before the Venetian attack on Pera of July, 1296. Pachymeres, II, 237. Cf. V. Grumel, *La chronologie: bibliothèque byzantine* (Paris, 1958), p. 481; and Georgiades-Arnakes, Οἱ πρῶτοι Ὀθωμανοί pp. 47–48.

Asia Minor

Having failed in his attempts to preserve Asia Minor through military action and through his personal presence, the emperor tried to institute some much-needed reforms from afar. It was clear that if the people of Anatolia were to fight, they needed a general they trusted and liked. It was also clear that the soldiers fighting against the Turks had to have some stake in the homeland they were defending. The fate of the peasant-soldier in Byzantium had been sealed long before the period we are discussing. Despite the efforts of John and Manuel Comnenus to revive small military holdings, despite the limited success of John Vatatzes (1222–1254) to create an army of small-holders in Nicaea, Byzantine social history after the Macedonian period was characterized by a progressive disappearance of the small freehold property and a progressive feudalization of the army.

Surprisingly, however, there were still, in the Asia Minor of the late thirteenth century, some free small-holders, some soldiers who were not great landowners and who served as free men in the imperial armies. The number of people in these categories was rapidly declining in the 1290's, because of the advance of the Turks and the activities of the great landowners. Their position may be compared to that of the allodial holders in France during another period of rapid feudalization, the tenth and eleventh centuries.[3] A similar lack of central control and state protection existed, a similar encroachment upon the property of the soldier small-holder by the large proprietor who was best equipped for the defense of his lands and his men against the external danger. On the other hand, the large pronoia-holders of Asia Minor contributed very little to the general defense of the area.

Philanthropenos had not done much to reform the social ills of the eastern provinces. Rather, he had depended on the support of the disaffected. The next man sent to Asia Minor tried to carry out the reform that was needed. He was the emperor's first cousin, John Tarchaneiotes, an able general, who went to Anatolia around September 1298, with little money and few soldiers.[4]

---

3. Marc Bloch, *La société féodale* (Paris, 1939), I, 266; Georges Duby, *La société aux XIe et XIIe siècles dans la région mâconnaise*, (Paris, 1953), chapter on "L'économie rurale et les transformations politiques et sociales." Rouillard, *La vie rurale*, pp. 164–165, adduces examples from monastic records of people selling their land to the church because of the poverty and insecurity under which they labored. These closely resemble western documents that show people giving up their properties in return for protection and the necessities of life.

4. Pachymeres, II, 257ff. Tarchaneiotes' mission probably began around September 1298, because according to Pachymeres it was nearly contemporary with Athanasios' letters of that date. It seems to be the same year in which negotiations for a peace treaty with the Serbians began: Pachymeres, II, 271ff.

The following simplified genealogical table shows the relationship between Andronicus II, John Tarchaneiotes, and Alexios Philanthropenos (from Papadopulos, *Genealogie*):

Megas Domestikos Andronikos Pal. *m.* Theodora Palaeol.

Martha (Maria) *m.* Nicephorus Tarchaneiotes   Michael VIII *m.* Theodora Vatatzes

John Tarchaneiotes   Michael Tarchaneiotes   Andronicus II

Alexios Philanthropenos

He found the situation most discouraging: some of the best soldiers had lost their lands and were unable, though willing, to serve in the army. Others had increased their holdings by bribing officials, and then proceeded to lead a life of indolence. John Tarchaneiotes reverted to the legal and, in this case, highly desirable Byzantine practice of *exisosis* ("equalizing"). In the case of military holdings, the official in charge of exisosis visited the pronoiai of a given area, increased the size of those lands which were too small to allow their holders to perform military service, and took lands away from those whose holdings were too large.

Tarchaneiotes appears to have "equalized" with some zeal the larger holding. The resilience which the population of Asia Minor still possessed is demonstrated by the fact that Tarchaneiotes' reforms made possible the formation of an army, even of a fleet, and the Byzantine position in Asia Minor rapidly improved.[5] The reported success of Tarchaneiotes' reforms would inspire skepticism if it had come from any source but Pachymeres. Pachymeres, however, had every reason to be hostile to Tarchaneiotes, the leader of the Arsenite party which threatened the status quo and the historians' patron, Andronicus. Nothing in Pachymeres' work creates suspicion of secret pro-Arsenite leanings; his sympathetic view of Tarchaneiotes must be ascribed solely to the man's military prowess and wise policy in Asia Minor.

As one might expect, Tarchaneiotes' measures were unpopular with the great landowners, who immediately set out to destroy him. The general had two things in his favor: he was related to Andronicus, and he was an Arsenite: a disadvantage at Constantinople, but a great advantage in Asia Minor with its history of pro-Arsenite sympathies. The imperial family itself continued to be split between pro-Arsenites and anti-Arsenites. The Tarchaneiotes branch of the family and their connections preserved their Arsenite sympathies. Andronicus wisely disregarded John's religious affiliation when it was a question of saving Asia Minor. John, however, did not finish his work in Asia Minor, for his enemies were strong and unscrupulous. Unable to let sleeping theological dogs lie, the patriarch, John XII Kosmas, and the orthodox party were violently opposed to having an Arsenite in a position of authority. In Asia Minor itself, the disgruntled pronoia-holders whose illegal increments Tarchaneiotes had taken away accused him of contemplating rebellion.

Had Tarchaneiotes really acted in ways overstepping his authority, as his opponents in Anatolia claimed? It seems doubtful: Andronicus' long refusal to listen to their accusations indicates that the general's actions were indeed legitimate and acceptable to the emperor. But in the end Tarchaneiotes had to face a coalition of the two hostile forces. The Asia Minor "soldiers"—the pronoia-holders—convinced the anti-Arsenite bishop of Philadelphia, Theoleptos, of the truth of their accusations. Tarchaneiotes shut himself up in a monastery, and shouted down to the bishop that he should be ashamed

---

5. Pachymeres, II, 259. Ostrogorsky, *Féodalité*, pp. 103–106. *Exisosis* was done periodically to nonmilitary holdings as well. Notice that some years later the megas domestikos and future emperor John Cantacuzenus also tried to use the same measure of *exisosis* in order to reform the army (Ostrogorsky, *Féodalité*, pp. 101ff).

of himself for associating with men of such low caliber as these particular pronoia-holders. He further accused the bishop of persecuting him for his Arsenite tendencies, although the emperor himself knew of them and had forgiven them. The whole business, Tarchaneiotes said, showed that not he but the bishop and his friends were traitors, for they hindered the work of an imperial official—Tarchaneiotes himself. He may have won the argument, but he lost the battle. Discouraged, and afraid for his life, he fled Asia Minor and joined Andronicus II in Thessalonica.[6] With his departure, his policy of social reform was abandoned, and so was the hope of saving Asia Minor from within.

The Byzantine clergy and its selfishness is often blamed for all the miseries of the empire. Unfortunately, this trite accusation holds true for the period under discussion. Several efforts at reconstruction were thwarted by the clergy. In the case of Tarchaneiotes, perhaps the dynatoi simply made use of the overexcited zeal of the orthodox and of the members of the established church. This was particularly easy to do, since the failure of Michael VIII's unionist policy and the existence of an anti-Palaeologan Arsenite faction had illustrated the instability of the established church and state. Perhaps the higher clergy, themselves landowners, found more in common with the rich pronoia-holders than with the less wealthy soldiers. It took a monk, Patriarch Athanasios I, a man despised for his puritanism and his lack of learning, to point out the corruption of the clergy. Athanasios complained time and again of the behavior of the prelates of Asia Minor who, instead of tending to their flocks, preferred to reside in the capital and indulge in endless disputes.[7] It may well be that such men had already written off the eastern part of the empire.

After the failure of Tarchaneiotes' campaign, Andronicus decided to use mostly mercenaries for the defense of Asia Minor. In 1301, 8,000 Alan warriors with another 8,000 dependents entered imperial territory from Bulgaria and asked for the emperor's protection. Andronicus decided to use them in Asia Minor, and he proceeded to strip his own army in order to equip them. He sent his tax collectors to search the properties of nobles and soldiers for money, weapons, and horses.[8] He raised taxes from the countryside, collected food from Thrace and Macedonia, and drew on the meager funds of the imperial treasury. Incredible though this procedure seems, it was used, "for he [the emperor] learned that this nation [*i.e.* the Alans] was well-behaved and obedient and also very warlike and bellicose. For this reason he despised the

6. Pachymeres, II, 261–262. Andronicus II was in Thessalonica from April 1299 to October 1300. Tarchaneiotes probably met Andronicus during the last part of the Emperor's sojourn in Thessalonica; the description of Tarchaneiotes' activities in Asia Minor suggests that he stayed there for some time, probably for two years. There may be a reference to John Tarchaneiotes in Maximus Planoudes' correspondence: Planoudes, *Epistulae*, letter 5.

7. Cod. Vat. Gr. 2219, fols. 13vo–14ro, 32vo–33ro, 41ro–42vo, 42vo–43ro (letters of Athanasios I to Andronicus II). Also, below, Appendix I, letter 1.

8. Pachymeres, II, 304, 307; Gregoras, I, 204, 205. Gregoras says that the Alans came in 1300.

Romans as having become effeminate and weakened both because of circumstances and because of their malevolent attitudes and disposition."⁹ The defenses of Thrace were stripped in order to provide for the Alans; so, when the Catalans came and decided to attack the empire, they had very little to fear from the Byzantines.

The Alans themselves had asked Andronicus II to be used in Asia Minor in the war against the Turks. Andronicus gave some of them to the grand heteriarch, Mouzalon, who was entrusted with the defense of Nicomedia. However, as soon as they had crossed into Anatolia they started to raid the area and to attack the Greeks. Around Easter 1302 (April 22), the young co-emperor, Michael IX, himself went to Asia Minor with the rest of the Alan mercenaries. He thought that "the affairs of the East needed the supervision of an emperor."¹⁰ He had a large army which, apart from the Alans, included Byzantines, whom he brought with him, and some native inhabitants who joined him. Michael and his retinue made their camp in Magnesia. The size of the army and the presence of the emperor frightened the Turks, who held back and for a time stopped their raids. Michael wanted a pitched battle that would confirm his control of the area. His generals, however, decided that such an act would be too dangerous for the precious life of the emperor, and persuaded him to abandon his plan. The Turks then took heart, resumed their attacks and kept Michael virtually under siege in Magnesia. The men of Asia Minor who had volunteered to serve under Michael left in disappointment and went to take care of their homes and properties, whose destruction they considered imminent. The people who lived around Magnesia fled before the Turks, and tried to reach the islands off Thrace.¹¹

Meanwhile, the Alans also abandoned Michael, and, despite Andronicus' opposition, returned to Thrace. Once there, however, they did give back their horses and arms, as the emperor asked them to do. Michael himself left Magnesia secretly, under cover of night and poor weather, and went to Pergamum. People followed his army in a desperate effort to reach Europe and safety.¹²

Further north, in Bithynia, another struggle was taking place that would have fatal results for the Byzantine Empire. In the summer of 1302, Osman, a Turkish chief from Bithynia, appeared outside Nicomedia with a large army composed of his own followers and of Turkish allies from Paphlagonia and the environs of the Meander River.¹³ Mouzalon, the defender of the city, was forced to fight Osman, although his army of two thousand men was inferior, and although the terrain was favorable to the light Turkish cavalry. The battle took place in the plain of Bapheus, on July 27, 1302, and the Byzantines

---

9. Pachymeres, II, 308: ἀπὸ κακοθελοῦς γνώμης καὶ προαιρέσεως. This sounds as if it were directed against the Arsenite opposition.

10. Pachymeres, II, 309–311; Gregoras, I, 205. ἐδέησε γὰρ καὶ βασιλέως ἐπιστασίας τοῖς κατ' ἀνατολὴν πράγμασιν (Pachymeres, II, 309).

11. Ibid., II, 310–315; Gregoras, I, 205–206.

12. Pachymeres, II, 314–322.

13. Ibid., II, 327, 333–335; Georgiades-Arnakes, Οἱ πρῶτοι Ὀθωμανοί, pp. 127–131.

suffered a terrible defeat. Modern historians consider this battle most important for the subsequent development of the Ottoman Turks, whose activities soon spread throughout Bithynia and to areas to the north, and eventually carried them to Constantinople. After Bapheus, most of the Anatolian hinterland was lost to the various Turkish chieftains. Contemporaries thought that it was no longer possible to defeat the Turks. Many of the inhabitants of Asia Minor who survived the battle and the massacres left their homeland forever and went as refugees to Constantinople and to the islands of the Propontis.[14]

The battle itself seems to have been recognized and remembered by the Byzantines as something of a milestone. Among other indications of this stands the testimony of a Frenchman who visited the area some seven years later. He gave the precise year of the battle, and described its results with such exactitude that he must have been repeating information given to him by the natives themselves: "Therefore, since they [the inhabitants of Asia Minor] did not want to give tribute to the Turks, the Turks devastated, depopulated, and impoverished all of the said land, seven years ago; and from this the power of the emperor of Constantinople has been greatly diminished."[15]

Osman's victories were not the only signs of the Turkish advance into Asia Minor. At about the same time, other Turkish leaders reached the Aegean and took to piracy. In 1304, Sasan, an old retainer of the emir of Menteshe and of the Aydinoglou, who were to found the emirate of Aydin, occupied Ephesus.[16] Soon, the coast of western Asia Minor, with the exception of Adramyttion and Phocaea, fell to the Turks; and the Genoese entrepreneurial family of Zaccaria of Phocaea occupied Chios, which Andronicus could not defend against the Turks (1305).[17]

By 1302 Asia Minor seemed lost. The Turkish invaders were very mobile; they could retreat when the Byzantines launched an attack, and return when the army left. This is what happened during the early stages of the campaign of 1302. The Byzantine army in Asia Minor was small, disorganized, and totally ineffective. Civil defense was nearly impossible, for the people were terrified, embittered, and lacked leadership. Economically, the life of Anatolia was completely disrupted. Turkish raids made property a useless asset, indeed a liability. Houses and crops were burned and people left in panic. The inhabitants of the country fled to the few well-fortified cities—Nicaea, Nicomedia, Brusa—or to Constantinople.[18] Naturally, they felt no great love for the government which had allowed them to suffer such losses in their families and their possessions. These people were to form the backbone of the Byzantine

---

14. Pachymeres, II, 327, 334–335, 344, 421; Gregoras, I, 214; Georgiades-Arnakes, Οἱ πρῶτοι Ὀθωμανοί, pp. 127, 133–134, dates the battle July 27, 1301. On the correct chronology, see Pia Schmidt, "Chronologie," p. 85.

15. Górka, *Anonymi Descriptio Europae Orientalis*, p. 7: "Unde quia dictis turcis noblebant reddere tributum, ab eisdem septimo anno transacto tota terra dicta fuit devastata, depopulata et depauperata et ex hoc est multum imperatoris Constantinopolitani diminuta potentia."

16. Lemerle, *L'Émirat d'Aydin*, pp. 20–25. Wittek, *Mentesche*, pp. 39ff.

17. Pachymeres, II, 558; Lemerle, *L'Émirat d'Aydin*, 24, 50 and n. 2.

18. Pachymeres, II, 310ff, 335, 390.

support for Charles of Valois when he sought to unseat the Palaeologi and recreate a Latin empire.[19]

Unable to provide for the defense of his people out of the resources of the empire, Andronicus turned to perhaps the most hardened and valiant body of mercenaries of the times. After the battle of Bapheus, he accepted the offer of the Catalan, Roger de Flor, and Berengar d'Entença to help against the Turks.[20] In September 1302 he made peace with Venice, and in the spring of 1303 he concluded a treaty with Roger de Flor.[21] With the arrival of the Catalans a new chapter opened in the relations of the Byzantine Empire with the West.

The efforts of Andronicus to save Asia Minor ended in complete failure. His reorientation of Byzantine policy had not achieved its desired aim and had in fact been self-defeating. He had alienated the papacy, he had done nothing to influence the Italian wars or to make allies against the day when the wars would end and potential invaders of the empire would have a free hand. He had done nothing, because he wanted to concentrate his time and resources on Asia Minor. And as a result of his failures in the East, in 1302 he turned to the very people of the West he despised, hated, and feared, and asked them to help him save Asia Minor.

One might well ask whether Andronicus had been misguided in his policy, whether particular errors of judgment can be ascribed to particular people, whether Asia Minor could have been saved and by what means. The easiest answer is that it could not be saved, that the empire was already too weak, too decentralized, too poor to withstand any of its enemies; Andronicus and his subjects were living on borrowed time, and nothing could have staved off the catastrophe. But such an answer is not satisfying; ineluctable historical forces are rarely quite that. Of course, the historian should not produce pat, foolproof plans and solutions which, he thinks, the men of another time should have elaborated. The historian, however, can suggest possibilities compatible with the personalities and the circumstances of the period he is discussing, which men of that period *could* have followed. Asia Minor was *not* inexorably doomed in 1296, but it was very nearly so in 1302. Surely, within that period there must have been mistakes that could have been avoided, and courses of action that Andronicus should have followed.

If only one could remake history, one might have made of Michael VIII a ruler more sensitive to the religious attitudes of his people and to the importance of Asia Minor. Had he been kinder to the population of Anatolia, would the early successes of the Turks have been possible? Andronicus II, on the other hand, had his heart in the right place, but he was too weak to follow his own convictions. Clearly, the appointment of John Tarchaneiotes was a step in the right direction: by a single action, Andronicus coopted the dangerous Arsenites, placed a competent general in the field, and launched a program of social reform. Perhaps if Michael IX had gone to Asia Minor with

19. H. Moranvillé, "Les projets de Charles de Valois sur l'Empire de Constantinople," *B.E.C.* 51 (1890), 83–84 (letter of "Constantinus Dux Limpidaris" to Charles of Valois).

20. Dade, *Versuche*, p. 81; Dölger, *Regesten*, no. 2246. Cf. below, Chapter V.

21. H. Finke, *Acta Aragonensia*, II, no. 431; Rubió y Lluch, *Diplomatari*, p. 17, no. 15.

Tarchaneiotes, things might have been different: the people would have been assured of imperial interest, the reforms would have had undisputed imperial sanction; Tarchaneiotes' enemies would not have been able to take advantage of distance to spread rumors about the general's loyalty to Andronicus.

Again, if Andronicus had been able to keep his patriarch under control, perhaps the staunchly orthodox would not have made quite so much trouble for Tarchaneiotes. Had Athanasios I been patriarch at the time, he probably would have behaved differently from John Kosmas. Athanasios too was against the Arsenites. But he might have subordinated his religious sentiments to his perception of the needs of the empire. Athanasios recognized the importance of preserving Asia Minor, and he believed in the need for internal reform. There was a bare possibility of saving Asia Minor through social and political reform: the population could have been made to feel part of the Byzantine state, part of the Palaeologan state. The fact that the rebels Lachanas and Philanthropenos could command a large following, and the fact that Tarchaneiotes was easily able to form an Anatolian army indicate that the fighting spirit of the population could be aroused in the proper circumstances. Asia Minor was lost not because of the superior power of a handful of Turks, but because of the mistakes of its rulers. This is why the years 1296–1302 are so important: during these years Andronicus gambled and lost, not only Asia Minor, but also the justification of his western policy of disengagement.

The Balkans

In the Balkans, Byzantium had to deal with three foreign powers. One was the relatively cohesive and organized state of Serbia, governed by Kral (King) Stephen Uroš II Milyutin (1282–1321). The Kingdom of Serbia was not yet civilized. Byzantine officials were horrified by the wild state of the terrain and of the inhabitants. Byzantine princes found the Serbian crown a very inadequate compensation for having to live there.[22] The king's subjects lurked in mountains and valleys, stole cattle, and often descended in destructive raids on the Byzantine part of Macedonia. However, the fact that Serbia was a recognized kingdom made negotiation possible. The Byzantines, unable to fight guerrilla war, could turn to diplomacy with Uroš and make agreements to end the war.

The two states had engaged in intermittent warfare from the beginning of Andronicus' reign. Stephen Uroš II allied himself with Charles of Anjou in the hope of gains in Macedonia. In 1282 he conquered the town of Skopje, where he often resided thereafter. In retaliation, Andronicus sent his father's Tartar mercenaries to attack Serbia.[23] Uroš replied with further raids. He also welcomed Byzantine refugees and used them against their country. One of them was Kotanitzes, once a robber and then a monk, who escaped from a monastery in Brusa and sought asylum at the Serbian court. He became one

---

22. K. Sathas, Μεσαιωνικὴ Βιβλιοθήκη, I, (Venice, 1872), 156–158, 170: Metochites' account of his embassy. Hereafter, this work will be abbreviated as Sathas, Μεσαιωνικὴ Βιβλιοθήκη. Pachymeres, II, 257, 272–273; Sathas, Μεσαιωνικὴ Βιβλιοθήκη, I, 164–165.

23. Mihailo Laskaris, *Vizantiske Princeze u srednjevekovnoj Srbiji. Prilog istoriji visantiskosrpskich odnosa odkraja XII do XV veka* (Belgrade, 1926), p. 53.

of the kral's lieutenants, and in 1296–1297 raided Macedonia with the Serbs.[24] By this time, the situation on the Serbian frontier had become dangerous. The Serbs were becoming expert in guerrilla warfare, for which they had most of the necessary prerequisites: a wild, almost inviolable hinterland to retreat into; small mobile bands of warriors; and the added advantage of having to deal with only a small Byzantine army. So they managed not only to make successful raids, but also to conquer parts of Byzantine Macedonia. In 1296 they also took the important Adriatic port of Durazzo.[25]

The only way for the empire to handle the situation was to maintain in the western Balkans an adequate army to guard the frontier and to act in small, mobile units wherever the Serbs attacked. In 1298 Andronicus sent a strong army to Macedonia under the grand constable Michael Glabas. But Glabas made Thessalonica his base, and Thessalonica was a long way from the frontier. The Byzantine army faced a typical guerrilla situation: "He [Glabas] launched many attacks, but not only did he not achieve anything, he was even defeated. For the Serbians did not invade openly but mostly behaved like robbers, and the Byzantine forces were unable to succeed."[26] Glabas realized that, even if he could get the Serbs to fight a pitched battle, one Byzantine victory would make no difference to the conduct of the guerrilla war. He advised the emperor to make peace. Andronicus agreed, for he was faced with pressing danger in Asia Minor, where John Tarchaneiotes was trying to reorganize the army and to check the Turkish advance. The insecure position of the empire in Anatolia made peace in the Balkans all the more important, as contemporaries realized.

The grand constable Glabas was no mean soldier; he knew the area and had successfully led the Tartars through it in 1283. Gregoras wrote that his military experience made the other generals look like children.[27] His advice to end the war was well-considered and based on his knowledge of the military

24. Pachymeres, II, 66–67, 257; Gregoras, I, 202.

25. Pachymeres, II, 270–273; Górka, *Descriptio*, p. 12; Laskaris, *Vizantiske Princeze*, pp. 60ff. On the main characteristics of guerilla waresfare, see C. W. Thayer, *Guerilla*, (London, 1964), foreword by Sir Fitzroy Maclean, pp. 11–13.

26. Pachymeres, II, 271–2: ὃς δὴ πολλάκις προσβάλλων οὐχ ὅπως ἤνυεν, ἀλλὰ καὶ προσηττᾶτο, ὅτι μηδ᾽ ἐκ τοῦ προφανοῦς εἰσβάλλοντες ἦσαν ἐκεῖνοι, ἀλλὰ λῃστείας τρόπον ὡς τὰ πολλὰ μετεχείριζον, καὶ οὐκ ἦν ὅλως ταῖς τῶν Ῥωμαίων δυνάμεσιν εὐοδεῖν.

27. Michael Tarchaneiotes Glabas had fought in the western part of the empire, where he had been responsible for the reconquest of Durazzo and Berat from the Angevins, sometime between 1281 and 1294. He had fought in Bulgaria against Lachanas, and in Thessaly: E. Miller, *Manuelis Philes Carmina*, II (Paris, 1857), no. 237; Gregoras, I 159. It is not known exactly who he was, or what connection he had with the imperial family. There was a family connection between the Palaeologi and the Tarchaneiotai, dating from the marriage of Michael VIII's sister Martha to Nicephorus Tarchaneiotes. But Glabas was not a son of that marriage. I do not know whether he was a nephew of Nicephorus Tarchaneiotes, or some other relation. However, it should be made clear that the genealogical information given in Papadopulos, *Genealogie*, no. 24, is wrong, since he confuses Glabas with the protovestiarios Tarchaneiotes. Glabas *did not* marry the daughter of Alexios Philanthropenos, nor did he have the title of protovestiarios, nor could he have the cursus honorum attributed to him by Guilland: "Études de titulature et de prosopographie." Guilland says that Glabas was promoted to the rank of protostrator during the first years of Andronicus II's reign, yet in 1299 he still had the title of grand constable, which is three places down in the hierarchy. The first time Pachymeres mentions him as having the title protostrator is during the Bulgarian campaign of 1304 (II, 445). The title 'protostrator' was both a high courtly title (eighth in the hierarchy), and carried with it high military office; the protostrator was, in effect, the commander of the army, and although

capabilities of the empire. Andronicus, in accepting that advice, was probably chiefly moved by diplomatic considerations. A few years earlier, he had finished an unsuccessful war with Nicephorus of Epirus, and the marriage of Thamar of Epirus to Philip of Taranto had not contributed to stability on the western frontiers of the empire. Byzantium was engaged in a war with Venice; Stephen Uroš could be a valuable ally in the Adriatic, or at least he could allow Byzantium to release its forces from the Macedonian front.

Andronicus not only agreed to make peace with Uroš, but he sought the best way of making the peace binding on a man he considered very unstable in his promises. Apparently both Byzantines and westerners agreed on this aspect of Uroš' character. An anonymous French author wrote, about 1308, that the kral "is a perverse man and one given to lying, not fulfilling any oath or pact."[28] Andronicus thought that a marriage alliance would be the best guarantee of Uroš' future behavior.[29]

Stephen Uroš was also interested in a marriage alliance; he required as his price for peace a Byzantine princess or a female member of the imperial family. His choice for what would be his fourth wife fell on Eudocia, Andronicus' sister and the widow of John II, emperor of Trebizond.[30] In order to marry her, Stephen was willing to abandon his Bulgarian alliance for a Byzantine one. He had married as his third wife, Anne, George Terter's daughter and Theodore Svetoslav's sister. He now claimed that his marriage to this Bulgarian lady was illegal, because his first wife had still been alive when the marriage was contracted. Gregoras reports that none of Stephen's three consorts had produced offspring, and that this was an additional reason for his wanting a fourth wife. This is not quite correct. Stephen had at least one daughter, Zorica (Little Dawn), by a Hungarian princess, although her legitimacy was open to question.[31] He also had illegitimate sons. It is, of course, quite possible

---

there *could* be several men with the same title and office (in different fields of operation), we know of only two protostratores during Andronicus II's reign: Glabas and John Philes Palaeologos. Alexios Philanthropenos Sr., had been Michael VIII's protostrator, and he survived Michael by a few years.

Michael Tarchaneiotes Glabas restored the twelfth-century monastery of the Pammakaristos in Constantinople, and added a chapel, where he was buried: P. A. Underwood, *The Kariye Djami*, (New York, 1966), I, 269.

28. Górka, *Descriptio*, p. 35: "Rex vero Urosius . . . homo est versutus et mendax, nullum iuramentum vel pactum . . . servans."

29. Pachymeres, II, 272.

30. Gregoras, I, 202; Pachymeres, II, 273–274; Laskaris, *Vizantiske Princeze*, p. 53. John II had died in August 1297.

31. Gregoras, I, 203; Górka, *Descriptio*, pp. 35–36. Westerners thought that Zorica was Uroš' legitimate daughter. Indeed, in 1308 there were negotiations between Charles of Valois and Uroš, who offered Zorica to Charles's son in order to cement their political alliance. According to the Byzantine sources, however, the girl was illegitimate, because Uroš' marriage to the Hungarian princess Elizabeth (daughter of Stephen V of Hungary, and sister of Andronicus II's first wife, Anne), was illegal. Pachymeres (II, 272ff), explicitly says that Stephen had an *adulterous* relationship with a nun, his brother's sister-in-law. His brother, Stephen Dragutin, had married the Hungarian princess Catherine, and her sister Elizabeth had been a nun (Pachymeres, I, 350–355, Górka, *Descriptio*, pp. 35, 36, 54). Gregoras says that Elizabeth was in fact married to Uroš. But both Byzantine historians agree that Uroš' first wife had been alive when he contracted his next two marriages, and that therefore these marriages were illegal. Stephen Uroš tacitly admitted this when he said that his third marriage was void because his first wife was alive at the time.

and even probable that he did want legitimate children, especially if they were to have a stake in the Byzantine Empire. If so, he would have had to wait for a long time, for the princess he finally married was only five years old. It would be at least eight years before she could bear children, and this was a long wait for a forty-year-old man in the fourteenth century. As a result of his own haste in consummating the union, he never did have any offspring from his Byzantine marriage.[32]

Eudocia, though pressed by Andronicus, would not hear of a Serbian marriage. The kral felt slighted by this and threatened the emperor, who then had to consider giving Stephen his own daughter.[33] Andronicus thought that a Serbian king was an unworthy husband for his beloved only daughter. His paternal feelings rebelled at the thought of marrying the young Simonis, whose life at birth had been miraculously preserved by the Apostle Peter, to an old man who had been his enemy.[34] But he dared not perpetuate the war with Serbia.[35] What his wife Irene thought of the marriage at the time is not known, though Gregoras, writing from hindsight, implied that she favored it, as part of her plan for her children's aggrandizement.[36] She certainly used her son-in-law for her own purposes subsequently; but in 1298 there were enough reasons of state for the marriage to make Irene's wishes unimportant.

Andronicus was to leave for Thessalonica, with Irene and Simonis, in the winter of 1298. There he was to receive the kral and the Byzantine defectors who were being exchanged for Simonis. The winter proved very severe; Constantinople was all but cut off from the West, and Thrace was particularly impassible. Horses could not be used because the ground was buried deep in snow, and the emperor was forced to postpone his trip. But the situation was urgent, and so he sent to Serbia an embassy led by Theodore Metochites. The embassy left Constantinpole at the beginning of the dreary winter, in late November 1298.[37] Metochites has left an account of his embassy, written in the early spring of 1299 and probably addressed to Nicephorus Choumnos.[38]

32. Gregoras, I, 243.

33. Gregoras, I, 203; Sathas, Μεσαιωνικὴ Βιβλιοθήκη, I, 165. Pachymeres, II, 274–275, does not mention the kral's anger; he simply says that the emperor could not afford to slight him, and so was forced to find another bride.

34. M. Treu, *Dichtungen des Metochites*, A, verses 571–578; Pachymeres, II, 276–277. When Simonis was born, Andronicus was afraid that she would not survive, for he had already lost two or three daughters in their infancy. Then "an experienced and good woman" advised him to take the following (apparently popular) measure. Twelve candles of the same length and weight were placed each before an icon of each of the twelve apostles. Then, psalms were sung before the icons, until all the candles save one had burned out. The girl was given the name of the apostle whose candle survived longest. That was Simon (Peter). From then on, she was under his protection.

35. Treu, *Dichtungen des Metochites*, A, verses 561–565.

36. Gregoras, I, 256ff. Cf. Constantinidi-Bibicou, "Yolande de Montferrat," pp. 425–442.

37. Sathas, Μεσαιωνικὴ Βιβλιοθήκη, I, 158–162; Pachymeres, II, 276–278. Metochites must have left late in November 1298, because, writing late in February of the following year, he said that he had left for Serbia about three months earlier: Pachymeres, II, 278–279; Sathas, Μεσαιωνικὴ Βιβλιοθήκη, I, 183; Ševčenko, *Métochite et Choumnos*, p. 140. Dölger, *Regesten*, no. 2209, places Metochites' embassy between July and early winter of 1298.

38. Treu, *Dichtungen des Metochites* A, verses 571–576; Ševčenko, *Métochite et Choumnos*, p. 10, n. 3. Choumnos was then ἐπὶ τοῦ κανικλείου, that is, head of the Imperial Chancery. On Simonis' marriage, see also the poem of Manuel Philes in A. E. Martini, "Manuelis Philae, Carmina

When the embassy reached Thessalonica, it was received with unusual honors by the inhabitants, who had already heard that Metochites was bound for Serbia to negotiate a peace treaty—"[bringing] peace . . . after a very long time and very long wars."³⁹

In Thessalonica Metochites met Glabas, the leader of the western army "and governor of [the western] cities and lands," who explained that the kral was becoming impatient with the slowness of the embassy. He himself had had to pacify the kral with excuses. Glabas presented a most discouraging report on the condition of the western provinces, which were virtually in a state of anarchy. He described the natives as wild men, warlike, fond of plunder, and "goat thieves" (αἰγῶν ἁρπακτῆρες) a term which then, as now, denoted a petty but unscrupulous sort of thief. The Byzantine deserters in the kral's camp were doing their best to obstruct the negotiations. There were rumors that the Bulgarians were planning to attack Serbia to erase the insult inflicted by Uroš on the daughter of their former king. The embassy also heard of Turkish attacks on Asia Minor and of Tartar depredations in Thrace.⁴⁰ Therefore there was every reason for the ambassadors to speed the peace negotiations with Serbia.

They stayed in Thessalonica for only three days and then left for Serbia. The kral had been for some time "in the middle of his land," but he traveled to the Byzantine frontier to meet the embassy with every possible honor and courtesy.⁴¹ Serbia in December or January would have been even more of a challenge to the Byzantine ambassadors than Macedonia and Thrace had been, and to this extent Uroš' travel to the frontier was indeed a courtesy. When the Byzantine ambassadors and the kral met, Metochites explained that Andronicus wished the marriage of his daughter to Stephen; the embassy had come to receive the solemn promises and oaths of the kral, his mother, his nobles, the Serbian church and the Serbian "patriarch." Other questions to be discussed were that of a frontier rectification—demarcation problems being almost chronic in the area—and the exchange of hostages.

The discussions were long and sometimes heated. Stephen Uroš had with him a strange character who appears to have been important in the discussions. His name was George, he was a Serb, and he had spent some time among the Byzantines as a prisoner of war. According to Metochites, it was this man George who had first suggested the Byzantine marriage alliance to Uroš. He now pursued the negotiations with great ardor, and brought Stephen and Metochites together for the final discussions which ended in agreement sometime in late February 1299. Metochites sent three men (one of them a Serbian

inedita," *Atti della Reale Academia di Archeologia, Lettere e belle Arti*, 20, (1900), supplement, poem 16. Also, L. Koukoules, «Συμβολὴ εἰς τὸ περὶ γάμου παρὰ Βυζαντινοῖς κεφάλαιον,» *Ε.Ε.Β.Σ*, 2, (1925). For comments on Metochites' Πρεσβευτικός, see P. Nikov, "Tatarobulgarski otnošenija prez srednite vekove" in *Godišnik na Sofiskija Universitet, Ist.-Fil. Fakultet*, 15–16 (1919–1920), 54–95.

39. Sathas, Μεσαιωνικὴ Βιβλιοθήκη, I, 163–165.
40. Ibid., I, 165–166, 191.
41. Ibid., I, 170–173; Treu, *Dichtungen des Metochites*, A, verses 583–585. Metochites mentioned especially the tasty Danube fish which the kral sent him, and which was hard to find in Constantinople: Sathas, Μεσαιωνικὴ Βιβλιοθήκη, I, 174.

priest named Tobrailo) to report success to Andronicus, whom they found midway between Constantinople and Thessalonica.[42]

There were many people who, for various reasons of their own, opposed the marriage between Stephen Uroš and Simonis. The Bulgarians sent an embassy to Stephen, accusing Andronicus of insincerity, and presenting the state of the empire as even more desperate than it was; they were trying to show Stephen what a bad bargain he was about to make. Trying to create as many difficulties as possible, they also told the Byzantines that Stephen's word was not very dependable. The Greek state of Thessaly also tried to obstruct the Serbian-Byzantine alliance. They accused Andronicus of duplicity and said that Serbian interests would be better served by an anti-Byzantine coalition with Thessaly, bolstered by a marriage alliance. In these circumstances, one can understand Andronicus' decision to give up his daughter. Metochites wrote to Choumnos to urge the emperor to hurry his decision and the marriage, in case the kral changed his mind.[43] An alliance between Bulgaria and Serbia or Serbia and Thessaly might have proved fatal to Byzantium in the years of the Venetian war (1296–1302) or of the Catalan invasion (1303–1311).

The other great and obstinate opponent of the marriage alliance was the patriarch John XII Kosmas (1294–1303) who found Stephen an undesirable son-in-law for the emperor, by reason both of his age and of his moral character. Andronicus managed to leave Constantinople, on February 6, and apparently he had hoped that the patriarch would not realize that he was on his way to Thessalonica. While Andronicus was lingering in Thrace, however, John Kosmas found out all about it, and followed the emperor, to bless his voyage, as he said. Andronicus met John in Selyvria, on March 7, 1299, and there the two discussed John's opposition to the Serbian marriage and his insistence that John Tarchaneiotes be recalled from Asia Minor. In the end, the patriarch consented to bless the bride and the marriage, but he refused to follow Andronicus to Thessalonica:[44] the patriarch had been defeated, but only temporarily, and he bided his time.

Andronicus, Irene, and Simonis reached Thessalonica before Easter 1299 (April 19); it was Andronicus' first visit to the second city of his empire. The kral, still somewhat suspicious of Byzantine intentions, decided that the exchange of Serbian hostages for Simonis should take place midway up the

---

42. Sathas, Μεσαιωνικὴ Βιβλιοθήκη, I, 176–179. The date of the agreement can be easily, if only approximately, deduced. We may assume that Metochites sent his emissaries to Andronicus immediately after the agreement was concluded. Andronicus left Selyvria for Thessalonica soon after March 8, 1299, and arrived in Thessalonica just before April 19. The emissaries probably met Andronicus between March 28 and April 1, 1299, and it must have taken them a good month to reach him. Therefore, the agreement between Metochites and the Serbs must have taken place at the end of February. Metochites wrote the account of his embassy after February 22: ibid., p. 184.

43. Ibid., pp. 188–193.

44. Pachymeres, II, 280–282. Notice that Andronicus II had taken important men with him to Thessalonica; among them was Phakrases, the logothete of the troops. Planoudes sent several letters to both Andronicus II and Phakrases, urging their swift return home: Planoudes, *Epistulae*, letters 1, 4, 11, 17.

Vardar River.[45] In late April 1299, Stephen received his child-bride. He was very gallant, honoring the emperor in her person. The whole group then went to Thessalonica where Andronicus had prepared suitable banquets and celebrations. Simonis' dowry consisted of large parts of Macedonia.[46] One year later, Andronicus gave his son-in-law the village of Kastrion (Gradac) on the Strymon River, to be donated to the Serbian monastery of Chilandar, on Mount Athos.[47] Stephen's marriage to Simonis provoked a rebellion by his elder, lame brother (Stephen Dragutin) and part of the Serbian nobility, but Andronicus lent Uroš soldiers to help put it down.[48]

During his residence in Thessalonica, Andronicus took some steps toward settling his other affairs in the West. He felt fortified by the imminent alliance with the Serbs, and he reaffirmed his good intentions toward his niece, Anne of Epirus, at her own request. Anne needed his assurances, for her husband Nicephorus had died (1295), and she had courted the displeasure of the Angevins by refusing to let her son Thomas perform homage to Philip of Taranto. At the same time, Andronicus tried but could not find the opportunity to deal conclusively with the state of Thessaly. In 1295 Andronicus had promised one of John I's brothers the city of Demetrias as the dowry of the Armenian princess Theophano, Rita-Maria's sister. Theophano died in Thessalonica before reaching Thessaly.[49] The sebastokrator had already taken possession of the city before the death of his bride, and he refused to abandon it. Demetrias had been taken by Glabas in 1283; now the emperor sent ambassadors asking that the city be returned to the Byzantines. The Thessalians were somewhat taken aback by Andronicus' presence so near their frontiers, but avoided giving him a definite answer.[50]

Andronicus II and his wife left Thessalonica in the fall of 1300 and reached the outskirts of Constantinople on November 22. What he had accomplished by his alliance with Serbia was an unquestioned second best. None of Stephen Uroš' conquests on Byzantine territory had been returned to the empire, while his dowry made him lord of a large part of Byzantine Macedonia. Although his Byzantine marriage might make Uroš less eager to attack Byzantium, he had not been suddenly transformed into a great friend of the Byzantines. On his western frontiers, then, Andronicus' policy was one of

45. Pachymeres, II, 283–285; Gregoras I, 203–204; L. Bréhier, *Vie et mort de Byzance*, (Paris, 1948), p. 415. Metochites was present on this occasion: Treu, *Dichtungen des Metochites*, A, 578. Cf. Dölger, *Regesten*, no. 2218; Pia Schmidt, "Die Diplomatischen Beziehungen zwischen Konstantinopel und Kairo zu Beginn des 14. Jahrhunderts im Rahmen der Auseinandersetzung Byzanz-Islam," Unpub. diss., Munich, 1956, p. 143.

46. Górka, *Descriptio*, p. 12: "Magnam partem istius provincie seu regni [the "kingdom of Thessalonica," which the author calls thesaliam] possidet rex rasie seu servie, et hoc nomine dotis, eo, quod filiam imperatoris qui nunc imperat duxit in uxorem." Górka, *Descriptio*, p. 35: "Habet [Uroš] nunc filiam imperatoris constantinopolitani, cum qua habet magnam terram in grecia circa thesalonicam." Cf. Górka, *Descriptio*, p. 37.

47. L. Petit and B. Korablev, "Actes de Chilandar," *Vizantiiskii Vremennik*, 17 (1911), no. 16; Dölger, *Regesten*, no. 2229.

48. Pachymeres, II, 286.

49. Hopf, *Griechische Geschichte*, p. 355.

50. Pachymeres, II, 284.

containing his enemies by giving in to some of their demands—at least he thought he had averted full-scale war. As it turned out, war was only postponed for a few years: at the time of the Catalan invasion, Stephen Uroš helped save Thessalonica, but also launched his own attack against the empire.[51] In 1300, however, the alliance seemed a triumph to the hard-pressed Byzantines, and Constantinople, fearfully expecting an attack from the Venetian fleet, welcomed Andronicus with relief.[52] The inhabitants poured out of Constantinople and all, Byzantines and foreigners, and especially the Italians, along with the nobles and the clergy except for the patriarch, welcomed the emperor and empress.

The patriarch, however, was still not reconciled to the marriage. On his return to Constantinople, Andronicus found that John XII had abandoned the patriarchal residence, was obstinately ensconced in the monastery of the Pammakaristos, which was under the protection of his sponsor, Michael Glabas, and was threatening to resign. In vain did Andronicus plead with him to come out and return to his house. Finally, in February 1301, Andronicus told his patriarch that if he insisted on resignation, the people would all think that he had resigned solely because of the Serbian affair, and great scandal would ensue in the church. If only the patriarch would come out of hiding, Andronicus would give in to all his demands.

This somewhat bizarre story ended with John XII visiting the emperor, and presenting a list of accusations and demands in front of a congregation of the high clergy. The first accusation was that Andronicus had surrendered his infant daughter to an old adulterer, despite John's opposition. The emperor answered in an apologetic tone; he had not wanted his daughter to leave his arms and marry "a barbarian lacking totally in tenderness." He had been forced to do it because his lands and his subjects were seized or taken captive or laid waste by a man whom he could not fight. The marriage was born of necessity.[53]

While the northwestern frontier of the Byzantine Empire seemed relatively safe by 1302, clouds were gathering in the northeast. Unlike Serbia, Bulgaria was not an organized state, but rather a chaotic assemblage of semi-independent rulers, under the loose overlordship of the Tartars, who directly governed the areas nearest the Black Sea. From 1292 until 1298 Bulgaria was ruled by Smilec, a man supported by the Tartar usurper, Nogai, Michael VIII's old ally.[54] In 1299, Nogai's son Tchaka took over. At first he was helped and supported by his brother-in-law, Theodore Svetoslav, the son of George Terter—the Bulgarian who had, in 1280, rebelled against the pro-Byzantine tsar John Ašen III. Svetoslav, however, nourished ambitions of his own and, like his father before him, he could count on the support of most of the Bulgarians. In 1300 he

51. J. F. Boissonade, *Anecdota Graeca*, II, 201; cf. below, Chapter VII, "The Catalan Campaigns of 1307–1311."

52. Pachymeres, II, 283–284, 290–291.

53. Pachymeres, II, 291–298. John Kosmas had originally been introduced to Andronicus by Glabas: Pachymeres, II, 183.

54. Pachymeres, I, 324, 525; II, 266, 268; Dölger, *Regesten*, no. 2201.

imprisoned Tchaka and ruled Bulgaria on his own. Some of his subjects rejected his rule and appealed to Andronicus II. The emperor supported two rebels against Svetoslav, but both failed miserably.[55] The new Bulgarian king had lived among the Byzantines for a long time in his youth, but this had not given him any feelings of loyalty toward the Empire. A few years after his accession to the throne, he would take advantage of the Catalan presence in Thrace to become more dangerous for Andronicus' empire than any Bulgarian had yet been.

The Venetian-Genoese War and the Byzantine Empire

Andronicus II's policy of securing his western frontiers in order to concentrate on Asia Minor was shattered by the second major war between Venice and Genoa (the first had taken place in 1256–1269), which developed into a costly war between Venice and the Byzantine Empire.[56] The Venetian-Genoese war of 1293–1299 had its origins in the commercial and colonial rivalry between the two Italian states. At the end of the thirteenth century, Genoa was at the apogee of her power. She had confirmed her mastery of the Tyrrhenian Sea by her victorious war over Pisa (1282–1288), and already she had begun her economic expansion westward into Spain and North Africa. Benedetto Zaccaria, the intrepid Genoese admiral and merchant, had helped build the fleet of Don Sancho of Castile, and in 1294 armed a fleet to help Philip IV of France in his wars against England. Genoese ships were already sailing to Flanders and England. In 1291, two Genoese brothers, the Vivaldi, attempted to reach Asia by circumnavigating Africa. Their ships were never heard from again after they had sailed through the straights of Gibraltar, but apparently their effort survived in legend, and a Venetian trader, writing from West Africa in 1455 was to have occasion to recall this legend.[57]

Naturally, Venice was uneasy at the increase in the power of her rival. What most concerned the Venetians, however, was not Genoese expansion westward, but rather the extraordinary economic power of Genoa in the East; in the Aegean, in the Byzantine Empire, in the Black Sea, in the empire of Trebizond. For, while Venice had by far the most extensive territorial possessions in the East—Modon, Coron, Crete, parts of Nigroponte, several islands in the Aegean—it was Genoa which had the greatest commercial privileges, and thus commercial superiority. After the fall of Acre to the Egyptians (1291), the Genoese preponderance became all the more evident, as the products of the Far East began to pour into the Black Sea ports where Genoa held an undisputed advantage.[58]

55. Pachymeres, II, 262–267.

56. Kretschmayr, *Geschichte von Venedig*, II, 60ff; Caro, *Genua*, I, 28ff, 193–209, 234–236.

57. Manfroni, *Marina italiana, 1261–1453*, pp. 189–192; letter of Antonio Usodimare in R. S. Lopez and I. W. Raymond, *Medieval Trade in the Mediterranean World* (New York, 1967), pp. 382–384.

58. Marino Sanudo Torsello, *Secreta Fidelium Crucis*, in J. Bongars, ed., *Gesta Dei per Francos*, II (Hanover, 1611), 230ff; Kretschmayr, *Geschichte von Venedig*, II, 64–65; Heyd, *Commerce*, II, 100.

Indeed, a later Venetian historian accused Genoa of helping the sultan take Acre, and ascribed the Venetian-Genoese war to the crusading spirit of an aroused Venice, seeking revenge for the fall of Acre.[59] That was not quite true; it *is* true that Genoa did nothing to avert the fall of that port, because Genoa had disengaged herself from the ports of Egypt, Syria, and Palestine, and instead had concentrated on the Black Sea outlets. By 1293 Genoa had a tight hold over the Black Sea trade, and Venice wanted her own share of that trade. Genoa, on the other hand, had ambitions in the Adriatic that she could only accomplish through a successful war with the power in control, that is, Venice.[60] A war between Venice and Genoa, then, was almost inevitable. When it came, it was a colonial war, waged for commercial and colonial dominance, and much of it was fought in the eastern Mediterranean, the area of colonial penetration.

The immediate cause of the war was a rather trivial and not unusual skirmish between Venetian and Genoese ships off Coron in July 1293.[61] Fights between privately owned ships and piratical attacks were quite common in the Aegean in those days, and in normal circumstances the incident would have been passed off with a routine letter of complaint and a request for reparations. But this time, Venice used the incident to accuse Genoa of breaking the truce between the two states, and of deliberately molesting Venetian shipping in the Mediterranean.[62] Both states prepared, as yet in a small way, for war. In late December 1293, Venice and Genoa alerted their ships in the Mediterranean to the danger of hostilities. In January and April 1294, Venice sent money and arms to Modon and to Crete; the substantial arms shipment to Crete cost 14,000 hyperpyra.[63]

The next incident took place in the Armenian port of Lajazzo, where some Venetian ships attacked the Genoese in retaliation for the fight in Coron (1294). The Venetians had a total of twenty-eight ships, including the usual merchant ships, their convoy of armed galleys, and an additional five galleys.[64] Now the hostilities snowballed. When the Lajazzo incident occurred, there were in Constantinople a number of Genoese ships, ready to make their annual voyage to the Black Sea. When they heard of the attack on their fellow-citizens, they proceeded to act in a way that held ominous consequences for Byzantium: "they unloaded their cargoes" in Pera, and from there sailed to Lajazzo. Their fleet consisted of eighteen galleys and two other ships, and the captain was Nicolo Spinola, member of one of the four most important Genoese families. Spinola was an envoy to the Byzantine court, and earlier in the same

59. Marin Sanuto, *Vitae Ducum Venetorum* in Muratori, *RIS.*, XXII (Milan, 1733), col. 578. He probably had in mind the commercial treaty which the commune concluded with the sultan in May 1290, after the fall of Tripoli: Caro, *Genua*, II, 133. Cf. Manfroni, *Marina italiana, 1261–1453*, p. 194.

60. Kretschmayr, *Geschichte von Venedig*, II, 65.

61. Ibid., II, 64; Caro, *Genua*, II, 182; R. Cessi, *Storia di Venezia*, chap. iv; Manfroni, *Marina italiana, 1261–1453*, pp. 197–198.

62. Andreae Danduli, *Chronicon*, in Muratori, *RIS.*, XII (Milan, 1728), col. 404.

63. Caro, *Genua*, II, 185; Cessi, *Deliberazioni del maggior consiglio*, pp. 354–355, no. 136; p. 357, no. 14.

64. Dandolo, col. 404; Jacopi de Varagine, *Chronicon Januense*, in Muratori, *RIS.*, IX, cols. 14–18, 55; Kretschmayr, *Geschichte von Venedig*, II, 65.

year he had negotiated with Andronicus certain privileges for Genoese merchants.[65] Spinola's campaign against the Venetians immediately placed Andronicus in a dangerous situation, because his treaty with Venice (1285) had stated that he would not allow anyone to arm in his empire against Venice.[66]

The Genoese were victorious in the fight at Lajazzo, but, of course, this was far from a decisive victory. Venice sent more ships to attack the enemy in various places, and in December 1294, the Venetian government closed Armenia and Cyprus to Venetian shipping.[67] For a while Venice concentrated her activities in Italy, trying to crush Genoa on home ground. All Venetian subjects were recalled from abroad, and Venice tried to build up a system of Italian alliances which would include the Catalans and the kingdom of Sicily. The Genoese too tried to adjust to war conditions. As usual, Genoa was in the midst of a civil war, theoretically between Guelphs and Ghibellines but actually between parties of the most important and ambitious aristocratic families. In January 1295 the Genoese put a temporary end to the ten-year old conflict, and set about rebuilding their army and navy. Both powers stepped up the production of warships, yet on the whole the war moved at a sluggish pace.[68]

In 1295 and 1296, after abortive peace negotiations, initiated by a rather harassed Boniface VIII, the Genoese continued their war preparations, while the Venetians provided for the defense of their colonies in the Aegean and formed a squadron of thirteen galleys to patrol the Adriatic.[69] But Genoa, in 1296, chose to shift the war back to the Aegean, and the Genoese fleet, which the Venetians thought was sailing back home from Sicily, went to Crete instead. It captured and burned Canea and left, carrying a number of prisoners. It was probably at this time that the Genoese tried to open negotiations with the Cretan rebel Alexis Kallergis and thus force the Venetians to fight on yet another front. Their effort failed, for Kallergis informed them that his quarrel with the republic was temporary and negligible compared to what he would do to the Genoese if he had the opportunity.[70] As a result of the Genoese expedition to Crete, the Venetian government placed Cretan affairs under the

65. Jacopo de Varagine, cols. 14–18; Dölger, *Regesten*, IV, no. 2160; Bertolotto, "Nuova serie," pp. 512, 536; Caro, *Genua*, II, 186–188.

66. Tafel and Thomas, *Urkunden*, III no. 378 (June 15, 1285); Cessi and Sambin, *Consiglio dei Rogati*, I, 3.

67. Dandolo, col. 404. In February 1296 the Venetian government discussed measures for compensating the Venetian merchants who had suffered damages in Armenia: Cessi, *Deliberazioni del maggior consiglio*, p. 394, no. 119.

68. Jacopo de Varagine, cols. 15, 17, 55; Caro, *Genua*, II, 200, 215. Dandolo, cols. 404 (1294), 405 (1295), 407 (1298). A fleet of 200 galleys was to be ready to leave Genoa in August 1295; Caro, *Genua*, II, 203–207. Cf. Manfroni, *Marina italiana, 1261–1453*, pp. 202–203.

69. Dandolo, col. 404; Manfroni, *Marina italiana, 1261–1453*, pp. 202–203.

70. Dandolo, col. 405, 410; Jacopo de Varagine, cols. 16–17; Pachymeres, II, 233; Caro, *Genua*, II, 201–203, 225–226. The historian Navagero claims that in 1303 the people of Crete again rose in revolt, and asked Kallergis to lead them. Kallergis, now loyal to the Venetians, informed them of the danger and then met the rebels and gave them advice. He explained that the revolt could not succeed without outside help. This could come from two quarters only: from the Genoese who hated Venice, or from the Catalans who were iniquitous and avaricious. Much better, he told them, to live under the moderate rule of the Venetians than to depend on either of the two powers (Muratori, *RIS.*, XXIII [Milan, 1733], col. 1012). This incident corroborates the information concerning Kallergis' attitude during the Venetian-Genoese war.

jurisdiction of the Council of Thirty, which had, since May 1294, assumed control of Venetian relations with Genoa.[71]

The war, especially when waged in the eastern Mediterranean, was potentially dangerous for the Byzantines. At first Andronicus II tried to preserve a cautious neutrality, but such a course was difficult indeed. Nicolo Spinola's expedition from Constantinople to Lajazzo had endangered the neutrality of the empire, and as the war continued it became quite clear that Andronicus was favorably disposed toward the Genoese. Of course, even if he had wished to, Andronicus could not have helped the Genoese in a war fought at sea; it is mostly through the evidence of diplomatic exchanges that the Byzantine involvement can be followed. In 1296 the first—still unofficial—Venetian attacks against Byzantine territories are noted: the bailo of Nigroponte and his corsairs, a force of over three-hundred men, attacked Byzantine ships near Chios. The corsairs of Nigroponte had mostly Genoese leaders, but Venetian crews, and their sympathies were with Venice.[72] Their action was probably connected with the Genoese war, and may have had the unofficial sanction of Venice. At this same time, two Venetian admirals, Ruggiero Morosini and Marco Michiel, were cruising the Aegean around Modon, Coron, and Chios.[73] Andronicus may have thought that they were involved in the attack of the corsairs; in any case, in the summer of 1296 he sent his friend and imperial official, Michael Lopardos, to Venice to complain of the activities of the corsairs.[74]

Despite such incidents, Byzantium and Venice were still on fairly correct terms. But in 1296 the Venetians broke an important article of the treaty of 1285, which had forbidden hostilities between Venice and Genoa in the waters from Abydus to the Black Sea. It was probably inevitable that the Venetians should carry the war into this sensitive area. This was primarily a colonial war, and the most important Genoese colonies were in Pera and on the Black Sea coasts. A Venetian fleet of approximately seventy ships under the command of Ruggiero Morosini attacked Pera on July 22, 1296.[75] Pachymeres' passionate eyewitness account of the incident shows how contemptuously the Venetians treated the emperor on this occasion, and how the Byzantines were finally roused from their torpor at the sight of the patent collapse of their authority in the capital itself.

The Venetian attack on Pera occurred on a Sunday. According to Pachymeres, the Venetian fleet appeared off Constantinople; its destination was unknown. The emperor, the megas domestikos, and some soldiers went to a port near the hippodrome, at the southern tip of the city, and stood watching the ships. Andronicus sent a Venetian nobleman to the fleet to enquire about

71. Cessi, *Deliberazioni del maggior consiglio*, p. 414, no. 89 (December 8, 1296).
72. Sanudo, *Istoria*, pp. 146–147, 176–177.
73. Dandolo, col. 406.
74. C. A. Marin, *Storia civile e politica del commercio de' Veneziani*, VI (Venice, 1800), document 1, pp. 305–307; Dölger, *Regesten*, no. 2186; Caro, *Genua*, II, 231.
75. Tafel and Thomas, *Urkunden*, III, 329. Pachymeres, II, 237 (75 ships); Dandolo, col. 406 (40 ships); Jacopo de Varagine, col. 56, (76 ships); Sanuto, *Vitae*, col. 578 (66 ships); Kretschmayr, *Geschichte von Venedig*, II, 65; Caro, *Genua*, II, 231–232.

their intentions; Morosini did not deign to answer. Apparently, Andronicus was afraid of an attack on the city itself, but his fears were not well founded. On this occasion the Venetians did not have adequate equipment for taking fortified cities; they could only burn undefended towns like Pera. In any case, the emperor filled Constantinople with soldiers, and he imprisoned the bailo, Marco Bembo, and all Venetian merchants found in the city, as a precautionary measure.[76] At this point, twenty-two Genoese long galleys appeared. Pachymeres and the Byzantines did not know, as the Venetian chronicle knew, that the Venetians had pursued these galleys all the way from Modon to Constantinople.[77] When the Genoese galleys appeared, the Venetians tried to capture them but were outmaneuvred.

Meanwhile, the Genoese of Pera scuttled their ships in the Golden Horn. They then requested the emperor's protection, and were allowed to enter the city from the northeastern side, near the palace of the Blachernai. The Venetians proceeded to land and burn some Greek houses situated outside the walls. They also destroyed Pera, and burned many Genoese and Byzantine ships lying in the harbour.[78] Andronicus was furious at this flagrant breach of the treaty of 1285, and at the Venetian contempt for his authority. This is one case in which the emperor's sense of dignity and honor prevailed over reason and moderation: "hating the arrogance of the Venetians," he entered the war, and immediately released his forces to fight on the side of Genoa.[79]

The Venetians could not undertake much more against Constantinople, and in the end they apologized to Andronicus. When they left for Venice, they took with them a Byzantine ambassador carrying the imperial protests against the breach of the truce and against the Venetian attack on Pera and Constantinople. The ambassador was the bishop of Crete, Nicephorus. It was hoped that the bishop would have more than the usual influence on the Venetians, since he came from a Venetian colony and knew their ways. When he arrived in Venice, the Major Council reissued its earlier directive to the Council of Thirty to treat all matters pertaining to Byzantium in the context of the war with Genoa.[80]

Meanwhile, in order to give compensation for the burned houses, Andronicus confiscated the property of Venetians in Constantinople, to the value of 80,000 hyperpyra. Pachymeres was right in saying that Andronicus took this

76. Pachymeres, II, 238. The main Venetian source, Dandolo, gives a different account of Bembo's imprisonment. He claims that Andronicus II had made a new treaty with the Genoese, in which he agreed to imprison Bembo and all Venetians resident at Constantinople! It was this incident, says Dandolo, which provoked the Venetian attack on Pera and Constantinople. This is very unlikely; Andronicus would have been quite mad had he made such an agreement. On this, see Dandolo, col. 406, and Manfroni, *Marina italiana, 1261–1453*, pp. 205–206.

77. Dandolo, col. 406. Cf. Pachymeres, II, 238–240; Gregoras, I, 207.

78. Jacopo de Varagine, col. 56; Dandolo, col. 406; Gregoras, I, 207; Caro, *Genua*, II, 232. The Byzantine ships found in the harbor were probably private boats for the most part, although some vessels had escaped the destruction of the imperial navy and still belonged to the emperor.

79. Pachymeres, II, 238–239; Marin, *Venezia*, VI, 308–309.

80. Pachymeres, II, 241–242; Tafel and Thomas, *Urkunden*, III, 373; Caro, *Genua*, II, 233–234; Marin, *Venezia*, VI, 309; Dölger, *Regesten*, nos. 2192, 2193; Cessi, *Deliberazioni del maggior consiglio*, p. 409, no. 71 (September 20, 1296).

measure primarily because he felt insulted; there is really no rational explanation of this action, which was almost certain to provoke further Venetian
hostilities.[81] The confiscation was of dubious legality. According to the treaty
of 1285, the emperor had a right to resort to it, in order to pay damages to the
Genoese, but only when all other measures had failed, only after he had
complained to Venice and Venice had not responded to his appeals. In any
case, it is unclear whether the treaty of 1285 was still valid. The treaty had
been concluded for ten years, but it was also stated that it would be valid even
after ten years, unless either party had decided to abrogate it and had given
six-months notice. Only after the expiration of the six-month period could
hostilities begin.[82] It is fairly certain that these niceties had not been observed,
and the actions of both the Venetians and Andronicus II in July 1296 violated
the provisions of the treaty.

After the Venetian attack on Pera, the empire was at war with Venice.
Worse was to come. At the end of December 1296, some Genoese, "many
against few and wild against quiet men," killed the Venetian bailo and as
many other Venetians as they could. They were then overcome by fear and
fled to Genoa.[83] This was the first Genoese action in the war not condoned by
Andronicus. He sent the monk Maximus Planoudes and the orphanotrophos
Leo Bardales to explain to the Venetian senate that he had not been involved
in these atrocities. The Venetians declined to send their own ambassadors in
exchange. It may be that they had planned to send an embassy, but that they
had had second thoughts after the report of the murders.[84] The Venetian
government deplored the impotence of imperial justice and refused to renew
the treaty of 1285 unless given compensation for the confiscated Venetian
property. The question of reparations was to be one of the stumbling blocks
in the future negotiations for peace.

Between 1296 and May 1299 Venice was at war with both Genoa and
Byzantium. On the whole, Venetian operations in the East were successful.
Ruggiero Morosini, after his attack on Pera, went south and attacked and
destroyed the Genoese town of Phocaea, whose valuable alum mines had made
the fortune of the Zaccaria family.[85] In the same year, 1296, the admiral,

81. Pachymeres, II, 242; Gregoras, I, 208; Dandolo, col. 406; Cessi and Sambin, *Consiglio
dei Rogati*, p. 5, no. 29.

82. Tafel and Thomas, *Urkunden*, III, 341.

83. Pachymeres, II, 242–243.

84. Ibid., II, 243; Tafel and Thomas, *Urkunden*, III, 373; Thomas, *Diplomatarium*, I, 12;
Caro, *Genua*, II, 234; Ihor Ševčenko, "Léon Bardales et les juges généraux," *Byzantion*, 19
(1949), 247–259 (1296); Dölger, *Regesten*, no. 2197; Cessi, *Deliberazioni del maggior consiglio*, p.
419, no. 7 (March 20, 1297). Thiriet, quite wrongly telescopes into one the two embassies, of
Nicephorus and Planoudes, and says that the embassy had been sent in reply to Delfino Dolphin's
representations of 1294: Thiriet, *Délibérations*, p. 70, n. 2. Maximus Planoudes referred twice to
his Venetian embassy in his correspondence. In a letter to Leo Bardales, he recalled that the
two ambassadors had feared for their safety in Venice, and that in fact they suffered greatly
while they were there: Planoudes, *Epistulae*, letter 5. Letter 29, to Demetrius Sgouropoulos, then
metropolitan of Thessaly, recalls that when Planoudes and Bardales returned from Venice, they
found that their horses and equipage had been seized by pirates.

85. Dandolo, col. 406; Sanuto, *Vitae*, col. 578; Jacopo de Varagine, p. 56; Caro, *Genua*, II,
233.

Giovanni Soranzo, with twenty-five galleys entered the Black Sea and burned the Genoese colony at Caffa.[86] Another Venetian, of much less illustrious lineage, Domenico Schiavo, was active both in the Black Sea and in the Aegean. Besides attacking Genoese possessions in the Black Sea, he also captured an imperial ship near Chios, and brought it to Nigroponte. The ship must have carried some particularly valuable cargo—perhaps mastic from Chios— because Andronicus later demanded the high compensation of 29,000 hyperpyra.[87] In Nigroponte, Bonifacio da Verona seized the castle of Carystos, which had been occupied by the Byzantines. There were hostilities between Venice and Genoa near Chios, near Macronesos, and in Modon. All the available information indicates that during the course of the war Greek opinion supported Andronicus' alliance with Genoa. Marino Sanudo reports that when the inhabitants of Macronesos saw the Genoese ships, they sailed out to them in their boats and sold bread and other provisions. When the same people saw the standards of Saint Mark, they were not nearly so eager to appear.[88]

The Venetian victories against Genoa in the Aegean and the Black Sea only increased Genoa's determination to fight on. It is not surprising that Venice should have had such a high rate of success, because Genoa was overexpanded in the East, and her colonies offered convenient points for attack. Politically, too, Venice was far more likely than Genoa to win a long war. Venice had already developed a relatively centralized form of government, in which the state controlled much of the shipbuilding and most of the foreign trade, and either owned or could commandeer all seaworthy ships. Venetian colonies were governed by officials sent from Venice and really existed for the benefit of the mother city. Genoa had not yet evolved and in fact never would evolve a stable political system. The city was governed by factions, always at one another's throats, and civil war was virtually endemic. The Genoese colonies were often quite detached from the mother city, and sometimes followed their own foreign policy. It was often a matter of chance whether a colony would follow a policy consistent with that of Genoa or one opposed to it. Finally, the Genoese government had virtually no control over the ships of private individuals, and had to ask individuals to contribute to the war effort. This loose political system would eventually prove the ruin of Genoa, and was already the commune's greatest weakness. But at this point, Genoa wanted desperately to win the war. Not only did she want to preserve her position in the East, but, says the Genoese chronicler, she insisted on proving to skeptical observers that her men and ships could, indeed, defeat Venice.[89]

In 1298 Genoa gave the command of her army and fleet to the capable new

---

86. Dandolo, cols. 406–407. The continuator of Jacopo da Varagine, in *RIS*, IX (Milan, 1726), 56B claims, wrongly, that the Venetians were unable to burn Caffa (hereafter, Cont. of Jac. d. Varag.). Cf. Caro, *Genua*, II, 233. Caffa was rebuilt, but in 1307 it was burned by the Mongol Tohtu; the Genoese and their Byzantine allies were unable to defend it (Cont. of Jac. d. Varag., pp. 500–501); Brătianu, *Recherches sur le Commerce*, p. 283.
87. Dandolo, col. 406; Dölger, *Regesten*, no. 2231.
88. Sanudo, *Istoria*, pp. 130–131; Dandolo, col. 406.
89. Jacopo de Varagine, cols. 14–18.

Captain of the People, Lamba d'Oria. The new commander-in-chief took his fleet up the Adriatic, and met the Venetian forces near the island of Curzola, the present-day Korčula, off the Dalmatian coast. Here, on September 7, 1298, a major naval battle took place. The fleets of the two states were nearly equal in number, but d'Oria exhibited superior strategy and managed to inflict a resounding defeat on his enemies. The disaster seemed complete for Venice: eighty-five of their ninety-five ships were destroyed, 7,000 men were killed, and many more were taken prisoner. Among the prisoners was the admiral, Andrea Dandolo, the son of a doge, who, rather than suffer the indignity of being jeered at by the Genoese mob, committed suicide by bashing his head against the sides of a ship. Marco Polo was also taken to Genoa as a prisoner, there to begin his career as a storyteller.

The Genoese victory at Curzola was dramatic, but its results were not nearly as beneficial as Genoa might have hoped. The aristocratic government of Venice tightened the reins and prepared to recover what had been lost; Genoa was unable to conceive and enforce long-term policies. Both belligerents were tired, and both had suffered. The battle of Curzola had taken its toll of Genoese ships and men, and, of course, the Genoese colonies in the Levant had been greatly damaged. In 1298 and 1299 a number of peacemakers persuaded the two parties to open negotiations, and the good offices of Charles II of Naples, Matteo Visconti of Milan and Pope Boniface VIII were rewarded by the conclusion of a peace treaty between Venice and Genoa on May 25, 1299.[90]

But if Genoa considered herself victorious, she must have felt cheated by the provisions of the treaty of Milan. There was a cessation of hostilities, and some readjustments in Italy. Venice also promised not to give Pisa any help against Genoa—an anachronistic promise, since Pisa was by now very weak. The situation in the East, which had really caused the war, was hardly mentioned. Indeed, Genoa made certain promises which at first glance seem detrimental to Byzantium alone, but which in fact damaged Genoa's power in the Byzantine Empire by reducing her active involvement. Genoa reserved her right to remain allied to the Byzantines, but agreed not to sail to Byzantine territory in the Adriatic. Genoa was not allowed to break the treaty by using as an excuse the Venetian occupation of Byzantine territories, even if Genoa was opposed to such occupation.[91] In effect, although not in principle, Genoa promised not to interfere in the continuing war between Venice and the Byzantines, and she kept to both the letter and the spirit of her promise.

Thus, the Byzantines were left after 1299 with a dangerous war which they

90. On the battle of Curzola and the treaty of Milan, see Jacopo de Varagine, col. 499; Dandolo, cols. 407–409; Manfroni, *Marina italiana, 1261–1453*, 208–216; *Liber Jurium*, II, 344–352; Tafel and Thomas, *Urkunden*, III, 391. Navagero, in *RIS*, XXIII (1733), col. 1011, gives a false account of the treaty which would leave Venice a much freer hand in dealing with Byzantium. For example, Venice could ask the emperor to pay reparations for any harm done to Venice "a instanza dei Genovesi," and the Genoese were not to sail in Byzantine waters or in the Adriatic while the republic was at war with the empire. See also T. O. Negri, *Storia di Genova*, pp. 426–429.

91. *Liber Jurium*, II, 344–352; Dandolo, col. 409; Marin, *Venezia*, V, 127ff; Tafel and Thomas, *Der Doge Andrea Dandolo und die von ihm angelegten Urkundensammlungen* (Munich, 1855), p. 115.

had only entered accidentally. The allies, on whose behalf Andronicus had interfered, had abandoned him completely. Venice now had a free hand, and immediately after the treaty of Milan adopted a tougher attitude toward the hapless Byzantines. In 1299 the Venetians had asked Andronicus for a renewal of the treaty of 1285. They even promised to leave to the emperor most of the goods he had confiscated in 1296. Pachymeres makes it quite clear that this took place before the treaty of Milan, when the Venetians were still faced with a dangerous situation in Italy.[92] Andronicus considered the Venetian offer acceptable, as indeed it was. But his greedy councillors thought that a short wait would force Venice to forego even the rest of the reparations. The Byzantines had just concluded their alliance with Serbia, and this no doubt increased their confidence in the future. Andronicus rejected the Venetian offer; neither he nor his advisers could have foretold the treaty of Milan, which was to entirely change the attitude of Venice.

In 1300 and 1301, Venice devoted herself to restoring the defenses of her colonies in the Levant. Crete, Modon, and Coron were sent men, arms, and money for wheat and biscuit. The disaster of Curzola had left Venice short of ships, and she had to delay both her trading expeditions and her war activities.[93] In September 1300, Venice authorized her representatives in the Romania to exchange war prisoners with the Byzantines, perhaps in an attempt to recover men for her army and navy. Finally, on February 18, 1301, the senate decided to send two flotillas to the east, which would leave as soon as they were ready, one at the end of February and the other one later. Their primary aim would be to fight the Byzantines in the Aegean, but some galleys were to be allowed to go to Armenia for trading purposes.[94]

Part of the war was fought in the Adriatic, but here the contest was between Venice and Stephen Uroš.[95] The Serbian kral, with his expansionist tendencies,

92. Pachymeres, II, 286–287; Dölger, *Regesten*, no. 2247. Cessi and Sambin publish the following document, the caption of a decision by the Venetian senate: "Ambaxator missus ad Imperatorem requirat satisfactionem yperperorum LXXX mille et yperperorum XIIII mille et aliorum," and they date this, tentatively, March 1299: Cessi and Sambin, *Consiglio dei Rogati*, p. 5, no. 29. If we accept Pachymeres' statement about Venetian concessions before the treaty of Milan, and I do, there are two possible explanations for the document: either the date is wrong, and the document should be dated *after* May 25, 1299, or else these were the preliminary instructions to the ambassadors and were later changed. I tend to accept the first possibility. Sambin accepts the date March 1299 in his article, "La politica mediterranea di Venezia alla fine della guerra del Vespro," *Istituto Veneto di Scienze, Lettere e Arti, Atti*, 104, (1944–1945), 978.

93. Cessi and Sambin, *Consiglio dei Rogati*, p. 12, no. 52; pp. 11–12, no. 50; Sambin, "Politica di Venezia," p. 979. This is a very important article, particularly with regard to Venetian foreign policy in 1299–1302. Sambin does not, however, use Byzantine sources and so on occasion makes minor errors.

94. Cessi and Sambin, *Consiglio dei Rogati*, p. 6, no. 35; pp. 17–18, nos. 69–71; Sambin, "Politica di Venezia," p. 980.

95. Cont. of Jac. d. Varag., p. 299. The Angevins also had interests in the Adriatic but these concerned Epirus, in which Philip of Taranto had a viceroy throughout this period. The war with the Aragonese prevented them from taking an active part in the conflict between Venice, Genoa and Byzantium. See Hopf, *Griechische Geschichte*, pp. 356–357. Sambin thinks that the Aragonese of Sicily may have tried to help Andronicus, and as evidence he adduces the heavy incidence of piratical attacks from Sicily against Venetian ships, in March 1301: Sambin, "Politica di Venzia," pp. 980–981.

created trouble for Venetians and Byzantines alike. In 1296, when he took Durazzo from the Byzantines, many Venetian traders suffered from the greed of the population of the city and of the conquering army. Venice immediately forbade her citizens from going to Durazzo, and sent an embassy to Uroš requesting reparations and the renewal of whatever privileges Venetian citizens had under the Byzantines.[96] After his alliance with Andronicus, Stephen Uroš attacked Ragusa, a Venetian dependency.[97] This shift in his attitude was one of the few benefits Byzantium reaped from the alliance.

In early April 1301 a Byzantine embassy, headed by the orphanotrophos Leo, arrived in Venice to seek peace.[98] It is most unlikely that Andronicus was prompted by the activities of the Venetian fleet, because that was still in Venice in March 1301. It is more likely that he thought, correctly, that the longer the war dragged on the more difficult it would be to negotiate. The Byzantine embassy requested the renewal of the treaty of 1285, and reparations for the Byzantine ship captured by Domenico Schiavo. The Venetians, however, were not eager to make peace. The Byzantines wanted a twenty-year truce, the Venetians would only accept a ten-year truce. The Byzantines asked for 29,000 hyperpyra as reparations; the Venetians offered 18,000. Time and again Venetian documents contain the formula: "and if the ambassadors will not be satisfied with this, tell them that they should go in peace." By April 29 negotiations had foundered, and the Byzantine ambassadors were told to go home—on a Venetian ship, naturally.

The war continued during the summer of 1301 and in 1302, with increasing activity on the part of the Venetians. A Byzantine embassy returned to Venice in May 1302, but whatever its proposals may have been, the Venetians refused to accept them.[99] The Venetians now took a drastic action which forced the complete capitulation of the empire. In the summer of 1302 thirteen Venetian ships under the command of Belleto Giustiniano, along with seven boats belonging to pirates from Crete and Nigroponte, entered the Golden Horn, stopped at Pera, and in full view of the palace of the Blachernai burned the fields of the peasants, rich with summer wheat. Andronicus wanted to oppose the attack, but he had virtually no ships, as the remains of the imperial fleet were engaged elsewhere.[100] The policy of disarmament was bearing evil fruit, as both the emperor and his subjects now realized.

96. Cessi and Sambin, *Consiglio dei Rogati*, p. 4, no. 11; Cessi, *Deliberazioni del maggior consiglio*, p. 400, no. 29 (June 19, 1296); Sanudo, *Istoria*, p. 129; Hopf, *Griechische Geschischte*, pp. 355–356; Jireček, *Geschichte der Serben*, pp. 338–339.

97. Jireček, *Geschichte der Serben*; F. Miklosich, *Monumenta Serbica spectantia historiam Serbiae Bosniae Ragusii* (Vienna, 1858), nos. 40, 41, 42, 45, 46, 51, 52, and so on for privileges granted to Ragusa by the kings of Serbia.

98. On the embassy and the negotiations, see Dölger, *Regesten*, no. 2231; Cessi and Sambin, *Consiglio dei Rogati*, p. 26, no. 95; pp. 28–29, no. 100; p. 32, no. 112; Sambin, "Politica di Venezia," p. 981.

99. Sambin, "Politica di Venezia," p. 984. Notice the peremptory note of the document in Cessi and Sambin, *Consiglio dei Rogati*, p. 55, no. 196: "Quod dicatur nuntio Imperatoris quod, si vult aliud dicere de eo quod dixit, potest dicere, sicut placet ei, alioquin potest ire in bona fortuna."

100. Pachymeres, II, 321ff; Gregoras, I, 208–210; Dölger, *Regesten*, no. 2237; Dandolo, col. 409; Navagero, col. 1011.

In 1296 it had been Andronicus who had felt personally slighted by the Venetian attack on Pera. This time his subjects too felt insulted, and begged him to give them orders, a little time, and a little money to rebuild a fleet. Others suggested building a bridge from the old city to Pera, using fishing boats, cargo boats, and any larger ships available. Their purpose was to transport armies to Pera, and fight the Venetians on land. Andronicus thought these proposals dangerous and, swallowing his pride, announced that he disliked fighting against other Christians. The Venetians, little concerned with such subtleties, had no scruples about attacking Christians; indeed they allowed the pirates to attack the islands of Propontis, which were crowded with refugees from the Turks. The emperor and his men were able to see from the city the plight of the poor refugees, who were killed if they had no money to give for their ransom.[101]

Andronicus sent the Venetian admiral 4,000 gold pieces to ransom the refugees and then, evoking the lapsed treaty of 1285, reminded Giustiniano that it was forbidden to cooperate with the pirates. Giustiniano, having already made his point, repented and proclaimed that he also was only interested in peace, provided the issue of compensation could be settled. The Venetians then departed, taking with them Andronicus' ambassadors (the protosynkellos Maximos and a certain George of Coron) who were to negotiate the peace treaty. On September 12 the Venetian senate appointed Giustiniano and three other men as its representatives in the discussions.[102] The discussions were terminated and the treaty concluded on October 4, 1302.[103]

The peace treaty of October 1302 between Venice and the empire was basically a renewal of the truce of 1285, which Venice accused the Byzantines of breaking. Some questions arose after it had been signed, and Byzantine ambassadors were dispatched to Venice to negotiate the disputed points and sign a new treaty.[104] The Byzantines had fared badly in the war at sea, and some large islands had been conquered by Venice. Of these, Venice kept Keos, Amorgos, Seriphos, and Santorin, returning the others. The Byzantines did not claim any damages from the expedition of Ruggiero Morosini. On the other hand, Venetian property confiscated by Andronicus as a result of Venetian attacks on the city and on Pera, to the value of 79,000 hyperpyra, would be returned. The Venetians did not claim any reparations either from Byzantium or from Genoa for damages done to them by the Genoese in the Sea of Marmora and the Black Sea. They had settled this with Genoa in the treaty of 1299. In any case, Venice had launched the attack on the Genoese colonies, and the Venetians had inflicted more damages on the Genoese than vice versa. The Genoese also waived their own rights to reparations from the Byzantine government. Venice would enquire into the claims of some of her subjects to reparations of 7,000 hyperpyra, which they said they had lost during

---

101. Pachymeres, II, 323–324, 326; Dandolo, col. 409.

102. Pachymeres, II 326–327. On Giustiniano's expedition, see also Sanuto, *Vitae*, col. 579; Cessi and Sambin, *Consiglio dei Rogati*, p. 69, no. 244.

103. Thomas, *Diplomatarium*, I, no. 7 (text of the treaty); Marin, *Venezia*, V, 276–280; Dölger, *Regesten*, no. 2247; Cessi and Sambin, *Consiglio dei Rogati*, p. 71, no. 253.

104. Thomas, *Diplomatarium*, I, 83; Pachymeres, II, 326; Dölger, *Regesten*, nos. 2250, 2251.

the Venetian attack of July 1302. If the claims were thought valid, Andronicus would have to meet them. On the positive side, Andronicus could subtract from the 79,000 hyperpyra he owed to Venice 24,000 hyperpyra as compensation for the ship destroyed by Domenico Schiavo near Chios. The Venetians also promised to abstain from their trade in salt and mastic throughout the empire.

The treaty was to remain in force for only ten years, unless renewed. On October 5, the Venetians decided to send to Constantinople a new bailo, and an ambassador who would discuss the payment of the reparations Andronicus had promised. On October 27 it was decided to release all Greek prisoners held in Venice. Discussions about the money payments continued, but by the end of October normal and normally uneasy relations had been restored between Venice and Byzantium.[105] Venice could not begin concerted efforts to reorganize her trade and her economy, both severely disrupted by the war.

If one were making a list of unprofitable wars, the war of 1293–1302 would be a good entry. It was long, it was destructive, and in the end no one really gained much. Certainly, the profits that accrued to any single party were not worth even a fraction of the human and material sacrifices that went into the war. On balance, Venice probably profited more than the other two belligerents, but that is saying very little. Venice's gains were mostly in the Aegean, where she needed them least; her gains in the Black Sea were nil, unless one counts as a Venetian gain the temporary weakening of the Genoese position in that area, and the destruction of Genoese properties in Caffa. Venice renewed again her treaty with Byzantium, but this could have been done without the war. And Venice and Byzantium still felt hostility and suspicion toward one another. Venetian complaints against the prejudiced attitude of Byzantine officials continued to stream into the Byzantine and Venetian chanceries. For these small gains Venice paid with the destruction of her fleet, the death or imprisonment of many of her citizens, and an immense expenditure of money. Trade too had suffered, as her subjects were not allowed to travel to Armenia, Cyprus, the Byzantine Empire, and Ragusa while hostilities were going on. Venice had to spend several years trying to reorganize her economy and recover from the effects of her war with Genoa.

For the Byzantine Empire the war was disastrous. Michael VIII's offensive in the Aegean had not completely stopped at his death. Now, during the war with Venice, Andronicus had lost most of what his father had gained. The Byzantines had suffered humiliation, loss of life, property, and territory—all because they had become involved in the war of an ungrateful ally. Finally, the war of 1296–1302 spelled the bankruptcy of the western policy of Andronicus II. He had depended on his friendship with Genoa, and Genoa had let him down. He had believed himself safe from Venice after the treaty of 1285, and he was sadly disabused. Venetian hostility toward Byzantium, far from decreasing, now took a new form. On July 17, 1301, Venice sent a formal embassy to Charles of Valois, brother of the king of France. The instructions of the

---

105. Cessi and Sambin, *Consiglio dei Rogati*, p. 71, no. 256; p. 72, nos. 257–262; p. 73, no. 265; pp. 75–78, nos. 272–273, 275–276, 278–282.

ambassadors have not survived; they may have discussed the possibility of an alliance against Byzantium, but even if they did not, a first contact had been made between the Venetians and the man who would soon emerge as the official western pretender to the Byzantine throne.[106]

Genoa, the victor of Curzola, reached its apogee in that famous battle, and then began a slow decline. Internal disorders erupted again, and Genoa's primacy in the Tyrrhenian Sea was soon to be challenged by Aragon. Its policy toward Byzantium was shortsighted beyond comprehension. The Genoese forfeited much of the power and prestige they had enjoyed in the empire, although this was not immediately apparent. In May 1303 Andronicus gave the commune a larger and better location on which to rebuild its colony of Pera.[107] Further privileges were granted to Genoa, at the commune's request, in March 1304, and Genoese merchants still received preferential treatment. Andronicus persevered in his effort to keep the Genoese friendly in order to have their help at sea, but his subjects were embittered. Immediately after the war, the Byzantines had to deal with the Catalan campaign, which soon developed into an invasion. When the Genoese of Pera failed their hosts yet again, the people of Constantinople expressed their anti-Genoese feelings through riots, anti-Latin propaganda, and an intense pressure on Andronicus to rebuild the fleet so that dependence on the Genoese might cease once and for all.

In yet another way the Genoese suffered from their ambivalent relations with Byzantium. Although they left the Byzantines to face the music after 1299 they did insist on reserving their right to help them against Venice. Sometime in late February or early March 1301, the Genoese began discussions with Venice, in an effort to conclude a tripartite treaty between Venice, Genoa, and the kingdom of Naples. The initiative probably had come from the Angevins of Naples, who wanted the maritime republics at peace with each other and allied to Naples in its war against the Aragonese in Sicily. Venice discussed the possibility of such an alliance for a short time. But on May 8, 1301, the Venetian senate wrote to its ambassador that if Genoa persisted in keeping its rights of interference in the Byzantine Empire, no alliance could be made.[108] Venice, of course, realized that she and Genoa had conflicting interests in the Levant, and that any alliance between them would be meaningless.

106. Ibid., p. 37, no. 132; Sambin, "Politica di Venezia," p. 991.

107. Georgii Stellae, Annales Genuenses, in L. A. Muratori, ed. *RIS*, XVII, 1021. Stella dates this concession 1304. See also Cont. of Jac. d. Varag., ed. V. Promis, p. 10, and the Italian translation, in G. Monleone, *Annali Genovesi* (Genoa, 1941), p. 69; A. Giustiniano, *Annali della Repubblica di Genova*, ed. G. B. Spotorno, II (Genoa, 1854), p. 6. This chronicle of Giustiniano, who lived from 1470 to 1535, is mostly an adaptation of Stella, as far as this period is concerned. Manfroni, "Relazioni," p. 609; Desimoni, "Quartieri," pp. 247ff; Sauli, *Colonia*, document 109; *Liber Jurium*, II, 435–438; L. T. Belgrano, "Prima serie di documenti riguardanti la colonia di Pera," *Atti della Società Ligure di Storia Patria*, 13 (1877–1884), 103; Heyd, *Commerce*, I, 454ff; E. Dalleggio d'Alessio, "Recherches sur l'histoire de la latinité de Constantinople," *Échos d'Orient*, 25 (1926), 21ff.

108. Sauli, *Colonia*, document 10; Belgrano, "Prima serie," document 10; Cessi and Sambin, *Consiglio dei Rogati*, p. 19, no. 79; pp. 32–33, no. 115; Sambin, "Politica di Venezia," pp. 972–976. E. Dalleggio d'Alessio, "Galata et la souveraineté de Byzance," *REB.*, (1961), 319.

The Venetian-Genoese-Byzantine war put an end to the halcyon years of Andronicus II. During the next few years he would be faced with the most pressing dangers from the West.

The Means of Defense

During the late Middle Ages, an aggressive foreign policy was a very expensive affair. Paying the fares of ambassadors and providing for their sustenance while they stayed abroad—and their residence in foreign countries might range from one month to over a year, depending on the nature of their instructions— was only the beginning. Bribes were very much the order of the day: bribes to foreign officials, to other states, or to dangerous tribes could accomplish much at the expense of considerable amounts of money. Yet even expensive bribes were cheaper than the cost of maintaining an effective army and fleet. The important maritime cities of Italy—Genoa and Venice—could maintain their large fleets only by converting their commercial fleets into military ones as the need arose. The new rising Mediterranean naval power, Aragon, depended for the most part for its fleet on the province of Catalonia, the aid of whose merchants could be enlisted in time of war. Armies too were difficult for a medieval state to maintain. Feudal levies were just becoming outmoded, and the kings of France, England, Castile, and Aragon were engaged in difficult and protracted efforts to get sufficient taxes voted to enable them to equip and maintain small armies. The hiring of mercenaries was a common expedient. But mercenaries, while often efficient, were dangerous people. Once a war was over, how could they live except by the method they had become accustomed to, pillage? The cost of maintaining independent states was rising. Yet without effective diplomacy, without an army or a navy, that is, without money, how could a state survive?

Byzantium in the 1290's was a poor state, and it was correspondingly weak. It is this basic fact that determined the foreign policy of Andronicus II, yet it does not justify particular errors of policy. The most striking aspect of Andronicus' foreign policy, and the most dangerous for the future, was his placing the empire in an entirely defensive position while neglecting to provide it with adequate means of defense. Indeed, such was the disintegration of the means of defense—the army and the navy—that is was no longer possible, at the end of this period, to defend Byzantine territories without outside help. Much less was an independent and positive foreign policy within the realm of possibility.

In some ways, the emperor and his advisers had willed this situation in the 1280's, when they scrapped the navy and gave important privileges to the Genoese. This can be seen as part of the policy of concentrating all available resources against the Turks: as yet, the war with the Turks was fought on land, and naval power was largely irrelevant. On the other hand, defense against the West depended on sea power. Michael VIII had recognized this, and had insisted on an efficient naval force, saying "it is impossible for the Byzantines to hold Constantinople securely without being masters of the seas." But at the time of Andronicus II the Byzantines apparently considered the western danger insignificant, and consciously or unconsciously depended on the Genoese to defend them at sea, should the need arise. During the Venetian-Genoese war, the folly of this policy became clear: the Byzantines had given Genoa the privileges she had asked, and by so doing had shown all their cards: they had kept no power of persuasion—or of blackmail. The historian Gregoras presented with some violence his views on the subject: "The Romans [Byzantines] threw the imperial office into bondage voluntarily, on purpose, and one may say with great art. This they did by emptying the seas of their ships, for hope of profit, a profit so small but pregnant with long and expensive and shameful loss. For if the Romans had remained masters of the seas, as they had been, then the Latins would not have grown so arrogant toward the Romans, nor would the Turks ever have gazed upon the sands of the sea, nor would the Romans have been driven to such extremities that they fear their neighboring nations, and those who live a great distance away as though these were Tantalus' stone, hanging over our heads by a thin thread. Nor would we have had to pay to everyone tribute every year."[109]

The demolition of the navy, far from being an isolated decision of a few greedy or misguided imperial advisers, was indicative of the trend toward a state with economic and political interests based on land. The rapid process of feudalization, the increasing power of the dynatoi, the gradual move away from an economy of exchange and the shift of the center of political interest from Europe and the seas toward Asia Minor and the Balkan hinterland were other concomitant manifestations of the same trend. The feudalization of the Byzantine state, that is the spread of the large pronoia holdings had adverse effects on both the organization and the morale of the Byzantine army. The developments described below were not new to the 1290's; some had begun under Michael VIII, some even at the time of the Comnenoi and the Angeloi, but they proceeded at a faster pace under Andronicus II as the central government lost power.

Feudalization in the army and decentralization in the administration proceeded concurrently, and both can be attributed largely to the impoverishment of the public treasury. All of these developments were interconnected, in the sense that if lack of money led to the distribution of lands in payment for services, so the proliferation of land grants undercut the state's sources of revenue. It is also evident that the twin process of decentralization and feudalization was self-perpetuating, unless checked by radical reforms. Decentralization of government meant that the central government could not, at any one time, control all of its provinces and the activities of all its provincial officials and generals.

In the years before 1302, the central administration had not yet become bankrupt. We know of only relatively minor cases of insubordination among imperial officials, such as the provincial officials who refused to execute imperial decrees regulating Italian commerce. But after 1303, the Empress

---

109. Pachymeres, I, 309–310; Gregoras, I, 208–209.

Irene was allowed to wield extraordinary powers in Thessalonica, where she resided, and from then on the decentralization of the Byzantine administrative system would proceed at a rapid pace.[110]

In the military field, decentralization led to a number of provincial rebellions, especially in Asia Minor, which was the threatened province par excellence and which more than any other was outside effective central control. There were mobile forces stationed in and around Constantinople, which presumably could be sent wherever trouble occurred. But by and large the central government depended for the defense of Asia Minor on the efficiency of the provincial general who was empowered to recruit from his own area, and to wage war as best he saw fit. This made him virtually independent of the government of Constantinople, and allowed generals like Philanthropenos to engage in dangerous rebellions.

The preservation of a good army depended on money and money was scarce from the beginning and became increasingly hard to get. In 1283 Andronicus had instituted a 10 percent tax on the pronoiai. In theory, the funds came from the revenues of the dynatoi; in practice, as Pachymeres noted, the money was collected from the paroikoi.[111] Indeed, the attitude of the dynatoi determined to a large extent the condition of the army and of the defenses of the Empire. Marxist historians have made a rather tenuous case for the treasonable cooperation between the Byzantine upper class, including landowners, and the Ottoman Turks, leading to the downfall of the empire.[112] A less dramatic but stronger case can be made against them: that they behaved in a completely selfish manner, and allowed the military and diplomatic defenses of the empire to disintegrate, to the eventual, but at first unforeseen, benefit of the Ottoman Turks. The central government must share part of the blame for the dissolution of the defensive system of the East: Michael VIII, pursuing his western ambitions and trying to break down the opposition of Asia Minor to his rule, had discontinued the pay of the *akritai*, the frontier guard, and moved the armed forces of Anatolia westward to fight his other wars.[113] In the later years of the thirteenth century, it was the provincial officials (ἡγεμόνες) who tried to make money by reducing the salary of the frontier soldiers.[114] The rapid advance of the Turks into Asia Minor indicates that very few of these frontier soldiers were left by the later 1290's.

Pachymeres attributed the disintegration of the Byzantine army partly to the mild, kind personality of Andronicus II, who found it difficult to punish anyone, even the men who appropriated the salaries and lands of his soldiers. The emperor was eventually forced to realize that reforms were necessary, but he instituted them in a halfhearted manner. Unable to bring his local officials under effective control, he tried to appoint honest men as heads of the provinces

110. Thomas, *Diplomatarium*, pp. 174–175. See below, Chapter VII, "Diplomacy in the Balkans."

111. Pachymeres, II, 69: ὃ δὴ καὶ συνήγετο μὲν ὡς δῆθεν ἐκ τῶν δικαίων τῶν δεσποτῶν, τὸ πᾶν δ' οἱ παροικοῦντες ἀπετίννυον δυναστευόντων ἐκείνων. Cf. Pachymeres, II, 209. The *paroikoi* were the peasants cultivating the *pronoia*-lands.

112. Francès, "La féodalité byzantine," pp. 69–90.

113. Gregoras, I, 138; Pachymeres, I 310.

114. Pachymeres, II, 208.

(εἰς κεφαλάς).[115] This was a step in the right direction, but it was not sufficient, since his new appointees had little power over the dynatoi, and he himself had little opportunity of judging the actions of the officials once they were at their posts.

His second remedy was disastrous: since the native army was small and ineffectual, he turned to more or less preorganized bodies of soldiers. In the 1290's, for example, he recruited Cretan soldiers who had fled the Venetian occupation, sent them to Asia Minor, and paid them an annual salary, financing it mostly out of the 10 percent tax on the pronoiai.[116] Most of the soldiers recruited in groups were mercenaries, and nearly all proved dangerous for the empire. This is understandable, since the bands of mercenaries had their own leaders, on whom they depended for sustenance, and to whom they gave an obedience far above the temporary allegiance they might grant to the state. Mercenaries, groups of people whose business was war and who existed as defined, organized groups were, in the end, a threat to any army and to any state. The Italian city states found this out, as did France during the Hundred Years' War. So did the Byzantines. Chortatzes led his Cretan mercenaries to serve under Philanthropenos, and then to rebel against him; in the Epirus campaign the Byzantine commander was obliged to draw back because his mercenaries obeyed not him but one of their own leaders. A few years later, partly as a result of Philanthropenos' rebellion, Andronicus was to rely on Alans, Turks, and Catalans, all of whom eventually turned against him.

The native Byzantine army consisted of two types of soldiers. Some were paid salaries, in cash. In 1272 Michael VIII, in a very important *prostagma* (decree), empowered his son and heir, Andronicus, to increase the salary of such soldiers. The Cretan soldiers of Philanthropenos, although "settled" in Asia Minor—which in earlier periods would imply that they were given land grants in payment—also received their pay in cash.[117] There is reference to special taxes, imposed at some time before February 1301, to provide money for the payment of soldiers. The patriarch, John XII, protested against these new demands for money, which is why the information has survived. It is not known whether the money went to a specially recruited force, or to a specific area. Since the emperor tried to justify the new taxes by recalling the pressing dangers to the empire, the money might possibly have been used to pay some of Michael IX's forces, which were subsequently defeated in Asia Minor. It is perfectly possible, of course, that Andronicus used this money not for native troops, but for the Alan mercenaries who appeared in 1301.[118]

Native soldiers of the second type had plots of land from which they drew their subsistence. Pachymeres calls all such men "pronoia-holders," which would indicate that they all had received from the emperor personal land grants. There is a slight possibility that Pachymeres was using this term loosely, to denote all soldiers with landed property, even if their land was allodial; but this possibility can probably be discounted, since Pachymeres insists that

115. Pachymeres, II, 208–209.
116. Pachymeres, II, 209.
117. Heisenberg, *Aus der Geschichte*, pp. 40ff, 70, 79–81; Ostrogorsky, *La féodalité byzantine*, pp. 96ff; Pachymeres, II, 209.
118. Pachymeres, II, 293, 307.

Michael VIII gave pronoiai to a great number of people, and since Pachymeres' subsequent discussion of the fate of the small pronoia-holder seems to refer to lands granted conditionally, not to allodial holdings.

The pronoia-holders of this transitional period, 1261–1302, must be separated into two distinct groups, those who held large pieces of land, and were rich and powerful, and those who held small plots. Some small pronoia-holders survived at least until 1302, when the great exodus from Asia Minor began. Michael VIII's prostagma of 1272 referred to such people, and he allowed Andronicus to augment their holdings, if he thought it necessary. Pachymeres also referred to them in connection with Michael IX's defeat at Magnesia, in 1302, saying that as a result of this defeat they became dispossessed: "The Roman forces had not only become weakened, but also the soldiers had lost their pronoiai, and so they left the East and came West, trying merely to keep alive; and it was not feasible to recruit others and pay them fixed salaries."[119] They abandoned their houses and their property and crossed the Hellespont in search of safety.

A few years later, during 1305–1307, some of them responded to Michael IX's efforts to reorganize an army against the Catalans and the Bulgarians, while others went further west and contributed to the defense of Thessalonica.[120] The passage of Pachymeres, quoted above, follows immediately upon his statement that the Byzantine armies in Asia Minor were dissolved, and is an explanation of that statement. The passage makes it clear—especially by the passing reference to the possibility of forming new, salaried armies—that until 1302 the defense of the province, such as it was, depended on fairly numerous and fairly small pronoia-holders. It would seem that the psychological and military—though not perhaps the social—basis of that system was quite similar to the system of the peasant soldier: the small pronoia-holders were given plots of land to sustain them while they gave military service, and they were expected to fight well, both in order to keep their holdings and because they had a stake in the lands they were trying to preserve.

There were other pronoia-holders in the area, with much larger domains. Michael IX himself was one of them, and, like others, he lost his holdings during the Turkish advance. He was given lands in Thrace instead.[121] Some of the big pronoia-holders owed their property to the gifts of Michael VIII; others had begun as small-holders, and had increased their domains by bribing the heads of the provinces (τοὺς ἡγεμονεύοντας).[122]

Before 1302 Andronicus tried to arrest the disappearance of the small

---

119. Pachymeres, II, 388–389: Αἱ μὲν Ῥωμαϊκαὶ δυνάμεις οὐχ ὅπως ἐξησθένουν, ἀλλὰ καὶ προνοίας ἀπολωλεκότες, ἀνατολὴν φεύγοντες ἐπὶ δύσεως ὥρμων, περιποιούμενοι ἑαυτοῖς μόνον τὸ ζῆν· ἑτέρους δ᾽ ἐγκαθιστᾶν ἐπὶ ῥητοῖς γέρασι ἀμήχανον ἦν. Cf. Ibid., pp. 316ff. On this, see also A. Andréadès, "Floraison et décadence de la petite propriété dans l'empire byzantin," *Mélanges offerts à Ernest Mahaiem*, (Paris, 1935), pp. 261–266; G. Ostrogorsky, "Les grands domaines dans l'empire byzantin," in *Recueils de la société Jean Bodin, IV, Le Domaine*, (Paris, 1949), pp. 35–50; H. Glykatzi-Ahrweiler, "La politique agraire des Empereurs de Nicée," *Byzantion*, 28 (1958), 51–67.
120. Pachymeres, II, 316ff.
121. Pachymeres, II, 407.
122. Pachymeres, I, 92, 97, 315–316; II, 258; Ostrogorsky, *La féodalité byzantine*, pp. 93–94; Cf. Rouillard, *La vie rurale*, pp. 155ff.

holding. John Tarchaneiotes was sent to Asia Minor in order to reorganize the army of the province, and the reorganization was based on a policy of supporting the small-holder. After Tarchaneiotes' failure, Andronicus made one further effort to restore the native defenses of Asia Minor. His intention seems to have been to take away from the churches and monasteries and his personal entourage (τοῖς βασιλεῖ παρασπίζουσιν) their lands and pronoiai, and to distribute them among the soldiers of Anatolia, thus creating the basis for a new army. He tried to do this sometimes between the battle of Bapheus (June 27, 1302) and the arrival of the Catalans in Constantinople (September 1303). Since the patriarch who permitted Andronicus' reform was Athanasios I, the reform must have been attempted after the abdication of John XII Kosmas, which took place on June 21, 1303.[123]

It was the first time since the reign of Manuel Comnenus (1143–1180) that an attack had been attempted on monastic properties, and the pious Andronicus was forced to take this unusual measure because of the desperate situation in Asia Minor: "it was impossible to defend ourselves and to counter them [the Turks] with an army, and it was neither proper to negotiate with the Persians [Turks], nor indeed possible, for they were many and they had different views." So, "because of the critical times and the circumstances, it appeared necessary to take the one measure still remaining: releasing from the overlords however much was given in pronoia to the monasteries, the churches, and the imperial entourage, to make everything—including even the lands attached to single monk's cells—into military holdings, so that people would stay and defend their own."[124] This would have been sound policy, and it would have set a precedent for the later efforts of John V and Manuel II, undertaken in 1367 and after 1408, under much heavier pressure.[125] To his credit, the patriarch Athanasios I did not, like later patriarchs, forbid the alienation of church property. Perhaps he could not openly commit himself to the emperor's policy, but "he sent the emperor an olive branch, without saying a word."[126]

---

123. Pachymeres, II, 390. For the chronology of the battle of Bapheus and the appearance of the Catalans, see Schmidt, "Chronologie," p. 85, and G. Caro, "Zur Chronologie der drei letzten Bücher des Pachymeres," *BZ*, 6 (1897), 116. On the abdication of John XII Kosmas see V. Laurent, "La chronologie des patriarches de Constantinople de la première moitié du XIVe siècle, 1294–1350," *REB* 7 (1949), 147.

124. Pachymeres, II, 389–390: καὶ τὸ μὲν γὰρ ἀνθίστασθαι καὶ ἀντιπαράγειν ἐκείνοις [the Turks] στρατεύματα ἄπορον ἦν· θεραπεύειν δ᾽ αὖθις ὁμολογίαις τὸ περσικὸν οὔτε τὸ πρέπον ἐδίδου, καὶ ἄλλως ἄπορον ἦν τόσων ὄντων καὶ διαφόρων τὰς γνώμας ... Ἐν τῶν ἀναγκαίων ἔδοξε τῷ καιρῷ καὶ τοῖς ἐφεστῶσι πράγμασι, τὸ περιλειφθὲν τέως, ὅσον ἐν προνοίαις ἐτάττετο μοναῖς τε καὶ ἐκκλησίαις καὶ τοῖς βασιλεῖ παρασπίζουσιν, ἀφεικότας τῶν δεσποτῶν, τάττειν εἰς στρατιωτικόν, πλὴν καὶ μονοκελλικόν, ξύμπαντας, ὡς ἐντεῦθεν αὐτοὺς ἐκείνοις ὑπὲρ τῶν ἰδίων προσμένοντας μάχεσθαι. On the correct translation of this important passage see Elizabeth Fisher, "A Note on Pachymeres' 'De Andronico Palaeologo'," *Byzantion*, 40 (1971), 230–235.

125. Ostrogorsky, *La féodalité byzantine*, pp. 160ff.

126. Pachymeres, II, 390: ἐστέλλετο τοιγαροῦν καὶ παρὰ πατριάρχου θαλλὸς ἐλαίας ἀναυδήτως τῷ ἄνακτι. Contrast this with the answer of Philotheos Kokkinos to a similar request made by John V (1367), found in Miklosich and Müller, *Acta et diplomata*, I, 507, 508: ἐγὼ οὐκ ἔχω ἄδειαν ἐκδοῦναι τινί τι τῶν τῆς ἐκκλησίας κτημάτων, φύλαξ γὰρ εἰμὶ τούτων ... εἰ δὲ βούλεται ὁ βασιλεὺς ὁ ἅγιος λαβεῖν αὐτὰ τῇ ἰδίᾳ ἐξουσίᾳ, ὃ βούλεται ποιῆσαι, ποιησάτω: "I am not permitted to give away any of the possessions of the church, for I have been appointed to guard them . . . But if the holy emperor wants to take them on his own authority, let him do whatever he wishes to do."

The whole reform plan, however, had no practical application, and its significance lies only in revealing imperial and patriarchal intentions. Charanis and Ševčenko discuss the reform as though it had indeed taken place, but Pachymeres is unusually clear on this point: "but all this was intentions only, for those who had been ordered to implement the decisions did not remain in office, and the Turks invaded from many places, and killed many people, while those who were able to flee . . . shut themselves up in Cyzicus."[127] Even though it had no practical application, the intended reform of Andronicus II must mitigate the usual accusation levied against him, that he enriched the monasteries with lands above all proportion.[128] At least with reference to Asia Minor, this was not entirely true. According to the surviving sources, all the lands he donated to monasteries lay in Europe.[129] In Asia Minor, both the emperor and the public-spirited patriarch tried to restore the small-holder and with him the defenses of the empire. These examples also suggest the need to modify Ostrogorsky's thesis on the negative role of the pronoia during the rule of the first Palaeologi. It is clear from the cases quoted above that until the time of the Catalan invasion the defense of Asia Minor remained largely in the hands of fairly small pronoia-holders, and not with the great feudal lords. It was precisely the rapid disappearance of the small pronoia that finally disrupted the defense of the area.

After 1303, the imperial army was very small, and inadequate to deal with the military problems of the state. The crisis in the ranks of the army had also been a crisis in leadership. It is a sad irony that at the time of its worst defeats the Byzantine army was led by some very able generals: Michael Glabas, John Tarchaneiotes, Alexios Philanthropenos. Perhaps it was, after all, unhealthy for the imperial family to have a monopoly in military leadership. These men, all closely related to the emperor, were haunted both by the possibility of rebellion and by the probability of being accused of contemplating rebellion. They also had to contend with the poisonous feelings of suspicion between soldiers and civil officials. Time and again soldiers and their leaders complain about the corruption and inefficiency of officials at Constantinople, to whom bribes spoke more loudly than valor.[130] The civil officials, on the other hand, lost no opportunity of accusing every successful general of planning to overthrow Andronicus. There were, of course, military attempts at rebellion; but on the whole, if one keeps in mind the welfare of the Byzantine Empire

127. Pachymeres, II, 390. Cf. Charanis, "Monastic Properties," p. 111; Ševčenko, "Anti-Zealot Discourse," p. 156. Meyendorff, *Palamas*, p. 36, recognizes that Andronicus' measure was not implemented.

128. Ostrogorsky, *La féodalité byzantine*, p. 173. Cf. Ševčenko, "Anti-Zealot Discourse," pp. 156–157.

129. This, of course, is partly due to the nature of the sources, which tend to come from the European parts of the empire. One assumes the loss of similar sources—mainly *praktika* of monasteries—from Asia Minor. See V. Mošin, *Akti iz Svetogorskich archiva. Spomenik der Kgl. Serb. Akademie*, 2d ser., 70, 5, (Belgrade, 1939); L. Petit and B. Korablev, "Actes de Chilandar," *Viz. Vrem.*, 17 (1911); L. Petit and W. Regel, "Actes d'Esphigmenou," *Viz. Vrem.*, 12 (1906); L. Petit, "Actes de Xenophon," *Viz. Vrem.*, 10 (1903); W. Regel, W. E. Kurtz, B. Korablev, "Actes de Philothée," *Viz. Vrem.*, 13 (1907); Regel, Kurtz, and Korablev, "Actes de Zographou," *Viz. Vrem.*, 13 (1907); Miklosich and Müller, *Acta et Diplomata*, I–VI.

130. Pachymeres, II, 208.

rather than the preservation of Andronicus on his throne, one cannot avoid the thought that any good general would have done more for Byzantium than the officials of Constantinople, whose numbers grew like a cancer on the weakened body of the empire. They hampered the work of the army, and the effect of their malpractices became evident in such vital matters as the administration of the army, appointments to office, the sale of goods, and the provisioning of Constantinople.[131] Despite difficulties, the Byzantine army could boast of some good generals, even after 1302, but it was becoming increasingly difficult for them to do their job properly.

The disintegration of the Byzantine army must have occurred quite rapidly in 1300–1303. Compare Tarchaneiotes' moderate success to the situation at the time of the Catalan campaign, when Andronicus found it impossible to oppose these faithless mercenaries because "prolonged poverty mocked the imperial army" (ἐνδείας μακρᾶς τὰ βασιλικὰ καταγελώσης στρατόπεδα).[132] In this case, ἔνδεια meant lack of soldiers rather than lack of money. Much later, in 1321, Andronicus, trying to restore the defenses of the empire, was thinking in terms of an army of 2,000 horse to be stationed in Thrace and Macedonia, and another of 1,000 men in Asia Minor. [133] It was very difficult to maintain an independent foreign policy with such small armies.

The Social Background

The material resources of a state ultimately depend on the material and psychological strength of the people who make up the society. The Byzantine state of the late thirteenth and early fourteenth century witnessed a progressive social disruption which sapped its resources. The gradual decline of imperial authority, primarily in Asia Minor but also, to a lesser extent, in the rest of the empire, inevitably had destructive repercussions on the lives of Byzantine subjects. Other historians have traced the growth of large ecclesiastical and secular domains in this period, a trend in itself indicative of the fragmentation of the empire. We are concerned here with the more general social background to the various political events of the period.

The subjects of Andronicus' empire suffered a number of devastating blows during the first twenty years of his reign. There were natural disasters, especially earthquakes. One occurred in June 1296 and another in August 1303.[134] They hit Thrace, Asia Minor, and Constantinople, whose inhabitants were suffering from other evils as well. In 1285 Thrace and Macedonia were under a triple threat from the pirates who ravaged the seacoasts, from the Tartars, and from the Vlachs, who were said to be contemplating an alliance with the Tartars.[135] Andronicus transferred the inhabitants of the coasts to the interior, and ordered those living in the threatened areas to repair to the fortified towns.

131. See the letters of Athanasios I, discussed below, Chapter VI, "The Cost of Byzantine Foreign Policy," and Appendix I.
132. Gregoras, I, 223.
133. Gregoras, I, 317–318.
134. Pachymeres, II, 391; Gregoras, I, 202, provides the date, June 1296.
135. Pachymeres, II, 105–106.

The Vlachs were forcibly moved from Vizyë to the Asiatic coast of the Bosphorus. The transfer of the Vlach population took place in winter and thus gravely disrupted their cattle-based economy. After the Tartar danger had passed, Andronicus allowed the Vlachs and the inhabitants of the coasts to return to their old homes. His actions in this crisis indicate that although he was still able to control his subjects in Thrace, and even to safeguard their lives, he could only do so by the most temporary measures, and could do nothing to save their property.

A few years later, during the Venetian-Genoese war, it was demonstrated that the emperor was quite incapable of protecting those of his subjects who had the misfortune to live near the coast or on the islands near the capital. The incursions of Stephen Uroš in Macedonia wrought even more extensive devastation. Andronicus himself admitted that "of the men and lands and chattels belonging to our empire, some were taken into miserable captivity, some were totally devastated and some were irreparably lost as spoils."[136]

In Asia Minor, devastation and social dislocation reached their peak. Metochites' two orations to Andronicus speak of the gradual destruction of the province, a destruction that Andronicus' two visits there failed to arrest. "Ἡρημώθη ἡ Ῥωμαΐς," "The land of the Romans has become deserted," was a usual cry among contemporary Byzantine witnesses, and Pachymeres used it to describe what happened in Anatolia after the rebellion of Philanthropenos.[137] Yet, whatever the troubles that had beset Asia Minor in the latter part of the thirteenth century, it was during Michael IX's unsuccessful campaign of 1302 that the real exodus of the population began. The first wave of refugees came after his retreat from Magnesia, in 1302. Michael's army was followed by men, women and children "who paid for the preservation of their lives with a long march and much sorrow." They fled toward Pergamum in a senseless and disorganized flight. Some fell behind and were trampled by horses, or were left to die of cold while the others pressed on. Some took refuge in the relatively secure cities of Asia Minor, but most of them crossed the Hellespont to reach the coast of Thrace, "without means, without clothes and without food," abandoning their houses and their properties, "the creations of famous men."

A second large wave of refugees, even greater than the first, came after the battle of Bapheus.[138] They left Asia Minor, with what cattle they could bring along, and went to Constantinople. Most of them had lost some relative, all of them had lost hope, and they wandered in the streets of the city telling a tale of woe. As refugees, they had still much to suffer from the lack of interest on the part of their compatriots in the capital. In the correspondence of the Patriarch Athanasios I, we find long and appalling descriptions of the lack of sympathy of the people of Constantinople for the refugees, who were left to die of cold and hunger.

---

136. Pachymeres, II, 293–294: ἀνδρῶν καὶ χωρῶν καὶ πραγμάτων προσηκόντων τῇ βασιλείᾳ τῶν μὲν ἀπαγομένων ἀθλίως, τῶν δ᾽ ἐρημουμένων ἐσχάτως, τῶν δὲ σκυλευομένων ἀνταποδότως.

137. Pachymeres, II, 232.

138. Pachymeres, II, 316ff, 335–337. Bekker in his notes on Pachymeres says that they went to Nicomedia, not to Constantinople. The text simply says "to the city," εἰς πόλιν, but talks of them crossing a πορθμός, which must be the Bosphorus.

The Social Background

One factor among the many that combined to oppress the Byzantine population was the burdensome taxation imposed on the poorer elements of town and country. The peasants in particular were heavily taxed, as all our sources testify. The extent to which the central government benefited from these taxes is debatable, since this depended on the control the emperor exercised in each province at any given moment. It is very difficult to determine which taxes went to the imperial treasury and which were appropriated by provincial officials. The people of Thrace paid their taxes to the central government, both now and later. Of course, the proximity of Thrace to Constantinople facilitated the task of imperial officials who wanted the money to go to the treasury. It appears that at the time of Metochites' embassy to Serbia, Macedonia also paid taxes which reached the imperial treasury.[139] A few years later, at least after the Catalans had cut off communications between Constantinople and Macedonia (1305), western Greece became almost independent of the capital in every respect.

The 10 percent tax on the pronoiai, which began as an extraordinary measure, was levied very frequently, and its burden was heavy on the paroikoi.[140] The Patriarch John XII made a formal complaint about the frequency of that tax. In 1301 taxes on the rural population increased to enable the emperor to meet the requirements of his Alan mercenaries.[141] The fate of the cultivator seemed to be to struggle with men and nature in order to raise his crop, and then to see most of the result of his labor disappear into the treasury of the pronoia-holders or the emperor. As Gregoras said, the peasants had to "work hard throughout their lives and to be worn down yearly by tax-collectors and tribute collectors."[142]

The taxes which fell on people other than peasants are less well documented. Venetian and Genoese documents indicate that there was an occupation tax on sailors, and there may have been a similar one on Jewish furriers and leather workers. There were import taxes levied on merchandise carried by Byzantine merchants or on Byzantine ships, and the state claimed part of the income of Byzantine shipowners who hired their vessels to the Italians. There were also purchase taxes levied on the corn sold by Venetians.[143] The patriarch John XII Kosmas complained in 1301 that "everything is sold for gold and silver [*i.e.* at a very high price]; salt, necessary for life, is being taxed, and so is iron. And even

139. His Serbian guide suggested that they live off the country through which they were passing. To this, Metochites answered that these people pay taxes and are consequently free φορτικῶν καὶ δυσχερείας ἁπάσης. Since, however, he had met his guide just outside Constantinople, we do not know exactly to what area he was referring; we only know that it lay between Constantinople and Thessalonica. Sathas, Μεσαιωνικὴ Βιβλιοθήκη, I, 156. For an enumeration of the taxes levied on the countryside in the late thirteenth century, see P. Lemerle, "Un chrysobulle d'Andronic II Paléologue pour le monastère de Karakala," *Bulletin de Correspondance Hellénique*, 60 (1936), 428–446.

140. Pachymeres, II, 209, 293.

141. Pachymeres, II, 307; Gregoras, I, 204.

142. Gregoras, I, 175–176: τὸ δὲ τὰ ὅπλα ἀποδόμενον πρὸς γεωργίαν ἐτράπετο, αἱρετώτερον ἡγησάμενοι οὕτω τε μοχθεῖν διὰ βίου καὶ τοῖς ἐτησίοις κατατρίβεσθαι τελώναις τε καὶ φορολόγοις, ἢ λιμῷ συνωθοῦντι πρὸς θάνατον . . . καταπροέσθαι.

143. Thomas, *Diplomatarium*, nos. 72–79; below, Chapter VIII, "The Italian Maritime Cities." On taxes levied on Byzantine shipping, see G. Rouillard, "Les taxes maritimes et commerciales d'après des actes de Patmos et de Lavra," *Mélanges Charles Diehl*, I, 277–289.

though he [the patriarch] has often requested that the just thing be done, he has been treated with contempt."[144] The patriarch was, at this point, presenting Andronicus with a list of complaints which had to be satisfied before John XII would consent to return to his throne; in answer Andronicus appealed to the patriarch's sense of public responsibility, in order to justify the heavy taxes. He explained that the needs of the state were great and that they could not be met without money. He himself was no lover of gold, he said, but other revenues had failed, and he needed money for the soldiers' wages. He even called a treasury official (λογαριαστής) as a witness, and adduced examples of previous emperors who had solved similar problems by similar means. He promised to heed John's future admonitions, and the patriarch was finally appeased.[145]

In this incident, John XII, playing the role of protector of the poor, was unfair to Andronicus who was not trying to enrich himself or his family. In this sense, he was one of the least selfish emperors, and both he and his son Michael would later use their private resources to finance the war against Bulgarians and Catalans. Andronicus was also right in telling the patriarch that other sources of revenue had disappeared, and in thus justifying his new taxes: the virtual loss of Asia Minor and the commercial concessions granted to the Italians had eliminated two important sources of revenue. However, the mere fact that Andronicus was acting out of necessity was not sufficient to justify his actions in the eyes of his harassed subjects, asked to finance foreign mercenaries whom they feared and hated. Their taxes were usually collected by the type of official whom they had come to regard as corrupt, and this too infuriated them.

Contemporary accounts all agree that the calibre of imperial officials was very low, and that their reputation was even worse. Bribes were commonplace and essential for any dealings with officials. Honest men who would not, or poor men who could not, make gifts, had no hope of advancement.[146] Corrupt or rich men could aspire to honors and to greater wealth by reason of the money they put into the pockets of imperial officials. This happened in Asia Minor, where John Tarchaneiotes found that the best soldiers had lost their pronoiai to those who could afford to offer bribes.[147] Athanasios I went to the root of the evil when he advised Andronicus to provide for his soldiers and deal personally with them instead of letting his officials treat them dishonorably

---

144. Pachymeres, II, 293: καὶ ὅτι χρυσολογεῖται τε καὶ ἀργυρολογεῖται τὸ πᾶν, τετιμιουλκημένου μὲν τοῦ χρειώδους ἅλατος τετιμιουλκημένου δὲ σιδήρου, συχνῶν δὲ καὶ συνδοσιῶν γινομένων, καὶ τρίτον ὡς καταφρονεῖται αὐτὸς ἀναφορὰς πολλάκις ὑπὲρ τοῦ δοκοῦντος δικαίου ποιούμενος.

145. Pachymeres, II, 295–298.

146. Pachymeres, II, 208. Theodore Palaeologus, Enseignements, Cod. Brux. 11042, fol. 82vo (on Metochites): "car il ne faisoit à nul rien sanz grant louier." Cf. fols. 83ro, 85vo, 86ro. See also the case reported by Planoudes to Phakrases, logothete of the troops: a friend of Planoudes had been unwise enough to become a tax-farmer. He then found that he was not a man "to rejoice in the tears of others, or to seek gain from the loss of others." He sought release from the remaining six months of his office as a tax-farmer, and Planoudes pleaded his friend's cause. Planoudes also reminded Phakrases that there were tens of thousands of other men who were very eager to assume the job, "and to fatten their bellies on the public money": Planoudes, *Epistulae*, letter 3.

147. Pachymeres, II, 258.

and appropriate their property; then, said the patriarch, would the army obey and honor its emperor, then could he depend on his soldiers. Athanasios was scathing about "your nobles" who, he said, "devour the poor like bread." The comparison was apt for, as we shall see later, one of the great abuses of power by imperial officials concerned their dealings in the black market for corn. According to Athanasios, the salvation of Asia Minor depended primarily on the repentence of the people, and in the second place on the removal of corrupt officials. He implored Andronicus to send good worthy men to Asia Minor. Only then, he insisted, would that province become free and rich once again.[148]

The gradual emergence of the patriarch as the spokesman for the weak and humble and as the guardian of the state was one of the interesting developments of this period. Perhaps such a development was inevitable, given Andronicus' weak personality, attested by both major Greek historians of the period, and given also the difficulty of the times and the corruption of officials. John XII (1294–1303) and Athanasios I (1289–1293, 1303–1309) were bitter enemies in their lifetimes, but they both viewed the patriarchate as protecting the interests of the people. Athanasios especially, that tough, self-righteous, severely virtuous monk, whose strictness aroused the hatred of ecclesiastics and laymen in high places imposed his dominant personality on the emperor during his time in office.[149] In his voluminous correspondence he returned again and again to what he considered an important aspect of his office, his role as the sole representative of the people to the emperor, his function as mediator between the oppressed subjects and the imperial officials. In return, the people of Constantinople gratefully recognized him as their protector, even their leader, and obeyed him on occasions where the imperial officials could hardly control them.

Most of Athanasios' letters were written during the second period of his patriarchate, although some belong to his first term in office (October 14, 1289–October 16, 1293). Gregoras reports that during this first term Athanasios' main concern was with the internal corruption of the church: greedy monks seeking the patronage of the rich, or prelates residing in Constantinople and engaging in disruptive discussions while their sees were neglected.[150] But he was also very much concerned with the preservation of justice and with the morals of people in high places. His real influence in public life becomes apparent in this passage by Gregoras: "He was consumed by such a great and illustrious zeal against unjust men that not only the emperor's relatives but even his sons feared his [Athanasios'] free and severe tongue and his reprimands more than they feared the emperor's commands. For his incorruptibility and the emperor's respect toward him made them all fear and respect him."[151] His

---

148. Cod. Vat. Gr. 2219, fols. 9vo–10ro: Appendix I, letter 6. Cod. Vat. Gr. 2219, fol. 10ro: τὸ κατεσθίειν ὡς ἄρτον τοὺς πένητας ἀδεῶς. Cod. Vat. Gr. 2219, fol. 17vo: παρακαλῶ καὶ τὰ ἴχνη κατασπάζομαι τῶν ποδῶν σου. Cf. Appendix I, letter 3.

149. Pachymeres, II, 519; Gregoras, I, 182–183.

150. Gregoras, I, 181–184.

151. Gregoras, I, 182, 15–21: ζῆλος κατὰ τῶν ἀδικούντων οὕτω πάνυ τι μέγιστος καὶ περιφανής, ὡς μὴ μόνον αὐτούς γε τοὺς ὅσοι τῷ βασιλεῖ κατὰ γένος προσήκοντες ἦσαν, ἀλλὰ καὶ αὐτούς γε τοὺς αὐτοῦ υἱέας δεδιέναι τὴν αὐτοῦ μετ' ἐκπλήξεως παρρησίαν καὶ τοὺς ἐλέγχους μᾶλλον ἢ τοῦ βασιλέως προστάττοντος· καὶ ἡ πρὸς αὐτὸν τοῦ βασιλέως αἰδὼς πολλὴν ἐδίδου τούτοις τὴν συστολὴν καὶ τὸ δέος.

great importance, both personal and in his role as patriarch, became clear during his second patriarchate (1303–1309), in circumstances of great danger for the empire.

The first twenty years of Andronicus II's reign ended on a solemn note. The empire was poor, the army dispersed, and imperial authority was undergoing a rapid fragmentation. A few bright tones relieved the generally gloomy picture. Good relations were at long last reestablished with Epirus, and Serbia was, for a moment, contained. But so weak was the empire that if any of its western enemies decided to launch a serious attack, they were not likely to meet with very effective resistence. As yet, the Byzantium of Andronicus II had clashed only once with a western power, and that only as an incident in the Venetian-Genoese war. But the next eight years were to be critical in the relations between Byzantium and the West, and crucial for the very survival of an orthodox Byzantine state.

V

Reaping the Whirlwind

In the year 1302, dangerous forces pressed the Byzantine Empire on all sides, upsetting the precarious equilibrium which Andronicus II had tried to maintain in his diplomatic relations with the West. The Byzantines had suffered two major defeats in Asia Minor, and Andronicus' efforts to preserve and reorganize that province had collapsed. He now had desperate need for help if he were to preserve even the small part of Anatolia still in Byzantine hands. But, unlike his father, he could not seek western help in the form of a crusade, assuming that he were so disposed. His renunciation of the union of the churches made it impossible for him to appeal to the papacy. Indeed, the West was, on the whole, hostile to Byzantium. Venice saw the peace of 1302 as only a temporary truce. The popes were still too involved in the internal European conflicts between Aragon and the Angevins to think about Byzantium very seriously; besides, Boniface VIII and Philip IV of France were engaged in a struggle for power over the control of the French clergy. Papal interest in the empire at this point was both small and negative. The house of Anjou-Naples had not yet quite abandoned its eastern ambitions, as had been proven by its involvement in the affairs of Corfu and Epirus.[1] If Sicily were to be lost to the Angevins, as seemed increasingly probable, they might be expected to become more interested in the East. And as for Aragon, the peace negotiations of 1293 had indicated that the Aragonese house too, especially its Sicilian branch, might be expected to join or even to initiate an attack against the Byzantine Empire.

In fact, what had kept Byzantium relatively free from western attacks in 1282–1302 was the war between Aragon and the Angevins. As soon as this war ended, in 1302, it was to be expected that some of the released western forces would launch an attack against Byzantium.

Surprisingly, the first western threat after 1302 came not from one of the claimants to the Byzantine throne, but from a body of Catalan mercenaries who had been fighting for the Aragonese in Sicily. The story of the Catalan expedition in the Byzantine Empire is strange and very complicated. Much has been written on it, but mostly by Italian and Spanish historians who were interested in the expedition from the viewpoint of the West. The most extensive and the best work on the subject has been done by the great Spanish historian, Antonio Rubió y Lluch. Several other writers have contributed studies, some good, some bad, but mostly inadequate.[2] The matter is fraught with controversy

---

1. Hopf, *Griechische Geschichte*, pp. 334–335, 354–355.
2. Instead of giving a detailed bibliography of the Catalan expedition here, I shall refer the reader to the bibliography, where the works of Antonio Rubió y Lluch, K. M. Setton, and William Miller are cited. Among the earlier contributions to the study of the Catalan campaign,

and tinged with the national pride of each historian. What follows is neither a detailed account of the Catalan expedition, nor a reopening of the various controversies regarding the moral or cultural contribution of the Catalans to the Byzantine Empire and to the Duchy of Athens which they held from 1311 to 1388. Rather, it is an effort to discover the aims of the Catalan Company from the moment it left Sicily to the moment it left Thrace for Macedonia (1307). It is also a discussion of the aims of other westerners who, from time to time, sought to ally themselves to the Catalans. But primarily it is an account of the Byzantine policy toward the Catalans and toward the other powers with whom the Catalans were, or seemed to be, allied. The Catalan expedition proved very costly to Byzantium, and the costs too should be described and assessed.

The Peace of Caltabelotta

The war for the domination of Sicily, which involved the royal houses of Anjou and Aragon, lasted intermittently for twenty years, from 1282 to 1302. After 1293 there were sustained efforts on the part of the papacy to end the war, but the complexity of issues and interests made peace a difficult enterprise. In June 1295 Boniface VIII managed to persuade the major contending parties, Charles II of Anjou-Naples, James II of Aragon, and Philip IV of France, to make peace. The treaty of Anagni, which in fact consisted of several separate peace treaties between the various parties, officially ended the war for Sicily. James II agreed to restore immediately to Charles II the parts of southern Italy which were held by the Aragonese, and Charles II agreed to give his daughter Blanche in marriage to James II, along with a substantial dowry. The king of France, Philip IV, and his brother, Charles of Valois, would renounce all their claims to the throne of Aragon. These claims went back to the time of Pope Martin IV, who had excommunicated Peter II of Aragon (1276–1285) because of his invasion of Sicily, and granted Aragon to Charles of Valois. The excommunication of the king of Aragon was also lifted in 1295. As for the island of Sicily, James promised that his officials would turn it over to the pope, at a time and in circumstances to be decided by Boniface VIII. There was, however, the possibility that the Sicilians might rebel; in such a

---

perhaps the most noteworthy is the work of Gustave Schlumberger, *Expédition des Almugavares ou routiers Catalans en Orient de l'an 1302–1311* (Paris, 1902). The work of Francesco Giunta, *Aragonesi e Catalani nel Mediterraneo, II: La Presenza Catalana nel Levante dalle origini a Giacomo II* (Palermo, 1959) places the Catalan expedition in the wider framework of Aragonese expansion in the Mediterranean, but does not study the expedition in any detail. An extensive bibliography on the Catalans can be found in the article of S. Tramontana, "Per la storia della 'Compagnia Catalana' in Oriente," *Nuova Rivista Storica*, 46 (1962), 58–95, which otherwise is of very limited value, being full of inaccuracies of fact and interpretation. The article by Ignatius Burns, S.J., "The Catalan Company and the European Powers, 1305–1311," *Speculum*, 29 (1954), 751–771, contributes very little. Among the works that we will not have occasion to note later, see Nicolae Iorga, "Ramon Muntaner et l'Empire byzantin," *Revue historique du Sud-est Européen*, 4 (1927), 355ff; Gustave Schlumberger, "Le sceau de la Compagnie des routiers Catalans à Gallipoli en 1305," *Comptes rendus de l'Académie des inscriptions et des belles lettres*, (1925), pp. 131–137.

case, James II would offer them no help, but neither would he fight against them, for, he said, he needed his forces to fight a possible war with Castile.[3] While James' sincerity in abandoning Sicily is still debatable, the implementation of the part of the treaty of Anagni which concerned Sicily was quite different from what the pope expected.

Muntaner describes in some detail the process of turning the island over to the pope. On a certain day, the officials of the king of Aragon announced that they were abandoning the castles they held in Sicily, and asked, in public, whether there was any papal official who would take over. Since the pope had not been informed of this action, no papal officials were in evidence; the Sicilian people took over on behalf of the infante Frederick, James II's brother, and Frederick's officials then resumed command. Frederick was a son of the king of Aragon, Peter III, and he claimed Sicily from his mother Constance, the daughter of Manfred of Sicily.[4] He had no intention of abandoning his heritage; he was crowned Frederick III, king of Sicily, on May 3, 1296, and the war with the Angevins continued. Although Charles II of Naples and his son Robert had papal support in the struggle, they were unable to win. In 1301 Boniface VIII asked Philip IV of France to help his Angevin relatives, rather as Urban IV had asked Louis IX to send Charles of Anjou to Sicily to help the papal forces (1264). Philip IV then sent his brother, Charles of Valois, with 4,000 soldiers, whose salaries were paid by the pope.[5] Charles of Valois, however, had no intention of fighting. He had good reasons to desire peace in Italy and Sicily, and so he saw himself as a mediator between Charles II and Frederick III.

Charles of Valois wanted to end the Angevin-Sicilian war in order to pursue his eastern ambitions. Through his marriage to Catherine of Courtenay, in January 1301, he was now the main western claimant to the throne of Constantinople. In the marriage contract, Catherine had separated her rights to Constantinople and Namur from those to Courtenay. Her imperial rights and possessions went to Charles of Valois and to his heirs, whether of this marriage or a future one: in effect, though not in theory, her imperial title became transferred to Charles of Valois. Her rights to Courtenay, on the other hand, would devolve onto her own children by Charles of Valois, and if no children were born the titles would return to her family after Charles's death.[6] Charles of Valois, then, had legally recognized claims to the Byzantine Empire.

---

3. Muntaner, chaps. clxxxiv–clxxxv. I am using the Catalan edition of Antonio de Bofarull, *Cronica Catalana de Ramon Muntaner* (Barcelona, 1860), and the English translation—not always accurate—of Lady Goodenough, *The Chronicle of Muntaner* (London, 1921). Cf. Finke, *Acta Aragonensia*, III, no. 20; V. Salavert y Roca, "El tratado de Anagni y la expansion Mediterranea de la Corona de Aragon," *Estudios de Edad Media de la Corona de Aragon*, 5 (1952), 209–360, especially 249–260.

4. Muntaner, chaps. clxxxiv, clxxxv; R. L. Wolff, "Mortgage and Redemption," pp. 56, 70, and notes 22, 60.

5. Muntaner, chap. cxcvii.

6. January 28, 1301. A.N. J 167 no. 4. Philip IV confirmed it in March, 1301; A.N., JJ 38, no. 64. On the occasion of Charles's marriage, Philip IV gave him, Catherine, and their heirs, an annual gift of 100,000 livres tournois. In June 1310, he confirmed this in favor of Charles and Charles's heirs in perpetuity: A.N. JJ, vol. 46, fol. 18.

But he was a very dutiful brother, who rarely took a step without the consent of Philip IV. In 1302 both Philip IV and Boniface VIII extracted from Charles the promise that he would not lead an expedition to Constantinople before fighting in Sicily.[7] The Sicilian expedition was a precondition of any help that Boniface and Philip might give him for the recovery of Constantinople.

Charles of Valois realized the dangers inherent in the continuation of the war in Sicily. If he kept his army in Sicily for a long time, he ran the danger of remaining a titular emperor forever. Therefore, he offered both sides his good offices as mediator. His two envoys, Thibaut de Chepoy and Aimeric de Sus, carried out the negotiations, and their efforts and Charles's were rewarded with the conclusion of a peace treaty between Charles II and Frederick III at Caltabelotta on August 31, 1302.[8] The treaty confirmed, more or less, the de facto possessions of the two opponents: Charles II kept his lands in southern Italy, while Frederick kept Sicily and promised to abandon his possessions in Calabria. The two enemies confirmed their new friendship by a marriage alliance: Frederick III married Eleanor, a daughter of Charles II. Four days after the conclusion of the peace of Caltabelotta, Frederick communicated its contents to the king of Aragon.[9]

Like the Sicilian Vespers, which had started the Aragonese-Angevin war, the treaty of Caltabelotta was a turning point in the relations between the Byzantine Empire and the West. The armies of Charles of Valois, Frederick III, and the Angevins were now released for possible action in the East. Almost immediately, Charles of Valois tried to ensure the preponderance of his own claims to the Byzantine Empire. As far as the Angevins were concerned, there was no problem: on March 11, 1302, Charles of Valois and Charles II of Naples renewed the treaty of Viterbo, which had been concluded in 1267 between Charles of Anjou and Baldwin II of Constantinople, and which had provided for the conquest of Byzantium.[10] On September 26, 1302, Charles of Valois and Frederick III concluded an agreement which discussed Charles's proposed expedition against Constantinople. Charles's aim was to ensure not only the tolerance, but also the active help of Sicily in this enterprise. In the document, Frederick III professed great love for Charles of Valois, and promised to help his expedition with twenty galleys and two hundred knights, all equipped at Frederick's own expense. This force would stay in the Romania

---

7. A.N. J 164A, no. 11: Charles of Valois promises to go to the help of Charles II of Italy, to return as soon as possible, and not to depart for Constantinople without Philip IV's permission. Cf. Du Cange and Buchon, *Histoire de Constantinople* (1826), II, 333; H. Moranvillé, "Les projets de Charles de Valois sur l'Empire de Constantinople," *BEC* 51 (1890), 63–86; A.N. J 164A, no. 11: Charles of Valois promises that he will not embark on his "crusade" against Constantinople without Philip IV's permission (1301). Cf. Muntaner, chap. cxcvii; also, Philip IV's expenses in B.N., lat. 9783, fol. 115 ro.

8. Michele Amari, *La guerra del vespro Siciliano*, 9th edition (Milan, 1886), II, 462ff. The Florentine historian Giovanni Villani entitled his chapter discussing the peace of Caltabelotta "Come messer Carlo di Valos passò in cicilia per fare guerra per lo re Carlo, e fece ontosa pace": *Cronica de Giovanni Villani*, ed. F. Gherardi Dragomanni, II (Florence, 1845), 54. See also Carlos de Caldas, *El Tratado de Caltabelotta* (Barcelona, 1943).

9. Finke, *Acta Aragonensia*, II, no. 81, September 4, 1302.

10. Du Cange, *Histoire de Constantinople* (1657), *Chartes*, pp. 44–45 (summary in the edition of 1826, II, 335).

for four months, and, if the war were not finished by then, for a further four months. Frederick even envisaged the possibility of personally joining Charles's forces; in such a case, he would add to his previous contribution ten ships and four hundred knights. Finally, he promised "that we will conclude no treaty with Andronicus . . . unless the said Lord Charles has previously made peace with him."[11]

It is not surprising that a member of the Aragonese royal family should be willing to abandon the old ties of his house with the empire, ties already loosened by Andronicus' abandonment of the union between the churches. It is more surprising that Frederick who, in 1293, had had aspirations to the Byzantine throne, should now appear to assist so complacently the ambitions of Charles of Valois in the East. In fact, the events taking place in Frederick's immediate entourage at the same time suggest that Frederick was consciously misleading Charles of Valois.

In his wars against the Angevins, Frederick had made use of a well-organized, valiant group of Catalan mercenaries under the command of Roger de Flor. Roger de Flor is a very interesting figure, one of the many soldiers of fortune to whom the expansion of Europe eastward had offered great opportunities for advancement. He was, however, a better soldier and of a more flexible character than most. He was the son of a German soldier, a falconer of Frederick II Hohenstaufen, who had died in the battle of Tagliacozzo. When Roger was a boy of eight, he caught the fancy of a sergeant of the military-monastic order of the Templars, who took him aboard his ship. The boy apparently loved the sea, and became an able and valiant sailor. When the Egyptians besieged Acre in 1291, Roger was already a well-known member of the Templar order. During the siege, he carried away in his ships several nobles and women, and a substantial treasure. Later, when he was accused of withholding part of the treasure from the Grand Master of the Templars, he abandoned the order and fled. At first he offered his services to Robert of Anjou-Naples, but when Robert indicated that he was not interested, Roger de Flor, his ship, and his men joined Frederick of Sicily. Soon he became the commander of a company of Catalans and Aragonese, and they all fought valiantly in Italy.[12] With the end of the Angevin-Aragonese war, both Roger and Frederick III found themselves in an embarrassing situation. The Templars still wanted to bring Roger to justice, and now that Frederick had made his peace with the papacy he would have to surrender Roger. Also, mercenary companies which were an asset in time of war became a terrible liability in peacetime. They knew only one trade, war, and they were used to living off the spoils. When there was no war to fight, what would such an organized, martial group do? Frederick was apprehensive. So, after the conclusion of the peace of Caltabelotta, Roger de Flor had good reason to leave the Kingdom of Sicily, and Frederick was no less eager to see him go.

Roger's thoughts turned to the East once again; he had had some experience

---

11. A.N. J 510, no. 18 (*Vidimus* of Philip IV, December, 1313); Du Cange, *Histoire de Constantinople* (1657), *Chartes*, p. 43. The edition of 1826, II, 335, gives only a summary of the document. Cf. Dade, *Versuche*, p. 76.

12. Muntaner, chap. cxciv.

there when he was with the Templars, and he claimed that he could speak Greek. After the peace of Caltabelotta, he sent messengers to Andronicus II, offering to help the empire against its Turkish enemies.[13] According to the Byzantine sources, the emperor was only too happy to receive the overtures of a man who was reputed to be "full of martial spirit": "The emperor, who had already started to hire foreigners because of necessity, seized [Roger's] message as though it were an unexpected gift."[14] Andronicus accepted Roger's proposals, and offered four months' pay for the Catalans. Roger was to have the title of megas dux, and to marry Maria, the daughter of John Ašen of Bulgaria, and the emperor's niece.[15]

The Catalans seem to have misinterpreted the significance of the emperor's offer. Muntaner wrote that the office of megas dux entitled its holder to all the islands and seacoasts of the Romania: "And grand duke is a title which means the same as prince and lord over all the soldiers of the empire, with authority over the admiral; and all the islands of Romania are subject to him, and also all the places on the seacoasts." Muntaner misunderstood the functions of the megas dux and interpreted them in the inappropriate terms of western feudalism. The office of megas dux in the thirteenth century could be both an honorary title and an effective command. It must have been a coveted title, since it was seventh in the hierarchy of court offices, and Andronicus probably meant to confer only the honorary title upon Roger de Flor. In itself, the honor done to a westerner aroused the anger of the Byzantines, and on June 1, 1305, the emperor had to defend his action; he responded to criticism by reminding his subjects that Michael VIII too had given the title of megas dux to an Italian, Licario. In any case, even if Andronicus had meant Roger de Flor to exercise the effective powers of a megas dux, these did not include the command of the islands and the coastal areas, as Muntaner thought. The best source on titles and offices of the Palaeologan period, Codinus Curopalates, gives this description of the office of megas dux: "the megas dux is the commander of all the naval forces, just as the megas domestikos is the commander-in-chief of all the armed forces."[16]

To the emperor who hired them, the Catalans seemed no more than another lot of mercenaries who, like the Alans, were to help save Asia Minor. Yet from

13. Muntaner, chaps. cxcix, cc; Pachymeres, II, 394–395; Gregoras, I, 220ff; Finke, *Acta Aragonensia*, II, no. 431; Dölger, *Regesten*, nos. 2252, 2258.

14. Pachymeres, II, 395: ὁ μέντοι γε βασιλεὺς διὰ τὴν ἀνάγκην ἀρξάμενος ἤδη ξενοτροφεῖν ὡς ἕρμαιον ἁρπάζει τὸ σύμβαμα. cf. Gregoras, I, 220.

15. Pachymeres, II, 395–397; Gregoras, I, 218–219; Muntaner, chap. cc.

16. Codinus Curopalates, *De officialibus palatii Constantinopolitani et de officiis magnae ecclesiae liber*, ed. E. Bekker (Bonn, 1839), p. 28. The passage from Muntaner, chap. cxcix, reads: "E magaduch es tal offici, que vol aytant dir com princep senyor de tots los soldaus del emperi, e que haja a fer sobrer almirall, e que totes les illes sien sotsmeses de la Romania a ell, e encara los llochs de les marines." Only four men are known to have held this office during the reign of Andronicus II, and three of them were Catalans: Roger de Flor, Berengar d'Entença and Ferran Ximenes de Arenos. In 1321 he conferred this dignity on Syrgiannes, a Byzantine of Cuman extraction. On the office of megas dux, see Rodolphe Guilland, "Études de titulature et de prosopographie byzantines. Les chefs de la marine byzantine: drongaire de la flotte, grand drongaire de la flotte, mégaduc," *BZ*, 44 (1951), 221–240, and Ernst Stein, "Untersuchungen zur spätbyzantinischen Verfassungs-und Wirtschaftsgeschichte," *Mitteilungen zur Osmanischen Geschichte*, 2 (1923–1925), 57.

the beginning the decision to accept the Catalan offers must have been recognized as the change in policy which it was. It was the first time that Andronicus II asked western Europeans into his empire to help him fight the Turks. Surely, this was a great departure from his earlier policy of trying to organize internally the defense of Asia Minor. Furthermore, the imperial treasury was really almost empty. Yet Andronicus was willing to promise Roger a substantial sum of money; when the Catalans arrived, he had to withhold the salaries of the palace employees in order to find money to pay them.[17] He would have done better to heed the advice of the eleventh-century writer Kekaumenos, or of his own contemporary, Thomas Magister, both of whom advised very strongly against using foreign mercenaries, and especially against spoiling them with high titles and large salaries.[18] Despite Andronicus' natural disinclination to use western forces, all the sources make it clear that he was pushed into this decision by the disastrous situation in Asia Minor.

After the battle of Bapheus, Michael IX and his army had retreated to Pegae, and Anatolia was left virtually undefended. Reports of disaster came daily from every part of Asia Minor. In Bithynia, Mysia, Phrygia, and Lydia only the cities had remained in the hands of the Byzantines, and they were desperate for help. Brusa and Nicaea lived in a state of siege. Only the coasts were still relatively safe, but the Turks had begun building ships to attack the islands of Chios, Samos, Rhodes, and even the Cyclades. The Ottomans had carried their invasions to the north of Asia Minor, across the Bosphorus from Constantinople, "as if the emperor had been asleep or not alive" (ὥσπερ ὑπνώττοντος βασιλέως ἢ μὴ ζῶντος); Constantinople itself was apprehensive, since only a narrow stretch of water separated it from the Turks.[19] Thus, Andronicus was reduced to the only measure he had not yet tried, hiring western mercenaries. It is quite clear that he expected the Catalans to achieve fast and magnificent results.

The motivations and involvement of Frederick III in the Catalan expedition are somewhat more difficult to understand. Certainly, Roger de Flor reached his decision to offer his services to Andronicus after consultation with Frederick. But at first, the king of Sicily did not send the Catalans to conquer the Byzantine Empire. His only help to the Catalans consisted of ships to transport them, and some money and food for each soldier. Trying to ensure himself against papal blame for letting Roger escape the justice of the Templars, Frederick "asked [Roger] to provide for his journey in such a manner that he [Frederick] would not be blamed."[20]

Some historians have been inclined to think that from the outset the Catalans

17. Pachymeres, II, 396–397; Gregoras, I, 222–223.

18. Kekaumenos, Στρατηγικόν and Νουθετητικόν, ed. B. Wassiliewsky and V. Jernstedt, in *Cecaumeni Strategicon et incerti scriptoris de officii libellus* (Petropoli, 1896), p. 95. In his Περὶ βασιλείας Thomas Magister advised Andronicus never to use foreign mercenaries, who were primarily interested in their own profit and were always ready to abandon the Byzantines when the fortunes of war went against them (an allusion to the behavior of the Alans at the battle of Apros?): Migne, *Patrologia Graeca*, CXLV, cols. 460, 461, 464.

19. Pachymeres, II, 388, 410, 412, 413, 391, 398; Muntaner, chap. ccii.

20. Muntaner, chap. cxcix: "li pregava que hi provelus en tal manera, que ell [Frederick] ne fos sens blasme." Cf. chap. cc, and Pachymeres, II, 396–397.

were allied to forces hostile to the empire and that they left Sicily as part of a crusading army. The possibility has even been raised that the Catalans were the force promised by Frederick III to Charles of Valois, and so that they constituted the first "crusading" contingent to be sent to the Romania.[21] But there is no reason to suppose this, and in fact the sequence of events seems to suggest that a different policy should be attributed to Frederick. If the sources are correct, Roger's offer to Andronicus II took place immediately after the peace of Caltabelotta, which was signed on August 31. So, when Frederick II promised his help to Charles of Valois, on September 26, he knew that he would soon have in the Romania an army composed of men who were still his vassals, who had fought for him, and whose leader was faithful enough to request Frederick's permission before placing himself and his troops under foreign command. Yet not a word was said about this in the agreement of September 26, 1302. In September 1302 Frederick III was playing a waiting game. He certainly had not taken the initiative in sending the Catalans to the East: the sources all agree that the initiative belonged to Roger de Flor. But Frederick said nothing to Charles of Valois about the expedition, because he was retaining a diplomatic weapon: in the event of an attack on Constantinople led by Charles of Valois, Frederick would be able to claim a substantial reward, backed by the Catalan force already in the Empire. But not until October 1303 is there any sign of Frederick III or James II planning to use the Catalans to conquer the Byzantine Empire.

The Catalan Campaign

"In September of the second indiction, the city of Constantine had the misfortune to see the Latin Roger, who came with seven ships of his own, and others belonging to the Catalans and the Almugavars, whose number was eight thousand."[22] Roger de Flor's army arrived at Constantinople in September 1303. It was made up of Catalans, Aragonese, and men from Calabria and Sicily. The exact size of the army varies in the sources. Muntaner, surely the most trustworthy source in this matter, speaks of 1,500 cavalry, 4,000 Almugavars and 1,000 foot, plus the various oarsmen who manned the ships. Most of these people, says Muntaner, had their wives or mistresses and their children with them. Pachymeres gives a total figure of 8,000 men, while Gregoras reduces the figure to 2,000.[23]

21. Dade, *Versuche*, pp. 79ff; Tramontana, "Compagnia Catalana," pp. 78–80; Giunta, *Aragonesi e Catalani*, II, 163–167.

22. Pachymeres, II, 393. The company led by Roger de Flor is usually called the "Catalan Company" because most of its members had come from Catalonia. However, the army also included men from other parts of Spain, and from Italy and Sicily. The most distinguishing and effective part of the army was made up of the Almugavars, that is, lightly armed infantry recruited in Spain—hence the Hispano-Arabic name "Almugavar." The Almugavars had been in Italy and Sicily from the time of Peter III, fighting in his wars, and they were considered among the most efficient mercenary groups of the Middle Ages. See the small book of Ferran Soldevila, *Els Almogàvers* (Barcelona, 1952).

23. Pachymeres, II, 393; Gregoras, I, 220; Muntaner, chap. cci; Dade, *Versuche*, p. 81. The date of the arrival of the Catalans at Constantinople has been established by Caro, "Chronologie," 115–116, 124, and has since been accepted by Dade, Rubió y Lluch, and most other good historians. Tramontana, "Compagnia Catalana," pp. 78–80, still adheres to the

The Catalan Campaign

The arrival of the army at the capital of the Byzantine Empire was marred by the first of many unpleasant incidents attending the Catalan expedition. Before leaving Sicily, Roger de Flor had borrowed money (20,000 hyperpyra) from some Genoese merchants of Pera, and he had also hired from them ships to transport him and his men to the Romania. Roger named the emperor as guarantor for this loan. When the Catalans appeared in Constantinople, the Genoese asked them to repay the loan. The Catalans appealed to the emperor to mediate, but before the imperial envoy could interfere, a quarrel broke out which soon acquired the dimensions of a small-scale war. Some Genoese, led by a certain Roso da Finar, came as far as the palace of the Blachernai in their pursuit of the Catalans. As casualties mounted—although Muntaner's figure of 3,000 Genoese dead is certainly exaggerated—Andronicus intervened. He asked the Catalans not to pillage the Genoese quarters: "If they sack Pera, the empire is destroyed, for the Genoese have much of our property and of that of our barons and other people of our empire."[24] This first quarrel between Catalans and Genoese in the empire arose out of incidental problems; soon, however, relations between the two would become very strained.

The Catalan army spent their first Byzantine winter in Cyzicus, on the Asia Minor coast of the Sea of Marmora. In the spring of 1304, they and the Alan mercenaries began their campaign in Asia Minor.[25] The years 1303 and 1304 were characterized by internal disagreements among the Catalans, and were marred by some unpleasantness with the Alan mercenaries and the Greek troops under Maroules. Even at the beginning of their campaign, the Catalans showed an incomplete loyalty to the empire, for they were ever ready to plunder Asia Minor for money, horses, or food. Still, the campaign of 1304 was successful, the Turks were defeated, and the inhabitants of the Greek fortified towns, especially Philadelphia, asked for the support of the Catalans. The Turks abandoned the siege of Philadelphia and fled. Two other Catalan leaders joined Roger de Flor late in the summer. Ferran de Ahones, the commander of the fleet, came to Anea (Ani), south of Ephesus, to meet Roger. About twelve days later another of the Catalan leaders who had remained in Sicily arrived at Ephesus. This was Berengar de Rocafort, a more than usually nasty, ambitious, and unscrupulous man, whom Roger immediately made seneschal of the Catalan host. Rocafort had refused to surrender the forts he held in Calabria, as he should have done according to the provisions of the treaty of Caltabelotta, and consequently his relations with Frederick III of Sicily were very uneasy.[26]

---

date September 1302, which researchers before Caro had used, without giving an explanation. On his way to Constantinople, on August 18, 1303, Roger de Flor attacked the Venetian island of Ceos; in 1319, the Venetians asked Andronicus II to pay them compensation for the damages done by Roger, since he was then an imperial official. This reference helps to establish the date of the Catalans' arrival at Constantinople: Rubió y Lluch, *Diplomatari*, nos. 111, 113, pp. 135–138.

24. Pachymeres, II, 397–399; Muntaner, chap. ccii.

25. Muntaner, chaps. cciii, ccv; Pachymeres, II, 425, 451.

26. Pachymeres, II, 413, 421–428; Muntaner, chaps. ccv, ccvi, ccvii, ccviii. Anaea or Ania or Ani is a town on the coast of Asia Minor, just opposite Samos, the modern Qadi-kalesi: W. Tomaschek, *Zur historischen Topographie von Kleinasien im Mittelalter* (Vienna, 1891), p. 35. Muntaner would have us believe that Roger de Flor stayed in Ani, went to Ephesus where he

By August 1304 the Catalans had achieved a certain amount of success in Asia Minor, and at the same time they had had the first serious troubles with their hosts. The Catalan source claims that the army became discontented because the Byzantines broke their contract and discontinued payment of the salaries of the army.[27] On the other side, the story is longer and more convincing. Pachymeres wrote in great detail, citing specific names and cases, of the constant depredations of the Catalans in the Anatolia they had come to liberate. And, surely, the composition of the Catalan company made it virtually unavoidable that they should displease their employers: the Catalans were a totally self-interested body of soldiers, who could not be expected to have any loyalty to Andronicus, but who could be expected to be greedy. Philadelphia, Pyrgion, and Ephesus were plundered, and their inhabitants were indiscriminately tortured so that they would surrender their money. Roger de Flor assembled a fleet which ravaged Chios, Lesbos, and Lemnos, seeking booty. The city of Magnesia was besieged because the people refused to succumb to Roger's demands for money.[28] Despite this flagrant disloyalty toward Andronicus, however, it does not seem likely at this point that either Roger de Flor or his army had any plans to attack the empire. Roger may have had vague dreams of keeping Asia Minor for himself: his trip through Asia Minor, his reluctance to leave it, his request in early January 1305 that he be granted the "Kingdom of Anatolia" all point at this direction.[29]

Meanwhile, it was becoming clear to Andronicus that the remedy he had offered to Anatolia was almost worse than the disease. In August 1304, he recalled Roger de Flor and his army to Europe, ostensibly to help his son Michael IX, who was in Thrace campaigning against the Bulgarian, Theodore Svetoslav. Roger answered the call only after his siege of Magnesia had failed. Muntaner, taking the Catalan side, considered the recall ill-advised, and hinted that it was due to Michael IX's jealousy at Roger's spectacular success.[30] In fact, Michael was less than enthusiastic about having to cope with Roger de Flor in Thrace: he told Andronicus that his Anatolian soldiers could not be trusted to behave properly if they were asked to cooperate with the Catalan army which had plundered their homeland.[31] Roger too voiced concern at being asked to leave the "Kingdom of Anatolia" before all its cities and forts had been delivered from the Turks. But even during his stay in Asia Minor

---

stayed four days, returned to Ani for a fortnight, and then went through all of southern Asia Minor to the Iron Gates in the frontiers of Cilician Armenia; then he returned to Ani and then to Constantinople. Simply in terms of time, and had Roger found no opposition from the Turks of Asia Minor, it would be impossible to believe that he did all this between July 1304, when Rocafort appeared in the East, and August, when Roger was recalled to Constantinople. On this, see also Antonio Rubió y Lluch, *Paquimeres y Muntaner*, *Memóries de la secció històrico-arqueològica del Institut d'Estudis Catalans*, 1 (Barcelona, 1927), 24.

27. Muntaner, chaps. ccx, ccv, ccvii; Finke, *Acta Aragonensia*, II, no. 431.

28. Pachymeres, II, 428, 436, 451ff, 500ff, 514–516; Gregoras, I, 222–223. Cf. Muntaner, chap. cciii. See also Jean Verpeaux, *Nicéphore Choumnos*, pp. 46–52.

29. Muntaner, chap. ccxxii.

30. Pachymeres, II, 451, 480–484; Muntaner, chaps. ccviii, ccix.

31. Pachymeres, II, 482–484, 500–505; Muntaner, chap. ccxiii. Schlumberger, *Almugavares*, p. 110, says that Andronicus' excuse was probably his real reason for recalling the Catalans.

the area had once more fallen into anarchy. The Turks overran the country-side, a Bulgarian vagabond appeared, had some small success, and faded out of the scene. The Alans left the Catalan host, preferring death to Roger de Flor, as they said.[32] The combination of all these things forced Andronicus to recall Roger de Flor. If the emperor had retained any illusions about the possible success of the Catalans, he would not have gambled the safety of Asia Minor for a Bulgarian campaign which was not, after all, nearly as vital to the empire.

Roger de Flor and his army returned from Asia Minor in late August 1304. According to Pachymeres, Roger de Flor did not return to Constantinople, but instead occupied the peninsula of Gallipoli, which is strategically very important and also easy to defend once one has control of the fortifications. At the same time, the Catalan fleet appeared at Madytos, near the southern tip of the peninsula. The peninsula was occupied by a fait accompli, and only later did Andronicus II "allow" the Catalans to remain there. If he thought that in this way he could keep them out of Thrace and so out of trouble, he grossly underestimated the strategic position of the peninsula; from Gallipoli, the Catalans could launch attacks against any part of Thrace, and then return to their virtually impregnable stronghold. Muntaner tells the story somewhat differently: he claims that Roger did indeed come to Constantinople, and that it was Andronicus who told him to stay with his army in Gallipoli.[33] But it is difficult to believe that the emperor was so lacking in common sense. The occupation of Gallipoli by the Catalans, coming as it did after the failure of their Anatolian campaign, was one more dramatic indication of the deterioration in the relations between the Byzantines and their mercenaries. Meanwhile, developments in Europe would change the character and the aims of the Catalan campaign.

Soon after the departure of the Catalans for Constantinople, both James II of Aragon and his brother, Frederick III of Sicily, began to dream of conquest. Neither had enough money, or indeed the intention, of attacking the Byzantine Empire with his own army. But since there was already an army on Byzantine soil, both James and Frederick thought of using it in order to conquer the empire for themselves. It was quite natural for Frederick III to preserve his connection with Roger de Flor, the man who had fought for him; it is more suspicious that James of Aragon should wish to keep in contact with the Catalans. A curious document of October 30, 1303, indicates that there was an early connection between James II and the leaders of the Catalan Company. This document contains James's answer to some proposals put forth by Roger de Flor and Berengar d'Entença, another of the Catalan leaders, who left for Constantinople a year after Roger. These proposals must have been put forth before Roger's departure for the Levant. Roger and Berengar seem to have promised to persuade Andronicus to help James II with money and ships for

---

32. Pachymeres, II, 442ff, 451–452.
33. Pachymeres, II, 480–484, Cf. Muntaner, chap. ccix.

the conquest of Sardinia.[34] In return, James II promised the two men to help them in anything they needed. The document is curious, because Roger de Flor must have been well aware of the fact that Andronicus II was in no position to help even himself, let alone anyone else.[35] Why then this preposterous promise to try for Byzantine help? Probably, James II, and Roger, and Entença were merely trying to preserve their connection with one another, and this document, in a way, made the two Catalan leaders almost into Aragonese envoys to the court of Constantinople.

James and Frederick became further involved in the affairs of the Catalans in 1304. An anonymous writer, who clearly reflected the Sicilian viewpoint, relates that a short while after Roger's arrival in Constantinople, some Catalans returned to Sicily as messengers, complained to Frederick that the emperor refused either to pay his soldiers or to let them go back to Italy, and that they had to resort to force in order to find food. If Frederick sent some ships, they said, the Catalans could be easily aroused against Andronicus, and the empire would be conquered. Frederick then began to consider the possibility of conquering Byzantium.

Sometime in the early summer of 1304 (before July), Frederick wrote to Pope Benedict XI that he desired to fight the enemies of the Catholic faith, for the honor of the church and for the love of Charles of Valois. Frederick then requested—and received—the pope's permission to send to the Byzantine Empire a fleet of ten ships, under the command of his half-brother Sancho of Aragon. Sancho's objective would be to make war on Andronicus, as far as possible, and especially to conquer and hold the islands of the Romania. Sancho would also try to judge the extent of the Catalans' disaffection with Andronicus, and if he found them ready to rebel he would help them conquer Constantinople "to the honor of the Roman church and of Charles, the son [sic] of the king of France." In his letter to the pope, Frederick also produced the statement that this occupation of the Greek islands might be a first blow against Egypt: if the Catholics held these islands, they could boycott Egyptian commerce and thus undermine the economic and political strength of the Egyptians. The Venetian Marino Sanudo Torsello was to develop this idea of a boycott into a consistent plan for the conquest of Egypt in 1306 and later.[36]

---

34. Rubió y Lluch, *Diplomatari*, no. 9; cf. no. 12; Pachymeres, II, 484–485; Gregoras, I, 222; Muntaner, chap. ccxi.

35. Muntaner, chap. cxcix. Once before, James II had tried to borrow money from Andronicus II: in 1297, he instructed his emissary to the Byzantine court to ask for as much money as he thought he could get. Marinesco, "Notes sur les Catalans," pp. 509–511.

36. Finke, *Acta Aragonensia*, II, 683–684: "transfretarent [the galleys] ad . . . partes Romanie et predictum Imperatorem niterentur offendere toto posse. Et specialiter deberent se conferre ad quasdam insulas, que sunt dicti imperatoris, ipsasque studerent invadere et habere: scito per dominum regem, admodum et perquam maxime fore utile, si habitarentur et tenerentur a catholicis christianis . . . si forte huiusmodi casus accideret [i.e., if the Catalans wanted to rebel] ipsi requisiti vel non requisiti a predictis armigeris insurgentibus, contra predictum imperatorem totum subsidium et sforcium, quod possent, ei impenderent et iuvarent eosdem." Cf. Pachymeres, II, 508; Rubió y Lluch, *Diplomatari*, no. 15; Dade, *Versuche*, pp. 83–93. Since Benedict XI died in July 1304, Frederick must have requested his permission in the early summer of 1304. See Marino Sanudo's *Secreta Fidelium Crucis*, in Bongars, *Gesta Dei per Francos*, II, (Hanover, 1611). Guillaume d'Adam also advocated taking Constantinople to put an end to Egyptian commerce: Delaville le Roulx, *La France en Orient*, I, 70ff.

Sancho of Aragon and his ships arrived in the Romania in the spring of 1305.[37]

While Frederick was holding discussions with Benedict XI, he also acquainted his brother, James II of Aragon, with his new plans. Sometime before July 1304 he sent Roger de Lluria to Tortosa, to inform James that he wanted to conquer the Byzantine Empire, and to ask whether James would advise this course of action.[38] James's reply was rather cautious: "since the affair of the Romania is full of doubt and uncertainty, we cannot give you proper advice." But should Frederick decide to go to war with Byzantium, and should he ask for Aragonese help, James promised to help the enterprise.[39] This reply seems surprisingly evasive. It is hardly possible that James really was not interested in Frederick's possible conquests; if only as the head of the senior branch of the Aragonese royal house, he should have shown more interest. Perhaps, James II was building up his links with the Catalans, behind Frederick's back; his negotiations with Berengar d'Entença support this conclusion. In the meantime, James wanted to discourage Frederick from taking unilateral action against Byzantium, and was trying to ensure that he himself would not be left out.

One of the tantalizing problems about the early plans and allegiances of the Catalan Company revolves around the person of Berengar d'Entença. If the nature of Berengar's allegiances in the summer of 1304 were known, the positions of James II, Frederick III, and perhaps Roger de Flor in regard to the question of the conquest of the Byzantine Empire could be clarified. Unfortunately, reports of Berengar d'Entença's activities are confusing, and this confusion seems to reflect the as yet unclear position of all parties. In June 1304 Berengar d'Entença was preparing to leave Sicily for the East, thus fulfilling his agreement with Roger de Flor. Before he left, he had become involved in negotiations with James II of Aragon. He had talked with Roger de Lluria, Frederick's emissary to James, and, on June 20, 1304, he acknowledged the receipt of certain letters written by James. In this letter to James, Entença said twice that he was leaving for the Romania "per cumplir lo dit manament"—"to execute your said orders." But Entença considered those orders too serious to repeat in a letter. An anonymous Sicilian source claims that Entença was sent to find out whether Andronicus had in fact broken his promises to the Catalans, and whether the mercenaries were ready for a rebellion—in other words, he was to investigate and establish whether there was cause and possibility of war between the Catalans and Byzantium.[40]

---

37. Sancho of Aragon was an illegitimate son of Peter III the Great. Dade, *Versuche*, p. 91, says that Sancho arrived in Romania in May, 1305, but Pachymeres (II, 522), mentions Sancho already active in Byzantine waters in April 1305.

38. Rubió y Lluch, *Diplomatari*, no. 11: On the "feit de Romania, ço es asaber de conquerirla, e sobre ço n a trames al senyor papa e enten lo dit Frederic aver sobra d aquest feit aiuda e consell del . . . rey d'Aragon." Cf. Rubió y Lluch, *Diplomatari*, no. 13, and Finke, *Acta Aragonensia*, II, no. 428.

39. Rubió y Lluch, *Diplomatari*, no. 13 (September 22, 1304); also in Finke, *Acta Aragonensia*, II, 678.

40. Entença's letter is published in the *Diplomatari*, no. 10. Cf. the earlier edition by E. Martin-Chabot, "Un document relatif à l'expédition de la Compagnie Catalane en Orient, 1304," *Moyen Age*, 2d ser., 23 (1910), 198–203. The anonymous Sicilian source is found in Finke, *Acta Aragonensia*, II, no. 431. Dade, *Versuche*, pp. 90–91, does not make the connection between this source and Entença's letter.

Berengar d'Entença then promised to do his best to fulfill the king's commands in this affair; he pledged himself to the king's service and promised to labor for James' benefit.[41]

So far, then, it appears that Entença was leaving for Constantinople as an emissary of James II, totally committed to his service—Dade, in fact, rather adopts this position; yet things are not quite so clear. Did Entença recognize James II as his sovereign? In the letter under discussion, he offered James "greetings with humble kissing of hands and with full reverence and honor, *as to a natural seigneur*" ("saluts ab homil besament de mans e ab tota reverencia e honor *com a senyor natural*"). Near the end of the letter, however, he also pledged himself to work for "the salvation and prosperity of the great lord, King Frederick III" ("la salut e prosperitat del alt senyor rey en Frederic terç"). Also, Pachymeres tells us that when Entença was in the Byzantine Empire, and finally consented to take an oath of fealty to Andronicus, he named Frederick III—not James II—as his liege lord.[42] If Pachymeres' choice of words ("φθάσας ὁρκήσεις... πρᾶξαι," "he had *just* sworn his oath to Frederick") has any real meaning, it suggests that Frederick had asked Entença to reaffirm his homage just before leaving for the Romania, as Frederick was to do later, with the infante of Mallorca Ferran, who went east as Frederick's personal representative and leader of the Catalan Company.

While, then, the exact position of Entença in relation to James II and Frederick III cannot be established, his activities in 1304 illustrate two developments: Frederick III was seriously thinking of using the Catalans to conquer the Byzantine Empire, and James II was seriously trying to build up his own links with the leaders of the Catalan Company. Thus, if Roger de Flor had gone to the empire on his own initiative and at the subsequent invitation of the Byzantines, Entença went at the invitation of Roger de Flor, and with the consent of both Frederick III and James II; he left Sicily in September 1304 and arrived at Gallipoli in October. Andronicus II was so far out of touch with these developments, that he did not at first know whether Entença had been properly invited.[43]

The arrival of Berengar d'Entença in the Byzantine Empire produced, or precipitated, a change in the relations of the Catalans to the empire. The Catalans became more ambitious and intransigent, perhaps because they were told of Sancho of Aragon's projected expedition, and were assured of the support of the kings of Sicily and Aragon. This support, however, was as yet cautious, because at the same time Charles of Valois was preparing his own "crusade" against Constantinople, and was seeking the cooperation of all the interested princes. Berengar d'Entença himself showed from the beginning that he had not come to Byzantium as a friend. He did not immediately go to

41. Rubió y Lluch, *Diplomatari*, letter 10: "a exequsio del dit fet e a cumpliment del vostre manament, en tal manera que venga a acabament, Deu volen, o que non venga per ren que yo per mi fer hi pusche e complir en serviy vostre e creximent de la vostra alta senyoria."

42. Pachymeres, II, 499.

43. Ibid., II, 485–486; Muntaner, chap. ccxi; Finke, *Acta Aragonensia*, II, no. 431. Entença had with him 1,000 Almugavars and 300 knights. In 1305 the Genoese considered Entença an Aragonese agent: below, Chapter V, "Byzantium, the Genoese, and the Catalans."

Constantinople. Instead, he stayed at Gallipoli, and received imperial emissaries who were trying to make him take an oath of allegiance to Andronicus. His whole behavior was a calculated insult to the Byzantines. On his way to Gallipoli, he had stolen an imperial ship, manned by Monemvasiots, and he had also forced a Venetian ship to give him wheat. He apologized to Venice, but not to Byzantium. Before consenting to appear at Constantinople, he demanded a hostage, Andronicus' son John. Despite these insults, Andronicus eventually agreed to all of Entença conditions, loaded him with gifts, and, on December 25, 1304, gave him the title of megas dux with the understanding that Roger de Flor would be promoted to caesar.[44]

The investiture of Entença as megas dux was the climax of a series of events which occurred during the autumn of 1304 and proved that Andronicus II had to deal with increasing hostility on the part of his mercenaries. In the autumn of 1304 Roger de Flor asked for money for his army. Money was hard to find, and Andronicus imposed a new tax on crops, the σιτόκριθον (sitokrithon), demanded one third of the revenues of the pronoiai of the West, and even tried to fool the Catalans with debased coins.[45] The Catalans, especially angered by this last measure, raided Thrace and then resumed negotiations with Andronicus. At the end of October 1304 they asked for 300,000 hyperpyra. Andronicus could not possibly pay, and even Roger realized the enormity of the demand. The presence of Berengar d'Entença made things more difficult for the Byzantines, for he was a greedy man, and his arrival had strengthened the Catalan army by 300 horsemen and 1,000 foot.[46] Andronicus II found himself in a position similar to that of Alexius I at the time of the first crusade. Alexius had asked for a small, more or less disciplined body of soldiers to help him deal with the Turks—a body similar to that given him by the count of Flanders.[47] He received the unruly, self-indulgent multitudes of the first crusade.

Andronicus II complained to the Catalans that he had asked for 500 knights and 1,000 foot to fight the Turks, "and not that you should collect and bring such a multitude."[48] But he was not in a position to support his arguments with force. Thus he was obliged to accept the services of Berengar d'Entença. On his appointment as megas dux on December 25, 1304, Entença took an oath of fealty to the emperor, and swore to be a friend of his friends and an enemy of his enemies, saving his liege homage to Frederick III.[49]

It appears that the Byzantines still regarded the Catalans as an isolated problem—although a very unpleasant and expensive one, and they continued to deal with the demands of the Catalans on a day-to-day basis. It was the

44. Pachymeres, II, 491–492, 496–500; 504–505; Rubió y Lluch, *Diplomatari*, nos. 12, 14, XIV (Entença's letters of apology to the Venetian Doge); Muntaner, chap. ccxi.

45. Muntaner, chap. ccx; Pachymeres, II, 492–496; below, Chapter VI, "The Cost of Byzantine Foreign Policy."

46. Pachymeres, II, 491–492, 500–505; Finke, *Acta Aragonensia*, II, no. 431; Muntaner, chap. ccxi.

47. Anna Comnena, *Alexias*, (Bonn, 1839), I, 360–361, 395.

48. Pachymeres, II, 487.

49. Ibid., II, 499.

Genoese of Pera who first realized how very dangerous the situation had become. In the late summer or early autumn of 1304, the post arriving from Genoa brought disquieting information: a great fleet was being prepared in Sicily, to invade the empire during the coming spring, and Sancho of Aragon with a smaller fleet was on his way. The Genoese reported this to Andronicus, and added that Roger de Flor and his army were behaving like spies, not like allies of the Emperor, and already they were in secret contact with the Sicilians. In time, said the Genoese, the Catalan army would form an overt alliance with the Sicilians, and all together they would attack the Byzantine Empire.[50] This information, as reported by Pachymeres, was surprisingly accurate. Genoese spies must have followed very closely the diplomatic moves of Frederick III.

Having presented their information to Andronicus II, the Genoese of Pera then offered to help the empire with money and ships. Their plan consisted of a preventive attack on Roger and the Sicilian fleet: Byzantines and Genoese would requisition Roger's boats, and Andronicus would prepare fifty ships of his own to match fifty ships armed by the Genoese. Then, the combined fleet would intercept the Sicilian naval forces. This was the first and most positive effort of the Genoese of Byzantium to help the empire against those who would soon become its most dangerous enemies, but Andronicus politely rejected their advances. Although he had been concerned enough to recall the Catalans from Asia Minor, he was still negotiating with them, and was not ready to provoke a real fight. The Genoese then started to prepare their own defenses. They surrounded their quarter with a deep moat, which they tried to fill with sea water for greater security. They brought machines which threw stones and arrows (πετροβόλα, ἰοβόλα) and barricaded the windows of big houses. They prepared their ships for action and called in admirals from Genoa. They even collected money, which would enable them to hire mercenaries if the need arose. They obviously expected to have to defend their part of Constantinople against a major attack.[51]

Although Genoese fears of a Sicilian attack were well founded, the leaders of the Catalan army were not yet ready to contemplate an attack on Constantinople. Berengar d'Entença was among those most hostile to Byzantium; but both he and the others were restrained by the more moderate Roger de Flor. None of the sources gives any indication that Roger desired to conquer the Byzantine Empire by taking Constantinople. On the contrary, he seems to have fallen into the usual Byzantine trap of neutralizing dangerous "barbarian" leaders by flattering them. Roger was doubtless very pleased with his high titles in the Byzantine hierarchy, as well as with the important family connections of his wife, Maria. Perhaps too, Roger wanted not the entire empire but Asia Minor, and this more or less depended on the continuation of a Byzantine regime in Constantinople. In any case, he adopted a conciliatory attitude. In

---

50. Ibid., II, 489–490. Dade, *Versuche*, p. 93, greatly telescopes the Genoese-Byzantine negotiations regarding the Catalans, and inaccurately speaks of an alliance at this point.

51. Pachymeres, II, 489–491; 494–496.

his negotiations with Andronicus II, he often promised to try to pacify his army, and he seemed almost reasonable in the matter of pay: it was he who suggested compromises, despite his soldiers' opposition—or at least so he said. Also, it was Roger de Flor who promised Andronicus that Entença would help Michael IX in his wars, and he then persuaded Entença to swear fealty to the emperor. Indeed, the anonymous Sicilian source claims that Roger de Flor was responsible for the failure of Frederick's plans of conquest. The same source considered Entença's oath of fealty to Andronicus as an act of treason—all of which indicates that the Sicilians were, at this point, much more eager than the Catalan leaders to launch an anti-Byzantine expedition.[52]

In early January 1305, Andronicus II received word of certain activities of Roger de Flor, which alarmed him considerably, especially since he was counting on Roger's loyalty, reinforced as it was by family ties. He learned that the Catalans were fortifying Gallipoli, and that Roger de Flor was collecting huge quantities of grain and meat, and loading it on his ships. Andronicus thought that something was distinctly amiss, and to test Roger he invited both him and his wife to come to Constantinople to celebrate the Feast of Lights ('Επιφάνεια, Φῶτα), which falls on January 6. But Roger refused to appear at the capital, and he allowed his army to raid Gallipoli and the surrounding territories, in order to blackmail Andronicus into paying the money the Catalans demanded.

The emperor now feared for the integrity of his European possessions, and he made an important offer to Roger. The Catalans were to go to Asia Minor, to save the city of Philadelphia which was once again besieged by the Turks. Roger would receive the title of caesar, and the offices of strategos (general) with full powers to govern Asia Minor, with the exception of the large cities.[53] The Catalans would receive 20,000 gold coins and 300,000 modii of grain as soon as they crossed the straits into Asia. Since the cities were the only part of Asia Minor still in Byzantine hands, Andronicus was, in effect, telling Roger to recover the Byzantine territory occupied by the Turks, and keep it. Thus, Roger would become an imperial governor of Asia Minor, but with a special authority: he would be virtually independent of the government of Constantinople (στρατηγὸς αὐτοκράτωρ). Andronicus was offering to Roger de Flor what Alexios Philanthropenos would have liked in 1295. Roger was invested with the title of caesar in a solemn ceremony on April 10, 1305. "Caesar" was a purely honorific title, and had been somewhat debased by Alexius I Comnenus. It was still, however, one of the highest titles, being third in the hierarchy, and so it represented a promotion for Roger de Flor. But Muntaner was wrong in saying that "there is no difference between the emperor and the caesar." Perhaps he was misled by the ceremony of investiture, which to a westerner

---

52. Finke, *Acta Aragonensia*, II, no. 431. The source's condemnation of Entença's action may perhaps indicate that Entença was closer to James II than to Frederick III, and that the Sicilian author knew it. Also, Pachymeres, II, 491–492.

53. Ibid., II, 506: παραδιδοὺς δὲ καὶ πᾶσαν χώραν Ἀνατολῆς πλὴν τῶν περιφανῶν πολισμάτων, καὶ αὐτοκράτορα στρατηγὸν καθιστᾶν ὑπισχνούμενος. Cf. ibid., II, 508.

would resemble a coronation, and by the fact that a caesar was variously addressed as "my lord Caesar" and "your majesty."[54]

In this discussion of the agreement between Roger de Flor and Andronicus, Pachymeres has been used as the authority. Muntaner gives a somewhat different account. He claims that the emperor gave Roger all of Anatolia and the "isles of the Romania," and told him to distribute the cities, towns and castles to his vassals.[55] Thus, Roger was invited to set up a feudal principality in Anatolia. But what is known of Andronicus' political theories and even of his actions, which did not always agree with his theories, argues against Muntaner's account. Desperate though he was, Andronicus would not surrender his theoretical sovereignty over Asia Minor, nor would he agree to the setting up of a complete feudal regime in Anatolia.

Yet even the partial surrender of Asia Minor to the Catalans was a desperate measure. It must have been especially painful to Andronicus, whose main concern for over twenty years had been the liberation of Asia Minor. He was probably prompted by his fear of an attack on Constantinople, and the rumors of Sancho of Aragon's impending arrival contributed to his desire to speed up the departure of the Catalans. Perhaps Andronicus had decided to take seriously the warning of the Genoese, who were already prepared for a long siege.

During and after the negotiations of January 1305, Roger began to behave in a manner designed to cause maximum trouble to the Byzantines and to secure his hold on the islands adjacent to Asia Minor. He sent help to the inhabitants of Chios against the Turks. Then he assembled some important Byzantines, "the most illustrious ones of each area," outside the fort of Gallipoli and spoke to them against Andronicus.[56] He told them how the emperor had accepted the Catalan offer of help against the Turks, how Asia Minor had been defended, and how the Catalans had been defrauded of their money and therefore were forced to plunder. He also asserted that he was ready to obey Michael IX, but that he would fight him to death if necessary. Roger clearly was playing some sort of game; his purpose seems to have been to extract as much money as possible and then to leave for Asia Minor. He kept repeating to the emperor that his men were not all completely obedient to him. In March 1305 he told Andronicus that only 1,000 Catalans were loyal to himself and would follow him to the East. The rest were ready to attack the empire unless they were given more money.[57] On April 10, when he accepted the title of caesar, he agreed to take 3,000 men to Asia Minor with him, and to dismiss

---

54. Ibid., II, 522. Muntaner, chap. ccxii: "And a Caesar is an officer who sits in a chair near that of the Emperor, only a half a palm lower, and he can do as much as the Emperor in the Empire . . . finally, all the Emperor can do, he can do also. And again, he signs 'Caesar of Our Empire' and the Emperor writes to him 'Caesar of Thy Empire.' What shall I tell you? There is no difference between the Emperor and the Caesar, except that the chair is half a palm lower than that of the Emperor and the Emperor wears a scarlet cap and all his robes are scarlet, and the Caesar wears a blue cap and all his robes are blue with a narrow gold border." Cf. Codinus, *De officialibus*, pp. 7, 15–16, 28, 101.

55. Muntaner, chap. ccxii.

56. Pachymeres, II, 510, 510–512: τοὺς ἐξ ἐκάστης χώρας ἐμφανεστέρους.

57. Pachymeres, II, 510–516; Dade, *Versuche*, pp. 96–97.

the rest. Immediately afterwards, he said that these last would not listen to him. Meanwhile, Sancho of Aragon and his fleet of thirteen galleys had arrived; Pachymeres first mentions the operations of this fleet in April 1305. Apparently, as soon as the fleet appeared, Berengar d'Entença joined Sancho, and together they attacked various islands. Roger, however, asked Sancho of Aragon not to sail north of the island of Lesbos.[58]

Roger's attitude toward Sancho illustrates his aims and those of his army. Sancho, of course, had arrived with the double mission of launching naval attacks on Byzantium and trying to investigate the possibility of a Catalan rebellion against the Byzantines. But almost immediately Roger indicated that his interests were not quite identical with those of the king of Sicily. Instead of cooperating with Sancho to attack Constantinople, Roger limited Sancho's attacks to a few islands. After Roger's death, at the end of April 1305, his army could not agree on the terms of cooperation with Sancho, who was reduced to attacking the islands on his own.[59] Therefore, it seems that the conflict between Roger and his army, which he constantly reported to Andronicus, was minimal: Roger probably exaggerated his army's desire to attack Constantinople in order to play up his own role as mediator. The only major conflict which existed in 1304–1305 was the conflict of interests between the Catalan army and Frederick III.

In the early spring of 1305, it appeared that Andronicus II and Roger de Flor had come to a shaky understanding. Roger became caesar, he received 33,000 hyperpyra and 100,000 modii of wheat, and he promised to go to Asia Minor with 3,000 men. At this stage, Roger took the strange and inexplicable decision of going to visit Michael IX at Adrianople. He took with him a mere 1,000 infantry and 300 knights. Muntaner insists that Roger was motivated by pure courtesy: "it would be a great disgrace for him to depart from Romania and go to the Kingdom of Anatolia with the intention of remaining to fight the Turks and not to take leave, and it would be taken in bad part . . . He [went] from the great loyalty of his heart and great love and fidelity towards the emperor and his son." Pachymeres explained that the deeper reason for Roger's visit was that he wanted to spy on Michael's camp—which hardly makes sense. Roger would have sent more expendable men to do this.[60]

Roger's visit is puzzling. Michael IX hated him bitterly for various reasons, among them, no doubt, Roger's greater success in war. Michael IX was, unlike his father, a soldier at heart. But he had had poor luck on his campaigns, and his defeats in Asia Minor had forced Andronicus to request the services of the Catalans. Roger's success in that very province must have rankled. In April 1305 Michael IX was trying to collect an army to fight the Catalans, and Roger knew it. Furthermore, Michael IX had with him refugees from Asia Minor who had no love for Roger. Also, he had the Alan soldiers who had, at first,

58. Pachymeres, II, 521–526.

59. Pachymeres, II, 527; Gregoras, I, 227ff.

60. Muntaner, chaps. ccxiii, ccxiv; Pachymeres, II, 523, says Roger went with only 150 of his most trustworthy men. Gregoras, I, 223, gives the figure 200. I have followed Muntaner, who was in a better position to know the real numbers.

operated in Asia Minor with the Catalans.[61] The Alans and the Catalans had fallen out, partly because a son of the leader of the Alans had been killed in Cyzicus by the Catalans. Muntaner would have us believe that Roger de Flor acted out of pure chivalry; but there are not many other instances where the chivalric part of his character came to the surface. One can only guess at Roger's real motives: perhaps he was indeed paying a courtesy visit, but to make a point. The key phrase in Muntaner is "gran vergonya li seria, que ell partis de Romania e entras el regne del Natuli . . . e que non presses comiat." He was leaving for the Kingdom of Anatolia—his province. Was he trying to make the point to Michael IX that now they were equal in rank and that he had come to take leave from his equal? Was he pressing the point home that now he was governor of Anatolia by imperial decree? If so, he miscalculated badly.

Michael was taken aback when he learned Roger's plans, but he soon recovered, and he recalled his Turkish and Alan mercenaries from the Bulgarian frontier where they were fighting.[62] On the night of April 30, 1305, Roger de Flor was assassinated by the Alan soldiers (or, according to Pachymeres, by their leader George), and his retinue fled to Gallipoli. The details of the assassination differ in the two major sources, as Muntaner sought to prove that Michael IX was responsible and Pachymeres sought to absolve Michael of all responsibility. On the whole, it seems reasonable to believe that Michael did engineer the assassination of Roger de Flor, although it is highly unlikely that the timid Andronicus—who would also have had an idea of the implications of this assassination—knew about Michael's plans.

The assassination of Roger de Flor opened an unbridgeable chasm between the Catalans and the Byzantines, although once again the two important chroniclers differ in their assessment of the situation. For Muntaner, the murder of Roger de Flor marked the point of no return between the Catalans and the Byzantines. For Pachymeres, the assassination was merely the result of the already existing and insoluble tensions. The judgment of Muntaner seems preferable, if only because what would have happened had Roger not been killed cannot be known, while after his murder the more anti-Byzantine elements among the Catalan army, such as Berengar de Rocafort, took over the leadership. Besides, there is no escaping the fact that Roger was one of the few Catalans who had begun to think in terms of a coexistence with the Byzantines. His murder removed a stabilizing, moderate element.

The contradiction in the chroniclers reflects the fact that there were a number of interests at play and that each interested party decided to break off negotiations at a different time. Since both Byzantines and Catalans were suspicious of each other almost from the beginning, each hostile action increased the suspicion of the other party until a final breach was inevitable. Certainly, most of Andronicus II's activity between the late summer of 1304 and April 1305 can only be explained by his uneasiness at the behavior of the Catalans.

61. Pachymeres, II, 525; Muntaner, chap. ccxv; A. Morel-Fatio, ed. *Libro de los Fechos et Conquistas del Principado de la Morea*, (Geneva, 1885), §530; Rubió y Lluch, *Diplomatari*, no. 14; Nicolaus Specialis, *Historia Sicula*, in L. A. Muratori, ed., *RIS*, X (Milan, 1727), books vi, xxi; Caro, "Chronologie," 129.
62. Pachymeres, II, 524–525.

After the death of Roger de Flor, the relations of Catalans and Byzantines degenerated very rapidly. The Catalans shut themselves in the fort of Gallipoli, killed all the Greeks there, and prepared for war with the empire.[63] The Catalan Company now did what Frederick III had tried to make them do some months earlier. They defied Andronicus in Constantinople, in the presence of Venetian envoys, and a few days later they raised the standard of St. Peter on the walls of Gallipoli, proclaiming that they were crusaders fighting for the church.[64] They did not, however, cooperate closely with Sancho of Aragon, who was left to raid the islands on his own. There is some evidence that Entença asked for Sancho's help, and that Sancho stayed around Gallipoli to give naval protection to the Catalans. He left for Sicily after the end of May 1305.[65] Meanwhile, Entença and his fleet ravaged the Byzantine coasts and tried to take Heracleia, a city on the Sea of Marmora, not far from Constantinople. Constantinople had to open its doors to refugees once again and Andronicus, afraid for the safety of the capital, requested and received the help of the Genoese (May 1305).[66]

Byzantium, the Genoese and the Catalans

During the years 1304–1308 the Byzantine Empire, threatened by the Catalans and by the possibility of an invasion from Europe, was forced to mobilize all its financial, military and diplomatic resources. For five years the empire was virtually under siege, and all its policies had one aim, averting the danger of annihilation. When trouble with the Catalans first occurred, Byzantium was diplomatically isolated. The only western friend the empire had was Genoa, and Genoese friendship had proven untrustworthy during the years of the Byzantine-Venetian war. Yet Genoa and Byzantium were now thrown into an alliance on which depended the preservation of the empire and the commercial greatness of the commune. The real Genoese colonization of the empire took place in the years 1304–1308, and corresponded with the mounting threat of the Catalans. Each state exhibited a substantial degree of ambivalence toward the other: for Genoa, alliance with the Byzantines entailed the hostility of the papacy, of the Catalans, and of their Aragonese protectors. At one point, in 1307, Genoa was even contemplating war with Venice, because of conflicting interests in the East. For the Byzantines, the Genoese alliance meant the abandonment of independence: the empire became dependent on Genoa for its naval defenses, for the provisioning and defense of the city, for the defense of the coasts and islands of Asia Minor. Because of these difficulties, the alliance was somewhat halfhearted, and it was opposed by people on both sides.

---

63. Ibid., II, 527.

64. Muntaner, chaps. ccvi, ccxix. The crusading aspect of the Catalan expedition is pointed out by Burns in his article, "Catalan Company." Tramontana, "Compagnia Catalana," greatly exaggerates both the chivalric and the crusading aspects of the Catalan adventure.

65. Pachymeres, II, 527; Finke, *Acta Aragonensia*, II, no. 431. Michael Lupi de Mendia, writing to Frederick III on June 24, 1305, said *Sancius . . . cepit unam insulam noviter, que dicitur Galipo.*

66. Pachymeres, II, 529; Muntaner, chap. ccxv.

In Genoa there was an anti-Byzantine, pro-Aragonese party, and in Byzantium there was a large and very vocal anti-"Latin" party. The patriarch Athanasios I thundered against the dependence of the empire on the greedy Genoese, the people of Constantinople murmured about it, and the historians deplored it in writing. What evidence there is suggests that Michael IX tried an alternative measure—internal reorganization. Yet the alliance did take place, because the immediate interests of both states seemed to require it.[67] As far as Genoa was concerned, there was a double danger inherent in the Catalan campaign: if the Catalans were successful, and if they should conquer Constantinople with the help of Sicily or Aragon, the Genoese commercial preponderance in the Aegean and the Black Sea would be severely threatened. Secondly, Genoa was becoming very apprehensive about Aragonese expansion in the western Mediterranean: Genoese and Aragonese interests clashed in Corsica and Sardinia, which had been granted to James II at the peace of Anagni in 1295. Genoa had annihilated her neighbor and rival, Pisa, in 1284. But now another power, Aragon, was expanding in the western Mediterranean, and threatening to expand in the Aegean as well. Genoa's economic power was being attacked on both fronts.

From the Byzantine side, the responsibility for the Genoese alliance falls on Andronicus II and perhaps on Theodore Metochites, whose political influence was rising until, in 1305 or 1306, he supplanted his rival, Nicephorus Choumnos, and became mesazon, thus acquiring one of the most influential political posts in the state.[68] Andronicus certainly, and Metochites possibly, preferred to base their anti-Catalan policy on an alliance with Genoa, rather than try to strengthen the fighting potential of the empire. But Andronicus II did not enter this alliance with a light heart or without realizing its dangers. His policy was cautious at first. Even after the arrival of Berengar d'Entença and the announcement of Frederick III's contemplated invasion, he seemed reluctant to give the Genoese more power than they already held. He succumbed because of the pressing Catalan danger.

Although Genoa had abandoned the Byzantine Empire during the Venetian-Genoese war, there was no immediate recrimination from the Byzantines. Relations remained friendly, although there were the usual complaints about illegal action taken by imperial officials against Genoese subjects and the usual reports of trouble between Byzantines and Genoese.[69] In May 1303, the

67. Previous students of the period have not discussed at any length the relations between Byzantium and Genoa during the years of the Catalan campaign. Dade, *Versuche*, pp. 93ff, has a short and quite inadequate discussion of the Genoese position. Burns, "Catalan Campaign," p. 753, mentions the Genoese policy very briefly, and does not distinguish the policy of Genoa from that of the Genoese of Pera. The studies of Sauli, Manfroni, and Belgrano are concerned with the Genoese in the Byzantine Empire during this period, but not within the context of the Catalan campaign, which so deeplya ffected both Byzantine and Genoese policy.

68. On Metochites' rise to power, see Ševčenko, *Métochite et Choumnos*, pp. 147–151. The office of mesazon is a somewhat nebulous one, but it is clear that his functions were very important: he was head of the imperial chancery, head of the passport office, and in some way intermediary between the emperor and his subjects. See Ševčenko, ibid., p. 6, n. 4, and Raymond Leonertz, "Le chancelier impérial à Byzance," *Orientalia Christiana Periodica*, 26 (1960), 275–300.

69. In 1300 and 1302: Belgrano, "Prima serie," no. 7 (February 7, 1302); Manfroni, "Relazioni," p. 688.

privileges of the Genoese in the empire were reaffirmed and extended. Since the Venetian fleet had destroyed the Genoese quarter in Galata in 1296, Andronicus granted the Genoese a larger and better situated portion of Pera, and carefully defined its extent and position.[70] Outside the Genoese area was a no-man's land where no buildings could be erected and no Greeks were allowed to live, except for the priests of the Greek church of St. Nicholas. But Greeks and Genoese often lived side by side in Pera, and their relations with each other were often friendly. Such was the exchange of cultures—or habits— that sometimes Genoese would offer votive offerings to Greek saints or churches.[71] When Michael VIII had made the original grant of a part of Pera to the Genoese in 1267, he had destroyed the fortifications of the area, for fear that Pera, if fortified, might become a city within a city and endanger the security of Constantinople. The Genoese quarter of Pera was still not fortified in 1303; the moat was built only in the autumn of 1304.[72]

Less than a year after issuing the chrysobull of 1303, Andronicus received two Genoese ambassadors, Guido Embriaco and Accursino Ferrari, who came to ask for more formal privileges, to match those granted to Venice in 1302. The emperor agreed to their request, and in March 1304 he granted them a chrysobull. In this, he confirmed the cession of Pera, and gave the Genoese merchants the usual privileges of a loggia, a church, permission to have their own butcher and their own weights and measures, to be used in the presence of imperial officials. Similar privileges were granted to the Genoese of Smyrna, which was still under Byzantine rule.[73]

By the same imperial decree, the persons and property of all Genoese shipwrecked in Byzantine waters were safeguarded, and the owners of that property could claim compensation if it were stolen. Genoese merchants were exempted from all imperial duties on any form and article of commerce, with the exception of salt and mastic—an aromatic gum which men and women chewed with great abandon, and which was also the basis for many perfumes. The Genoese could also buy and export Byzantine grain and other agricultural produce, and any commodity from the Black Sea area, without paying duty. Alum, tar, and wood were especially mentioned as duty-exempt commodities.

The Byzantines promised to punish all Latin or Greek pirates who attacked the Genoese and who did not come "from the parts . . . of those who have made pacts and sworn treaties with us." "Those who have made pacts . . . with us" probably referred to the Venetians, and this article must be interpreted as Byzantine unwillingness to repeat an accidental involvement in another war between Venice and Genoa. The Genoese, in return, promised to suppress their own pirates. Finally, the chrysobull included regulations on the hearing of cases that involved Byzantine and Genoese subjects.

70. Above, Chapter IV, notes 107, 108 for full bibliography; Sauli, *Colonia*, no. 109; Desimoni, "Quartieri," pp. 247ff; Manfroni, "Relazioni," p. 689.

71. Brătianu, *Recherches sur le Commerce*, 108ff; G. I. Brătianu, *Actes des notaires génois de Péra et de Caffa de la fin du XIIIe siècle*, Académie roumaine, Études et Recherches, II (Bucharest, 1927), passim.

72. Pachymeres, II, 489.

73. Sauli, *Colonia*, no. 10; also in Belgrano, "Prima serie," no. 10.

The privileges of the chrysobull of 1304 were extended only to genuine Genoese subjects, and no one else was allowed profit from them, although this provision was not implemented. There were a number of Byzantines who claimed Genoese citizenship for reasons of convenience, but whom the empire considered to be its own subjects. Some of these people were Greek merchants who were eager to adopt Genoese citizenship in order to avoid paying customs duties; but some were Greek women, whose primary interest cannot have been a commercial one. Apparently, even some Venetian merchants bought charters of citizenship from Genoa, in order to facilitate their commercial transactions in the empire. The Genoese consuls of the Black Sea colonies made a profitable business out of issuing charters of Genoese citizenship, and their abuses had to be corrected in 1308.[74]

The privileges of 1304 were in many respects similar to those granted to Genoa by Michael VIII in 1275.[75] But the omission of certain basic clauses in 1304 illustrates the progression of Byzantine-Genoese relations. In 1275 the emperor had had the right to ask Genoese subjects to stay and defend his empire in times of danger, and he could also obtain from them, at the current market price, any ships he needed for defense. This right was relinquished by Andronicus; when he needed the help of Genoa, as he did in the summer of 1305 and again in 1306, he had to ask for it specifically. Michael VIII had had the right to detain in port the ships of the Genoese if he feared that they might give his enemies information about the movements of his fleet. This article was also omitted in the decree of 1304. This was the most understandable omission, because the imperial fleet was almost nonexistent, and in any case could not undertake any large-scale, offensive operations. Finally, it had been stipulated in 1275 that any wheat exports authorized by the emperor could be carried only to Genoa and not to the territory of any of the enemies of the empire. This provision also was omitted in 1304.

Since the text of the negotiations between the emperor and the Genoese envoys has not survived, the reasons the Genoese requested a formal grant of privileges and Andronicus assented are not known. The presence of the Catalans in the East, resented so heartily by the Genoese, probably made them eager to have their privileges reaffirmed and increased. Andronicus, although hopeful for the results of the Catalan expedition in Asia Minor, must have found it impolitic to deny the requests of the Genoese. His reason for letting the important defense clauses of 1275 lapse may be ascribed to the feeling of false security generated by the early stages of the Catalan campaign: in the spring of 1304 the Catalans had just embarked on their Anatolian campaign and he had no reason to fear an attack from them. Charles of Valois had not yet completed his system of alliances, and in any case the new important position of the Genoese in Pera made it probable that they would defend their interests, and by that token the empire.

The Genoese of Pera viewed the arrival of the Catalan army with great

74. Thomas, *Diplomatarium*, p. 104 (1317). Cf. Belgrano, "Prima serie," no. 12, p. 110; V. Promis, *Magnum Statutum Peyrae*, in *Miscellanea di Storia Italiana*, 11 (1870), 513–780.

75. Bertolotto, "Nuova serie," no. 19; *Liber Jurium reipublicae Genuensis*, II, 440ff; Manfroni, "Relazioni," p. 690.

misgivings. Their new "magnificent" quarters in Pera and the privileges granted them in 1303 and 1304 had increased both their prosperity and their arrogance, both their power and their stake in the Byzantine Empire and the Black Sea. They considered the empire their private backyard where no other westerner was suffered to play.[76] They were particularly interested in preserving their supremacy in the Black Sea. For this reason, they entered an unsuccessful war against the Comnenoi of the empire of Trebizond, who did not repeal their customs duties as the Genoese demanded.[77]

Apparently the Genoese of Pera feared that if the Catalans were successful in their campaign against the Turks they would become very influential in the Byzantine Empire. Should such an eventuality occur, the Genoese anticipated, at least according to Muntaner, that Andronicus "who had dared do nothing but what they wished" would scorn their advice. This, in fact, happened during the first stages of the Catalan adventure, when the emperor brushed aside the efforts of the Genoese of Pera to discredit his new mercenaries.[78] His ambivalent feelings toward the people on whom he depended, the Genoese, are clearly indicated by the fact that he granted them extensive privileges in 1303 and 1304, but disregarded their advice in the fall of 1304.

Realizing, perhaps, the emperor's ambivalence, the Genoese tried to ingratiate themselves with him and to increase their diplomatic contact with Byzantium. The chrysobull of 1304 may have been the result of the Genoese quest for reassurance. But during the negotiations between Andronicus and the government of Genoa, we also find a concomitant effort by the Genoese of Pera to get closer to Andronicus. Suddenly, in 1304, they began to take into account the deteriorating political condition of the empire, and they offered their help. They particularly regretted their failure to help in Asia Minor, now virtually lost, "from which they had become rich through commerce."[79] They promised that in future they would be faithful allies of the Byzantines and would contribute in the defense of the empire. Others, such as the Zaccaria family of Phocaea, who had traditionally been friendly and useful to the Byzantines, were as alarmed as the inhabitants of Pera.

In the winter of 1304 Andronicus II came to understand that the Catalans had become as dangerous as the Genoese had warned him that they would be. He also began to realize that the Catalan affair would be resolved at sea, as much as on land. At this time, a Genoese sailor, Andrea Morisco, who had been a very successful pirate and had fought against Turks and Venetians, came with his two ships and placed himself at the emperor's disposal. Andronicus made him a vestiarios and the Venetians, upset at his success, attacked and burned one of his ships.[80] The arrangement with Morisco was personal, and did not yet mean a common Byzantine-Genoese policy against the Catalans, but the utility of the Genoese offers became obvious as the situation

76. Muntaner, chap. ccii. Muntaner's chronicle shows a great deal of hostility toward the Genoese.
77. Pachymeres, II, 448–450. Date: this event took place in the same year as Michael IX's first campaign against Svetoslav. See below, Chapter VI, "Toward a Byzantine Defense."
78. Pachymeres, II, 489–491; Muntaner, chap. ccii.
79. Ibid., II, 490–491.
80. Ibid., II, 495–496.

deteriorated after Christmas 1304. After the murder of Roger de Flor, the fear of war with the Catalans increased. In Constantinople, both the patriarch and the people demanded that Andronicus take the necessary measures to protect his subjects. The emperor tried to prepare a small fleet of mercenaries and "Italians" under the command of the Catalan leader, Ferran de Ahones, who had joined the Byzantines. Suspicions arose as to the loyalty of Ahones; and he was imprisoned. Then the indignation of the inhabitants of Constantinople took the form of bitter recriminations against those who had advised that the imperial fleet be dismantled, thus placing the empire at the mercy of even its weakest enemy.[81] Andronicus was forced to realize the importance of sea power in the conflict with the Catalans.

Although it was becoming clear to the Byzantines that they needed an ally with naval power, the next incident of Byzantine-Genoese cooperation was the result of personal arrangements between Andronicus and a private Genoese citizen, Benedetto Zaccaria, the master of Phocaea. Soon after the departure of the Catalans from Asia Minor, in the late summer of 1304, the Turks once more overran the area they had occupied. The Byzantines were unable to defend the islands close to the Anatolian coasts. In January 1305, Chios was plundered by thirty Turkish ships, and its inhabitants fled to Skyros. Roger de Flor, claiming the island as his own, tried to defend it against the Turks.[82] But the initiative had already passed to another man. Benedetto Zaccaria sent an embassy to Andronicus demanding that either the islands be effectively defended, or else that he be allowed to defend them himself. Phocaea, situated on the southeastern coast of Asia Minor, was very important to the Genoese both because of its good commercial position and because of the production of alum, necessary to the Genoese textile industry.[83] Zaccaria wanted to keep the seas free of the Turks so that his communications with Genoa would remain open and his alum fleet could sail without difficulties. This is not expressly stated as his reason, but Chios was just to the north of Phocaea, and could be very dangerous in the hands of a hostile power. Its good position made this island the center of the alum trade and the entrepôt of Genoese trade with the East in the fifteenth century. Besides, Chios was rich in wine, oil, beautiful women, and mastic, in all of which Zaccaria was most interested.

Chios became a part of Zaccaria's far-flung commercial empire, and he made immense profits out of mastic. He showed quite outstanding flexibility in changing his business techniques to acquire the maximum possible profit out of mastic. Until then, the cornerstone of his fortune had been alum, a mineral product which had to be sold in great quantities and at a low price, and Zaccaria had been very successful in undercutting his competitors by

81. Ibid., II, 531–533.

82. Ibid., II, 510–516, 558.

83. Phocaea was given to Benedetto and Manuele Zaccaria by Michael VIII in 1275: Lopez, *Genova marinara*, p. 12. On Phocaea and the alum trade, see Lopez, *Genova marinara*, pp. 23–50; Charles Singer, *The Earliest Chemical Industry, An Essay in the Historical Relations of Economics and Technology Illustrated from the Alum Trade*, (London, 1948); M.-L. Heers, "Les Génois et le commerce de l'alum à la fin du Moyen-Age," *Revue d'histoire économique et sociale*, 32 (1954), 31–53.

lowering the costs of production and transportation of alum from the mines of Phocaea. Mastic was a luxury product of which he had an absolute monopoly since it was produced only on Chios. Zaccaria recognized that in this case he needed to maintain as high a price for his product as the market would bear. He set a target figure of production, based on his calculations of what the market would absorb at the high price he desired, and he and his family realized extremely high returns.[84]

Benedetto Zaccaria occupied Chios in 1305 and subsequently received it from Andronicus to hold for ten years; he would pay no tribute, but he was obliged to fly the imperial banner and mention the emperor's name on official occasions. Usually, the cession of Chios to Zaccaria is placed in the autumn of 1304, on the assumption that it was precipitated by the Turkish attacks which followed the evacuation of Asia Minor by the Catalans.[85] Since Pachymeres does not mention the presence of the Genoese when writing of the major Turkish attack of January 1305, the island was probably given to Zaccaria soon after that date. If this is true, then Zaccaria was defending Chios not only against the Turks but also against the ambitions of Roger de Flor. It is possible that the Catalans remembered this and bore a grudge against the lords of Phocaea and Chios. They soon found occasion to take some small revenge. Benedetto Zaccaria died in 1307, leaving Phocaea to his son Nicolino. Nicolino found the castle of Phocaea under the control of his cousin Ticino, who had held it for five years. Ticino's accounts were found wanting; he was thrown out of Phocaea and was in danger of being sent to Genoa to defend his behavior. He went to Gallipoli instead, asked Ramon Muntaner, the Catalan leader and historian, for help, and in return promised to remain loyal to him. The Catalans sailed to Phocaea, took the castle, pillaged the town, which was populated by Greeks working in the alum mines (Easter Sunday, 1307—March 26), and returned to Gallipoli. This was a mission of revenge rather than of conquest; the Zaccaria continued to rule Phocaea until 1314. Ticino Zaccaria took the castle of Thasos, where he settled, bound in eternal gratitude to Muntaner.[86]

Zaccaria's intervention in Chios was the first major Genoese contribution in the war against the Catalans and the Turks. Soon, the Genoese would get more deeply involved. In the late spring of 1305, Andronicus II, afraid of the activities of the Catalans and especially of Berengar d'Entença, finally requested Genoese help.[87] At the end of May 1305, sixteen (or eighteen) Genoese ships

84. Heers, "Génois et le commerce de l'alum," p. 42; Lopez, *Genova marinara*, pp. 224–227.

85. The cession of Chios was renewed after ten years, and then twice at five-year intervals: Cantacuzenus, I, 370; R. Lopez, *Storia delle colonie genovesi nel Mediterraneo* (Bologna, 1938), p. 283. Lemerle, *L'Émirat d'Aydin*, pp. 50–52, 51 n. 5. Lemerle adopts the date 1304. Cf. Heyd, *Commerce*, I, 430ff; W. I. Miller, "The Zaccaria of Phocaea and Chios, 1275–1329," *Journal of Hellenic Studies*, 31, (1911), 42–55 Ph. Argenti, *Bibliography of Chios from Classical Times to 1936*, (Oxford, 1940); K. Amantos, «Συμβολὴ εἰς τὴν Μεσαιωνικὴν ἱστορίαν τῆς Χίου,» Ἐπιστημονικὴ Ἐπετηρὶς Φιλοσοφικῆς Σχολῆς Πανεπιστημίου Ἀθηνῶν, 2d ser., 5 (1954–1955), 153–164. Lopez, *Genova marinara*, pp. 224–227, gives no precise date, but seems to place this event in 1303.

86. Muntaner, chap. ccxxxiv; Rubió y Lluch, *Diplomatari*, no. 35; also in Rubió y Lluch, *Contribució a la biografía del infant En Ferràn de Mallorca*, Estudis Universitaris Catalans, VII (Barcelona, 1915), no. 39.

87. Pachymeres, II, 532–533.

arrived at Constantinople a few days earlier than they were due, and were met by Berengar d'Entença who, with five ships, was plundering the seacoast around Rhegium and Heracleia in the Propontis.[88] After the death of Roger de Flor, Entença had, at least in his own mind, assumed command over the Catalan army, and appropriated the title "dominus Natulii ac insularum . . . Imperii [Romanie]". He was now expecting reinforcements from Sicily to launch an attack against Constantinople, and he was mildly taken aback to realize that the ships he saw were Genoese. Even so, he hoped that he could persuade these ships to join him in an attack against the empire.[89]

Entença had become aware of the ambivalences inherent in the relations of the Byzantines to the Genoese of Pera, and he was trying to take advantage of them. Some of the inhabitants of Pera had shown themselves disposed to cooperate with the Catalans, and a number of Catalans hid in Genoese houses. The Catalans of Pera loaded a ship with provisions and sent it to the men at Gallipoli; when Andronicus' admiral intercepted it, certain Genoese tried to kill him. Andronicus was rightly furious. Further incidents in Pera had poisoned relations between the emperor and his supposed allies. There was the matter of the friars who had, at the request of Athanasios I, been deprived of a certain area previously granted to them for the purpose of building a monastery. They asked for Genoese support; Andronicus, angry at the intervention, dismissed the Genoese podestà from his presence, and the matter was still pending when the Genoses fleet appeared.[90]

Because of these disagreements between the Byzantines and the inhabitants of Pera, Entença thought he could persuade the Genoese to cooperate with him. But the commander of the Genoese fleet, Egidio D'Oria, preferred to help Andronicus, for he considered this the best way of defending Genoese interests in the empire. The emperor sent D'Oria men and arms, and the joint enterprise ended with the capture of the Catalan ships and of Entença himself, on May 31, 1305. Entença was kept in the custody of two Genoese ships for four months, and was then taken back to Genoa.[91] He was not handed over the the Byzantines, because Genoa was anxious not to provoke Aragon more than absolutely necessary. This became clear in the negotiations which followed Entença's

88. Finke, *Acta Aragonensia*, II, 685; Muntaner, chap. ccxviii; Pachymeres, II, 540–542; Gregoras, I, 227ff.

89. On this incident, see Pachymeres, II, 533–540, and Muntaner, chap. ccxviii. Dade, *Versuche*, p. 101, does not discuss this inciuent except for a one-sentence mention. Manfroni, *Marina italiana, 1261–1453*, p. 226, places this incident in 1306, which is manifestly wrong, especially after the publication of Rubió y Lluch's *Diplomatari*. Entença designated himself with the title "magnus dux . . . imperii Romanie ac dominus Natulii [Anatolia] ac insularum eiusdem imperii" in a letter to the doge of Venice, written on May 10, 1305. In a previous letter, of September 10, 1304, he had simply called himself "Berengarius de Entença miles": *Diplomatari*, nos. 12, 14.

90. Pachymeres, II, 532, 536–538.

91. Muntaner, chap. ccxviii; Pachymeres, II, 540–542, 554, 478; Rubió y Lluch, *Diplomatari*, nos. 16, 17, 18, 19; Finke, *Acta Aragonensia*, no. 431; Caro, *Genua*, II, 308; Pachymeres, II, 554, 478. He was probably sent back to Genoa at the end of August or the beginning of September. The exchange of letters between James II and the Genoese, concerning Entença's capture starts on September 4, 1305: Rubió y Lluch, *Diplomatari*, no. 16. Cf. Caro, *Genua*, II, 357.

capture. Genoa, although forced by her interests to oppose the expansion of the Catalans, insisted that she was also eager to preserve her friendship with Aragon.[92] James II protested very strongly against Entença's capture and the loss of his property. The Genoese gave various answers, some more sincere than others, and most, though not all, were conciliatory.

The Genoese said that they did not want to abandon their friendship with James and Frederick III, but "they did this [the arrest of Berengar] in the service of the emperor."[93] For they saw that "he [Berengar] wanted to invade the empire of the Romania, which greatly affects the Genoese . . . who have affairs with and debts to the emperor of the Greeks." Genoa, said the ambassadors to James II, "has old and great agreements with Andronicus, and she loves and must love the emperor and the empire because the Genoese need this empire and hold franchises in it." The Genoese asked James to send messengers to the Catalans in Byzantium, ordering them to leave.[94] They also sent ambassadors to Frederick III of Sicily, in an effort to persuade him to tell the Catalans "to leave the said empire . . . by the road of peace in such a way as would result in honor for the said emperor and salvation for the said Catalans." The king of Aragon answered that the Catalans were not under his orders.[95]

On the other hand, the Genoese claimed that those who had captured Entença were men of no consequence, and did not act on the orders of the Commune.[96] They also said that after this event, orders had been sent to Pera to release any Catalan captives and to abstain from any further attacks on the Catalans (September 1305).[97] The government of Genoa, then, was oscillating between a strong position, manifested in their request that the Catalans leave the empire, in which the Genoese had a predominant sphere of influence, and a weak position, which took the form of apologies to the king of Aragon. Perhaps the Genoese did not want to precipitate a full-scale war with Aragon, and certainly the capture of Entença had already made their point. They had removed from the Byzantine empire the man they had most feared, for they had from the beginning considered Entença as an agent of the Aragonese government. The fact that they presented their apologies to James of Aragon rather than to Frederick of Sicily further illustrates the fact that for the Genoese Entença was an Aragonese, not a Sicilian agent. It is probable, then, that the official Genoese position was conciliatory to the degree of wishing to avoid war with Aragon, but that it was ambivalent only in appearance. Genoa lost nothing by apologizing to James, and she had succeeded in removing his most dangerous agent, Entença, from the Levant. But it is also possible that the changing attitude of the Genoese of Pera was affecting official Genoese policy.

92. Rubió y Lluch, *Diplomatari*, nos. 18, 19.

93. Finke, *Acta Aragonensia*, II, 685; this is an account of the exploits of the Catalans up to 1305; probably a Sicilian source. Rubió y Lluch, *Diplomatari*, no. 18; cf. Manfroni, "Relazioni," p. 692.

94. Finke, *Acta Aragonensia*, II, 686; Rubió y Lluch, *Diplomatari*, no. 17 (September, 1305).

95. Rubió y Lluch, *Diplomatari* no. 19. James' answer to the proposals of the Genoese ambassadors (October 21, 1305).

96. Ibid., no. 19 (October 31, 1305).

97. Ibid., nos. 17 (September, 1305), 11, 19.

As we have seen, the Genoese merchants of Pera were willing to find a modus vivendi with the Catalans, and although officially they opposed the company, they cooperated sufficiently to be safe from Catalan attacks. This, perhaps, was the reason why Muntaner accused the commune of perfidy when D'Oria captured Entença.[98]

The Genoese did not follow the capture of Entença with any large-scale operation against the Catalans. On May 31, 1305, Andronicus II asked the Genoese fleet to stay and fight against those Catalans who still remained in Gallipoli. D'Oria agreed in principle, but demanded 6,000 hyperpyra as payment. Andronicus did not have this amount in cash, so he sent the Genoese the equivalent in unminted bullion. The Genoese weighed it, found it inadequate, returned it, and decided to leave. The short weight was clearly only an excuse. Pachymeres claims that they were persuaded by their compatriots in Pera not to help the emperor further. In any case, their trading interests called them to Trebizond; they sailed there, after having dispatched one ship to carry the news of Entença's capture to Genoa[99]

After Michael IX's defeat at the hands of the Catalans at the battle of Apros (July 10, 1305), Andronicus became desperate for help. Thirteen Genoese ships returned from Trebizond, and once more he offered them an alliance. They were not overwhelmingly eager to help. Two ships, the best ones, left for Genoa, while the others prepared to sail to places where their commercial interests took them.[100] Finally, two ships agreed to stay for two months, hoping to find an opportunity to attack "the common enemy of the emperor and of their illustrous commune." For this they were paid 6,000 hyperpyra. The other nine ships decided to stay gratis for a few days and then left.[101] Although the instructions they had from the government in Genoa are not known, their actions appear to mirror the policy reflected in the Genoese

98. Pachymeres, II, 534; Muntaner, chap. ccxviii.

99. Ibid., II, 541, 542, 544–545.

100. Ibid., II, 554, says that the first two ships left with Entença. But, on p. 578, he claims that Entença stayed in Pera, and only left after the two months of the Genoese service had elapsed. This agrees better with Muntaner's statement that Entença stayed in Pera for four months after his capture (chapter ccxviii). For the date of the battle of Apros, see Dade, *Versuche*, pp. 103–104.

101. Pachymeres, II, 554. The pirate Andrea Morisco, with his two ships, made some effort to help Byzantium. He caught and massacred some Turks who had been with the Catalan army, had quarreled with them, and now were returning to Asia Minor. For this doubtful success, which caused the Turks to stay on and contribute to the destruction of Thrace, he was made an admiral, and he and his brother Ludovico were given the islands of Rhodes, Kasos and Karpathos: Dölger, *Regesten*, no. 2287, summer 1305; Muntaner, chap. ccxxvii; Hopf, *Griechische Geschichte*, p. 393; Hopf, *Chroniques Grécoromanes*, p. 491. Andrea Morisco remained admiral until at least 1319–1320. The Venetians were very upset at the cession of these islands, which in fact extended the Genoese sphere of influence into the Dodecannese. Ludovico Morisco "attacked" Karpathos, presumably in order to take possession of it. The Venetians then considered him a pirate, captured him and imprisoned him (1309?, Thomas, *Diplomatarium*, I, 130). Andronicus said that Ludovico was his vassal, one of his barons and the brother of his admiral, and asked Venice to hand him over to the Byzantines (Thomas, *Diplomatarium*, I, 143, no. 77, 1319; cf. Dölger, *Regesten*, no. 2427). The isolated activities of the Morisco brothers should not be seen as part of a Genoese policy of cooperation with Byzantium. In any case, their motives were not free of thoughts of personal gain, and they were accused by the Byzantines of being more interested in piracy than in the welfare of the empire (Pachymeres, II, 584–585).

letters to James II. Genoa wanted to foil the attempts of the Catalans to conquer the Byzantine empire and disrupt Genoese commerce, yet she was not ready to provoke a complete break with the Catalans, Sicily, and Aragon.

Andronicus also found himself in a dilemma in 1305, for he was unable to decide between different policies for dealing with the Genoese and the Catalans. At times he hoped to depend on his own soldiers, led by his son Michael, to oppose the Catalans and their Turkish allies. He tried to obtain the help of the Genoese. But he was apparently disingenuous in the matter of pay; he also allowed the patriarch to precipitate a quarrel over the friars of Constantinople, and almost broke off relations with the Genoese of Pera. The Byzantine people were willing to defend the empire, but had not found the means or the leadership which would enable them to do so.[102] Although anti-Latin feeling was very strong, Andronicus was not able to harness it effectively, and use it against the Catalans or to encourage the Genoese to adopt a more positive policy. His son, Michael IX, tried to do just that. Instead of depending on foreigners, he tried to use native men and resources to oppose the Catalans.

102. Pachymeres, II, 546.

VI

The Catalan Attack and the Byzantine Defense, 1305–1309

If the assassination of Roger de Flor marked a turning point in the relations between the Byzantines and their Catalan mercenaries, the capture of Berengar d'Entença served to tighten the discipline of the Catalan Company and forced them to define their aims. Realizing that they were confronting two enemies, Byzantium and Genoa, the Catalans behaved like strong but cornered animals. The conquest of Thrace became their aim, and the possibility of attacking Constantinople was never far from their minds. Secure in their fort of Gallipoli, they launched constant raids in Thrace. To counter them, the Byzantines followed two different but complementary policies. Andronicus II persevered in his effort to form a Genoese alliance, while his son and co-emperor, Michael IX, tried to oppose force by force: his policy was to exploit the internal resources of Thrace, and to reorganize his army to fight the Catalans. Although it is difficult to apply labels to policies which were, in the end, not pursued with spectacular ability, for purposes of differentiation it can be said that Andronicus II depended on diplomacy while Michael IX depended on the military action of a native army augmented by Alans and Vlachs.[1] Although Michael IX's policy does not fall within diplomatic history narrowly defined, it must be discussed here because it offered an alternative to diplomacy. Moreover, in terms of the history of the Byzantine state, Michael IX's policy presented a very interesting experiment, which has not been studied by modern historians.

Toward a Byzantine Defense

When Michael IX was crowned co-emperor, on May 21, 1295, he was presented with a panegyric which both voiced the desires of a large number of Byzantines and, to some extent, predicted the young emperor's future policy.[2] The writer realized that the restoration of the empire was still unfinished. Michael VIII's successors must reestablish their authority over the rest of the empire and over the islands, and clear the sea of pirates. For this, a navy was absolutely necessary. He told Michael IX that some ships and money were already available in the empire and that Michael commanded the loyalty of the Byzantines. The young co-emperor should make use of these advantages. He should collect a large army, recruiting even shepherds and peasants.[3] In other words, the writer urged Michael IX to embark on an aggresive policy, making full use of the available native resources.

---

1. This is another way of saying that Andronicus II retained control of foreign affairs, while his co-emperor was limited to domestic affairs.
2. P. Lamma, "Un discorso inedito," pp. 49–69.
3. Ibid., 61–62, 67.

Michael IX did follow just such a policy after the arrival of the Catalan army in Byzantium. Like Alexios Philanthropenos and John Tarchaneiotes a few years earlier, the co-emperor tried to exploit the fighting power and will of the Byzantines. Michael IX was haunted by the failure of his Anatolian campaign, which had not only cost him the loss of his lands in Asia Minor, but had also made it necessary for Andronicus II to accept the help of the Catalans. But this was not the sole reason for the co-emperor's turn to a new policy. He was a soldier, and he had lived constantly among soldiers after 1302; indeed, he was considered one of the most accomplished knights in the world, although this claim had more than its fair share of exaggeration.[4] He now chose a soldier's way to fight the Catalans. His policy presupposed the concentration of forces in Thrace, and the temporary abandonment of Asia Minor. His way, had it been more ably pursued, might have proved the salvation of the empire; in any case, it commanded the support of the people more than Andronicus' actions did.

Was Michael IX's policy realistic, in view of the impoverished condition of the Byzantine state? One is tempted to answer that the state of the imperial treasury would have precluded any large-scale reorganization of the armed forces. But this is not the right way to look at Michael's efforts. What he tried to do, what his panegyrist had advised, was to use the resources of the empire, not those of the emperor. He tried to galvanise people, to make them fight for their lands, perhaps even for their country, and this did not necessitate the expenditure of vast sums of money. He counted on the cooperation of the peasants and the urban dwellers; and their strong antiwestern feelings, their realization of the need for self-defense, made up in part for the disadvantages of an impoverished state. As for his soldiers, they had incentives other than money, at least at first.

Michael IX's army consisted mostly of soldiers from Anatolia who had lost their land-holdings and had been transferred to Thrace.[5] They were eager to fight the Catalans, whom they considered partly responsible for the destruction of their homeland, and at times they were joined by volunteers from Thrace and Macedonia who had similar feelings.[6] The army fought pitched battles, and tried to contain the southward pressure of the Bulgarians. But after 1305, the day-by-day defense of Thrace came to depend almost entirely on the local inhabitants. Sometimes they joined Michael's army; at other times they fought on their own, perhaps with the help of Michael's officers. In all cases, they were moved by their fear and contempt of the westerners, and by the wish to save their homes. The numerous examples of greedy or cowardly Byzantines who benefited from the Catalan campaign should not blind us to the great battle for life that went on in Thrace and later in Macedonia. The townsmen and even the peasants of the empire, although they rarely joined an organized army, proved a great force for the preservation of the state.

The oscillation of Byzantine policy between negotiations and armed defense,

4. Muntaner, chap. cciii.
5. Pachymeres, II, 446.
6. Ibid., II, 482–483.

between reliance on western allies and on a Byzantine army, was not a sign of conflict between Andronicus II and Michael IX. It was an uncertain, often shifting, double effort to assert the identity of the Byzantine empire against its various enemies and to preserve, even to create anew, a self-sufficient state out of the shambles of Michael VIII's empire. Perhaps the real tragedy of these years was that neither Andronicus II nor Michael IX had a clear enough notion of the state they *could* create, and thus could not make use of the vital forces released during the Catalan troubles.

Michael IX's hostility towards the Catalans was manifest from the beginning. After the failure of his Anatolian campaign, Michael spent some time at Pegai, in northern Asia Minor, recovering from a long illness. While he was at Pegai, he refused to give audience to Roger de Flor, because he found objectionable the behaviour of the Catalans at Cyzicus, where they were spending the winter of 1303–1304.[7] On January 23, 1304, Michael arrived at Constantinople, as the most important refugee from Anatolia. Before him, many other Greeks from Asia Minor "had been dispersed in the West"; many were soldiers, who roamed about Thrace looking for work and food.[8]

As soon as he came west, Michael IX reorganized his army and once again embarked upon military action. His first efforts were directed against the Bulgarians who, under their king, Theodore Svetoslav, had taken advantage of the weakness of the empire to attack its defenses near Mount Haemus. Some of the forts in that area had surrendered, others had been taken by force. Andronicus, having, as he thought, provided for Asia Minor by sending the Catalans there, decided to oppose the Bulgarians strenuously. He sent soldiers to the threatened areas, and started negotiations with the Bulgarian Eltimir who ruled at Crounai. Andronicus pleaded with him not to attack the empire, and promised him pronoiai in Byzantium. At first Eltimir did not respond to this offer, and in the summer of 1304 he cooperated with Svetoslav, who repaid Eltimir with the Byzantine forts of Yamboli and Lardaia. Together, Eltimir and Svetoslav took Ktenia, Rosokastron, and other forts in the Haemus, and then bore down toward the towns of Sozopolis, Mesembreia, and Anchialos (summer, 1304).[9]

Andronicus sent an army led by Michael IX and the protostrator Michael Tarchaneiotes Glabas to oppose the invasion.[10] Apparently, Glabas had some success and, according to the poet Philes, he retook Rosokastron and Mesembreia, rebuilt Anchialos, and forced the Bulgarians to abandon Mt. Haemus. The reports of his exploits, coming from a panegyric, are probably exaggerated;

7. Ibid., II, 405–406.
8. Ibid., II, 395.
9. Ibid., II, 401–410; Geronimo Zurita, *Los Anales de la Corona de Aragon*, (Barcelona, 1852), VI, 3; Dölger, *Regesten*, no. 2264.
10. Pachymeres, II, 444–447; Miller, *Philes Carmina*, II, no. 237, pp. 246–253; Martin, *Philes Carmenia inedita*, no. 63. Cf. P. Petrov, "Les relations bulgaro-byzantines au cours de la seconde moitié du XIIIe siècle, reflétées dans le poème de Manuel Philès 'Les exploits du célèbre protostrator'" (in Bulgarian, with French summary), *Izvestija na Instituta za Bulgarska Istorija*, 6 (Sofia, 1956), 545–576. On the title and office of protostrator, see R. Guilland, "Études de titulature. Le protostrator."

in any case, the valiant general was taken ill and had to return to Constantinople, leaving Michael IX to fight alone. The co-emperor then proceeded to reorganize his army in a way which indicates that he took the Bulgarian campaign very seriously indeed. He assembled a large army of soldiers from Anatolia and Adrianople, and in order to pay them enough money to live on, he melted down the family gold and silver plate

Like his father, Michael IX was not a greedy man, and like his father he was quite willing to sacrifice his personal wealth in order to serve the state. In this case, Michael IX hoped to achieve several aims. By raising the effective strength of his army, he hoped to defend Thrace and its inhabitants from the Bulgarians—and he recruited soldiers from Thrace, hoping that they would recognize their stake in this enterprise. But he also meant to provide employment for his Anatolian soldiers, and to protect his new pronoiai in Thrace. At the end of August 1304, Michael and his new army launched a large and successful campaign against the Bulgarians, and returned safely to their camp at Adrianople.[11]

Michael's Bulgarian campaign had provided Andronicus with an excuse for recalling the Catalans to Thrace.[12] But Michael's army reacted violently when they heard that the Catalans might soon join them. They were in no mood to accept as allies the men who had ravaged Asia Minor, and when they heard that the Catalans had committed new atrocities near Madytus and Lampsacus, a near-rebellion broke out. They would never cooperate with the Catalans, the soldiers declared; indeed, they threatened to leave Michael and go to Asia Minor to defend their country and their relatives against the mercenaries. In September 1304, Michael wrote to his father, advising him of the temper of the army, and asking that no Catalans be sent to the Bulgarian front. Furthermore, he promised his Anatolian soldiers that after a certain period he would release them to return to Anatolia. Andronicus II, still hoping that Roger de Flor would behave properly, suggested a compromise: one thousand Catalans would join Michael IX's army, while the rest would go to Asia Minor, "for he had not originally requested such a large number of men, nor was the empire capable of feeding them all." Perhaps it is lucky that the arrival of Berengar d'Entença put a stop to this plan, since Michael IX had warned his father that if any Catalans appeared in his camp, the soldiers would rebel and the empire would have to deal with a civil war on top of all its other problems.[13]

In these circumstances, it is not surprising that Roger de Flor should have been assassinated when he visited Michael's camp at Adrianople: everyone, including Roger, had been forewarned. Immediately after the assassination, Michael IX prepared for certain war with the Catalans. One of his first actions was to sign a truce with Theodore Svetoslav, thus freeing his army for action on a different front. At the same time, the temper of his soldiers was rising. The

11. Pachymeres, II, 446–448; Lamma, in "Discorso," pp. 55–56, erroneously dates this expedition 1305.

12. Pachymeres, II, 480–481; Muntaner, chaps. ccviii, ccix.

13. Pachymeres, II, 481–482.

Thracian soldiers now became incensed as the Catalans raided fields and burned houses in Thrace.[14] Between April and July 1305, there were small skirmishes between the Catalans and the Byzantines. While Andronicus II was cooperating with the Genoese in the moves that culminated with the capture of Berengar d'Entença, Michael IX sent three of his lieutenants along with part of his army to attack the Catalans at Gallipoli. But the Catalans ambushed the Byzantine forces, and this first attack failed. The Catalans' victory enabled them to send messages to Asia Minor and to recruit a number of Turks, who joined them at Gallipoli.[15]

In June and July 1305, Michael tried to launch a decisive attack against the Catalans. He assembled as many men as he could, both professional soldiers and volunteers. He collected the Thracian forces, the Macedonian army, and the army of the East, under the command of his uncle, Theodore. He included Alan and Turkish mercenaries, and Vlach and Greek volunteers. Muntaner gives the number of the combined army as 100,000 foot and 17,000 cavalry, but these figures should not be taken seriously. Michael's first objective was Gallipoli, where the Catalans had their headquarters; he hoped to besiege and take the fort. But the Catalans managed to avoid the siege of Gallipoli by meeting the imperial army on the plain of Apros. There a great battle took place on July 10, 1305. The Turkish "allies" of the Byzantines defected, and the Catalan cavalry wrought disaster on Michael's army. The young emperor fought bravely and well; telling his men that now death was better than life, and living a more bitter fate than dying, he rode into the midst of his enemies. At least one of his generals, Chandrenos, fought equally bravely. But the emperor was wounded and his army was routed. While he fled to Didymoteichon, the Catalans pursued his retreating army and spent the following day ravaging Thrace. The Alans, whose cowardice during the battle had been a primary factor in the Byzantine defeat, also plundered the environs of Apros.[16]

Everyone, from contemporary witnesses to modern historians, has recognized the importance of the battle of Apros. Michael's army was destroyed. Muntaner tells us that the Byzantines lost 2,000 cavalry, and countless infantry. The Byzantine defeat was due not to lack of courage on the part of the Greek contingent, but rather to the collapse of the front lines, which consisted of the Turkish and Alan mercenaries. Also, it seems that the Byzantines had failed to learn from the Catalan manner of fighting and to change their tactics accordingly, which they should have done after their defeat at Gallipoli. But now they learned how difficult it was to defeat the Catalans, and no further pitched battle was fought in Thrace. As for the Catalans, they realized that the field was now theirs: "And from that hour all Romania was conquered and

---

14. Gregoras, I, 228. Pachymeres, II, 528–529, 543; Muntaner, chap. ccx, claims that the truce with Svetoslav was concluded immediately upon Roger de Flor's return to Constantinople, in the autumn of 1304. Cf. Dölger, *Regesten*, no. 2621.

15. Pachymeres, II, 543–545, 591; Muntaner, chaps. ccxv, ccxxix; Gregoras, I, 228–229; Dade, *Versuche*, p. 106.

16. Pachymeres, II, 549–551; Gregoras, I, 229–233; Muntaner, chaps. ccxv, ccxx–ccxxi; Boissonade, *Anecdota Graeca*, II, 195. Dade, *Versuche*, pp. 103–104, establishes the date July 10 for the battle of Apros.

we had so put fear into their hearts, that we could not shout 'Franks' but they were at once prepared to flee. . . . And every day we made raids and raided as far as the gates of Constantinople." The conquest of Thrace was within reach, and it was undertaken almost immediately.[17]

The Greek inhabitants of the countryside also recognized the importance of the battle of Apros. Although it was harvest time, they left their fields and crowded to the gates of Constantinople, seeking safety. In order to enable them to return to their villages, Andronicus II created a kind of gendarmerie under whose protection the peasants went on with the harvest: "He wanted to form an indigenous army and attack, but had to delay because he was distracted by many [other] necessities. So, he prepared some forces to be sent to the fields and the peasants, taking courage from this, did their summer work fearlessly."[18] He also made a truce with the Catalans, and tried to conclude an alliance with the Genoese ships involved in the capture of Berengar d'Entença.[19] This failed, as did his effort to lure the Alans back into his service.[20]

Michael IX was very discouraged by his defeat at the battle of Apros. Both Byzantine and Catalan sources agree that he was a proud soldier, and the results of the battle must have cut him very deeply. Nor did Andronicus help by reproaching his son for endangering his life at the battle. While Michael stayed at Didymoteichon, nursing his emotional and physical wounds, his army disintegrated. The soldiers, whom he had gathered with so much effort and at so much personal expense, dispersed, partly because there was no money to pay them, and partly perhaps because they too were discouraged.[21]

In the meantime, the Bulgarians had repudiated their truce with Michael. Theodore Svetoslav had already tried to negotiate a marriage alliance with Andronicus, asking for the hand of Theodora, the nine-year-old daughter of Michael IX. Andronicus refused, and Svetoslav invaded Thrace, seeking revenge not only against Andronicus but also against Eltimir who had once again changed sides and joined the Byzantines after the battle of Apros.[22]

The Catalans too overran all of Thrace east of the Marica River and west of Constantinople. They met with little opposition, for the inhabitants had deserted the countryside, probably seeking safety in the fortified towns; the the story of Asia Minor was being repeated in Thrace. Andronicus II tried to negotiate a settlement with the Catalans, so that they would leave his empire; they answered with extravagant demands for money. They also demanded the release of all Catalan prisoners, payment for any horses they might leave behind, and the return of the Catalan ships captured by the Genoese. Quite apart from the fact that the Catalan demands were very steep, there was also a disagreement

17. Pachymeres, II, 552; Gregoras, I, 232, 244ff; Muntaner, chaps. ccxxi–ccxxiii.
18. Pachymeres, II, 552–553.
19. Ibid., II, 554. Cf. above, Chapter V, "Byzantium, the Genoese, and the Catalans," and Dade, *Versuche*, pp. 103–106.
20. Pachymeres, II, 574–575. Cf. Pachymeres, II, 601ff, Muntaner, chap. ccxxvi.
21. Pachymeres, II, 562, 576.
22. Ibid., II, 559–562. Cf. below, Chapter VI, "The Defense of Thrace." Svetoslav's marriage proposal was probably made in 1305 after Roger de Flor's murder and before the battle of Apros, when the position of the Byzantines seemed relatively hopeful.

in principle. Each side insisted that the other had broken the original agreements, and should make amends. But Andronicus had prefaced his request for peace by the argument that the Catalans had first broken their agreement with the Byzantines. Because of these disagreements, no peace was concluded, and the Catalans remained in Thrace.[23]

Thus, Michael IX's original attempt to defeat the Catalans through military action ended in unqualified failure. If anything, it probably made the situation worse, since his defeat made the Catalans think that they were invincible, and persuaded the Byzantines too that they could not win a pitched battle against these mercenaries. The defeat at Apros also give the Bulgarians an opportunity to reopen hostilities, but it did not spell the end of Michael IX's policy. On the contrary, it was only after July 1305, that the struggle began for the defense of the cities, if not of the countryside, of Thrace against the Catalans, and in the struggle Michael IX and the urban populations of Thrace emerged as valiant heroes.

Andronicus II had been persuaded to contribute to the policy of indigenous defense against the Catalans. The people of Constantinople, furious at the Catalan success, and no doubt fearful as well, violently denounced Andronicus' demolition of the fleet. Sometime in May 1305, the mob of Constantinople arose in a near-riot, "because it was not possible for them to live in security unless ships were armed according to the old customs of the Romans." Despite the efforts of the patriarch, Athanasios I, to appease the mob, feelings ran high, and soon the unrest turned into an anti-Latin riot. The people were convinced that because of the destruction of the Byzantine fleet the evil Italians held the empire captive. It was very easy to translate into action the deep hatred of the Byzantines against the Latins: the rioters attacked and burned the houses of some Genoese where Catalans were hiding, and killed the Catalans.[24] It is not clear from Pachymeres' account whether the people of Constantinople were motivated by sheer emotion or by a reasoned belief that a fleet was essential to the safety of the city. Probably, both factors were present. Anti-Latin emotion was always there, whether dormant or active, and now more than ever before the decision to dismantle the fleet was seen to have been disastrous. The remnants of the empire were very much exposed to maritime attack, and most of its enemies were relatively strong at sea. Even in Asia Minor, which traditionally had been defended by wars on land, the Turks were becoming a maritime power.

Whether the people of Constantinople realized it or not, in May 1305, the creation of a new Byzantine fleet was not only necessary, it was also feasible. All that was required was a policy centered on the defense of Constantinople and aimed at throwing the Catalans out. With the Bulgarians still at peace, the northern frontiers could be defended with a minimal force. Macedonia could be cut off temporarily, and men and resources could be diverted to man a fleet to protect Thrace and the adjacent islands. Even a small imperial fleet might sever or at least impede Catalan communications with Sicily, and in these

23. Pachymeres, II, 562–572. For the Catalan demands, see ibid., II, 572.
24. Ibid., II, 531–533. According to Pachymeres, this took place between the time of the murder of Roger de Flor (April 30, 1305) and the capture of Entença (May 31, 1305).

circumstances the Catalans would probably prove more amenable to negotiations.

Later in May 1305, the people of Constantinople once again demanded that a fleet be built. Andronicus, fearing the activities of the enraged mob, brought an army into Constantinople to forestall a possible rebellion. On June 1, he addressed a speech to "the first men" of Constantinople, in which he tried to justify his acceptance of the Catalan offer to fight for him. He said that it had been necessary to depend on Latin mercenaries since the Byzantine army was so weak, and in order to prove that he had not innovated in this respect, he adduced the examples of John III Vatatzes and Michael VIII, both of whom had used Latin mercenaries. As for the decline of the empire, which had been at the root of the whole problem, he ascribed that to the sins of those in power, and to divine anger. Then, he asked these men to quell all rebellious sentiment and to tell the people to attend each to his business; rebellion in the city would be the worst possible evil. Finally, he made them swear on the Bible to remain loyal to the two emperors, to abstain from all revolutionary activity and to persuade all others to do the same. Andronicus sent his officials throughout the city to administer the oath of loyalty to the inhabitants. This rather surprising action indicated the explosive nature of the situation.[25]

Andronicus, however, did not stop at this negative action. The temper of his people, combined with the untrustworthy behaviour of the Genoese in the summer of 1305, convinced him that it was, indeed, necessary to rebuild the fleet he had demolished. He decided to finance the new fleet by using some of the money he had collected to pay the Genoese. According to Pachymeres, "the emperor . . . gave the salary [intended for the Genoese] to his own men, and prepared ships, trying to correct his defeat."[26] There is ample evidence elsewhere that an imperial fleet was being built at the end of 1305 or the beginning of 1306. In the spring of 1306, Berengar de Rocafort went on an expedition to the Black Sea coast, to the town of "Lestanayre" (Neorion), "where all the ships and terides and galleys of the Romania are made"; one hundred and fifty ships are said to have been destroyed on this expedition.[27] The timing of Rocafort's attack, which just preceded the arrival of a second Genoese fleet at Constantinople, makes it clear that this was no minor skirmish but rather a conscious effort to prevent the creation of a Byzantine fleet. In spite of the success of Rocafort's expedition, it seems that some ships were built. Thus, we are told that approximately two years after Irene's arrival in Thessalonica (thus, in 1305 or 1306), Andronicus' ships were patroling the Dardanelles to keep the Turks from crossing into Thrace and joining the Catalans.[28] About

25. Pachymeres, II, 546–549.

26. Ibid., II, 545.

27. Muntaner, chap. ccxxv; A. Rubió y Lluch, *La companyía Catalana sota el Comandament de Teobald de Çepoy, 1307–1310*, Institut d'Estudis Catalans (Barcelona, 1923), p. 20; A. Rubió y Lluch, "Notícia geografica de l'Orient segons En Muntaner," *Butlletí del Centre Excursionista de Catalunya*, 1 (Barcelona, 1891), 227.

28. Pachymeres, II, 557. On the date, see Ševčenko, *Métochite et Choumnos*, Appendix 3 and pp. 6, 275–277: John married Irene Choumnos in 1303 or early 1304, and the Empress Irene left for Thessalonica soon after the marriage.

1307 the Byzantine general Maroules was given ten ships, "belonging to the emperor," in order to harass Ticino Zaccaria in Thasos. In 1309 a body of Turkish mercenaries under Chalil left the Catalans and hoped that by pledging faith to Andronicus they would be allowed to leave for Asia Minor on imperial ships. However, when a few of these Turks were allowed to cross, they did so on ten Genoese ships with the consent of Andronicus (1312–1313).[29] Perhaps the new Byzantine navy did not last much longer than Michael's army had done.

The Defense of Thrace

With the imperial army disorganized and Michael IX ill at Didymoteichon, the Catalans were free to attack Thrace. The countryside was easy to take, but in terms of the aims and the military techniques of the Catalan company this meant very little. They had no desire and no possibility of holding the countryside. Their army was too small to occupy every part of the country, and if they dispersed they might be easily vanquished. The strength of the Catalan company lay in its ability to launch concerted attacks, in which the mounted knights were supported by the formidable lightly armed infantry, the Almugavars. Thus, although the Catalans were masters of the Thracian countryside, in the sense that they were able to attack any part of it without much opposition and without reprisals, they could do this only because they had a fortified area, Gallipoli, to which they could retreat for safety.

Michael IX realized the double aspect of the Catalan position: Gallipoli was indispensable to them as a fort, but the Thracian countryside was necessary for their survival, since their food came from their raids outside Gallipoli. In the summer of 1305 Michael conceived a new plan, and communicated it to his father. Michael suggested that Andronicus II collect a new army and come to Rodosto. Pachymeres says that Andronicus was to come "west, to Rodosto and further." The choice of words as well as the choice of city permits a reconstruction of Michael's plan. Rodosto was the great granary of Thrace, where grain was collected and stored in warehouses, to be then shipped to Constantinople and elsewhere.[30] By making his camp at Rodosto, Andronicus would secure this city and repulse the attack which the Catalans were already launching against it. Byzantine occupation of Rodosto would presumably secure eastern Thrace from Catalan raids. If that side were secured, and Michael was able to recover some strength at Didymoteichon, then the Byzantines could hope to enclose the Catalans in Gallipoli, where they could not survive for long.

This plan seems feasible, despite the disruption which affected Michael IX's army after the battle of Apros. Even in July 1306, Michael had with him some soldiers from the western army.[31] Perhaps more such men could have been

29. Pachymeres, II, 638; Gregoras, I, 254; Muntaner, chap. ccxli; below, Chapter VII, "Diplomacy in the Balkans."

30. Pegolotti, *Pratica*, p. 42; Muntaner, chap. ccxxii; Rubió y Lluch, *Diplomatari*, no. 31; Heyd, *Commerce*, I, 177; II, 243.

31. Pachymeres, II, 608; Dölger, *Regesten*, no. 2623.

collected at Didymoteichon, if a concerted effort were made. But the Constantinople part of the operation never began. The imperial treasury was empty and could not sustain the expense of equipping the army Michael wanted. Andronicus II tried to raise funds by public subscription, but although many people contributed, the money he collected was not sufficient, and the plan had to be abandoned.[32] Perhaps the richer inhabitants of Constantinople found it unnecessary to give money for this enterprise.

The Catalans too realized the importance of conquering the cities of Thrace, for only thus could the countryside be securely held. Every fortified city they held would become a small Gallipoli, where they could retreat after their forays, and from where they could defend themselves against Byzantine attack. But for the same reason that it was easy to hold a city, it was difficult to conquer it. And the inhabitants of the cities of Thrace displayed quite magnificent and unexpected tenacity in defending themselves against the Catalans. Their courage can only be explained in terms of a protonationalism: they hated all westerners, and therefore also the Catalans, so much that they were willing to die in defense of their city. Through the dry, archaic style of Pachymeres can be followed the heroic defense of the towns of Thrace. This was heroism on a small level, but heroism it was.

For obvious reasons, one of the first cities to suffer the attack of the Catalans was Rodosto. In the summer of 1305, while Ferran Ximenes de Arenos with part of the Catalan army raided Thrace up to the walls of Constantinople, Berengar de Rocafort attacked Rodosto. The city itself fell easily, but the fort resisted. The Catalans tried to besiege it and failed; they tried to take it by negotiation, and also failed. Contemporary testimony differs as to what happened after that.[33] Most probably, Rocafort occupied the suburbs, while the fortified part of the town continued its resistance for one whole year. It seems that Rodosto was defended mainly by its own population. That is why, in the summer of 1306, Andronicus sent two ships to relieve the city of those incapable of fighting, so that the rest could wage war more efficiently.[34] This incident also helps to answer the question of provisioning for goods other than grain: if Rocafort had surrounded the city by land, the sea was still relatively clear. Andronicus may have sent provisions to Rodosto, but he cannot have sent many soldiers, since only three hundred men defended the fort. Later in the summer of 1306, the fort could be held no longer. Rocafort was pledged to take it, and his attacks became increasingly persistent. After a year's resistance, the inhabitants of Rodosto decided to surrender. Rocafort at first tried to reject their offer, which would entail lenient treatment of the captives. In the end, however, he allowed them to surrender, and to either live under him or leave the city, as they willed. Rocafort made Rodosto his granary, and there he collected wheat and other provisions from the surrounding area. It seems

---

32. Pachymeres, II, 576; cf. Dölger, *Regesten*, no. 2622 (summer 1305).
33. Pachymeres, II, 586; Muntaner, chaps. ccxii, ccxiii. Muntaner claims that Rocafort made Rodosto his headquarters, while Pachymeres said that he abandoned it. The document published in Rubió y Lluch, *Diplomatari*, no. 31, supports Pachymeres' testimony (that Roger abandoned the city), for it speaks of the conquest of Rodosto in 1306.
34. Pachymeres, II, 613–614.

that his army was getting ready for a long war in Thrace, for at the same time his Turkish allies occupied the area around Ganos to the south of Rodosto, and cultivated it.[35]

Adrianople was one of the most important cities of Thrace, second only to Constantinople. Situated at the confluence of three rivers, the Hebrus (Marica), the Arda, and the Tonzus, commanding communications with Bulgaria, it had always played a major role in the defense of Thrace and of Constantinople itself. It was also an important trading center. Its population was large and varied, and the city usually held a large garrison. Its geographical position made it, throughout Byzantine history, the center of many key events. John Tzimiskes started his Bulgarian expedition from Adrianople, Nicephorus Bryennios was proclaimed emperor there in 1077, and Frederick Barbarossa conquered it on his way to Jerusalem. Since Michael IX had been particularly interested in the Bulgarian war, he too had made Adrianople his headquarters during the campaign of 1304. It is therefore surprising to find it suffering from the same lack of organized defense as the rest of Thrace.

In the late spring of 1306, the Catalans and their Turkish allies attacked Adrianople, on their return from an attack on the Alans who were then in Bulgarian territory.[36] Since the city did not have an adequate garrison, the Catalans were able to cut down the vines and burn the wheat in the fields outside the city. Then they occupied the suburbs and proceeded to lay siege to Adrianople itself. Adrianople was well fortified and its inhabitants were willing to defend themselves. They set fire to the suburbs and retreated into the fortified town. Two of Michael's lieutenants came in to help with 150 soldiers from Anatolia. The city held for eight days, and on the last day the Catalans brought ladders and began to climb onto the wall. They tried, it seems, to set fire to a section of the wall, but the wind changed, and the fire burned their ladders. The Byzantine soldiers took the opportunity to kill many of the Catalans and the siege was abandoned. Adrianople was saved by a combination of luck and courage.

On this occasion, the small Byzantine army contributed to the defense mounted by the inhabitants of the city. Although it is a sad comment that only 150 soldiers could be mustered for the defense of such an important place, there was a lesson in this for the Byzantines. The Catalans could not afford drawn-out sieges. They had neither the time, nor the machines, nor yet the intention to starve the cities of Thrace into submission, as the Turks were doing in Asia Minor.[37] A determined effort, and a little help from the imperial government would have saved many a Thracian city. Even though there was no money to maintain a real army, small mobile forces like the 150 men who went to Adrianople were not beyond the capabilities of the imperial treasury. Yet

---

35. Ibid., II, 621–623; Rubió y Lluch, *Diplomatari*, no. 31.

36. Pachymeres, II, 602–604; Miller, *Philes Carmina*, II, no. 216 = Martin, *Philes Carmina inedita*, no. 44, verses 51–56 (this is very similar to Pachymeres' account). Cf. Miller, *Philes Carmina*, II, nos. 226, 288; Muntaner, chap. ccxxvi. Pachymeres, II, 603, says that the Catalans burned young wheat outside Adrianople; therefore, the attack took place in the late spring.

37. Georgiades-Arnakes, Οἱ πρῶτοι Ὀθωμανοί, pp. 85–86.

many cities were forced to surrender because they despaired of help. Philes attributed the salvation of Adrianople to a miracle of the Virgin.[38]

It is clear from the conquest of Rodosto and the siege of Adrianople that in 1305 and 1306 the war in Thrace developed into a series of small attacks and counterattacks. It is also clear that the imperial army contributed very little to the defense of the Thracian cities. In the autumn of 1306 there were curious incidents of guerrilla-type harassment of the Catalan army. At that time, Rocafort was pressing the Byzantines hard and brought his army near Constantinople. While he was thus engaged, the minute Byzantine army attacked his rear-guard, in an effort to create a diversion. At the same time, the inhabitants of the town of Tzurulon (Chorlù) made a raiding expedition against Rocafort's army, collected some booty, and returned to their city.[39] All of this took place in an area less than fifty miles outside Constantinople. The action of the men of Tzurulon is particularly worthy of notice. It was one thing for the inhabitants of the fortified cities to stay inside their walls and defend their homes. Attacking the Catalan army *outside* the cities, in the countryside, was a more difficult and more courageous action.

The defense of the other cities followed patterns similar to that of Adrianople and Rodosto. In the case of Vizyë, the heroism of the inhabitants was even greater. Ferran Ximenes de Arenos and his army attacked this city in the spring of 1307.[40] Vizyë had a guard of two hundred soldiers under the command of Umbertopulos. They thought that since the Catalans were much more numerous, the best thing to do was to shut themselves up in the fort, and defend that. "But then, the mob of Vizyë was seized by martial spirit, and, making frequent representations to the leader [Umbertopulos] they said that if he attacked the foe they would fight with him. And he, seduced (καταγοητευθείς) by their courage and their great numbers (for they increased by thousands the strength of the infantry), made a sortie with them and with all the cavalry." Unfortunately, the city people were unused to fighting; they lost heart and fled in an unruly retreat, and the Catalans "falling in great numbers against the infantry, killed many of them, like sheep." Those inside the city watched the massacre and feared for their fate. The women were then disguised as men, took up arms, and stationed themselves on the walls of the city, to keep the Catalans away. Andronicus, moved by these sad events, sent some reinforcements, while the patriarch held a litany to beseech God to forgive the sins of his people and deliver them from the Catalans.

---

38. Martin, *Philes Carmina inedita*, no. 44, verses 45ff. There are a few exceptions to the statement that the Catalans were not interested in lengthy sieges. Ferran Ximenes de Arenos besieged Madytos for a long time. It was a well-fortified city, and Andrea Morisco was able to provide its inhabitants with food. Ximenes tried to starve them into submission and succeeded in the end. (Pachymeres, II, 583–584, 578; Muntaner, chap. ccxxiii). He adopted the same technique in the city of Aenos, which was defended by its inhabitants (summer 1307? Pachymeres, II, 639–640). His policy may be explained by the fact that these operations were undertaken quite late in the campaign, when food supplies in Thrace were so low that starving a city would seem an easy enterprise.

39. Pachymeres, II, 626–627. For the date, see Rubió y Lluch *Diplomatari*, no. 31.

40. Pachymeres, II, 629–630, places the attack on Vizye at approximately the same time as the Byzantine treaty with Svetoslav—so, in the spring of 1307.

In such a way the inhabitants of Thrace fought the most important enemy of the empire. City after city, Rodosto, Adrianople, Vizyë, Madytos, Aenos and perhaps others that have not been recorded, mobilized its human and material resources in an effort to defend itself.[41] The defense was confined to the city dwellers; the countryside did not participate. Constantinople did very little to help the cities in their struggle, for it had its own internal battle to fight out. Michael himself, although he set the pattern, did not contribute much to the defense of the cities. That was left to his lieutenants, some of whom distinguished themselves in this war.

The Bulgarians, the other enemy of the empire in Thrace, were not opposed by the local inhabitants. Here, a combination of military activities and diplomacy achieved results which, although not very favourable to Byzantium, were not disastrous. One great danger of the Catalan campaign in Thrace was the possibility that the Catalans and the Bulgarians would form an alliance and enclose the province in a pincer attack. Fortunately for the Byzantines, if there was ever a Catalan–Bulgarian alliance, it was short-lived.

Theodore Svetoslav, although an enemy of Byzantium, was also hostile to the Catalans in 1305. Perhaps he realized that his sphere of interests conflicted with theirs, and he took advantage of the Byzantine defeat at Apros to take the ports of Anchialos, Mesembreia, and Agathoupolis with their surrounding territories. These conquests gave him control of some of the most important grain outlets of the Black Sea area, and virtually ended Byzantine control over that part of the Black Sea coast. In the summer of 1306, the Alan mercenaries defected from the Byzantines, and offered Svetoslav their services against their erstwhile employer. The Catalans, who still harbored a deep hatred against the Alans, attacked them and massacred them in Bulgarian territory.[42]

It is possible that the Catalans were motivated by political considerations as well as by a desire to pay off old scores. Svetoslav was already very strong, and he would become stronger if the Alans became an effective part of his military force. If this was the reason for the Catalan attack against the Alans, Svetoslav reacted in the way the Catalan leaders must have wished. Soon after the massacre of the Alans, he sent an embassy to Berengar de Rocafort, asking for a treaty and an offensive alliance against Byzantium. Rocafort would marry Svetoslav's sister, and the two men would combine their attacks on Thrace. Rocafort accepted these offers, but nothing else is known about the negotiations.[43] They seem not to have been pursued further.

Seeing that his negotiations with Rocafort produced no tangible result, Svetoslav asked Andronicus II for peace shortly before April 1307.[44] The peace treaty was very favorable to the Bulgarians. There was to be a simple cessation of hostilities, not a restoration of the status quo ante bellum. In return, Svetoslav finally secured (1308) the Byzantine marriage he had been negotiating

---

41. Pachymeres, II, 583–584, 578, 639–640; Muntaner, chap. ccxxx.
42. Pachymeres, II, 601–602; Muntaner, chap. ccxxv; Gregoras, I, 232–233.
43. Pachymeres, II, 606. Cf. Jireček, *Geschichte der Bulgaren*, p. 288 (he dates the embassy 1308).
44. Pachymeres, II, 628–629; Dölger, *Regesten*, no. 2303 (before April 1307).

since 1305. He married Theodora, one of the daughters of Michael IX and Maria of Armenia; she was then twelve years old.[45] Andronicus was not eager to accept Svetoslav's terms. But there was one deciding factor in favor of the Bulgarian king. Constantinople and all of Thrace was starving, and Svetoslav had been holding back the Bulgarian wheat supplies. To overcome Andronicus' hesitation, he allowed Black Sea grain to be shipped to Constantinople; the famine in the city was relieved, and Svetoslav received his bride. From that time until Svetoslav's death in 1322, Andronicus and the Bulgarian king maintained friendly relations. Svetoslav also entered into an alliance with Stephen Uroš II and relative peace reigned in the Balkans.[46]

Diplomatic Efforts

While Michael IX had been organizing the local defense of Thrace, Andronicus II made other efforts to stave off the many enemies of his state. He thought the situation desperate, and with good reason. Not only were the Bulgarians and the Catalans attacking Thrace, but in Asia Minor the inhabitants of the forts were starving; some rebelled against the imperial authority, while others defected and joined the Catalans. The Catalan company received reinforcements from Sicily and from the Turks. On the other hand, the Empress Irene, who had offered to come from Thessalonica bringing Serbian help, was stopped by the insecurity of the roads. Constantinople seemed threatened, its inhabitants were in despair, and even religious processions did not help. In these circumstances, Andronicus was again forced to seek help from foreigners.[47]

Although Genoa had not been a very cooperative ally, it was once again called to the rescue. This time, Andronicus negotiated with the Genoese government itself, and not with the inhabitants of Pera. In the autumn of 1305 he sent an embassy to Genoa asking for ships to come to Constantinople in the spring of 1306.[48] They arrived on time, but although Constantinople was threatened by the Catalans, neither the Genoese nor Andronicus were overly eager to fight. The Genoese fleet was not much different from any other commercial expedition; in September 1305, before Andronicus' request for help, Christiano Spinola (one of James II's Genoese supporters and informants) had anticipated the fact that Genoese ships would go to the Romania in June 1306, presumably on a trading expedition.[49] In this period, both warships and many merchant ships were great galleys, and as qualified to serve in war as in trade.

45. Gregoras, I, 283; Cantacuzenus, I, 186 and passim. F. Dölger, "Einiges über Theodora, die Griechin, Zarin der Bulgaren, 1308–1330," *Mélanges Henri Grégoire*, I (Paris, 1949), 211, 220–221 (Theodora born in 1296), 215 and n. 2 (married in 1308). On the Byzantine peace treaty with Svetoslav, see also Laiou, "Provisioning," pp. 102–103.

46. Cantacuzenus, I, 169; Djuro Daničić, *Životi kraljeva i archiepiskopa Srpskich, napisao Danilo i Drugi* (Zagreb, 1866), p. 141 (hereafter, Daničić, *Danilo*); Dölger, "Žarin." p. 215 and n. 2; Jireček, *Gesch. der Bulg.*, pp. 288–289.

47. Pachymeres, II, 558–561, 581–585, 588–590.

48. Ibid., II, 590; Dölger, *Regesten*, no. 2290. On this expedition, see also A. Laiou, "A Byzantine Prince Latinized: Theodore Palaeologus, Marquis of Montferrat," *Byzantion*, 38 (1968), 386–410.

49. Rubió y Lluch, *Diplomatari*, no. 16.

What probably happened in the spring of 1306 was that the Genoese government increased slightly the number of the ships making their annual commercial voyage to the Black Sea, armed the seamen, and gave the command to an important man, Antonio Spinola. It is an established fact that the Genoese were, on the whole, motivated by economic rather than political factors, and it would have been too much to expect them to send a whole fleet—always an expensive enterprise—to Byzantium for political purposes only. Pachymeres accused the Genoese government of perfidy, since they had sent ships which were to participate in war, if Andronicus should so ask them, but which otherwise were to engage in their normal trading activities. In the circumstances, however, Pachymeres' complaint was totally unrealistic. The Genoese government committed itself to the extent of ordering Antonio Spinola to give priority to the alliance with Andronicus, and to serve him at a low salary; for Genoa this was a substantial commitment.[50]

In fact, Andronicus had been engaged in negotiations with the Catalans just before he sent his embassy to Genoa.[51] His request for Genoese ships may, therefore, be interpreted as an effort to intimidate the Catalans and force them to leave the empire without any more bloodshed; if negotiations failed, he would then ask the Genoese to help him in an attack. As soon as the fleet arrived, the emperor started negotiating with the Company once again. As usual, the talks failed on the question of money. The Catalans asked for 300,000 hyperpyra, while Andronicus offered 100,000 and no more. The Catalans were clearly not very interested, for when the emperor's ambassadors went to Gallipoli they found that most of the army had gone inland, leaving Muntaner with a few soldiers.[52]

A question of strategy was now posed: was Gallipoli worth taking, even though the bulk of the Catalan army was away? Against the benefits to be reaped from such a conquest was the possibility that the infuriated Catalans might launch an attack on Constantinople. In that case, the Byzantines would have to fight alone, for the Genoese could not fight on land, while the Catalans would be reduced to fighting only on land. While he was negotiating, Andronicus allowed the Genoese ships to go to the Black Sea for twenty days. Only four ships remained, to guard the straits. Andronicus adopted an indecisive solution to this strategic problem. When the Genoese fleet returned from the Black Sea, he asked them to attack Gallipoli, "to do something valiant, if they could, and then to sail for home." The Genoese fleet along with seven Byzantine ships did attack Gallipoli, in mid-July 1306, and they were defeated. In any case, the engagement was not conceived very seriously, since the Genoese planned to leave for Genoa immediately thereafter, whatever the outcome.[53]

What did Andronicus II wish to accomplish by his appeal to his Genoese

50. Pachymeres, II, 597–598. Cf. Muntaner, chap. ccxxvii; Pachymeres, II, 601.
51. Pachymeres, II, 592.
52. Ibid., II, 599–605; Muntaner, chap. ccxxvii.
53. Pachymeres, II, 605–606; cf. Muntaner, chap. ccxxvii. In my discussion of the Genoese expedition of 1306, I have followed Pachymeres' account, because it agrees both with the attitude of the Genoese before and after the expedition, and with the information we have from Genoese and Aragonese documents. Muntaner, in chap. ccxxvii, gives a slightly different account, which seems to exaggerate the fierceness of the Genoese attack on Gallipoli.

allies, and why did he not order the Genoese to launch a really effective attack on Gallipoli? Perhaps he thought a Genoese victory in Gallipoli not worth the effort; since the Genoese could not and would not fight on land, how could he have followed up a victory? On the other hand, he may have hoped that a show of strength would deflect the Catalans from the siege of Didymoteichon in which they were engaged, and make them amenable to the discussions which he reopened immediately.[54] But if this was his plan, he should have detained the Genoese ships in harbor while he pursed the negotiations. Andronicus' policy is hard to interpret and its indecisive character cannot be explained simply by the weakness of his personality and his political immaturity. Perhaps he feared getting too deeply in the debt of the Genoese, or perhaps he was yielding to anti-Genoese pressures.

If Andronicus had to deal with anti-Latin sentiment, this probably came from the patriarch Athanasios I. The patriarch's position toward the Latins was made clear in a letter he wrote to Andronicus II in late May or early June 1305.[55] This letter was occasioned by a development which became directly linked with the Genoese expedition of 1306. In January 1305, the Empress Yolanda-Irene inherited the marquisate of Montferrat, following the death of her brother, John I. When envoys came from Montferrat to acquaint her with the news, she told them that she herself did not want to return to her homeland, but she would send instead her eldest son, the despot John. As soon as Athanasios I heard of this, he wrote Andronicus II a strongly worded letter, in which he presented at great length the dangers of this project: John was a young man, and if he were sent to dwell "among barbarians, among a most arrogant and irrational people," ("ἀλλοδαπῆ γῆ βαρβάροις κατοικουμένη καὶ ἔθνει κατάκρως ὑπερηφάνω καὶ ἀπονενοημένω τὰ μέγιστα"), he might lose his piety and his true religion, thus endangering the salvation of his immortal soul. Once he had lost that, what was to prevent him from harboring hostile feelings against the empire itself?

Athanasios went further, and gave expression to ideas which would later become the usual argument of the anti-western party in Byzantium: "Or is it that we expect from there [the West] military help? Let us rather be persuaded by the counsel of those who love God. This counsel clearly shows that human help is vain, so that we may rather become strong through confidence in God. For in this way He derides and will confound those who desire to destroy us."[56] So, even in times of extreme peril, the patriarch considered western help unnecessary, indeed potentially dangerous, and preferred to depend on salvation from heaven. It was irrelevant to the patriarch, as it was to the historian Nicephorus Gregoras, that at this time the empire was in desperate need of Genoese help to defend the capital itself.[57] From the thirteenth to the fifteenth century, as the fortunes of the empire declined, so

54. Pachymeres, II, 605–606.

55. This letter is published in Laiou, "Theodore Palaeologus," pp. 404–410. The article discusses the negotiations which culminated in the election of Theodore as marquis of Montferrat and in his marriage to Argentina Spinola, daughter of the Genoese captain of the people. These events will therefore only be summarized here.

56. Laiou, "Theodore Palaeologus," p. 409.

57. Gregoras, I, 237–238.

the pride of the Byzantines in their heritage and in their contracting world increased.

Athanasios was able to block the appointment of the despot John to the throne of Montferrat. Instead, Irene's second son, Theodore, was chosen. In the summer of 1306, when the Genoese ships left Constantinople for Genoa, they took with them the young marquis of Montferrat. By the time he left, Theodore had become engaged to Argentina Spinola, the daughter of Opicino Spinola, one of the captains of the People of Genoa.[58] For Spinola, the marriage had obvious social advantages and was also useful in terms of internal Italian politics. From the Byzantine side, the usefulness of this marriage was less obvious; perhaps the Genoese negotiated the marriage as payment for the limited help they gave Andronicus in 1306.[59]

The departure of the Genoese fleet left the empire nearer than ever to a state of collapse. Michael IX was ill, and his army had been very much reduced. The remaining parts of Bithynia (Mesothinia) revolted when Andronicus sent his tax collectors to collect the usual land tax for the army. The Catalans and their Turkish allies proceeded with the conquest of Thrace.[60] At this point, the Genoese of Pera decided to seek peace with the Catalans so that they could navigate in the Hellespont and the Propontis. Since they had lately received from home a new *abbate del popolo*, it is probable that the government of Genoa urged them, or at least allowed them to proceed with these negotiations. Andronicus was angry and fearful of the consequences. The Genoese involvement in the war, nominal though it was, had appeared as his only protection against total defeat.

Andronicus tried to deflect the Genoese from their purpose, but they refused to be persuaded. The emperor then tried to make the best of the inevitable and asked the *abbate* to act as an imperial envoy; on the emperor's behalf, he was to offer the Catalans money, honors and high office, in return for peace.[61] The *abbate* talked with both Berengar de Rocafort and Ferran Ximenes de Arenos, who was then in Madytos. Ximenes apparently was rather conciliatory. The Catalan Company was already splitting into factions, and Ferran Ximenes de Arenos' faction may be considered a moderate one. It included many of the Aragonese nobles and the cavalry, and its aim was to establish relatively friendly relations with Byzantium. Berengar de Rocafort, on the other

58. On the election and marriage of Theodore, see Pachymeres, II, 598–599; Muntaner, chap. ccxxvii; "Chronica illorum de Solario," Vincenzo Promis, *Miscellanea di storia Italiana*, 9, (1870), 135; Benvenuto di San Giorgio, cols. 408–413. Cf. D. A. Zakythinos, «Ὁ Μαρκίων τοῦ Μομφερράτου Θεόδωρος Α' Παλαιολόγος καὶ ὁ βασιλεὺς τῆς Γαλλίας Φίλιππος ΣΤ'» Ε.Ε.Β.Σ., 11 (1935), 16–18. In part, Spinola desired this marriage because of internal Italian politics, having to do with the rivalry between the Spinola and the D'Oria, and with the war between the marquisates of Montferrat and Saluzzo: see Stella, *Annales Genuenses*, col. 1022; *Cont. of Jac. d Varag.*, p. 11; A. Giustiniani, *Annali della Repubblica de Genova*, ed. G.B. Spotorno, (Genoa, 1854), pp. 7–8.

59. Muntaner, chap. ccxxvii; Caro, "Chronologie," p. 121. For this reason, although Andronicus had offered substantial rewards for their help, they said they would serve for very little (Pachymeres, II, 592, 598).

60. Pachymeres, II, 608, 618–619, 621–623.

61. Ibid., II, 623. Rubió y Lluch, *Diplomatari*, no. 31: Christiano Spinola, who wrote this letter to James II (October 19, 1306), said that Andronicus offered the Catalans 80,000 hyperpyra.

hand, exhibited the same ambition and rapacity which had aroused the hatred of his Sicilian master, Frederick III. He had the support of most of the Almugavars, and he wanted the undisputed leadership of the Company and probably the conquest of the empire.[62]

The Genoese abbate del popolo held unprofitable discussions with Rocafort. The Catalan leader demanded that Andronicus pay 200,000 hyperpyra for the "services" of the Company. Along with this preposterous demand, he also offered to sell back to Andronicus the lands and castles he occupied, as well as his Byzantine prisoners! If Andronicus refused, Rocafort threatened to attack and conquer the rest of the empire (September 1306). Ximenes de Arenos, whom Pachymeres considered milder (ἡμερώτερος) wrote to the emperor in September, dissociating himself from Rocafort's threats.[63] Meanwhile, Rocafort tried to make his point by moving his army up to the walls of Constantinople. As the patriarch appealed to divine Providence once again, the people who lived outside the capital and some of the inhabitants of Pera rushed into the city seeking refuge. It was at this point that the leader of the small Byzantine army, Ducas, and the inhabitants of Tzurulon produced their timely diversion, and Rocafort was deflected from the siege of Constantinople.[64]

Along with his Genoese alliance, Andronicus II also turned to the east to seek allies against his two enemies, the Turks and the Catalans. In 1305–1306 he sent an embassy composed of Manuel Philes and others, to the king of Georgia, to ask him for an army against the Catalans. The Georgians promised to help, with no recompense other than their expenses, but subsequent negotiations failed, and only a few men came to Constantinople.[65] Although fruitless, this appeal to Georgia is of some interest. The Byzantines had maintained close relations with Georgia in the days when the empire was strong, and Georgian soldiers had been among the most valiant in the Byzantine armies. Now, when Byzantium was so weak that even its capital seemed in danger, the Georgian promise of help is touching evidence that in this remote area the glory of the empire was still remembered, and could evoke a certain amount of emotion.

Byzantine negotiations with the Mongols of Persia, although less tinged with emotion, were more extensive and had a more solid basis: the opposition of both states to the power of the Turks. These negotiations also were hallowed by tradition: Michael VIII, continuing the policy of the emperors of Nicaea, had made treaties with Hulagu, the khan of Persia. In 1304 Andronicus II decided to renew the alliance, and solidify it with a marriage contract. He offered one of his illegitimate daughters to Gazan, the khan of Tabriz, and

---

62. Pachymeres, II, 625–626; Dade, *Versuche*, pp. 108–110.

63. Pachymeres, II, 625–626; Rubió y Lluch, *Diplomatari*, no. 31.

64. Pachymeres, II, 626–627. Date: late September 1306? On October 14, Genoese ships carried the news back to Genoa: Rubió y Lluch, *Diplomatari*, no. 31.

65. Pachymeres, II, 592, 620; Miller, *Philes Carmina*, II, no. 18; Dölger, *Regesten*, no. 2292, gives the date 1305–1306. Cf. M. Treu, "Athanasios Chatzikes," *BZ*, 18 (1909), 481; K. Kokylides, «Γεωργιανοὶ ἢ Ἴβηρες ἐν τοῖς Ἁγίοις Τόποις,» Νέα Σιών, 15 (1920), 249; Ihor Ševčenko, "The Imprisonment of Manuel Moschopoulos," *Speculum*, 27 (1952), 145, 153.

after Gazan's death (May 14, 1304), to his successor, Olĝäitü (Charbanda).[66] Asia Minor was then experiencing its most severe incursion of Turks; the Asiatic coast of the Hellespont was thrown into confusion; Nicaea and Nicomedia were besieged, and the inhabitants of Chalcedon had fled to Constantinople (1304).[67] It was, therefore, understandable that Andronicus should seek the help of the khan; but negotiations took a long time.

In the early summer of 1304, while the emperor was engaged in discussions with the Mongol ambassadors, Umur, a Turkish emir, asked for "the area between the rivers near Sangarios" to hold from Andronicus.[68] Thus, even the rumor of a Mongol alliance and, perhaps, the Catalan campaign in Anatolia, began to have some effect on Byzantine relations with the Turks. Yet in 1305, while the situation in Bithynia was steadily deteriorating, the alliance had still not been concluded. In the spring of 1305, Andronicus sent another embassy to request help from Olĝäitü.[69] The help was to be used against the Ottomans and perhaps against Sasan who had taken Ephesus (October 24, 1304).[70] Soon afterwards, Andronicus received an embassy from Persia, and the information that the khan was preparing to send 40,000 men; another 30,000 were already around Iconium and were awaiting instructions.

In 1307 Andronicus was still discussing the future marriage of Olĝäitü. At that time, he sent to Nicaea his sister Maria, the widow of Olĝäitü's grandfather, Abaga.[71] She had instructions to promote the marriage and to try to persuade the Ottomans to accept Andronicus' authority. She would use the impending arrival of the Mongols as a weapon of persuasion. Her efforts provoked Osman's ire, and he mounted an even more determined siege of Nicaea. In the early summer of 1307, news came to Constantinople that Olĝäitü's 30,000 soldiers had started to attack the Turks. Pachymeres, finishing his history, thought that the Byzantines, with Mongol help, would be able to recover all their old possessions in Asia Minor. Later historians make allusions

66. Pachymeres, II, 402, 588; Dölger, *Regesten*, no. 2265 (embassy to Gazan, May 1304); 2280 (spring 1305, embassy to Olĝäitü); Georgiades-Arnakes, Οἱ πρῶτοι ᾿Οθωμανοί, p. 152; Wittek, *Mentesche*, p. 63. Andronicus had two known illegitimate daughters: One was Maria, who married Toḫtu (Toktai), khan of the Golden Horde, in 1292. As Toḫtu did not die until 1313, the negotiations cannot have concerned her. The other daughter was Irene who eventually married John II of Thessaly, and it was probably Irene whom Andronicus offered first to Gazan and then to Olĝäitü.

67. Pachymeres, II, 410ff; Geordiades-Arnakes, Οἱ πρῶτοι ᾿Οθωμανοί, pp. 142ff. The date given by Georgiades-Arnakes (1308) is wrong.

68. Pachymeres, II, 459–460. The date is determined by the fact that at the time, Gazan's ambassadors were in Constantinople, where they learned about his death (spring, 1304).

69. Pachymeres, II, 588ff; Georgiades-Arnakes, Οἱ πρῶτοι ᾿Οθωμανοί, p. 146.

70. Gregoras, I, 214; Lemerle, *L'Émirat d'Aydin*, p. 20 and n. 4; S. Lambros, «Μιχαὴλ Λουλλούδης ὁ ᾿Εφέσιος καὶ ἡ ὑπὸ τῶν Τούρκων ἅλωσις τῆς ᾿Εφέσου,» Νέος ῾Ελληνομνήμων, 1, (1904), 209–212.

71. Pachymeres, II, 620, 637. Date: Maria's departure seems from Pachymeres' account, to follow the death of Meliteneiotes. He died in April 1307: V. Laurent, "La date de la mort de Jean Beccos," *Échos d'Orient*, 25 (1926), 316–319. Maria was the "Lady of the Mongols" (Κυρὰ τῶν Μουγουλίων) who endowed a monastery at Constantinople. After her husband's death, she became a nun, with the name Melane, and her portrait survives in one of the most appealing mosaics of Kahriye Djami. On Maria, see Steven Runciman, "The Ladies of the Mongols," Εἰς μνήμην Κ. ᾿Αμάντου, (Athens, 1960), pp. 46–53.

to the Mongol force, but there is no precise information about its further activities. The fact that the Ottomans were unable to take Brusa until 1326 and Nicaea until 1331 has been taken as proof that their plans were disrupted by the Mongol intervention.[72]

Andronicus' negotiations with the khans of Tabriz indicate that even during the worst moments of the Catalan invasion the emperor did not entirely abandon Asia Minor. Even as he offered Anatolia to Roger de Flor, he was also trying to save it through the help of the Mongols. It is true that in 1305–1309 most of his energy was directed toward saving his European possessions from the Catalans; yet his negotiations wih the Mongols show that his policy of those years was not entirely defensive, or entirely forgetful of Anatolia.

The Catalans and Europe

Before the threat, however feeble, of a Byzantine–Genoese alliance, the Catalans stepped up their diplomatic activity in an effort to get help from Europe in what had become a real war against Byzantium. Apparently, it was the capture of Berengar d'Entença by the Genoese that galvanized the Catalans into action. In the summer of 1305, the Byzantines captured a Catalan secretary who had been on his way to Sicily to tell Frederick III that the Company had great need of his help; if there were no reinforcements from Sicily, the Catalans would have to make peace with Byzantium.[73] There is evidence that in January 1306 the Catalans appealed to the pope, to Frederick III, and to James II of Aragon. On January 22, two men, sent by the Catalan Company, addressed a letter to James II, telling him that they had come west to bring the messages of the Company to Sicily and the pope and the king of Aragon. The two men designated themselves as "naturales humiles et fideles" of the king of Aragon. They then reported that Berengar d'Entença, released from his Genoese prison, had appeared before the pope (Clement V), and before Charles of Valois, "de mandato, licencia et voluntate dominacione vestra [sic]," to ask them for help against the Byzantines. Entença was going to send James II a written report, and meanwhile he urged the two Catalan emissaries to hurry to the pope.[74]

Entença, then, kept fast his ties with Aragon, and once again behaved as an agent of both the king of Aragon and the Catalans. Furthermore, the Catalan Company itself was requesting help from Europe, although it would seem that the two emissaries considered their ties with Aragon more tenuous than did Entença. James II also retained his interest in the affairs of the Company,

---

72. Pachymeres, II, 637–638, 651; Dervis Ahmed Ašikpašazade, *Tevarikh-i al-i Osman*, ed. Ali (Constantinople, 1916), p. 25; V. Bratutti, *Chronica dell'origine e progressione della casa ottomana*, (transl. of Sa'deddin) I, (Vienna, 1649), 27 (from Georgiades-Arnakes, Οἱ πρῶτοι Ὀθωμανοί, pp. 154–155).

73. Pachymeres, II, 563–572. On the subject treated in this section, see the somewhat limited discussion of Dade, *Versuche*, pp. 111ff.

74. Rubió y Lluch, *Diplomatari*, no. 23; cf. no. 33; Finke, *Acta Aragonensia*, II, 686–687; Muntaner, chap. ccxxix; *Regestum Clementis, Papae, V*, (Rome, 1885–1888), no. 1444 (Entença acts as witness of James II, on May 28, 1306). Cf. Caro, *Genua*, II, 356–357.

to the extent of commissioning Entença to negotiate with Charles of Valois and Clement V on the matter of an attack on Byzantium. Another fragment of evidence supports the theory that James II retained his interest in Byzantium. On August 16, 1306, the Empress Constance, illegitimate daughter of Frederick II Hohenstaufen and widow of John Vatatzes, transferred to James II, her closest male relative, all her rights to the Byzantine empire. These consisted of her dowry, money, jewels, and some lands in Asia Minor whose rent she estimated at 30,000 hyperpyra per year.[75]

Entença's representations to Clement V and Charles of Valois remained fruitless, for both men had other plans: Charles of Valois was planning his own expedition to Byzantium, and the pope was supporting him. As Muntaner put it, "[Entença] went to the Pope and to the King of France, to arrange that the Company should get succours from them. But much might he labor; I do not believe that the Pope nor the House of France wished that all the infidels of the world should be conquered by the followers of the Lord King of Aragon; and so both denied him succours."[76]

In the summer of 1306, the Catalans of Gallipoli asked Berengar d'Entença to join them again. He mortgaged his lands, and returned to the East with five hundred men, sometime between August 29 and September 25, 1306. James II's only help appears to have consisted of a certain quantity of biscuit that he gave Berengar. Before leaving, Berengar wrote to James II, reaffirming his loyalty as "vesayl natural" to his "senyor natural," and promising that he would work for the king's honor and prosperity.[77]

Although the Catalan Company was trying to obtain help from Europe, it seems to have still considered itself independent of any formal ties to either Sicily or Aragon. Entença's homage to James II was a personal affair. The Company itself acted for the most part as an independent agent. Modern historians cannot make a completely persuasive argument to prove either the complete independence or the complete dependence of the Company on any outside power, and this is probably due to the fact that the various leaders of the Company had divergent aims. Berengar de Rocafort was in all likelihood opposed to any formal dependence upon Sicily, with whose king he had quarreled, while Entença was certainly, by 1306, an Aragonese agent.

In Gallipoli itself, the Company took action which seemed to establish its independence while retaining informal ties with Sicily and Aragon. After Entença's capture, four flags were made: "And I had at once a great banner made of Saint Peter of Rome, to place on our tower; and I had a royal banner made of the lord king of Aragon, and another of the king of Sicily, and another of Saint George; and these three we were to carry in battle and that of Saint

75. In 1316 James II asked Andronicus II to give him satisfaction on these rights: J. Miret y Sans, "Tres princesas Griegas en la corte de Jaime II de Aragon," *Revue hispanique*, 15 (1906), Appendix 1, (pp. 717–719) and pp. 693–697; Miret y Sans, "Nuevos documentos de las tres princesas Griegas," *Revue hispanique*, 19 (1908), 112–134; Wolff, "Mortgage and Redemption," p. 58 and n. 26.

76. Muntaner, chap. ccxxix.

77. Muntaner, chap. ccxxix; Rubió y Lluch, *Diplomatari*, nos. 27, 29, 30. No. 31 proves that the Catalans were then acting against the empire, not, as Muntaner (chap. ccxxix) would have us believe, against the Turks. Cf. Caro, *Genua*, II, 336; Finke, *Acta Aragonensia*, II, 683.

Peter was to be put on the principal tower." The battle cry of the Company was "Aragon! Aragon! Saint George! Saint George!"[78] In the summer of 1305 it also made, for the first time, its own seal, the "segell de la host dels franchs que regnen lo regne de Macedonia." The latest researcher on the subject, David Jacoby, thinks that Muntaner, who reports this event, was confusing his dates, for the Catalans could not have talked of the Kingdom of Macedonia while they were still in Gallipoli, which is in Thrace.[79] Mr. Jacoby confuses modern geographical designations with medieval ones. In 1305 "Macedonia" was a perfectly proper name for modern Thrace, and the Byzantine theme of Macedonia originally designated Thrace east of the Nestos (Mesta) River. In the fourteenth century, the theme of Macedonia consisted of Thrace from Constantinople to the Marica River. Muntaner was very consistent in his terminology: he always spoke of Thrace as the Kingdom of Macedonia, while modern Macedonia (which is the same as ancient Macedonia) he designated as "the Kingdom of Thessalonica."[80] The seal of 1305 is an interesting indication that the Catalans, having broken even their tenuous ties with the Byzantines, now considered themselves independent rulers of Thrace.

The Catalan Company, then, seems to have tried to bolster its military superiority in Thrace with a degree of legitimacy. They claimed for themselves the title of defenders of the Catholic faith against the schismatics. In the summer of 1306, before the Genoese attacked Gallipoli, there was an interesting exchange of letters between the Genoese commander, Antonio Spinola, and Muntaner. Spinola wrote that the Catalans should leave: "he defied us in the name of the Commune of Genoa" ("desafians de part del comu de Genova"). Muntaner replied that the Commune of Genoa was a friend of the House of Aragon, Sicily, and Mallorca, and therefore the Genoese should not challenge the Catalans. Muntaner added that since the Catalans were crusaders, the Genoese were required to join them in the fight against the schismatic Byzantines: "and so we required him, in the name of the Holy Father and of the King of Aragon, and of the King of Sicily to help us."[81] None of these pieces of evidence tells unequivocally whether the Catalan Company considered itself

---

78. Muntaner, chaps. ccxix, ccxx.

79. Muntaner, chap. ccxxv. David Jacoby, "La 'Compagnie catalane' en Grèce," *Journal des Savants*, (1966), pp. 80–82. Mr. Jacoby maintains that the Company remained independent until 1312, and I agree with his thesis in general, although I disagree on several details.

80. See, for example, Muntaner, chap. ccxxiv, where he speaks of "Ser Jordi de Cristopol," as coming from the "reyalme de Seledonich." Christopolis (modern Kavala) was just to the west of the frontiers of the old Byzantine theme of Macedonia, and so part of the theme of Thessalonica. Cf. Stein, *Untersuchungen*, p. 26. On the fourteenth century themes, see St. Kyriakides, Βυζαντιναί Μελέται, II–V (Thessalonica, 1939). The Byzantines themselves thought of "Macedonia" as designating both the ancient province and the contemporary theme, although geographically the two areas were quite different. See, for example, Codinus, *De officialibus*, p. 55, where it is said that the eastern barbarians pay homage to the Byzantine Emperor as to the successor of Alexander of Macedonia, because the Romans (Byzantines) now hold Macedonia. See also a curious series of coins issued by Andronicus II and Michael IX, on which the inscription reads Αὐτοκράτορες Ῥωμαίων (Emperors of the Romans) and on the reverse τῆς Μακεδονίας (of Macedonia): Tommaso Bertelé, "Autocratori dei Romani, di Constantinopoli e della Macedonia," *Numismatica*, n.s., 2 (1961), 75–82.

81. Muntaner, chap. ccxxviii.

legally bound to the pope, the king of Aragon or the king of Sicily. Its words and actions indicate that while it was not formally, legally, bound to anyone, the Company considered itself morally (and vaguely) bound to these three powers. The ambivalence of the stand was made clear in the spring of 1307, when the Catalans were asked to give full and formal allegiance to the king of Sicily.

Frederick III's involvement with the Company became much more obvious than that of his brother James. As early as March 1306, Frederick discussed with his cousin, the infante of Mallorca Ferran, the possibility of sending Ferran to the Romania.[82] Ferran of Mallorca was first cousin to James of Aragon and to Frederick of Sicily. He was the son of James I of Mallorca, who was the brother of Peter III of Aragon, father of James and Frederick.[83] Frederick of Sicily was thus following the established tradition of the House of Aragon, that is, the tradition of sending members of the cadet branch of the family to rule over conquered provinces. This fact in itself would indicate that Frederick III was taking seriously the claim of the Catalan Company, that it was "reigning over the Kingdom of Macedonia." By sending Ferran to the Romania, Frederick would be legitimizing and bringing under his control the de facto rule of the Catalans over Thrace. James II also may have been involved in this: in March and April 1306, Ferran appealed to him, requesting the help James had promised for Ferran's "voyage."[84] It is possible that in these documents Ferran was referring to his projected voyage to the East. Finally, on March 10, 1307, Frederick of Sicily and Ferran of Mallorca signed a formal pact by which Ferran undertook to lead the Catalan Company, in Frederick's name.[85]

There are several interesting points in this document. Frederick III unequivocally designated the Catalans as "the people of our lord the king [of Sicily] who are in those parts [of the Romania]" ("gentem dicti domini nostri regis in eiusdem partibus [Romanie] existentem"). More specifically still, Frederick assumed that the Catalans owed him fealty and homage, and this they would now swear to Ferran, Frederick's lieutenant and viceroy. So, Frederick III now, for the first time, formally treated the Catalan Company

---

82. Rubió y Lluch, *Ferrán*, nos. 2, 3, 5.

83. This simplified genealogical table shows the relationship: (A = Aragon, M = Mallorca, S = Sicily)

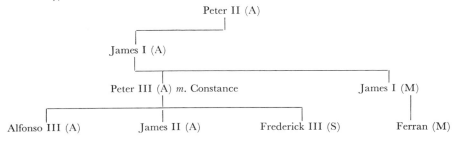

84. Rubió y Lluch, *Ferrán*, nos. 2–5.

85. Rubió y Lluch, *Ferrán*, no. 7; Rubió y Lluch, *Diplomatari*, no. 32. Burns, "Catalan Company," p. 767, calls this the "masterstroke" of Frederick III's policy.

as his vassals, and assumed command over them through his viceroy. Ferran of Mallorca promised to always remain friendly to Frederick, and to execute his will in the Romania. And for all these things "the lord Infante Ferran swears fealty by hands and mouth, and performs homage in the hands of the said lord our king" ("dominus infans Ferandus fecit fidem et manibus et ore homanagium in manibus dicti domini nostri regis"). Of course, Ferran also promised that he—and therefore, the Company under his command—would not make peace or conclude a treaty with anyone, except with the permission and at the command of Frederick III. So far, then, it appears as though the Catalans had finally acquired a formal feudal suzerain, the king of Sicily. Frederick was probably eager to accomplish this, because Charles of Valois was preparing to go the the East.

The real situation, however, did not conform to this theoretical assumption of suzerainty on Frederick's part. Ferran of Mallorca arrived at Gallipoli with four ships, on May 20, 1307.[86] Upon his arrival, the already existing split among the Catalan leaders became clearer. Muntaner, Entença, Ferran Ximenes de Arenos, and their followers accepted Ferran as their leader, and swore fealty to him and to Frederick III. But Berengar de Rocafort balked. He suggested that the Company pay homage to Ferran in his own right, not in his role as the personal representative of the king of Sicily. Here, no doubt, Rocafort was motivated by his personal dislike for the king of Sicily. But there were other, more profound reasons for his disagreement. An interesting social split existed within the Catalan Company.

According to Muntaner, Rocafort thought to himself "If this lord [Ferran] remains here as lord and chief thou art lost, for En Berenguer de Entenza and Ferran Ximeno have accepted him before thou didst, and both are nobles . . . and they have mortal hatred against thee." On the other hand, Rocafort thought he had his own considerable strength, which consisted of "the greater part of the Franks, horse and foot, . . . and the Turks and the Turcopoles who, here, acknowledge no other lord but thee." So, he assembled these people and persuaded them not to swear homage to Frederick III. It appears that while the nobles were ready to do their feudal duty, and had a sense of feudal obligation to the king of Sicily, Rocafort and the Almugavars did not accept Frederick's contention that they were "his men." Finally, it is interesting that when he voiced his repudiation of Frederick, Rocafort also urged the conquest of the "Kingdom of Saloniki."[87] Perhaps he had already conceived the idea of becoming king of Thessalonica, in which case he would want to retain his independence from Sicily. Ferran agreed to let the matter rest until the conquest of Thessalonica.

By this time the Catalans were ready to leave Thrace.[88] Hunger drove

---

86. Rubió y Lluch, *Diplomatari*, p. 41. Muntaner, chap. ccxxx; cf. Dade, *Versuche*, pp. 125ff.
87. Muntaner, chap. ccxxx.
88. Pachymeres, II, 650–652; Gregoras, I, 244–248; Muntaner, chaps. ccxxxi, ccxxxii; Rubió y Lluch, *Diplomatari*, no. 33 (June, 1307); Boissonade, *Anecdota Graeca*, II, 219 (letter of Thomas Magister to the philosopher Joseph); Paul Lemerle, *Phillippes et la Macédoine orientale à l'époque chrétienne et byzantine* (Paris, 1945), I, 189–194; «Τοῦ πατριάρχου Κωνσταντινουπόλεως κυροῦ Φιλοθέου Βίος καὶ πολιτεία τοῦ ὁσίου καὶ θεοφόρου πατρὸς ἡμῶν Σάβα τοῦ Νέου,» A. Papadopoulos-Kerameus, ed. Ἀνάλεκτα Ἱεροσολυμιτικῆς Σταχυολογίας, V (St. Petersburg, 1898), XI, 210.

them west, for they lived off the land like locusts, without engaging in humiliating activities like agriculture. Their incursions had been so terrible that most of Thrace in the environs of Gallipoli had been destroyed.[89] The Marica (Hebrus) River was the western boundary of the Catalan raids, and the land east of that river was depopulated. The fields lay fallow, since fear of Catalans kept the peasants away. By the summer of 1306 there is already evidence that the Catalans were beginning to feel the effects of the devastation of Thrace. They tried to collect grain and other victuals in the city of Rodosto, while in the autumn their Turkish allies began to cultivate the land, "so that they could wage war against the emperor infinitely."[90]

Then, sometime in October 1306, Andronicus II took a bold and very unpopular measure. He forbade the peasants of Thrace to cultivate their fields, with the express purpose of starving the Catalans out of Thrace.[91] Surprisingly, the normally weak emperor showed great singleness of purpose here. Although his people at Constantinople were severely threatened by famine, and although the patriarch Athanasios was very much opposed to Andronicus' measure, the emperor persevered. The very desperate nature of his action proves that he expected the Catalans to try to conquer Constantinople.

In the end, Andronicus was vindicated: in the summer of 1307, the Catalans found that "food . . . is very expensive and [they] suffer from very great lack of food," and they then decided to move into Macedonia.[92] Constantinople was saved because Andronicus II did, for once, adopt an unpopular but successful policy, and also because, in the spring of 1307, King Svetoslav of Bulgaria allowed grain from the Black Sea to come into Constantinople, thus relieving the famine.[93] But the danger under which the emperor labored should not be underestimated. Had the Catalans persevered another winter, had they had the unity and the patience to organize food-gathering expeditions into northern Thrace, they would probably have conquered Constantinople, whose population was already driven by hunger into opposition to Andronicus. Byzantium was saved by the devastation of Thrace and by Andronicus' purposefulness.

When the Catalans decided to move further west, they first tried to take the town of Palaiokastron, west of the Dardanelles. If they were successful in that enterprise, they would then march toward the "Kingdom of Thessalonica."[94] Macedonia was still rich enough to feed the Catalan army, and so, some hoped, the internal disputes of the various leaders might disappear before the likelihood

89. Muntaner, chap. ccxxxi, claims that the Catalans had destroyed everything in an area of ten days' journey in each direction from Gallipoli. This may be an exaggeration, for such an area would extend beyond the Marica River in the west, and perhaps into Bulgarian territory in the north. Cf. Gregoras, I, 244–247; Pachymeres, II, 562, 639–640.

90. Rubió y Lluch, *Diplomatari*, no. 31.

91. Pachymeres, II, 628. For a full discussion of this see Laiou, "Provisioning," pp. 91–113. Two letters of the patriarch Athanasios I, referring to this measure and the ensuing famine, are published in the above article.

92. Rubió y Lluch, *Diplomatari*, no. 33: victualia sint valde cara . . . [the Catalans] habent victualium indigenciam valde magnam.

93. Pachymeres, II, 628–629.

94. Rubió y Lluch. *Diplomatari*, no. 33. For the identification of Asperosa (Palaiokastron), see Konrad Kretschmer, *Die italienischen Portolane des Mittelalters* (Berlin, 1909), p. 639.

of booty.[95] Mount Athos, with its wealthy monasteries, was one of the objectives of the Catalans, and Thessalonica, the second city of the empire and the residence of the two empresses (Irene and Rita-Maria) was the second objective.[96]

The Catalans left for Macedonia in the early summer of 1307, and by July major changes had taken place in the army. The leaders had fought among themselves, Entença had been killed, and Ferran Ximenes de Arenos had fled to join the Byzantines; he was given the title of megus dux, and married Theodora, a niece of Andronicus II. Rocafort now remained the only effective leader of the Catalan army.[97] Ferran of Mallorca, realizing that he could not fulfill his mandate, left the host, along with Muntaner, and began his long and adventurous journey back to Sicily.[98] With his departure, the formal tie of the Catalan Company to Frederick III of Sicily was dissolved. Berengar de Rocafort now turned to another man, who was useful as an overlord because he was far away, and perhaps because he could keep a check on Frederick of Sicily, should Frederick wish to take forceful measures to reestablish his control over the Catalans. This man was Charles of Valois.

The Byzantine–Genoese Agreement of 1308

The departure of the Catalans from Thrace relieved Constantinople from the immediate danger of conquest. While the emperor tried to take stock of his forces, and while he made an effort to organize the defense of Macedonia, he also reexamined his relations with Genoa. During the years of the Catalan presence in Thrace, the Genoese of Genoa and Pera had been able to defy all Byzantine regulations and all Byzantine authority. While they made an effort to help Byzantium fight the Catalans, the Genoese of Pera soon discovered that they could make use of the difficulties of the empire in order to increase their power and their wealth. Indeed, during the years of the Catalan adventure, the Genoese behaved as though the state to which they were bound in alliance and on whose sufferance they were supposed to live had already been dissolved. Until 1307 Andronicus had depended on them both for defense and for the provisioning of Constantinople, since most of the ships bringing grain from the Black Sea belonged to Genoese merchants. But even the emperor was not wholeheartedly pro-Genoese, and at the same time the people of Constantinople

95. Muntaner, chap. ccxxxi.

96. Pachymeres, II, 650–652; Gregoras, I, 244–248.

97. Muntaner, chaps. ccxxxii, ccxxxiii; Rubió y Lluch, *Diplomatari*, nos. 33, 35; Finke, *Acta Aragonensia*, II, 688; Gregoras, I, 232; Rubió y Lluch, "Companyía Catalana," p. 20. According to the *Libro de los Fechos*, #535, Arenos' followers were opposed to the Catalan collaboration with the Turks, and for that reason they defected to Constantinople. These events took place early in July, 1307: Dade, *Versuche*, pp. 126–127. Gregoras says that the Theodora who married Arenos was Andronicus' niece by his sister. We know of only one Theodora who fits this description, the daughter of Irene Palaeologina and Ivan (John) III Asên: Papadopulos, *Genealogie*, no. 44. Papadopulos does not mention Theodora's marriage to Arenos.

98. Rubió y Lluch, *Diplomatari*, pp. 43, 44 and n. 3; Muntaner, chaps. ccxxxi, ccxxxii, ccxxxiii; Rubió y Lluch, *Ferrán*, no. 9. Ferran started back in the early summer of 1307; he and Muntaner were captured by the Venetians near Nigroponte in July 1307 (Rubió y Lluch, *Ferrán*, no. 10).

became bitter and vocal enemies of the rich "Italians" who lived in their midst. The patriarch Athanasios, giving expression to these feelings, wrote bitterly against these Italians who made their profits by selling victuals in the black market and in return received precious gold or even Greek women.[99]

As soon as the Catalans moved into Macedonia, Andronicus II changed his attitude towards Genoa. Whereas in the past he had generally considered himself a friend and ally of the Genoese, in 1308 he presented them with a long list of complaints that explains just how much the Genoese had mis- behaved. They had done their best to defraud the imperial treasury of even the meager revenues it had from certain duties that the Genoese were still required to pay. They had built houses outside Pera, although this was not allowed. Genoese merchants had brought to Genoa and sold as slaves Byzantine boys and girls. Two Genoese pirates had planned an attack against the empire, while Genoese ships attacked various parts of the empire with the intention of securing them for Genoa. All of these activities reflect a state of anarchy in the empire. Andronicus II's empire was admittedly a weak state, weaker in 1305– 1307 as a result of the Catalan campaign. Significantly, the most serious charges against the Genoese were not repeated in the next list of Byzantine complaints, in 1317.[100]

In 1308 Andronicus felt in a stronger position toward Genoa. Genoa ap- parently arrived at a similar estimate of the situation, because in the Genoese– Byzantine agreement of 1308 the Commune agreed to almost all the conditions made by the emperor, and promised to meet all of his complaints. The meek- ness of the Genoese must have been due in part to developments in the Black Sea area: in 1307 the khan of the Golden Horde, Toktai, angered at the arrogance of the Genoese, had ordered an attack against them, and Genoese traders were killed in Sarai and Soldaia. The colony of Caffa was defended until May 1308, when it was abandoned for eight years.[101]

According to the Byzantine–Genoese agreement of 1308, Andronicus was to be given reparation for the duties which Genoese merchants had refused to pay. The right to grant charters of Genoese citizenship was to be restricted to the podestà and council of Pera. This right, which carried immunity from most imperial duties, had been grossly abused, and some Genoese officials of the Black Sea colonies granted charters to people who had no right to them. All these charters were to be examined by the podestà and council of Pera, and if found fraudulent were to be revoked. The merchants who had been involved in fraudulent practices designed to cheat the imperial officials would have to pay double the amount of the proper duty. The Genoese had bought land out- side their quarters in Pera, and from there attacked the empire. This was now forbidden. It was agreed that the Byzantines would be granted the same

---

99. Cod. Vat. Gr. 2219, fol. 75vo: Appendix I, letter 9, and below, "The Cost of Byzantine Foreign Policy," in Chapter VI.

100. Belgrano, "Prima serie," no. 12 (March 2, 1308), no. 14 (February 14, 1317); Sauli, *Colonia*, no. 12. Genoese and Byzantines had long bought and sold Christian slaves: Brătianu, *Actes de Péra et de Caffa*, nos. 193, 194, 238.

101. Belgrano, "Prima serie," no. 12, pp. 113–115; *Cont. of Jac. d. Varag.*, pp. 10–11.

privileges in Genoa that the Genoese enjoyed in the empire, and that all Byzantine subjects who had been sold as slaves in Genoa would be set free.[102] Andronicus also requested that the Genoese be forbidden to carry wood, iron, and slaves to Egypt or, if they did carry them, that they pay duty to Byzantium. This request was disputed by Genoa. Finally, the government of Genoa ordered that all Genoese sailing to the empire in armed ships, should give a security of 4,000 livres génois and promise that they would not attack Byzantine lands. Although this was a far cry from the promise Genoa had made to Michael VIII to defend the empire with her ships, it nevertheless indicates that a measure of order was slowly being established in Byzantine waters.

Thus, as soon as the Catalans left Thrace some of the worst results of Byzantine dependence on Genoa were corrected. The Genoese were still the best western friends and closest western allies of the Byzantines, but their excessive privileges had been curbed, and the emperor was once again master in his capital.

The Cost of Byzantine Foreign Policy

The Catalan expedition proved very expensive, both financially and in the destruction of human and natural resources. The original purpose of the enterprise was not fulfilled. The rapid reconquest of Asia Minor by the mercenaries was a temporary affair. The subsequent outbreak of hostilities between Greeks and Catalans enabled the Turks to recover most of their losses, while the emperor had to spend money, men, and energy for four years in an almost hopeless effort to defend his state against the men he had invited. Almost all independent Byzantine foreign policy stopped during these years. Negotiations with foreign powers—Genoa, the Serbs, the Bulgarians, the Mongols—took the form of requests for help against the Turks or the Catalans, with the promise of rewards of one sort or another. The Catalan adventure disoriented Byzantine diplomacy, paralyzed the system of taxation, disrupted the finances of the empire, precipitated the disorganization of the army, caused the displacement of the most productive classes of the empire—the peasants—and made Constantinople into a center of political discontent. Foreign policy depends as much on the internal affairs of a state as it does on external diplomatic conditions; a look at the economic and social condition of the empire in 1303–1307 facilitates an understanding of Andronicus' foreign policy during the Catalan invasion.

In purely fiscal terms, the money paid out to the Catalans was more than the empire could afford; according to Gregoras, the imperial treasury was soon emptied because all the money was given to the mercenaries.[103] By collating the various sources, an approximate estimate of the payments Andronicus II made to the Catalans can be obtained. When the Catalans arrived at Constantinople, they received a certain amount of money, computed as per capita

---

102. Belgrano, "Prima serie," no. 12, pp. 110–115; renewed in 1317, ibid., no. 14, p. 118.
103. Gregoras, I, 220; cf. Pachymeres, II, 397.

payment for the next four (or three) months of service.[104] We do not know what each soldier was given then, but we do know that later, in the spring of 1304, Roger de Flor required "two and three ounces of gold a month for his Italians."[105] This must mean that monthly payments were three ounces of gold for each cavalry soldier, and two ounces for each infantry man. The first payment, that made in September 1303, was probably on a similar scale.

As for the numbers of the Catalans, Muntaner was in a better position than the Byzantine sources to know. According to him, the army of Roger de Flor originally (before the summer of 1304) consisted of 1,500 cavalry, 4,000 Almugavars, and 1,000 other soldiers.[106] The first installment, accordingly, would be 58,000 gold ounces if it was paid for four months. If, as Pachymeres wrote, the Catalans received only three months' pay, this would come to 43,500 gold ounces. The second installment, paid in the spring of 1304, is more difficult to compute, since the appropriate passage in Muntaner is not clear. The Catalan chronicler writes that in the spring of that year, Roger de Flor went to the emperor, who gave him enough money to pay the company for four months. Then Roger returned to Cyzicus, and gave money to his army, which had incurred great debts during the winter: "it was the most handsome gift a lord had made to his vassals for more than a thousand years. Altogether he gave them pay for eight months, one with another, the pay of the horsemen amounted to fifty thousand onzas and that of the men afoot to nearly sixty thousand onzas . . . And when he had done this, . . . he commanded that, on the next day, every man . . . should . . . receive pay for four months in fine gold."[107] Possibly, Muntaner's memory may be confused here. The words "four months pay" keep recurring in his narrative, and probably in the spring of 1304 Roger did obtain and give to his men money equivalent to four months pay. The "eight months pay" mentioned by Muntaner must refer to the original payment, of September 1303, plus the new payment of spring 1304. The additional four months pay which Roger then gave his soldiers may be a figment of Muntaner's imagination.

If the Catalans received four months pay in the spring of 1304, and if Pachymeres' figures for the per capita salaries are correct, the payments totaled 58,000 gold ounces (18,000 for the cavalry and 40,000 for the infantry). The 1,000 Alan mercenaries, paid on a lower scale than the Catalans, received 12,000 hyperpyra in the spring of 1304. These were immense sums of money.[108]

Andronicus was not forced to have recourse to special taxes in order to make

104. Pachymeres, II, 395–397 (he says they received only three months' pay); Muntaner, chap. ccii (four months). Cf. Dade, *Versuche*, p. 81; Georgiades-Arnakes, Οἱ πρῶτοι Ὀθωμανοί, pp. 136, 200.

105. Pachymeres, II, 420.

106. Muntaner, chap. cciii.

107. Muntaner, chap. cciv.

108. See Pachymeres, II, 420, 422–424. The total payments in 1303 and early 1304 according to our computation would be 36,000 gold ounces for the cavalry, and 80,000 for the infantry. Muntaner, chap. cciv, says that the eight-month payment to the Catalans amounted to 50,000 gold ounces for the cavalry and 60,000 for the infantry, not including the gifts Andronicus made to the leaders.

In 1274 one gold ounce of Naples was equivalent to approximately 63.96 pre-1914 francs gold, while the normal equivalent for the hyperpyron in the early fourteenth century was 7.57 francs gold. In 1304 the hyperpyron was equivalent to 7.44 francs gold: Zakythinos, *Crise*, pp. 25–26.

the first two payments to the Catalans. He had tried since 1296 to build up his treasury for military purposes, and apparently it contained a large enough sum to satisfy the first demands of the Catalans. His revenues came in part from the tenth taken from the revenues of each pronoia; much of this, however, especially the money collected in Anatolia, was usurped by the local magnates. Some money must also have been raised from the excise duties on salt and iron. This was a relatively recent measure, for John Kosmas treated it as an innovation when he complained to the emperor about it (1301). Even in the spring of 1304, however, the emperor was forced to revert to some unusual measures in order to meet the claims of the Catalans: he stopped paying the Byzantine soldiers and the palace staff.[109] Obviously, the resources of the treasury were running very low. It is therefore not surprising that later in the same year Andronicus was unable to meet Roger de Flor's new demands and had to take unhealthy economic measures.

The conflict between Catalans and Byzantines on the question of money became acute in the fall of 1304, when Roger de Flor was ordered back to Thrace. In October 1304, after Berengar d'Entença's arrival in Constantinople, Roger demanded 300,000 hyperpyra; only then would he fulfill his promise of sending 1,000 men to fight with Michael IX while the rest returned to Anatolia. Andronicus complained that the demand was excessive and Roger, aware of the emperor's difficulties, decided to accept a portion of that sum. To this Andronicus consented. Some of the money then paid to Roger came from the Emperor's own purse, but most if it was raised by a new tax, the σιτόκριθον (tax on wheat and barley). Andronicus ordered that each peasant should give to the treasury six modii of wheat and four modii of barley per *jugum*. This was sold at the current, near-famine price, and the revenue was given to the Catalans.[110]

Two factors made the creation of this new tax imperative. First, the destruction and depopulation of Asia Minor had changed it from an important source of revenue into a burden for the imperial treasury. The truth of this statement is borne out by the fact that in the spring of 1305 Andronicus had to collect what wheat he could from the big monasteries in Constantinople and send it to Bithynia. In the same year, a revolt erupted in Bithynia, triggered by the presence of an imperial tax collector who had come to collect the usual land

---

Converted into hyperpyra, with the gold ounce equivalent to 8.59 hyperpyra, the payments made to the Catalans would be: (in 1303) 498,220 hyperpyra according to Muntaner, or 372,665 hyperpyra according to Pachymeres. In 1304, the Catalans probably received 498,220 hyperpyra. The total for the two years was either 996,220 or 870,885 hyperpyra. In their later requests for money, the Catalans never asked for over 300,000 hyperpyra at any one time. We cannot compare this information to Andronicus' revenues in 1303–1304, because these are unknown to us. Given the source of revenue, mostly land taxes, some of which were in theory temporary, his revenues must have varied from year to year. We do know that ca. 1321 Andronicus managed, after determined efforts to improve his finances, to achieve the large annual revenue of 1,000,000 hyperpyra: Gregoras, I, 317. His normal revenues in 1303 may have been lower—they probably were. But here one can only give conjectures, not facts.

109. Pachymeres, II, 209, 262, 290–294, 397.

110. Pachymeres, II, 481, 484, 491–493; Muntaner, chap. ccx. A *jugum* is the area cultivated with one pair of oxen. Ostrogorsky, *La féodalité byzantine*, p. 284; L. Bréhier, *Les institutions de l'Empire byzantin* (Paris, 1929), p. 275; Hopf, *Griechische Geschichte*, p. 384; Dölger, *Regesten*, no. 2271 (November 1304).

tax for the salary of the soldiers stationed there. Since no revenues came from Asia Minor, new taxes had to be imposed on the European provinces. Second, it was necessary to raise money to meet the further demands of the Catalans as well as the needs of the remaining parts of the empire.[111] As yet, the European part of the empire ("Macedonia and the entire West") had not been laid waste by the Catalans. Corn was plentiful here, and relatively expensive because of the influx of refugees from the eastern part, and this is where the *sitokrithon* was most productive.

Apart from introducing this new tax, Andronicus II took other emergency measures at the same time. The salaries of the palace staff were stopped once more, and the emperor demanded one third of the revenue of every pronoia in Thrace and, presumably, Macedonia.[112] He also had recourse to a measure used by his father, Michael VIII, to find money to pay his Italian mercenaries. The Byzantine coinage which had already suffered one devaluation during Andronicus' reign was further devalued, so that only half of the hyperpyron now consisted of gold.[113] According to Muntaner, the situation was even more grave, for Andronicus minted some coins, which he expected to be current at 2.6 times more than their real value. Since these coins were to be used within the empire, those of the emperor's subjects who had trade relations with the Catalans would suffer. Eventually, of course, the imperial treasury, insofar as it still received taxes in cash, would feel the effects of the devaluation. In the spring of 1305, the emperor gave the Catalans six months pay in this new coin.[114] The Catalans accepted it because they planned to spend it all in Thrace and, since they were preparing to leave for Asia Minor, they would escape the wrath of the people to whom they gave it.

The devaluation of the Byzantine coinage had the usual bad financial results. It encouraged hoarding, jeopardized internal trade, and made dealings with other powers depend on foreign currency.[115] Within the context of the Byzantine economy, it meant one more step toward a closed economy based on land. In this particular case, it had other potentially dangerous consequences. Surely Andronicus could not hope to send the Catalans away without giving them a considerable amount of money which would be negotiable in Italy or Spain. Equally, the Catalans would use the devalued currency only for their expenditures in the empire. The fact that they accepted it at all, indicates that they took the "cession" of Asia Minor quite seriously, and that they expected to go and live there.

Between November 1304, and the assassination of Roger de Flor in April 1305, the Catalan Company made a number of further requests for money. Just before his fatal trip to Adrianople, Roger de Flor accepted 33,000 hyper-

---

111. Pachymeres, II, 492–493, 588, 618–620. Pachymeres wrote about the collection of wheat for Asia Minor as contemporary with the first embassy to Olğäitü. This would place it at about the spring of 1305, not as Georgiades-Arnakes thought, 1308: Οἱ πρῶτοι Ὀθωμανοί, pp. 146–147, 151.

112. Pachymeres, II, 493: τῶν κατὰ δύσιν προνοιῶν.

113. Pachymeres, II, 493–494; Zakythinos, *Crise*, pp. 8–10, 18–19.

114. Muntaner, chap. ccx. Cf. Tramontana, "Compagnia Catalana," p. 93.

115. Pachymeres, II, 502; Zakythinos, *Crise*, pp. 25–39, 41–43. Cf. R. S. Lopez, "The Dollar of the Middle Ages," *Journal of Economic History*, 11 (1951), 216–217.

The Cost of Byzantine Policy

pyra and 100,000 modii of wheat, and agreed to leave for Asia Minor with 3,000 men. He even did the emperor the indignity of sending his own men to collect the wheat alongside the imperial officials.[116] But even when properly remunerated, the Catalans took the matter of provisioning into their own hands. While staying in Cyzicus, during their first winter in the empire, they took money and provisions from the inhabitants and held people to ransom. During the Anatolian campaign of 1304, they plundered many of the areas recovered from the Turks. While they were at Gallipoli, they justified their frequent raids in the Thracian countryside with the excuse that they were merely collecting their salary—in kind. After Roger de Flor's death, no large sums of money were given to the Catalans, mainly because the two parties could not agree on how dearly peace could be bought.[117] But between plunder, the sale of Greek slaves, and the salaries they had been paid earlier, the Catalans collected great sums of money. A frugal Catalan in Byzantium could have amassed considerable property during the four years from 1303 to 1307. When Muntaner presented his demands for the restitution of his property taken by the Venetians in July 1307, he estimated the total value of that property at 25,000 gold ounces. That was after he had already given some money to Ferran, the infante of Mallorca.[118]

One of the important results of the Catalan campaign was the virtual disappearance of cash from the imperial treasury. This is confirmed by Andronicus' inability in 1305 to pay the Genoese 6,000 hyperpyra in currency. He was obliged to offer them unminted bullion; when they refused to accept it, he used it to pay for ships and thus eventually paid it to his own subjects. This gold must have come from private sources. All the available evidence (especially the letters of Athanasios I) indicates that the rich men of the empire were more concerned with filling their own purses than with helping the state.[119] On the other hand, Andronicus had already given his own money to the Catalans in November 1304. His son, Michael IX, used his and his wife's gold and silver plate to equip an army against the Bulgarians. It is probable that on this occasion also, in 1305, the emperor used gold belonging to himself or to his immediate family.[120] The two emperors' financial contribution to the defense of the

---

116. Pachymeres, II, 522–523; Gregoras, I, 232, says that at the beginning of 1305 Andronicus offered Roger de Flor Asia Minor, 20,000 hyperpyra, and 300,000 modii of wheat.

117. Pachymeres, II, 399, 413, 428, 435–436, 510–512, 623; Rubió y Lluch, *Diplomatari*, no. 31.

118. Muntaner, chaps. ccxxi, ccxxxi, ccxxxv, ccxxxvii; Rubió y Lluch, *Diplomatari*, no. 31; Rubió y Lluch, *Ferrán*, no. 10, pp. 42–44.

119. Pachymeres, II, 529–533, 542, 544–545, 554. Cod. Vat. Gr. 2219, fols. 39ro–40ro, 44vo: below, Appendix I, letter 4. Cf. Górka, *Descriptio*, pp. 21–23.

120. Pachymeres, II, 447, 492. A contemporary writer advocated this same measure in preference to raising taxes to meet the expenses of the state. Thomas Magister (Theodulos Monachos), Περὶ βασιλείας, Migne, *Patrologia Graeca*, CXLV, col. 481 (hereafter, Thomas Magister, Περὶ βασιλείας). He thought that the personal possessions of the emperor were accumulated out of the surpluses of the state, and therefore were in the form of an investment, to be used for the commonweal when the need arose. But he also thought that such resources should be used to maintain a national Byzantine army (col. 461). Thomas Magister would have disapproved of melting the imperial treasures to pay the Catalans and the Genoese. Later, about 1321, because of the Turkish invasions, Andronicus was forced to sell the imperial jewels. Apparently, although his increased taxes produced an annual revenue of 1,000,000 hyperpyra, this did not suffice to meet the expenses of the state (Gregoras, I, 351, 317–318).

empire was not unique in the history of Byzantium. Yet it shows that the rulers of the empire, like the empire itself, were reduced to their last resources in the fight against the Catalans.

Less than four months later, Andronicus agreed to give two Genoese ships another 6,000 hyperpyra.[121] That payment was probably made in cash. A whole summer had elapsed between the first negotiations (end of May 1305) and the return of the Genoese from Trebizond. Although the peasants near Constantinople fled into the city at the time of the harvest, and the area around Apros was ravaged by the Catalans, we can assume that enough grain was harvested so that the σιτόκριθον could be collected and the imperial coffers replenished.

As soon as it became clear that the Byzantine army was unable to deal with the Catalan threat, the people of Thrace and, later, Macedonia were forced to provide for their own survival. The challenge was immense, and their response varied. The study of the Byzantine efforts to survive yields some interesting information about the social structure of the empire in this period. A large number of feudal military leaders, especially those lately arrived from Anatolia, joined Michael IX's army and distinguished themselves in battle. But most of the aristocracy, particularly the office-holders in Constantinople, behaved discreditably, continuing to exploit the people. In the capital, the patriarch had to wage continuous war against the influence of those who sought to use for their own purposes the troubles generated by the Catalans.

The real struggle for defense and survival took place in the countryside and in the towns outside Constantinople. The problems of the countryside were the most pressing and the most serious for the fate of the empire as a homogeneous state. Asia Minor was devastated before the arrival of the Catalans. By 1303 the whole coast of Anatolia across the Bosphorus was overrun by the Ottomans and deserted by the inhabitants, who fled to the cities and castles. Some came to the islands and to Constantinople. Nicaea and Nicomedia were cut off from the surrounding countryside and the towns suffered from famine and epidemics. The Catalan "liberation" of Asia Minor did not bring security or the repopulation of the area. Particularly during and after the siege of Magnesia by Roger de Flor, Anatolia presented a sad spectacle. Those who could, went west, into Thrace, Constantinople, and the islands; only a few people crowded into the fortified towns.[122] Similar events took place in Gallipoli and Thrace, even before the assassination of Roger de Flor.

With the indifference typical of mercenaries, the Catalans took wheat, money, horses, and killed animals—even the oxen used in the fields (autumn 1304). In late May 1305, they enlarged the circle of their activities to include the islands of the Bosphorus and the area around Perinthus. The local inhabitants, many of them refugees from Anatolia, flocked into Constantinople with whatever they could carry. In the summer of 1305, following Michael IX's defeat at Apros, more peasants came into Constantinople, abandoning the crops they had just harvested. From that time until the summer of 1307

121. Pachymeres, II, 554, 551–552.
122. Ibid., II, 285, 410ff, 441.

Thrace was terrorized by the Catalans; the word "Franks" was enough to cause the flight of the local population. As the situation deteriorated, with Catalans, Alans, and Bulgarians at large in Thrace, the inhabitants of the suburbs of Constantinople also moved into the city.[123] Those remaining outside were exposed to the greatest dangers: loss of property, loss of life, or loss of freedom. The Catalans sold many of their Greek prisoners as slaves, especially in Sicily, but also in Aragon. The first notarial notices of such Greek slaves in Sicily appear in 1307.[124]

As the countryside became deserted, the towns too began to fall to the Catalans. All the towns, wrote Muntaner with some measure of exaggeration, had been pillaged, except for Constantinople, Adrianople, Christopolis, and Thessalonica.[125] As anarchy prevailed in the countryside, brigandage became endemic, as it would become in Macedonia when the Catalans moved there.[126] Thrace lay open to conquest; which explains why Theodore Svetoslav was able to persuade so many towns to capitulate.[127]

The peasants' reaction to the Catalan invasion was, on the whole, defeatist; most of them left their fields and sought refuge in the cities. In general, no local defense took place, as it did in the cities of Thrace and would later in Macedonia, in Mount Athos, and in western Greece. There were a few exceptions. Michael IX had a number of dispossessed peasant-soldiers from Anatolia. On a more popular level, there was the incident of the Bulgarian John Choirovoskos (pigherd), whose exploits in Asia Minor form the second episode (the first being that of pseudo-Lachanas) in the class-struggle which Marxist historians see in late-Byzantine Anatolia.[128]

While Michael IX was still in Asia Minor, John (or Ivan) collected about three hundred men, "ignorant and unwarlike people," and proposed to transport them to Anatolia to fight the Turks. The government became apprehensive, presumably fearing a larger uprising of the population. John was imprisoned for nine months. He then escaped, sought the asylum of the church, and eventually collected various Anatolian refugees and went to Asia Minor. There he had some encounters with the Turks, and in the last he was taken prisoner. He escaped, and traveled to Michael IX's camp in Thrace. At the time, the Catalans were already making trouble in Thrace. With Michael's permission, he collected 1,000 peasants, ostensibly to fight the Catalans'

123. Ibid., II, 482, 484, 529, 552, 590; Muntaner, chap. ccxxi.

124. Tramontana, "Compagnia Catalana," pp. 87–95; Charles Verlinden, *L'esclavage dans l'Europe médiévale*, I: *Péninsule Ibérique-France* (Bruges, 1955), p. 322; M. Gaudioso, *La schiavitù domestica in Sicilia dopo i Normanni* (Catania, 1926), pp. 20–24; Rubió y Lluch, "Mitteilungen zur Geschichte der griechischen Sklaven in Katalonien im XIV Jahrhundert," *BZ* 30 (1930), 462–468. Gaudioso attributes the sudden influx of Greek slaves into Sicily after 1304 to the Catalan raids in Thrace, and claims that after 1308 more Greek than Saracen slaves came into Sicily. Rubió y Lluch mentions a document of Frederick III, which provides for the liberation of Greek slaves after seven years of servitude, and after they have been converted to Roman Christianity (Finke, *Acta Aragonensia*, I, 698). The Catalans continued to sell Greek slaves after their establishment in the Duchy of Athens.

125. Muntaner, chap. ccxxviii.

126. Boissonade, *Anecdota Graeca*, II, 223.

127. Pachymeres, II, 562, 601.

128. E. Francès, "La féodalité byzantine et la conquête turque," esp. p. 71.

Turkish allies. His army quickly degenerated into a company of brigands who terrorized the area around Thessalonica.[129] This incident cannot be interpreted as reasoned defense against the Turks, or the Catalans. Whenever there was a spontaneous rising of peasants, whether led by pseudo-Lachanas or by Ivan, it degenerated before it could offer any real defense. These were the disorganized movements of a hopeless populace; rather than considering them as "nationalist" elements trying to save their country from the Infidel, the peasant "armies" of this period should be viewed as the counterpart of the *pastoureaux* who invaded southern France at approximately the same time.[130]

The inhabitants of the towns, whether local men or refugees, adopted a very different attitude from that of the rural population. It is here that any reasoned and "nationalistic" opposition to the Catalans must be sought. It was certainly much easier to defend a walled city against what often were guerrilla-type attacks. But this was only one of the reasons that enabled the towns of Thrace and Macedonia to provide their own defense. The issues here are very large, and have not yet been adequately studied.[131] Perhaps the most important is the question of town autonomy, which raises the problem of determining the motivation of those who fought to save their towns against the Catalans.

The beginning of the political influence of the towns is, perhaps, as old as the eleventh century;[132] but the rigors of the Catalan wars gave that influence form and expression. There is no evidence that the defense of the towns against the Catalans was undertaken by certain classes of inabitants and not by others. Far from experiencing a class struggle between the feudal landowners resident in the towns and an emerging bourgeoisie, during the critical years the towns seemed to be united against the Latins by the common bond of nationality.[133] It cannot be too strongly emphasized that in 1305–1307 the individual towns of Thrace acted as united bodies, as communities, with a civic responsibility. Nowhere is there anything to suggest that the rich inhabitants took a different course of action from the poorer ones, or the "bourgeoisie."[134] The activity of

129. Pachymeres, II, 442–445.

130. E. Lavisse, *Histoire générale de la France*, III, pt. 2 (by C.-V. Langlois) (Paris, 1901). On the Byzantine peasantry, see also G. Ostrogorsky, *Quelques problèmes de la paysannerie byzantine* (Brussels, 1956), *Corpus Bruxellense Historiae Byzantinae*, Subsidia II; B. T. Gorjanov, "Vizantiiskoe Krest'janstvopri Paleologach," *Viz. Vrem.*, 3 (1950), 19–50; A. P. Každan, *Agrarnye otnošenija v Vizantii XIII-XIV vv.*, (Moscow, 1952); D. Angelov, "Prinos Kŭm Pozemlemte otnošenija vŭv Vizantija prez XIII vek," *Godišnik na Filosof.-Ist. Fak.*, 2 (Sofia, 1952), 1–103; Charanis, "Social Structure," pp. 94–153.

131. On this, see Charanis, "Social Structure"; G. I. Brătianu, *Privilèges et franchises municipales dans l'Empire byzantin*, (Paris and Bucharest, 1936); L. Bréhier, *Les institutions de l'Empire byzantin* p. 214; E. Francès, "La féodalité et les villes byzantines au XIIIe et au XIVe siècle, *Byzantinoslavica*, 16 (1955), 76–96; B. T. Gorjanov, *Pozdnevizantijskij Feodalizm.* (Moscow, 1962), and the review by V. Hrochová, *Byzantinoslavica*, 26 (1965), 140–144.

132. Charanis, "Social Structure," passim.

133. For the interpretation based on the idea of a class struggle, see Francès, "Féodalité et les villes," pp. 87–88, 89.

134. This is implied in the discussion by Francès, "Féodalité et les villes," pp. 87–88, 91. In the same article, the distinction between the activities of the Byzantine and the Western aristocracy is based on an erroneous concept of late medieval feudalism. The parallel should have been drawn between the consuls of the southern French towns and those Byzantine "feudal lords" who resided in the cities and took part in the political activities of the cities.

the towns indicates that they already had a sense of autonomy, later reinforced by formal privileges.[135]

This view is supported by the writings of Thomas Magister, who both described and advocated town autonomy. He presented the city as an entity in itself. All its inhabitants should learn the art of war, so as to be able to defend themselves when the need arose. Then they would not be dependent on the emperor's unreliable soldiers. Meanwhile, all the soldiers must learn a craft, so as to be self-sufficient. True, he said that only property owners should be entrusted with the defense of the city, but this was not the result of a class conscience in the modern sense. He simply thought that only those who could identify with the physical entity of the city and who had property to give as guarantee of their good behavior could be trusted to give their life for the city. Although he did recognize the emperor's authority and responsibility for the whole realm, he tended to speak of the towns as if they were almost autonomous entities.[136]

The only city in which the action of the inhabitants can be studied in detail is Constantinople. But here developments were quite different from those in the cities of Thrace and Macedonia. Several special factors were operating in the capital. The refugee problem, always a disruptive factor, was more acute than anywhere else. The city was an emporium, with a large Italian population whose presence both aggravated the people's rage against all "Italians" and caused problems like provisioning to develop into bitter quarrels. More important, it was the center of government and the seat of the patriarch. Most of the imperial officials lived here, and their lack of public spirit is well attested. A contemporary western observer wrote that the imperial officials, the nobles, and the emperor's family dressed themselves in rich habits, and were much addicted to pomp and luxury.[137] Their greed and selfishness provoked popular reaction, and at Constantinople mob action could influence policy. The existence of a large, angry and hungry population gave the patriarch powers of persuasion which often determined the emperor's actions.

Living conditions in Constantinople were far from pleasant, and not conducive to order. The city was overcrowded, for the refugees from Asia Minor were soon joined by others from Thrace. By all accounts, the Greeks of the capital behaved very badly toward their more unfortunate compatriots who had fled from the Turks. The Catalans found some of these men when they first arrived at Constantinople. They lived "among the rubbish heaps in Constantinople," and went hungry. The Greeks remained unresponsive to their cries for food; the Catalans took pity on them and helped them. For this reason, says Muntaner, when the Catalans left for Asia Minor, they were joined by 2,000 refugees.[138] The figure may be excessive, but the defection

135. The privileges granted to Janina are discussed below, "The Papacy, the Angevins, and Byzantium," in Chapter VIII.

136. Thomas Magister, Περὶ βασιλείας, cols. 464, 477, 484, Περὶ πολιτείας, Migne, *PG*, CXLV, cols. 509, 512–513, 520–521; on Thomas Magister, see Karl Krumbacher, *Handbuch*, pp. 548–549.

137. Górka, *Descriptio*, pp. 21–23.

138. Muntaner, chap. cciii.

probably did take place. Some time later, Greeks from Anatolia crossed over to Europe along with some Turks and joined the Catalan forces.[139]

The letters of Athanasios I confirm Muntaner's information about the treatment of the refugees. The patriarch complained that those who had escaped from the hands of Turks and Catalans were mercilessly denuded of all their goods by their fellow Byzantines. In the winter of 1305–1306 or 1306–1307, he tried to make use of the wealthy people of the city to solve the refugee problem. He asked Andronicus to read to all the δυνάμενοι (powerful) assembled in the palace, an encyclical letter, requesting that each one take into his home for the duration of the winter as many refugees as possible; failing that, the rich citizens should give as much money as they could toward the support of the refugees. Apparently these δυνάμενοι were not very numerous for Athanasios also wrote to each of them separately.[140]

The patriarch Athanasios I emerged as the most important figure in Constantinople during the period of the Catalan threat. He took it upon himself to protect the inhabitants of the city against the imperial officials, against all those who wanted to exploit them, even against themselves. His letters give a priceless first-hand impression of conditions in Constantinople in 1304–1307.[141] Much of his energy during those years was spent in trying to deal with the all-important problem of food. There were rich men in Constantinople who, not unlike the large monasteries, collected great quantities of wheat in their warehouses; this they then sold at very high prices, without considering the harm they were doing to the state.[142] This happened during the early period of the hostilities, while it was still possible to buy wheat in Thrace. At first, the patriarch appealed to the emperor in somewhat vague terms; Andronicus should act, dispense justice, and punish all malefactors. The people he accused of "considering the destruction of the nation as beneficial to them" were imperial officials, for he also said that they defrauded the imperial treasury and enriched themselves out of the taxes they collected. Against these people he fulminated that they "wanted to devour the Lord's people and used bread for this purpose."[143]

Under pressure from the populace, Anthanasios was soon obliged to request specific measures. Sometime in 1304 he threatened to excommunicate all those who made money out of the sale of wheat and wine.[144] The profiteers, he said, were accursed by the people, for they enriched themselves out of the people's disasters and profited no one but themselves. He invited Andronicus to use the

139. Pachymeres, II, 585–586. According to Caro, "Chronologie," this would be in 1305.

140. Cod. Vat. Gr. 2219, fol. 79ro.

141. On Athanasios, see below, Appendix I. There is an anonymous life of Athanasios, published by the Archimandrites Athanasios Pantokratorinos, «Βίος καὶ πολιτεία τοῦ Ἀθανασίου Α΄ οἰκουμενικοῦ Πατριάρχου (1289–1293 καὶ 1304–1310) συγγραφεὶς ὑπὸ Ἰωσὴφ Καλοθέτου μοναχοῦ,» Θρᾳκικά, 13 (1940), 56–107. Hereafter, this edition will be referred to as *Vita*.

142. Pachymeres, II, 461.

143. Cod. Vat. Gr. 2219, fols. 39ro–40ro, 44vo: below, Appendix I, letter 4. All these accusations refer to the imperial officials rather than to the "aristocracy" as a whole. Discontent with such officials was very widespread. See Thomas Magister, in Migne, *PG*, CXLV, cols. 464, 476–477.

144. Pachymeres, II, 461; Cod. Vat. Gr. 2219, fol. 81ro.

power of the state to curtail their activities. Otherwise, the patriarch would use the powers of the church to end this injustice, unthinkable in a Christian society and unacceptable even among pagans.

Both the patriarch and the emperor took some effective steps against the profiteers and toward easing the lot of the city's poor. The patriarch was brought very close to the problem: "when, in the past, we [Athanasios] went through the streets, different paupers asked for different things. But now they are all crying for wheat, asking piteously that it should not be allowed to leave the city. And they make me promise by solemn oaths to speak to your Imperial Majesty about wheat before any other matter."[145] Clearly, the problem was complicated, for not only were prices inflated, but the supply of wheat was becoming very uncertain. Athanasios did appeal to the emperor. He asked that the profiteers either change their ways or be punished. He stressed the point that this was a matter requiring the emperor's interference, and lamented that Byzantium was a state which allowed its rich and powerful men to persecute its poorer subjects. He then asked that no one be allowed to sell wheat without the patriarch's permission; an obvious effort to control the behavior of those who dealt in wheat.[146]

The winter of 1306–1307 was the hardest to endure. The weather was harsh, and the problem of food was worse than ever. For two years the agricultural activities of the peasants of Thrace had been disrupted, so that little wheat had been harvested. Svetoslav had cut off the supply of wheat from the south-western part of the Black Sea coast, and in October Andronicus II had forbidden the peasants to cultivate their fields. The biographer of the patriarch wrote: "Famine had struck Constantinople, famine more terrible than any ever recorded, so that whole families were entirely extinguished. Dead people were lying in piles in the streets. So weakened were men by this famine that those who carried the dead fell themselves into the tombs."[147] In this situation, Athanasios behaved more than ever as the father of the people. He indirectly accused the emperor and the rich men of gorging themselves while the poor were dying of hunger and cold, and then he actively interfered to alleviate the famine. After the battle of Apros, Athanasios had taken away the livings (οἰκονομίαι) of the Constantinopolitan high clergy, despite their protests.[148] Now, in the winter of 1306–1307, he set up "soup kitchens" on various street corners, and probably financed them with the money yielded by the confiscation of those οἰκονομίαι. After a while, his kitchens could no longer operate because he did not have enough fuel. He then appealed to the emperor to

145. Cod. Vat. Gr. 2219, fols. 53ro–vo: below, Appendix I, letter 7.

146. Cod. Vat. Gr. 2219, fols. 53vo–54vo, 54vo: below, Appendix I, letters 8, 10.

147. *Vita*, §105, p. 101. I place these developments and Athanasios' measures in the winter of 1306–1307, because this was the hardest winter Constantinople saw during the course of Athanasios' Patriarchate. All the internal evidence I can find in his letters supports my dating. See Laiou, "Provisioning," pp. 101, 106–107.

148. Pachymeres, II, 559–561. In 1307 the high clergy of Constantinople appealed to Andronicus, asking him to persuade the patriarch to give them some money in place of the benefices he had confiscated. Athanasios refused, "indicating that times were hard," and finally he decided to give them six or eight hyperpyra per year! The sum was rightly considered to be ridiculously small, and the conflict continued: Pachymeres, II, 642–650.

allow him to collect wood, "not as much as we need, but as much as the lords will consider proper."[149]

The patriarch's letter implied more than it actually said. Athanasios deplored his own lack of sympathy and his reluctance to give the poor even the crumbs from his table, "all the while reading the Bible." He may, in his humility, have thought that he was not doing enough for the poor; but by extension he was castigating the wealthy men of Constantinople who were far more guilty than he of indifference. When Athanasios wrote that the patriarch and the emperor had a duty to help the indigent, he was including Andronicus among those who did not do all they could to ease the crisis. The manner of his request shows how little he thought he could depend on Andronicus. The real malefactors were the δεσπόται, the ἄρχοντες, the lords. But Andronicus seemed to be under their influence.

To the same period must be attributed the letters in which Athanasios attacked the Italians who dealt in food-stuffs, and urged the emperor to bring the sale of wheat under his own control. The uncontrolled wheat trade, among other evils, brought about the transfer of Byzantine gold from the Greeks to the Italians. These Italians—presumably Genoese from Pera—were dealing in wheat, probably imported from the Black Sea, which they sold in exchange for gold or even for the wives of the Greeks of Constantinople.[150]

The old system of imperial control which regulated by a guild system the wheat trade and the baking of bread had lapsed long before. The wheat that came into Constantinople was kept in warehouses until the price rose; then it was sold to the bakers or even exported from the city. If the bakers were still organized in corporations, these must have been very loose and outside the control of the government. In times of crisis there was a seller's market for grain, and prices were very high.[151] In order to remedy the situation, Athanasios took upon himself one of the main functions of the old prefect of the city, the control of provisioning.[152] He insisted that the prices of bread and wheat be subjected to imperial control. For the office of controller of sales, Athanasios suggested Sebastos Dermokaites, "one of the most pious of men." His job would be to find out exactly what ships brought what quantities of wheat into Constantinople. He should also find out how many bakers there were in Constantinople, where and how they bought their wheat; the object of this probably was to discover any hidden sources of supply. Then, Dermokaites would make sure that the wheat brought into the city from the Black Sea (it came by ship) did not disappear into the hands of the hoarders of wheat or the profiteers; instead, it should be distributed to those bakers who needed it. Finally, he and his assistants would check the various weights and measures used in Constan-

149. Cod. Vat. Gr. 2219, fols. 57ro–58vo; see Laiou, "Provisioning," letter 2.
150. Cod. Vat. Gr. 2219, fols. 75ro–vo: below, Appendix I, letter 9.
151. Pachymeres, II, 493.
152. J. and P. Zepos, *Jus Graecoromanum*, II (Athens, 1934), 371–392. Michael VII Parapinakes and the logothete Nikephoritzes had tried to reestablish an imperial grain monopoly in the late eleventh century. However, their efforts must not be seen in the same light as those of Athanasios, for they aimed at increasing imperial revenue, and Athanasios at lowering the consumer price of bread.

tinople. All this was dictated in detail by Athanasios. Sebastos Dermokaites was duly appointed, and given two assistants, whom Athanasios chose. When all these steps had been taken, Athanasios implored the emperor to order these men to work conscientiously, and he hoped that Constantinople would be saved as a result.[153]

Surrounded by the Catalans and in danger of being conquered, Constantinople was also troubled by social tensions. The inhabitants of Constantinople and those of the countryside did not share a common purpose. The city dwellers did not welcome the refugees—most of them peasants—in spite of the common ties of language and religion. Some peasants, on the other hand, joined the enemies of the empire, Catalan or Turk, in the depredation of the countryside and the pillage of cities. The lack of sympathy between country and town, which those fleeing Constantinople after the Latin conquest experienced (1204), appears here in a much more advanced degree. In addition, the people were gradually alienated from their rulers. In Asia Minor the people hated and despised the rulers in Constantinople who did not defend Anatolia against the Turks. The inhabitants of Constantinople hated those who were able to make money out of the common sufferings. They disagreed with Andronicus' foreign policy and voiced their sentiments loudly. In fact, the only person able to calm them on both issues was the patriarch. He took their side and was able to achieve some concessions from the emperor. The patriarch's carrying out of duties which properly belonged to the civil authority is another facet of the process which led to the decentralization and eventually to the communalization of the empire.

The greatest internal challenge to the authority of Andronicus in Constantinople came during the cold and miserable winter of 1305–1306. A certain John Drimys, who had "come from the West" hoping to become a priest, rose in revolt. Trying to capitalize on the pro-Lascarid, anti-Palaeologan feeling which still existed, he pretended to be a descendant of the deposed Lascarids.[154] It seems that even before the rebellion, Andronicus feared lest the Arsenite and the pro-Lascarid factions should take advantage of the problems created by the Catalans. Motivated by this fear, he made a determined if unsuccessful attempt to come to terms with John Tarchaneiotes and the other Arsenite leaders (September 1304). When he saw that they were intransigent, he ordered them to at least abstain from inflaming the passions of the people.[155]

John Drimys was supported by the Arsenite faction, who launched attacks on the church and the patriarch. Athanasios I answered with a letter of his own, in which he excommunicated the rebels. The other supporters of Drimys, who appear to have come from the lowest socioeconomic strata, were even more dangerous. They, and Drimys, tried to obtain the support of the Jews of Constantinople, the Catalans, and the Bulgarians. Two military men, operating in conjunction with Drimys, also wrote to the Catalans, inciting them to battle.

---

153. Cod. Vat. Gr. 2219, fols. 78vo, 75ro–vo: below, Appendix I, letter 9.
154. Pachymeres, II, 592–593; Migne, *PG*, CXLII (1885), 484–492: letter of Athanasios on Drimys' rebellion.
155. Pachymeres, II, 461–480.

The rebels were soon discovered and imprisoned, and the rebellion failed. The incarcerated Arsenite leaders were then transported outside the city, where, it was hoped, they could create less trouble.[156] The fact that he was not secure even in his own capital must have contributed to Andronicus' half-hearted defense against the Catalans, and to his willingness to depend on the help of outsiders, namely the Genoese.

At the time of the Catalan crisis, Athanasios I was one of Andronicus' principal advisers and, according to all the sources, the man who had the most moral influence on Andronicus. It is instructive to look at the long correspondence of the second term of his patriarcate. It contains a strange brew of mystical and practical advice, so well conforming to the religiosity and superstition of Andronicus. The patriarch ascribed all the evils which had befallen the Romania to Andronicus II's, or Michael VIII's, or the people's neglect of God and the true faith. The lack of justice and order in the empire had also contributed to its downfall. His remedies for the situation included prayers and litanies, which the people considered effective.[157] Fortunately, he also had some very practical suggestions about organizing the defense and the provisioning of the city. He advised Andronicus, for example, to speak to the people sweetly and pleasantly. The emperor should take particular care of the army, and make sure that the soldiers had enough food so that they would not live off the people. Apparently, the patriarch subscribed to the view that a peaceful emperor should be very good at making war, in order to achieve peace.[158] He advised Andronicus to make frequent visits to the city walls and gates, without regard for his own safety. Presumably, the purpose of this exercise would be to make certain that the walls were adequately manned, and to give a good example to the soldiers.

For the safety of Constantinople, Athanasios advised Andronicus to forbid the entry into the city of anyone carrying arms; this was to apply more severely to the Italians. He wrote at length and repeatedly against the court officials who "love presents, seek compensation and do not judge fairly the cases of orphans."[159] Indeed, he urged Andronicus to tell his officials at the time of their appointment and before witnesses, to mind their ways because the patriarch would examine their actions to ensure that the emperor's orders were being carried out. In another letter, Athanasios told the emperor to remove from the city and from the empire those who indulged in luxury, cultivated injustice and disobeyed the laws.[160]

The patriarch advocated that Byzantium should stand on its own feet, should reform its ways, and try to restore itself to its former glory. Help from Europe was not only unnecessary but potentially harmful. Soon after his

---

156. Ibid., II, 593; Migne, *PG*, CXLII, 484–492. It is not quite clear what help Drimys could expect from the Jews. Perhaps Athanasios was carried away by his dislike of the Jews in giving us this information.

157. Cod. Vat. Gr. 2219, fols. 9vo–10vo, 17ro–vo: below, Appendix I, letters 3, 6; Pachymeres, II, 614, 627–628, 631.

158. Cod. Vat. Gr. 2219, fol. 9vo: below, Appendix I, letter 6. Cf. Thomas Magister, Περὶ βασιλείας, *PG*, CXLV, cols. 457–460.

159. Cod. Vat. Gr. 2219, fols. 10ro–vo; Pachymeres, II, 559–561.

160. Cod. Vat. Gr. 2219, fols. 10ro–11ro.

return to the patriarchate in June 1305, he wrote: "I say again, before God, that even if it were possible for the entire West to assemble to our aid" (we would not achieve anything). The only way to salvation was through repentence and justice.[161] "For this reason I have proposed that someone be sent to the East, even though I was not heard; and again I ask, and I kiss the prints of your feet." He ascribed the decline and loss of Anatolia to the reluctance of the high clergy of that area to remain in their sees. In a symbolic sense, this was true, for Asia Minor had fallen from neglect as much as anything else. And Athanasios never tired of asking the emperor to send all the bishops and archbishops to their proper areas, instead of letting them stay in Constantinople and create "scandal."[162]

Athanasios I was not popular with the higher clergy or with the highly placed laity of Constantinople. But seen with the advantages of hindsight, he must be placed first in the long line of late-Byzantine patriarchs who were strong-minded, strong-willed, interested in the welfare of the people, and who eventually, in the fifteenth century, supplanted the Palaeologan fainéant emperors in the essential functions of government, particularly justice.

Athanasios reflected as well as aided the transformation of the Byzantine state from a European to a Balkan one. He consistently opposed any appeal to the West for help. He pleaded with the emperor to divorce himself and his state from the barbaric, schismatic, and arrogant "Italians." Byzantium would be saved by its orthodoxy, in God's good time. Meanwhile, it subjects should reform their moral and religious practices, so as to deserve the divine salvation which was sure to come. It is interesting that Athanasios' program of internal reform agreed with Michael IX's aims and policies rather than with those of Andronicus II.

Although Andronicus repudiated his father's religious policy, and shifted the focus of his interest from the West to the East, he remained the heir of that most able of thirteenth-century diplomats to this extent: throughout the years of the Catalan campaign, he did persevere in his efforts, however indelicate and finally unsuccessful, to solve his many problems through diplomacy.

161. Cod. Vat. Gr. 2219, fols. 17ro–vo: Below, Appendix I, letter 3.
162. Cod. Vat. Gr. 2219, fols. 8vo–9vo, 12vo, 13vo–14ro, 32ro–33ro, 41ro–42vo, 47ro–50vo.

VII

The Catalans, Charles of Valois, and Byzantium, 1302–1313

While the Catalans were occupied in the East, important developments were taking place in Europe. Charles of Valois, brother of Philip IV of France and husband of Catherine of Courtenay, decided to reclaim his wife's empire. On paper his plans were impressive, for he contracted alliances with all the European states which might help him. In reality, the success of his efforts depended on the support of his brother, the king of France, who at this point was too poor and too preoccupied with other affairs to seriously consider an expedition to Byzantium. Philip IV did give Charles assurances of his support and a little money, but he could do no more. Thus, it was unlikely during this period that a large French force, led by Charles of Valois, should appear before Constantinople. On the other hand, the state of the Byzantine empire was such that a small army would have sufficed to conquer, if not to hold it. Although in retrospect the plans of Charles of Valois appear futile, at the time there was a possibility that he might succeed, especially so since he managed to ally himself with the Catalans and with discontented elements within the Byzantine empire. The Byzantine response to these threats was, for the most part, passive; there were, however, some interesting diplomatic developments.

The Plans of Charles of Valois

Charles of Valois had taken a first step toward the fulfillment of his eastern ambitions by acting as a mediator in the Italian wars. But even after the conclusion of the peace of Caltabelotta, he could not consider leaving for Constantinople for a long time. He was one of the most important peers of France, and he could not, would not and was not allowed to leave the French kingdom in times of crisis. Several important affairs kept him in France. The French war with Flanders was at a critical point. The battle of Courtrai (July 11, 1302), a major disaster for the French, was followed by two campaigns in 1303 and 1304. Peace was temporarily restored by the treaty of Athis-sur-Orge, in July 1305.[1] Not only was France unable to sustain a crusade while the war with Flanders was going on, but the great conflict between Philip IV and

---

1. Lavisse and Langlois, *Histoire de France*, III, pt. 2, pp. 302–305; Henri Pirenne, *Histoire de Belgique*, II (Brussels, 1947). A number of books have been written on various aspects of the western attempts to retake Constantinople. Dade, *Versuche*, the most important of these works, says nothing of Byzantine policy. Joseph Petit, *Charles de Valois*, 1270–1325 (Paris, 1900) is valuable but includes too many faulty references and dates. Ch. DuFresne du Cange, *Histoire de Constantinople sous les Empereurs françois* (Paris, 1657), is too old an account, but valuable because it is based in part on some lost documents. This and the edition by Buchon (Paris, 1826) includes the texts of some important documents. General works on crusading projects, such as Joseph Delaville le Roulx, *La France en Orient au XIVe siècle* (2 vols.; Paris, 1886), and A. S. Atiya, *The*

Boniface VIII erupted in the year 1302. In November 1302, Boniface VIII published the bull *Unam sanctam,* asserting the supremacy of the papacy and precipitating the final crisis. Philip IV produced forged papal letters (dated December 5, 1302) in order to arouse the national feelings of the French clergy and people. In March and June 1303, in two assemblies of the French prelates and nobles in Paris, Philip IV and his officials, Guillaume de Nogaret and Guillaume de Plaisians, denounced the pope. The "outrage of Anagni" followed, and after a short while the death of Boniface VIII.[2]

Charles of Valois had to return from Italy to France for these affairs. But he continued his efforts to create a situation conducive to the realization of his eastern ambitions. He tried once again to act as a mediator, this time between Philip IV and Boniface VIII. At the same time, he prepared the ground for his expedition, by negotiating with men who might be willing and able to help him. He and the king of Naples confirmed and renewed the anti-Byzantine treaty of Viterbo, on March 11, 1302, and since 1301 the Venetians had been holding discussions with Charles, discussions whose content is unknown but which may have had something to do with the conquest of Constantinople.[3]

Charles then tried to get the support of the duke of Burgundy, a strong French prince who also had some rights in the Byzantine empire. In 1266 Baldwin II of Constantinople had conferred on Duke Hugues IV the Kingdom of Thessalonica—although the marquis of Montferrat still kept his own titles to it. In 1303 Duke Robert II of Burgundy once more became interested in his "kingdom."[4] His son Hugues swore allegiance to the titular empress of Constantinople, Catherine of Courtenary, thus reviving the pretensions of his house to Thessalonica. On March 24, 1303 he was affianced to Catherine of Valois, the daughter and heiress of Count Charles and Catherine of Courtenay. The young man promised to recover his "kingdom," and this was considered a necessary condition of the projected marriage. Catherine of Courtenay and Charles of Valois confirmed Hugues in the possession of the Kingdom of Thessalonica in January 1305.[5] This confirmation and the Valois marriage were very important to the House of Burgundy, so long as there was any chance that Charles might really recover Constantinople; in that case, Hugues, as the husband of Catherine of Valois, might eventually become emperor. As for Charles of Valois, he needed the support of Burgundy, for money and for soldiers. In 1303 Charles also approached the duke of Athens, Gui II de la Roche, and

Crusade in the Later Middle Ages (London, 1938), are important but do not treat this period in great detail. Other books and articles of varying importance and relevance will be mentioned in context.

2. Lavisse and Langlois, *Histoire de France*, III, pt. 2, pp. 153–166; *Cambridge Medieval History*, VII, 305–339.

3. Lavisse and Langlois, *Histoire de France*, III, pt. 2, p. 115; Petit, *Charles de Valois*, p. 89; A. N. J509 nos. 12, 15; J512, no. 21. Charles was in Paris in 1303, for the affairs regarding Boniface VIII.

4. Dom Plancher, *Histoire générale et particulière de Bourgogne* (Dijon, 1741), II, 33.

5. A. N. J510, nos. 19, 20; Petit, *Charles de Valois*, pp. 90–91; Jean de Saint Victor, in *Recueil des historiens des Gaules et de la France*, XXI (Paris, 1855), 645; Plancher, *Bourgogne*, II, 109; Du Cange, *Histoire de Constantinople*, *Chartes*, pp. 45, 49; Du Cange and Buchon, *Histoire de Constantinople*, II, 336–341.

letters were exchanged between the two with regard to the expedition against Constantinople.[6]

In order to proceed with his plans of conquest, Charles of Valois, like Charles of Anjou before him, found that the help of the papacy was absolutely necessary. If his enterprise were declared a crusade, he would not only obtain money from crusading subsidies, but his followers would receive all the privileges and indulgences attached to a crusade, and thus would be more eager to go with him. Finally, any other would-be conqueror of Constantinople would find it hard to compete with or openly oppose a holy enterprise.

From the time of Innocent III the papacy had been willing to treat the conquest of Constantinople on the same basis as a crusade. The Greeks were heretics and schismatics, and the conquest of the empire, which would heal the schism, was thus a desirable enterprise. Some people also thought that the conquest of Constantinople would facilitate the recovery of Jerusalem. On the whole, then, papal policy was more favorable than not to an expedition against Constantinople. After the capture of Acre by the Egyptians in 1291, the zeal of western Europeans for the liberation of the Holy Lands revived, and crusading projects were endlessly discussed from the 1290's until the 1330's.[7] To the popes who took part in such discussions the recovery of Jerusalem was the primary aim of a crusading expedition. The return of Byzantium to communion with Rome was a secondary objective, and an armed conquest of Byzantium was a peripheral enterprise. Thus, there was a difference in purpose between the popes and the westerners who wanted to conquer the Byzantine empire, and for this reason long negotiations with the papacy were necessary. For this reason also, men like Charles of Valois or his son-in-law Philip of Taranto, eventually found that in order to receive papal help they had to link their specific Byzantine plans to more general French crusading plans.

Papal policy, as Charles of Anjou had found out, could not be taken for granted. The papacy was a great European power, and the Roman pontiffs operated in a complex world, with many varied political factors. While Boniface VIII was alive, his quarrel with the king of France made it unlikely that he would support fully Charles of Valois' plans. After Boniface's death, Charles requested the aid of the new pope, Benedict XI.[8] Originally, Benedict XI refused to order the collection of a tithe for the expedition of Charles of Valois, unless this campaign were to form part of a general crusade. This attitude was, by now, traditional. At the same time, he wrote, as other popes

---

6. H. Moranvillé, "Les projets de Charles de Valois sur l'Empire de Constantinople," *BEC.*, 51 (1890), 78: gift of Charles of Valois to Richard, messenger of the duke of Athens (hereafter, this work will be referred to as Moranvillé, "Projets").

7. Delaville le Roulx, *France en Orient*, passim; Atiya, *The Crusade in the Later Middle Ages* passim.

8. Moranvillé, "Projets," p. 70; Charles Grandjean, *Les Registres de Benoît XI* (Paris, 1905), no. 1008, June 27, 1304 (hereafter, Grandjean, *Registres*). Benedict XI has received Charles's envoys, Guillaume de Perche and Pierre de Herbouville, who came to the pope to ask him to allow men who had sworn to go on a crusade to fulfill their obligations by following Charles to Constantinople.

had done during Michael VIII's reign, on the difficult position of the Byzantine empire, which could not oppose the Turks for long. It was, he felt, the duty of good Christians to bring the schismatics back to the Catholic church, and at the same time prevent the conquest of a large and ancient part of Christendom by the Turks.[9] Later, he agreed to grant those who would join Charles of Valois all the usual crusading privileges and indulgences.[10] On June 27, 1304, he granted Charles of Valois a tithe to help his enterprise; that was to be paid to Charles of Valois, unless a general crusade preceded his trip to Constantinople.[11]

Insofar as the success of Charles of Valois' plans depended on the attitude of the pope, his reconquest of Constantinople became more likely after the election to the papal throne of Clement V in January 1305. Here was a French pope, well disposed toward the French royal house and eager to restore good relations with Philip IV and his family. Peace and cooperation replaced once again the uncomfortable hostility between the papacy and France.[12] Charles of Valois was present at Clement's elevation to the papal throne on November 14, 1305, in Lyons. During the next two years he prepared his expedition, which now finally seemed possible. Clement V did desire the reconquest of Constantinople, and attributed great importance to this enterprise within the context of a general crusade.

On January 14, 1306, the new pope wrote a letter to the bishop of Senlis, in which he urged Catholic bishops to support the plans of Charles of Valois to recover his wife's empire. Concerned with the spread of the true faith, Clement deplored the fact that the Byzantine church had been separated from the Christian community "by one Michael Palaeologus and after his death by his son Andronicus and their schismatic fellow-conspirators and supporters." This "noble empire" should be reunited to the rest of Christendom and Charles of Valois, as eager to serve the Apostolic See as he was to recover his wife's patrimony, was the person most likely to succeed in this holy enterprise. All good Christians should support him. The matter was all the more urgent since the empire was in grave danger of being conquered by "Turks and other Saracens and infidels" from whose hands it would be very difficult to recover.[13] Thus, Clement V used Andronicus' repudiation of the church union and the failure of his policy in Asia Minor to justify western plans to take Constantinople.

Finally, Clement V linked the reconquest of Constantinople to the liberation of Jerusalem, but the connection was almost an afterthought: "Desiring that

9. Grandjean, *Registres*, no. 1006 (May 1304).

10. Ibid., no. 1007 (June 20). In this letter, Benedict urged the faithful to help Charles of Valois, promising the same indulgences as for a crusade.

11. Ibid., no. 1008 (June 27, 1304): Benedict writes to Charles of Valois, granting him the commutation of the crusading oaths. Cf. August Potthast, *Regesta Pont. Rom.*, II, no. 25445; Raynaldus, *Annales Eccl.*, 1304; Dade, *Versuche*, pp. 78–79. Dade discusses Charles's negotiations after 1305 (pp. 112ff).

12. Lavisse and Langlois, *Histoire de France*, III, pt. 2, pp. 171–173.

13. *Regestum Clementis Papae V* (Rome, 1885–1888), no. 243 (hereafter, this work will be abbreviated as *Reg. Clem. V.*).

this enterprise, which concerns not a little both the Apostolic See and all faithful Christians . . . , be successful, and expecting that its happy consummation could prove helpful to the affair of the [liberation of the] Holy Land . . ." In theoretical terms, then, Clement V had justified Charles of Valois' projected expedition. In practical terms, he granted Charles a crusading subsidy, which in France would be collected for the next two years by the bishop of Senlis;[14] in the Kingdom of Sicily, the tithe was to be collected for three years. Clement V also recommended that Charles request the help of the naval cities of Venice and Genoa, and demanded that the "emperor's" future subjects return to the Roman faith.[15]

After the pope had proclaimed the projected expedition of Charles of Valois a crusade, Charles was in need of suitable allies and of a favorable opportunity. His brother, the king of France, was in favor of the enterprise, if and when he did not need Charles in France. James of Aragon and Frederick of Sicily were far from eager to help, although they paid lip service to the idea of the reconquest of the Byzantine empire by its rightful owner. Charles II of Naples continued to be favorable to the Valois crusade. In 1306 Philip IV of France confirmed the treaty of 1302 between Charles II and Charles of Valois. Philip IV also confirmed the treaty of Viterbo (1267).[16] Clearly, Philip IV and Charles of Valois were counting on the support of the Angevins of Naples. Although this support was precious, Charles of Valois was more immediately concerned with the problem of transport, for which he needed the help of the naval cities of Italy.

Both Clement V and Charles of Valois tried to win the cooperation of Venice and Genoa. On January 14, 1306, Clement wrote to the doge and commune of Venice, urging them to help Charles, and offering them the privileges of crusaders, should they participate in this enterprise.[17] He sent a similar letter to the abbate del popolo and the commune of Genoa, advising them that the time had come to bring the Greeks back to the true faith.[18] In his letters, the

---

14. Ibid. This was a continuation of the tithe granted by Benedict XI. Clement V also granted Philip IV the tenth of the revenues of ecclesiastical benefices in France, for the needs of the kingdom. Since it was not possible to collect both these taxes at once, Charles's two-year tithe was prorogued. Then Charles of Valois asked his brother to allow him to collect his tithes first, in priority for the affair of the crusade (1307). Philip agreed; Charles promised to remain under his brother's command, and Clement ordered another year's collection to be given to Philip: *Reg. Clem. V*, no. 1757 (June 3, 1307); Cod. Par. Fr. 2838 fols. 42vo–43ro. The French document is an act of Charles of Valois, dated 1308 and confirming Philip's grant. In 1307 Philip IV lent Charles 30,000 livres tournois, with the tithe as guarantee: Petit, *Charles de Valois*, p. 109, n. 7. Charles obtained further funds for the crusade from Philip IV and Philip V; he also received loans from popes, but there is no evidence that he collected the tithe for Constantinople: Petit, *Charles de Valois*, pp. 323–325.

15. *Reg. Clem. V.*, nos. 243, 244; Dade, *Versuche*, p. 112.

16. A. N. J509 no. 12; J512, no. 21. Both are *vidimus* of Philip IV, made at the request of Philip of Taranto, Charles of Valois, and Catherine of Courtenay (1313; so these letters were confirmed twice, in 1306 and 1313); A. N. J509, no. 15 (a *vidimus* of Philip IV, 1306, of the treaty of Viterbo); Geanakoplos, *Michael Palaeologus*.

17. *Reg. Clem. V.*, no. 248; Thomas and Predelli, *Diplomatarium*, I, no. 21; A. N. J509, no. 16bis; Dade, *Versuche*, p. 114.

18. A. N. J509, no. 16 (*vidimus* of Philip IV, December 13, 1313, confirming his own confirmation (1306) of the Pope's letter). This letter has not been published in Clement's Registers, although it presents some interest.

pope emphasized the schismatic nature of the Greek church and the need to force the Byzantines to return to obedience to the Catholic church.

In his letter to the Genoese, Clement V discussed at some length the Turkish danger to the Byzantine empire, and made of this the primary justification of Charles of Valois' plans. It is striking that he insisted on impressing upon the Genoese the Turkish threat, while his letter to the Republic of Venice simply mentioned this argument.[19] This difference can be explained by the special position of the Genoese in the Byzantine empire. At that time, Genoa had vested interests in Byzantium, was the only state helping Andronicus II against the Catalans, and had most to lose from the reestablishment of a Latin empire. Venice's hostility to the Byzantine emperor was, on the other hand, well known. Therefore, the pope very intelligently insisted on the one thing the Genoese feared above all, the possible Turkish domination of the East.

Clement V had every reason to be uncertain of Genoa's response to his appeal. On the other hand, Genoa could become an invaluable ally to a potential conqueror of the Byzantine empire. Not only did she have ships to transport the crusaders, but her established position in the Levant made her cooperation more desirable than that of Venice, the other great Italian sea power. For this reason, Charles of Valois appealed to Genoa for assistance before writing to Venice.[20] Among other things, his emissaries to Genoa (who were accompanied by the embassadors of Clement V and Philip IV), wanted to know how many ships were necessary for the conquest of the empire, and whether Genoa was prepared the allow Charles to hire these ships. In return, Charles would give the Genoese "every liberty" in the empire, "and everything which will seem best for the commune." The Genoese debated Charles's request, and finally refused it, sometime between October and December 1306.[21]

Genoa had, by this time, closely identified her interests with those of the empire. In order to defend both, she had been willing to risk the hostility of the Catalans, James II of Aragon, and Frederick III of Sicily. It was inevitable, therefore, that she should be unwilling to support Charles of Valois in a scheme which aimed at the destruction of that empire. Apparently, only some Genoese Guelphs, opposed to the communal government, were eager to cooperate with the anti-Byzantine forces. The other Genoese adopted the same position they took with the Catalans; the Catalans in the empire, they said, "are allied with the infidel Turks, the enemies of the Christian faith, and they are also hostile to Genoa and the Genoese in the Romania."[22] Genoa felt

19. Clement V, however, insisted on the Turkish danger in his letter to the archbishop and bishops of Venice on March 10, 1307: Thomas and Predelli, *Diplomatarium*, I, no. 28.

20. January 1, 1306: Moranvillé, "Projets," pp. 72, 78; Finke, *Acta Aragonensia*, III, no. 69, James II had sent an ambassador to Genoa to request help against Sardinia. The ambassador reported that Thibaut de Chepoy had come secretly to ask Genoa's help in Charles's expedition in the Romania. Cf. Finke, *Acta Aragonensia*, II, no. 431, p. 687; J. Petit, "Un capitaine du règne de Philippe le Bel, Thibaut de Chepoy," *Moyen Age*, 2d ser., II (1891), 237–239.

21. Finke, *Acta Aragonensia*, II, 687; Rubió y Lluch, *Diplomatari*, no. 31. This is a letter to James II from Christiano Spinola who was James's friend and informer (October 19, 1306). The Genoese had not yet reached a decision when this letter was written, but Spinola thought that Genoa would finally decline Charles' offers. Cf. Caro, *Genua*, II, 379.

22. Rubió y Lluch, *Diplomatari*, no. 19 (James' answers to the Genoese ambassadors, October 21, 1305).

compelled to defend the empire against the Catalans, and did not want to participate in Charles of Valois' enterprise, which was certain to have the support of Venice, was said (wrongly) to have the support of James II and Frederick III, and whose avowed aim was to destroy the Byzantine empire and with it Genoa's position in the East.

Before waiting for the answer of the Genoese, Charles of Valois began negotiations with Venice on January 28, 1306.[23] Venice, of course, was much more eager than Genoa to cooperate. Despite the Venetian–Byzantine truce of 1302, and despite the fact that Andronicus II was involved with the Catalans and so could present no danger to Venice, things were far from calm in the Romania. Apparently, hostilities in Nigroponte continued, probably carried out on the Byzantine side by local Greeks, but without the active involvement of Constantinople. In March 1305, the bailo of Nigroponte reported his fears of increased Byzantine aggression, and later, in June 1307, the bailo was allowed to contract a loan of 4,000 hyperpyra in order to fortify the city of Chalkis.[24] All of this, along with the generally hostile attitude of Venice toward the Palaeologi, made the Venetian government responsive to the advances of Charles of Valois.

Some sort of alliance was concluded on June 22, 1306. It was probably not a definitive arrangement, for on July 28, Charles of Valois sent from Paris to Venice Thibaut de Chepoy, Pierre le Riche, and Pierre de Herbouville, a knight, to discuss with the Venetians the matter of the expedition to Constantinople.[25] A treaty was signed between the doge Pietro Gradenigo and the French plenipotentiaries on December 19, 1306.[26] On June 3, 1307, Clement V excommunicated Andronicus II and warned any Catholic powers allied to him that they would share the excommunication and forfeit their property to the church. The excommunication would not be raised until Andronicus II had returned to the Catholic church and sought absolution.[27]

The treaty between Venice and Charles of Valois confirmed with a few modifications the treaty of 1281 between Venice and Charles of Anjou. The number of ships and cavalry, which had been specified in 1281, could be reduced if both parties agreed. Charles of Valois could ask Venice for all the ships he needed to transport his soldiers, so long as he did so before the following Easter. Venice promised to rent the ships at current prices.[28] The expedition was to leave from Brindisi between March 1307, and March 1308. Meanwhile, the allies would send a joint force of ten galleys, with a Venetian captain, to attack the imperial lands and waters. Anyone who tried to prevent or oppose

---

23. A. N. J509, no. 15; Romanin, *Storia di Venezia*, III, 8–10; Moranvillé, "Projets," p. 72; Thomas and Predelli, *Diplomatarium*, II, no. 27.

24. Thiriet, *Délibérations*, pp. 108–109, no. 109; p. 113, no. 132.

25. Moranvillé, "Projets," p. 72. On Thibaut de Chepoy, see Petit, "Un capitaine."

26. Thomas and Predelli, *Diplomatarium*, I, no. 27; Romanin, *Storia di Venezia*, III, 8–10.

27. Thomas and Predelli, *Diplomatarium*, I, nos. 33, 34; Raynaldus, *Annales Eccl.*, 1307, §7; *Reg. Clem. V.*, no. 1759; Moranvillé, "Projets," p. 77.

28. Tafel and Thomas, *Urkunden*, III, 287ff. Venice did build some ships for Charles of Valois, as she had promised: Louis de Mas-Latrie, *Commerce et expéditions de la France et de Venise au moyen-âge* (Paris, 1880), pp. 73–78.

the "crusade" would be treated as an enemy; presumably, this article referred to Genoa. Philip IV of France was also drawn into the negotiations: Charles promised to try to persuade the king to treat as enemies all those hostile to the expedition. This again was a reference to Genoa and, possibly, to Aragon.

A few difficulties arose shortly after the treaty had been signed. In the spring of 1307, Venice sent an embassy to Charles of Valois, complaining about the delay of the expedition and asking him to reconfirm the treaty of 1306. Charles was forced to equivocate: he wrote that neither he, a vassal and a peer of Philip IV, nor any French noble or baron could leave the French kingdom while there was danger of war. These reservations notwithstanding, he asserted that he was keeping the treaty of 1306, and expected Venice to do the same.[29] On May 27, 1307, Philip IV, at the instance of Charles of Valois, exempted the Venetians from the royal taxes levied on all foreign merchants who engaged in trade in France.[30] This was probably a bribe, to keep Venice happy—also, there were not many Venetian merchants in France. Similarly, a question arose about the relative expenses of each party. Charles of Valois was having problems, since he could not yet levy his crusading tithe in France: Philip IV was collecting that for his own purposes, for two years, and Charles's interests would have to wait. Perhaps for this reason he complained to Venice that the sum he had agreed to pay for the transport of his men was excessive. In their reply, on June 28, 1307, the Venetians said that "the campaign that Charles of Valois will lead will cause great damage to Venetian possessions in the Romania, and this obliges Venice to arm her own men, since Charles's forces are not sufficient." If all that were taken into account, Venice said, the sum demanded for transport was far from excessive.[31]

The treaty between Venice and Charles of Valois caused great offense to Genoa. The Genoese probably had expected such an alliance. But it seems that they misinterpreted one of its articles, which stated that ten ships, maintained jointly by Venice and Charles of Valois, would be sent to the Romania before and during the actual attack, "in order to guard the seas and the land, and to molest their common enemies in the empire."[32] This article reminds one of the idea, prevalent in contemporary crusading propaganda, that a large crusade should be preceded by a limited naval enterprise ("passagium particulare"), whose aim would be to molest enemy shipping. The Genoese, perhaps rightly, interpreted this article to mean that the ten galleys would attack Genoese possessions in the Romania, and they claimed that the article "allowed the Venetians to send twelve galleys to the Black Sea."[33] Any threat to Genoese predominance in the Black Sea aroused the ire of Genoa, and feelings ran so high that in May 1307, one Genoese predicted that "the war will turn into one

---

29. Thomas and Predelli, *Diplomatarium*, I, no. 32.

30. Mas-Latrie, *Commerce et expéditions*, pp. 59–61; Moranvillé, "Projets," p. 78. This grant was renewed in 1320, at the request of Charles of Valois: Mas-Latrie, pp. 60–61.

31. Thiriet, *Délibérations*, I, pp. 113–114, no. 133; Thomas and Predelli, *Diplomatarium*, I, no. 32.

32. Thomas and Predelli, *Diplomatarium*, I, 51.

33. Finke, *Acta Aragonensia*, II, 687. The Genoese made a mistake over the number of the ships.

between Genoa and Venice."[34] As soon as he heard of the Venetian treaty, the captain Opicino Spinola, who was by then related to Andronicus II by marriage, asked the nobles and the people of Genoa whether they would be willing to defend the empire against Charles of Valois and Venice. He received an affirmative answer.[35]

Along with his European alliances, Charles of Valois tried to support his plans by winning the alliance of various elements in the East. At this point, the Catalans were one of the most important powers in the Balkans. In terms of a projected military campaign, they were *the* most important power, since they had already demonstrated, and repeatedly, both their ability and their willingness to fight the Byzantines. Since they called themselves crusaders, Charles of Valois, as the declared leader of the crusade against Constantinople, appeared to have a good chance of getting them to acknowledge his leadership, so that he could conquer Byzantium inexpensively. After the departure of Ferran of Mallorca and the liquidation of Entença and Arenos, the Catalan Company was composed of the most intransigent elements, those who cared nothing about their Sicilian allegiance and those who wanted to conquer a part at least of the Byzantine empire. Although their attacks on Constantinople had failed, and they had been forced to abandon Thrace, they were now moving into Macedonia in order to take Thessalonica.[36] Charles of Valois was almost forced to seek the support of this redoubtable army: he could not afford to have the Catalans as his enemies in the Romania, and he hoped to profit by having them as his friends. So, he sent ambassadors to Rocafort, and, by-passing Frederick III of Sicily, he negotiated with James II, whom he considered the overlord of the Catalan Company.

Thibaut de Chepoy, Charles's envoy, appeared in Nigroponte with some Venetian galleys, sometime in 1307.[37] While on their way to Macedonia, the Catalans under their new leader, Berengar de Rocafort, opened negotiations with Thibaut. These probably took place just after the departure of Ferran of Mallorca in the early summer, and before the Catalans reached Cassandreia.[38] The Catalans became vassals of Charles of Valois in the summer of 1307. Berengar de Rocafort and the Company swore fealty to the "emperor of Constantinople" and to his representative Thibaut who became their leader, if only in name.[39] The earliest reference to this arrangement is in a document of August 31, 1307, in which the Catalans referred to Charles of Valois as their emperor ("nostre senyor emperador micer Xarles").[40] This document was

34. Ibid.

35. Ibid.: letter of Christiano Spinola to James II, January 5, 1307.

36. Muntaner, chap. ccxxx; Gregoras, I, 245.

37. Probably in the spring of 1307: Rubió y Lluch, "Companyía Catalana," p. 17.

The date 1308, adopted by Schlumberger and others, has been proved wrong by the discovery of new documents. Cf. Dade, *Versuche*, pp. 118, 127–128.

38. Finke, *Acta Aragonensia*, II, 688.

39. Muntaner, chap. ccxxxv.

40. Rubió y Lluch, *Diplomatari*, no. 34; cf. ibid., no. 35. Christiano Spinola, writing on September 16, 1307, mentioned Rocafort's negotiations with Thibaut while the Catalan army was moving toward Macedonia (Ibid., no. 35). G. Schlumberger says that Thibaut left Paris in September 1306, was in Venice in 1307, and left Brindisi for the East early in 1308:

addressed by Rocafort to Muntaner, and contained a promise that Charles of Valois would repay all the expenses which Muntaner had contracted in the service of the Company.

Venice apparently cooperated with Charles of Valois in his effort to secure the allegiance of the Catalans. Thibaut de Chepoy travelled to Nigroponte on Venetian ships, and the Venetians captured Ferran of Mallorca and Muntaner, who were on their way back to Sicily. A little later, they sent Ferran to Robert of Naples, the inveterate enemy of the Aragonese royal family.[41] Clearly, the Venetians as well as Charles of Valois wanted to destroy the influence of the house of Aragon over the Catalan Company. James I of Mallorca asked Philip IV of France and Charles of Valois to intervene so that Ferran would be freed, and in the summer of 1308 the infante returned to his father.[42]

The alliance between Rocafort and Charles of Valois was only as strong as Thibaut's power of enforcing it. Rocafort did not take it very seriously. Yet the presence in Macedonia of a strong army which not only had ambitions of its own but was also allied to the leader of what was to be a much larger expedition, influenced the attitude of the Serbs, the other important power in the area. In 1308 the Catalans, under Thibaut de Chepoy, made Cassandreia their stronghold and launched several attacks on the fortified monasteries of Mount Athos and on Thessalonica; apparently, they controlled the whole area around Thessalonica, except for the city itself.[43] Charles of Valois, strengthened by his Catalan alliance, established connections with Stephen Uroš II, and with malcontents in the Byzantine empire: genuine unionists, enemies of Andronicus, or men who feared the Turk more than the Frenchman. Charles' negotiations and alliances have been discussed by J. Petit and Dade, among others. But these historians examined the negotiations from the western viewpoint and not within the framework of the general Balkan situation.

Charles of Valois concluded only one formal alliance in the Balkans. On March 27, 1308, his representatives and the envoys of Stephen Uroš signed the treaty of Lys.[44] Stephen had initiated the negotiations and his ambassadors,

---

Schlumberger, *Almugavares*, p. 303. J. Petit, "Un capitaine," p. 233, also accepts these dates which are based on the *Comptes de Chepoy* and on the accounts of Charles of Valois published by Moranvillé. These dates are obviously wrong. On p. 72 of the accounts published by Moranvillé, it is clearly stated that Thibaut de Chepoy stayed in the Romania for three years and eight months, from September 9, 1306 to April 29, 1310, but Petit and Schlumberger interpreted "Romania" rather broadly, to include Venice. Thibaut must have left Venice early in the spring of 1307. Unfortunately, Muntaner is not clear on whether Rocafort reached an agreement with the Valois envoys while he was in Thrace or in Macedonia (chap. ccxxxv).

41. Muntaner, chaps. ccxxxv, ccxxxviii; Rubió y Lluch, *Diplomatari*, nos. 34, 35; Rubió y Lluch, *Ferrán*, no. 8.

42. Rubió y Lluch, *Ferrán*, no. 9 (Perpignan, July 2, 1308); Muntaner, chap. ccxxxix.

43. Gregoras, I, 245; A. Papadopoulos-Kerameus, Ἀνάλεκτα Ἱεροσολυμιτικῆς Σταχυολογίας, V (St. Petersburg, 1898), 211; Górka, *Descriptio*, p. 37. N. Iorga, "Encore un traité de croisade, 1308," *Bulletin de l'Institut pour l'étude de l'Europe sud-orientale* (1921), pp. 59–64.

44. Du Cange, *Histoire de Constantinople* (1657), *Chartes*, pp. 59ff. Buchon, *Histoire de Constantinople*, II, 350–351, 351–352 (Stephen's confirmation, July 25, 1308); A. Ubičini, *Ougovor o savezou i priateilstvou medjou Karlom od Valoa i poslanitzina Srbskog Kralia Ourocha* (Belgrade, 1870);

Marco Lucari and Tripho de Cattaro, had come to France with full powers to negotiate a treaty with Charles and an agreement concerning church union with Clement V.[45] The Uroš–Valois alliance of 1308 was both offensive and defensive, and was mainly directed against the Byzantine empire. Stephen Uroš promised to help Charles of Valois recover the empire in whole or in part. He would participate in person, and pay his own way. If the state of his kingdom did not allow Stephen to leave, he promised to send men to fight for Charles. He also promised not to give asylum to any "rebels" or enemies of Charles. This clause referred to possible Byzantine refugees, and because of Stephen's ties with the imperial family of Constantinople, perhaps to Andronicus himself. After the empire had been conquered, in whole or in part, Charles of Valois promised to help Stephen against any enemy or invader. This promise did not hold in the case of a Serbian attack against the conquered imperial lands, or against the lands of Philip of Taranto. Charles would remain neutral if war erupted between Stephen and Philip.

In return for the help he promised, Stephen received in full possession some imperial lands he held in Macedonia. These included the area between Prilep and Prosêk, the areas between Ovčepolje and Štip, between Debar and the River Mat in Albania, and Kičeva near Lake Ochrid, up to the area inhabited by the Goge tribe. The annual rent from these lands was not to exceed 5,000 florins, and Charles's envoys would inspect the area in order to ascertain its true value. Stephen Uroš promised to return to the Catholic church and to swear obedience to the pope. At Stephen's request, Clement V sent Egidi of Grado, Gregory of Cattaro, and Henry of Arimino to Serbia, to convert Stephen and his subjects to Catholicism. If Stephen did return to the true faith, he was to be under the special protection of the Catholic church.[46] After the conversion, Charles, son of Charles of Valois, would marry "Stephen's only daughter," Zorica, allegedly his child by Elizabeth of Hungary.[47] In case that marriage did not take place, both parties agreed that the treaty would still be valid, unless Zorica married Andronicus or any of his relatives, friends, and allies. The envoys of Clement V left some time around June 13, 1308,[48] and Stephen Uroš confirmed the treaty of Lys on July 25 of the same year.

Stephen Uroš took the first steps toward concluding this alliance. He was the first to send ambassadors to the pope and to Charles of Valois, and the text of the treaty reflects the fact that Stephen was eager to court Charles's

---

reviewed in *BEC.* (1873), 116–118; Moranvillé, "Projets," p. 76. Jireček, *Geschichte der Serben*, p. 345; Dade, *Versuche*, pp. 137–146; Petit, *Charles de Valois*, pp. 110–112; Rubió y Lluch, "Companyía Catalana," p. 15; Stojan Novaković, *Srbi i Turci XIV i XV veka* (Belgrade, 1893), pp. 63ff (hereafter, Novaković, *Srbi i Turci*). Burns, "Catalan Company," p. 759, mentions the documents, but does not analyze them.

45. A. N. J510 no. 17; *Reg. Clem. V.*, no. 3559 (April 1, 1308) = Augustin Theiner, *Vetera Monumenta Slavorum Meridionalium*, I (Rome and Zagreb, 1863), 127–130.

46. *Reg. Clem. V.*, nos. 3559, 3560, 3561, 3563, 3564, 3565, all dated April 1, 1308.

47. Zorica was *not* legitimate as the text of the treaty claimed. If Uroš was ever married to her mother, that marriage was illegal, because his first wife was alive at the time. See above, Chapter IV, n. 31.

48. *Reg. Clem. V.*, no. 3566 (April 1, 1308, not April 30, as in Rubió y Lluch, "Companyía Catalana," p. 15; cf. Du Cange, *Histoire de Constantinople, Chartes*, p. 62.

friendship. In this way, Uroš temporarily abandoned the Byzantine camp, and returned to the policy of his predecessor, Stephen Dragutin, a policy of cooperation with the western pretender to the Byzantine throne. Stephen's opportunistic attitude was partly the result of his desire to secure some of the spoils of a western victory. Serbia was to become one of the successor states of the Byzantine empire. At the time, this made good political sense. In normal circumstances the difficult nature of the terrain protected Serbia from the possible ambitions of a western force landing on the Adriatic coast of Greece or in Dalmatia. It seems, however, that at least one advocate of Charles of Valois was certain that Charles would try to conquer Dalmatia, both for its silver mines and because this would make his passage into the Byzantine empire easier. The inhabitants of Dalmatia being Catholic, the conquest might be made easier. The real fear, however, was that Charles's invading force would have the support of the Catalan Company, then in the vicinity of Thessalonica. By itself, Rocafort's "Kingdom of Macedonia" would have been a dangerous neighbor for Serbia. In alliance with Charles of Valois, the Catalans would be even more formidable. So, "fearing that he would not be able to resist this army, and that his kingdom was in danger, he [Uroš] asked for peace and alliance."[49]

Thus, the presence of the Catalans in Macedonia and their alliance with Charles of Valois prompted Stephen Uroš II to offer Charles his cooperation. But it would be wrong to assume, as A. Rubió y Lluch does, that Stephen joined the Valois camp wholeheartedly. A French contemporary, writing in 1308, a little while after the treaty of Lys, realized that fear motivated Stephen and that for this reason Stephen's promises were meaningless: "He [Stephen] persecutes and hates the Catholics excessively, but because of fear of the Lord Charles he has striven to show some sign of devotion toward the Catholic church, so that the Roman church would forbid the Lord Charles to attack him, and for this reason he [Stephen] asks for Charles's friendship."[50] When the Catalans attacked Thessalonica, in the spring of 1308, there were Serbians defending the city; and in 1307 Stephen had sent men to defend Chilandar. Presumably, these men defended the monastery during the "three years and three months" that it was in danger. Stephen Uroš was playing a double game in accordance with the double aim of his policy. He did not want a strong Catalan state in Macedonia and apparently he opposed it; on the other hand, he believed that the Byzantine empire would be unable to withstand the combined attack of Venetians, Catalans, and Charles of Valois, and so he joined the anti-Byzantine camp in order to receive part of the spoils.

Charles of Valois seems to have made no effort to engage in direct negotiations with the Bulgarians, who since 1307 had been allied to the Byzantines. Perhaps Charles considered Bulgaria too remote and not important enough to

49. Górka, *Descriptio*, p. 37. Dade, *Versuche*, pp. 144–146, says that Stephen Uroš feared Philip of Taranto more than he did Charles of Valois. Philip had pretensions to Albania, and in 1307 he had become Prince of Achaia and had gone to his principality to fight the Greeks. Dade, however, also agrees that Stephen feared the Catalans.

50. Górka, *Descriptio*, p. 36.

warrant an alliance. It is also possible that he had listened to the theories of the anonymous author of the *Descriptio Europae Orientalis*. This French author, whose geographical description is sprinkled with advice to Charles of Valois, judged the Bulgarians to be "not bellicose, nor are they used to arms." Therefore, he thought that Charles could easily conquer Bulgaria once he had taken the Byzantine empire; for this, the help and alliance of the king of Hungary would be necessary: "Bulgaria and Ruthenia and Rasia are between Greece and Hungary, and since the Lord Charles will have had the empire of the Greeks, a confederation having been made with the king of Hungary, this same Lord Charles on one part, and the king of Hungary Charles on the other, will easily take and subjugate all these schismatic and barbaric nations which occupy such rich and delightful kingdoms as unjust possessors."[51]

The alliance of Charles of Valois with the Catalans gave him control—at least nominal control—over the most efficient army in the Romania. However, the Catalan campaign in Thrace had proven more than the efficiency of that army; it had also proven that the conquest of the Byzantine empire could be a very lengthy operation. The Byzantine state had degenerated into a collection of fortified towns which defended not only themselves but also, in part, the countryside. The Thracian campaign had shown that the fortified cities could and would put up considerable resistance. A Venetian fleet and a French army—should such an army ever be collected—could no doubt take Constantinople, and perhaps most of Thrace. But the conquest of western Thrace and Macedonia, even with the help of the Catalans, would be a long and tiring process if the Greeks should decide to defend themselves. In other words, western pretenders to the Byzantine throne needed the cooperation of the Greeks not only in order to preserve the empire once they had conquered it, but even in order to carry out the initial military conquest. It is not clear that Charles of Valois realized this; on the whole, it seems that he did not. But certain Greeks understood how valuable they could be to Charles, and they approached him, offering their help and requesting in return that Charles fight the Turks.

The documented negotiations between Charles and his Byzantine supporters lasted from the summer of 1307 until the spring of 1310. The Greek "collaborators," if an anachronistic term be permissible, were not traitors to the Byzantine cause in the broad sense. Their primary aim was to defeat the Turks, and they felt that the government at Constantinople could not or would not take adequate action against the Turkish enemy. In turning to Charles of Valois they were, of course, traitors to the legitimate government of their state, but they were also acting in accordance with what they took to be the best interests of the state. These men were in high positions, and had certain common characteristics. Four of the five known by name—John Monomachos, his brother Constantine, Constantine Limpidaris, and the monk Sophronias—came from Asia Minor. They said that they had the support of a large number

---

51. *Ibid.*, pp. 40, 42.

of their compatriots who resided in and around Constantinople, or who formed part of the guard in Thessalonica, and of other Greeks who were in command of various towns in Macedonia.[52] Monomachos claimed that others, greater than he, shared his pro-Valois sentiments, and this has been taken to refer to the Empress Irene; but no one has proved that the reference is, in fact, to Irene, or that she was in any way involved.[53]

The Greek negotiations with Charles of Valois are known through a number of letters.[54] In the first of these letters, John Monomachos assures Charles of Valois of his long-standing loyalty to the Valois cause. As proof of this loyalty, he mentions his discussions with Philippo Marchiano and Matteo Balbo, who are also charged with transmitting the letter. He deplores the fact that Charles of Valois has been forced to postpone his expedition for so long, and describes the desperate situation of the Byzantine empire, devastated by "pagans and other enemies." He acknowledges Charles of Valois as his "natural lord," by virtue of Charles' marriage to Catherine of Courtenay, and urges Charles to arrive soon, pledging his support and that of others, refugees from Asia Minor, who had fled with Monomachos. The second letter is addressed to Catherine of Courtenay; Limpidaris assures her that he is working for her cause, and urges the swift conquest of the Byzantine empire, before the land and the people are completely in the hands of the barbarians.

John Monomachos is the most interesting of the Greek collaborators. He was from Asia Minor ("ego sum de parte orientis Romanie"). In the Latin text of the letter to Charles, he called himself "capitaneus . . . fortilicie [thessalonicensis]." Dade and Moranvillé translate this as "commander" or "gouverneur" of Thessalonica, but do not define the terms. All the evidence points to his being the commander of the armed forces of Thessalonica, but not the governor of the city. Many of the soldiers from Asia Minor who had lost their pronoiai had come west and joined Michael IX's army. They were an embittered group and some of the best generals were recruited from among them. Monomachos, presumably, was one such general. He said he was in close contact with other men from the East who were in Thessalonica. These can hardly have been civilian refugees settled so far from Constantinople.

52. See the letters published by H. Omont in Moranvillé, "Projets," pp. 83–84, and the first letter published below, Appendix II.

53. Constantinidi-Bibicou, "Yolande de Montferrat," 437–439; Burns, "Catalan Company," pp. 760–776.

54. The letters are found in the French national archives, series J510 no. 25. All of these letters have been published, originally by Du Cange in 1657, and later by Omont and Miklosich and Müller: Du Cange, *Histoire de Constantinople, Chartes*, pp. 50–53; Miklosich and Müller, *Acta et Diplomata*, III, 242–245; Omont, in Moranvillé, "Projets," pp. 82–86. Two of the letters have not been republished since Du Cange, although they are among the most interesting of the group. In his edition of Du Cange, Buchon gives only summaries of these letters: Du Cange and Buchon, *Histoire de Constantinople*, II, 344. In particular, the letter of John Monomachos to Charles of Valois is very important, since it is the only letter which provides some clues as to the date of the negotiations. Dade has correctly dated this letter 1307 (*Versuche*, pp. 149–150), but he did so for the wrong reasons, and more modern researchers, like Burns ("Catalan Company," p. 760), continue to use the older dating, 1308. Two letters appear in Appendix II—one from Monomachos to Charles of Valois, and one from Limpidaris to Catherine of Courtenay. A careful scrutiny of these two letters firmly establishes the date of the negotiations, which is the summer of 1307.

They must have been soldiers under his command. One other piece of evidence speaks against Monomachos' being the civil governor of Thessalonica. Andronicus was so concerned with preserving the allegiance of the city, especially after his wife Irene had gone to live there, that he sent his two principal advisers to govern it: Theodore Metochites was there for two years after 1303, and Nicephorus Choumnos was made governor of the city about 1309 or 1310.[55] It is unlikely that in between Andronicus had sent a relatively unknown man like Monomachos to replace a highly political man like Metochites. Indeed, it is unlikely that he sent any civilian governor after 1306 and before 1309, for the Catalan occupation of Thrace made communications difficult.

As military commander of Thessalonica, Monomachos was an important person, and his help would be indispensable once Charles of Valois launched his attack. In the first letter published in Appendix II, Monomachos promised to surrender the city of Thessalonica, and also urged Charles to produce a document, promising to treat as his faithful men all those Greeks who decided to surrender their cities, or to render their services to the pretender. This action, Monomachos thought, would persuade many ambivalent Greeks to cooperate with Charles. In another letter, to Catherine of Courtenay, he repeated that he and his friends expected Charles to arrive soon, with a large army. He sent two envoys to Charles, Matteo Balbo and Philippo Marchiano, both his relatives, and he also sent along his own brother, Constantine, whom apparently he thought he could trust more than the two other envoys.[56]

Charles received the envoys, and in the early spring of 1308 he sent them along with his own envoy, Simon de Noyers, to Thibaut de Chepoy in Cassandreia.[57] Although his message to Thibaut has not survived, it is reasonable to suppose that Charles urged the Catalan army to besiege Thessalonica, which they did without success.[58] It is also possible that Charles put some store by the cooperation of his Greek friends. Certain French knights who had promised to follow Thibaut de Chepoy to Macedonia later decided not to go; it may be that Charles of Valois considered himself sufficiently strong because of his alliance with the Catalans and with the Greeks.[59]

The other important military man who cooperated with Charles of Valois was Constantine Limpidaris or Limbidaris. Also a native of Asia Minor and apparently still living there, at least until a short time before his letter was written, he called himself *dux*, and was obviously important in Anatolia. "I was sent by the towns of the East to the emperor who is [in Constantinople] against nature, in order to get some kind of help from him, for they have been besieged for four years because of his poor council." He failed in this mission.

55. Ševčenko, *Métochite et Choumnos*, pp. 6–7, and Appendix 3; Verpeaux, *Nicéphore Choumnos*, pp. 50–52; V. Mošin, *Supplementa ad Acta Graeca Chilandarii* (Ljubljana, 1948), p. 17.

56. Moranvillé, "Projets," pp. 74, 77, and letter 1.

57. Ibid., pp. 74, 76. Moranvillé's theory that this proves the letters were written in the beginning of 1308 is not convincing.

58. Boissonade, *Anecdota Graeca*, II, 226–227.

59. Du Cange, *Histoire de Constantinople*, *Chartes*; Du Cange and Buchon, *Histoire de Constantinople*, II, 349–350.

But, he said, "your imperial majesty should know that my army is as if you had a great army here, and I have been working for a long time and have caused many to become your majesty's servants." So certain was he of his influence in the remaining parts of Asia Minor, that he promised Charles of Valois that Asia Minor would surrender as soon as he appeared. Not only Asia Minor, but Constantinople as well, "for there are so many men from the East outside the city that they and we will cross [the Bosphorus?] and give the city to you as to our common lord."[60] In other words, he promised to attack the city with the support of the Anatolian refugees. Presumably, he did not think much of the defenses of Constantinople.

The important position of Limpidaris in Asia Minor suggests that he was the megas stratopedarches and protovestiarios Livadarios who had suppressed the rebellion of Philanthropenos. The text of his letter, written in colloquial Greek, indicates that the author was a man of no learning; Livadarios and Limpidaris could easily be the learned and the colloquial form of the same name. Dade considered the possibility of this identification, but then rejected it, because Livadarios had shown that he was faithful to Andronicus in 1295.[61] But this sort of reasoning would not apply to a man of the mentality of Livadarios during this period. He was ambitious and self-serving, and he set great store by his power in Asia Minor. In 1295 his interests moved him to fight Philanthropenos—not because Philanthropenos was opposed to Andronicus but because, as the sources tell us, he was threatening the power of Livadarios. In 1307 the great danger came from the Turks who were busy conquering precisely the areas which Livadarios had governed. There is no incompatibility between his actions in 1295 and his efforts to ally himself to Charles of Valois in 1307; both were undertaken to serve his own best interests. Like Monomachos, Limpidaris, too, claimed that he had been in contact with Matteo Balbo and Philippo Marchiano for many years, which suggests that these two were agents of Charles of Valois operating in the empire, probably after his marriage to Catherine of Courtenay.

The third collaborator whose letters have survived was a monk named Sophronias. His letter to Charles of Valois was more flattering than those of the other two, and sounds less sincere; this was probably the result of his florid monastic style.[62] He also must have come from Asia Minor. He did not say so explicitly, but there is one passage supporting this theory. He was asking the help of Charles of Valois because "much darkness and obscurity has covered our affairs" ("πλείστη γὰρ σκοτία καὶ ζόφος κατέλαβε τὰ ἡμέτερα"). This darkness was "the invasions of the barbarians (τῶν ἐθνῶν), the captivities, the destruction of cities, forts, and lands." This could only refer to the Turks,

---

60. Moranvillé, "Projets," letter 2, pp. 83–84. ληπὸν ἐγὼ ἀπεστάλην ἀπὸ τὰ κάστρι τῆς Ἀνατολῆς πρὸς τὸν εὑρικόμαινων παραφίσην βασιλέα ὅπως εὕρουσιν τῆ πωται ἐξ αὐτοῦ βοήθηαν, ὅτι χρόνους τέσαρι ἕναι ἀποκλησμαῖνα διὰ τὴν κακὴν τοῦ βουλήν . . . Ἀσπληροφωρίθη δὲ ἡ βασιλεία σου ὅτι ὅσπερ νὰ ἦχες μέγαν φουσάτον ἐνταῦθα ἔναι καὶ ὁ ἔδηκον μου σῶμαν, πλὴν ἐγὼ ἀπὸ πώλου τω ἐργάζομαι καὶ πωλοὺς ἐκατήφερα καὶ ὑποδουλόθησαν ἠς τὴν βασιληὰν σσου . . . διότι τοσούτοι ἀνατολικοὶ εὑρισκώνται ἀπέσω ὅτη καὶ ἐκείνη καὶ ἡμοῖς νὰ περάσωμεν καὶ να σε τὴν παραδοσωμεν ὁς γονηκὸν μας αὐθέντην.

61. Dade, *Versuche*, p. 153.

62. Moranvillé, "Projets," letter 3.

since the Catalans, also engaged in destructive activities, were assumed to be in the service of Charles of Valois; and in 1307 the Turks were active mostly in Asia Minor. It is possible that the term "τὰ ἡμέτερα" ("our affairs") applied to the empire as a whole; that was quite a common use of the expression. But it seems much more probable that it referred to Asia Minor, his birthplace or at least his major concern.

Sophronias wrote in a much more familiar way than either Monomachos or Limpidaris. Unlike the others, he did not find it necessary to introduce himself or to tell Charles of his long dedication to the Valois cause. On the contrary, his was almost a letter of introduction for the two envoys: "these two most honest and wise men who are coming to see your imperial majesty and who are faithful to your imperial majesty will speak the truth in everything they tell you concerning the affairs of the Romania, and the things they tell you should be accepted." Sophronias also wrote of the possibility of seeing Charles in France, as if he were accustomed to such trips. From these pieces of evidence it is tempting to conjecture that Sophronias—who has not yet been identified— was the same as the monk Sophonias who had been sent by Andronicus II to Italy in 1294, and who had come into contact with Simon Constantino-politanus, the Dominican friar.[63] The difficulty, of course, lies in the fact that the two names, Sophronias and Sophonias, are quite different, and one would be reduced to discussing far-fetched possibilities, for example, that Sophonias disguised his name when writing to Charles of Valois. It is also possible that Sophronias and Sophonias were the secular and monastic forms of the same name.

The archbishop of Adrianople, Theoktistos, was also involved in the negotiations with Charles of Valois.[64] His role must have been important, for he stayed in Paris for over five months and cost Charles of Valois a considerable amount of money. Unfortunately, his precise activities are not known. He was brought to France by a merchant whose expenses were later defrayed by Charles. On October 10, 1309, he came from Crépy to Paris, where he stayed until March 28, 1310. Charles paid for the bishop's clothes, his horses, his lodgings, and his general expenses.[65] One assumes that Theoktistos was engaged in discussions concerning the union of the churches. His action cannot be ascribed to the same sense of immediate danger which motivated the other collaborators. No Turks were yet in Thrace, except for those allied to the Catalans, and Adrianople, though it suffered as much as any Thracian city during the

---

63. In the early fourteenth century, Simon Constantinopolitanus wrote not only to Sophonias, but also to the poet Manuel Holobolus, then a monk with the name Maximus. While Holobolus' theological ideas were very fluid—he was pro-unionist in 1272, and anti-unionist in 1285—his primary political attachment, for which he lost his nose, his lips and, for a time, his freedom, was to the deposed Lascarids: Pachymeres, I, 192, 282, 374, 392–394; II, 25, 90. So, in the early fourteenth century we find, along with the pro-Valois movement, an effort by the church of Rome to capitalize on the anti-Palaeologan, pro-Lascarid sentiment within the Byzantine Empire.

64. Moranvillé, "Projets," p. 77, n. 4. See Planoudes' letter and laudatory poem to Theoktistos, in Planoudes, *Epistulae*, letter 9 and p. 204.

65. Moranvillé, "Projets," p. 77. This is a document containing the expenses of Charles of Valois "pour le voiage de Constentinoble."

Catalan invasion, had been able to defend itself successfully. Besides, the Catalans had left Thrace some time before the archbishop's trip to Paris. Thus, he must have belonged to the unionist party which had existed among the Byzantine clergy ever since the time of John Beccos. The cooperation of this party would be very valuable to Charles of Valois, if he were to fulfill his promise to the pope to return the empire to the Catholic fold. The archbishop was probably not a paid agent: the amount of money entered under his name in Charles of Valois' accounts must have genuinely just covered his expenses.

What was the motivation and the aims of these Byzantines who, at a moment when the empire needed all its resources to combat its numerous enemies, were ready to welcome and to help an outside conqueror? One element pervades the available evidence—the loss of Asia Minor, the inability of the Byzantine emperors to save it, and the desperate need for someone who was strong enough to take over and defend the empire and its subjects. John Monomachos wrote, "this country is widely ravaged by the pagans and by other enemies because of the inertia of this unnatural lord, and the rest [of the empire] is in danger of being lost." Limpidaris complained that Asia Minor had been living in a state of siege for years, and no help came from Constantinople.

Alongside the despair and bitterness of the Anatolian refugees one can see their patent contempt for the bureaucrats and imperial officials of the capital who, because of "inertia" or poor advice, had let these things come to pass. No doubt personal considerations also existed. Monomachos urged Charles of Valois to bribe, in effect, the Greek commanders of various towns in order to win them over to his side. Both he and Limpidaris were concerned with the fate of their lands, which were overrun by the Turks. They wrote to Charles of Valois and to Catherine of Courtenay to hurry, because the population of the empire was being exterminated by the infidels, and a land without its inhabitants was worth nothing. At a time of rapid depopulation, this was a very proper sentiment for a landlord. A feudal landlord, and an impoverished one like Charles of Valois, would understand the argument.

Yet the desire to save Asia Minor and the empire from the Turks predominated. The hour of decision seemed near. "The people, unable to bear any more such persecutions, will receive with joy not only your imperial majesty, who is their natural overlord, but also anyone else who would fight for them and defend them." "We need someone who will save us . . . He is the one whom God will elevate and raise to His right side. We wish that you will be that man." And Limpidaris wrote that, unless help came soon, many of the remaining Christians of Asia Minor would defect to the Turks and embrace Islam.[66]

Charles of Valois seemed the best choice to defend the Anatolian homeland against the Turks. He was planning to conquer the empire in any case. By cooperating, the Byzantines could ease his task and in return they hoped that they might be allowed to indicate to him the best course to take against the

66. Ibid., letters 2, 3.

Turks. They thought Charles would be strong enough for their purposes, since he had the support of his brother, of the pope, and, they thought, of the Catalans. Finally, he had rights over Constantinople which, if they accepted the legitimacy of the first Latin empire, overshadowed the rights of the Palaeologi. John Monomachos especially was very careful to point out that Charles's rights derived from his marriage to Catherine of Courtenay, and that John's allegiance to Charles dated from the time of the marriage. Limpidaris was more pragmatic; he said that he had turned to Charles of Valois when the emperor refused him the help he had sought on behalf of the Greeks of Asia Minor.

The Byzantine supporters of Charles of Valois, then, were landlords and soldiers from Asia Minor, who were trying to save their patrimony from the Turks. But surely these considerations do not provide a sufficient explanation of their appeal to Charles. Other Byzantines too, as we have seen, were concerned with Asia Minor, and they found other ways to try to preserve it: Metochites counseled the reconciliation of the inhabitants to their government, Athanasios I preached that prelates and people should mend their ways and return to a religious life, Andronicus II appealed to western mercenaries and then to the Mongols. The fact that these pro-Valois Greeks could so swiftly abandon their allegiance to the ruling dynasty suggests that they may have had Arsenite or pro-Lascarid sympathies.

These people were from Asia Minor, where pro-Lascarid and Arsenite sentiments were strongest, as the expeditions of both Philanthropenos and Tarchaneiotes had proved. The pro-Lascarids, of course, felt no allegiance to the Palaeologi, and could easily prefer a French dynasty to them. When Limpidaris wrote that Andronicus held Constantinople "against nature," he was referring to Michael VIII's usurpation of the Lascarid throne.[67] As for the Arsenites, they too opposed the Palaeologan church, and by extension the Palaeologan dynasty. Nor should it seem unlikely that they might invite a foreign, western pretender into the empire—witness the well-attested precedent of the rebellion of Drimys in 1305–1306. At that time the Arsenites sought the support of westerners by appealing to the Catalan army. In this connection, it is fair to assume that when Limpidaris wrote of the men from the East who resided just outside Constantinople and who were eager to surrender the city, he was referring not only to simple Anatolian refugees but also to those Arsenite leaders whom Andronicus had sent outside Constantinople after Drimys' rebellion.[68]

These sources, by their nature, may well exaggerate the number of those who were so inimical to the Palaeologan dynasty that they were eager to help a westerner to conquer Constantinople. By contrast, the other Byzantine sources say nothing of a pro-Valois movement. It is particularly vexing to find that the narrative sources do not discuss John Monomachos, or his activities during the siege of Thessalonica by the Catalans. Even the sources concerned

67. Ibid., p. 84.
68. See "The Cost of Byzantine Foreign Policy" in Chapter VI.

with the history of that city, Thomas Magister and St. Savvas the Young, do not mention the existence of a pro-Valois party in those years.[69] Their silence perhaps indicates that Monomachos and his followers had been replaced by the time of the Catalan attack on Thessalonica (spring 1308). A clue is found in Thomas Magister's oration in defense of the general Chandrenos. According to Thomas, when Chandrenos arrived in Macedonia, he was placed under the command of Angelus Palaeologos, who had been sent there by Andronicus. Moreover, Angelus had found that he could not depend on his lieutenants before Chandrenos' arrival.[70] This probably means that after the Catalans invaded Macedonia, Andronicus sent Angelus Palaeologos to Thessalonica, where he superseded Monomachos as commander of the armed forces, and perhaps dismissed Monomachos of his charge.

One also wonders whether the Empress Irene was aware of the plot being hatched in Thessalonica, and, if so, whether she supported it. One phrase of Monomachos' has been thought to hint at her active involvement: "And others, greater ones, who think in the same way as I, would write as I am writing, were they not afraid of being thought ungrateful."[71] This may or may not refer to Irene. But the sum total of her activities during the Catalan attack on Thessalonica indicate that she tried to contribute to the defense of the city. She was known not so much for her pro-Latin sympathies as for her strong maternal ambitions. Her main purpose in life seemed to be providing for her children. Unless evidence of her negotiations with Charles of Valois is discovered, it should be assumed that she thought she could achieve more as empress and wife of a reigning emperor, than as the ally of the man who would replace her husband in Constantinople.

It is interesting that the collaborators of 1307–1310 did not once mention the union of the churches, although it is probable that the archbishop of Adrianople discussed it. Remembering the first Latin empire of 1204–1261, they must have known what would happen if the Byzantine people were forced to accept the supremacy of Rome. Being mostly military men, perhaps they did not care very much about the religious implications of their political attachments. But if they also had Lascarid and Arsenite tendencies, they were far from faithful to Arsenius' principles: he had been one of the staunchest anti-unionists.

In general, Charles of Valois seems to have let the other side take the initiative in the East. Stephen Uroš initiated the negotiations leading to his alliance with Charles, and the Greek supporters of the Valois were at least as eager as Charles to come to an agreement. The same can be said about Charles' alliance with the Kingdom of Armenia. In May 1307, the "unionist" party of Armenia, which had developed, like its Byzantine equivalent, because of the Turkish and Egyptian menace, met at the council of Sis and decided to make some concessions to the Roman church. A few days later, King Leo IV

---

69. Thomas Magister in Boissonade, *Anecdota Graeca*, II, 188–228; Papadopoulos-Kerameus, Ἀνάλεκτα, V, no. 11: Τοῦ πατριάρχου Κωνσταντινουπόλεως κυροῦ Φιλοθέου Βίος καὶ Πολιτεία τοῦ ὁσίου καὶ θεοφόρου πατρὸς ἡμῶν Σάβα τοῦ Νέου.

70. Boissonade, *Anecdota Graeca*, II, 196–197.

71. Below, Appendix II, letter 1.

sent ambassadors to Europe to report this event and to ask for help. The Armenians also sent messengers to Philip IV, to the same purpose.[72] Charles of Valois sent an embassy "to the king of Armenia who has shown himself to be the friend of my lord [Charles]."[73]

The Catalan Campaigns of 1307–1311

The Catalan campaign in Macedonia had two related main objectives: the conquest of Thessalonica, and the creation of a kingdom of Macedonia, with its capital at Thessalonica. At the same time, the Catalans planned to attack and plunder the monasteries of Mount Athos, which were famous for their wealth. Andronicus' defense of Macedonia and Greece was conditioned by his lack of resources and influenced by his experience of the Catalan campaign in Thrace. Once again, Byzantine policy depended on the self-defense of the inhabitants, supplemented by Serbian help.

As soon as it became obvious that the Catalans would move west, Andronicus started to prepare the defense of Macedonia. His first concern was with Mount Athos, which he wanted to protect because of its importance to Orthodox Christianity. Since he could not send armies or equipment, he used other means. He wrote to the monks, instructing those who resided in badly fortified or depopulated monasteries to move into the cities or into cloisters which would be able to repel an attack. He gave the same instructions to those monks who were living on the mountain, but outside the monasteries. The monks were very worried at the prospect of the Catalan invasion; still, some of them preferred to trust in God and stay in their huts or monasteries. Others went to Thessalonica and other fortified cities and islands. In effect, the defense of Mount Athos was left to the monks, who rose admirably to the occasion.[74]

Soon after the Catalans entered Macedonia, Andronicus decided to cut off their retreat into Thrace by building a fort at Christopolis. This fulfilled its purpose so that after Macedonia became untenable, the Catalans could not return to Thrace but had to move south. At the same time, the emperor sent into Macedonia a number of Byzantine generals "not ignorant of the arts of war."[75] The generals were to collect an army in Macedonia—obviously from among those inhabitants who did not yet belong to the armed forces.

---

72. Ch.-V. Langlois and Charles Koehler, "Lettres inédites concernantes les croisades," *BEC.*, 52 (1891), document no. 6, to Edward I. Cf. *Historiens des croisades, Historiens arméniens*, vol. I, LXX; *Archivio Veneto*, (1890), p. 29 (Venetian embassy to Armenia, September 11, 1302); *Reg. Clem. V.*, no. 748, July 2, 1306: Clement writes to Patriarch Gregory and King Leo III of Armenia. He has learned of the troubles of Armenia through the Armenian ambassadors, sympathizes, and hopes to be able to help them by a small crusade.

73. Du Cange and Buchon, *Histoire de Constantinople*, II, 355.

74. A. Papadopoulos-Kerameus, Ἀνάλεκτα, V, 210–212; Dölger, *Regesten*, no. 2300, dates Andronicus' letter 1306–1307. It must have been written in 1307, for Andronicus could not have known any earlier that the Catalans would move toward Macedonia.

75. Gregoras, I, 246; Cantacuzenus, I, chap. vi; P. Lemerle, *Philippes et la Macédoine orientale à l'époque chrétienne et byzantine*, I (Paris, 1945), 189–194; G. Bakalakis, «Τὸ περὶ τὴν Χριστούπολιν τείχισμα,» Ἑλληνικά, 10 (1938), 307–318; Rubió y Lluch, "Companyía Catalana," pp. 3–4.

They would also make sure that the cities were able to withstand long sieges; to this purpose, they were to bring in both soldiers and food.[76]

Among the generals sent to Macedonia was Angelus Palaeologos, the megas stratopedarches and leader of the Greek army in Macedonia.[77] Perhaps his most important, and certainly most famous, lieutenant, was Chandrenos.[78] Chandrenos came from an old family of landowners in Asia Minor, and according to his apologist he had fought valiantly to defend his lands and towns. He had inspired fear and respect in the Turks who "live in arms" and who considered it more glorious to be defeated by him than to defeat other, less valiant, men. Fighting with only a few soldiers, he had won considerable victories, but in the end he was unable to save his patrimony. He left after Asia Minor was virtually occupied by the Turks, and came to Europe, where he joined Michael IX's army. He was in Thrace at the time of the battle of Apros, where he is said to have distinguished himself and to have won the only Byzantine victories. Although this is only attested by his apologist Thomas (Theodulos) Magister, it must be true, for subsequently Chandrenos was sent to Angelus Palaeologos, to help defend Macedonia. He did a good job, and managed to contain the Catalan attacks on Thessalonica and the surrounding countryside.[79]

The defense of Mount Athos and Thessalonica is relatively well attested and provides valuable information about conditions in Macedonia and in the Byzantine Empire as a whole. The holy mountain, with its numerous monasteries, was the first to suffer from the Catalan attacks. Their stronghold in Cassandreia, easy to defend, provided a perfect base of operations against Athos. We do not know how many monasteries were attacked, and for how long. The Serbian monastery of Chilandar was besieged at least twice, and the Catalans terrorized the environs "for three years and three months."[80] Since the monastery was well fortified, the Catalans tried to starve it into submission. During the first siege, in the early summer of 1307, it was defended by its own monks. Later, the abbot Daniel went to Skopje to ask Stephen Uroš II for help. Then, "came a great number of men with arms to the holy mountain to fight against the pagans."[81]

76. Gregoras, I, 246. Notice that Thomas Magister, in the Περὶ βασιλείας suggested that the emperor should always have granaries full of food in the cities, for just this purpose (Migne, *PG*, CXLV, col. 484).

77. Martin, *Philes Carmina inedita*, no. 20. Martin dates this poem 1310, but I think this date is erroneous. The poem was written on the occasion of Angelus' departure for Thessalonica, and Thomas Magister wrote that Angelus was in that city before the arrival of Chandrenos (Boissonade, *Anecdota Graeca*, II, 196), who was already in Greece in 1309–1310; so, the poem was probably written in 1307. Cf. Miller, *Philes Carmina*, II, nos. 193, 218.

78. Boissonade, *Anecdota Graeca*, II, 188–211.

79. Ibid., 193–195, 226–227.

80. Rubió y Lluch, "Companyía Catalana," pp. 34–36; L. Mirkhović, *Životi kraljeva i archiepiskopa Srpskich* (Belgrade, 1935), p. 258. This is an edition of Danilo, and will hereafter be abbreviated as Mirkhović, *Danilo*.

81. Boissonade, *Anecdota Graeca*, II, 223–224. Mirkhović, *Danilo*, pp. 257–265; Djuro Daničić, *Životi kraljeva i archiepiskopa Srpskich, napisao Danilo i Drugi* (Zagreb, 1866), pp. 340–355. This is the earlier edition of Danilo, hereafter, Daničić, *Danilo*. Since both this and Mirkhović' edition are quite rare, it has been thought useful to refer to both. Cf. Novaković, *Srbi i Turci*, pp. 40–52. The "pagans" were the Turkish allies of the Catalans. Cf. Rubió y Lluch, Companyía Catalana, p. 40.

Whether Serbian soldiers or Macedonian volunteers came to fight is unclear. Given Uroš' constant concern over the welfare of Chilandar, the first seems more probable. It might be the reason for Stephen's increased influence in the affairs of Mount Athos a few years later. In 1311 he asked Andronicus to confirm certain possessions of the Russian monastery of St. Panteleemon.[82] That monastery had a special relationship with Chilandar: the abbot Daniel, on his return from Skopje in 1307, visited the monastery to warn it of the Catalan danger.[83] A few years later, in 1319, Andronicus granted certain possessions to Chilandar, at the request of the Serbian king, to whom the emperor was said to be indebted for help given in battle. This may refer to the Serbian help against the Turk Chalil in 1313, but may also refer to Uroš' help during the Catalan invasion.[84] Stephen's help to Chilandar is also implied in the monks' present to him of Catalan arms and other spoils of their eventual victory. A nineteenth-century fresco at Chilandar is thought to represent a sea-attack by the Catalans, repulsed by a miracle.[85]

The Catalan army also attacked the rich monastery of Lavra. Again, the monks appealed for help not to their emperor, the defender of the faith, but to the man they thought best able to exercise a restraining influence on the Company: James II of Aragon. The monks sent two emissaries to him in the early summer of 1308.[86] They requested a royal letter ordering the Catalans to refrain from attacking the monastery. It is probable that they also asked for Clement V's intervention, for the emissaries were in Avignon before going to Valencia. James granted their request, and gave them a royal rescript, by which he ordered the Catalans not to attack Lavra or its monks, who lived outside the monastery, or the property and the serfs belonging to the monastery. The rescript was issued through the mediation of Arnau de Villanova, James' envoy in the papal court, who convinced the king that such an action would be pleasing in the eyes of God. Whether the Catalans obeyed James' orders or not is unknown, but there is no evidence of any further attack on Lavra. According to tradition, some Catalans were converted to orthodoxy and remained at Mount Athos as monks. One of them may be the saint who rejoiced in the appropriate name of St. Barbaros.[87]

82. J. and P. Zepos, *Jus Graecoromanum*, III (Athens, 1934), no. 31; Mošin, *Akti iz Svetogorskich archiva*, pp. 219–223. Andronicus granted the request: Dölger, *Regesten*, no. 2333.

83. Rubió y Lluch, "Companyía Catalana," pp. 37–38; Mirkhović, *Danilo*, p. 265; Daničić, *Danilo*, p. 341.

84. Dölger, *Regesten*, no. 2416 (March, 1319); Petit and Korablev, *Chilandar*, no. 41. The chrysobull of October, 1313, giving privileges to Chilandar, mentioned specifically Uroš' help against the Turks. See Boissonade, *Anecdota Graeca*, II, 63; Petit and Korablev, *Chilandar*, no. 26; Dölger, *Regesten*, no. 2348. Cf. K. Jireček, "Staat und Gesellschaft in Mittelalterliches Servien . . ." *Denkschriften den Kais. Akad. der Wissenschaften* (Vienna, 1914), p. 67; S. Lambros, «Τὸ ἅγιον Ὄρος καὶ οἱ Καταλώνιοι,» Νέος Ἑλληνομνήμων, 6 (September, 1909), 317; S. I. Papadatos, «Ἡ διοικητικὴ ἀνεξαρτησία τοῦ Ἁγίου Ὄρους ἐπὶ Βυζαντινῶν,» Ε.Ε.Β.Σ., 32 (1963), 427–483.

85. Rubió y Lluch, "Companyía Catalana," p. 39, says that the result of the monks' appeal to Uroš is unknown. For traditions relative to the Catalan attack on Mount Athos, see R. M. Dawkins, "The Catalan Company in the Traditions of Mount Athos," *Homenatge a A. Rubió y Lluch*, I (Barcelona, 1936), 267–270.

86. Rubió y Lluch, *Diplomatari*, no. 40 (Valencia, July 1, 1308); Finke, *Acta Aragonensia*, II, 876. Cf. Rubió y Lluch, "Companyía Catalana," 40. Verpeaux, *Nicéphore Choumnos*, pp. 39–50.

87. Dawkins, "The Catalan Company in Traditions of Mount Athos," pp. 269–270.

All the contemporary evidence indicates that Mount Athos suffered greatly from Catalan and Turkish depredations, and was almost occupied. It was saved by the self-defense of the monks, encouraged by Andronicus, and with the help of the kings of Serbia and Aragon. It was also helped by the forays of Chandrenos, who eventually forced the Catalans to remain in Cassandreia, stopped their devastating incursions into the surrounding territory, and cut off their sources of food. His contribution was indirect and probably came after the siege of Thessalonica (1308). In the early days of the Catalan invasion, communications between Mount Athos and Thessalonica, where Chandrenos operated, were virtually nonexistent.[88]

Essentially the same combination of forces saved Thessalonica, which Roca-fort coveted for himself. Thessalonica was the main Catalan objective in Macedonia; it was rich, it was essential for the occupation of the rest of Macedonia, and it was the residence of the Empresses Irene and Rita-Maria who had been unable to make their way back to Thrace. A first attack was made in the spring of 1308.[89] Earlier, the Catalans had burned the countryside between Mount Athos and Thessalonica, and spread chaos and terror; the monastery of Chortaites (near Thessalonica) was among the many that suffered from these attacks.[90] The people of Macedonia took the one possible course to defend themselves. They fled into the fortified cities, taking their flocks with them, and leaving the countryside empty.[91] Apart from thus cutting off an important source of food supply for the Catalans, this action mitigated the refugee problem in the city, since the refugees took provisions with them.

The Catalans asked the inhabitants of Thessalonica "not only, as their ancestors had done, for earth and water"; they demanded the immediate surrender of the city, threatening total destruction and massacre in the event of resistance.[92] Thessalonica was besieged by land and sea; the adjoining areas were as good as taken over by the Catalans.[93] The inhabitants of the city, terrified though they were,[94] defended themselves intelligently and valiantly. They armed five boats in order to disrupt the Catalans' communications with Thessaly, which had become the main source of food for the Company. Thibaut de Chepoy was forced to keep two Venetian galleys and one *lignum* (smaller boat) to oppose the threat presented by this action of the men of Thessalonica. He also paid a Genoese ship to transport bread from Thessaly to Cassandreia.[95]

---

88. Boissonade, *Anecdota Graeca*, II, 198–199; 223–224; A. Papadopoulos-Kerameus, Ἀνάλεκτα, V, 214.

89. Gregoras, I, 245–248; Pachymeres, II, 586–587; Muntaner, chap. ccxxxv.

90. Martin, *Philes Carmina inedita*, no. 61 (pp. 79–81); Boissonade, *Anecdota Graeca*, II, 222–223; A. Papadopoulos-Kerameus, Ἀνάλεκτα, V, 214; G. L. Tafel, *De Thessalonica eiusque agro*, (Berlin, 1839), pp. 252ff.

91. Gregoras, I, 246.

92. Boissonade, *Anecdota Graeca*, II, 226. The quotation refers to Xerxes' demands on the people of Athens, recounted in Thucydides, II, 19.

93. Górka, *Descriptio*, p. 60; Iorga, "Un traité," pp. 59–64. On the Catalan fleet, see Comptes de Chepoy, in Du Cange and Buchon, *Histoire de Constantinople*, II, 356.

94. Boissonade, *Anecdota Graeca*, II, 227: Ἕστηκεν οὖν ἡ πόλις ἐν ἀγρυπνίᾳ τε καὶ φροντίσι, καὶ πλήρης θορύβου καὶ μεστὴ ταραχῆς...

95. Comptes de Chepoy, in Du Cange and Buchon, *Histoire de Constantinople*, II, 355–356.

The Empress Irene, whose relations with the Serbs were better than her husband's also contributed to the defense of the city. In 1305 or 1306 she tried to bring into Thessalonica an army of "Serbians who were Byzantine subjects," and of other Serbians, the subjects of her son-in-law.[96] If she succeeded, perhaps the investment of imperial money in Serbia, of which Nicephorus Gregoras complained, had not been entirely wasted.[97] There is an indirect confirmation of the assumption that Stephen Uroš II helped the Byzantines defend Macedonia. The author of the *Descriptio Europae Orientalis* was very bitter in his description of Stephen's duplicity, insincerity, and hatred of the Catholics. Since the book was written sometime in 1308, the only evidence of duplicity which could possibly be available to the writer would be Stephen's help to the Byzantines at a time when he was allied to Charles of Valois.[98] Stephen's part of Macedonia, which he had received as Simonis' dowry, had been occupied by the Catalans; it was but natural that he should fight them. But these defense measures were not sufficient in themselves. It was necessary for the general Chandrenos, acting, one must assume, from the outskirts of the city, to divert the Catalans and make them raise the siege of Thessalonica (1309).[99]

In the meantime, important developments had taken place inside the Catalan Company. From the beginning, relations between Berengar de Rocafort and Thibaut de Chepoy had been strained. Thibaut had come to Cassandreia in August 1307, with a number of French knights; a few more Frenchmen arrived in 1308. Charles of Valois also sent money for provisions, for horses, for hiring ships, and for paying the Catalans.[100] But Rocafort was too arrogant to take seriously his oath of allegiance to Charles of Valois. He continued to give orders to his army as if he were their leader, and expressed his intention of becoming "king of Saloniki" (1308).[101] He also hoped to marry Jeanette de Brienne, the sister of Gui II, duke of Athens, and thus receive the Duchy of Athens as well as Thessaly, over which Gui exercised a protectorate. Gui was not averse to the idea. He sent two representatives to Cassandreia to discuss the marriage and, in the late summer of 1308, Rocafort became a vassal of the duke of Athens.[102]

96. Pachymeres, II, 557: two years after her arrival in Thessalonica, see Boissonade, *Anecdota Nova*, pp. 25–29.

97. Gregoras, I, 241–243; Rubió y Lluch, *Companyía Catalana*, p. 33; Stojan Novaković, *Strumska oblast u XIV veku i car Stephan Dušan*, (Belgrade, 1893); Novaković, *Srbi i Turci*. There is an undated chrysobull of Andronicus II, which gives to Irene in perpetuity certain possessions (Miklosich and Müller, *Acta et Diplomata*, V, 268–270). The emperor justifies his donation by saying that Irene "is helping our affairs by contributing money for the common needs and she is neglecting to use her own money . . . for her necessities, preferring to spend it for the public good." It seems to me that this is the only period in which Irene helped the empire, and that the chrysobull was issued during or soon after the Catalan attack on Thessalonica.

98. Górka, *Descriptio*, pp. v–xi, 35–37; Iorga, "Encore un traité," pp. 59–64; below, Sources.

99. Boissonade, *Anecdota Graeca*, II, 199–200; Rubió y Lluch, "Companyía Catalana," p. 33 (Spring, 1309).

100. Du Cange and Buchon, *Histoire de Constantinople*, II, 352–356; J. A. C. Buchon, *Chroniques étrangères relatives aux expéditions françaises au XIIIe siècle* (Paris, 1840), p. 468; Rubió y Lluch, "Companyía Catalana," pp. 11ff.

101. Muntaner, chap. ccxxxv; Rubió y Lluch, "Companyía Catalana," pp. 20ff.

102. Du Cange and Buchon, *Histoire de Constantinople*, II, 355 (Comptes de Chepoy).

One of the terciers of Nigroponte, Bonifacio da Verona, and the Venetian bailo of Thessaly, Antonio Flemingo, advised Rocafort to attack and take Nigroponte. At this point, Venice saw the danger presented by the Catalans and decided to act. On September 23, 1308, the Venetian government, having learned of Rocafort's intentions, wrote to the bailo of Nigroponte, Bellctto Falier, ordering him to request arms and men from the duke of Crete, should the need arise. Another letter, to the duke of Crete, Guido dal Canal, confirmed a previous order that the Cretans should help Nigroponte in time of need. Because of the general insecurity in the waters of the Aegean, Venice ordered the castellans of Modon and Coron, the captain of the galleys of Cyprus and Armenia, the captain of the galleys of Cyprus, and the captain of the galleys guarding the Venetian colonies of the Romania (Marco Morosini) to coordinate their activities for the defense of Venetian interests in the Aegean.[103]

Thibaut de Chepoy had also realized the instability of the Catalan alliance, and his reports to Charles of Valois made Charles uneasy. In 1308 (before May), Charles wrote to Blanche, the wife of James II of Aragon, appealing to her to persuade her husband to write to Rocafort that he, James, "has our [Charles's] need and our honor and our profit at heart." In that way he hoped to persuade the Catalans to keep the agreements and work for the cause of the Valois, not for their own. At the end of his letter, Charles hinted strongly that the long-desired return of the Val d'Aran to Aragon depended on James' complying with his request.[104] James II rose to the bait, sent two ambassadors to Paris to negotiate on the matter of the Val d'Aran, and wrote a letter to Rocafort and the Catalans whom he called "our subjects and vassals . . . who are acting in the Romania for the affairs of . . . Charles."[105] James urged the Catalans, in the name of the fidelity they owed him, to pursue fervently Charles's affairs in the empire.

Whatever influence James thought he had over the Company did not extend to its leader, Rocafort. In the summer of 1308 Rocafort tried to make alliances that would increase his personal power and would certainly conflict with the interests of Venice and of his overlord, Charles of Valois. Thibaut de Chepoy, with the help of the Venetians and using money dispatched by Charles, conspired with the malcontents in the Catalan army to dispose of Rocafort (end of 1308).[106] Rocafort was captured and was turned over to Thibaut who left

103. Rubió y Lluch, *Diplomatari*, no. 43; Hopf, *Griechische Geschichte*, pp. 388–389; Mas-Latrie, *Commerce et expéditions*, p. 240; Hopf, *Chroniques Gréco-romanes*, p. 372. Jeannette had been discussed as a possible bride for Theodore of Montferrat: Hopf, *Griechische Geschichte*, p. 387; Gregoras, I, 233–237, 240; Constantinidi-Bibicou, "Yolande de Montferrat," pp. 425–442. For the Venetian activities, see Giomo, *Lettere di Collegio*, nos. 37, 38, 43, 44, 45, 50 (September 23–25, 1308).

104. Petit, *Charles de Valois*, document no. 11, pp. 384–385. On the question of the Val d'Aran, see Lavisse and Langlois, *Histoire de France*, p. 291. The Val d'Aran was returned to Aragon in 1312, although not as a result of Charles's pressure; here, as in everything else, it was Philip IV who decided on policy.

105. Rubió y Lluch, *Diplomatari*, no. 39 (May 10, 1308): "dilectis suis Bernardo de Rocaforti militi ac societate sue ceterisque naturalibus et fidelibus ac agentibus nostris pro negociis . . . Karoli . . . in partibus Romanie agentibus."

106. Muntaner, chap. ccxxxix; Rubió y Lluch, "Companyía Catalana," pp. 21–22.

secretly in the autumn of 1309 and took him to Calabria to die of hunger in the prison of King Robert of Naples.[107]

After Thibaut's departure, the Catalans would serve Charles of Valois no more. The paths of the Catalan Company and Charles of Valois had crossed momentarily. In theory, the alliance might have had beneficial short-term effects for Charles of Valois. In the long run, it would have been useless or even detrimental had it survived Charles's projected conquest of the empire. For the Greeks had learned to fear and hate the Catalan "barbarians," and the Catalans themselves had been too long without discipline and without a real master.

The Catalans in Athens

Unable to take Thessalonica, and without ties to Charles of Valois, the Catalans decided to leave Macedonia. To the south was Thessaly, which they knew to be rich, for they had been buying food from there.[108] In fact, their contacts with Thessaly during 1308 must have been very numerous, for a fairly keen observer made the mistake of thinking that they had conquered it.[109]

John II Angelos (1303–1318), who ruled Thessaly, was a sick man and a weak ruler. He had married Irene, Andronicus II's illegitimate daughter, but he had no heirs and was, for all practical purposes, under the tutelage of the Duchy of Athens. In the spring of 1309, realizing that the fort of Christopolis made a return to Thrace impossible, the Catalans decided to invade Thessaly. They stayed there for one year, plundering, but were constantly harassed by the Byzantine army under Chandrenos.[110]

In the spring of 1310 they found another master. After the death of Gui II of Athens (1308), the Byzantines, Anne of Epirus, and John II of Thessaly took combined action against the influence of the Duchy of Athens in Thessaly.[111] The new duke of Athens, Walter of Brienne, who spoke Catalan, invited the Company to defend his interests.[112] Within six months, they had

---

107. Date from Dade, *Versuche*, p. 156. Schlumberger, *Almugavares*, p. 357, gives the date 1310. We know that Chepoy returned to Paris in 1310. See Petit, "Un capitaine."

108. Gregoras, I, 244–248; Du Cange and Buchon, *Histoire de Constantinople*, II, 355–356.

109. Górka, *Descriptio*, pp. 12–14. The editor thinks that this passage refers to the area of Macedonia that surrounds Thessalonica (ibid., pp. v–vi) and uses this as one of his reasons for dating the book 1308. However, it is clear that the author is talking of Thessaly: "inter machedoniam, achayam et thesalonicam est quidam populus valde magnus et spaciosus qui vocantur blazi. This, as the editor himself indicates in n. 2 of p. 13, refers to the Vlachs of Thessaly.

110. Gregoras, I, 244–248, 249–254; Boissonade, *Anecdota Graeca*, II, 199; Morel-Fatio, *Libro de los Fechos*, §535; Muntaner, chap. ccxl; Delaville le Roulx, *France en Orient*, I, 45; K. M. Setton, *The Catalan Domination of Athens* (Cambridge, Mass., 1948); Lemerle, *Philippes*, I (Paris, 1945), 189–198.

111. Constantine of Thessaly died in 1303, precipitating an Epirote invasion caused by Anne's desire to extend her influence on Thessaly. The duke of Athens and his allies from Achaia came to defend Thessaly and carried their attack into the Byzantine part of southern Macedonia. See *La chronique de Morée*, §873ff.

112. Boissonade, *Anecdota Graeca*, II, 199. Muntaner, chap. ccxl; Morel-Fatio, *Libro de los Fechos*, §536; Setton, *Catalan Domination*, pp. 7–10; Hopf, *Griechische Geschichte*, p. 390; *Chronicle of the Morea*, verses 5930–5960.

won a number of victories, taken thirty Thessalian towns including Demetrias, Zeitouni, Domokos, and Halmyros, and caused the allies of the Byzantines to ask for peace. At this point, Walter of Brienne realized the dangerous position in which he had placed himself. He had promised the Catalans pay for six months' service at the beginning, and to keep them in his service afterwards. When his main purpose in Thessaly was achieved, he decided to keep only two hundred knights and three hundred foot in his service, and dismissed the rest. The Catalans then moved on to attack the Duchy of Athens; they descended into Boeotia through Phthiotis and Lokris, and met Walter's army, which was reinforced by the army of the principality of Achaia. The encounter took place in the marshes of what was once the Lake of Kopais; the Catalans used the treacherous terrain to their advantage, and the flower of Frankish chivalry fell there, on Monday, March 15, 1311.[113]

The Catalans now took over the Duchy of Athens, and a number of smaller baronies in the western part of Greece as well.[114] In this way, they achieved their old aim of carving out for themselves a state in Greece. From that time on, they were settled in Athens, still considering themselves as crusaders. In 1312 they asked Frederick III of Sicily for his protection. He accepted their allegiance, and sent as their commander Berengar Estañol, who ruled them until 1316. In 1316 Frederick's illegitimate son, Don Alfonso Fadrique, succeeded Estañol and ruled over the Catalans as the representative of the duke of Athens, William II of Aragon (1317–1338).[115] The Catalans of the Duchy of Athens became fearsome pirates, whose activities provoked the verbal and active opposition of Venice, the pope, and Mathilda de Hainaut, princess of Achaia. They were accused of cooperating with Turks and even with Greek pirates. In general, they were one of the primary contributors to the perils of travel in the Aegean at that time.

As in Thrace and Macedonia, so in the threatened provinces of Greece, Andronicus II could not count on an organized army of his own. When the Catalans started to launch attacks into Phokis and the western parts of Greece, Andronicus had to ask the local inhabitants to contribute heavily to their own defense. In return, the men of these provinces, who had probably not seen very many officials from Constantinople in their lifetime, received privileges which almost abolished imperial control.

In 1309 or 1310 the emperor sent letters to the inhabitants of the Morea and southwestern Greece, asking that young and old arm themselves and come

---

113. Muntaner, chap. ccxl; Gregoras, I, 249–254; Boissonade, *Anecdota Graeca*, II, 201; *La chronique de Morée*, §500, p. 402; Morel-Fatio, *Libro de los Fechos*, §551; Setton, *Catalan Domination*, pp. 8–13; G. T. Kolia, «Ἡ μεταξὺ Καταλάνων καὶ μεγάλου Δουκὸς τῶν Ἀθηνῶν μάχη,» ΕΕΒΣ, 26 (1956), 358–379.

114. Such a barony was Salona which they took from the Stromoncourt. K. Sathas, Χρονικὸν Ἀνέκδοτον Γαλαξειδίου (Athens, 1865), p. 205; Setton, *Catalan Domination*, p. 13.

115. Muntaner, chap. ccxliii; Rubió y Lluch, *Diplomatari*, no. 53; Marino Sanudo Torsello, in J. Bongars, ed. *Gesta Dei per Francos*, II (Hanover, 1611), no. 16 (hereafter Sanudo in Bongars); Miller, *The Latins in the Levant*, pp. 236, 241–242; Setton, *Catalan Domination*, p. 27; D. Jacoby, "La Compagnie Catalane en Grèce," *Journal des Savants* (1966) 84–89; R.-J. Loenertz, "Athènes et Néopatras, Regestes et notices pour servir à l'histoire des duchés catalans (1311–1394)," *Archivum Fratrum Praedictorum*, 25 (1955), 103.

to fight against the Catalans.[116] Presumably, they were to join the Byzantine army under Chandrenos, who, at the request of the Thessalians and at Andronicus' orders, made incursions into Thessaly in order to fight the Catalan army. So glorious was his campaign that Thomas Magister, writing some time later, says, "until today the Thessalians are singing about it, and almost all men sing about it."[117] All the areas that obeyed the imperial order would receive exemption from imperial taxation and become self-governing. The importance of the first promise should not be underestimated; at times, the emperor considered the payment of taxes to his representatives as proof of the taxpayers' citizenship.[118] At first, the inhabitants of Phokis answered Andronicus' call. Three thousand men from Galaxeidi, Loidoriki, and Lepanto started against the Catalans. In Lamia (Zeitouni), they disagreed on the question of leadership, and dispersed. The men from Loidoriki joined Chandrenos and, after winning two victories, returned to their villages with imperial gifts.[119]

The Catalan invasion contributed to the dismemberment of the Byzantine empire in a number of significant ways. Constantinople was, for all purposes, cut off from the rest of the empire for over two years. In Thrace itself, the authority of the emperor was recognized, but ineffective. The Catalans effectively ruled the countryside and a number of towns, while the remaining Byzantine towns had to depend on their own inhabitants for their defense. The parts of Asia Minor which were still under Byzantine rule rebelled during the Catalan occupation of Thrace. Rhodes was, at first, given to the Morisco brothers and, after they and the Byzantines had proved unable to defend it, was taken by the Knights Hospitallers on August 15, 1308.[120] Andronicus tried to protect Macedonia from the Catalans, but his entire defense policy depended on the cooperation of the inhabitants and, to a smaller extent, of the Serbs. The same comment applies to the rest of Greece.

The physical fragmentation of the empire also accelerated the process of fragmentation of authority which had begun in the late twelfth century. The reign of Andronicus II saw the emergence of the walled town as a self-governing and often self-financed entity. The privileges granted to Galaxeidi and the other towns of Greece, if they are accurately recorded, were the earliest

116. Sathas, Χρονικὸν τοῦ Γαλαξειδίου, pp. 204–205, dates this event 1310. As it took place during the period of the Catalan invasions from Thessaly, it can have happened at any time between the spring of 1309 and the spring of 1310. Cf. Hopf, *Griechische Geschichte*, p. 389.

117. Boissonade, *Anecdota Graeca*, II, 199–200, 220; Gregoras, I, 249–250.

118. The case of Salamis is an example of such thinking on Andronicus' part. The emperor sent ambassadors to Venice in 1319 to request compensation for damage done by Venetians to the Byzantines. Among other Byzantine territories to have suffered was Culuri (Salamis). Culuri, said the imperial ambassadors, belonged to Monemvasia (since 1317), for its inhabitants paid the ἀκρόστιχον (land tax) to the imperial officials there. See Thomas and Predelli, *Diplomatarium*, I, no. 72; Dölger, *Regesten*, no. 2423; Lemerle, *L'émirat d'Aydin*, pp. 85–86.

119. Sathas, Χρονικὸν τοῦ Γαλαξειδίου, pp. 225–226, identifies the «'Ανδρέας» of the text as 'Ανδρηνός=Χανδρηνός. Schlumberger, *Almugavares*, identified «'Ανδρέας» as Andrea Morisco. The geographical position of the towns in question speaks against the second identification. Morisco operated at sea; Lamia, toward which the inhabitants of western Greece went, is situated inland.

120. Pachymeres, II, 618–619, 634–637; Grumel, *La chronologie*, p. 402.

formal imperial concessions of authority in such an extreme form. In the late part of his reign, Andronicus II granted equally extensive privileges to towns or groups of individuals. As the central government was losing its power, it transferred its authority to particular groups; the growth of particularism is a fundamental aspect of the Palaeologan period. As for the walled town, its importance as a self-governing entity increased during the last years of Byzantine rule, and it played a significant role during the four hundred years of Turkish occupation. The Catalan campaign, by forcing the town inhabitants to provide for their own defense, contributed to the development of local government, with the towns as a focus.

Diplomacy in the Balkans

While the Catalans were in Thrace, Andronicus II's diplomatic activities had been geared to the Catalan problem, and had been restricted to efforts to defend the most threatened provinces. His alliance with Genoa against the Catalans and his negotiations with the Georgians and the Mongols, which aimed at halting the Ottoman successes in Asia Minor, are the only recorded contact with foreign powers. Although Andronicus had no diplomatic contacts with other powers from 1303 to 1307, other members of the imperial family did. It is a measure of the fragmentation of authority, which the Catalan campaign precipitated, that Andronicus' wife, Irene, was able to engage in diplomatic activities of her own, quite independently of her husband.

The Empress Irene had great ambitions for her children. She had tried to persuade her husband to give her sons appanages, in the western manner, and Andronicus had indignantly refused, telling her that it was not in his power to change the Roman mode of governing, and to create a multiplicity of authority (πολυαρχία) where unity (μοναρχία) existed. She cried, threatened suicide, and appealed to her husband's affection. Andronicus would not be moved, and at the end he became so angry that he refused her his bed.[121] Her original plans thwarted, she then tried to provide for her sons through appropriate marriage alliances. Between 1297 and 1301, she tried to negotiate the marriage of her eldest son, John, to Isabeau de Villehardouin, Princess of Achaia and widow of Florent of Hainaut. This failed, as did her effort to make John "lord of the Aetolians and the Akarnanes and the whole area adjacent to Epirus."[122] Instead, Andronicus II married John to Irene Choumnos, the daughter of Nicephorus Choumnos, who was then head of the imperial chancery and mesazon.

The marriage took place in 1303, and Irene was furious, for she thought the bride of too lowly a rank for her son. She had planned earlier to go to Thessalonica in order to meet Simonis, her daughter and the wife of Stephen Uroš II; now, because of her disagreement with Andronicus she decided to leave for

---

121. Gregoras, I, 235.
122. Ibid., I, 246; Constantinidi-Bibicou, "Yolande de Montferrat," pp. 432–433; J. Longnon, in Setton, Wolff, and Hazard, *A History of the Crusades*, II, 265.

Thessalonica, and to stay there.[123] It is not known what powers of government, if any, Andronicus granted her, but Theodore Metochites, who had already acquired some diplomatic experience in two foreign embassies, to Armenia and Serbia, and who enjoyed the confidence of the emperor, was asked to stay with her in Thessalonica. Presumably, he was to be her adviser, and perhaps to report her activities to the emperor. He stayed with Irene for two years.[124]

Irene's estrangement from Andronicus continued, and she did her best to discredit the emperor in the eyes of her entourage: the monks, the noble ladies-in-waiting, and her son-in-law, King Stephen. From her secure base in Thessalonica, she hurled vulgar accusations at her husband, and insinuated unpleasant things about his sexual habits. Andronicus then changed his previous strict attitude toward her, and tried to soothe her in every possible way. This change of heart, encouraged by the patriarch Athanasios I, was probably the result of political factors.[125] For Irene had increased her political activities from Thessalonica. She tried to negotiate the marriage of her second son, Theodore, to the daughter of Gui II de la Roche, the duke of Athens, who was then to help Theodore to conquer the land of the weak John II Angelos of Thessaly (1303–1318).[126] The duke of Athens rejected these proposals, and it is probable that Andronicus himself would have opposed the creation of an appanage under Irene's influence in Thessaly, which he had long hoped to unite to the empire. In fact, John II finally married Irene, Andronicus' illegitimate daughter.[127] In that sense, the empress' plans had worked against those of her husband.

Irene's most active diplomatic involvement was with Serbia. When she first reached Thessalonica, she invited Stephen Uroš there, and showered him with

123. Gregoras, I, 235; Pachymeres, II, 378–379; Treu, *Dichtungen*, A, verses 722–755. The date of her departure is disputed. I prefer 1303 to late 1304 or 1305: S. Runciman, "Thessalonica and the Montferrat Inheritance," Γρηγόριος ὁ Παλαμᾶς, year 42, 32, n. 12. The best discussion of the date is in Ševčenko, *Métochite et Choumnos*, pp. 6–7, 275–279. See also Constantinidi-Bibicou, "Yolande de Montferrat," pp. 432–433; Cognasso, "Crisobolla," p. 42.

124. Treu, *Dichtungen*, A, 764–765. On his return to Constantinople from Thessalonica he received honors from the emperor, and the office of mesazon: Ševčenko, *Métochite Cethoumnos*, pp. 245ff, 275. Nicephorus Choumnos was governor of Thessalonica in 1310: Ševčenko, *Métochite et Choumnos*, 278–279.

125. Gregoras, I, 235–236, 242; Pachymeres, II, 557–559; Cod. Vat. Gr. 2219, fols. 77vo–78ro.

126. These negotiations must have taken place between 1303 and the early summer of 1306, when Theodore was betrothed to Argentina Spinola. Metochites claims that one of Irene's two main reasons for going to Thessalonica was «πραγμάτεων ἔνεκ᾽ ἐς τά ᾽πὶ Θετταλίαν βελτίστων, τῷ τότ᾽ ἀδέσποτον οὖσαν»: Treu, *Dichtungen*, A, verses 725–726.

127. Mrs. Constantinidi-Bibicou says that the marriage took place in 1315, and is supported by Papadopulos, *Genealogie*, no. 67. Soloviev, "Fessalijske arkhonti," p. 162, adopts the same date without explaining his reasons. It is true that Gregoras (I, 278) says that John II lived only three years with Irene, and then he died. This would, indeed, place the marriage in 1315. But Gregoras begins this particular passage by saying he will not pay great attention to it: "let us talk now about Thessaly and its affairs, so that having disposed of that subject, we may then turn to discuss greater and more important things." In a previous passage (I, 249), he wrote explicitly that John of Thessaly was married to Irene when the Catalans descended into his area, and since this passage is lengthier and more detailed than the one mentioned earlier, I would discount the date 1315 as an error on the part of Gregoras. Cf. Hopf, *Griechische Geschichte*, p. 389.

presents and with so much money, wrote Gregoras, that "it would have been enough to arm one hundred galleys, which would have been to the perpetual benefit of the Romans." Gregoras also claims that Irene hoped that one day the Serbs would overrun and conquer the empire, to the benefit of her daughter Simonis and her heirs.[128] Soon, however, Irene learned that Simonis had suffered injuries which made it impossible that she would ever have children. The empress then tried to make Stephen Uroš adopt one of her own sons as his heir. Her youngest, Demetrius, traveled to Serbia sometime after 1303, and Theodore undertook the same voyage sometime around 1316. The kral was sympathetic to these plans, but neither of the Byzantine princes could bear life in Serbia. Irene continued to send extravagant gifts to Uroš, and such was her influence over him that Andronicus was forced to treat her gently, for fear she would arouse the Serbs against the empire.[129]

Gregoras may have exaggerated the sinister aims of the empress. At the time of the Catalan campaign in Macedonia she certainly used her good relations with her son-in-law to get Serbian help. Perhaps she was acting only for her own preservation, since if the Catalans took Thessalonica she would be captured or killed. Not only did she get some Serbian soldiers to help defend Thessalonica, but Gregoras mentions rumors of a possible anti-Catalan coalition between Serbs, Albanians, Thessalians, and Akarnanians in 1308; if that was at all contemplated, it must have been with Irene's knowledge.[130] And her friendly relations with the Serbs precipitated a chain reaction in the Balkans, culminating in an anti-Turkish coalition between Byzantium, Serbia, and Genoa (1313).

In this way, Irene behaved almost as a head of state in Thessalonica, forming her own foreign alliances. Stephen Uroš, who was so well disposed toward his mother-in-law, meanwhile exhibited a characteristic opportunism in his relations with Andronicus II. Perhaps the one clear factor in his policy was his fear of the Catalans, which led him to form alliances with both Irene (and the monks of Chilandar), and Charles of Valois. He had not abandoned his hopes of getting part of the northern Byzantine frontier. He tried to secure these

128. Gregoras, I, 241–244.

129. Ibid., I, 237. Demetrius' trip to Serbia took place some time after 1303, because Gregoras' narrative indicates that these negotiations took place while Irene was in Thessalonica, therefore after 1303 or 1304. It is probable, again from the tone of the narrative, that they took place after the Catalan invasion. Theodore's trip took place after his twenty-fifth year (Benvenuto di San Giorgio, col. 455), so sometime after 1313 (Papadopulos, *Genealogie*, no. 62, places his birth at about the year 1288). Cognasso, "Crisobolla," p. 43, says that the trip took place between 1316 and 1319. There are discrepancies in the sources as to the chronology of Theodore's trip. Gregoras wrote that Theodore came to see his mother, went to Serbia, returned to say goodbye to his mother, and left for Montferrat. In his autobiography, on the other hand, Theodore claims that his mother had invited him to Byzantium, but that he left only after she was dead, and indeed that he undertook his trip "tam causa mortis dicte domine matris mee, quam dicte mee nationi serviendi." Cognasso resolves the difficulty by saying that Gregoras has given a confused account of events. But he does not see another inconsistency: Theodore says that he stayed in the empire for about two years, and since we know that he left Constantinople in November 1318 he must have reached the empire *before* his mother's death, in 1316. He does not mention the trip to Serbia—perhaps he was concealing it, while Gregoras, who disliked Theodore, made of this trip the sole cause of Theodore's presence in the Byzantine Empire.

130. Gregoras, I, 247.

territories from Charles of Valois, and when Charles' conquest of Byzantium seemed to have been indefinitely postponed, and as soon as the Catalans had left Macedonia for Thessaly, Uroš attacked the empire. In 1309 he had accepted a force of 1,500 Turks who, under the leadership of Malik, abandoned the Catalans and sought refuge in Serbia. Stephen Uroš accepted them on condition that they live peaceably, except when he needed them in time of war.[131] He used them to attack the Byzantine empire (1309), but they found a formidable opponent in Chandrenos. For once, the Byzantines had on their side the advantage of knowing the terrain, and for once they made a frontal attack which succeeded: the Serbians and the Turks retreated.[132] In 1310 Stephen Uroš changed sides again. His good relations with the Empress Irene had provoked the reaction and rebellion of his brother, Stephen Dragutin, and of the Serbian nobility, supported by the Turkish mercenaries. This rebellion brought Uroš much closer to Byzantium. The kral sent the abbot of Chilandar to request Andronicus II, Michael IX, and the patriarch Niphon to mediate in the Serbian dispute.[133] In return, in 1313 he answered his father-in-law's request for help against the Turks of Chalil.

The Byzantines also had trouble with Turkish soldiers who had left the Catalans in the spring of 1309. One body of 1,300 mounted soldiers and 800 foot, under Chalil, asked to be allowed to cross the fort of Gallipoli and then return to Asia Minor. Andronicus, suspicious of their movements through Macedonia, sent one of his generals with 3,000 cavalry to escort them from Macedonia to the Hellespont.[134] When the Turks reached eastern Thrace, the Byzantines decided to attack them; the Turks, emulating the Catalans, then captured a fort and shut themselves up in it. Some time passed without much activity on the Byzantine side: "for it is a habit, I know not why, among those who direct the affairs of the Romans, to deal slowly with important things."[135] The Turks received reinforcements from Asia Minor, and they began to make incursions into Thrace. Michael IX collected an army of virtually unarmed peasants and was defeated (1311). The whole Catalan story was being repeated—the Turks remained in Thrace for two years, further devastating the already ravaged countryside.

Finally, Andronicus decided to act. He relieved Michael IX of his office as commander-in-chief of the Thracian army. Andronicus decided that God was withholding His favor from Michael because of the sins of his ancestors (*i.e.* Michael VIII's unionist policy), and he gave the command of the army to

---

131. Ibid., I, 254.

132. Boissonade, *Anecdota Graeca*, II, 201; Gregoras, I, 248; Mirkhović, *Danilo*, pp. 107–109; Novaković, *Srbi i Turci*, pp. 53, 65–67; Dölger, *Regesten*, no. 2344; Jireček, *Geschichte der Serben*, p. 345.

133. Mirkhović, *Danilo*, pp. 107–109; Daničić, *Danilo*, pp. 143–144, 357; Jireček, *Geschichte der Serben*, pp. 346, 347ff; Constantinidi-Bibicou, "Yolande de Montferrat," p. 434; Novaković, *Srbi i Turci*, pp. 53, 65–67; I. Dujčev, "La conquête turque et la prise de Constantinople dans la littérature contemporaine," *Byzantinoslavica* 16 (1955), 321–322; V. Laurent, "Une famille turque au service de Byzance, les Mélikès," *BZ*, 69 (1956), 349–368.

134. Gregoras, I, 248, 254; Muntaner, chap. ccxli; Dölger, *Regesten*, no. 2318 (1310–1311).

135. Gregoras, I, 255.

the valiant protostrator Philes Palaeologos.[136] Then, having no money to hire foreign mercenaries, he appealed to the Serbs for help.[137] Two thousand nobles on horseback, royal kinsmen, and friends came from Stephen Uroš. The Genoese of Pera lent eight ships and some machinery for attacking the Turkish fort. This coalition of forces defeated the Turks, most of whom were massacred trying to cross into Asia Minor.[138]

This was Stephen Uroš' most important help to Andronicus II. It symbolized his return to a pro-Byzantine policy, which he followed until his death in 1321. Although his attitude during the Catalan invasion had been ambivalent, it should be acknowledged and emphasized that on the whole he did oppose them, and that he did contribute to the defense of both Macedonia and Mount Athos. That this was enlightened self-interest is another matter. This same self-interest spoke for the creation of a Balkan alliance against the Catalans, but apart from Gregoras' single mention of such an effort, a policy of full cooperation was not adopted by either the Serbians or the government of Constantinople.

Charles of Valois, Venice, and Byzantium

During the years 1306–1308, Charles of Valois had built up a system of alliances which included the pope, the king of France, Venice, Serbia, the Catalans, the king of Armenia, and a number of important Greeks eager to support his cause. He also had the apparent acquiescence of James II of Aragon and Frederick III of Sicily. Charles's expedition was to leave for Byzantium between March 1307 and March 1308. Yet after 1308 there was a diminution of diplomatic activity and a gradual abandonment of his plans of conquest. His biographer, J. Petit, suggests that Charles lost interest in the eastern empire after he was offered the candidature to the throne of the Holy Roman Empire (1308).[139] That is not quite accurate. Catherine of Courtenay died in 1308, and after her

---

136. Ibid., I, 262–269. According to Gregoras, this event took place one year before Niphon I's eviction from the Patriarchate of Constantinople. Niphon was evicted on April 11, 1314. See Grumel, *La chronologie*, p. 437; see also Grumel, "La date de l'avènement du Patriarche de Constantinople Niphon," *REB.* 13 (1955), 138–139; Dölger, *Regesten*, nos. 2344, 2346, adopts the date end 1312–1313.

137. Gregoras, I, 262–269. Daničić, *Danilo*, p. 145: Stephen Uroš II then called his relatives and friends and sent them against the Turks; Cf. Dujčev, "Conquête turque," p. 323.

138. Mirkhović, *Danilo*, pp. 109–110; Daničić, *Danilo*, p. 145. The Serbian victory, wrote Danilo, aroused the admiration of those on the other side of the sea. Dujčev, "Conquête turque," p. 323, thinks that "those on the other side of the sea" were the Byzantines. Since the victory was won in Thrace, this is highly unlikely. On the other hand, we know that the Genoese participated in this enterprise, and they must have brought word back to Genoa. So, this remark probably refers to Italy. Daničić, *Danilo*, pp. 145–146, speaks of a second request for help from Andronicus II to Stephen, a short time after the first victory. Stephen sent a large army under Novak Grebostrek, who fought in Anatolia, won, and completely destroyed the Turks! (Daničić, *Danilo*, pp. 146–148; Mirkhović, *Danilo*, pp. 110–112). No other source mentions what, from Danilo's account, appears to be a major event. Danilo was somewhat given to exaggeration, and this second Serbian attack against the Turks is probably a figment of his imagination. Cf. Dujčev, "Conquête turque," pp. 323–325; Novaković, *Srbi i Turci*, pp. 59ff, 67–68, 82–94.

139. Petit, *Charles de Valois*, pp. 120ff.

death Charles of Valois changed his tactics, but the change had been prepared by the events of the years 1306–1308.

It was impossible for him to leave in March 1307 as planned. He was, after all, a vassal of his brother, and a faithful vassal at that, and the affairs of France were not in good order. Flanders had capitulated, in theory, in 1305, with the treaty of Athis-sur-Orge, but the Flemish cities did not accept this treaty until 1309. Even that did not solve the Flemish problem. There was danger of war in 1313 and 1314, and Philip IV tried to raise taxes for the war, thus provoking a reaction from French nobles and cities, and leaving an explosive situation for his successor. Because of the looming Flemish danger, neither Charles nor any of the French nobility could leave on a lengthy expedition in 1307. Moreover, Charles could not levy the tithes given him by the pope without the permission of Philip IV; but Philip was levying his own tithes, for two years, and would not grant his permission while there was danger of war. Furthermore, Philip IV faced chronic financial difficulties, as evidenced by the expedients he used—heavy taxes, and the confiscation of the property of Jews, Lombards, and Templars.[140] In 1308, other problems confronted France and its royal family. Albert of Austria, the Holy Roman Emperor, was assassinated, and Philip IV was very much involved in the problem of succession.[141] Finally, the king had to deal with the affair of the Templars, in which also he needed the support of his nobility.

The plans of Charles of Valois thus lay dormant until they were transferred to another prince in 1313. Meanwhile, his most important ally, Venice, had become so disturbed by his equivocations, that it broke the Valois alliance by signing a truce with Andronicus in 1310. In fact, one of the most interesting aspects of the project of Charles of Valois is that, after the conclusion of the Venetian–Valois treaty in 1306, it was Venice who insisted on assurances that the expedition would in fact take place, and it was Venice who kept goading Charles of Valois. No doubt, the Venetians rightly saw the plan as a replay of the abortive schemes of Charles of Anjou, and wanted to avoid incurring the same damage they had suffered in the years before 1285.

In February 1308 the Venetians gave Charles of Valois until Easter (April 14) to reply to them concerning the expedition; Charles had had some trouble with the pope on the question of crusading subsidies. Venice sent a similar letter, *mutatis mutandis*, to Philip IV of France.[142] More letters were exchanged in 1309, and in July of that year Charles of Valois, answering the Venetian complaints about the delay, found it necessary to defer the expedition once again, to February 1, 1310.[143] At the time, he was at the papal court, trying to obtain further financial help; but he made it clear that his "crusade" depended on the disposition of the pope and of the king of France, both of whom thought that it could not be undertaken for the time being. The Venetians realized

140. Thomas and Predelli, *Diplomatarium*, I, no. 41 (July 6, 1309); J. R. Strayer and C. H. Taylor, *Studies in Early French Taxation* (Cambridge, Mass., 1939), pp. 3–94.
141. Lavisse and Langlois, *Histoire de France*, p. 315.
142. Giomo, *Lettere di Collegio*, nos. 159–160, p. 305.
143. Thomas and Predelli, *Diplomatarium*, I, no. 41.

that circumstances had changed and the opportunity to attack the empire had really been lost.

On September 10, 1309, the doge Pietro Gradenigo wrote to Charles of Valois setting out the Venetian position.[144] He regretted the repeated postponements of the expedition and the pope's preoccupation with other affairs. He wrote of the great hardship inflicted upon the Venetian merchants by the fact that Venice was at war with the empire, without actually fighting that war. He made it clear that the Venetians could not support the expense and peril to which they were exposed by the continuation of this uncertain state of affairs. And he concluded that for love of Charles of Valois they would accept one further deferment, to February 1310. This letter was forwarded by the pope to Philip IV.[145] Venice was clearly impatient and wanted either to carry out the project soon, or else abandon it.

Meanwhile, Venice had already begun to take stock of her position in the Levant, where her interests were in danger. Even before her treaty with Charles of Valois, Venice had experienced difficulties in the Byzantine empire. In January 1304 the Venetian senate had decreed that no single ships should go to the empire; only convoys were allowed to sail in those parts.[146] In 1306 an embassy was sent to Constantinople to request reparations for damage done by Roger de Flor and the Catalan Company. But navigation in the empire and the Black Sea was still permitted in 1306.[147]

In 1307 and 1308 things became more difficult for Venice in the Romania. Apparently Byzantine sailors inflicted damage on Venetian shipping in and around Nigroponte. These attacks were probably by private persons, not taking their orders from Constantinople. But the Genoese sailor, Andrea Morisco, who was in the pay of the emperor, was also molesting Venetian shipping off the western coast of the Peloponnesus, and other Genoese pirates were active in the same area. As a result, Venice began to take measures for the defense of her possessions. In March 1307 two captains were sent to the East, one to lead the galleys which protected Venetian possessions in the Romania, and the other to patrol the Asia Minor coast. In 1308 and 1309 Venice sent a number of her best admirals to the East, and repaired the fortifications of Modon, Coron, and Nigroponte.[148]

In May 1309, Venice decided to send to Andronicus the embassy he wanted, in order to discuss the outstanding problems between the two states; in September of that year, an order went out to the Venetian representatives in the Levant not to molest Andronicus' subjects.[149] In other words, Venice

---

144. Ibid., no. 42; Du Cange and Buchon, *Histoire de Constantinople*, II, 139–140. On Venetian losses through the continuation of unfriendly relations with Byzantium, see Marino Sanudo Torsello, *Fragmentum*, ed. R. L. Wolff, p. 153.

145. On October 22, 1309: Thomas and Predelli, *Diplomatarium*, I, no. 43.

146. Cessi and Sambin, *Consiglio dei Rogati*, I, 108, no. 70.

147. Thiriet, *Délibérations*, I, no. 118; Cessi and Sambin, *Consiglio dei Rogati*, p. 118, nos. 181–183, 187–188.

148. Thiriet, *Délibérations*, I, no. 138 (severe damages inflicted by Byzantines on Venetians); cf. nos. 146, 168–169; Giomo, *Lettere di Collegio*, nos. 38, 40, 41, 43–45, 50–53, 63.

149. Thiriet, *Délibérations*, I, nos. 174, 181; Cessi and Sambin, *Consiglio dei Rogati*, p. 133, no. 70.

was already, in 1309, breaking the spirit of her treaty with Charles of Valois by exchanging ambassadors with Byzantium. In the early 1280's, before the truce of 1285, Venice had forbidden all navigation in the waters of the empire, while now her ships sailed yearly to the Romania. Thus it would appear that Venice was being careful not to cut off all relations with the Byzantine empire, and was unwilling to start a war with Byzantium, unless Charles of Valois also participated.

In 1309 a new threat appeared to Venetian shipping in the Aegean. The Knights Hospitallers, who had conquered the island of Rhodes in 1308, were preparing a fleet with which to attack the Venetian possessions. On November 29, 1309, the Venetian government sent letters to its representatives in the colonies of the Romania, acquainting them with this danger: Venetian inform-ers in Genoa had reported to Venice that the Grand Master of the Hospitallers, Foulkes de Villaret, had armed several galleys in Genoa, and had been seen off Naples, en route to Rhodes. It was rumored that the Hospitallers planned to attack and conquer the islands of Mytilene, Cyprus, and perhaps even Crete. In 1309 and 1310, Venice sent men and ships to the Levant, and sent instruc-tions to her representatives to prepare to withstand the attacks of the Hospi-tallers, and of the Genoese who had sent a fleet of forty galleys. In fact, the Hospitallers did not launch an attack on Venetian possessions, although their ships did attack particular Venetian ships; one of them, a ship belonging to Marino Falier, lost a cargo of 330 pounds of pepper, about 20 pounds of saffron, and a certain quantity of sugar. But in May 1310, Venice was exchang-ing ambassadors with Rhodes, and relations became less tense.[150]

The Venetian discussions with Andronicus (1309) were continued in 1310. When the promise made by Charles of Valois to give the Venetians a definite answer by February 1310 was not carried out, the Venetians moved decisively toward the reestablishment of normal relations with Byzantium. In April 1310 the senate added to the terms of the proposed treaty the stipulation that either party could break it, after giving six months' notice. On April 27, the major council decided to select an ambassador, who would leave for Byzantium soon thereafter. In June the senate urged that the truce be signed quickly, and in the meantime it decreed that no Venetian ships could sail to Thessalonica, to the Dardanelles, or to the Black Sea. And in July the Venetian senate decided that if disputes arose between Byzantines and Venetians on the ques-tion of reparations, the ambassadors, Jacopo Quirino and Gabriel Dandolo, would accept a compromise.[151]

A twelve-year treaty finally was signed on November 11, 1310, at the palace of the Blachernai.[152] The treaty confirmed the previous treaties and agree-ments between Andronicus II and Venice, and added only a few new articles. The first article that was expressly stated in the text of the treaty was not new, but rather a confirmation of the article which had been incorporated in all treaties with Venice since 1277. It was restated that no Venetian could buy

150. Thiriet, *Délibérations*, I, nos. 192–195, 197, 200–201, 210, 212, 213.
151. Ibid., nos. 207, 208, 214–216; Cessi and Sambin, *Consiglio dei Rogati*, pp. 133–134, nos. 73, 77–79, 82, 84; Giomo, *Lettere di Collegio*, no. 564.
152. Thomas, *Diplomatarium*, I, nos. 145, 146.

Byzantine wheat or export it, if its price was more than one hyperpyron per modium. That article had probably been violated, hence the explicit reconfirmation. Also, Andronicus forbade his subjects to molest any of the Venetian possessions in the Aegean. Again, it is clear that some had done so, for Andronicus was forced to pay reparations amounting to 40,000 hyperpyra, for damages done by his subjects to the Venetians; he waived his right to similar payment for damages done by the Venetians to his subjects.

The most important new article had to do with the Catalans. Already Venice was beginning to feel the effects of the establishment of the Catalans in Greece, and on October 27, 1310, the government had complained to the king of Aragon that the Catalans had pillaged some Venetian ships. Venice had demanded compensation.[153] In the treaty of 1310, the Venetians and the Byzantines treated the Catalans as their common enemy. The Venetians would forbid their subjects to sail or trade in those parts of the empire, or in the lands of those vassals of the empire (Thessaly) which were held by the Catalans. This economic boycott would last for the period of Catalan domination over these lands. Once the Catalans left, the Venetians could go to these parts and engage in trade as freely as they did in all the other parts of the Byzantine empire.

By 1310 the forces of Charles of Valois had weakened, and the danger he presented to the Byzantine empire had correspondingly diminished. Venice was no longer an active member of his system of alliances, and the king of Serbia was growing more friendly toward the Byzantines. The Catalans too had thrown off their allegiance to Charles of Valois. Thus, this particular danger to the integrity of the Byzantine empire lapsed, not because of any diplomatic activity on the part of Byzantium, nor because of any defeats the Valois forces suffered, but simply because Charles of Valois was forced to stay in France and participate in French affairs. He did not totally abandon his Byzantine ambitions, and while it had become clear that crusading zeal was no longer an effective motivating factor, Charles of Valois seems to have thought that Byzantium could still be conquered—not by himself, but by his daughter's husband.

Catherine of Valois, the issue of the Courtenay–Valois marriage, inherited the titles to the throne of Constantinople after the death of her mother in 1308. Suitors for the hand of the heiress had appeared when she was still a baby. In 1303 she was promised to Hugues, the son of the duke of Burgundy.[154] In 1306 Hugues succeeded to the ducal throne, and confirmed the engagement. One year later, however, he had to abandon his claim to the hand of the young heiress. Clement V and Philip IV, meeting at Poitiers, decided that the duke was not strong enough to recover his future wife's inheritance, and that Catherine should marry Philip of Taranto. Since Charles of Valois was wary of breaking his agreement, it was decided that Hugues should be persuaded to

153. *Thiriet, Délibérations,* I, no. 227.

154. Du Cange and Buchon, *Histoire de Constantinople,* II, 100. On June 3, 1304 Benedict XI permitted the double marriage of Philip (Charles of Valois' son) to Beatrice (daughter of Robert of Burgundy), and of Hugues of Burgundy to Catherine of Valois: Grandjean, *Registres,* no. 740.

renounce his rights voluntarily. Some lengthy and complicated transactions followed, in which the king of France played a principal role, and through which a compromise acceptable to all was reached. In theory, the engagement was broken by Catherine, with the consent of Clement V and Philip IV, on the pretext that Hugues had not tried to recover his Kingdom of Thessalonica.[155]

Philip of Taranto, who had divorced Thamar of Epirus in 1309, was the most eligible husband as far as Charles of Valois was concerned. Charles II of Naples, Philip's father, had transferred to him in 1294 the suzerainty of Achaia, Athens, Albania, and Thessaly; he also received Corfu and Butrinto. From his marriage to Thamar he had the four fortified towns of Lepanto, Vonitza, Angelokastron, and Vrachori, and the promise, broken by Anne of Epirus after her husband's death, that he could become the suzerain of the despots of Epirus. When Anne refused him this suzerainty, Philip tried to seize the despotate of Epirus with the help of John I of Cephallonia and the prince of Achaia, Philip of Savoy (1303).[156] Philip of Savoy was not very enthusiastic in the cause of his suzerain. In 1307 he and his wife, Isabeau de Villehardouin, were dispossessed of the principality of Achaia because they refused to help Philip of Taranto in his second campaign of 1306. Philip of Taranto then became prince of Achaia, although Isabeau did not recognize this, and left the principality to her daughter Mathilde or Mahaut.[157]

Philip of Taranto married Catherine of Valois on April 6, 1313, and thus the two western personages with the strongest claims to the Byzantine empire were united.[158] Philip IV promised to give Philip of Taranto five hundred

155. On these negotiations, see Du Cange, *Histoire de Constantinople, Chartes*, pp. 65–67, 71–80; Du Cange and Buchon, *Histoire de Constantinople*, II, 344–346, 357–360. A. N. J510 nos. 19, 20; JJ 49 no. 59; KK 549 fols. 17ro–19ro (June 1313); JJ 59 nos. 56, 77, 75, 78 (Philip IV's confirmation and approval, 1313).

156. Du Cange and Buchon, *Histoire de Constantinople*, II, 62–64. Anne then married her son Thomas to Anne, daughter of Michael IX and Rita-Maria: Miller, *Latins in the Levant*, p. 202.

157. Morel-Fatio, *Libro de los Fechos*, §527–529; Miller, *Latins in the Levant*, p. 204. Philip of Savoy was the third husband of Isabeau de Villehardouin, and prince of Achaia (1301–1307).

158. Du Cange, *Histoire de Constantinople*, p. 246. Philip of Taranto and Catherine of Valois were doubly related to each other: Charles of Valois had married Catherine of Courtenay, who was the daughter of Philip of Courtenay and Béatrix of Anjou, Charles of Anjou's daughter. Philip of Taranto was the son of Charles II of Naples, eldest son of Charles of Anjou and brother of Béatrix. The other family link came through the relationship of Charles of Anjou and Charles of Valois: Charles of Anjou, Philip of Taranto's grandfather, was the brother of Louis IX of France, who was Charles of Valois' grandfather. This simplified genealogical table shows the relationship:

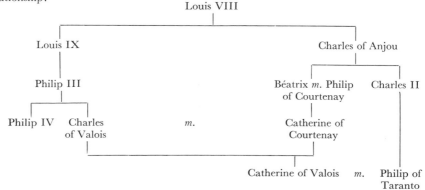

knights for one year, or the equivalent in money. Philip of Taranto was to use this gift to help Charles of Valois recover the empire of Constantinople. The enterprise was envisaged as part of a general crusade, whose final aim would be the recovery of the Holy Lands. In 1321 the king of France, Philip V, paid Philip of Taranto 70,000 livres tournois, which was estimated as the money equivalent of the five hundred knights promised in 1313.[159]

It was almost inevitable in 1313 that the reconquest of Constantinople should be linked with a crusade to Jerusalem. Perhaps the principal reason for this was the failure of previous plans, which had exasperated the Venetians and filled with suspicion those who had been ready in 1302 or in 1306 to join Charles of Valois. Also, since December 19, 1312, a general crusade had been proclaimed by the church council of Vienne, and a six-year tithe had been imposed on church property in order to provide funds for this crusade. The aim of the crusade was the recovery of Jerusalem, while an attack on Constantinople was also contemplated. Indeed, on November 22, 1311, James II's representatives at the council of Vienne sent him a letter in which they said that the pope was contemplating a plan for a general crusade, by which the Catholics would conquer the Byzantine empire, then go through Asia Minor to Armenia, and from there to the Holy Lands. Apparently, the papal vice-chancellor who discussed this plan with the Aragonese ambassadors also said that the Catalans would be an invaluable help to this crusade, for they had already proven successful in wars against the Greeks, and they held large portions of Greece.[160]

The decision of the council of Vienne, to proclaim a crusade, had been prepared by a long series of propagandists of the crusade, who suggested various more or less practical ways of recovering Jerusalem. Most of them agreed that the success of their plans depended on the prior conquest of the Byzantine empire and on the disruption of Egyptian trade; sometimes the one was thought to depend on the other.

Fidenzio of Padua considered the conquest of Constantinople and Asia Minor necessary mainly because this would facilitate the passage and provisioning of the crusading army. Guillaume d'Adam, in his *De modo Saracenos extirpandi*, wrote that the Byzantine emperor, as well as Genoa, the Catalans, and, to a lesser degree, Venice and Pisa had commercial relations with Egypt; in order for this to stop, the Byzantine empire should be conquered. The conquest would be very easy, for the Greeks were effeminate cowards (a very old idea), as proven by the fact that even the Turks could defeat them.[161]

159. A. N. J510 no. 21, 21bis no. 2, 21ter. Philip V made the same promise. Payments: JJ 268 no. 21, fol. 37vo, JJ 64 no. 222 fol. 125vo–126ro. Cf. *Reg. Clem. V.*, nos. 7759–7765 (April 30, 1312), 8863 (July 15, 1312).

160. *Reg. Clem. V.*, nos. 8781, 8782 (April 22, 1312), 8783 (April 25); Delaville le Roulx, *France en Orient*, I, 59ff. C.-J. Hefele, *Histoire des Conciles*, VI, 2, (Paris, 1915), 642ff; Charles Samaran-G. Mollat, *La fiscalité pontificale en France au XIVe siècle* (Paris, 1905), pp. 14ff; Rubió y Lluch, *Diplomatari*, no. 52.

161. Delaville le Roulx, *France en Orient*, I, 19ff, 55ff, 62–63, 70ff; Atiya, *The Crusade*, pp. 36–43, 64–66; Fidenzio of Padua, a Franciscan, wrote his *Liber Recuperationis Terre Sancte* before the fall of Acre (1291). Guillaume d'Adam was a Dominican friar who had visited Constantinople. The *De modo Saracenos extirpandi* was written in 1313 and has been published by Koehler, *Recueil des historiens*, II. The author of the *Descriptio* expressed the same contempt for the effeminate Greeks, and was certain that the conquest of the empire would be very easy: Górka *Descriptio*, pp. 23–25.

Marino Sanudo, whose ideas more than those of any other such writer developed to suit the times, advocated the subjection of Egypt. More clear-sighted than the Venetian government of the time, he believed that the crusaders should not attempt the preliminary conquest of the Byzantine empire, so difficult to hold. On the other hand, he thought that after the fall of Egypt, a few ships molesting the seacoasts of the empire and of Asia Minor would so weaken Byzantium that it would soon fall.[162]

Finally, the Frenchman Pierre Dubois had, since 1300, developed a theory of the crusades aiming at the greater glory of the French royal family. In his *De recuperatione Terrae Sanctae* (written between 1306 and 1308), he advised Charles of Valois among other things to learn the Greek language before the proposed expedition; the Greeks hated the Franks, and would accept more easily a man who spoke their language.[163] This was one of his more practical suggestions. In 1308 he suggested that one of the sons of the king of France, Philip the Tall (later Philip V), be made king of an eastern kingdom, to consist of Egypt and Syria.[164] The result of a crusade, then, would be the domination of the French in the Byzantine empire, Asia Minor, Egypt, and Syria.

Immediately after the council of Vienne proclaimed a crusade, a kind of crusading frenzy struck the French nobles. In the summer of 1313, in Paris, several high-born young men, among them Hugues of Burgundy and Philip the Tall, then count of Poitiers, were knighted, and immediately took the crusading oath as well. As the French chronicler put it, "fu faite si grande croiserie que c'estoit merveille de la dévocion que tout le peuple avoit." The fervor continued, and in 1316 another group of nobles, led by Louis of Clermont (later duke of Bourbon), took the oath. The French crusaders were constantly enthusiastic, but rarely translated their zeal into action.

Philip IV, and French kings after him were very hard pressed for money and could not finance a crusade. This probably accounts for the discrepancy between enthusiasm and action. Indeed, the crusading subsidies granted by Clement V, and especially by John XXII, may be regarded as loans to the kings, rather than as real efforts to finance a crusade.[165] It is in this light that one must see Philip IV's attitude toward Charles of Valois and Philip of Taranto. He appeared to support both wholeheartedly, although his support was, in

---

162. The first book of his *Secreta Fidelium Crucis* was presented to the pope in 1309. See Bongars, *Gesta Dei per Francos*, II; Arturo Magnocavallo, *Marin Sanudo il Vecchio*, (Bergamo, 1901), pp. 44, 71. On Sanudo, see Atiya, *The Crusade*, pp. 53–55.

163. Petit, *Charles de Valois*, pp. 95–96; Atiya, *The Crusade*, pp. 48–52; Charles-V. Langlois *Collection des textes pour servir à l'étude et l'enseignement de l'histoire* (Paris, 1891), pp. 284ff: *Libellus super abreviatione guerrarum et huiusmodi provisionibus*, written ca. 1300. Similar views were expressed by Guillaume de Nogaret, a close friend of Philip IV and vice-chancellor of the kingdom. His memoir was written in 1310. See Boutaric, *La France sous Philipe le Bel*, pp. 411–413.

164. Delaville le Roulx, *France en Orient*, p. 53; Langlois, *Collection*, appendix, pp. 131–140: "Oppinio cuiusdam suadentis regi Francie ut regnum Jerosolymitanum et Cipri pro altero filio suorum ac de invasione regni Egipti."

165. On Philip IV's taxes and resources, see G. Picot, *Documents relatifs aux États généraux sous Philippe le Bel* (Paris, 1901); G. Dupont-Ferrier, *Institutions financières de la France à la fin du moyen-âge*, (Paris, 1930-1932), I; Strayer-Taylor, *French Taxation*, pp. 3–105.

fact, limited. In May 1312 he forgave Charles of Valois all debts owed to the royal treasury because of Charles's great expenses, "and especially because we think that he provides with pains and diligence for the recovery of the Holy Land."[166] In August of the same year he gave Charles of Valois money, again for the recovery of the Holy Land.[167] In 1313 Philip IV also confirmed various documents which the count of Valois had obtained on several occasions, and which pledged the support of Sicily, Naples, the papacy, and Venice to the expedition against Constantinople. The reissue of these documents was probably a sort of guarantee to Philip of Taranto that his rights to the Byzantine empire were being safeguarded.[168]

Finally, in his will, Philip IV left 100,000 livres tournois to be used for the expenses of the crusade. The money was to go, in the first instance, to Philip the Tall, who had taken the crusader's oath in 1313. If Philip was unable to go to the East, the money was to be given to Charles of Valois or, in the last instance, to Louis, count of Évreux.[169] This particular sum was clearly meant for the purposes of a general crusade rather than an expedition to Constantinople.

The documentary evidence of the years 1308–1314 suggests that Charles of Valois was still concerned with the reconquest of the Byzantine empire, although a number of factors had changed his plans slightly. So much was this the case, that Charles refused an offer of Andronicus II to marry a Byzantine prince to the heiress of the Latin empire, Catherine of Valois. Andronicus sent one of his bishops to Clement V, then at the council of Vienne, to Philip IV, and to Charles of Valois, to request Catherine's hand for one of his sons (May–June, 1311). Only Demetrius can have been single at the time. It is possible, however, that the document referred to one of Michael IX's sons, either Manuel, or the future Andronicus III.[170] Charles of Valois answered that his daughter was going to marry Philip of Taranto.

Then, the imperial envoys tried to get in touch with James II of Aragon, in order to obtain one of *his* daughters for the Byzantine prince. James requested further information about the proposals, but knew that they did not have much chance of success. Andronicus II viewed this proposed marriage as a way of keeping western armies, especially that of Charles of Valois, out of his empire. To this purpose he was apparently willing to sacrifice his earlier religious policy: we are told that "the emperor, his son, and all the people of

166. A. N. J164 A. no. 25 (May 21, 1312). Philip said he did this because of "les granz et agreables soins [?] que [Charles] a faiz en noz besoignes et es besoinges de nostre royaume et que nous esperons que il doie faire de ci en avant plus curieusement et diligentement et especiaument pou ce que nous cuidons que il meite peine et diligence a l'ordenance et la pourveance du passage de la Terre Saincte."

167. A. N. J164 A. nos. 26, 27. The gift was of 100,000 livres tournois to be given within two years. In 1313 Clement V granted tithes to both Charles of Valois and Philip IV for the crusade: Samaran-Mollat, *Fiscalité*, pp. 14–15.

168. A. N. J510 nos. 16, 18; J509 nos. 12, 16bis; Du Cange and Buchon, *Histoire de Constantinople*, II, 366–370.

169. A. N. R⁴*799, I, fol. 68ro–vo. Philip V left the same amount, for the same purpose, in his will: P. Lehugueur, *Histoire de Philippe le Long*, I (Paris, 1897), 196.

170. Finke, *Acta Aragonensia*, II, no. 465, pp. 748–749; Marinescu, "Tentatives," pp. 14–15.

his empire would recognize and obey the Catholic faith and would obey the Lord Pope like any Catholic Christian." If that report is true, Andronicus must have very deeply feared the proposed French expedition. As it was, the expedition did not take place, and Andronicus did not repeat his offer to recognize the Catholic church until 1324. His initiative of 1311 must be seen as the first important change in his relations with western Europe and with the papacy.

The years 1303 to 1313—from the arrival of the Catalans at Constantinople to the marriage of Catherine of Valois—were decisive for the Byzantine empire. During these years, the first aim of the Palaeologan policy, the preservation of the dynasty at Constantinople, was severely challenged. The challenge was strongest in 1308, when what must have seemed a formidable alliance threatened Byzantium: Charles of Valois—with the pope and the king of France behind him—Venice, the Catalans, the Serbs, the disgruntled Greeks. Had Charles of Valois launched an attack in 1308, who could have stopped him? And where would the Byzantine imperial family have fled, now that Asia Minor was in the hands of the Turks? The Byzantine state would have been obliterated. The threat was grave, and it must have seemed imminent. Yet Andronicus II could do nothing to stave it off. The already weakened resources of his empire had been spent in his fight against the Catalans. Indeed, the greatest contribution Andronicus made to the preservation of the Byzantine empire was his success in getting the Catalans to move out of Thrace, and into Macedonia. For the rest, it was not so much the emperor as his subjects who put up a real defense against the Catalan forces.

Perhaps the most telling difference between the state of Michael VIII and that of Andronicus II is this: in 1282, Michael VIII faced as formidable a coalition of western forces as did Andronicus II in 1308. But Michael was fully aware of the complexities of European politics, and he encouraged all the anti-Angevin forces. Thus, he contributed to the uneasy situation in Italy and Sicily which kept Charles of Anjou out of the empire. By contrast, Andronicus II had nothing to do with the failure of Charles of Valois' plans. These failed because Charles became involved in intra-European affairs, and because he could not receive enough real support for his enterprise. Andronicus II's attitude is reflected in the Byzantine sources, where Charles's plans are not mentioned. No doubt this lack of concern in the sources was due to the much more immediate preoccupation of the Byzantines with the Catalans, the Turks, the Serbs. But it also illustrates the isolation of the Byzantines from western Europe.

Andronicus II's peace treaty with Venice in 1310, the establishment of the Catalans in the duchy of Athens in 1311, and the emperor's offer to marry a Byzantine prince to Catherine of Valois and unite the Greek and Latin churches are all symbolic of the end of an era in the relations of Andronicus with the West. No longer threatened by Europe, Andronicus II would draw closer to it.

VIII

After the Storm, 1311–1321

In 1311 Andronicus II was fifty-one or fifty-two years old. He had just gone through an ordeal so heavy that it might have destroyed even a younger and bolder man. Yet, surprisingly, during the ten-year period 1311–1321 both his foreign and his domestic policies showed signs of a new political maturity. His relations with western Europe assumed a less convulsive and more coherent tone. No longer under immediate threat from the West, he could afford to ignore the Franco-papal crusading plans which, although potentially dangerous to Byzantium, never actually resulted in a campaign. As his father had done, Andronicus tried to bring some balance into his relations with westerners, particularly with Venice and Genoa. His pro-Genoese policy had proved disappointing; he now entered into long negotiations with Venice, seeking to resolve the outstanding differences between the two states. He worked slowly and with dignity, unwilling to yield on any point, yet eager to reach an agreement with the Venetians. At the same time, he reestablished friendly contact with Aragon, Serbia, and Bulgaria.

Andronicus II used the diplomatic détente to rebuild the strength of his empire. The Catalan campaign had underlined with painful clarity the weaknesses of his state: the lack of money, the disintegration of the armed forces, the disaffection of the Arsenites and pro-Lascarids. Now, after 1311, Andronicus II set about putting his house in order: he ended the Arsenite schism, he replenished his treasury, and he created a small but efficient army. He had already achieved two of the aims of the policy his father had initiated: the Palaeologan dynasty was firmly established on the throne of Constantinople, and the western efforts to reestablish a Latin empire had failed. The third aim of Palaeologan policy, the recovery of Epirus, Thessaly, and the Morea, now seemed within his reach.

In Greece, Andronicus II was able to claim a measure of success: his northern frontiers were peaceful, and parts of the Morea, of the state of Thessaly, and of the Despotate of Epirus came under his control. But in Asia Minor, there is no evidence of Byzantine military activity, nor is there evidence that Andronicus II made any effort to defend Anatolia against the Turks, as he had done during the first twenty-two years of his reign. Perhaps this inactivity in Asia Minor makes Andronicus II's foreign and domestic policy begin to resemble that of Michael VIII. For the first time, Andronicus concentrated his activities on the western part of his empire, and showed a greater interest in the affairs of Europe. Was it because his earlier policy, focused on the recovery of Anatolia, had failed?

Given the condition of the Byzantine empire after the Catalan campaign, it was remarkable that Andronicus II found the stamina to embark upon a reorganization of the state. Unfortunately, his achievements went up in the flames of the civil war which began in 1321 and ended with his dethronement in 1328.

While the sources make it possible to study the Byzantine foreign policy of the years 1311–1321 in detail, domestic developments are much less well documented. There is very little detailed information about economic and social developments, about the state of the army, and still less about conditions in Asia Minor. This is the result of a hiatus in the Byzantine narrative sources: Pachymeres ended his account in 1307, while Cantacuzenus began his with the year 1320. Gregoras is the only narrative source for the period between 1307 and 1320, but his account is very short and very selective. He devotes a mere thirty-six manuscript pages to the years 1311–1321, pages which are mostly concerned with his discussions with his mentor, Theodore Metochites, and with Andronicus II, whom he was trying to cultivate. His account can be supplemented with information from other sources, but on the whole less is known about this decade than about any other period of Andronicus II's reign.

Domestic Policy of Andronicus II

Soon after the Catalans left Macedonia, Andronicus II was able to turn once again to the turmoil inside the Byzantine church. In 1309 the discontent of the higher clergy with the patriarch Athanasios I forced the patriarch to abdicate for the second and last time. The most serious accusation against Athanasios was that one of his subordinates, Theophanes, had been found guilty of simony. Athanasios insisted that he was in no way guilty of collusion with the man, and indeed he himself had written a letter to the emperor accusing Theophanes of simony. The synod of Constantinople, however, was eager to believe any calumny against Athanasios. In his letter of resignation, the patriarch wrote that he would have preferred deposition; but, not wishing to disrupt the ecclesiastical hierarchy and perhaps start a new schism, he chose to resign (September 1309).[1] His successor, Niphon I (1310–1314), was, even more than Athanasios, innocent of formal learning—according to Gregoras he could not even write—and was also a very greedy and worldly man.[2] Despite his

1. This letter is published in Migne, *PG*, CXLII (Paris, 1885), cols. 496–501. Nicephorus Choumnos reports that Athanasios I was deposed by the synod because Theophanes was guilty of simony, with Athanasios' knowledge and consent: «Νικηφόρου τοῦ Χούμνου ἔλεγχος κατὰ τοῦ κακῶς τὰ πάντα πατριαρχεύσαντος Νίφωνος ἀνανεχθεὶς παρὰ τοῦ Νικομηδείας καὶ τοῦ Μυτιλήνης πρὸς τὴν Ἱερὰν Σύνοδον,» Boissonade, *Anecdota Graeca*, V, 255–283. V. Laurent accepts this statement without comment: "Les grandes crises religieuses," p. 284. But Migne publishes the letter of Athanasios I to Andronicus II, in which the patriarch denounced Theophanes' simoniac practices: *PG*, CXLII, col. 504. Gregoras, I, 258–259, gives a more lurid account of Athanasios' resignation. He says that Athanasios' enemies appropriated the patriarch's footstool, and painted on it a representation of Christ flanked by two men: Andronicus II who held a bit in his mouth, and Athanasios I who held the harness. They then showed this to the emperor, claiming that Athanasios I viewed their relationship in this fashion. Andronicus II did not believe them, but the patriarch heard about the plot and was so disgusted that he decided to resign.

2. Gregoras, I, 259–262. For the dates of Niphon's patriarchate, see Laurent, "Chronologie," pp. 149–150, and V. Grumel, "Mélanges," *REB* 13 (1955), 138–139.

faults, Niphon I rendered a great service to the empire: during his occupation of the patriarchal throne, the Arsenites were finally, and formally, reconciled to the established church.

There was little hope of peace with the Arsenites while Athanasios I was patriarch. He was an uncompromising man, and he would not easily come into an agreement with the people he considered perpetrators of schism. Besides, he and the Arsenites drew their support from the same source: the monks, some of whom were Arsenites, while others supported Athanasios.[3] As soon as Niphon ascended the patriarchal throne, the Arsenites made the first move toward reconciliation. Their movement had become sterile and negative, and all their years of opposition to the established hierarchy had accomplished nothing. Now, they asked to be taken back into the body of the church. They presented a list of six demands, some quite reasonable, and all acceptable to emperor and patriarch.[4] For the first time, the Arsenites dropped their most controversial demand: they no longer insisted that the only way to union was the election of an Arsenite patriarch. Thus, they implicitly recognized the legitimacy of the Palaeologan church hierarchy and of the Palaeologan dynasty.

Andronicus II responded with alacrity. On September 14, 1310, the emperor and the patriarch participated in a bizarre ceremony of union in the church of Sancta Sophia. The corpse of Arsenius (who had been dead for thirty-seven years) was dressed in patriarchal robes and seated on the throne; it its hands, it held a formula of absolution, forgiving those whom Arsenius had once anathematized. The emperor read the charter of union between the Arsenites and the official church, and then Niphon took from Arsenius' hand the formula of absolution and read it to the congregation.[5] The Arsenites participated in the celebration of Mass, and the schism was ended.

The ceremony in Sancta Sophia was given content by one imperial chrysobull, two imperial decrees, and an encyclical letter of the patriarch Niphon, all proclaiming the end of the schism and the reinstatement of Arsenite clergy.[6] This did not result in the immediate restoration of peace and unity in the Byzantine church. As so often in the past, there were intransigents who wanted no conciliation with the schismatics. The more extreme of the "orthodox" opposed the practice of *oikonomia* (accommodation) which both the patriarch and the emperor were following; the extremists insisted that the Arsenites, being schismatics, should not be allowed to rejoin the body of the church without having formally recanted their errors. Sometime after the official promulgation of union, Andronicus II was forced to reaffirm his original chrysobull at the request of the metropolitans of Chalcedon, Monembasia, Patras, Serres, and Christopolis, who were not convinced of the emperor's sincerity.[7] As late as 1315, we find evidence of persecution of the Arsenites by

3. Laurent, "Les grandes crises religieuses," pp. 249–251, 275–279.
4. Ibid., document 2, pp. 289–292.
5. Ibid., documents 4, 5, pp. 297–304.
6. Ibid., documents 2, 3, 4, 6, pp. 289–302, 306–311.
7. Ibid., document 7, pp. 311–312.

the intransigent clergy. An Arsenite priest from one of the provinces spent a year in Constantinople pleading his cause before Andronicus II and Niphon I. The priest claimed that, despite the imperial and patriarchal decrees of conciliation, his bishop had forbidden him to exercise his priestly functions, because he had been an Arsenite.[8]

Despite occasional difficulties, the reconciliation of the Arsenites removed an element which, because of its hostility toward church and state, could be very dangerous to both. The Arsenite faction was large even as late as 1310. Gregoras wrote that when the emperor and the patriarch indicated their willingness to negotiate with the Arsenites, these appeared from everywhere; as though springing out of the earth, they streamed to Constantinople, dressed in rags, but proud in their arrogance.[9] Being, for the most part, monks, they could exercise a great deal of influence over the populace, and they did not hesitate to seek alliances with the enemies of the empire in order to bring down the Palaeologan establishment. Their return to the church was a major factor in the reorganization and stabilization of the empire.

The establishment of peace within the Byzantine church was followed by a gradual improvement in state finances. Here too the sources are inadequate, so that only the end-result is known of what must have been a long, concerted effort. Despite the loss of Asia Minor, despite the many fiscal privileges Andronicus II granted to communes, monasteries, Byzantine and foreign merchants, he had so managed his financial affairs that by 1321 the treasury could count on an annual revenue of 1,000,000 hyperpyra.[10] Although Gregoras hailed this as a great achievement, the empire still faced grave financial problems. In 1317, for example, there was a famine, and it is highly likely that taxes that year did not yield anything like 1,000,000 hyperpyra.[11] Besides, the value of the hyperpyron continued to decline during the decade 1311–1321.[12] Yet on the whole, it seems that Byzantine finances had much improved by the end of this period. At the time of the Bulgarian and Catalan campaigns, both Andronicus and Michael IX had been forced to liquidate their personal assets in order to provide for the needs of the state. In 1321, when Andronicus II wanted to remove John Cantacuzenus from the capital, he ordered the young general to go to Thessaly to fight the Catalans of the Duchy of Athens, and was able to give him immediately 50,000 hyperpyra from the treasury.[13]

Andronicus II wanted to use his increased revenues for the defense of the state. In 1321 he was planning to equip a standing army consisting of 1,000 cavalry stationed in Asia Minor, and 2,000 cavalry stationed in Thrace and Macedonia.[14] He had sent a substantial army to Epirus, in 1313–1314, and

8. J. Gouillard, "Après le schisme arsénite. La correspondance inédite du pseudo–Jean Chilas," *Académie Roumaine, Bulletin de la section historique*, 25 (1944), 174–211.

9. Gregoras, I, 261.

10. Gregoras, I, 317–318.

11. Thiriet, *Délibérations*, I, 174, no. 389.

12. Zakythinos, *Crise*, pp. 26–27; Thomas and Predelli, *Diplomatarium*, I, 118.

13. Cantacuzenus, I, 88.

14. Gregoras, I, 317–318.

the fact that he was able to do this probably indicates that his finances had already improved by 1313.[15]

Some of this money came from customs duties, as the Byzantines enforced more strictly the administration of commercial treaties with westerners. Unfortunately, in order to replenish his treasury, Andronicus II had also been forced to tax heavily those people who had most suffered from the Catalan invasion, and who were still suffering from the periodic incursions of the Tartars: the peasants and townsmen of Thrace and Macedonia. The tax collector became once again a hated figure, particularly since tax farming was an established practice and overenthusiastic tax collectors tried to outdo each other in the performance of their duties. As a result, the population of Macedonia, and especially of Thrace, became alienated from Andronicus II and his officials, and was ready to rebel against the central government. Ironically, Andronicus II's efforts to raise money in order to protect his state caused such discontent that they proved a major reason for the success of his grandson's rebellion.[16]

Very little is known about developments in Asia Minor during this period. The Byzantine sources provide virtually no information about the progress of the Turks, and the Ottoman sources, written at a later period, are not very reliable. For some reason, Ottoman progress in Bithynia was interrupted between 1307 and 1317; Georgiades-Arnakes thinks that Andronicus II's Mongol alliance of 1304–1307 may have contained the Ottomans and forced them to abandon the siege of Brusa and Nicaea.[17] Around the year 1317 the Ottomans became active once again. Sultan Osman sent his son and heir, Orkhan, to complete the conquest of the last Byzantine forts on the northern bank of the Sangarius River. In the same year, the Ottomans unsuccessfully besieged the city of Brusa.[18]

Byzantine political control of Asia Minor was by now virtually limited to northern Bithynia. At the same time, the Byzantine church was losing control of the Christian population of Asia Minor, both in Bithynia and in the more remote provinces. The Christian population rapidly declined in numbers, either because people converted to Islam or because they fled into the empire of Trebizond and into the European possessions of the Byzantine empire. The metropolitan sees of Asia Minor were impoverished, and the patriarchal synod of Constantinople adopted the practice of granting the bishops of Anatolia for their sustenance lands outside their diocese. A series of such grants documents the abandonment of Asia Minor by the Byzantines. In 1317 a monk named Kallistos was granted the see of Amaseia, which had remained vacant for years. But, "because of the great poverty of his see, and because the barbarians rule over it," Kallistos was also granted the see of Limnion, situated in the

---

15. Thomas and Predelli, *Diplomatarium*, I, 135–136, no. 76; 146, no. 77; and below, "The Papacy, the Angevins, and Byzantium," in Chapter VIII.

16. Gregoras, I, 319; Cantacuzenus, I, 93–94.

17. Georgiades-Arnakes, Οἱ πρῶτοι Ὀθωμανοί, p. 185.

18. Joseph von Hammer, *Geschichte des Osmanischen Reiches*, I (Budapest, 1827), 72–83. H. A. Gibbons, *The Foundations of the Ottoman Empire* (Oxford, 1916), p. 42.

empire of Trebizond. The new bishop would live in Trebizond, and somehow exercise his authority over the Christian population of Amaseia.[19] The preamble of the synodical letter announcing Kallistos' appointment indicates that many of the Christian inhabitants of Amaseia, "a great and renowned see which has now been destroyed," had either been converted, or had somehow disappeared: "The Christian flock, that is, those members of the flock who have remained there, and those who, having remained, have not been converted by the barbarians who rule over them, had no spiritual leader, and lacked spiritual guidance."

In 1318 the patriarchal synod recorded that the bishopric of Melitene, in eastern Asia Minor (Cappadocia), had been captured by the "barbarians" a long time ago, "and is, even now, surrounded and occupied by them," and granted another see to the nominal bishop of Melitene. In 1318 the bishop of Smyrna, Xenophon, "whose see has been occupied and surrounded by the barbarians for a long time," was granted the vacant bishopric of Chios. The Christian population of Brusa was much reduced before the occupation of the city by the Ottomans. In 1318 the synod gave to the resident metropolitan bishop of Brusa the see of Apameia in Phrygia, along with a monastery in Brusa which had been under direct patriarchal control. The bishop could not survive on the revenues of the see of Brusa, because his flock was very small.[20]

This picture of desolation is not relieved by any report of activity from Constantinople. Only the scantiest information exists concerning Andronicus II's attitude toward Asia Minor. Georgiades-Arnakes makes a curious mistake in saying that in 1307 Andronicus II's grandson, the future Andronicus III, "asked his grandfather for 1,000 soldiers, saying that he could hold the cities of Bithynia . . . But his suggestion was not accepted, probably because the suspicious old emperor was already afraid that his grandson might turn against him and covet the throne."[21] In 1307 Andronicus III was all of ten years old, and Andronicus II would have been suspicious indeed to have feared him. The incident took place at a much later date.

There are only two references to Andronicus II's Anatolian policy, if policy it may be called. Apparently, the Turkish advances in Asia Minor were one of the main reasons for the heavy fiscal burdens the emperor imposed on the population of his western provinces; and he was planning to send a permanent garrison of 1,000 men to Bithynia.[22] Also, the synodical letter to the newly appointed bishop of Amaseia states that Andronicus wanted bishops to be appointed to the vacant sees of Asia Minor, to help restore it to Christianity

19. Miklosich and Müller, *Acta et diplomata*, I, 35–37, 39–41, 69–71. See also George Georgiades-Arnakes, «Ἡ περιήγησις τοῦ Ἴμπν Μπαττούτα ἀνὰ τὴν Μικρὰν Ἀσίαν καὶ ἡ κατάστασις τῶν Ἑλληνικῶν καὶ Τουρκικῶν πληθυσμῶν κατὰ τὸν ΙΔ´ αἰῶνα, ΕΕΒΣ, 22 (1952), 142–143.

20. Miklosich and Müller, *Acta et Diplomata*, I, 80–83, 92–93. Smyrna was occupied by the emir of Aydin, Umur, in 1317. The fort of the city was then taken and defended by the Zaccaria; it fell to Umur in 1329: Lemerle, *L'Émirat d'Aydin*, pp. 40–62. A. Wächter, *Der Verfall des Griechentums in Kleinasien im XIV. Jahrhundert*, (Leipzig, 1903), 54; Georgiades-Arnakes, Οἱ πρῶτοι Ὀθωμανοί, p. 159.

21. Georgiades-Arnakes, Οἱ πρῶτοι Ὀθωμανοί, p. 151.

22. Gregoras, I, 317–318.

and so, presumably, to the empire.[23] Whether Andronicus II had, in effect, abandoned Asia Minor, which he had so loved and cherished in the past, or whether his activities have not been recorded simply cannot be learned.

The Papacy, the Angevins, and Byzantium

In 1313, as Europe seemed ready to go on a crusade, there was a possibility that the crusade might be diverted to Constantinople. But Philip IV of France and Pope Clement V died in 1314, and for the next few years the would-be crusaders were immobilized by both domestic and intra-European problems. France, which traditionally played an important role in crusades, was faced with a rebellion in Flanders, and the efforts of Louis X (1314–1316) to raise money to combat the rebellion resulted in the movement of the Charters, which kept France in turmoil for almost two years. Then, Louis X and his son, John, died, and the problems of succession kept the peers of the realm occupied for another two years. Only in the spring of 1318 was the question of succession regulated, and Louis X's brother, Philip of Poitiers, who had been regent, was able to overcome his opponents and become king of France (Philip V, the Tall, 1316–1322).[24]

The papal throne, too, remained vacant from the time of the death of Clement V, on April 10, 1314, until the election of John XXII, on August 7, 1316. John XXII was one of the most influential and strong-willed Avignonese popes and, like Clement V, he wished to lead a crusade to liberate the Holy Lands. Like Clement V also, John was an enemy of the Byzantines, whom he considered schismatics.[25] But during the early part of his pontificate, John XXII focused his attention not on Byzantium but on Egypt, and on the kingdom of Lesser Armenia, in Cilicia. This Christian state was hard pressed by Egypt, and at frequent intervals Armenian ambassadors required help from Avignon.[26]

A crusade, any crusade, needed a strong secular leader. John XXII's

23. Miklosich and Müller, *Acta et diplomata*, I, 69.

24. Lavisse and Langlois, *Histoire de France*, pp. 264–271, 308–309; Artonne, *Le mouvement de 1314 et les chartes provinciales de 1315* (Paris, 1912). Lehugueur, *Philippe le Long*, I, 92–105, 54ff, 122.

25. On John XXII, see J. Asal, *Die Wahl Johannes XXII* (Berlin and Leipzig, 1909); B. Aistermann, *Beiträge zum Konflikt Johanns XXII mit dem deutchen Königtum* (Bonn, 1909); G. Mollat, *Les papes d'Avignon, 1305–1378* (10th ed., Paris, 1964), pp. 39–71, 157–200, 343–360. On John XXII and France, see G. Tabacco, *La casa di Francia nell'azione politica di Papa Giovanni XXII* (Rome, 1953). On his crusading policy, see Gottfried Dürrholder, *Die Kreuzzugspolitik unter Papst Johann XXII (1316–1334)*, (Strassburg, 1913), pp. 11–30. On his anti-Byzantine attitude, see Norden, *Papsttum und Byzanz*, 676–705.

26. In 1317–1318, Armenian ambassadors asked John XXII to help their country. He heard them with compassion, and sent them on to Philip V, who "soupira . . ., fist faire ung concille, et illec . . . fut fait ung decreit que les terres de Flandrez, d'Escosse et d'Angleterre appaisées, se il peust estre fait, en l'an suivant, aprez la Pasque, grant secours de Chrestiens en la Terre Saincte envoiraient": *Chronique parisienne anonyme*, ed. A. Hellot, in *Mémoires de la société de l'histoire de Paris*, 11 (1884), 28–29, 35, 37; Auguste Coulon, *Jean XXII, Lettres secrètes et curiales relatives à la France*, I, (Paris, 1906), nos. 238, 667. A daughter of Philip of Taranto, Jeanne, had married the Armenian king in 1316, and Armenia came under papal authority in October 1324.

closest friends and allies in Europe were the French royal house and its Italian connection, the Angevins of Naples. Successive French kings, Philip V, Charles IV (1322–1328), were eager to see French power and influence extended to the East—if it could be done without much expense—while Robert of Anjou, king of Naples (1309–1343) and his brother, Philip of Anjou-Taranto, hoped to conquer the Byzantine empire. However, conditions in France, Italy and western Europe in general made it very difficult for any European prince to undertake conquests overseas.

France had foreign wars to fight and a process of internal organization to complete, whereas in Italy, Robert of Naples was locked in war with Frederick III of Sicily, and it was the recovery of Sicily, not Robert's eastern ambitions, which formed the basis of his policy.[27] Since the beginning of the century, the Italian peninsula had been rocked by civil wars, which pitted the Guelphs, led by Robert of Naples and the pope, against the Ghibellines in virtually every city. This meant that Robert was forced to remain in Italy in order to make his forces available to the Guelph party.

Finally, after 1313, all of western Europe became involved, in one way or another, in the intrigues surrounding the election of a Holy Roman Emperor, and in the subsequent conflict between Lewis IV of Bavaria (1314–1347) and John XXII. In Italy, especially in Lombardy and Tuscany, the contested German election lent new virulence to the Guelph–Ghibelline conflict. The struggle of papacy and empire, entailing emperor Lewis' excommunication by John XXII, the deposition of John XXII by Lewis, and the election of an anti-Pope, continued throughout the life of John XXII, and created an unstable situation in Europe.

This general background explains why the French crusading projects and the Byzantine plans of Philip of Taranto did not succeed. Yet the French spoke of a crusade constantly, and Philip of Taranto was no less persistent in claiming various parts of the Byzantine empire. Indeed, there were crusading assemblies in France in 1319, 1320, and 1321, and Philip V was still discussing his plans for a general crusade when he died in 1322.[28] But by then his subjects had begun to see these assemblies for what they really were, that is, excuses by which the king hoped to raise money, and they refused to be duped by these excuses.[29] Pope John XXII also indicated his displeasure at the French crusading plans. In 1320 and in June 1321, he wrote Philip very coldly that if France was, at the moment, relatively peaceful, the rest of Europe was in turmoil, and a crusade was not advisable.[30]

The only crusading plans which might have seemed dangerous for a moment

27. Romolo Caggese, *Roberto d'Angiò e i suoi tempi*, in 2 vols. (Florence, 1922, 1930); II, 304–305. Cf. Luigi Salvatorelli, *L'Italia comunale, del secolo XI alla metà del secolo XIV* (Milan, 1940), pp. 755–774.

28. *Archives historiques du Poitou*, 13 (1883), 67–68, 68–69; C. H. Taylor, "The Composition of Baronial Assemblies in France, 1315–1320," *Speculum*, 29 (1954), 433–459; H. E. Hervieu, *Recherches sur les premiers États Généraux*, (Paris, 1879), p. 156.

29. C. H. Taylor, "French Assemblies and Subsidy in 1321," *Speculum*, 43 (1968), 217–244, esp. 234–244.

30. Coulon, *Jean XXII*, I, nos. 1227, 1262.

were those of Philip of Taranto and Louis of Clermont, later duke of Bourbon, who, in 1321, acquired an interest in the Principality of Achaia. In 1316, the French princes were assembled in Paris, to discuss the question of the succession to the French throne. On July 23, 1316, Robert of Clermont and his sons, Louis of Clermont and Jean of Charolais, *cum aliis multis*, renewed the crusading oath they had taken in 1313, and received the cross from Peter, patriarch of Jerusalem and bishop of Rouen.[31] A letter to James II of Aragon refers to five thousand nobles who followed Louis of Clermont to Avignon, and there took the crusading oath again, in September 1316.[32] The crusade of Louis of Clermont was conceived as a *passagium particulare*, a preliminary expedition, which would prepare the way for a general crusade.[33] It was to be a sea-voyage, and it would begin in the spring of 1318.[34]

Louis of Clermont then asked the city of Marseilles to prepare an estimate of the ships, men, and provisions he would need for his passagium particulare. The resulting document, the *Informationes civitatis Massilie pro passagio transmarino*, was a detailed and serious piece of work.[35] It concerned a small expeditionary force, whose main purpose would be to boycott Egyptian commerce, ravage the coasts of Egypt, and then repair to Cyprus and Rhodes, so that its leaders could cooperate with the kings of Cyprus and Armenia, and with the master of the Hospitallers. On March 21, 1318, John XXII asked Philip V, whom he acknowledged as the leader of the crusading movement, to appoint for the preliminary expedition a captain, "who should be neither soft nor delicate, but strong and accustomed to work and to the hardships of the sea"; in September 1318, Philip V found such a man in Louis of Clermont.[36] Earlier in 1318, Philip V had promised to go on a crusade within two years, and requested from the pope additional grants of crusading subsidies.[37]

Philip V and John XXII did prepare ten galleys for the preliminary expedition in 1318–1319. Five of these were built in Narbonne, and five were purchased at Marseilles. All ten, fully equipped, were at anchor at Marseilles in August 1319. But in the summer of 1319, Robert of Naples had appeared at Avignon,

---

31. *Chronique parisienne*, pp. 25–26; Continuator of Girard de Frachet, in *Receueil des historiens des Gaules et de la France*, XXI (1855), 45–56. Continuator of John of St. Victor, *H.F.* XXI, 657. The major secondary work on the crusading projects of Louis of Clermont is de Boislisle, "Projet de croisade du premier duc de Bourbon, 1316–1333," in *Annuaire-Bulletin de la Société de l'histoire de France*, 9 (1872), 230–236, 246–255. His treatment of the early plans of Louis of Clermont is inadequate, and the whole French crusading movement of these years needs to be studied afresh. It is discussed very briefly in Delaville le Roulx, *La France en Orient*, pp. 78–85.

32. Finke, *Acta Aragonensia*, I, 223, no. 145.

33. At the same time Philip V also was holding vague discussions on the crusade: Coulon, *Jean XXII*, nos. 23, 27, 265, 300, 1261. The most instructive comment is that by an Aragonese observer: "de istis non debet credi, nisi quod videtur" (Finke, *Acta Aragonensia*, I, 244, no. 145).

34. Luc d'Achéry, *Spicilegium* (2d ed., Paris, 1723), III, 709. All the sources agree that the expedition was to leave in 1318, not in 1317 as Dürrholder, de Boislisle, and Lehugueur thought. See for example, Finke, *Acta Aragonensia*, I, 223, no. 145.

35. It has been published by de Boislisle, "Projet de croisade," pp. 248–255. B. de la Roncière, "Une escadre franco-papale, 1318–1320," *Mélanges archéologiques et historiques de l'école française de Rome*, 13 (1893), 399, dates this document 1316–1317.

36. Coulon, *Jean XXII*, no. 511; J. L. A. Huillard-Bréholles, *Titres de la maison ducale de Bourbon* (Paris, 1867), no. 1509, p. 259.

37. Finke, *Acta Aragonensia*, I, nos. 314, 315; Coulon, *Jean XXII*, nos. 471, 472.

seeking help against the Ghibellines of Genoa who, from their exile, were threatening the Guelph government of the city. John XXII decided that August was too late in the year for the ten galleys to sail overseas, and gave them to Robert of Naples instead. Since the Ghibellines managed to capture all ten ships, the preliminary expedition to the East was abandoned for the time being.[38]

The fate of the crusading squadron of 1318–1319 was typical of the moves which led to the failure of the French crusading plans. Everyone involved found that other issues, in this case the conflict between Guelphs and Ghibellines, had a higher priority than the crusade. Even the pope himself was unwilling to see the leaders of the Guelph party sail for Egypt or Syria while serious matters were pending at home. On the other hand, insofar as Philip V and John XXII supported the eastern ambitions of the Angevins, there was still a potential danger to Byzantium.[39]

In response to the western crusading projects of this period, of which Andronicus II was probably aware because of the great number of westerners in his capital, he tried to strengthen his ties with the Ghibelline forces in Europe. He allied himself with Genoa. Going beyond Italy, he also sought the alliance of anti-papal forces in Germany. In 1317, he married his eldest grandson, Andronicus III, to the sister of the duke of Brunswick-Grubenhagen, Adelheid, who was renamed Irene.[40] At the time of his marriage, Andronicus III was twenty years old.

The Brunswick alliance was desirable for two reasons. First, the duke, Henry II, was a supporter of Lewis of Bavaria, and so an opponent of the Guelph powers—the pope, the king of France, and the Angevins. Second, the house of Brunswick already had family ties with another Ghibelline state, the marquisate of Montferrat. Adelheid's maternal grandmother was Alessina of Montferrat, daughter of the marquess Boniface III.[41] The alliance with the house of Brunswick-Grubenhagen does not seem to have brought any immediate benefits to

---

38. Coulon, *Jean XXII*, I, nos. 784, 852, 865, 927, 983; de la Roncière, "Escadre franco-papale," pp. 397–418, considers the construction of this flotilla as part of the Capetian policy of building up the fleet. On Genoa and Robert of Anjou-Naples, see below, "The Italian Maritime Cities," in Chapter VIII. At least one French source resented the influence of Robert of Anjou on the pope: "Rex Robertus Avinioni cum Papa residebat, ita eum circa sua negotia occupatum detinens, ut non solum aliena sed etiam propria negotia Papa negligere videretur": Continuator of Guillaume de Nangis, *H.F.* XX (1840), 624.

39. Dürrholder, *Johann XXII*, p. 29.

40. Gregoras, I, 277. The date of the marriage (October 23, 1317) is given in the short chronicle published by R.-J. Leonertz, "La chronique brève de 1352," *Orientalia Christiana Periodica*, 29 (1963), 333, no. 11. Werner Ohnsorge, "Eine Verschollene Urkunde des Kaisers Andronikos III. Palaiologos für Heinrich, dictus de Graecia, Herzog zu Braunschweig (-Grubenhagen), vom 6. Januar 1330," in his *Abendland und Byzanz* (Darmstadt, 1958), pp. 492–493, dates the marriage 1318, because Gregoras says that it was celebrated in the year following the death of Irene of Montferrat, which is usually placed in 1317. However, there is no discrepancy between the Gregoras passage and the short chronicle. The short chronicle places the marriage in October of the Byzantine year 6826. If Irene died before September, 1317 (when the new Byzantine year began), the two sources are in perfect agreement.

41. See Wilhelm Karl, Prince von Isenburg, *Stammtafeln zur Geschichte der europäische Staaten*, I (Berlin, 1936; 2d ed., Hamburg, 1953), table 68. See also Georg Max, *Geschichte des Fürstentums Grubenhagen*, I (Hannover, 1862), 214–226; Paul von Zimmermann, *Das Haus Braunschweig-Grubenhagen* (Wolfenbüttel, 1911), pp. 10ff.

Byzantium. After 1321, however, Andronicus III's army contained a substantial number of German soldiers who played a major part in the Byzantine civil war. They were probably sent by Henry II of Brunswick-Grubenhagen, although it is impossible to guess whether he sent them to Andronicus II or to Andronicus III. Adelheid-Irene bore one son, who died at the age of eight months; she herself died in August, 1324.[42]

If the French and papal crusading plans threatened Byzantium only indirectly, the eastern ambitions of Philip of Taranto were somewhat more dangerous. He was able to engage in warlike activities in the Romania while still thinking of a large-scale attack on Byzantium. Philip's larger plans were ruined by the realities of the political situation in Italy. He was a faithful vassal of his brother, Robert of Anjou-Naples, and Robert, much as he might like adventures in the East, could rarely release Philip from his obligations in Italy. In April 1318 the king of Naples sent Philip of Taranto to the papal court at Avignon to request papal help for the Guelph party. Philip stayed at Avignon at least until the summer 1320, and all available information indicates that his activities concerned Italy, not Byzantium.[43]

Only in June 1320 did Philip of Taranto engage in negotiations concerning the possible reconquest of the Byzantine empire. From Avignon he sent an ambassador to Venice, to urge the renewal of the anti-Byzantine alliance of 1307, which Venice had contracted with Charles of Valois. Venice answered in November 1320, but the content of the response is unknown.[44]

The French royal house seems to have become marginally involved in these negotiations. In September 1320 Philip V relieved the Venetian merchants, retroactively and for the future, of the tax of one denier per livre tournois, which the Venetians had been obliged to pay on their commercial transactions. This privilege was granted at the request of Charles of Valois, and it may have been meant as an inducement for Venice to agree to the Byzantine policy of the Angevins. Charles of Valois was rewarded for his service to Venice with a gift of 2,000 florins. Venice, however, was carefully disengaging herself from the Angevin plans which had proved so fruitless in the past: on October 4, 1320, the republic reached an agreement with Charles of Valois, in which he abandoned all claim to the six ships which had been equipped in Venice for use in his expedition against Byzantium. In return, he received a payment of 5,000 florins.[45]

Although Philip of Anjou-Taranto as titular Latin emperor of Constantinople did not form extensive anti-Byzantine alliances comparable to those contracted by his father-in-law, he did in fact undertake campaigns in the East, which Charles of Valois had never been able to do. The Angevins and the Byzantines clashed in the Morea (Achaia) and in Epirus.

In the Morea, a period of relative peace between the Byzantines and the Franks came to an end in 1307, when Philip of Savoy was dispossessed of the

42. Cantacuzenus, I, 98, 119, 193, 301; Gregoras, I, 383–384.
43. Coulon, *Jean XXII*, I, 862, and nos. 1170, 1199.
44. Thomas and Predelli, *Diplomatarium*, I, 170–171; Mas-Latrie, *Commerce et expéditions*, pp. 72–73; Cessi and Sambin, *Consiglio dei Rogati*, p. 226 (book 6, nos. 62, 66).
45. Mas-Latrie, *Commerce et expéditions*, pp. 60–61, 73–78; Marin, *Venezia*, V, 309.

principality. Both the suzerainty and the effective possession of Achaia now passed to Philip of Taranto who, at some time in 1309, disembarked and began a short series of operations against the Byzantines. He soon returned to Italy, leaving a viceroy to continue the struggle.[46]

In 1313 the situation in the Morea changed, as titles to the principality became the subject of a complicated legal tangle. On his marriage to Catherine of Valois, Philip of Taranto had given his rights in the principality of Achaia to Mathilde of Hainaut, the eldest daughter of Isabeau de Villehardouin. Mathilde then married Louis of Burgundy, the younger brother of the duke of Burgundy, Hugues V. This arrangement was by way of compensation to Hugues for the fact that his engagement to Catherine of Valois had been broken. Louis of Burgundy, prince of Achaia and king of Thessalonica, actually resided in his principality, and enjoyed friendly relations with the Byzantines.[47]

Louis of Burgundy died in August 1316, and his death opened once again the question of suzerainty over the principality of Achaia, as his brother, Duke Eudes, claimed Louis' inheritance.[48] The issue was settled by the marriage of Mathilde of Hainaut, Louis' widow, to John of Gravina, a brother of Robert of Naples; although the marriage was never consummated, the Angevins and the pope recognized John as the new prince of Achaia.[49] As such, of course, he owed hommage to Philip of Taranto, emperor of Constantinople. The royal house of Naples now resumed operations in Achaia. In 1317, Robert of Naples sent a viceroy to Achaia, while in 1321 Philip of Taranto, preparing for an expedition against Byzantium, sent provisions to his forts in Corfu and in Achaia.[50]

In 1321 another development linked the eastern policy of the Angevins to the French crusading plans. For in that year, Louis of Clermont, who was planning to lead the preliminary expedition against Egypt, became interested in Achaia and the Kingdom of Thessalonica. He first tried to purchase the titles of one of the claimants to Achaia and Thessalonica, Eudes, duke of Burgundy. Later, in May 1321, Louis concluded a marriage alliance with Philip of Taranto, whose eldest son, Philip, despot of the Romania, wed Louis' daughter, Béatrix. In October 1321 Philip of Taranto purchased the rights of Eudes of Burgundy to Achaia and Thessalonica.[51] The interest of

46. Morel-Fatio, *Libro de los Fechos*, §§519–523; cf. Buchon, *Nouvelles recherches historiques*, II, 339–343; Hopf, *Griechische Geschichte*, pp. 367–369; Miller, *Latins in the Levant*, pp. 203–206; Dürrholder, *Johann XXII*, p. 16; Norden, *Papsttum und Byzanz*, p. 673, dates this expedition 1312–1313.

47. Morel-Fatio, *Libro de los Fechos*, §578–579; and Zakythinos, *Despotat*, I, 70—an excellent two-volume work on the Greek possessions in the Morea.

48. Dom Plancher, *Histoire de Bourgogne*, II, 170–171.

49. Hopf, *Griechische Geschichte*, pp. 402–403; Morel-Fatio, *Libro de los Fechos*, §635.

50. Caggese, *Roberto d'Angiò*, II, 306–309.

51. Huillard-Bréholles, *Titres*, I, nos. 1589, 1590, 1604. The last document proves that Louis of Clermont had not in fact completed the purchase of the principality as some modern historians have thought (see, for example, Longnon, *Empire latin*, p. 320). Cf. Dürrholder, *Johann XXII*, pp. 24–25; Coulon, *Jean XXII*, II, no. 1354. For payments to Eudes, see A. N. J510 no. 21; JJ 64 no. 222 fols. 125vo–126ro; JJ 268 no. 21, fol. 37ro; Jules Viard, *Les journaux du Trésor de Charles IV le Bel* (Paris, 1917) nos. 414, 6449, 9515, 2719, 1753, 2220, 2927, 3456, 5326, 1530.

Louis of Clermont in the principality of Achaia (and the Kingdom of Thessalonica) shows that in 1321 he had not abandoned his plan to lead an expedition to the East: indeed his projected expedition against Egypt might well have been diverted to the Morea, or even to Constantinople itself.

Western operations in the Morea met with strenuous opposition from the Byzantines. As part of his policy of reorganizing his empire, Andronicus II consolidated his position in the Morea; under two able governors, Cantacuzenus and John Asên, the Byzantines extended their possessions in the peninsula, and laid the foundations for what would become the Despotate of the Morea, the wealthiest and strongest part of the late Palaeologan empire. Andronicus II realized that the system of appointing a new governor of the Morea every year, while it had the virtue of inhibiting the possible ambitions of the governors, did not permit them to establish and follow a coherent policy. This problem was compounded by the fact that the pirate-infested Aegean made communications with Constantinople hazardous; therefore, it seemed advisable to appoint governors for longer terms and allow them greater independence of action.

The first two governors appointed under the new system were both of illustrious families, and good soldiers. In 1308, Andronicus II appointed Cantacuzenus, the father of John Cantacuzenus, the later emperor and historian.[52] Cantacuzenus was able to hold his own against the Franks of Achaia, and to maintain good relations with Louis of Burgundy, whom he helped against an invasion by Ferran of Mallorca, in the summer of 1315.

Ferran of Mallorca had retained his interest in the East after the failure of his effort to assume the leadership of the Catalan army. In 1313 he married a young girl of fourteen, Isabelle de Sabran, the daughter of Marguerite, lady of Akova, sister of Isabeau de Villehardouin. Marguerite had her own claims to the principality, and although they were of very doubtful legality, Ferran adopted them. The combined forces of Louis of Burgundy and the Byzantines defeated Ferran, who was killed at the battle of Manolada, on July 5, 1316.[53] Cantacuzenus died in the same year, also in battle.[54]

He was succeeded by Andronicus Palaeologus Asên, son of the former king

52. Morel-Fatio, *Libro de los Fechos*, §528, erroneously mentions Andronicus Asên as the first governor of the Morea under the new system. It is obvious that the author made a mistake, because later, §641, he mentions anew the appointment of Andronicus Asên, in 1320. Andronicus Asên reached the Morea in 1316: Zakythinos, *Despotat*, I, 69–70. Actually, the date of the appointment of Cantacuzenus as governor is not at all certain. As D. M. Nicol, *The Byzantine Family of Kantakouzenos* (Dumbarton Oaks, 1968), pp. 27–30, n.52, points out, all we know is that Cantacuzenus held his office for eight years, and died at the age of twenty-nine: Cantacuzenus, I, 85. Nicol places Cantacuzenus' term in office at approximately 1286–1294. Zakythinos' date is based on the fact that the next *known* governor of the Morea, Asên, arrived in 1316.

53. On Ferran of Mallorca as "Prince of Achaia," his marriage, and his activities in the principality, see Morel-Fatio, *Libro de los Fechos*, §§555, 558, 587–619; Rubió y Lluch, *Diplomatari*, nos. 74 (pp. 91–92), 80 (pp. 99–100); Rubió y Lluch, *Ferrán*, pp. 291–379; Miller, *Latins in the Levant*, pp. 252–256; Hopf, *Griechische Geschichte*, pp. 399–401; Setton, *Catalan Domination*, p. 120; Zakythinos, *Despotat*, I, 70–71; S. V. Bozzo, *Note Storiche Siciliane* (Palermo, 1882), pp. 338–344.

54. Cantacuzenus, I, 85; according to Nicol's dating, Cantacuzenus died in 1294.

of Bulgaria John III Asên, and grandson of Michael VIII on his mother's side. Asên too proved able, took several fortresses held by the Franks of Achaia, and repulsed an invasion of the Catalans of the Duchy of Athens.[55] So successful was he in the Morea that, in June 1321, some of the most important barons of Achaia, including the chancellor, wrote to Venice to request the help of the republic against the Greeks and the Catalans: "These men, because they cannot defend themselves against the great onslaughts of the Greeks, and because their own lord does not seem to be very concerned with these affairs, not wishing to be utterly destroyed, deliberated deeply the best way to give themselves up to another lord."[56] The barons offered themselves and the principality of Achaia to Venice, whose reply is not known. In the same year, 1321, Asên returned to Constantinople to participate in the civil war which broke out between Andronicus II and his grandson, and thus the Byzantine offensive in the Morea was interrupted.

The Byzantine reconquest of the lost provinces of the Morea, Epirus, and Thessaly was characterized by the progressive decentralization of government. In each of the three areas, the Byzantine authorities at Constantinople had to abandon a great deal of power to local elements: feudal lords, or communes. In the second volume of his excellent work on the Despotate of the Morea, D. A. Zakythinos has described in detail the process of fragmentation, and the groups which took over the prerogatives and obligations of government. One aspect of the fragmentation, privileges granted to communes, is of particular interest here.

The Catalan campaign in Thrace, Macedonia, and Greece had indicated that much of the strength of the empire was now concentrated in the towns and cities. The weakness and impoverishment of the central government had enhanced the importance of the fortified towns as units of administration and defense. Andronicus II had found it necessary to give fiscal privileges to the towns of Greece in order to induce them to fight the Catalans. The importance of these towns, and the formal or informal recognition by the central government of their importance increased in the years following the Catalan campaign.

In the Morea, because of the fragmentary nature of the Byzantine reconquest, the process of decentralization was accelerated. The town of Monembasia, situated at a strategic point, is a well-documented example of the fragmentation of authority in Andronicus II's empire. Imperial chrysobulls granted by Michael VIII and Andronicus II gave the inhabitants and merchants of Monembasia immunity from all imperial taxes on their persons and properties. By 1316 the Monembasiot merchants could trade freely all over the empire, paying no port duties, no road duties, no taxes on the building and possession of ships; only at Constantinople was a commercial tax (kommerkion) levied at the rate of 1 per cent ad valorem of their merchandise. In their own city they did not even pay the "tax for building castles" (καστροκτισία),

---

55. Morel-Fatio, *Libro de los Fechos*, §§641–654; Gregoras, I, 362–363; Miller, *Latins in the Levant*, p. 259; Zakythinos, *Despotat*, I, 71–73, II, 63–64.
56. Mas-Latrie, *Commerce et expéditions*, p. 56.

which was one of the few taxes some pronoia-grants reserved to the emperor.[57]

Except for the commercial tax of one per cent, the privileges of the Monembasiots approximated very closely the commercial privileges granted to the most favored Italian merchants. As far as the imperial fisc was concerned, the inhabitants and merchants of Monembasia were almost outside its authority. No doubt, Andronicus II wished to encourage the trading activities of the Monembasiots, particularly since the chrysobull indicates that they were mostly involved in trade in food products. In the process, however, he was undercutting his own sources of revenue; not only had he enfranchised foreign merchants, he was now granting similar privileges to his own subjects. The burden of imperial taxation thus fell more heavily on land and the peasantry, while the number of privileged groups increased. The privileges granted to the inhabitants of Monembasia are but one example of the decentralization of fiscal and political authority; other instances occur in the parts of Epirus recovered by Andronicus II.

In the splinter states of Epirus and Thessaly, Andronicus II was able to use other favorable circumstances to bring some areas under his control. In Epirus the ruling despot, Thomas Angelos (1295–1318), was engaged in constant warfare with the armies of Philip of Taranto. Philip claimed suzerainty over the despotate of Epirus, basing his claims upon the agreement concluded between Charles II of Anjou (Philip's father) and Nicephorus Angelos in 1294 on the occasion of Philip's marriage to Thomas' sister, Thamar. After Nicephorus' death his widow repudiated the agreement. Philip divorced his Epirote wife in 1309, but neither then, nor after her death in 1315, did he abandon her claims to the despotate. He and his lieutenants, from their strongholds in Corfu and Durazzo, regularly attacked Epirus.[58]

In order to defend his state, Thomas turned to Byzantium. He married Michael IX's daughter, Anne, in 1313, and in the same year Andronicus II and Michael IX sent to Epirus a considerable army, under the command of John Lascaris.[59] The imperial army had a number of successful engagements

57. Miklosich and Müller, *Acta et diplomata*, V, 154–155, 161–165. On this, see St. Binon, "L'histoire et la légende de deux chrysobulles d'Andronic II en faveur de Monembasie," *Échos d'Orient*, 27 (1938), 306–307. The kommerkion was a tax, levied on the import and export, sale, distribution, and circulation of goods; it could be both a sales tax and a port duty: J. Danstrup, "Indirect Taxation at Byzantium," *Classica et Mediaevalia*, 8 (1946), 139–167, esp. 144–155. On the numerous and varied taxes levied on private ships and their cargoes, see Germaine Rouillard, "Les taxes maritimes et commerciales d'après des actes de Patmos et de Lavra"; *Mélanges Charles Diehl* (Paris, 1930), I, 277–289. On the privileges granted to Monembasia, see G. I. Brătianu, *Privilèges et franchises municipales dans l'Empire byzantin* (Paris and Bucharest, 1936), p. 111. The chrysobull of 1316 is published in Miklosich and Müller, *Acta et diplomata*, V, 165–168, with the date November 1317. It is reproduced in Ioannes Phrantzes, *Chronicon*, ed. I. Bekker, (Bonn, 1838), pp. 400–405. For the date, see Zakythinos, *Despotat*, I, 83–85; II, 116–118; Dölger's review of Zakythinos is in *BZ* 34 (1934), 126–127. Dölger accepted the date 1336 but has since revised his opinion. In his *Regesten*, no. 2383, he accepts the date 1316, with reservations as to the authenticity of the chrysobull. See also J. B. Papadopulos, "Über 'Maius' und 'Minus' des Georgios Phrantzes und über die Randnoten des Angeblichen Pachomios," *BZ* 38 (1938), 323–331.

58. Morel-Fatio, *Libro de los Fechos*, §§524–525, 569; Finke, *Acta Aragonensia*, II, 706–707, no. 445; Buchon, *Nouvelles recherches historiques*, I, p. 406; Hopf, *Griechische Geschichte*, p. 417.

59. Gregoras, I, 283; Cantacuzenus, I, 13.

with the Angevins, and the years 1314–1319 saw intensive Byzantine activity in that part of Greece. The Byzantine garrison of Valona launched small-scale attacks against Corfu, captured some Neapolitan ships sailing in the Adriatic, and even attacked the Venetian squadron which patrolled there. The Byzantine governor of Berat, the pincernes John Syrgiannes, also participated in engagements in Epirus: in 1314, he and his army appeared in the capital of the despotate, Arta, where they burned some property belonging to Venetian merchants.[60]

The Byzantine army of John Lascaris stayed in Epirus until 1317. In the following year, Thomas began peace negotiations with his former brother-in-law, Philip of Taranto. Before peace could be concluded, Thomas was assassinated by his nephew, the count of Cephallonia, Nicholas, who married the widowed Anne and governed the despotate until 1323.[61] At this point, the inhabitants of the town of Janina (Ioannina), who had hated Thomas' despotic government, asked the Byzantine governor of Berat to occupy their city. This important town now came under Andronicus II's authority.[62]

Andronicus II used feudal ideas to justify his claims to the Despotate of Epirus. In 1294 Anne of Epirus had mentioned in somewhat vague terms that she considered the emperor at Constantinople as the natural overlord of the despots of Epirus. In 1319 Andronicus II himself argued that the despots of Epirus were bound to him by the tie of vassalage ("iuramento vassallagii"). So long as they behaved as faithful vassals, he would in return extend his favor to them. But if they behaved contumaciously, then he was within his rights to make war against them "as against apostates and infidels."[63] This statement, which he made to Venice in order to justify his operations against both Thomas and Nicholas of Cephallonia, is a striking example of the influence of western political concepts on the traditional Byzantine theories of sovereignty. It would have been interesting to study the Greek phraseology of this statement, but unfortunately, only the Latin text has survived.

In 1318, the same year in which Thomas of Epirus was assassinated, the sickly "duke of Neopatras," John II Angelos of Thessaly, also died. He had no children, and with his death Thessaly dissolved into chaos. The Catalans of the Duchy of Athens attacked the southern part of the state, and by 1319 they had occupied Neopatras, Siderocastron (near the ancient city of Heracleia), Domokos, Pharsalus, and Karditsa. Part of northern Thessaly reverted to Andronicus II, while the central area was governed by local feudal lords.[64]

60. This information comes from lists of complaints presented by the Venetian government to Andronicus II in 1319–1320: Thomas and Predelli, *Diplomatarium*, nos. 76, 77, 79, pp. 135–137, 146–147, 161–162.

61. Morel-Fatio, *Libro de los Fechos*, §§628–630.

62. Hopf, *Griechische Geschichte*, pp. 417–421.

63. Thomas and Predelli, *Diplomatarium*, no. 77, p. 146: "ipsa terra iurisdictionis est Imperii nostri et qui tenent ipsam terram iuramento vassallagii adstringuntur Imperio nostro et servitia consueverunt facere pro ipsa, et cum complerent et facerent, ut vassalli, in requie et quiete erant, ab Imperio habentes favorem et amorem; quando vero contraria faciebant, monebatur necessario Imperium facere guerram contra ipsos, ut contra apostates et infideles."

64. Gregoras, I, 279; On the Catalan conquests, see Marino Sanudo Torsello, letter 3, p. 293, in Bongars, *Gesta Dei per Francos*; cf. Setton, *Catalan Domination*, p. 29.

Thessaly had become a feudalized state long before 1318. Since 1290, it had been dominated by Greek "barons," "great lords, Greek noblemen of great standing," who remained under restored Byzantine rule.[65] Apparently, in 1318, the patriarch and the synod of Constantinople wrote several letters to the Thessaliot lords who had chosen independence, exhorting them to return to obedience to the emperor, "so that there would be one Roman state as in the past"; but they did not obey.[66] In Byzantine Thessaly, the feudal lords retained important fiscal and judicial privileges. In 1342 John Cantacuzenus had to promise the *archontes* (lords) of Thessaly that he would preserve their rights.[67] Six years later, Stephen Dušan of Serbia, who conquered them, gave them the same assurances.[68] Within Thessaly, smaller units had rights and privileges of their own, which were respected by the feudal lords.[69]

In 1320 Andronicus II and Michael IX were preparing an offensive which they hoped would result in the recovery of the whole of Thessaly and Epirus.[70] But Michael IX died in 1320, and the civil war between Andronicus II and Andronicus III put an end to all Byzantine operations in Greece.

The Byzantine reconquest of Epirus and Thessaly was characterized by the abandonment, on the part of the central government, of certain essential functions and rights. In Thessaly the feudal lords had inherited the exercise of effective authority, in Epirus, town independence had been growing. In February, 1319, an imperial chrysobull granted to the town of Janina privileges that allowed its inhabitants a very considerable degree of self-government. When the inhabitants of Janina invited the Byzantine governor, Syrgiannes, to take possession of their town, they also asked Andronicus to confirm their old rights and possessions. Andronicus did so willingly: in effect, in his chrysobull he promised to guard Janina in his personal capacity as ruler, not as an embodiment of the state.[71]

The chrysobull of 1319 made Janina not only a walled town but a commune in the medieval sense of the term: that is, a town enjoying certain privileges and a degree of self-government. There was still an imperial governor, but the head men of the city (κεφαλατικεύοντες) had the right to appeal from the governor to the emperor, and the right to confiscate the properties of traitors. The inhabitants of Janina were released from the obligation to serve in the imperial army—but they still had to defend their own city. As in pronoia-grants, the emperor relinquished the collection of taxes, with two exceptions:

65. Buchon, *Recherches historiques*, I, 416.
66. Gregoras, I, 279.
67. Cantacuzenus, II, 309ff.
68. I. Soloviev, "Fessalijske arkhonti v XIV v," *Byzantinoslavica*, 4 (1932), 158–174.
69. See the privileges which Michael Gavrielopoulos confirmed to the town of Phanari in 1342: Miklosich and Müller, *Acta et Diplomata*, V, 260–261. For the dating of this document see N. Bees, in *BZ* 21 (1912), 170; *Viz. Vrem.* 20 (1913), 57.
70. Gregoras, I, 278; Hopf, *Griechische Geschichte*, p. 422.
71. Published by Miklosich and Müller, *Acta et Diplomata*, V, 77–84; cf. E. Francès, "La féodalité et les villes byzantines au XIIIe et XIVe siècle," *Byzantinoslavica*, 16 (1955), 91; "N. Bees, Uebersicht über die Geschichte des Judentums von Janina," *Byzantinisch-Neugriechische Jahrbücher*, 2 (1921), 159–177; Hopf, *Griechische Geschichte*, pp. 418–419; Brătianu, *Privilèges et franchises*, p. 110.

he retained the right to levy a tax for building castles (καστροκτισία) and the right to treasure trove (θησαυροῦ ἀνεύρεσις).[72] The merchants of Janina, like those of Venice and Genoa, paid no duties anywhere in the empire.

By the fourth decade of his reign, then, Andronicus II had been forced to abandon the concept of full and absolute sovereignty. Instead, he had to establish or deal with the system of extraneous rights and privileges which is characteristic of feudal societies. The decentralization of authority affected Byzantine foreign policy in that grants of fiscal immunity to individuals and groups impoverished the state, and the state exercised effective control over an increasingly diminishing territory. Thus, the recovery of Epirus and Thessaly contributed very little to the wealth or to the political power of the empire, and so did not enhance its position relative to other powers. Foreign policy was still made at Constantinople; but it was rapidly becoming the only important state function still carried out by the central government.

The Italian Maritime Cities

Relations between Byzantium and Genoa after 1308 may be described by the term "restrained friendship." Between 1308 and 1318, the Byzantines were, indeed, on good terms with the Genoese, while at the same time trying to diminish the excessive power acquired by the Genoese during the years of the Catalan campaign.

Contacts between the Byzantine government and the Genoese took place mostly at the local level, with the inhabitants of the Genoese colonies. Genoese traders were still predominant in the Aegean and the Black Sea, although they had suffered a terrible blow in 1307–1308 when the Tartar Khan Toktai ordered the destruction of Caffa. Sailing in the Black Sea was dangerous for another reason: the Turkish emir of Sinope, Zarabi (or Zalabi), was notorious for his piratical attacks against Genoese shipping in those waters. But after 1313, Caffa was rebuilt, and Genoese supremacy in the Black Sea was restored.[73]

In 1314 the government of Genoa created a special office to deal with the affairs of the Black Sea colonies, and this office was known, after 1341, as the *Officium Gazarie*. In 1314–1316, the government took a series of measures specifically designed to help the colony of Caffa: Caffa was designated as the primary trading center of the Black Sea, and its consul became the head of the Genoese administration in the Crimea. All Genoese merchants sailing from Constantinople to the eastern part of the Black Sea, or sailing out of the Sea of Azov were obliged to stop at Caffa for at least one day, and pay a special tax for this doubtful privilege. In order to ensure that the colony would be sufficiently populated, the government ordered every man who acquired land in Caffa to build a house within eighteen months. No Genoese trader

---

72. Miklosich and Müller, *Acta et Diplomata*, V, 82; Ostrogorsky, *Féodalité*, pp. 92ff, 109, 116. Thomas Magister wrote against the emperor's right to treasure-trove: Περὶ βασιλείας, in Migne, *PG* CXLV, cols. 477–480.

73. Continuator of Jacopo da Varagine, ed. V. Promis, pp. 10–11; Gregoras, II, 683–685.

was allowed to stay in the rival ports of Tana and Soldaia for more than three days, or spend the winter there, or acquire property. The most severe of these restrictions were later lifted, but in the meantime they had achieved their purpose, and Caffa became once again a populous and prosperous trading colony.[74]

Benedetto Zaccaria, the great merchant and admiral, died in 1307, and was succeeded by his son, Paleologo Zaccaria. The Genoese possession of the island of Chios was confirmed by Andronicus II, who renewed the original grant twice, in 1314 and 1319.[75] In 1314 the brother-in-law of Paleologo Zaccaria received the right to govern New Phocaea, which now probably replaced Old Phocaea as the center of the alum trade.[76] As for the colony of Pera, this too was large and prosperous. Several houses, including the government building, were destroyed in a great fire, in 1315, but the colonists took advantage of the fire to rebuild their colony, and protect it with land walls.[77]

In the eyes of outsiders, the power and influence of the Genoese in the Byzantine empire remained supreme. In 1317 the Venetian bailo of Constantinople, Marco Minotto, wrote to the doge that "in Romania semper diminuimus et Januenses semper crescunt."[78] He explained that so extensive were the Genoese privileges in the Byzantine empire, that many Greek and Venetian merchants bought charters of Genoese citizenship. In this way, the numbers of "Genoese" swelled. The bailo explained that the Venetians would be stronger and more formidable if their number increased, and so he asked the doge to see to it that all Venetians in the Byzantine empire accept the bailo's judgment concerning their citizenship. He added that Andronicus II shared his opposition to the Genoese, and that the emperor would be pleased to see more Venetian merchants.

Marco Minotto astutely recognized Andronicus II's growing concern about the predominant position of the Genoese in his empire. Andronicus' attitude became clear in an agreement he reached with Genoa in February 1317.[79] The text of this document indicates that the agreement was preceded by negotiations between the emperor and the commune, and that Andronicus II had initiated the negotiations: almost every article curtails some Genoese privilege or abuse of privilege.

The agreement of 1317 dealt with the question of citizenship, and in parti-

74. *Historiae Patriae Monumenta. Leges Municipales*, I (Turin, 1838), 378–409; Heyd, *Commerce du Levant*, II, 170–171. In 1318, the colony of Caffa was given its first bishop, the Catalan Hieronymus: Sauli, *Colonia*, I, 220.

75. Cantacuzenus, I, 371; Dölger, *Regesten*, nos. 2349, 2409; W. Miller, *Essays on the Latin Orient* (Cambridge, 1921), pp. 287–290. The dates 1314 and 1319, are usually computed from the short passage of Cantacuzenus which says that the original ten-year grant of Chios was renewed for five years when it expired, and then was renewed again. If we accept my dating of the occupation of Chios by Benedetto Zaccaria (early in 1305), then the dates of the renewal should be corrected to 1315 and 1320 respectively: above, "Byzantium, the Genoese, and the Catalans," in Chapter V.

76. Cantacuzenus, I, 389; Gregoras, I, 526; Dölger, *Regesten*, no. 2350; Miller, *Latin Orient*, p. 289; Lemerle, *L'Émirat d'Aydin*, pp. 66–67.

77. Continuator of Jacopo da Varagine, p. 10.

78. Thomas and Predelli, *Diplomatarium*, no. 59, pp. 103–105.

79. Published in Belgrano, *Prima serie*, no. 14, pp. 116–123, and in Sauli, *Colonia*, II, no. 10.

cular the question of people who were not Genoese, but who wanted to travel and trade in the Byzantine empire as Genoese subjects. This issue had been raised by Andronicus II in 1308, when he complained that the Genoese officials in the colonies issued too many charters of Genoese citizenship; it had then been decided that the podestà and council of Pera would have sole authority to issue such charters. In 1317 it was agreed that within eight days of his arrival at Pera, the podestà would call the council of twenty-four men which advised him on major issues and they would elect six "good and wise" men, three nobles and three non-nobles. These would have authority to discuss with imperial officials any issues concerning persons of disputed citizenship. If this council declared a man to be Genoese or to have the rights of a Genoese, its decision would be final.[80]

A second group of articles concerned the behavior of Genoese in the empire, or in parts of the empire that were temporarily alienated. The Genoese were forbidden to erect any buildings on land outside the limits prescribed by the treaties, except with the emperor's knowledge and permission. If anyone broke this stipulation, he would be judged by imperial officials acting in conjunction with the council of six. Furthermore, the Genoese were absolutely forbidden, under pain of a heavy fine, to build any castles in imperial territory, or in those territories controlled by the infidels, i.e., in Asia Minor ("in terris subditis domino Imperatori que possidentur per inimicos fidei christiane et in preiudicium Imperii sui"). This article may indicate that Andronicus II, who had little power left in Asia Minor, was still trying to preserve his theoretical sovereignty over it.

The rights of the imperial treasury were safeguarded, as much as possible, from abuse by the Genoese. It was forbidden, on pain of double the ordinary commercial tax, for Genoese to take through customs merchandise belonging to non-Genoese merchants. The commune twice repeated the provisions of this article, presumably to impress its importance on the podestà. As soon as a Genoese ship docked at Pera, the podestà should tell the captain of the ship to report immediately to the Byzantine customs officials any non-Genoese merchandise on board, so that the emperor would not be defrauded of his legitimate customs duties: "ut dominus Imperator non fraudetur suo comerchio." The Genoese officials in charge of weighing merchandise were forbidden to weigh and measure any goods not belonging to Genoese traders. If they came across any such goods, they were to declare them immediately to the Byzantine customs officials.

The agreement also redefined and curtailed somewhat the trading activities of Genoese merchants in the empire. They were permitted to buy salt in the Black Sea area and transport it to the West, but they were only allowed to bring such merchandise to Constantinople and Pera in transit. It was absolutely forbidden to them to unload or sell salt in Constantinople, Pera, or any other part of the Byzantine empire. In case of a storm, Genoese ships carrying salt were allowed to stop in Byzantine ports, but were forbidden to sell their salt

80. Belgrano, "Prima serie," pp. 111, 113–114, 116–117; and below, pp. 118–120.

there. The Genoese were also forbidden by their own government to bring and sell in Constantinople any wheat from Varna and Anchialos, while these cities, on the western coast of the Black Sea, were in the hands of the Bulgarians ("durante rebellione"). They could, however, transport and sell this wheat in all other parts of the Byzantine empire, outside Constantinople.

The commercial clauses of the agreement aimed at reestablishing the imperial salt monopoly, and at regulating the sale and distribution of grain in Constantinople. The salt monopoly in particular must have become a source of considerable revenue for the Byzantine state.[81] Andronicus' effort to revive the system of state monopolies, combined with a stricter enforcement of customs regulations must have contributed to the improvement of his finances.

Jurisdictional questions concerning court cases between Genoese and Byzantine subjects were clarified in the agreement of 1317. In 1304 Andronicus II had given the podestà and council of Pera authority to judge all Genoese criminals and all other cases involving Genoese subjects; Byzantine courts had retained the authority to judge all Byzantine subjects and anyone else who was not Genoese. In 1308 the ambassadors of Andronicus II complained that an innovation had occurred, and that the Genoese had created special officials to judge cases involving Greeks and Genoese. Andronicus II then requested that such cases be judged by Genoese judges, in the presence of Byzantine officials, and the government of Genoa assented.[82] In 1317 the problem was further discussed, at the request of the Byzantine ambassadors. All cases in which the plaintiff was Genoese and the defendant was Greek would be tried by two imperial officials, who swore to judge impartially, according to the habits and rites of the Greeks. But if these judges should be misled by the difference in language and customs, and if the Genoese were not happy with the decision of the Byzantine court, the podestà could appeal the case to Andronicus II, whose decision would be final.[83]

The Byzantine–Genoese agreement of 1317 represents an interesting stage in the relations of the two states. In 1308, immediately after the retreat of the Catalans from Thrace, Andronicus II had been able to demand, and receive, assurances that the Genoese would not repeat the most offensive abuses they had committed at the time of the Catalan campaign. In 1317, with his state relatively at peace, he went further, and sought to regulate the activities of the Genoese in his state, so as to undermine their power and predominance. But normal relations between Byzantium and Genoa were interrupted in 1318, and Andronicus II was forced to change his policy yet again.

A new factor was interposed in Byzantine–Genoese relations. In Genoa, a long factional war between Guelphs and Ghibellines culminated in the overthrow of the Ghibelline government. In November 1317 the Guelphs came to

---

81. The career of Alexis Apokaukos illustrates the importance of the salt monopoly as a source of revenue. Apokaukos was a poor man, from an inconspicuous family, but he was able to create a huge private fortune out of the salt monopoly, which Andronicus II allowed him to exploit: Cantacuzenus, I, 117–118.

82. Belgrano, "Prima serie," no. 10, p. 108; no. 12, pp. 112, 114.

83. Ibid., pp. 121–122.

power with the election of Carlo Fiesco and Gaspare Grimaldi as captains of the people of Genoa.[84] At the same time, the two major Ghibelline families, the Spinola and the D'Oria, went into exile. Supported by the Visconti of Milan, they occupied the small coastal town of Savona, to the west of Genoa, and from there they launched their attacks against the city.[85] Both the Guelph government and the Ghibelline exiles now moved to form foreign alliances. Pope John XXII and Robert of Naples gave their help to the Guelphs.[86] The exiles, on the other hand, reconstituted in 1318–1319 a Ghibelline league, consisting of approximately the same powers which had opposed papal schemes ever since the time of Frederick II Hohenstaufen and his successors: Sicily, the marquisate of Montferrat, the cities of Venice, Lucca, and Pisa, and the Byzantine Empire.

The participation of Byzantium in the Ghibelline league is of particular interest. Neither Genoese nor Byzantine sources provide any detailed information, except for the fact that Andronicus II's major contribution to his allies came in the form of a subsidy. Giovanni Villani, the Florentine chronicler, and the anonymous continuator of Jacopo da Varagine, both mention the Byzantine–Genoese alliance, but with no details. Giorgio Stella does not seem to know about the participation of Byzantium in the alliance against the Guelphs. Gregoras did know about the civil war in Genoa, and about the Guelph victory. He wrote that news of this conflict brought chaos to all the Genoese colonies, as they too became divided into warring factions. But he did not mention Andronicus II's help to the Ghibelline exiles.[87]

Despite this dearth of evidence, it is certain that Andronicus II did become involved in the Genoese civil war on the side of the Ghibellines. Even the date of the alliance can be discovered, as well as the intermediaries Andronicus II employed. This information comes from a source that has not yet been used in this context: a list of complaints presented by the Venetian government to Andronicus II, with the emperor's answers. These documents link the Byzantine–Ghibelline alliance with the journey of Theodore of Montferrat to the East.[88]

Theodore of Montferrat came to visit his parents at the end of 1316, and he stayed in the Byzantine empire until November 1318.[89] According to his auto-

84. On Genoese politics between 1309 and 1321, see M. G. Canale, *Storia politica commerciale e letteraria della Repubblica di Genova dall'origine fino all 1340*, IV (Capolago, 1851), 188–199. Agostino Giustiniani, *Annali della Repubblica di Genova*, ed. C. G. B. Spotorno, II (Genoa, 1854), 8–33, is, for the most part, an abbreviated version of Giorgio Stella. Other secondary sources which discuss briefly the civil war in Genoa are T. O. de Negri, *Storia di Genova* (Milan, 1968), pp. 435–445 and V. Vitale, *Breviario della storia di Genova*, I (Genoa, 1955), 96–104.

85. Continuator of Jacopo da Varagine, pp. 12–13; Stella, cols. 1029–1034; Giovanni Villani, *Cronica*, ed. F. G. Dragomanni, II (Florence, 1845), 204–205, 206 (book 9, chaps. lxxxii, xc).

86. Villani, II, 208 (book 9, chap. xciv). On the involvement of Robert of Naples see Caggese, *Roberto d'Angiò*, II, 26–48.

87. Continuator of Jacopo de Varagine, p. 13; Villani, II, 208–209 (book 9, chapter xcv); Stella, col. 1033; cf. Raynaldus, *Annales Eccl.*, 1318, §XXII; Manfroni, "Relazioni," pp. 697–698; Gregoras, I, 286–287.

88. Thomas and Predelli, *Diplomatarium*, nos. 72, 73, 77, 79, pp. 125, 130–131, 143, 154–156.

89. Cognasso, "Crisobolla," p. 43; above, Chapter VII, n. 129.

biography, the purpose of his visit was to see his mother and father, to place himself at his mother's service, and help his father and brother in their struggles against Turks, Tartars, and other barbarians.[90] But it is also possible that Theodore mentioned to Andronicus II the civil war in Genoa, and discussed the plight of the Ghibellines. Not only was Montferrat traditionally a Ghibelline state, but Theodore had family ties with the Spinola, who had been the first to suffer from the overthrow of the traditional power-structure in Genoa. All the Italian sources mention that Theodore was allied to the Ghibellines in 1318, and it is probable that he brought messages from them to Andronicus II as early as 1316.

In October 1318 Theodore of Montferrat was preparing to return to Italy. Unlike his earlier trip, which had brought him by ship to Genoa and from there to Montferrat, he now traveled by way of Venice.[91] Andronicus II wrote letters to the Venetian government, asking them to facilitate his son's journey, and commending to them his emissary, Stephen Syropoulos. Venice, at this time, was trying to restore good relations with the Byzantines; the republic was also pro-Ghibelline, although its contribution to the league was very limited. The Venetian government responded very courteously to Andronicus' letter. In November 1318 they offered to send to Constantinople two galleys to bring the marquis to Venice, from where he could travel by land to Lombardy.[92] In the end, Andronicus II preferred to use one of his own ships, and one which belonged to a Ghibelline Genoese captain, Napoleone Del Mar. The Venetians sent Giovanni Michiel, the captain of the galleys patrolling the Adriatic, to meet Theodore off Corfu and escort him to Venice, which he reached in December 1318.[93]

Along with Theodore, Andronicus II sent an emissary, Stephen Syropoulos, to Italy, to contract the alliance with the Ghibellines. In a letter to Venice, Andronicus II wrote that at that time (1318), he wanted to send help to "our Genoese Ghibellines" ("nostris Januensibus Ghibellinis"), that he had made his intention known to Venice, and that Venice had been pleased. So, he asked Napoleone Del Mar to take aboard his galley the Byzantine ambassador, Stephen Syropoulos. Del Mar would bring Syropoulos to Venice, and from there, presumably, the imperial emissary would travel by land. Syropoulos did, in fact, reach Venice, at the same time as Theodore of Montferrat, while Napoleone Del Mar sailed on, launching incidental attacks on Venetian ships.[94]

All the sources indicate that the Byzantine help took the form of monetary subsidies, but none tells how much money was sent. In October 1318 Andronicus II wrote that he had paid a certain Venetian the sum of 10,000 hyperpyra, which was to be changed into florins, and given either to Theodore or to an

90. Benvenuto di San Giorgio, col. 455.
91. Thomas and Predelli, *Diplomatarium*, nos. 68, 69, pp. 117–120 (October 5, 1318).
92. Thiriet, *Délibérations*, I, 178, no. 408.
93. Thomas and Predelli, *Diplomatarium*, no. 73, pp. 130–131, no. 79, pp. 154–156; Thiriet, *Délibérations*, I, 179, no. 409. For the date, see Cessi and Sambin, *Consiglio dei Rogati*, pp. 198–199 (book 5, nos. 256, 257).
94. Thomas and Predelli, *Diplomatarium*, nos. 72, 73, 77, 79, pp. 125, 130–131, 143, 154–156.

imperial envoy in Venice and in Milan.[95] If the imperial envoy in question was Stephen Syropoulos, then it is probable that the 10,000 hyperpyra was granted to Theodore not so much for his personal needs as for the needs of the Genoese Ghibelline exiles.

Stephen Syropoulos attended a parliament of Theodore's vassals at Montferrat, on September 3, 1319. Montferrat had gone through a period of unrest during Theodore's absence in Byzantium, and now an effort was made to reconcile the marquis and his vassals. Syropoulos spoke to the assembly, as a representative of the emperor, and he also read Andronicus' letter to Theodore's vassals. Both the letter and Syropoulos' speech present an interesting picture of Andronicus' concern with the affairs of Montferrat. He saw Montferrat as an extension of the Byzantine empire, and promised its inhabitants that, if they obeyed and served Theodore, Andronicus would extend his protection over them: "si fideles se haberent . . . dictum Marchionatum sui Imperii defenderet et gubernaret." In his letter, Andronicus II promised those who showed "constancy, perfect loyalty, and due obedience to our empire and to our very dear son" that they would receive every favor from both God and the emperor. He would withdraw his favor from all those who showed disobedience: "ab indignis revocabit Imperium nostrum omne beneficium suum."[96] The letter proves Andronicus II's interest in the affairs of Italy. Although Montferrat was a particular case, since it was governed by Andronicus' own son, perhaps the authoritative tone of the letter was also due to the fact that Andronicus II already had an alliance with one Ghibelline power, the Genoese exiles.

When Theodore reached Italy, the Ghibellines were besieging the city of Genoa. The siege itself was unsuccessful, but in July 1319 the exiles were able to capture several Genoese suburbs. In October, ten Guelph galleys came from Constantinople, bringing food to the starving population of the city; neither Andronicus II nor the inhabitants of Pera had yet made it impossible for Guelph ships to trade in the Romania and pass through the Dardanelles and the Bosphorus. In 1320 John XXII excommunicated the city of Milan, the strongest ally of the Genoese Ghibellines. In the same year, the war between Guelphs and Ghibellines extended to the sea, as Frederick of Sicily armed forty-two galleys against the Genoese government, and Robert of Naples built his own fleet in Genoa, Naples, and Provence, in order to attack Sicily. In 1321 Frederick III was also excommunicated.[97]

The civil wars in Germany and Italy, and more specifically the expulsion of the Ghibellines from Genoa, changed Andronicus II's relations with that city. Until then, he was reasonably friendly with the government of Genoa, and indeed, his relations with that government were often better than with the Genoese colonists. Now, however, he was faced with a hostile government in Genoa, and in the 1320's this would serve to tighten his relations with the Ghibelline colony of Pera. In 1318, he reacted to the Italian situation by form-

95. Ibid., no. 69, p. 118.

96. Benvenuto di San Giorgio, cols. 432–435.

97. Stella, cols. 1034–1037, 1039–1044; Villani, II, 211, 216–217, 219–222, 232–233 (book 9, chaps. xcix, cix, cxii–cxvi, cxxxiv).

ing an alliance with the Ghibelline exiles. No doubt he understood that a Guelph Genoa would be extremely dangerous to him, allied as it was to John XXII, a known advocate of forcible church union, and to Robert of Naples, the head of the hated house of Anjou.

One well-informed source, Giovanni Villani, thought that the Byzantines gave very considerable help to the Ghibellines. Discussing the outbreak of the civil war in Byzantium, in 1321, Villani wrote: "And this (the civil war) was a major reason for the weakening of the Genoese exiles, because the said emperor, in order to reduce the strength of the church and of King Robert, had constantly, with his money subsidies, helped the Genoese exiles and those of Savona to make war against the city of Genoa and against King Robert; and because of his own war, he abandoned this enterprise."[98]

Andronicus II's interference in the affairs of Italy forms an interesting contrast with his virtually complete diplomatic inactivity during the years of the war of the Sicilian Vespers. For the first time in his long reign, he plays the game of Michael VIII, and supports his Ghibelline friends with apparently substantial sums of money. This is the beginning of a new form of foreign policy, which Andronicus II would pursue during the 1320's. It was characterized by involvement in the affairs of Europe, and by an effort to influence the course of European events, so as to prevent the victory of forces hostile to his empire.

Toward Venice, Andronicus II exhibited a more flexible attitude after the conclusion of the treaty of 1310. Both he and the Venetian government changed their policy of hostility and suspicion, and slowly the two states set about normalizing their diplomatic and commercial relations. The two states found it in their common interest to deal with each other as friends: Venice abandoned her hopes of seeing a Latin emperor on the throne of Constantinople, and Andronicus II tried to build up his friendship with Venice in order to counteract the power of Genoa. Between 1314 and 1325, the Venetians and the Byzantines exchanged several embassies, which debated at length the outstanding problems between the two states: the question of Byzantine subjects in Crete, problems arising from piracy, and disputes concerning the rights of Venetian colonists and traders in the Byzantine empire.

These exchanges have not been studied in any detail, either by the historians of Venice or by the historians of Mediterranean trade.[99] Yet the relevant documents yield interesting information, both for Venice and for Byzantium. Venice changed from a policy based on an effort to destroy the power-structure in the Black Sea and the Aegean, to a new attidue based on alliances with the states of the Black Sea and the Byzantine empire. As for Byzantium, the

---

98. Villani, II, 232 (book 9, chap. cxxxiii).

99. See R. Cessi, *Politica ed economia di Venezia nel trecento* (Rome, 1952); Cessi, *Storia di Venezia*; Marin, *Venezia*; S. Romanin, *Storia documentata di Venezia*, 10 vols. (Venice, 1853–1861, reprinted in 1925); Gino Luzzatto, *Studi di storia economica veneziana* (Padua, 1954); Luzzatto, *Storia economica di Venezia dall XI al XVI secolo* (Venice, 1961). There is a brief discussion of this subject in Heyd, *Commerce*, I, 466–469.

negotiations with Venice shed light on the operation and implementation of commercial treaties with westerners.

Andronicus II had good reasons to seek better relations with Venice. Since he no longer had aspirations in the Aegean, a potential source of conflict with Venice, in Crete and Nigroponte, had been eliminated. The establishment of the Catalans in the Duchy of Athens presented a danger to both Venetians and Byzantines, and the two states could cooperate against the new threat. Moreover, Andronicus II's empire had expanded westward. The annexation of parts of the despotate of Epirus had increased his power in the Adriatic, and brought him into closer proximity to Venice. While not so strong in the Adriatic that he could seek conflict with Venice, Andronicus was interested enough in the western part of his empire to suggest that the Dalmatian coast should be designated as an area where the treaties should not apply. That is, he suggested that the situation on the Dalmatian and Epirote coasts was so fluid that Venetians and Byzantines should not be able to demand compensation for any damages they might suffer; similar provisions had applied to Nigroponte in the treaty of 1285.[100]

Finally, Andronicus II was already beginning to exhibit a certain diplomatic flexibility toward the West, a flexibility discernible in his involvement in the Genoese civil war, and in his willingness to listen to pro-unionist arguments, as expounded, late in 1317, by the first Catholic bishop of Caffa, Hieronymus.[101] While this new agility will become clearer during the last six years of Andronicus' reign, he was already assuming an active role in his relations with Europe, instead of waiting for each dangerous western wind to blow over. It is possible that he adopted a more friendly attitude toward Venice in order to precipitate the republic's disengagement from its traditional allies, the Valois, the Angevins, and the pope.

Venetian willingness to improve relations with the Byzantine empire formed part of a larger picture. From 1308 to 1310, Venice had suffered one of the most difficult periods of its history. The republic became involved in a war with Ferrara, which cost a great deal in money and men, and which caused Pope Clement V to excommunicate the doge, Pietro Gradenigo, and place the republic under interdict (March 27, 1309). Within Venice, the interdict served to polarize political opinion, and in 1310 a dangerous plot was hatched. Members of the influential "Guelph" houses of Quirini, Tiepolo, and Badoer planned to depose the ruling doge, and replace him with one of the men involved in the conspiracy, Bajamonte Tiepolo. The government discovered and exposed the plot, severely punished the conspirators, and communicated the news to all Venetian representatives abroad, as well as to the other European states.[102] One such communication, to the castellans of Modon and Coron,

---

100. Thomas and Predelli, *Diplomatarium*, no. 76, p. 135; no. 77, pp. 146–147.
101. Girolamo Golubovich, *Biblioteca Bio-Bibliografica della Terra Santa e dell' oriente Franciscano*, III (Quaracchi, 1919), 40–41, 53.
102. Dandolo, *RIS*. XII, col. 410; Villani, II, 147–148 (book 9, chap. ii); Romanin, *Storia di Venezia*, III, 5–46.

the bailo of Nigroponte, the duke of Crete, the bailos of Cyprus and Lesser Armenia, the count of Ragusa, the Venetian ambassador to Constantinople, and Frederick III of Sicily, has been published by Giomo.[103]

Doge Pietro Gradenigo died in 1311, and his successor, Marino Zorzi, ruled for only one year. Under Giovanni Soranzo (1312–1328), Venice disentangled itself from the expensive war of Ferrara and was again admitted into the body of the Catholic church. A rebellion in Zara was extinguished, and Venice began to put her house in order. The Genoese had taken advantage of the troubles in Venice, and Genoese pirates had repeatedly attacked Venetian shipping in the eastern Mediterranean, especially off Lajazzo, in Armenia. In 1313 the Venetians were able to retaliate. They armed a squadron of forty galleys which, under the command of Giustiniano Giustiniani, attacked Genoese ships and raided the Genoese colony of Pera. After this show of strength, the Genoese capitulated, and paid Venice eight thousand ducats in compensation. In order to protect Venetian possessions in the Aegean, and especially in Nigroponte, Soranzo sent several galleys to patrol that sea.[104]

Under the able guidance of Giovanni Soranzo, Venice entered the most prosperous period of her history. Venetian commerce expanded both in the East and in western Europe, aided by the conclusion of commercial treaties and subsidies from the government. In 1317 the Venetians renewed their commercial treaty with Tunis, and in 1320 they signed treaties with France and Brabant. Agreements with Bruges and England, in 1322 and 1326, gave Venice new markets, and from this time on the volume of her trade with the Atlantic seaboard increased considerably. Trade with Flanders was subsidized by the state, which, in 1317–1318, allowed private merchants to make free use of state galleys for travelling to Flanders.[105]

In order to sustain the western part of her commercial operations, Venice had to have a sufficient supply of the Asian commodities in which she specialized—mainly spices, silks, and jewels. The major problem here was to find secure outlets where she could purchase the merchandise. After the loss of her colonies in the Latin kingdom of Jerusalem and after the papal prohibition of trade with Egypt, Venice had been forced to seek outlets in the ports of Cyprus, Lesser Armenia, and Asia Minor.[106] She was well established in Cyprus and Armenia, and in 1320 or 1321 she renewed her commercial treaty with the king of Armenia. In 1320 also, she signed an agreement with the

103. Giomo, *Lettere di Collegio*, letter no. 630 (June 27, 1310), pp. 376–377.

104. Dandolo, col. 411–412; Thomas and Predelli, *Diplomatarium*, no. 49; Marin, *Venezia*, VI, 4ff; Romanin, *Storia di Venezia*, III, 80–105. On Zorzi and Soranzo, see Andrea da Mosto, *I Dogi di Venezia*, (Milan, 1960), pp. 101–106.

105. Thomas and Predelli, *Diplomatarium*, nos. 20, 57, pp. 33–38, 101–102; Cessi, *Politica ed economia*, pp. 86–100; Luzzatto, *Storia economica*, pp. 35–56; F. C. Lane, "Merchant Galleys, 1300–1334: Private and Communal Operations," *Venice and History* (Baltimore, 1966), pp. 193–198, 108–109.

106. Barbara Flemming, "Landschaftsgeschichte von Pamphylien, Pisidien und Lykien im Spatmittelalter," *Abhandlungen für die Kunde des Morgenlandes*, 35 (Wiesbaden, 1964), 62–66; Heyd, *Commerce*, I, 534–547; II, 5–18, 73–83.

Ilkhanid khan of Persia, who safeguarded the passage of Venetian traders and merchandise through his state.[107]

Although Venice had outlets in Cyprus and Armenia, and could send merchants to Persia, she still did not have sufficient contacts with the Black Sea area. Not only did many of the products of China and India reach the sea at the Black Sea ports, but here also came the products of Russia and Bulgaria: wax, furs, salted fish, and wheat. Venice always found it difficult to feed her population, and she could not fulfill her needs with Italian wheat alone. A glance at Venetian documents shows that every year the government took measures concerning the import of wheat from Crete, Greece, and the Black Sea area.[108] Because of this double importance of the Black Sea, Venice tried in this period to establish friendly relations with the powers controlling the ports, and in this she was largely successful.

On the northern coast of the Black Sea, which was under the control of the Tartars of the Golden Horde, Venice already had trading privileges: the port of Soldaia was especially important.[109] In 1319 Venice concluded a commercial treaty with the empire of Trebizond, which until then was open only to Genoese merchants. The privileges granted by the emperor to the Venetians stated specifically that Venetian merchants would now pay exactly the same amount of duty as their Genoese counterparts. Thus, the ports of the empire, Samsun and Trebizond itself, were opened to the Venetians, who could buy there not only the products of the Far East, but also the food products and embroidered cloth, the alum and silver of the empire of Trebizond and Asia Minor.[110] The first Venetian consul was already in Trebizond in August 1320, and by 1322 there were annual journeys to Trebizond.[111] In the same period, Venetian merchants replaced the Genoese as the predominant foreign element in Bulgaria.[112]

Venetian negotiations with Byzantium must be seen as part of the effort of Doge Giovanni Soranzo to improve his relations with the powers of the Black Sea and the Aegean—a highly successful effort. In the 1320's, Venetian trade with the East was so brisk that she was faced with the possibility of an over-supply of eastern commodities. To counteract this danger, the Venetian senate established, in 1324, the *officium de navigantibus*; this office regulated sea trade, and issued a decree forbidding anyone to import by sea merchandise of higher

107. Thomas and Predelli, *Diplomatarium*, no. 86, pp. 176–178, no. 85, pp. 173–176; Heyd, *Commerce*, II, 107ff, esp. pp. 122–128. On Venetian embassies to Persia preceding the treaty of 1320, see Cessi and Sambin, *Consiglio dei Rogati*, pp. 222–223 (book 6, nos. 16, 22, May-June 1320). In 1319, Venice tried to convince Pope John XXII to allow her to resume trade with Egypt: Cessi and Sambin, *Consiglio dei Rogati*, p. 200 (book 5, no. 277).

108. Thiriet, *Délibérations*, I, nos. 268, 272 (1312), 285, 289 (1313), 312 (1314), 329 (1315), 345–346, 351 (1316), 376, 389 (1317), 418 (1319), 434 (1322), 440 (1323), 452 (1326).

109. Thiriet, *Délibérations*, I, no. 388 (1317); G. Heyd, *Le colonie commerciali degli Italiani in Oriente nel Medio Evo*, II, (Venice, 1868), 25.

110. Thomas and Predelli, *Diplomatarium*, no. 71, pp. 122–123; Heyd, *Commerce*, I, 552–553; II, 92–94, 100–103, 182; Claude Cahen, *Pre-Ottoman Turkey* (London, 1968) pp. 317–325.

111. Thomas and Predelli, *Diplomatarium*, no. 83, pp. 171–172; Cessi and Sambin, *Consiglio dei Rogati*, 206 (book 5, no. 338), 212 (book 5, 415; 1319), 241 (book 6, no. 238: 1322). Cf. Lane, "Merchant Galleys," p. 211.

112. Heyd, *Commerce*, I, 530.

value than his total taxable private property.[113] In general, Venice reached her economic zenith in the years 1319–1340, as evidenced by the very high price of shares in the Venetian public debt.[114]

The first diplomatic contacts between Venice and Byzantium, subsequent to the treaty of 1310 and not pertaining to its implementation, occurred in 1313. In November of that year, Venice sent to Constantinople an ambassador, Fantino Dandolo. Another embassy was sent to Byzantium in February 1314. Dandolo stayed on as bailo of the Venetian colony of Constantinople, and he still held that post in 1315.[115] He had been sent to negotiate about certain matters affecting Byzantine subjects living in Crete. The doge requested that Andronicus II should not give any of his subjects resident in Crete as serfs to Venetians, and the emperor granted the request.[116] It is probable that the doge wished to avoid the trouble which might arise from such complex loyalties. In order further to simplify the situation in Crete, the Venetian senate had voted, in February 1314, to allow all Byzantine subjects to leave the island.[117]

In November 1316 the Venetians sent an ambassador to Constantinople with instructions to conclude a treaty of friendship with Andronicus. The Byzantine emissaries found in Venice in May 1317 may have been sent in response.[118] Yet the condition of Venetian merchants in the Byzantine empire was still unsatisfactory. In 1317 the bailo of Constantinople, Marco Minotto, sent to the doge a long letter describing the state of Venetian colonies in the empire, and complaining about the practices of some Venetian merchants who did not show a proper regard for the authority of the bailo.[119] Much of this letter is concerned with the difficulties of governing the colonies. Venetian councillors did not always obey the bailo, did not accompany him in his visits to the emperor, refused to sit with him on Mondays, Wednesdays and Fridays when, according to custom, the bailo and the councillors had to judge the cases brought before them by Venetian merchants and colonists.

Minotto described a state of anarchy, partly attributable to the awkward relations between Byzantium and Venice. He complained that many Venetians pretended to be Genoese in order to profit from the privileged position of the Genoese in the empire. It was his understanding that Andronicus II would be pleased to see this situation rectified, and he asked his superiors to take the appropriate measures to this end. Minotto also brought to the doge's attention the problem of gasmuloi whose fathers had abandoned Venetian citizenship

113. Cessi and Sambin, *Consiglio dei Rogati*, pp. 286–287 (book 8, nos. 39, 42, 45, 54: 1324); Cessi, *Politica ed economia*, pp. 23–61; Luzzatto, *Storia economica*, pp. 123ff.

114. Luzzatto, *Storia economica*, pp. 135–155.

115. Cessi and Sambin, *Consiglio dei Rogati*, p. 140 (book 3, no. 152), 145 (book 4, no. 1); Thomas and Predelli, *Diplomatarium*, no. 54, p. 98 (1315): "Fantinus Dandulo, ambaxator illustris Ducis et comunis Venetiarum et nunc baiulus Venetorum."

116. Thomas and Predelli, *Diplomatarium*, no. 54, p. 98. Date: before May, 1315, when Dandolo was elected duke of Crete: Thiriet, *Délibérations*, I, 158, no. 325. Cf. Thomas and Predelli, *Diplomatarium*, nos. 55, 56, pp. 99–101.

117. Cessi and Sambin, *Consiglio dei Rogati*, p. 145 (book 4, no. 2).

118. Cessi and Sambin, *Consiglio dei Rogati*, p. 168 (book 4, no. 262); Thiriet, *Délibérations*, I, 170, no. 372.

119. Thomas and Predelli, *Diplomatarium*, no. 59, pp. 103–105.

at the time of the Venetian–Byzantine war, and who now wished to be regarded as Venetians. The bailo thought that his government should interfere on behalf of those gasmuloi who had been born before their fathers' change of citizenship.

In 1318 and 1319 the Venetians and the Byzantines drew closer. Theodore of Montferrat was well received when he reached Venice, and the senate voted to send him a solemn embassy and a cash gift.[120] Andronicus had sent his interpreter, Stephen Syropoulos, along with Theodore to negotiate the Byzantine alliance with the Genoese Ghibellines. But Syropoulos had also been to Venice in 1310 to discuss the Venetian–Byzantine treaty signed in that year, and he was something of an expert in Venetian affairs. In 1318 his commission included Venice: Andronicus II wrote to the doge that Syropoulos was to acquaint the Venetian government with developments in Byzantium. Andronicus assumed that Giovanni Soranzo would like to hear about these developments, being a sincere and special friend.[121]

Events in the Aegean underlined the need for Byzantium and Venice to resolve their differences. Always troubled by pirates, the Aegean had become particularly unsafe in 1318–1319. The Catalans of the Duchy of Athens increased their piratical activities, and an unholy alliance was being forged between them and the Turkish inhabitants of the maritime emirates of western Asia Minor. In 1318 the Venetians and the Catalans fought near Nigroponte.[122] In 1318–1319, Venice was engaged in long negotiations with Frederick III of Sicily, who acted as the Catalans' overlord. A six-month truce was finally signed between Venice and the Catalans on June 9, 1319, and the Catalans agreed to dismantle their entire fleet. The agreement was renewed in 1321, but it does not seem to have put an end to the Catalan attacks on Venetian lands and shipping.[123]

The first Turkish activities against Venetian possessions and against Venetian shipping on the high seas are also recorded in the year 1318. Turkish ships attacked the Venetian islands of Carpathos and Santorini (Thera), and the duke of Crete wrote that he was expecting a piratical assault by the joint forces of the Turks and the Catalans. In July 1318 he reported that the Turks were planning to launch an attack against Nigroponte with twenty-four ships of their own, and two Catalan galleys.[124] The threat presented by the Turks would become increasingly obvious to Venice in the 1320's. Even in 1318–1319 the combined Catalan–Turkish attacks must have served to bring Venice closer to Byzantium.

In 1319–1320 the Byzantines and the Venetians began a series of negotiations designed to resolve the differences between the two states. Several long letters

---

120. Thiriet, *Délibérations*, I, 179, no. 409; Cessi and Sambin, *Consiglio dei Rogati*, p. 198.

121. Thomas and Predelli, *Diplomatarium*, no. 69, p. 119: "ut amico sincero et speciali."

122. Thiriet, *Délibérations*, I, 176, no. 399.

123. Cessi and Sambin, *Consiglio dei Rogati*, pp. 198 (book 5, nos. 255, 260, 271), 215 (book 5, nos. 445–446); Thomas and Predelli, *Diplomatarium*, no. 70, pp. 120–122; Marino Sanudo Torsello, letter 5, in Bongars, *Gesta Dei per Francos*. Cf. Setton, *Catalan Domination*, pp. 26–27, 34–35.

124. Thomas and Predelli, *Diplomatarium*, nos. 61–63, pp. 107–110.

were exchanged, touching on important matters: specific grievances against Venetian or Byzantine officials and individual citizens, problems arising out of the privileges granted to Venice, questions regarding the sale of Black Sea grain in the Byzantine empire.

The first document that remains consists of a list of complaints presented by the ambassadors of Andronicus II, Gregory Cleidas and Andronicus Gerakites, to the doge and the senate of Venice, sometime in or before September 1319.[125] Some of Andronicus' requests and complaints arose out of the complex situation in the Aegean, where Greeks and Latins lived close together and sailed on the same pirate-infested sea. He asked that the Venetians allow all Byzantine subjects resident in Crete to leave that island, with all their possessions. Andronicus' request and the Venetian answers indicate that there were two types of Byzantines living on Crete. First were those who were considered hostile by Venice and who, after 1302, were allowed, indeed forced, to leave the island. But there were also others, some being refugees from Asia Minor, who had settled on the island and were productive, and therefore taxable, subjects. These were probably the people to whom Andronicus II referred in 1319, complaining that the duke of Crete refused to let them leave the island, despite the treaties.

Andronicus II also complained about the piratical activities of several Venetians who had harmed his subjects or their ships, and he demanded compensation. Most of the Venetian pirates sailed from Crete, and most of the Byzantine ships involved came from Monembasia; Venetian pirates had sold several Byzantines into slavery in Rhodes and Cyprus. Andronicus particularly wanted to settle a matter concerning Lodovico Morisco, brother of Andronicus' Genoese admiral, Andrea Morisco. The Venetians had captured Lodovico in 1309, and were holding him in a Cretan jail. Andronicus claimed that Lodovico was his man ("homo est . . . serenissimi imperatoris"), and asked the Venetians to liberate him. The Venetians, on the other hand, considered Lodovico a pirate, because he had attacked the Venetian island of Carpathos. As a pirate, Lodovico would fall outside imperial protection. Later, after September 27, 1319, Andronicus II repeated that Lodovico was his *vassalus*, and not a pirate. Moreover, Lodovico was reckoned a Byzantine subject: "computatus [est] ut Grecus." The Venetians rejected Andronicus' requests with regard to his subjects resident in Crete, and to Lodovico Morisco. As for the damages Andronicus mentioned, and the reparations he demanded, the Senate agreed to examine each request and answer it later.

The most important question Andronicus II raised concerned the sale of Black Sea grain to Byzantine subjects by Venetian merchants. The treaty of 1285 had stated that Venetians could buy Black Sea grain freely, and transport

---

125. The letters exchanged between Venice and Byzantium have been published by Thomas and Predelli, *Diplomatarium*, nos. 72–79, with the general dating 1319–1320. The approximate date of the first document can be established from a decision of the Senate which refers to it (September, 1319): Cessi and Sambin, *Consiglio dei Rogati*, p. 212, (book 5, no. 414). The names of the Byzantine ambassadors are found in the doge's answer: Thomas and Predelli, *Diplomatarium*, no. 73, p. 128. Cf. Dölger, *Regesten*, no. 2423.

it through the Byzantine empire, but had made no specific provision for its sale within the empire. The Venetians, apparently, had taken to selling this grain to the Byzantines. In 1319 Andronicus II asked the Venetians not to sell Black Sea grain to his subjects, save with his special permission. The Byzantines who bought such grain should pay the normal purchase tax to the imperial treasury.

The question of Black Sea grain became one of the points on which the emperor and the Venetians could not agree. In September 1319 the senate passed a resolution to remain firm on the matter of Black Sea grain.[126] Obviously, there was a financial principle involved, which neither party wanted to abandon. Black Sea grain was probably cheaper than Byzantine grain in the early fourteenth century, especially after the collapse of Thracian agriculture during the period of the Catalan and Bulgarian invasions. Andronicus II was trying to protect the native grower by forbidding the sale of cheaper foreign grain. His agreement with Genoa in 1317 had also forbidden the sale of wheat from the Bulgarian coast in Constantinople. Andronicus was also trying to build up his finances, and for this reason he had to insist that his subjects pay the regular sales and purchase taxes, and all other duties to which he was entitled. The Venetians saw the problem otherwise: to them, the purchase tax levied on the Byzantines violated the trading privileges Andronicus had granted to Venice.

The question of Black Sea grain thus transcended purely fiscal considerations, and touched on a much deeper issue, the issue of imperial authority over Byzantine subjects. The special privileges granted to Italian merchants put such merchants beyond imperial authority insofar as duties, taxes, and justice were concerned. Now the Venetians were trying to interpret the treaties in such a way that Byzantines also would fall outside the imperial fiscal system, when they engaged in commercial transactions with the Venetians.

The doge raised precisely these points in his answer to Andronicus' letter. He insisted on keeping the letter of the treaties:

> The Venetians, according to the form of the treaty, may sell to whomever they wish, and buy from whomever they wish, in every part of the Empire, all merchandise with the exception of salt and mastic and wheat grown in the empire . . . Therefore, since Black Sea grain is *not* grown in the empire, nor is it salt or mastic, it is permitted to the Venetians to trade in it, and sell it, and export it, however they wish, and the lord emperor may not impose any *commercium* or duty or imposition on anyone who buys from the Venetians.[127]

Andronicus understood the immense implications of the Venetion position, and in his reply he insisted that while the letter of the treaty of 1285 said nothing about the sale or otherwise of wheat grown in the Black Sea, the *spirit* of that treaty clearly indicated that such sales were not permitted. The emperor was

126. Cessi and Sambin, *Consiglio dei Rogati*, p. 212 (book 5, no. 414): "stemus firmi super capitulos frumenti de Mare Maiori et aliis pluribus capitulis et que commissa fuerunt Domino, Conciliariis et Capitibus."
127. Thomas and Predelli, *Diplomatarium*, no. 73, p. 129.

willing to allow the Venetians to sell Black Sea grain, but only if he could levy the regular purchase tax. He was not, he wrote, violating the privileges of the Venetians, but rather exercising an old imperial privilege over his own subjects.[128] To this the doge responded that he had no idea whether the emperor's ancestors had, indeed, levied such duties as part of their imperial privilege; in any case, purchase taxes were illegal, because they annulled the Venetian privileges. The Doge reiterated the pertinent clause of the treaty of 1285, and insisted that the emperor adhere to the letter, not the spirit, of that treaty.[129]

While answering Andronicus' complaints, the Venetians issued three long lists of their own grievances.[130] The first list discussed violations of the treaties by Byzantine officials. Imperial officials sometimes levied port duties on Venetian ships and merchandise, and when the merchant tried to recover his money, he came up against the Byzantine bureaucracy, which sent him from office to office and wasted his time. But the most interesting items on the list challenged, once again, the emperor's authority over his subjects. The doge complained that Byzantine customs officials did not allow the Venetians to sell sails and cloth in Constantinople; when such transactions were allowed, the buyer was taxed. As with grain, Venice argued that this purchase tax infringed on Venetian privileges and franchises.

Venetian needs for Byzantine manpower gave rise to equally interesting conflicts. Venice had always found it difficult to recruit enough free seamen for her ships, and by 1320 the problem was compounded by the change from biremes to triremes, which required larger crews. The Venetians recruited some sailors in Dalmatia, freed prisoners on condition that they work as crew, and, in Byzantium, depended on Byzantine sailors.[131] But the imperial treasury insisted on levying a trade tax on the wages of Byzantine seamen employed by Venetian captains. Since this practice made employment with a Venetian captain less attractive, the Venetians complained that their privileges were being violated. Andronicus II answered that he had made the Venetians, not his own subjects, privileged (*liberos*). He explained that these taxes were a normal, ancient Byzantine practice, and that if he were not allowed to levy them he would not be the lord of his vassals and his subjects.[132] In 1320 the Venetian bailo of Constantinople, Marco Minotto, wrote that Venetian ships

128. Ibid., no. 77, p. 141: "secundum autoritatem et libertatem imperialem." Actually, since the time of John II Comnenus the Byzantine emperors had exempted from the *commercium* those of their subjects who had business dealings with the Venetians: Danstrup, "Indirect Taxation," pp. 146–148.

129. Thomas and Predelli, *Diplomatarium*, no. 78, pp. 151–153. On wheat and the provisioning of the Byzantine Empire, see G. I. Brătianu, "L'approvisionnement du blé à Constantinople" and "L'étatisme des Paléologues et des colonies latines," in *Études byzantines d'histoire économique et sociale* (Paris, 1938); P. Charanis, "On the Social Structure and Economic Organization of the Byzantine Empire in the 13th Century and Later," *Byzantinoslavica*, 12 (1951), 94–153; A. Andréadès, "Byzance," 178.

130. Thomas and Predelli, *Diplomatarium*, nos. 74, 75, 76.

131. Lane, "Merchant Galleys," pp. 219–220, n. 85; Lane, "From Biremes to Triremes," *Venice and History*, pp. 189–192.

132. Thomas and Predelli, *Diplomatarium*, no. 77, p. 145: "non erimus domini vassalorum et subiectorum nostrorum."

could not sail without Greek sailors: Andronicus II had not granted the Venetians what they wanted, and the issue of Byzantine manpower was still open.[133]

The second list of complaints presented by Venice to the Byzantines specifically referred to the activities of Byzantine officials in Thessalonica. Thessalonica was important to Venice as an outlet of Macedonian and Balkan grain; a Venetian colony had begun to flourish there after 1310.[134] But the doge complained that imperial officials gave the Venetian merchants very small houses. Customs officials would often refuse permission to the Venetians to unload their merchandise, until the appropriate bribe had been paid. Sometimes also, these officials confiscated the cargoes of Venetian ships, and gave the merchandise to Genoese traders. The third list of Venetian complaints, dated September 27, 1319, dealt with specific grievances of individuals, and is interesting chiefly insofar as it reveals Byzantine activities in the Despotate of Epirus, western Greece, and the Morea in the years 1313–1319. One other complaint led to some nice diplomatic finessing on both sides.

In 1318 the Genoese of Pera armed some galleys and attacked the Venetians. Venice asked Andronicus II to pay compensation, because of the article in the treaty of 1285 stating that the Venetians and the Genoese were forbidden to engage in hostilities in the waters between Abydos and the Black Sea; if such hostilities occurred, the emperor would compensate the innocent party from his own treasury.[135] Andronicus replied that this article had been specifically rescinded in the treaty of 1302.[136] There was another article of the treaty of 1285 which the Venetians could invoke: "also, we forbid that any expedition against the Venetians be equipped in the territory of our empire"; if this was violated, Andronicus II was bound to make reparations.[137] The emperor claimed that this article referred to *Greek* fleets, and therefore was not applicable to the Genoese fleet of 1318. The Venetians replied that the article was an ancient one, and that it applied in *general* to all hostile action against them, if it occurred in Byzantine waters.[138] Therefore, they demanded that Andronicus II pay them compensation from his own treasury, while he wanted simply to mediate between Venice and Genoa. His interpretation of the treaty of 1285 seems to have been correct, but there was sufficient lack of clarity, so that the Venetians could present an entirely different argument.

Most of these issues remained unresolved until the end of the period, because neither party was willing to compromise on what were, after all, important

---

133. Ibid., no. 80, p. 166: "nostri marini non possunt navigare cum lignis, que habent, sine marinariis grecis." A very similar argument between the emperor and the Venetians concerned the hire of Byzantine boats by Venetian sea-captains. Andronicus insisted on taxing the rent paid by the Venetians: ibid., no. 77, p. 145, no. 80, p. 166.

134. F. Thiriet, "Les vénitiens à Thessalonique dans la première moitié du XIVe siècle," *Byzantion*, 22 (1952), 323–332.

135. Tafel and Thomas, *Urkunden*, III, 329; Thomas and Predelli, *Diplomatarium*, no. 76, p. 137.

136. Thomas and Predelli, *Diplomatarium*, no. 7, p. 14.

137. Tafel and Thomas, *Urkunden*, III, 333: "item, non permittet fieri Imperium nostrum aliquod armamentum in terra nostri Imperii contra Venetos."

138. Thomas and Predelli, *Diplomatarium*, no. 79, pp. 162–163. This article is found in the Venetian-Byzantine treaty of 1277: Tafel and Thomas, *Urkunden*, III, 145.

fiscal questions and sometimes questions of principle. On March 3, 1320 the Venetian bailo of Constantinople, Marco Minotto, sent to the doge a letter, reporting further violations of the Venetian–Byzantine agreements.[139] He complained that the Venetians, who should have been free and privileged throughout the empire, were never left in peace. Greeks and gasmuloi maltreated them in Constantinople, Thessalonica, Aenos, and the islands, and the emperor did nothing about it. Then there was the problem of justice. When a Venetian brought judicial action against a Greek, the case had to be judged in a Byzantine court. But the Venetians understood little of what was being said in a foreign tongue, and never won a case. If a Greek brought action against a Venetian before the bailo's court, and the bailo found for the defendant, the Greek would immediately appeal to a Byzantine court, which would reverse the decision.

Minotto wrote that the Venetians were becoming impatient with Byzantine bureaucrats, who so delayed their every decision, that the Venetian petitioner rarely saw his case reach its conclusion. He accused imperial officials of making difficulties for the Venetian merchants, who were forced to pay duty at the gate of Constantinople before they could bring their merchandise into the city. Venetians were not allowed to export any legumes, nor were Venetian butchers and fishmongers able to sell their merchandise in the general marketplace. The bailo also complained that the Anconitans and the Genoese were much favored in the empire, to the detriment of Venice.[140] Specifically, he argued that Byzantines who bought merchandise from a Pisan, an Anconitan, or a Genoese, did not have to pay a purchase tax, while they did if they bought anything from a Venetian. It is not possible to establish the truth of this last accusation, but it seems improbable that Andronicus II would have abandoned this particular form of revenue.

Discussions between Venice and Byzantium continued in 1321. Venice compiled a list of reparations which the emperor should pay to individuals; they totaled 14,135 hyperpyra and the senate decided to send another embassy to Constantinople.[141] The ambassadors were still in Venice on July 5, 1321, and when they did arrive at Constantinople they would have found the empire engaged in civil war.[142]

Aragon

Byzantine–Aragonese relations in the years 1311–1321 were limited, and revolved around two issues which arose during the Catalan campaign. James II

139. Thomas and Predelli, *Diplomatarium*, no. 80, pp. 164–168.

140. The city of Ancona had been granted an imperial chrysobull in July 1308. Anconitan merchants paid a 2 percent import and export tax ad valorem: Miklosich and Müller, *Acta et Diplomata*, III, xvi–xviii; Dölger, *Regesten*, no. 2314. In 1320 Andronicus II granted to the Dalmatian city of Ragusa, then a Venetian dependence, the right to trade freely in his empire, in exchange for a yearly payment of 1,000 hyperpyra: *Chronica Ragusina Junii Restii*, in *Monumenta spectantia historiam Slavorum meridionalium, Scriptores*, II (Zagreb, 1893), 111; Dölger, *Regesten*, no. 2433; K. Jireček, "Die Bedeutung von Ragusa in der Handelsgeschichte des Mittelalters," *Almanach der Kaiserlichen Akademie der Wissenschaften*, 49 (1899), 395 and n. 83.

141. Thomas and Predelli, *Diplomatarium*, no. 88, pp. 181–186.

142. Cessi and Sambin, *Consiglio dei Rogati*, pp. 221, 234–235 (book 6, nos. 5, 158, 171); Thiriet, *Délibérations*, I, 183, no. 431, July 5.

of Aragon tried to recover for the merchants of his realm the trading privileges
they had held in the empire, which had lapsed during the Catalan campaign.
He also claimed a certain amount of money in lieu of the rights of Constance of
Hohenstaufen to parts of Asia Minor—rights she had transferred to James II
in 1306. Andronicus II agreed to the first request, but not to the second.

Andronicus had first granted commercial privileges to Aragon and the lands
subject to the crown of Aragon in 1296.[143] The chrysobull of 1296 relieved the
merchants of Aragon, Sicily, Valencia, Barcelona, Catalonia, Tortosa, and
Mallorca of all duties and taxes, except for a 3 percent import and export duty,
payable at the ports of entry and exit. In case of shipwreck, the Aragonese and
other merchants were assured that the Byzantines would not confiscate their
property. No source states specifically that these privileges lapsed during the
Catalan campaign, but all of the internal evidence suggests that they did.[144]
The Catalan merchants of Constantinople had joined the Catalan Company
at Gallipoli in attacking the empire, and thus must have made it imperative
for the emperor to rescind the privileges he had granted them.

In 1315, or before, James II of Aragon opened negotiations which led to the
grant of a new chrysobull by Andronicus II in 1315.[145] The opening sentence
of that chrysobull stated that "the king of Aragon, Valencia, Sardinia, Corsica,
count of Barcelona, my beloved uncle,[146] the Lord James, sent to my Majesty
letters . . . asking . . . that the traders be granted permission and privileges to
trade in my empire." Normally, when Andronicus II renewed the trading
privileges of Venetians or Genoese, he mentioned explicitly the privileges granted
to them earlier; in this chrysobull, there is no mention of the privileges
of 1296. Instead, the chrysobull of 1315 reads like a first grant of privileges,
and in form it closely resembles that of 1296. The only difference is that in
1315 Andronicus II reduced the duty levied on Aragonese and Catalan merchandise to two percent on exports and two percent on imports. Andronicus II

---

143. The chrysobull has been published in Miklosich and Müller, *Acta et diplomata*, III,
97–98, and in Antonio de Capmany y Monpalau, *Memórias históricas sobre la Marina, Comercio y
artes de la antigua Ciudad de Barcelona*, II (Madrid, 1779; republished in Barcelona, 1962), 467–
468. For the correct date, see C. Marinesco, "Notes sur les Catalans dans l'empire byzantin,"
Mélanges offerts à M. F. Lot (Paris, 1925), 502–503; and F. Dölger, "Die Urkunden des Byzantinischen Kaisers Andronikos II für Aragon-Katalonien unter die Regierung König Jakobs
II," *Festschrift für A. Rubió y Lluch*, (1933), republished in *Byzanz und die Europäische Staatenwelt*
(Speyer, 1953), pp. 132–133; cf. Brătianu, *Recherches sur le Commerce*, pp. 100–104.

144. Dölger, *Byzanz*, p. 134, accepts that the privileges lapsed; Marinesco, "Notes sur les
Catalans," p. 502, does not.

145. The chrysobull has been published in Greek in Miklosich and Müller, *Acta et diplomata*,
III, 98–99; in Latin in Capmany, *Memórias*, II, 468–471; and in Rubió y Lluch, *Diplomatari*,
no. 115, pp. 140–141. All these editions date the chrysobull 1320, as does N. Nicolau d'Olwer,
in his "Note sur le commerce catalan à Constantinople en 1380," *Byzantion*, 49 (1927–1928),
193. Dölger, *Byzanz*, pp. 134–137, has proved conclusively that the correct date is 1315. See
also Dölger, *Regesten*, no. 2366, and Bănescu's review of Marinesco's "Notes sur les Catalans,"
in *BZ* 26 (1926), 449–450.

146. The term "uncle" is here used loosely, probably to refer to the following relationship:
James II's mother was a daughter of Manfred of Hohenstaufen, and this made him the great-
nephew of Constance of Hohenstaufen, who had married the Byzantine Emperor John III
Vatatzes. Michael VIII had married a niece of John III, and he called Constance his "aunt."
Andronicus II probably extended the title to James II, without tracing the relationship very
carefully. On this, see Dölger, *Byzanz*, pp. 134–135, n. 9.

and James II were reestablishing friendly relations, without referring to the Catalan campaign.[147]

Despite the fact that the subjects of James II were privileged once more after 1315, there is only limited evidence of their commercial activities in the Byzantine empire. Not even the names of Catalan consuls at Constantinople in the fourteenth century have survived. Most of the Aragonese subjects who traded with the East were Catalans, and no doubt they found that the activities of their countrymen of the Duchy of Athens predisposed the Byzantines unfavorably toward all Catalans. Furthermore, neither Venice nor Genoa was eager to see another trading power become active in the eastern Mediterranean. The rivalry between Aragon and Genoa, which was strong in the western Mediterranean, must have been specially detrimental to Aragonese commerce in the East. Yet there were some Catalan merchants in Constantinople, and in 1325 they became involved in a dispute with Venetian traders.[148]

On May 27, 1320, the "councillors and good men" of the city of Barcelona asked James II to intercede for them before Andronicus II.[149] Imperial officials were already violating the provisions of the chrysobull of 1315: they often forced the Catalan merchants to pay a two percent import and export tax every time they moved their merchandise from one Byzantine city to another.[150] The Catalans asked James II to express their grievances to Andronicus through the merchant William Carbonell who was sailing for the Romania.

Although Andronicus II was willing to reestablish friendly relations with Aragon, he completely rejected James' advances over the rights of Constance of Hohenstaufen. Constance, who was the widow of the emperor John III Vatatzes (1222–1254), had transferred her rights on parts of Byzantium to James II in 1306.[151] These rights included three cities in Asia Minor, with the country places attached to them, from which she claimed an annual income of 30,000 hyperpyra. She had been granted these lands by her husband, partly as gifts and partly in return for her dowry. She said that when she left Byzantium for Sicily and then Aragon, in 1262, she had been forced to abandon her possessions, but not her claims on them. Indeed, she said that Michael VIII had given her a written guarantee that should she return to the empire, she would have these lands for her sustenance.[152] In July 1316 James II decided

147. On August 15, 1316 James II wrote to Andronicus II, to introduce his ambassador, Bonanat Reig. James began by thanking Andronicus II for the privileges granted to James's subjects: C. Marinesco, "De nouveau sur Constance de Hohenstaufen," *Byzantion,* 1 (1914), 465–466.

148. Golubovich, *Biblioteca Bio-bibliografica,* III, 56–57; Heyd, *Commerce,* I, 479, n. 2; Nicolau d'Olwer, "Note," p. 193; Nicolau d'Olwer, *L'expansió de Catalunya en la Mediterránea oriental* (Barcelona, 1926), pp. 124–125.

149. Rubió y Lluch, *Diplomatari,* no. 114, pp. 138–139. This document lends further support to Dölger's dating of the imperial chrysobull of 1315, for it mentions the export-import duties of 2 percent as a well-established fact. See also, Marinesco, "Notes sur les Catalans," p. 506, and Dölger, *Byzanz,* p. 138.

150. The Byzantine officials were probably levying the commercium as it applied to the internal circulation of goods.

151. See above Chapter VI, n. 75. On Constance see also C. Diehl, *Figures byzantines,* II (Paris, 1921), chap. vii; G. Schlumberger, *Le tombeau d'une Impératrice byzantine à Valence en Espagne* (Paris, 1902).

152. Marinesco, "Constance," pp. 460–462, and p. 454.

to send ambassadors to Constantinople to ask that Andronicus honor Constance's transfer of her rights, and that he give James compensation for her property. This compensation was probably conceived as a cash settlement. On July 4, 1316, James II wrote to one of his palace officials, asking for the document which proved Constance's claims. Unfortunately for him, this document, an imperial chrysobull, had been lost.[153]

On August 15, 1316, James II gave his instructions to his ambassador, Bonanat Reig, who had also negotiated the chrysobull of 1315. Reig was instructed to assure Andronicus II of James' good-will and friendship, and then to recount the story of Constance's claims. If Andronicus should ask to see the charters which proved Constance's assertions, Reig should answer that one charter had been lost in the battle of Benevento, but that the other might be in the imperial archives at Constantinople. In any case, James II thought that Andronicus should be able to remember the whole affair.[154]

Andronicus II received Bonanat Reig well, and in August 1317 he sent his reply to James.[155] The emperor acknowledged James' thanks for the chrysobull of 1315, confessing his surprise that he should be thanked not once, but twice, for such a small thing. He also expressed his amazement that such a great lady as Constance of Hohenstaufen should have told James such tales.[156] He said that Constance had chosen to leave the Byzantine empire, although she had been treated honorably after her husband's death. On her departure, she took with her all her goods and possessions. Although she subsequently sent several ambassadors and messages to Byzantium, never once did she mention her "claims." Andronicus even wrote that one of Constance's ambassadors, a certain Bernard, was still alive at the court of Frederick III of Sicily, and could, presumably, bear witness as to the truth of the emperor's statements. James II did not pursue this matter any further. He had too many other interests—wars with Genoa, the conquest of Corsica, his interest in the crusade—to become very involved with the Byzantine empire. It may well be that his effort to receive restitution for Constance's "rights" was a long shot, which he attempted because of the success of his request for trading privileges.

In general, Andronicus II's relations with the kingdom of Aragon fits what is known of his western policy during these years. While James II took the initiative in restoring good relations, Andronicus II responded eagerly, but with dignity. Both the chrysobull of 1315 and his letter to James II in 1317 bespoke the emperor's friendship toward the king. Indeed, Andronicus II also recalled the fact that there were remote family connections between the two families: in 1315 he wrote that James II was his uncle, and in 1317 he

153. Rubió y Lluch, *Diplomatari*, no. 81, pp. 100–101; J. Miret y Sens, "Tres princessas griegas en la corte de Jaime II de Aragon," *Revue hispanique*, 15 (1906), 693–694.

154. Miret y Sens, "Tres princessas griegas," pp. 695–697; Rubió y Lluch, *Diplomatari*, no. 82, pp. 101–103; Marinesco, "Constance," pp. 457–458.

155. The letter, in Latin, is published in Marinesco, "Constance," pp. 466–468. Cf. Dölger, *Regesten*, no. 2391, and Dölger, *Byzanz*, pp. 137–138.

156. Marinesco, "Constance," p. 467: "mirati sumus nec immerito, si videlicet per talem et tantam dominam, extractam de magno et alto genere et que sortita fuerat talem et tantam dignitatem, talia fuerint dicta et ordinata."

wrote that he desired to have close and friendly family relations with the king.[157] On the other hand, he could be very firm when his interests were threatened: hence his refusal to consider James' claims on Constance's property. Byzantine–Aragonese relations are characterized by the same traits that recur in Andronicus II's foreign policy of these years: competence, firmness, and a willingness to minimize the potential sources of conflict.

The Northern Neighbors

After the departure of the Catalans from Macedonia, Andronicus II was at last able to enjoy the political results of his matrimonial alliances with the kings of Bulgaria and Serbia. Theodore Svetoslav of Bulgaria had accomplished his aims by the conquest of the Byzantine towns of Anchialos and Mesembreia, and by his marriage to Andronicus' granddaughter, Theodora.[158] Until his death in the summer of 1322 he maintained good relations with his Byzantine neighbors. The only danger the Byzantines had to face from the north came from the Tartars, who, although they inhabited Bulgarian territory, acted independently of the Bulgarian king. In 1320 a Tartar army marched through Bulgaria and Thrace, reaching Andrianople. Despite their substantial numbers, they were not able to inflict great damage on the population. The Tartars over-ran Thrace again in 1321, but again they found that the inhabitants had learned to defend themselves against such invasions: they simply abandoned the countryside, along with all their movable goods, and hid in the fortified cities, until the danger had passed.[159]

The Byzantine–Serbian frontier also seems to have remained stable during this period. Byzantine garrisons were established in Ochrid, Melnik, Prilep, Strumica, Prosêk, and Berat in Albania. While the population of these frontier areas was mixed, and the Slavic element probably predominated, they were under firm Byzantine control.[160] Stephen Uroš II Milyutin had fallen deeply and obsessively in love with his young Byzantine wife, and this is one reason why he stopped his incursions into Byzantine territory.

A more mundane factor also contributed to the stability of the Serbian–Byzantine frontier. During the later part of his reign (1317–1321), Stephen Uroš II had to fight against the forces of Philip of Taranto in Albania, and against the army of Charles of Hungary (1301–1342) on his northern frontier. In 1318 Uroš was faced with a dangerous coalition consisting of Philip of Taranto, Charles of Hungary, the Ban of Bosnia, Mlad, and a number of Albanian nobles. Pope John XXII lent his support to the coalition, and

157. Ibid., p. 468: "karam habere propinquitatem parentele vestre Regie Potestatis."

158. Jireček, *Geschichte der Bulgaren*, pp. 288–289; Cantacuzenus, I, 169; F. Dölger, "Einiges über Theodora, die Griechin, Zarin der Bulgaren, 1308–1330," *Mélanges Henri Grégoire*, I (Brussels, 1949), 217.

159. Cantacuzenus, I, 188–189.

160. Cantacuzenus, I, 37, 100, 184, 210; Gregoras, I, 373–383. Byzantine influence on Serbia was particularly obvious during this period. See F. Dölger, "Die byzantinische und mittelalterliche serbische Herrscherkanzlei," *Actes du XIIe Congrès international d'études byzantines*, I (Belgrade, 1963), 83–103.

encouraged the Albanian nobles to join the fight against the schismatic king of Serbia.[161] In 1320 John XXII tried to interest Frederick of Austria in the "crusade" being waged in Serbia by Charles of Hungary. The king of Poland, the king of Bohemia, and the duke of Carinthia were also urged to help the Hungarians.[162] Fortunately for Serbia, the king of Hungary had problems in his own kingdom, and Frederick of Austria was still involved in his war against Lewis of Bavaria. Thus, the war against the Serbs was waged only sporadically, and Stephen Uroš II was able to defend his kingdom.[163]

Only a few incidents marred the friendly relations between Serbia and Byzantium, and these were caused by personal, not political, problems. In 1317 the Empress Irene died in the town of Drama. Her daughter Simonis, Stephen Uroš' wife, came to Constantinople to attend her mother's funeral, and stayed far too long for her husband's liking.[164] Stephen sent ambassadors to Constantinople to demand that his wife return at once, and to threaten war if she did not. But if Simonis' charms had enslaved Stephen Uroš, she was less appreciative of the old man's affections. Knowing his jealous temperament, she proclaimed that she was afraid to return to him. Andronicus II, once again sacrificing his daughter in the interests of peace, forced her to leave, in the company of the Serbian ambassadors. But as soon as she reached Serres, she secretly assumed the habit of a nun; she had refrained from doing so at Constantinople, for fear she might embarass her imperial father. The Serbian ambassadors were nonplussed. They dared not lay hands on a nun, but neither did they dare face Uroš' wrath. Their problem was solved by Simonis' half-brother Constantine, who was governor of Thessalonica.[165] He probably feared that Uroš would invade Macedonia if Simonis did not return at once; so, Constantine tore off Simonis' habit, and gave the tearful girl to the Serbs to take back to Skopje.

In 1321 Stephen Uroš II sent to Constantinople a monk by the name of Kallinikos to demand that Andronicus II return a force of 2,000 Cuman soldiers whom Uroš had lent to the Byzantines. While he was at the capital, Kallinikos realized that trouble was brewing between the emperor and his grandson; Andronicus III, on the other hand, thought that an alliance with the Serbs would be useful to him, should civil war break out. He sent Kallinikos to Stephen Uroš, with proposals concerning such an alliance, and Stephen accepted enthusiastically. Andronicus III would meet the king in Macedonia and, as Cantacuzenus realized, Stephen Uroš would then launch his own attack against Byzantium, using his alliance as an excuse. But before any of this could occur, Stephen Uroš II died on October 29, 1321. Gregoras praised divine Providence, which had carried off the enemies of the empire, so that the

161. Raynaldus, *Annales Eccl.* 1318, §35; Augustin Theiner, *Vetera Monumenta Historica Hungariam Sacram Illustrantia*, I (Rome, Paris, Vienna, 1859), 830–831.

162. Raynaldus, *Annales Eccl.*, 1320, §1–3.

163. Jireček, *Geschichte der Serben*, pp. 348–353.

164. Gregoras, I, 273–275; Cognasso, "Crisobolla," p. 43. Simonis probably stayed in Constantinople for approximately one year, since Gregoras discussed the incidents attending her sojourn *after* his discussion of the Genoese civil war of 1318: Gregoras, I, 287–288.

165. Gregoras, I, 293.

civil war could be fought without external dangers! After her husband's death, Simonis returned to Constantinople, where she ended her days as a nun.[166]

Had it not been for the disasters in Asia Minor, the ten-year period 1311–1321 could have been called the most productive decade of the reign of Andronicus II. The church was, at last, pacified, and so was the state. In the Morea, in Thessaly, and in western Greece, the Byzantine armies slowly recovered territory which had not belonged to the central government since 1204. Andronicus II dealt with western European powers with more flexibility and competence than ever before. Trying to break the stranglehold of the Genoese on his state, he embarked on a series of negotiations with the Venetians and the Aragonese. And, for the moment, western pretenders to the Byzantine throne were too busy to launch an attack against Byzantium.

In fact, Andronicus II's easy relations with the West are reminiscent of the policies of Michael VIII. Perhaps the crux of the matter lies precisely in the virtual loss of Asia Minor. As long as Asia Minor was the focus of Andronicus II's interest, he had neither the time nor the possibility to develop an effective western policy. Now that Asia Minor seemed as lost as it must have appeared to Michael VIII, Andronicus II could concentrate on building up the resources of the remaining part of his empire, while at the same time drawing slowly closer to the West. The civil war which began in 1321 destroyed most of his accomplishments, but not his new western policy.

166. Cantacuzenus, I, 36–37; Dölger, *Regesten*, nos. 2468, 2497; Jireček, *Geschichte der Serben*, p. 354; Gregoras, I, 318; Papadopulos, *Genealogie*, no. 65; M. Laskaris, *Vizantiske princese u srednjevekonoj Srbiji* (Belgrade, 1926), p. 81; and Dölger's review of Laskaris, in *BZ* 27 (1927), 132.

IX

Seizing the Crown, 1321–1328

Civil War

The civil war between Andronicus II and his grandson, Andronicus III, which lasted intermittently for seven years, from April 1321 until May 1328, destroyed the old emperor's careful plans for the reconstruction of his state. When the war ended, Andronicus II had lost his throne, and the empire had been disrupted politically, economically, and socially. Surprisingly, although the civil war endangered Andronicus II's throne and indeed his very life, it only affected the intensity, not the direction of his foreign policy with regard to western Europe. Yet Andronicus II's western policy during the last eight years of his reign comes out in sharper relief if seen against the background of the civil war.

The conflict between the two Andronici was, primarily, a struggle for power. A new generation, represented by Andronicus III and his closest adviser, John Cantacuzenus, fought to wrest control of the empire from men who had grown old in its service, Andronicus II and Theodore Metochites.[1] The two historians of the civil war, Gregoras and Cantacuzenus, provide a striking picture of the differences in the personalities and preoccupations of the two protagonists. Andronicus II was sixty-one or sixty-two years old in 1321, and had been ruling for thirty-nine years. Age had increased his religiosity, and it was now reinforced by a strong element of superstition. He spent a considerable amount of his time in the company of Metochites, Gregoras, and the other intellectuals of whom he was the patron. He delighted in long discussions of philosophy and astronomy, and with Metochites he tried to determine the future by reading the messages of the stars, or of various omens. To the younger generation, it must have seemed that two old men, closeted together in the palace, were running the state on the basis of messages from the supernatural.[2] This picture was far from accurate, but it served its purpose.

Andronicus III, twenty-five years old in 1321, was impatient to succeed a grandfather who seemed to have no intention of dying. He was intelligent, bellicose, fairly well educated, he needed money, and he craved power. Gregoras claimed that Andronicus III was ambitious; the young emperor disclaimed any such commonplace motivation, and instead said that he desired

---

1. The civil war has not been discussed fully by modern historians nor has it been placed in its proper context, which is the development of the Byzantine state. The most detailed descriptions of the events of the civil war are in Valentin Parisot, *Cantacuzène, homme d'état et historien* (Paris, 1845), and U. V. Bosch, *Kaiser Andronikos III. Palaiologos. Versuch einer Darstellung der byzantinischen Geschichte in den Jahren 1321–1341* (Amsterdam, 1965). The two major sources, Cantacuzenus and Gregoras, are apologists for Andronicus III and Andronicus II respectively. Some of the difficulties created by this situation can be overcome by carefully collating the two authors.

2. Gregoras, I, 272–273, 274–275, 303–306, 321–339; Rodolphe Guilland, *Essai sur Nicéphore Grégoras; l'homme et l'oeuvre* (Paris, 1926), pp. 6–9.

power only to save the declining empire.[3] That too, of course, is ambition, but of a worthier sort. Cantacuzenus and Gregoras both agreed that Andronicus III was impatiently awaiting his grandfather's death. Gregoras mentioned another reason for the younger man's discontent: "he did not want to be forever treated as a child by his imperial grandfather, and forever to do as he was told."[4] Andronicus II, who had become an authoritarian and moralizing man, had no desire to abdicate: "How could I entrust so much power and authority to my grandson, a man so young and inexperienced that he cannot even take good care of his own affairs? . . . I will not, willingly, betray either my subjects or my own self."[5]

Andronicus III had been proclaimed co-emperor in 1316, and even Cantacuzenus admits that the old emperor doted on his grandson.[6] Suddenly, an unsavory incident poisoned the relations of the two men. According to Gregoras, Andronicus III had developed into a spoiled young man, who spent his grandfather's money (and money which he borrowed from the Genoese of Pera) on wine, women, and hunting. One night, while Andronicus III was at the house of his latest paramour—a lady of higher birth than morals—his brother Manuel came looking for him with a message from the palace. Andronicus III's bodyguard killed Manual, mistaking him for the lady's discarded lover. This incident took place in 1319 or 1320, for we are told that Michael IX died of sorrow soon thereafter.[7] Andronicus II suffered one of his violent reversals of emotion, and began to contemplate by-passing Andronicus III in the line of succession.

Soon after Michael IX's death, Andronicus II asked the governors of the provinces to renew their oath of allegiance to him alone, without mentioning the young co-emperor.[8] Andronicus III realized that his position as heir to the throne was unsafe. He thought he knew, too, who would replace him. Andronicus II's second son, the despot Constantine, had an illegitimate son named Michael Katharos. When the boy was half-grown, Constantine tired of his concubine, and fell in love with another woman, whom he later married. The young Michael was abandoned to his own devices, and Andronicus II took him to Constantinople, sheltered him, educated him, and planned to use him eventually as bridegroom for some barbarian chieftain's daughter.[9] Michael Katharos, however, soon captured the old emperor's affection, and became the favorite grandson. This development too was consistent with Andronicus

3. Gregoras, I, 284, 399, 400–401; Cantacuzenus, I, 220–221, and passim.

4. Gregoras, I, 285: μηδὲ γὰρ θέλων ὑπὸ τῷ πάππῳ καὶ βασιλεῖ καθάπερ ὑπὸ παιδαγωγῷ παιδοκομεῖσθαι καὶ ἄλλων λατρεύειν βουλήμασιν ὥσπερ παιδίον ἀεί.

5. Gregoras, I, 404: Πῶς ἂν δυνηθείην τῷ ἐγγόνῳ πιστεῦσαι τοιαύτην ἀρχήν, νέῳ τε ὄντι καὶ τοσαύτην ἀπειρίαν ἀσκοῦντι, ὡς μηδὲ τὰ κατ᾽ αὐτὸν εἰδέναι διαθέσθαι καλῶς . . . ; ἀλλ᾽ οὐκ ἂν ποτ᾽ ἔγωγε προδότης ἑκών γε εἶναι γενοίμην, οὔτε τῶν ὑπηκόων, οὔτ᾽ ἐμαυτοῦ.

6. Papadopulos, *Genealogie*, no. 68; Cantacuzenus, I, 13–14.

7. Gregoras, I, 284–286. Cantacuzenus suppresses the story of Manuel's murder, but he does attribute Michael IX's death partly to sorrow over the loss of Manuel: Cantacuzenus, I, 13–14; cf. Bosch, *Andronikos III*, p. 14. On the date of Michael IX's death (October 1320), see Gregoras, I, 277; Loenertz, "La chronique brève de 1352," p. 333.

8. Gregoras, I, 295–296; Cantacuzenus, I, 16–23.

9. Gregoras, I, 293–295; Cantacuzenus, I, 14–16; Bosch, *Andronikos III*, pp. 14–16.

SERBIA

BULGARIA

Danube River

Varna

ADRIATIC
SEA

Sliven
Mesembreia
Anchialos
(Bulg. 1307)
Sozopolis

Skopje

Philippopolis

Adrianople

Debar

Štip

Melnik

Didymoteichon

Durazzo
(S. 1296)

Prilep

Strumica

Ochrid

Prošek

Serres

Christopolis

Aenos

ITALY

Berat

Edessa

Avlona

Kastoria

Veroia

Thessalonica

Thasos

Abydos

Corfu

Janina

Larisa

Lemnos

KARASI

EPIRUS

THESSALY

Domokos

AEGEAN

SEA

SARUKH

Lesbos

Lamia

Phocaea (G)

Mag

CATALAN

NIGROPONTE
(V)

Chios
(G)

Sm

Thebes

DUCHY

(T. 1

OF ATHENS

Athens
(V)

Andros
(B)

Ephesus
(T. 1304)

Samos

AYD

PRINCIPALITY

Keos
(V)

Ikaria

Miletus

OF ACHAIA

Seriphos
(V)

Naxos

Kalymnos

Modon (V)

Mistra

Amorgos
(V)

Kos

Coron (V)

Monembasia

Astypalaia

Santorini
(V)

Rh
(Hospita

Cerigo
(Kythera)

Karpathos
(V)

M E D I T E R R A N E A N

Canea

CRETE
(V)

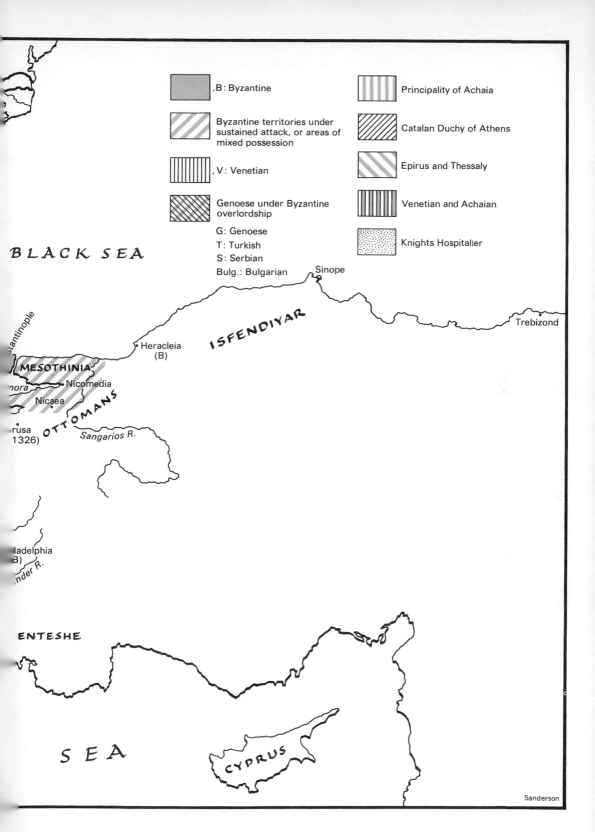

,B: Byzantine

Byzantine territories under sustained attack, or areas of mixed possession

,V: Venetian

Genoese under Byzantine overlordship

G: Genoese
T: Turkish
S: Serbian
Bulg.: Bulgarian

Principality of Achaia

Catalan Duchy of Athens

Epirus and Thessaly

Venetian and Achaian

Knights Hospitaller

BLACK SEA

Sinope

ISFENDIYAR

Trebizond

antinople

Heracleia
(B)

MESOTHINIA

nora   Nicomedia

Nicaea

rusa   OTTOMANS
1326)

Sangarios R.

adelphia
3)

nder R.

ENTESHE

SEA

CYPRUS

Sanderson

The Byzantine Empire, 1328

II's personality. He had treated Andronicus III as a son, and he had been disappointed. Now he was repeating the process, grooming another grandson for the imperial office, a young boy who owed everything, perhaps even his life, to the old emperor.

In 1320, as a consequence of Andronicus II's attitude, a number of men began to advise Andronicus III to rebel. Among them was the dark, scheming figure of Syrgiannes who would become the most evil presence in the civil war. Defecting from one emperor to the other, urging them both to continue fighting, he tried to serve his personal ambitions, whatever the cost to anyone else.[10] Meanwhile, Andronicus II realized that he had precipitated a crisis. He feared that his grandson might escape to western Europe and seek help from the Latins in order to launch a joint attack on Constantinople. Memories of the fourth crusade still haunted the Byzantines, and Andronicus II obviously feared that his grandson would play the role of an Alexius IV Angelus. In order to avoid such an eventuality, Andronicus II stopped demanding the oath of loyalty which Andronicus III had found so offensive.[11]

Andronicus III was not satisfied. He had already collected around him a small group of important people who were to remain with him throughout the next eight years. It included John Cantacuzenus, Theodore Synadenos, governor of Prilep, and John Apokaukos. This group began to deliberate on possible courses of action. They all thought Andronicus III should leave Constantinople, but they could not agree on whether he should go to Adrianople or to Christopolis. For the moment, the decision was postponed. Syrgiannes went to Thrace, where he had been appointed governor by Andronicus II, and there he proceeded to assemble an army.[12]

The two co-emperors stayed in Constantinople, in apparent peace, but both biding their time. Early in April 1321, Andronicus II tried to destroy his grandson's coterie. Andronicus III was made to affirm his loyalty to his grandfather, before a court consisting of the patriarch and the high clergy.[13] Andronicus II then ordered John Cantacuzenus to assume the command of the Byzantine forces in the Morea, but Cantacuzenus refused, claiming that his father's death in the Morea had given him a traumatic dislike of the peninsula. He could not cite the same excuse when he was asked to go to Thessaly to protect the Byzantine possessions against Catalan attacks, but he procrastinated, saying that he needed time to put his affairs in order, to assemble the soldiers, to collect

---

10. Syrgiannes was the son of the megas domestikos Syrgiannes, and of Eugenia, a sister of Michael VIII. In 1315 he had been sent to govern a Macedonian province near the Serbian frontier; there, he took it upon himself to attack Serbia and Epirus, in defiance of the existing treaties. He was relieved of his command, rebelled, and was imprisoned. Sometime before 1320, he was released from prison, and just before the opening of the civil war he was entrusted with the government of Thrace: Gregoras, I, 296–299; Cantacuzenus, I, 18–19; Bosch, *Andronikos III*, p. 14; Papadopulos, *Genealogie*, nos. 34a, 34b. According to Gregoras (I, 299), Syrgiannes planned either to seize part of the empire and govern it independently, or even to seize the throne.

11. Cantacuzenus, I, 18–20; Gregoras, I, 296–302.

12. Cantacuzenus, I, 23–40, 42–50, 54–55; Gregoras, I, 301–312; Bosch, *Andronikos III*, pp. 16–17.

13. Cantacuzenus, I, 56–92; Gregoras, I, 312–316; Parisot, *Cantacuzène*, pp. 42–47.

their pay from the treasury. Synadenos, who had been ordered to return to Prilep, used similar excuses. Finally, on the night of April 19–20, Andronicus III left Constantinople from the gate leading to Adrianople; he pretended that he was going hunting, and this surprised no one. He reached Adrianople within two days. The rebellion had begun.[14]

From Adrianople, Andronicus III built up support for his cause. He "promised the Thracian cities and towns that he would release them from all taxes, and immediately he had their obedience."[15] All of Thrace, up to the wall at Christopolis, joined the rebellion, mostly because people were exhausted by the fiscal exactions of the old emperor. Tax collectors in Thrace were hunted down, and the money they had already collected was taken from them. The partisans of Andronicus II saw their properties confiscated and their lives in danger. While Thrace was rising in rebellion, Andronicus II requested the prelates at Constantinople formally to pronounce his grandson a rebel; priests carried the Bible through the streets of the capital, asking the population to swear loyalty to Andronicus II.[16]

Somehow, Andronicus III collected a large army in Thrace. Although Cantacuzenus' estimate of 50,000 cavalry must be an exaggeration, both Gregoras and Cantacuzenus agree that the young emperor's armed forces were considerable. Only a small part of the army was made up of regular soldiers, while the rest consisted of men eager to benefit from the war, and to whom Andronicus III promised—or gave outright—the pronoiai of Andronicus II's followers.[17] Andronicus III appeared outside Constantinople at the head of a large army, and the old emperor, fearing rebellion in his capital, sent ambassadors to negotiate a peace treaty. The treaty was signed at Rhegion, between Selyvria and Constantinople, in early June 1321.[18]

The treaty of Rhegion divided the empire and the imperial authority into two parts. Thrace from Selyvria to Christopolis would be governed by Andronicus III, while the old emperor would retain his authority in the rest of the empire, including Constantinople. Foreign affairs too would remain within the jurisdiction of Andronicus II, as they had been when Michael IX was co-emperor. Gregoras wrote that Andronicus III preferred hunting and fighting to the long deliberations required by foreign policy.[19] Apparently, the treaty of Rhegion satisfied Andronicus III, but not his grandfather.

Four months after the signing of the treaty, sporadic hostilities began anew in Thrace. Syrgiannes joined Andronicus II, and during the winter Andronicus

14. Cantacuzenus, I, 84–89; Loenertz, "Chronique brève de 1352," p. 334, no. 13; p. 350; Bosch, *Andronikos III*, 19; D. M. Nicol, *The Byzantine Family of Kantakouzenos (Cantacuzenus), ca. 1100–1460*, (Dumbarton Oaks, 1968), pp. 36–37.

15. Gregoras, I, 319: οἱ δὲ περὶ τὸν νέον βασιλέα Ἀνδρόνικον ἐλευθερίαν κηρύξαντες καὶ ἀτέλειαν ταῖς ἐν Θρᾴκῃ κώμαις καὶ πόλεσιν ἅπαντας εἶχον εὐθὺς εὐπειθεῖς πρὸς ἅπαν δὴ τὸ τῆς γνώμης βουλόμενον. Cf. Cantacuzenus, I, 101.

16. Cantacuzenus, I, 93–102; Gregoras, I, 319–320; Parisot, *Cantacuzène*, pp. 47–52; Bosch, *Andronikos III*, pp. 21–25.

17. Cantacuzenus, I, 108; Gregoras, I, 352.

18. Loenertz, "Chronique brève de 1352," p. 350; Dölger, *Regesten*, nos. 2461, 2462; Bosch, *Andronikos III*, pp. 25–27.

19. Cantacuzenus, I, 108–119; Gregoras, I, 320–321.

Palaeologus, who held Stenimachos and other forts in the Rhodope range, also defected from Andronicus III.[20] The old emperor conceived the plan of enclosing his grandson in Thrace, and attacking him from both east and west. Syrgiannes attacked Andronicus III from the East. The Macedonian army, under the command of Andronicus II's son, the despot Constantine, did reach Thrace—tearing down part of the wall at Christopolis in order to pass through. But Andronicus III, pretending that he had already captured Constantinople, persuaded his uncle Constantine to retreat to Thessalonica (end of winter, 1321–1322).[21] Early in the spring of 1322, revolution broke out in Thessalonica, and the city was taken over by the followers of Andronicus III. With a stalemate, the two emperors met again, in July 1322, at Epibatai, and again they made peace. This time, it was agreed that Andronicus II would reestablish his authority over Thrace, but that Andronicus III's soldiers would be allowed to retain the pronoiai they had acquired here.[22]

With the treaty of Epibatai, a period of peace began, which lasted until 1327. The peaceful interlude allowed the Byzantines to deal successfully with the Bulgarians who, in 1322, opened a series of hostile moves in Thrace. Theodore Svetoslav, who had been a faithful ally of the Byzantines, died in the summer of 1322, and was succeeded by his son, George Terter II. The new king attacked several Byzantine towns in Thrace, occupied Philippopolis, and, in August 1322, appeared outside the suburbs of Adrianople.[23] His victories were short-lived, for in the autumn of the same year Andronicus III launched an offensive into Bulgaria. He then returned to Constantinople, to celebrate his first triumph against the "barbarians".

In November or December 1322, George Terter II died, and the Bulgarian nobles chose as his successor the governor of Vidin, Michael Šišman (1323). But Šišman was faced with a state in rebellion. Immediately after Terter's death, the strip of territory from Mesembreia to Sliven rebelled, and its inhabitants invited the Byzantines to take over the government. Meanwhile, the Byzantines had found a Bulgarian prince who was willing to rule under their guidance. Vojisil, Svetoslav's brother, had been living in Byzantium; now, in 1323, Andronicus II gave him the title "despot of Mysia," and with Byzantine help Vojisil took over certain Bulgarian lands, from Sliven to a place named Kopsis.[24]

Michael Šišman attacked the rebel territories in 1323. At the same time, Andronicus III was engaged in the siege of Philippopolis, which he soon

20. Cantacuzenus, I, 135–138; Gregoras, I, 353–355; Bosch, *Andronikos III*, pp. 28–31. On the second phase of the war, see also Parisot, *Cantacuzène*, pp. 54–58.

21. Gregoras, I, 354–356.

22. Ibid., I, 351, 356–360; Cantacuzenus, I, 152–169; Loenertz, "Chronique brève de 1352," pp. 334, 350; S. Lambros, «Βραχέα Χρονικά,» ed. K. I. Amantos, Μνημεῖα τῆς Ἑλληνικῆς Ἱστορίας, I (Athens, 1932–1933) 7; Bosch, *Andronikos III*, pp. 33–34; Nicol, *Kantakouzenos*, p. 38; Dölger, *Regesten*, no. 2479; Parisot, *Cantacuzène*, pp. 58–60.

23. Cantacuzenus, I, 172–188.

24. Bosch, *Andronikos III*, p. 56; Nicol, *Kantakouzenos*, p. 38; A. K. Burmov, *Istorija na Bulgarija prez vremeto-Šišmanovci (1323–1396)*. I. Godišnik na Sofiskija universitet, Istor. Filol. Fakultet (43, 1946–1947), pp. 5–18; Dölger, "Einiges über Theodora," p. 217. Jireček, *Geschichte der Bulgaren*, pp. 289–290.

recovered. After the fall of Philippopolis to the Byzantine forces, Andronicus
II and Andronicus III together decided to continue the war in Thrace in order
to further the interests of the state as well as those of individuals who happened
to have pronoiai there. But in mid-1324, word came from Bulgaria that
Šišman had married Theodora, Svetoslav's widow and Andronicus III's sister.
With this marriage, hostilities between the two states ceased.[25]

While Byzantium and Bulgaria were still at war, Thrace experienced the
worst of a series of Tartar invasions. A large Tartar army—the reported figure
of 120,000 men must be an exaggeration—passed through Bulgaria and came
into Byzantine territory. They were able to pillage Thrace for forty days,
because Andronicus III's forces were dispersed elsewhere, mostly on the northern
frontier of the empire. Eventually, Andronicus III was able to reorganize the
defenses, and after two major battles in the spring of 1324 the Tartars retreated.[26] Cantacuzenus reported a rumor that Andronicus II had invited
the Tartars into Thrace, in order to use them against his grandson. He mentioned this rumor only to refute it with indignation. Indeed, there is absolutely
no evidence that Andronicus II contemplated such a course of action. Using
foreign mercenaries against domestic enemies was a well-established practice.
But inviting into the empire a group such as the Tartars, who were known
for their greed and harshness, would have been an extremely unwise decision.[27]

So great was the destruction wrought by the Tartars, that word of it reached
Italy, and the Florentine historian, Giovanni Villani, devoted a chapter to it:

> In the same year (1324), during the month of February, the Tartars of
> Gazzaria and Russia, with an army of 300,000 horse, came to Greece up to
> Constantinople, during several days, laying waste and destroying whatever
> they found before them. And they stayed until the following April, and
> wrought great damage and destruction upon the persons and the property
> of the Greeks, so that more than 150,000 men were killed or taken into
> slavery . . . And this event shows once again that God's whip is visited upon
> those who are not his friends, whom he allows to be persecuted by those
> worse than they.[28]

During the interlude of peace the Byzantine government of Andronicus II
made its last faint effort to send help to Asia Minor. Andronicus II had already
made use of Turkish mercenaries in the civil war, thus initiating the process
which, during the wars between John V Palaeologus and John VI Cantacuzenus would allow the Ottomans to establish themselves in Thrace. But
the Turkish mercenaries of Andronicus II had been defeated by Andronicus

25. Cantacuzenus, I, 187; Bosch, *Andronikos III*, p. 60; Dölger, "Einiges über Theodora,"
p. 218; Burmov, *Istorija na Bulgarija*, pp. 21ff.
26. Cantacuzenus, I, 188–193; Burmov, *Istorija na Bulgarija*, p. 20; Parisot, *Cantacuzène*, p.
65, no. 3. One of the battles took place between Adrianople and Didymoteichon, and the other
on the banks of the Tunza river.
27. Bosch, *Andronikos III*, pp. 65–67, considers it very likely that Andronicus II called in the
Tartars to defeat his grandson. Her argument rests on conjecture.
28. Villani, II, 293–294 (book 9, chap. ccxli).

III near Tzurulon in 1321, and they left Thrace, returning to Asia Minor.[29] In 1323, the Turks of southern Anatolia besieged Philadelphia. On the advice of the patriarch Isaias (1323–1334), Andronicus II sent Alexios Philanthropenos, now a blind old man, to the defense of the city. Alexios went east without money and without an army, but the Turks, remembering the kindness and valor he had displayed in 1295, flocked to him, abandoning the siege of Philadelphia. The city remained in Byzantine hands until 1391.[30]

The worst blows in Asia Minor came from the Ottomans. Gregoras writes that during the period of hostilities between the two emperors (1321–1322), the Turks had begun to build ships, and they attacked Macedonia, Thrace, and the adjacent islands.[31] These were still raids rather than concerted attacks, but even so they properly aroused the fear of the Byzantines. The Ottomans achieved a major success on April 6, 1326, in Bithynia, when they captured the city of Brusa, which they had been trying to take ever since 1317.[32] The city had been able to withstand their attack during these nine years, but it could not defend itself forever without the help of the central government. Strangely enough, it was not Andronicus II but rather Andronicus III and his entourage who appeared concerned about the fate of this major Bithynian city. John Cantacuzenus campaigned in Bithynia, probably in 1325.[33] At approximately the same time, Andronicus III asked his grandfather to allow him to sail to a port near Bithynia, carrying provisions to the city. He and his army would attack the Turks, bring the food into Brusa, and then, presumably, they would leave: "If this had been done, then it could be hoped that they [the inhabitants] would have resisted the siege for a long time. For the city is well prepared in every other [except for provisions]." Later, in 1327, Andronicus III accused his grandfather of not concurring with this plan, and thus allowing the city to fall by famine.[34]

29. Cantacuzenus, I, 149–152.

30. Gregoras, I, 360–362. On Philanthropenos, see above, "Asia Minor," in Chapter III. The Turks besieging Philadelphia were from the emirate of Mentesche or the emirate of Aydin: Wittek, *Mentesche*, pp. 42–43; Lemerle, *L'Émirat d'Aydin*, p. 106.

31. Gregoras, I, 351. Gregoras is probably referring to the Ottomans here, for he speaks of small Turkish ships which were built just then (1321–1322) and began attacking Thrace. The Turkish maritime emirates possessed naval forces before 1321: see above, "The Italian Maritime Cities," in Chapter VIII.

32. For the date of the fall of Brusa, see P. Charanis, "An Important Short Chronicle of the Fourteenth Century," *Byzantion*, 13 (1938), 341ff; Lambros, «Βραχέα Χρονικά,» nos. 15, 4; 52, 5; Loenertz, "Chronique brève de 1352," p. 334, no. 16, and p. 353. Cf. V. Laurent, "La chronique anonyme du Cod. Mosq. Gr. 426 et la pénétration turque en Bithynie au début du XIVe siècle," *REB* 7 (1949), 208.

33. Cantacuzenus' campaign is mentioned only in one source, two letters of Theodore Hyrtakenos: "Theodore Hyrtakenos, Correspondance," ed. F. J. G. de la Porte-du Theil, in *Notices et extraits des manuscrits de la Bibliothèque nationale*, VI (1800), no. 54 (p. 18), no. 55 (p. 19). Hyrtakenos declared that Cantacuzenus was Byzantium's answer to Xerxes, and wrote that the Turks had all been killed or taken captive, and that "all of Asia is now subject to Europe!" For the probable date of this expedition, see Nicol, *Kantakouzenos*, p. 37, no. 5.

34. Cantacuzenus, I, 220; Gregoras, I, 384. Georgiades-Arnakes, Οἱ πρῶτοι Ὀθωμανοί, p. 156, makes a curious mistake here. He writes that Andronicus III "was able to land at Trigleia, and from there to bring some corn into Brusa; this raised the inhabitants' morale for the rest of the siege." Cantacuzenus, I, 220 says quite clearly that this was what Andronicus III *had planned* to do, but was unable to, because of his grandfather's lack of enthusiasm. Cf. Parisot, *Cantacuzène*, p. 70.

Andronicus III also claimed that he had asked his grandfather for a force of 1,000 soldiers to save Asia Minor, and that the old emperor had refused.[35] These accusations, presented in 1327, may have some truth in them. But in any case, Andronicus III's plans for Anatolia were minimal; surely, had he wanted to, he could have raised his own army to fight the Turks, as he had raised his own army to fight his grandfather. But the end result was that the Byzantines did nothing to help Brusa, and the Turkish sources may be correct in attributing the fall of the city to the alienation of the inhabitants from their government, and to the treason of the city's governor, Kiose-Michael.[36] The fall of Brusa was the crowning event of the reign of Sultan Osman. He died in the same year, and his son Orchan, the conqueror of Brusa, transferred his residence to that city. Ottoman Bithynia now became a state. Brusa was the first sizable city the Ottomans had taken, it was well populated and strategically situated, and it was a commercial and administrative center of no mean importance.[37] Only two Byzantine cities still survived in Bithynia: Nicaea which fell in 1331, and Nicomedia, which held out until 1337.[38]

Andronicus II and Andronicus III gave formal expression to their reconciliation at the coronation of the younger emperor, in Constantinople on February 2, 1325. The magnificent ceremony is described by Cantacuzenus in a pompously written passage.[39] But the proceedings were marred by an unpleasant incident. As the two emperors were riding to the church of Sancta Sophia, Andronicus II's horse missed his footing in a muddy puddle, and fell.[40] This was considered an evil omen, and indeed, new clouds soon began to gather.

The third phase of the civil war began in 1327. The two major sources again differ in their interpretation of the causes for the new outbreak of hostilities. Cantacuzenus accused Andronicus II of calling on his western army to prepare to attack Andronicus III; Gregoras, on the other hand, blamed the young emperor for having appropriated money in Thrace, and for having made an alliance with Michael Šišman of Bulgaria against Andronicus II.[41] This phase of the war, fought for the most part in Macedonia, was characterized by the active involvement of Serbia and Bulgaria.

Serbia supported Andronicus II, after its new king, Stephen Uroš III Dečanski, had allied himself by marriage to the old emperor. Stephen Uroš II had died in 1321, and the problem of succession had created a chaotic situation in Serbia. There were three contenders to the throne: Stephen Uroš II's illegitimate son, Stephen Dečanski; his other son, Constantine; and their

---

35. Gregoras, I, 401. This reference is to the years of the civil war, not to ca. 1307, as in Georgiades-Arnakes, Οἱ πρῶτοι Ὀθωμανοί, p. 151.

36. Georgiades-Arnakes, Οἱ πρῶτοι Ὀθωμανοί, p. 157, n. 76. Francès, "La féodalité byzantine," p. 70, calls Kiose-Michael a collaborator of Sultan Osman.

37. Georgiades-Arnakes, Οἱ πρῶτοι Ὀθωμανοί, pp. 162–163; von Hammer, *Geschichte des Osmanischen Reiches*, I, 85.

38. Lambros, Βραχέα Χρονικά. no. 26, 4; no. 52, 6; Loenertz, "Chronique brève de 1352," pt. 2, *OCP* 30 (1964), 40, no. 24; Georgiades-Arnakes, Οἱ πρῶτοι Ὀθωμανοί, pp. 187, 195–197.

39. Cantacuzenus, I, 196–204. For the date, cf. Loenertz, "Chronique brève de 1352," 334, no. 15.

40. Gregoras, I, 373.

41. Cantacuzenus, I, 208–215; Gregoras, I, 390–392; Bosch *Andronikos III*, pp. 39ff; Parisot, *Cantacuzène*, pp. 74ff.

cousin Vladislav, son of Stephen Dragutin, the older brother of Stephen Uroš II.[42] Constantine was elected king in the Zeta, but most of the Serbian nobles supported his half-brother, Stephen Dečanski. In the ensuing struggles, Dečanski won, and he was crowned king on January 6, 1322; his young son, Stephen Dušan, was crowned along with him. The new kral still had to fight for his throne, primarily against his cousin Vladislav, who was supported by the Angevins and their Hungarian and Bosnian allies.[43]

In order to destroy Vladislav's Angevin alliance, Stephen Dečanski, a widower, offered to marry Blanche, the daughter of Philip of Anjou-Taranto and Thamar of Epirus (1323). Should the marriage take place, Dečanski promised that he and his people would join the Roman church, and he would help Philip of Taranto to recover the Byzantine empire. Philip communicated this news to John XXII, who pronounced himself overjoyed, and immediately sent to Philip of Taranto the archbishop of Brindisi, Bertrand, Bernard of Parma, and John Dominici, a Dominican friar. They would go to Serbia to instruct Stephen Dečanski, his clergy, nobles, and people, in the Catholic faith. John XXII also sent Stephen Dečanski a profession of the faith, which he should recite in a public ceremony. After this had been done, the kral would be received into the Church, and would be recognized by the papacy as the legitimate king of Serbia.[44] These negotiations were strikingly similar to Stephen Uroš II's offers to Charles of Valois and Clement V.[45] But they failed, because the Angevins persisted in supporting Vladislav. Blanche eventually married Raymond Berengar of Aragon.

When his efforts to contract an Angevin alliance had failed, Stephen Dečanski turned to the Byzantines; in 1325 or 1326, when he was fifty years old, he married a twelve-year-old girl named Maria. Her parents were Irene, daughter of Theodore Metochites, and the panhypersebastos John, son of Andronicus II's brother, Constantine the Porphyrogenitus.[46] The immediate results of this alliance were not beneficial to Byzantium. The panhypersebastos John, governor of Thessalonica, suddenly remembered that Michael VIII had preferred Constantine the Porphyrogenitus to Andronicus II; now, in 1326, John decided that the empire was his by inheritance.[47] If he could not seize the throne, at least he could, he thought, independently rule the western part of the empire—Macedonia. He plotted with his brothers-in-law, who were

42. Jireček, *Geschichte der Serben*, I, 347, 354–355. The fact that Stephen Uroš III Dečanski was illegitimate is clearly stated in a letter of Pope John XXII: Augustin Theiner, *Vetera Monumenta Historica Hungariam Sacram Illustrantia*, I (Rome, 1859), 492, no. 748. Constantine too must have been illegitimate, for Stephen Uroš II had no legitimate sons at the time of his marriage to Simonis, in 1299, and she had no children: above, "The Balkans," in Chapter IV.

43. F. Miklosich, *Monumenta Serbica spectantia historiam Serbiae, Bosnae, Ragusii* (Vienna, 1858), p. 90; Villani, II, 257 (book 9, chap. clxxvi).

44. Raynaldus, *Annales Eccl.*, 1323, §§15, 17–18; Theiner, *Monumenta Hungarica*, I, 488–492, nos. 746–748. In 1323 the city of Ragusa voted to send its own ambassadors to Philip of Taranto; n support of Dečanski's proposals: *Monumenta spectantia historiam Slavorum Meridionalium; Monumenta Ragusina*, I (Zagreb, 1879), 90. Cf. Jireček, *Geschichte der Serben*, I, 359–360.

45. Above, "The Plans of Charles of Valois," in Chapter VII.

46. Papadopulos, *Genealogie*, nos. 38, 39; Cantacuzenus, I, 210–211; Gregoras, I, 271, 373; Jireček, *Geschichte der Serben*, I, 360; Bosch, *Andronikos III*, p. 84; F. Dölger, review of M. Laskaris, *Vizantiske Princeze*, in *BZ*, 27 (1927), 132–133.

47. Gregoras, I, 374: ἅτε κλῆρον οὖσαν αὐτῷ πατρικόν.

governors of Strumica and Melnik, and also appealed to Dečanski for help. John and the Serbian forces attacked Macedonia, and reached the city of Serres. Andronicus II, trying to appease his nephew, sent him the insignia of a caesar; John assumed them in Skopje, but he died soon thereafter.[48]

In the early spring of 1327 (around March), Andronicus II sent an embassy to Stephen Dečanski, led by Nicephorus Gregoras. The ambassadors had a double aim: to bring Irene, John's widow, back to Constantinople, and to discuss with Dečanski several other matters, which are not mentioned specifically in the sources. Gregoras has left a detailed account of his embassy; it was written in the form of a letter to his literary friend, Andronicus Zaridas, and was reproduced in full in Gregoras' *Histories*.[49] It is an amusing account, studded with interesting information about Macedonia. The western part of Macedonia, around the river Strymon, and particularly the frontier areas such as Strumica and its environs were wild, inhabited by lawless men. Brigandage was endemic. The inhabitants spoke not Greek, but Slavic of some sort—a dialect probably related to Bulgarian.[50]

The Byzantine ambassadors, having spent a dull Easter in Strumica, met the kral in the vicinity of Skopje. Gregoras was satisfied with the results of the embassy, and the group returned to Byzantium, taking with them Irene, John's widow. In spite of Gregoras' secrecy as to the aim of the embassy, Andronicus II probably had sought Stephen Dečanski's friendship, and an alliance against Andronicus III. From this moment on, Dečanski was on the side of the old emperor, and Andronicus III knew it.

In May, 1327, the young co-emperor formed a Balkan alliance of his own. While staying at Didymoteichon, he invited the king of Bulgaria, Michael Šišman, to visit him. Andronicus III said that this was to be a family visit, since he wanted to see his sister Theodora, and his new brother-in-law. Šišman met Andronicus III at Černomen, and they formed a mutual-assistance pact against Andronicus II and the Serbs.[51]

The empire was moving rapidly into the third phase of its civil war.

48. Cantacuzenus, I, 208–215; Gregoras, I, 374; Dölger, *Regesten*, no. 2552; Nicol, *Kantakouzenos*, p. 37; Bosch, *Andronikos III*, pp. 39–40.

49. Rodolphe Guilland, *La Correspondance de Nicéphore Grégoras*, I, (Paris, 1927), no. 12, pp. 30–51; Gregoras, I, 374–383; Dölger, *Regesten*, no. 2562; Guilland, *Nicéphore Grégoras*, pp. 11–12; Bosch, *Andronikos III*, pp. 40–41; Laskaris, *Vizantiske Princeze*, pp. 83–85; Jireček, *Geschichte der Serben*, I, 360.

50. Gregoras, I, 378, called the inhabitants ἄποικοι Μυσῶν.

51. Gregoras, I, 391–392, says that Andronicus III promised that when he became sole emperor he would give Šišman many Byzantine lands and cities. Cf. Cantacuzenus, I, 207–208. The date of the meeting at Černomen is variously given as May 1326 (Bosch, *Andronikos III*, p. 62; Dölger, *Regesten*, no. 2680) and May 1327 (Nicol, *Kantakouzenos*, p. 39). The date 1327 is the correct one. The short chronicle published by Loenertz, "Chronique brève de 1352," p. 335, no. 18, gives precisely that date. The internal evidence of Gregoras and Cantacuzenus leads to the same conclusion. Gregoras places the meeting after his own Serbian embassy, and Cantacuzenus gives the following sequence of events: February of the ninth indiction (1326), Anne of Savoy arrives at Constantinople (Cantacuzenus, I, 204, and below); Andronicus III marries her in October of the tenth indiction—still 1326 (ibid.). After the wedding, Andronicus went to Didymoteichon, having been wounded on the way in a minor skirmish with a Turkish force; he stayed at Didymoteichon for a long time, and met Šišman "around the time of harvest of the same year" (p. 207). The "same year' is the same *Byzantine* year, i.e. the tenth indiction. By our reckoning, with the year starting on January 1, this would be 1327.

Andronicus II, accusing his grandson of having broken the treaty of Epibatai, sent letters to his son Demetrius who was governing Thessalonica, to the kral of Serbia, and to the governors of Berat and the Macedonian towns (July and September, 1327). He ordered his Macedonian forces to secure the western towns, and then to come to Thrace, along with the Serbian auxiliary force.[52] In October 1327 Andronicus III requested permission to enter Constantinople and plead his cause. His request was rejected, and instead, Andronicus II sent a delegation of members of the clergy and the senate, and a delegation of the people of Constantinople to hear Andronicus III. The younger emperor refuted all the accusations presented by his grandfather, and disclaimed all personal ambition: he rebelled, he said, in order to give better government to the empire.[53]

Andronicus III had already proclaimed to the towns of Thrace and Macedonia that he would abolish all taxes, and he had received promises of support from these provinces. Several senators and many lesser people at Constantinople worked for the success of his cause, and Theodore of Montferrat, who was again in the empire, joined his nephew. The patriarch Isaias refused to excommunicate and anathematize Andronicus III, and was forced by the old emperor to retire to the monastery of the Mangana, where he stayed under guard.[54]

Andronicus III tried to enter Constantinople at night, and when this attempt failed moved his army toward the west. The Macedonian army and the Serbian auxiliaries, under the command of Andronicus II's son Demetrius, had already reached Thrace, and were deployed around Drama and Philippopolis.[55] Andronicus III outmaneuvred them, and in January 1328 reached Thessalonica. The city surrendered joyfully, but the fort resisted. It was defended both by soldiers and by civilian inhabitants of the city. A minor civil war now took place within Thessalonica; Andronicus III's army and its civilian supporters besieged the fort and took it. Thus, Andronicus III became master of the greatest Macedonian city. In a short while, the towns of Edessa, Kastoria, Veroia, and Ochrid also surrendered to Andronicus III: the dynatoi and the people, acting as though they were totally independent powers, with no attachment to the central government, gave up their towns. The governor of Melnik, however, resisted until the end of the war. Stephen Dečanski did not oppose Andronicus III's progress; he did, however, help the Byzantine exiles who had fled Macedonia, and sent them to the fort towns of Prilep, Prošek, and Strumica, which he considered impregnable. The one pitched battle of the war took place in the spring of 1328, at Mavropotamos, and Andronicus III won. By this time, he was master of virtually all of Macedonia, while part of his army was holding Thrace. Now, he decided to return to Thrace, where his position was threatened by the Bulgarians.[56]

52. Dölger, *Regesten*, no. 2567, 2572; Gregoras, I, 394; Cantacuzenus, I, 230–239; Bosch *Andronikos III*, pp. 42–43.

53. Gregoras, I, 297–303; Cantacuzenus, I, 257–267.

54. Gregoras, I, 395–397, 403–407; Cantacuzenus, I, 248–252, 257ff; Bosch, *Andronikos III*, p. 44.

55. Gregoras, I, 407–409; Jireček, *Geschichte der Serben*, I, 360–361.

56. Cantacuzenus, I, 267–288; Gregoras, I, 409–415; Bosch, *Andronikos III*, p. 47.

While Andronicus III was in Macedonia, his presumed ally, Michael
Šišman, offered Andronicus II his help. The old emperor welcomed this offer,
"as though he had found a harbor unexpectedly and after a great storm."[57]
But Gregoras realized that Šišman only wanted a chance to plunder Thrace
and perhaps to attack Constantinople. Gregoras wrote that the Bulgarians
"would make one state, extending from Constantinople to the Danube"—
as old a Bulgarian plan as it was a Byzantine fear.[58] When the Bulgarian and
Tartar army of three thousand men arrived, Andronicus II himself realized
that he was faced with a dangerous foe, not with an ally. Circumstances were
particularly perilous because a minor dispute between the Venetians and the
Genoese had resulted in a Venetian blockade of the port of Constantinople.
While Genoese ships loaded with Black Sea grain and salt fish lay idle in the
sea, the population of the city slowly starved. Andronicus II did not allow the
Bulgarian army to enter the city; only their generals were welcomed. Šišman
then changed sides once again, and withdrew his forces.[59]

The city of Constantinople was in turmoil in the spring of 1328. The subjects
of Andronicus II, threatened by famine, tired of the emperor and resented
his inefficiency, his heavy fiscal exactions, and the imprisonment of the
patriarch. Theodore Metochites, thoroughly hated for his malpractices and
his appropriation of government money, so feared for his life that he abandoned
his house and moved into the palace. There, he and Andronicus II, afraid to
face the irate population of the city, hid and awaited the end.[60]

On the night of May 23–24, Andronicus III's soldiers scaled the walls and
entered the city of Constantinople. With dawn, a great noise was heard at the
palace of the Blachernai where Andronicus II and Theodore Metochites were
spending a sleepless night. The grand logothete thought that the noise came
from people shouting in the streets, and he went off to sleep. Andronicus II
was left alone, lying on his bed, in a palace deserted by everyone but a few
young servants. Soon, the tumult came nearer, and Andronicus III and his
friends swarmed into the palace courtyard.[61] The younger Andronicus was,
once again, proclaimed emperor, and then he listened to his grandfather's
pathetic plea:

> My son, since God has this day taken the scepter away from me and granted
> it to you, I ask one grace of you, in return for the many I have given you
> since the day of your birth: grant me my life; spare the head of your father;
> do not shed violently the blood from which you have sprung . . . Respect

57. Gregoras, I, 411: ὁ δὲ βασιλεύς, ὥσπερ ἐκ μεγάλου ναυαγίου καὶ κλύδωνος ἀπροσδοκήτως λιμένι
περιτυχών, ἀπρὶξ ἐπελάβετο τούτου. Cf. Cantacuzenus, I, 288; Dölger, *Regesten*, no. 2596.

58. Gregoras, I, 415: μίαν ἀρχὴν καταστήσωσι τῷ σφῶν αὐτῶν ἀρχηγῷ τὴν ἀπὸ Βυζαντίου μέχρι τοῦ
Ἴστρου.

59. Gregoras, I, 415–420; Cantacuzenus, I, 294–295, 298–300; Continuator of Jacopo da
Varagine, p. 17. The appearance of a Tartar force near Constantinople, at the invitation of
Andronicus II is, of course, not comparable to the Tartar invasion of 1324. In 1328 only a small
Tartar force came, and it was part of the Bulgarian army—not an independent group, as the
large Tartar army of 1324 had been.

60. Gregoras, I, 411–412, 425–426.

61. Gregoras, I, 419–423; Cantacuzenus, I, 302–306; Loenertz, "Chronique brève de 1352,"
pt. 2, pp. 39, 43, no. 19; Bosch, *Andronikos III*, pp. 48–52.

these hands which held you many times when you were still a baby . . . , respect the lips which kissed you so often, with such warm love. Pity a broken reed, thrown about by fortune, and do not break it a second time. Being but a mortal, have no faith in momentary fortune. Observe how uncertain and everchanging things are, beginning with my own fate. Observe the end of my long life. Watch with wonder how one night has found me emperor for so many years, and left me the subject of another.[62]

Andronicus III entered the palace, kissed his grandfather, and ordered that no one should molest him or say unkind things to him. Then, the conqueror went to the monastery of the Mangana and released the patriarch Isaias. The long civil war was over, and with it the reign of Andronicus II, who now spent his days in the palace, reviled by all, including his own servants. He became a monk, with the name Antonios, on January 30, 1330; and on February 13, 1332, he died, a broken, unhappy man. Gregoras pronounced his funeral oration.[63]

The civil war had been destructive. The loss of life was relatively minor, but the loss of property, especially state property, was tremendous. Individuals appropriated tax money, and the whole system of taxation, so painfully organized by Andronicus II, was disrupted forever. The treasury was rifled during the first days of the occupation of Constantinople by Andronicus III's troops.[64] The Serbs and the Bulgarians had been invited to participate in the fratricidal war, and Thrace, the province which had endured so much during the Catalan occupation, became once again a battleground, where life and property were uncertain. The war had proved beneficial to certain military men, who realized they could sell their allegiance in return for money or lands in pronoia: civil war would become endemic in the empire after 1341.

Asia Minor had been left unaided during the period of the civil war, while resources were squandered in Thrace and Macedonia. Operations in Thessaly and Epirus stopped, and the Byzantine offensive was reversed. Thessaly in particular almost completely escaped imperial control. Whereas Andronicus II and Michael IX had planned to send an army against the Catalans who were invading Thessaly, and whereas as late as 1321 Andronicus II had tried to send John Cantacuzenus to protect the province, by 1325 most of Thessaly had been taken over by the Catalans. Those parts of the region which were still in the hands of Greeks were held independently, with no regard for the government of Constantinople.[65]

62. Gregoras, I, 423–424: ἐπειδὴ τήμερον ὁ θεὸς ἀφελὼν ἐμοῦ τὸ βασίλειον, υἱέ μου, σκῆπτρον σοί τοῦτ' ἐχαρίσατο, μίαν ταύτην αἰτῶ παρὰ σοῦ χάριν ἀντὶ πολλῶν, ὧν ἐξ αὐτῆς σοι γενέσεως ἐδεδώκειν αὐτός . . . : χάρισαί μοι τὴν ἐμαυτοῦ ζωήν· φεῖσαι πατρικῆς κεφαλῆς· μὴ βίαιον ἐπενέγκῃς αἵματι σίδηρον, ἀφ' οὗ σὺ τὰς πηγὰς ἐδέξω τοῦ ζῆν . . . αἰδέσθητι χεῖρας, αἵ σε πολλάκις ἐν σπαργάνοις ὄντα καὶ γάλαξιν ἠγκαλίσαντο. αἰδέσθητι χείλη πολλάκις μετὰ θερμοῦ σε τοῦ φίλτρου φιλήσαντα . . . κάλαμον ἐρριμένον ὑπὸ τῆς τύχης οἴκτειρον καὶ μὴ αὐτὸς ἐθελήσῃς δευτέραν ἐπενεγκεῖν συντριβήν. μὴ ταῖς παρούσαις ἄνθρωπος ὢν πίστευε τύχαις· ἀλλ' ὅρα τὸ τῶν πραγμάτων ἀβέβαιον καὶ ἀστάθμητον ἀρξάμενος ἐξ ἐμοῦ. ὅρα μακροῦ βίου τέλος. θαύμασον, πῶς μία δὴ νὺξ αὕτη με βασιλέα παρειληφυῖα πολυετῆ βασιλευόμενον οἴχεται καταλιμπάνουσα.

63. Gregoras, I, 424–427, 431–432, 441–446, 460–474; Cantacuzenus, I, 304–306, 399–414, 473; Loenertz, "Chronique brève de 1352," pt. 2, p. 40, nos. 22, 26.

64. Gregoras, I, 425.

65. Marino Sanudo Torsello, letter 3, in Bongars, *Gesta Dei per Francos*, II, 293 (hereafter, Sanudo in Bongars). Cf. Setton, *Catalan Domination*, p. 29, n. 32.

In the long run, the worst effect of the civil war lay in the impetus it gave to the centrifugal forces in the empire. More than anything else, this was a war for and from the cities. Only one pitched battle took place, in the spring of 1328. For the rest, the war was a struggle for the control of the cities of Thrace and Macedonia. Andronicus III particularly coveted the largest towns— Adrianople, Thessalonica, Rodosto, Serres, Christopolis, Edessa—and the frontier towns—Ochrid, Prilep, Strumica, Melnik. He was able to take most of these towns—except for Melnik, Prošek, and Strumica, which resisted, and except for Apros, which fell by assault—because they surrendered to him. And once the towns surrendered, the countryside too was his.

The development of town independence had created a situation in which only the towns exhibited any significant military and political activity. The countryside might as well have been empty. The towns, centers of defense and administration, were the political and military foci. Cantacuzenus, who admittedly was influenced by ancient Greek stylistic modes, spoke repeatedly of the need to "occupy the towns of Macedonia," or to "gain the affection of the town populations." The vitality of the towns and their ability and willing-ness to engage in military activities now became deleterious to the state. This element of strength, the last one Byzantium had, became dissipated in civil wars. Furthermore, the city populations became used to rebellion during 1321–1328. In the absence of central control, the trend toward local indepen-dence, coupled with very real social and economic inequalities, would lead the Byzantine cities and towns into the sociopolitical rebellions which plagued the empire during the 1340's.

During the last eight years of his reign, Andronicus II was more committed than ever before to an active western policy. Despite the fact that the civil war limited the resources of his state, he was able to pursue a foreign policy which was at once traditional and novel. Traditionally, he was allied to the Ghibelline powers, and especially to Genoa. He maintained this alliance, and gave what help he could to the Genoese. He strengthened his links with the Ghibellines by marrying Andronicus III to a princess of the house of Savoy, and by forming an alliance with Lewis IV of Bavaria. But at the same time, he made his first serious effort to improve his relations with the Guelph coalition: he became involved in serious and, I think, spontaneous negotiations for the union of the churches, through which he planned to court the friendship of the pope, the king of France, the king of Naples, and Philip of Taranto. Thus, during the last few years of his reign, his attitude toward the orthodox Byzantine church and toward the West underwent a complete reversal.

Although Andronicus II was thus negotiating simultaneously with two op-posed systems of alliance, his western policy was neither vacillating nor self-contradictory. The basic element of his policy in these last years was a desire to establish contact with western European powers, and to become more closely involved in the affairs of Europe. While he dealt with both the papal and the imperial party, he committed himself fully to neither. This flexible approach was probably the best Byzantium could follow at this point. It was also very similar to Michael VIII's diplomatic policy, which had explored all possible avenues to his main aim: the preservation and expansion of the Byzantine state. Not surprisingly, the most active diplomatic years were those of the interval of peace during the years of civil war: Andronicus II's western policy evolved most fully between 1324 and 1327.

In western Europe, the continuing struggle between papacy and Holy Roman Empire formed the background against which political alliances and alignments must be viewed. Lewis IV of Bavaria had established his predominance in Germany after his victory over Frederick of Austria in 1322. But he now became the target of papal and French opposition. He was supported by the traditionally Ghibelline powers, and also by the Spiritual Franciscans who fought the Avignonese papacy on the issue of Christ's poverty. In 1323 he lost one of his most valuable German allies, John of Bohemia: John married his sister, Mary of Luxemburg, to the king of France, Charles IV. The French king coveted the imperial throne, and in 1324 he tried to persuade several German princes to elect him Holy Roman Emperor; but in the end his electors failed him, and his designs were thwarted.[66]

On March 23, 1324, Pope John XXII excommunicated Lewis of Bavaria, ostensibly because Lewis had assumed the imperial title without having secured papal confirmation. In the bull of excommunication, Lewis was denounced as a schismatic, and, because of his association with Marsilio of Padua, as a heretic. By 1327, however, Lewis had brought relative order to his affairs in Germany, and he felt ready to undertake a visit to Italy. He could resist neither the attraction of the Eternal City, nor the call of the Ghibellines of Lombardy who needed substantial help. He appeared in Italy in 1327, and in the spring he received the iron crown of Lombardy in Milan. On January 17, 1328, he was crowned emperor in Rome, and in May he created an anti-pope, a Spiritual Franciscan who took the pontifical name of Nicholas V.[67] In 1329 he left Italy and returned to Germany.

Byzantium and the Ghibelline Powers

Andronicus II had become involved in the conflict between Guelphs and Ghibellines in 1318–1319, when he had formed an alliance with the Genoese exiles against the Guelph government of that city. His own civil war had forced him to stop his financial assistance to the Genoese, but he remained allied to the inhabitants of Pera and of the Black Sea colonies, which were still in the hands of the Ghibellines.[68] The government of Genoa made an effort to break this alliance, to defeat Andronicus, and to force the colonies into submission. In April 1323 a force of ten galleys, under the command of Carlo Grimaldi, was sent to Byzantium, to attack both the Genoese of Pera and the

66. Villani, II, 255, 297, 308–309 (book 9, chaps. clxxii, ccxlviii, cclxvii).

67. Villani, II, 307–308 (book 9, chap. cclxiv); III, 19–21, 49–53, 68–69 (book 10, chaps. xviii–xix, liv–lv, lxxii); Continuator of Jacopo da Varagine, pp. 16–17.

68. Continuator of Jacopo da Varagine, p. 15; Stella, col. 1049: two galleys belonging to the Spinola and the D'Oria sail from Byzantium with merchandise, and are captured by the ships of Robert of Naples (1322).

Byzantines. Grimaldi spent a few days in the Bosphorus, burned some Ghibelline ships, and then sailed into the Black Sea and plundered the Genoese colonies. Villani estimated that the expedition yielded a plunder of 300,000 gold florins.[69]

When Grimaldi tried to return to the Bosphorus, he found that Andronicus II and the inhabitants of Pera had formed a fleet of sixteen galleys, and were ready to fight him. The Guelph commander thought he had found an ally in the Turkish emir of Sinope, Zarabi, who promised to help him against Pera. So, in July 1323, Grimaldi and his ships sailed to Sinope. Zarabi invited his new allies to a grand banquet, in the course of which he ordered his men to attack the Genoese. Many were killed, and virtually all the captains, members of the nobility, were captured; they remained in captivity for eight years. Three or four galleys escaped, but there were too few sailors left to man them properly. While these ships sailed through the Bosphorus secretly and at night, the Genoese of Pera pursued them, and captured one galley. The other ships reached Genoa, and the sad failure of their expedition convinced the Guelph government to leave the colonies unmolested.[70]

The fact that the Genoese colonies in the East were firmly in Ghibelline hands, and were allied to the Byzantines, made it possible for Genoese ships belonging to the exiles of Savona to sail in Byzantine waters. Even the Genoese pirates of the Aegean were Ghibellines. In 1327, Genoese pirates pillaged Venetian ships in the Aegean and the eastern Mediterranean, and took three hundred prisoners. Venice was, at that point, on the side of the Ghibelline powers; yet she armed sixty galleys, and prepared to go to war with the Genoese of Savona. Open conflict was averted through the intervention of Castruccio of Lucca, who said that two Ghibelline allies should not fight one another.[71] But in September and December 1327, Venice increased her naval strength in the Aegean, probably in order to defend her colonies and her shipping against another piratical attack.[72]

In 1328 it was the Genoese of Pera who attacked Venetian ships in the Aegean, and in April 1328 a Venetian fleet appeared before Constantinople, to demand reparations. When the inhabitants of Pera refused to comply, the Venetians blocked the port of Hieron, on the northern side of the Bosphorus, so that no ships could sail to or from the Black Sea. Four Genoese round ships, ready to go into the Black Sea, were seized by the Venetians, but their cargoes were left intact. The blockade continued for fifteen or twenty days, in the course of which Andronicus II tried to form an alliance with the Venetians

69. Stella, cols. 1051–1052; Villani, II, 291 (book 9, chap. ccxvii); Manfroni, "Relazioni," pp. 698–699.

70. Continuator of Jacopo da Varagine, pp. 15–16; Stella, col. 1052; Villani, II, 281 (book 9, chap. ccxvii); Cessi and Sambin, *Consiglio dei Rogati*, I, 253 (book 10. no. 76), on the capture of two Venetians by Zarabi.

71. Villani, III, 60–61 (book 10, chap. lxiv); Cessi and Sambin, *Consiglio dei Rogati*, I, 349 (book 10, no. 278), December, 1327: "Sapientes electi super facto navigiorum captorum per Ianuenses extrinsecos."

72. Cessi and Sambin, *Consiglio dei Rogati*, I, 344 (book 10, no. 222); 348, 349 (book 10, nos. 270, 279).

against his grandson. But Andronicus III's army was already at the gates of Constantinople, and no doubt the Venetian commander was too practical to help a lost cause. Finally, the Genoese decided to pay the reparations Venice demanded, and the Venetian fleet returned to Italy.[73]

Although Andronicus II's alliance with the Ghibellines of Pera is well attested, there is no evidence that he was in close contact with the Genoese exiles at Savona. In 1325, however, he reinforced his ties with the Ghibellines of northern Italy through a marriage alliance with the house of Savoy.

Andronicus III's first wife, Adelheid-Irene of Brunswick, died on August 16, 1324. Her loving husband mourned her for fifteen days, at the end of which Andronicus II reminded his grandson that he should marry again—especially since that first union had produced no heirs to the throne. As the two men pondered over the question of suitable brides, it was brought to their attention that there was a marriageable princess in Savoy. She was Johanna, daughter of the great count Amedeo V, who had died in October, 1323, and half-sister of the ruling count, Edward.[74]

This information was probably given to the two co-emperors by Andronicus II's son, Theodore of Montferrat, who was, once again, in the Byzantine empire.[75] Theodore had come to Constantinople to visit his relatives and to request money for his Italian wars; he had left Savona in March 1325, and he must have reached the empire in June or July.[76] Andronicus II must have been considering a western bride for his grandson, as he had done in 1318; this search for European matrimonial alliances was a constant factor in his policy. It was natural, therefore, that he should consult Theodore of Montferrat, who lived in Europe and was acquainted with the possibilities. The houses of Savoy and Montferrat were already connected, both by family ties and by political cooperation. Theodore's predecessor, the marquis John I, had married Johanna of Savoy's half-sister, Margaret, in 1297. Montferrat, Savoy, and most of the Piedmontese states were predominantly Ghibelline, and together they fought against the armies of Robert of Naples.[77] Theodore

73. Gregoras, I, 416–418; Continuator of Jacopo da Varagine, p. 17.

74. Cantacuzenus, I, 194–195.

75. Anne of Savoy's biographer, Dino Muratore, has made a very persuasive case of Theodore's involvement; according to Muratore, Theodore was responsible for the marriage alliance between Savoy and Byzantium: D. Muratore, "Una principessa Sabauda sul trono di Bisanzio: Giovanna di Savoia imperatrice Anna Paleologina," *Mémoires de l'Académie des sciences, belles-lettres et arts de Savoie*, 4th ser., 11 (1909), 245–249. Muratore's work is based on a number of unpublished documents. Bosch, *Andronikos III*, pp. 106–107, gives a brief account of the marriage and of the negotiations preceding it.

76. Gregoras, I, 395–396; Benvenuto di San Giorgio, cols. 449–450, 456–457; Galeotto del Carretto, *Cronica di Monferrato, Monumenta Historiae Patriae, Scriptorum III* (Turin, 1848), 1176–1177; Muratore, "Principessa Sabauda," p. 245; D. A. Zakythinos, «Ὁ Μαρκίων τοῦ Μομφερράτου Θεόδωρος Α΄ ὁ Παλαιολόγος καὶ ὁ βασιλεὺς τῆς Γαλλίας Φίλιππος ὁ ΣΤ΄,» Ε.Ε.Β.Σ., 11 (1935), 16–18, 27.

77. See genealogical table in Muratore, "Principessa Sabauda"; also, Wilhelm Karl, Prince von Isenburg, *Stammtafeln zur Geschichte der europäischen Staaten*, II (Berlin, 1936; 2d ed., Hamburg, 1953), table 136. Galeotto del Carretto, cols. 1167–1175. See also a document of Theodore of Montferrat issued in Savona, on March 22, 1325: he wrote about giving help to Manfred IV, marquess of Saluzzo—at the request of Lewis of Bavaria—so that Manfred could recover some castles from the Guelphs: A. Tallone, "Regesto dei Marchesi di Saluzzo (1091–1340)," *Biblioteca della Società Storica Subalpina*, 16 (Pinerolo, 1906), 252, no. 877.

of Montferrat was also a friend and ally of Philip, count of Savoy and Piedmont, who had been married to Isabeau de Villehardouin, and who still retained the title of prince of Achaia, although he had been dispossessed by Philip of Taranto in 1307. In June 1325, while Theodore was on his way to Constantinople, Philip of Savoy and Piedmont helped Theodore's wife, Argentina, to withstand an attack by the Guelph forces.[78] In these circumstances, Theodore would be very likely to advise his father to consider a matrimonial alliance with the house of Savoy; thus, the ties between Savoy and Montferrat would be strengthened, and Byzantium would forge a connection with one of the most powerful Ghibelline states in Italy.

Andronicus II and Andronicus III reached their decision soon after the arrival of Theodore of Montferrat at Constantinople. They sent an embassy to Savoy which consisted of Andronicus Tornikes, a high court official, and John of Gibelet, member of one of the most important noble houses of Cyprus, who was then an officer in the Byzantine army.[79] The two ambassadors left by sea, probably in July 1325, and in mid-August they were in Savona. Soon thereafter they left for the county of Savoy, and Savoyard nobles met them and provided a guard of honor along every stage of the journey. The Byzantine embassy reached Chambéry early in September, and there they met Count Edward and the prospective bride.[80]

The formal part of the discussions between the Byzantines and the count of Savoy ended on September 22, 1325, when the marriage contract was drawn up and signed. The princess, who would be renamed Anne, left Savoy at the end of September 1325. She stayed in Savona for a long time, from October 18 until the end of November, and she was royally fêted by the Genoese Ghibelline exiles who ruled that city. Several members of the Spinola family were among the magistrates of Savona who demonstrated their friendship toward the Byzantine empire by welcoming the future empress. Anne of Savoy sailed for her new home probably at the end of November 1325, and arrived at Constantinople in February 1326. She was escorted by her chaplain, three Franciscan friars, and several knights and ladies-in-waiting. Her elegant entourage

---

78. Ferdinando Gabotto, *Asti e la politica sabauda in Italia al tempo di Guglielmo Ventura, Biblioteca della Società Storica Subalpina*, XVIII (1903), 427–433. Gabotto speaks of a double marriage alliance between the house of Montferrat and that of Philip of Savoy, in 1325 (pp. 427ff). This, however, is false. Theodore's daughter Yolanda did marry Aimone, a son of Count Amedeo V of Savoy, but the marriage took place in 1330: von Isenburg, *Stammtafeln*, II, table 137. The counts of Savoy-Piedmont were closely related to the counts of Savoy: the head of the house of Savoy-Piedmont was Thomas II (1199–1259), a second son of Thomas I of Savoy (1177–1233): von Isenburg, *Stammtafeln*, II, table 111.

79. Cantacuzenus, I, 195; Dölger, *Regesten*, no. 2533. John of Gibelet was of the Syrian noble house, which had emigrated to Cyprus. Muratore, "Principessa Sabauda," p. 248, n. 2, thinks John may be the same John of Gibelet who in 1306–1310 had joined a rebellion against the king of Cyprus, Henry II (1310–1324), who had been exiled, and who returned to Cyprus sometime after the accession of Hugues IV (1324–1359) to the Cypriot throne: Louis de Mas-Latrie, *Histoire de l'île de Chypre sous le règne des princes de la maison de Lusignan*, II (Paris, 1852), 173–174; III (Paris, 1861), 700–701.

80. Muratore, "Principessa Sabauda," p. 249; p. 250, n. 1; p. 251, n. 1, 2. Muratore has gleaned this information from unpublished documents, especially from the accounts of towns and castles where the expenditures of the Savoyard escort are recorded. See also Gabotto, *Asti*, pp. 433–435.

impressed the Byzantines, who greeted her with similar magnificence.[81] The long journey, undertaken in the wintertime, must have been unpleasant and left the young princess very weakened. She fell ill immediately upon her arrival at Constantinople, and her marriage to Andronicus III was not celebrated until October 1326. After the wedding ceremony she was crowned empress.[82] Anne of Savoy was destined to play a very significant role in Byzantine politics after her husband's death in 1341.

Most of the knights and noble ladies who had accompanied Anne to Byzantium returned home after the wedding festivities. But every year thereafter, says Cantacuzenus, Savoyard nobles would travel to Byzantium, so that Andronicus III was never without their company. What attracted them to the empire was Andronicus III's fascination with western forms of armed entertainment, especially jousting and tournaments. Cantacuzenus claims—quite wrongly—that these novelties were introduced to Byzantium for the first time by Anne of Savoy's compatriots.[83] The young co-emperor participated in the games, and he so excelled in them that, wrote Cantacuzenus, he was considered as a great champion, not only by the Savoyards, but also by the French, the Germans, and the Burgundians "who are the greatest students of these things." Andronicus III proved less adept in other forms of warfare: soon after his wedding, he was defeated by a Turkish force in Thrace.[84]

Within the context of Andronicus II's foreign policy, the primary purpose of the Savoyard alliance was to strengthen Byzantine ties with the Ghibelline coalition in Italy, and it thus followed a pattern similar to that of Andronicus II's own marriage to Yolanda-Irene of Montferrat. Certainly, Pope John XXII considered Anne's Byzantine marriage as an act of hostility toward the papacy. He was informed of the arrangement only late in 1325, when the princess had already left Savona, and he responded with an angry letter to Count Edward (December 31, 1325). The pope wrote that Edward should have found a good, Catholic prince for his half-sister, instead of allowing her to wed a schismatic, and he added that such marriages were forbidden by canon law. In his letter to the pope, Edward of Savoy had expressed the hope that Anne might be able to convert her husband to Catholicism; John XXII answered that such hopes were laudable, but probably vain. For his part, the pope thought that the husband, as the stronger of the two, would probably impose his own faith upon the wife, and thus Anne would be lost to the Catholic church.[85]

Although the Savoyard alliance formed part of Andronicus II's pro-

81. Muratore, "Principessa Sabauda," pp. 257–272; p. 267, n. 2; Cantacuzenus, I, 204. Muratore's documents even give the cost of Anne's trousseau.

82. Cantacuzenus, I, 204–205; Gregoras, I, 383–384; Muratore, "Principessa Sabauda," pp. 273–277.

83. Cantacuzenus, I, 205: καὶ τὴν λεγομένην τζουστρίαν καὶ τὰ τερνεμέντα αὐτοὶ πρῶτοι ἐδίδαξαν Ῥωμαίους οὔπω πρότερον περὶ τῶν τοιούτων εἰδότας οὐδέν.

In fact, the Byzantines had been exposed to jousting at least since the time of Manuel I Comnenus (1143–1180): John Cinnamus, *Epitome rerum ab Ioanne et Alexio Comnenis Gestarum,* (Bonn, 1836), p. 125; S. Lambros, «Ἔκφρασις τῶν ξυλοκονταριῶν τοῦ κραταιοῦ καὶ ἁγίου ἡμῶν αὐθέντου καὶ βασιλέως,» Νέος Ἑλληνομνήμων, 5 (1908), 3ff.

84. Cantacuzenus, I, 205: ἐν οἷς μάλιστα σπουδάζεται τὰ τοιαῦτα; Cantacuzenus, I, 206–207.

85. The letter is published in Muratore, "Principessa Sabauda," pp. 253–254.

Ghibelline policy, it may also be seen as an effort to build a bridge between his state, the papacy, and the French royal house. For Savoy was not fanatically Ghibelline, and Count Amedeo V, Edward's and Anne's father, had tried, in the last two years of his life, to forge ties of friendship with Charles IV of France and with Robert of Naples. In 1322 Amedeo V, Philip of Savoy-Piedmont, and Robert of Naples negotiated the terms of a possible peace-treaty.[86] In May 1322 Amedeo brought two of his daughters to Paris, to present them to Charles IV. The French king had just divorced his wife, Blanche of Burgundy, and several daughters of royal and princely houses had flocked to the royal court to seek his favor. Amedeo tried to persuade Charles IV to marry a Savoyard princess, "promising [to give] the king the dominion of Italy, insofar as that depended on the Ghibelline party."[87] Charles IV, however, spurned the Savoyard alliance for what he thought would be a more profitable one, and he married Mary of Luxemburg.

In January 1323 the count of Savoy appeared at the papal court at Avignon to continue his discussions with Robert of Naples. The pope treated him very well, and while he was at Avignon Amedeo V tried to negotiate yet another matrimonial alliance with the leaders of the Guelph party: he tried to marry one of his daughters to Charles, duke of Calabria, son of Robert of Naples. All of these negotiations were interrupted by Amedeo's death, in October 1323, and Charles of Calabria married Mary, a daughter of Charles of Valois, in 1324.[88] Yet the fact remains that as late as the fall of 1323 the count of Savoy had seriously considered the possibility of abandoning the Ghibelline party. The political ambivalence of Savoy must have weighed heavily in Andronicus II's decision to seek a Savoyard alliance. For in the 1320's the emperor himself was engaged in a policy which both supported the Ghibellines, and brought him closer to the pope and to the royal houses of France and Naples.[89]

One of the most striking points about the foreign policy of Andronicus II during the years 1321–1328 is the fact that the emperor acted completely independently of his grandson. Even between 1325 and 1327, when the two emperors reigned jointly, none of the documented negotiations were undertaken in the names of both emperors. In fact, during the last years of his reign, Andronicus II emerged as a diplomat, while Andronicus III saw himself primarily as a soldier. This observation has particular bearing on the last Ghibelline alliance formed by Andronicus II, which was dissolved by Andronicus

86. Gabotto, *Asti*, pp. 388ff.

87. Finke, *Acta Aragonensia*, I, 480, no. 320: "iste comes promitit regi dominium Italie, quantum ad partem Guebellinam." Cantacuzenus, I, 195, claimed that the king of France wanted to marry Anne of Savoy, but that her brother Edward found the Byzantine alliance more profitable!

88. Gabotto, *Asti*, pp. 388–395; Finke, *Acta Aragonensia*, I, 493, no. 327, (May 28, 1323), on negotiations with Charles of Calabria. On Charles's subsequent marriage, see von Isenburg, *Stammtafeln*, II, table 118.

89. Below' "The Unionist Approach." See also Muratore, "Principessa Sabauda," p. 245, and Bosch, *Andronikos III*, p. 106. They mention that Andronicus II must have found the Savoyard alliance useful because of the links of the house of Savoy to both the Ghibellines and the Guelphs; but they do not relate this to Andronicus II's general European policy. In 1335 Theodore of Montferrat made liege homage to the king of France, Philip VI—excepting his homage to the pope and to the Holy Roman Experor: Zakythinos, «Θεόδωρος Α΄.» pp. 21ff.

III. In 1328, in the last year of his reign, Andronicus II allied himself to the leader of the Ghibelline forces, the Holy Roman Emperor Lewis IV.

Two independent sources mention this alliance. On March 7, 1328, the Aragonese representative at the papal court, a certain Gondissalvo Zapata, reported to James II the latest news concerning Lewis of Bavaria and the continuing struggle between papacy and empire. Zapata wrote that the pope was greatly upset about Lewis' coronation in Rome, which had taken place on January 17. The pope was urging Frederick III of Sicily and Robert of Naples to make peace between them, so that the war against Lewis could be waged more efficiently. Then, Zapata reported various rumors concerning the movements of the kings of Sicily and Naples, and mentioned that it was being said that the inhabitants of Rome had sent an embassy to the pope, urging him to return to the city; otherwise, they and Lewis IV would depose him and elect another pope. Finally, wrote Zapata, "the emperor of Constantinople, according to what is being said, has made a very great fleet to help the Bavarian."[90]

By itself, this information might be dismissed as mere rumor. Yet there is another piece of evidence indicating that Andronicus II and Lewis of Bavaria had, indeed, held some sort of discussions. In October 1328 an embassy from Lewis IV appeared in Constantinople. The ambassadors came with specific instructions to see Andronicus II. Finding that the old emperor had been deposed, they appeared before Andronicus III, and presented their case. They said that the Byzantine emperors and the Holy Roman emperors had traditional ties of friendship and alliance; the Byzantines and the Ghibellines always helped one another in times of trouble. The Emperor Lewis, being in need of money, now appealed to this traditional friend, the Byzantine emperor.[91]

Andronicus III listened to the imperial envoys and referred them to Cantacuzenus, who proceeded to offer them not money, but an army. The ambassadors replied, as though offended, that they had many and valiant soldiers: they lacked money, and that was what they were seeking. Seeing that it was not forthcoming, they left. Cantacuzenus, who reports this event, declared himself proud of the way in which he had tricked Lewis' ambassadors. He and Andronicus III decided that, should another German embassy arrive, and should that embassy accept the offer of an army, the Byzantines would reply that Italy was far away, and much time would be needed to prepare such a force.[92] Thus, Andronicus III and John Cantacuzenus refused to cooperate with Lewis of Bavaria.

The appearance of an imperial embassy at Constantinople in the autumn of 1328 is a well-attested fact. The ambassadors came to Andronicus II, with a specific commission. This fact, together with Zapata's report, indicates that negotiations between Andronicus II and Lewis of Bavaria had already taken

90. Finke, *Acta Aragonensia*, I, 435, no. 290: "El emperador de Constantinople, segunt se diçe, façe muyt grant armada en ayuda del Bauaro." Cf. Bosch, *Andronikos III*, pp. 109–110.
91. Cantacuzenus, I, 335–336.
92. Ibid., 336–337.

place in the late winter or early spring of 1328. That Cantacuzenus should say nothing of such negotiations is not surprising: neither he nor Andronicus III had any connection with the government at Constantinople from the late summer of 1327 until the fall of Andronicus II from power. On the other hand, it does seem unlikely that the Byzantines should have sent Lewis of Bavaria "a very large fleet," as Zapata had heard. This would have been nearly impossible to do, even if there were no civil war in the empire. It is much more probable that Andronicus II had promised some money to Lewis of Bavaria, and that the envoys who came to Constantinople in October 1328 sought increased subsidies.

The probable intermediaries of the Byzantine–German alliance can only be guessed at, but there are several candidates. Perhaps the most likely intermediary would be one of the numerous Genoese Ghibelline merchants who traveled from Constantinople to Italy and back. Since the Genoese exiles were particularly interested in the swift victory of the Ghibellines, one of them may have suggested an alliance to Andronicus II, or to Lewis of Bavaria, or to both. I also think it possible that Lewis IV was given the idea of a Byzantine alliance by Henry II, duke of Brunswick–Grubenhagen, who had been Andronicus III's brother-in-law. Henry had been in Rome with Lewis of Bavaria at least since February 1328.[93] Subsequent events prove that Henry had not forgotten his Byzantine connection, and it is possible that in 1328 he had worked for a German–Byzantine alliance. In 1329 he left Rome for Constantinople, to visit Andronicus III who still addressed him as "brother-in-law." Henry then continued his eastern tour, which took him to Mount Sinai and Cyprus.[94] On January 6, 1330, Andronicus III gave Henry, his *cognatus carissimus*, a chrysobull, which was in effect a letter of introduction addressed to all kings, nobles, and lay and ecclesiastical princes of all the parts Henry was to visit. Andronicus III requested that these rulers give Henry II all aid and council.[95] The duke of Brunswick returned to his state in 1331, and from then on he adopted the title "Henricus dux dictus de Graecia."

Andronicus II's alliance with Lewis IV of Bavaria is by no means surprising. It came at a moment when the Byzantine civil war had made union negotiations with the papacy impracticable, and so had forced Andronicus to return to an unequivocally Ghibelline policy, much in the same way that Michael VIII had formed an alliance with Peter III of Aragon, after his unionist plans had failed.[96] The very fact that the emperor, fighting for his throne and for his life, should have found time to consider foreign alliances which were not immediately beneficial to him, proves that in the last years of his reign relations with Europe dominated his political thinking.

93. On March 18, 1328 Lewis of Bavaria wrote to Otto, Henry II's brother, who was ruling Brunswick in Henry's absence, responding to Otto's letter of February 15: J. F. Böhmer, *Regesta Imperii: Die Kaiserurkunden Ludwigs des Baiern* . . . (Frankfurt, 1838), no. 973.

94. W. Ohnsorge, *Abendland und Byzanz* (Darmstadt, 1958), p. 494.

95. The letter has been published in Ohnsorge, *Abendland und Byzanz*, pp. 506–507; H. Meibomius, *Opuscula Historica varia* (Helmstadt, 1660), pp. 185ff; Meibomius, *Rerum Germanicarum Scriptores*, I (Helmstadt, 1688), 472. Cf. Dölger, *Regesten*, no. 2756.

96. Geanakoplos, *Michael Paleologus*, pp. 344–351.

The Unionist Approach

While intensifying his contacts with the Ghibellines of western Europe, Andronicus II also tried to improve Byzantine relations with powers which had, traditionally, been hostile to his empire. The union negotiations he undertook in the years 1324–1327 form the climax of this policy. Had these negotiations been successful, the Palaeologi, the papacy, the Angevins, and the royal house of France could have been reconciled at long last. The emperor had already prepared the ground for such a policy with his attitude toward Venice: the long discussions in which he and the Venetians had been involved since 1319 resulted in an agreement in October 1324. In fact, Andronicus' Venetian policy may be considered as an intermediary step between his pro-Ghibelline and his unionist approach to European affairs. Venice, in the 1320's, considered itself an ally of the Italian Ghibellines. But to the Byzantines, Venice was also the power which had been involved in every crusading plan against Constantinople. The improvement of relations with Venice was thus doubly beneficial to Byzantium.

In practical terms, however, the agreement of 1324 was much less of a victory than Andronicus II might have hoped for. Negotiations with Venice had gone on for a long time, beginning in 1313 and becoming intensive in 1319. The exchange of embassies continued in 1322, as Venice and Byzantium sought solutions to the problems they had been discussing since 1319. In June 1322 the Venetian senate decided that the embassy leaving for Constantinople should demand the reparations of 14,000 hyperpyra claimed by Venice in 1321. Only then could the ambassadors proceed to discuss a comprehensive treaty. In November, the Venetians selected three experts (*sapientes*) who would discuss several matters with the Byzantine ambassadors already in the city. The experts would be assisted by Fantino Dandolo and Marco Minotto, both of whom had served as bailos of Constantinople. Presumably, the discussions occupied one month, for in December 1322 preparations were being made for the departure of the Byzantine ambassadors from Venice.[97]

The advice of the commission of experts to the doge and the senate survives in three documents which deal with the demands of both Venice and Byzantium.[98] Besides reiterating their state's position as presented in 1319–1321, the Venetian ambassadors were also to make a new demand: since merchants in the empire found themselves in constant danger from the Byzantines, and since Venetian properties were frequently threatened by fire and plunder, the ambassadors should request from Andronicus an enclosed residential quarter, specifically reserved to Venetians. The experts advised that the bailo and councillors of Constantinople should decide on the best position for the new quarter; it is likely, then, that this proposal applied to Constantinople alone. The Venetians were trying to create for themselves an enclave similar to the one the Genoese had at Pera, and to the one they had themselves inhabited from 1081 to 1261.

97. Cessi and Sambin, *Consiglio dei Rogati*, pp. 254–255, 262, 263 (book 7, nos. 93, 102, 202–203, 219–220).
98. Thomas and Predelli, *Diplomatarium*, 187–191, nos. 90–92.

In the matter of compensation to particular Venetians for particular damages, the experts examined each case, and sometimes found that the Venetian demands were unfair. They then mentioned that a number of articles of the treaties of 1285 and 1302 were in need of clarification and confirmation. In general, these articles concerned the privilege of Venetian merchants to engage in trade in the Byzantine empire freely and without any fiscal impediment, and their right to buy and sell within the empire all commodities with the exception of salt, mastic, and Byzantine grain. The Venetians particularly insisted that they be allowed to sell Black Sea grain in the Byzantine empire without a purchase tax being levied on the buyer, be he Greek or Latin. They also demanded confirmation of their right to live freely anywhere in the empire, and to practice their crafts and professions. They wished to sail freely in Byzantine waters, and to be free to hire Byzantine sailors. Finally, they demanded that if any Greek or Latin equipped armies or fleets on Byzantine territory that were subsequently used against Venetians, the emperor himself should pay reparations within three months.

Embassies were exchanged in 1323 and 1324, presumably in order to negotiate these points. The last Byzantine embassy was headed by Stephen Syropoulos, and its deliberations resulted in a preliminary treaty, signed in Venice on June 11, 1324.[99] This was a simple document, containing guidelines for the formal treaty. The Byzantine ambassadors and the Venetian representatives stated that the treaties of 1285 and 1302 should be renewed, and that the new treaty would last for a period of five years; they stated that Venice was satisfied with the payment of 14,000 hyperpyra, which Syropoulos had brought with him. On June 28, 1324, the doge acknowledged receipt of this payment.[100] Thus, Venice won her first demand as formulated in 1322: that no treaty would be signed until the Venetians had received full compensation for the damages done to her traders by Byzantine pirates or other Byzantine subjects.

When the preliminary treaty was signed, most of the significant points of dispute had been resolved. Only minor matters were still under discussion. In August 1324 the Venetian bailo at Constantinople, Thomas Soranzo, was instructed to examine carefully the question of citizenship of the sons of gasmuloi—presumably, of those gasmuloi who had assumed Byzantine citizenship during the Venetian–Byzantine war of 1296–1302. This problem was still being discussed in March 1326. The senate also agreed in August 1324 that Venetian merchants should not transport goods belonging to Greeks, and instructed the duke of Crete, the bailo of Nigroponte, and the castellans of Modon and Coron to levy no commercial duties on Byzantine merchants.[101]

A formal Venetian–Byzantine treaty was signed in October 1324. It was

99. Cessi and Sambin, *Consiglio dei Rogati*, pp. 269, 272–273 (book 7, nos. 282, 325, 313, 335): 1323; pp. 277, 284, 286 (book 7, no. 393; book 8, nos. 21, 22, 46): 1324; Thomas and Predelli, *Diplomatarium*, no. 94, pp. 194–195.

100. Cessi and Sambin, *Consiglio dei Rogati*, p. 284 (book 8, nos. 21, 22); Thomas and Predelli, *Diplomatarium*, no. 95, pp. 195–196.

101. Cessi and Sambin, *Consiglio dei Rogati*, pp. 287, 314 (book 8, nos. 56–58; book 9, no. 187).

in the form of a chrysobull, granted by Andronicus II to the Venetians, and it exists in the Greek original and in a Latin copy, made in the imperial chancery.[102] The treaty of 1324, which would be in effect for five years, confirmed the pacts of 1285 and 1302, and clarified and extended some of their articles. Its terms were a diplomatic defeat for the Byzantines. The lengthy negotiations and heated discussions resulted in a treaty which granted almost every important Venetian demand. It was decided that the Venetians could buy and sell Black Sea grain throughout the empire—except in Constantinople—without any fiscal impediment. The treaty explicity stated that Venetian merchants could sell Black Sea grain in the Byzantine empire, and the words "libere et sine aliquo gravamine vel impedimento" ("ἄνευ τινὸς βάρους ἢ ἐμποδισμοῦ") implicitly granted the second Venetian demand, that no purchase duty be levied on the buyer. The Venetians were also permitted to buy, sell and export all cereals and legumes; the conditions for purchase and export of wheat grown in the empire remained the same as in 1285. Of the major Venetian demands for economic privileges, only one was not satisfied: the conditions under which Venetians could hire Byzantine sailors was not discussed in the treaty of 1324.

Andronicus II also capitulated on an important political point. He agreed to pay compensation to Venice from his own treasury if anyone in his empire attacked any Venetians. In the conditions of anarchy which prevailed in the empire, especially during and after the civil war, and given the notoriously independent attitude of the Genoese colonists, this article was a very dangerous one for the Byzantines.

Venice was released from all obligation to pay for damage done to imperial subjects by Venetian merchants and officials. Andronicus II, on the other hand, agreed to pay to Venice within three years the sum of 12,000 hyperpyra; part of this money covered a loan which his nephew Andronicus Palaeologus had contracted with Venetians and had not repaid. The first Byzantine payment of 4,000 hyperpyra was made on time, before July 30, 1325.[103]

Andronicus II sent an embassy to Venice to receive the doge's confirmation of the treaty of 1324. The Byzantine ambassador, Constantine Physcomallos, was in Venice in February 1325; on April 30, Giovanni Soranzo formally confirmed the agreement.[104]

Considering the Venetian–Byzantine treaty of 1324–1325 in the light of the negotiations preceding it, the virtually wholesale capitulation of the Byzantines is striking. In 1319–1320, Andronicus II had appeared intransigent about his imperial privileges, both fiscal and political. Indeed, it had been he who began the long exchange of letters and privileges, and he who had raised the issue of Black Sea grain, claiming that the Venetians had no right to sell it within

102. The Greek text is in Miklosich and Müller, *Acta et Diplomata*, III, 100–105. Latin text in Thomas and Predelli, *Diplomatarium*, no. 98, pp. 200–203. Andronicus II gave the chrysobull to the Venetian bailo, Thomas Soranzo.

103. Thiriet, *Délibérations*, I, 187, no. 450.

104. Cessi and Sambin, *Consiglio dei Rogati*, p. 296 (book 8, no. 172); Thomas and Predelli, *Diplomatarium*, no. 99, pp. 203–204.

the empire.[105] At that time, the Venetians had reacted cautiously. They complained about the unpleasant conditions under which they lived and worked in the Byzantine empire, and countered each imperial complaint with one of their own. Yet the document Andronicus II signed in 1324 hardly even carried the signs of compromise: he received nothing in return for the privileges he granted to the Venetians.

It is clear that between 1321 and 1325, the relative positions of Venice and Byzantium had been reversed, and that Venice, during these years, negotiated from a position of strength. To a large extent this is probably the result of the Byzantine civil war. While in 1319–1321 Andronicus II acted as the undisputed head of a state in the process of reconstruction, by 1325 his authority had been gravely undermined. He needed peace with Venice, not only as a diplomatic coup, but also to help him with the rest of his western policy. Constantine Physcomallos, who received Soranzo's confirmation of the treaty in 1325, was also carrying imperial letters to a Venetian, Marino Sanudo Torsello; these letters concerned Andronicus II's negotiations for a church union with the West.[106] Thus, the treaty of 1324–1325 was the result both of the Byzantine civil war and of Andronicus II's desire to establish friendly relations with western Europe, including the pope, the French, and the Angevins.

With the treaty of 1325, the long period of suspicion which had characterized the relationship of Venice to the Palaeologan empire came to an end. Venice was now a friend of the Byzantines, and her commerce in the Aegean and the Black Sea was greatly facilitated. The change of attitude occurred partly because of conditions in the Byzantine empire: Andronicus II and his successors were too weak to invite Venetian hostility, and Andronicus III (1328–1341) and John VI Cantacuzenus (1347–1354) preferred to fight the Genoese, whose commercial expansion held Constantinople itself in a stranglehold. But in part, the amelioration of Venetian–Byzantine relations after 1325 was due to a change in Venice's policy.

Ever since 1261, Venetian attitudes had determined the tenor of Venetian–Byzantine relations. Venice, by hoping to restore a Latin empire at Constantinople, by allying herself to western pretenders to the Byzantine throne, by promising her help to Charles of Anjou and Charles of Valois, had ensured that her contacts with the Byzantine empire would remain hostile. But in the 1320's, Venice changed her aims. The fact that crusading projects against Constantinople had, until that point, failed unequivocally forced Venice to reconsider the feasibility of any new crusading plans and of her own desire to see a Latin emperor in Constantinople. Venice must also have realized in the 1320's that the Angevins, Charles IV of France, and the pope, were much too preoccupied with the wars in Italy and Germany to seriously undertake a successful war against the Byzantine empire. In fact, after 1320 there is no

105. Thomas and Predelli, *Diplomatarium*, no. 72, p. 124.
106. The treaty of 1324–1325 was not, as Muratore claimed, "the first step toward friendlier relations with the West, which would develop under Andronicus III": Muratore, "Principessa Sabauda," p. 245. We have seen clear evidence of a change of attitude on Andronicus II's part before 1325.

evidence of any Venetian involvement in the Byzantine projects of Philip of Taranto.

In a small work, a supplement to Villehardouin's *Conquête de Constantinople*, Marino Sanudo Torsello voiced the Venetian disillusionment with western crusading plans. When Catherine of Courtenay died, he wrote, Charles of Valois abandoned his plans for the recovery of Constantinople; but the Venetians continued to sign truce after truce with Andronicus II, because they were unwilling to make peace. As a result, the Venetians only held sway over those parts of the Romania which they already ruled, while the Genoese, both those of the commune and the exiles, were able to control the rest of Greece, *contra deum et omnia jura*. Genoa thus amassed great wealth, while the Venetians suffered grave losses and expenses, particularly for the preservation of Nigroponte and of other Frankish territories.[107]

The Venetians were realistic men, and their government had little use for outdated attitudes. The predominant aim of John Soranzo, in particular, was to further the commercial power of Venice. When he wrote to Andronicus II that Venice was a commercial power, and so she preferred the territories in which she operated to be at peace rather than torn by wars, he was voicing a primary tenet of the policy which made Venice great in the fourteenth century.[108] All these considerations argued for the establishment of friendly relations with the Byzantines.

Another factor too intervened in the 1320's, and made Venice seek cooperation with the Byzantines. That factor was the power of the Turks—not the Ottoman Turks, who had seized the northern part of Byzantine Asia Minor, but the inhabitants of the maritime Turcoman emirates, Aydin, Mentesche, Sarukhan.[109] Turkish pirates now attacked shipping in the Aegean, and launched small-scale but destructive raids on the neighboring coasts and islands. Venice was particularly vulnerable to such attacks, because she had extensive possessions in the Aegean. Also, much of her eastern trade was carried out in Rhodes, Cyprus, Asia Minor, and Lesser Armenia. That meant that her ships returned home through the southern Aegean, which was open to the attacks of the Turkish pirates. Crete, Modon, and Coron, where Venetian ships stopped for provisioning and trade, also suffered from Turkish raids. In the 1320's Venice became increasingly perturbed by the Turkish threat, and sought allies to help her fight the pirates. Constantinople was no longer a source of danger for Venice, but the southern Aegean was rapidly becoming one; so, the Venetians became friendlier toward the Byzantines and more hostile toward the Turks. In March 1325 the senate selected several experts (*sapienti*), to discuss the formation of a league (*societas*) against the Turks; this would culminate in an interesting proposal in 1327.[110]

An unofficial, but very instructive, source for the study of Venetian policy

107. R. L. Wolff, "Hopf's So-Called 'Fragmentum' of Marino Sanudo Torsello," *The Joshua Starr Memorial Volume*, (New York, 1953), p. 153.
108. Thomas and Predelli, *Diplomatarium*, no. 79, p. 161.
109. On this, see Lemerle, *L'Émirat d'Aydin*, and Wittek, *Mentesche*.
110. Cessi and Sambin, *Consiglio dei Rogati*, p. 296 (book 8, no. 175).

in Byzantium and the Aegean is the work of Marino Sanudo Torsello. Sanudo, born in 1270, was a member of a very important Venetian family, and his father had been a senator. He was a relative of the Sanudi who governed Andros and Naxos, and he had spent a considerable portion of his life in the Romania: the Byzantine empire and in those parts of Greece under Latin rule. He was an expert on the affairs of the Romania, and his *Istoria del Regno di Romania* is an excellent source for the history of Frankish and Venetian Greece down to 1310.[111]

Marino Sanudo Torsello is best known for his activities as a crusading propagandist. His major work, the *Secreta Fidelium Crucis*, written between 1306 and 1321, advocated a widespread commercial boycott of Egypt, which would weaken both the economic and the political power of that state, and permit its easy conquest by the crusaders. Once Egypt had fallen, the Holy Lands would be liberated.[112] Sanudo thought it highly impractical for the crusaders to travel to Jerusalem by land, or to conquer the Byzantine empire before freeing the Holy Lands. But he believed that the subjection of Egypt would bring about the fall of the Byzantine empire, as its more or less natural consequence. The *custodia* of ten galleys, cruising the Mediterranean to enforce the boycott against Egypt, would also interrupt Byzantine commercial and diplomatic relations with Egypt. And later, the crusaders could raid the Byzantine coasts from Syria, until the empire was so weakened that the crusaders could easily take it; its schismatic inhabitants would then return to obedience to the Catholic church.[113]

Sanudo's letters are of particular interest to us here.[114] Since he considered himself an expert in the affairs of the Levant, he gave the benefit of his knowledge to the pope and his cardinals, to the king of France, to Robert of Naples, to Andronicus II, and to other influential laymen and ecclesiastics. As Venice changed her eastern policy in the 1320's, he too changed his attitude from one of hostility toward Byzantium to one of cooperation: in the late 1320's, and especially in the 1330's, he would become one of the strongest western proponents of church union. The change in Sanudo's attitude is clearly traceable to his fear of the Turks, and for that reason his work is a valuable guide to the reasons behind the official policy of the Venetian government.[115]

In 1325, when the Venetian government first mentioned the possibility of forming a *societas contra Turchos*, Marino Sanudo Torsello wrote a letter to the bishop of Capua and chancellor of the kingdom of Naples. In this letter he

---

111. On Marino Sanudo's life and work, see Arturo Magnocavallo, *Marin Sanudo il Vecchio e il suo progetto di crociata* (Bergamo, 1901). The *Secreta Fidelium Crucis* is published in Bongars, *Gesta Dei per Francos*, II. The *Istoria* is published in Hopf, *Chroniques Gréco-romanes*.

112. *Secreta Fidelium Crucis*, in Bongars, II, especially book 1, pt. 1, chap. i; pt. 4, chap. vii; book 2, pt. 2, chap. i.

113. *Secreta Fidelium Crucis*, in Bongars, II, 32, 47, 81–82, 94.

114. His correspondence has been published by Bongars, as a sequence to the *Secreta*; by F. Kunstmann, "Studien über Marino Sanudo den Aelteren mit einem Anhange seiner ungedruckten Briefe," *Abhandlungen der Historischen Classe der Königlich Bayerischen Akademie der Wissenschaften*, 17 (1855), 753–819; and by L. Dorez and C. de la Roncière, "Lettres inédites et mémoires de Marino Sanudo l'ancien," *BEC.*, 56 (1895), 21–44.

115. On this, see Laiou, "Marino Sanudo Torsello," pp. 381–392.

referred at some length to the Turkish attacks on the islands of the Romania, especially Nigroponte, where they took many prisoners, and Naxos. In 1326, in a letter to various (unnamed) prelates, lords, and knights, he wrote bitterly that a crusade was unlikely in the near future; he suggested a series of compromises with Egypt, and then he turned to the Turkish problem. He stressed the danger the Turks presented to the islands of the Aegean, and urged that action be taken immediately.[116]

Sanudo was probably the first European to see the Turkish problem in its entirety. He explained that the Turks did not consist of just a few people who inhabited the coasts of Asia Minor. Turkish tribes held all of Anatolia, a territory larger than Spain, and this geographical strength formed the basis of their power. He wrote that if it were not for the desperate efforts of the Genoese of Chios, Nicolo Sanudo of Naxos, and the Hospitallers of Rhodes, the Aegean islands would have already been lost to the Turks. He had heard that the Turks threatened to send against Nigroponte six galleys and thirty smaller ships, a force which could scarcely be contained. The Turks and their allies, the Catalans of Athens, were dangerous to all other powers in the Aegean. He pleaded for help from the pope; Venice, in the meantime, had sent two galleys to Nigroponte, and continued to prepare reinforcements.[117]

Facts confirmed Sanudo's fears. In 1326 the Turks of the emirate of Aydin laid siege to the fortress of Smyrna, which had been held by the Genoese since 1304.[118] Venice, fully aware of the danger to her own possessions, proceeded to implement the decision of 1325 as to the formation of an anti-Turkish league. In July 1327 the senate decided to send letters to the duke of Crete and the bailos of Nigroponte and Constantinople, commissioning them to discuss with Andronicus II, the master of the Hospitallers, Martino Zaccaria of Chios, and others the formation of a league against the Turks. In December 1327 a Byzantine embassy was expected in Venice, and the senate voted that no fare should be paid by the ambassadors. Was this embassy perhaps connected with the discussions concerning the anti-Turkish alliance? We do not know, nor do we know what the Venetian representatives said to the Byzantine ambassadors who were in Venice in February 1328.[119]

The developments of 1327 represent a major indication of the change in Venice's attitude toward Byzantium. Far from being hostile to the schismatic Byzantines, the Venetians now suggested a common alliance against the common enemy, the Turks. Andronicus II was in no position to enter such an alliance in 1327–1328, for he was, again, in the midst of civil war. But if his earlier policy toward Asia Minor is taken into consideration, it can be assumed that had he been able, he would have been very happy to join this alliance. Presumably some arrangement could have been made so that Byzantine help against Aydin would be reciprocated by Venetian help against the Ottomans.

116. Bongars, II, letters 3 (pp. 291–294), and 5 (esp. p. 298).

117. Ibid., letter 5 (p. 298).

118. Lemerle, *L'Emirat d'Aydin*, p. 54.

119. Cessi and Sambin, *Consiglio dei Rogati*, pp. 341–342 (book 10, nos. 194, 202): "de faciendo societatem contra Turchos pro defensione locorum nostrorum"; p. 349 (book 10, no. 284); p. 351 (book 10, no. 315).

Such an alliance would have been a splendid reward for Andronicus II's new policy of rapprochement with the West. But the civil war and the subsequent deposition of Andronicus II caused Byzantium to lose this opportunity in 1327–1328.

An anti-Turkish League was, in fact, formed in 1332–1334. But the Byzantines, who had promised to cooperate, broke their word at the last minute. In any case, by that time the Byzantines had suffered further major reverses in Asia Minor: Andronicus III had been defeated at the battle of Pelekanon, in 1329, and Nicaea had fallen into the hands of the Ottomans in 1331.[120]

The slow evolution of Andronicus II's western policy gave place to a revolutionary shift in the years 1324–1327. For the second time in his long reign, the emperor envisaged the possibility of reuniting the Greek and Latin churches, of returning to what had been the cornerstone of Michael VIII's policy after 1271. Andronicus II had first considered such a possibility in 1311, when he sought to marry a Byzantine prince to Catherine of Valois, and held out the promise of church union. But that was a single and singular effort, which he abandoned when he saw that Europe was not interested. On the contrary, in 1324–1327, he initiated sustained negotiations toward union: in 1324, the Catholic bishop of Caffa, Hieronymus, told the West of Andronicus' willingness to join the Roman church, and for the next three years the emperor, the pope, the king of France and Marino Sanudo Torsello discussed the Byzantine proposals.

Until now, the scholars who have mentioned the union negotiations of the 1320's have linked them directly to the western crusading projects. With slight variations, their argument is that Andronicus II suddenly began to fear a crusade which might be deflected to Constantinople, and that he sought to avert the danger by promising to unite the Greek and Latin churches. According to this interpretation, Andronicus II's western policy during the 1320's had no coherence or significance, being a mere response to the European threat: it was a passive, not an active policy. The most important modern proponent of the passive theory concerning the union negotiations of the 1320's is Walter Norden; and subsequent investigators have accepted his interpretation, without reexamining it.[121] The theory, however, rests on the faulty interpretation of a small number of sources. In the absence of a detailed study of Andronicus II's foreign policy, it was quite understandable that historians should look for an extraordinary interpretation of his activities of the 1320's, for these were diametrically opposed to his policy as formulated in 1282. But his unionist plans were not the result of a sudden reversal of the policy he had followed during the first years of his reign; rather, that policy had changed over the intervening years.

120. Lambros, «Βραχέα χρονικά,» p. 154; Laurent, "La chronique anonyme du Cod. Mosq. Gr. 426," p. 209.

121. Raynaldus, *Annales Eccl.*, 1324, §39; Norden, *Papsttum und Byzanz*, pp. 684ff, 688–689; Muratore, "Principessa Sabauda," pp. 239, 279; M. Viller, "La question de l'union des églises entre Grecs et Latins depuis le concile de Lyon jusqu' à celui de Florence (1274–1438)," *Revue d'histoire ecclésiastique*, 17 (1921), 276; T. Käppeli, "Benedetto di Asinago da Como († 1339)," *AFP*, 11 (1941), 85. Dürrholder, *Johann XXII*, p. 37, makes less of this theory.

No source, Byzantine or western, clearly states that Andronicus II's overtures to the West resulted from his fear of a European crusade. Therefore, Norden's theory can only survive if the crusading projects of 1321–1328 are considered to have been more serious than those of the previous decade, and if contemporaries saw a clear danger that the crusade might be diverted to Constantinople. In fact, the French and papal crusading plans of these years were no more effective than they had been during the reign of Philip V. It is true that between 1322 and 1324 everyone was still discussing a crusade: John XXII, Charles IV of France, Charles of Valois, and Louis of Clermont were loath to abandon their plans to recover the Holy Lands. Early in the reign of Charles IV, the pope wrote to him urging him to follow Philip V's example and prepare to liberate Jerusalem; John XXII promised to support the expedition with crusading subsidies. Charles IV pronounced himself eager to undertake such a journey, and on December 18, 1324, the pope renewed the French crusading tithes for two years.[122]

A new crusading fervor seemed to be pervading France, as it had after the council of Vienne and during the reign of Philip V. Yet there was a major difference in the aims of the crusaders of the 1320's: John XXII was now primarily concerned not with a general crusade, but with the fate of the Christian kingdoms of Armenia and Cyprus. Armenia, under severe threat from Egypt, joined the Catholic church in 1323, and John XXII had a firmer commitment to defend its inhabitants against the Muslims.[123] From 1323 on, John XXII's letters about the crusade mention specifically that the first aim of such an enterprise would be to give aid to Cyprus and Armenia. He wrote to Charles IV and Charles of Valois, trying to impress upon them the needs of Armenia, and urging them to rush to its salvation. On December 20, 1322, the pope wrote that if Armenia and Cyprus were helped, the way to Syria would become much easier; and he promised that those who undertook the journey to Armenia would receive crusading subsidies and all the spiritual benefits which accrued to crusaders.[124]

In January 1323 the king of France, his uncle, Charles of Valois, and an assembly of nobles and prelates discussed the crusade in Paris; also present were Robert of Naples, Marino Sanudo Torsello, and representatives of the king of Armenia.[125] The assembly discussed the technical problems of a crusade: how many men and what equipment were necessary, and how much the jour-

122. Dürrholder, *Johann XXII*, pp. 30–51; Delaville le Roulx, *France en Orient* I, 75–83; Coulon, *Jean XXII*, nos. 1562 (December 5, 1322), 1682–1689 (February-May 1332); nos. 2311, 1323. On Charles IV's crusading plans, see F. Lot, "Projets de croisade sous Charles le Bel et sous Philippe de Valois," *BEC*, 4th ser., 5 (1859), 503–509.

123. The best discussion of John XXII's Armenian plans is in Dürrholder, *Johann XXII*, pp. 34–50; Norden, *Papsttum und Byzanz*, p. 683, does not show that Armenia was one of John XXII's primary concerns. Cf. Raynaldus, *Annales Eccl.*, 1323, §§4–6.

124. Raynaldus, *Annales Eccl.*, 1322, §30, 32, 33–39; 1323, §§4–6; Coulon, *Jean XXII*, nos. 1431 (June 22, 1322), 1571, 1682–1689 (February-May 1323); Finke, *Acta Aragonensia*, I, 489, no. 325 (April 23, 1323).

125. *Chronique parisienne anonyme*, ed. A. Hellot, in *Mémoires de la société de l'histoire de Paris*, XI (1884), 77; Sanudo, letter 7 in Bongars (p. 299); Dürrholder, *Johann XXII*, pp. 37–43. Sanudo did not attend the assembly as Andronicus' representative, as Petit claims: Petit, *Charles de Valois*, p. 201.

ney would cost. In April 1323 Charles IV and Charles of Valois reported the estimates of the assembly to the pope, who responded by halving the number of men he thought necessary for the crusade; he also estimated that the crusading subsidies he was giving France were much higher than Charles IV thought.[126]

Far from being concerned with a diversion to Constantinople, the assembly of 1323 was clearly discussing a crusade to save Armenia. An Aragonese emissary at the papal court referred on April 23, 1323, to "the messengers of the king of France who are here for the journey to Armenia."[127] Sometime in April, representatives of the kings of Armenia and Cyprus advised Charles IV on the crusade they had heard he was about to undertake: they spoke of a sea journey to Cyprus, Armenia, and then to Syria. Certain cardinals also gave Charles IV the benefit of their advice at approximately the same time; they spoke of a crusade to Armenia, and no mention was made of a possible diversion of the crusading fleet to Constantinople. In 1324, there were again Armenian ambassadors at Avignon, and John XXII recommended them to Charles IV, Charles of Valois, Louis of Clermont, and Alphonce of Castile.[128]

Thus, in 1323–1324 the most important proponents of the crusade, that is, the pope, and the king of France, had a major political objective: the preservation of Armenia. Although it is conceivable that a crusading expedition to the Holy Lands, such as the one under discussion in 1313–1321, might have attacked Constantinople, it is very unlikely that a crusade which aimed to save Armenia could be so deflected. For in Armenia time was of the essence, and everyone was well aware of the fact that an attack on Byzantium would be a lengthy enterprise. Only Raynaldus mentions at one point that the question of an anti-Byzantine crusade was raised: he says that in 1324 kings and princes discussed in closed councils whether they should go to Syria by sea, or by land, through the Byzantine empire. But the discussions, he wrote, were futile, and no one moved.[129] The crusade being planned in 1323 never materialized, and by 1325 Charles IV had abandoned his intention to go overseas: he was fighting the English, and, like John XXII, he had become too deeply involved in the wars against Lewis of Bavaria.[130]

It is clear, then, that the Byzantines had little to fear from the crusading plans of the pope and the king of France. Nor were the projects of other would-be crusaders—Charles of Valois, Louis of Clermont, Philip of Taranto—much more dangerous. Charles of Valois was, until 1323, one of the leading proponenents of the crusade—but he spoke of an expedition to the Holy Lands, not to Constantinople. John XXII commended Charles of Valois for his zeal

---

126. Petit, *Charles de Valois*, documents 19, 20; Finke, *Acta Aragonensia*, I, 492–493, no. 327; Coulon, *Jean XXII*, no. 1710.
127. Finke, *Acta Aragonensia*, I, 489, no. 325: "Les misatges del rey de França, qui eren aci per lo passatge Darmenia."
128. Coulon, *Jean XXII*, nos. 1690, 1692; Raynaldus, *Annales Eccl.*, 1324, §§42–43; Sanudo, letter 8 in Bongars.
129. Raynaldus, *Annales Eccl.*, 1324, §41.
130. Petit, *Charles de Valois*, pp. 202–218; Delaville le Roulx, *France en Orient*, I, 83–84; Dürrholder, *Johann XXII*, pp. 51–58.

in defense of the faith, and placed him under the command of the king of France.[131] Soon thereafter, Charles acquired German ambitions, as he had done in 1308. In 1324 King John of Bohemia, brother of France's new queen, decided to create a kingdom of Arles and Vienne, with Charles of Valois as its king. Although this plan miscarried, it aroused Charles's interest for a while. In 1323–1325 Charles of Valois helped his king with the war against the English; and on December 16, 1325, he died, probably from an attack of gout.[132]

As for Louis of Clermont, who became duke of Bourbon in December 1327, his crusading plans had deteriorated even before 1325. Charles IV, on his accession to the throne, had renewed all of Louis' rights and privileges with regard to a preliminary crusading expedition; in April 1322, the king promised Louis of Clermont the captainship of any such expedition.[133] But in 1323, when Charles IV, Viscount Amaury of Narbonne, and the bishop of Mende were preparing a crusading flotilla of twenty galleys, nothing was said of the rights of Louis of Clermont.[134] Subsequently, Louis abandoned his plans, though not without loud protestations. In 1325 he called together the men who were to go on a crusade with him, and told them that he was obliged to postpone the expedition until the spring of 1326; at that time, he planned to set sail for the East, from Lyons. His words met with ridicule, and his disgruntled followers went home.[135] In 1326 the more hardy among them returned, to hear Louis say that he was still not ready to go East, but that he felt mortally insulted because people did not take him seriously as a crusader. He told the people of Paris that he intended never to return to the capital, unless he had first fulfilled his crusading oath. "And so," write the chroniclers, "he left Paris, but he did not go very far; for he stayed near Paris, but outside the walls, that is, at the Temple, or the Louvre, . . . or near Vincennes."[136] From this quarter, then, the danger to Byzantium was minimal.

The plans of Philip of Taranto did involve a potential danger to the Byzantines. Since 1321, when Philip had sent provisions to his castles in Corfu and Achaia, he had been considering an invasion of Byzantium. More provisions were sent to the same castles in October 1322, and John XXII granted to Robert of Naples and to his son, the duke of Calabria, three years' crusading subsidies for the needs of the kingdom of Naples, and for those of Philip of Taranto.[137] The pretender's projected alliance with Stephen Uroš III of Serbia also mentioned the possibility of an attack against the Byzantine empire. John XXII applauded Stephen's promise to become Catholic, and his intention to help

131. Coulon, *Jean XXII*, no. 1711; Petit, *Charles de Valois*, pp. 201–204, and document 19.
132. Petit, *Charles de Valois*, pp. 201–220.
133. Huillard-Bréholles, *Titres*, no. 1633; de Boislisle, "Projet de croisade du premier duc de Bourbon, 1316–1333," *Annuaire-Bulletin de la Société de l'histoire de France*, 9 (1872), 232.
134. Sanudo, letters 4, 8, pp. 297, 300, in Bongars; Delaville le Roulx, *France en Orient*, I, 79.
135. Continuator of Guillaume de Nangis, *H.F.*, XX, 639: "quod dictum multis versum est in scandalum, nonnullis etiam in derisum, et sic fraudati ab intento ad propria vacui redierunt." Cf. *H.F.* XX, 719; *H.F.* XXI, 66, 686.
136. Ibid., XX, 644, 723; XXI, 69, 687, 688; de Boislisle, "Projet de croisade," 233–234.
137. Caggese, *Roberto d'Angiò*, II, 302–307.

Philip of Taranto against the Byzantines, but after 1323 nothing more was heard about the Serbian–Angevin alliance.[138]

Philip's expedition, scheduled to leave for the Romania in the spring of 1323, was grounded because of lack of funds; in 1324, he was again ready to depart for the East, but he had no soldiers.[139] Lacking the support of Venice, such an expedition had little chance of success in any case. In 1325 Philip of Taranto and his wife, Catherine of Valois, made a grant which was as magniloquent as it was devoid of any real meaning. Acting as emperors of Constantinople, and concerned with the prosperity and tranquillity of their subjects, Philip of Taranto and his wife constituted Asia Minor a kingdom; its "king and despot" was Martino Zaccaria, lord of Chios.[140] Martino was, of course, ruling Chios only at the sufferance of the Byzantine emperor, but he had also acquired strong ties with the principality of Achaia: he had married into the barony of Veligosti and Damala, and purchased the barony of Chalandritza.[141] Now, in 1325, he was granted not only the "kingdom of Asia Minor," but also the islands of Chios (which he already held), Lesbos, Samos, Kos, Tenedos, Icaria, Oenoussai, and Marmara. In return, Martino Zaccaria promised to give Philip or his successors five hundred knights and six galleys a year, after Philip had conquered the Byzantine empire, and after Martino had taken possession of his kingdom.[142] Norden thinks that this document proves Philip of Taranto's continuing concern with the recovery of the Byzantine empire.[143] In effect, however, this was an empty grant of titles over territories which Philip of Taranto did not control; the elevation of Asia Minor to a kingdom was a particularly futile act.

Philip of Taranto never undertook his expedition against the Romania; the Italian wars kept him at home. His brother, John of Gravina, prince of Achaia, did go to his principality in 1325.[144] But this did not particularly influence the policy of the Byzantines.

In these circumstances, the threat of a western attack cannot constitute a sufficient explanation of Andronicus II's western policy in the 1320's. Although the plans of Philip of Taranto in 1323 may have entailed some danger to Byzantium, surely by 1324–1326, when Andronicus II pursued his negotiations most diligently, the danger from the West was smaller than it had ever been since 1302.

Norden has singled out one French plan as a major cause of Andronicus II's conciliatory policy toward the papacy. He has ascribed great importance to Charles IV's plan to create a flotilla of twenty galleys, with the help of Amaury of Narbonne. Norden identifies Louis of Clermont as the future captain of that flotilla, and argues that, given Louis' interest in the principality of Achaia,

138. Raynaldus, *Annales Eccl.*, 1323, §§14–18.
139. Caggese, *Roberto d'Angiò*, II, 316.
140. C. Minieri-Riccio, *Saggio di Codice Diplomatico*, supplement 2, (Naples, 1883), pp. 75–77.
141. Hopf, *Chroniques Gréco-romanes*, p. 502; Miller, *Essays on the Latin Orient*, p. 290.
142. Minieri-Riccio, *Saggio*, p. 76; Hopf, *Griechische Geschichte*, p. 408.
143. Norden, *Papsttum und Byzanz*, p. 674.
144. Caggese, *Roberto d'Angiò*, II, 317; Hopf, *Griechische Geschichte*, pp. 407–408; Norden *Papsttum und Byzanz*, pp. 674–675.

it was likely that the flotilla would be diverted to Constantinople; Louis would follow the opinions of the bishop of León, who advocated the conquest of Byzantium.[145] No source, however, says that the flotilla would be led by Louis of Clermont, who had, in any case, lost his interest in Achaia.

The only sources that discuss the flotilla are two letters of Marino Sanudo Torsello, written in 1324 and 1326, and a close reading of the appropriate passages produces a very different interpretation from Norden's. In 1324, Marino Sanudo wrote to the bishop of Caffa that he might go East if the flotilla which, in 1323, was being prepared by the king of France, the viscount of Narbonne, and the bishop of Mende, was now ready to sail. But he added that "these men have no other intention but to destroy the infidel Mohammedan sect."[146] Sanudo thus gave a specific guarantee to the bishop of Caffa, who would transmit it to Andronicus II: the flotilla of 1323 would not attack Byzantium. It is true that in 1326, writing to the bishop of Mende, Sanudo said that the flotilla would, among other things, have saved Armenia and "defeated the schismatic Greeks." But this was a letter in which Sanudo deplored the fact that the flotilla had never materialized, because no one had seen fit to give enough money; and he probably exaggerated the potential results of this small expedition.[147] Even if Sanudo lied to the bishop of Caffa in 1324, and the flotilla was, indeed, partly aimed at Byzantium, still this has no bearing on Andronicus II's policy: Andronicus knew only what Sanudo told him through the bishop of Caffa, and Sanudo disclaimed any plans hostile to Byzantium.

As for the bishop of León, he was, as the bishop of Mende was, one of the many people who advised Charles IV of France on the crusade, its aims and the optimal routes. But the bishop of Mende—and it was he, *not* the bishop of León who sponsored the flotilla of 1323—advocated a *general* crusade which would send two fleets East: one would go to southern Asia Minor and Armenia, and the other to Syria. Neither would go to Byzantium. The bishop of León preferred the land route: he thought that the crusaders should make an alliance with the Tartars, defeat the Byzantines, and then proceed to fight the Muslims.[148] Even assuming that his views were favored, his plan necessitated a large expedition, traveling *by land*; it could not be carried out by the flotilla of 1323. Finally, since it was soon clear that the flotilla would not be finished, the plan of 1323 can hardly have influenced Andronicus II's policy in 1326–1327.

The union negotiations make it clear that Andronicus II acted on his own initiative, and not in response to western plans. The first documents concerning

145. Norden, *Papsttum und Byzanz*, pp. 683–684. Louis of Clermont's interest in Achaia diminished after 1322.

146. Sanudo, letter 8, in Bongars, p. 300: "ipsi non intenderent ad aliud quam ad consumptionem infidelium sectae Mahumeticae."

147. Sanudo, letter 4 in Bongars, p. 297: "quae armatura magna esset si sufficientia stipendia solverentur: sed nimis parum de pecunia dabant pro armatura tanta. Unde nihil postmodum est secutum."

148. Delaville le Roulx, *France en Orient*, I, 81–83.

the union of the churches date from 1324. In December of that year, Marino
Sanudo Torsello addressed a letter to the emperor in which he said that he
had stayed for a long time at the courts of Paris and Avignon, where he had
discussed the crusade: "And I have heard from the religious men who have
come from your majesty, and primarily from the lord bishop of Caffa, that your
majesty . . . desires the union of the churches, which made my heart rejoice;
for I know that the union of the churches supplements the crusade to the
Holy Land."[149] Sanudo then added that he had spoken of Andronicus II
to many French nobles and cardinals, to the papal legate in France, and to
Robert of Naples, all of whom showed themselves well-disposed toward the
empire. Sanudo offered his services to the emperor in the matter of church
union, and mentioned the letter he was writing to the bishop of Caffa.

The letter to Hieronymus of Caffa was also written in Venice, in December
1324.[150] Sanudo asked the bishop to recommend him to Andronicus II,
and to acquaint the emperor with Sanudo's work as a crusading propagandist.
He insisted that the emperor should know that the *Secreta Fidelium Crucis*,
unlike other crusading propaganda, did not consider the conquest of the
Byzantine empire as a necessary prerequisite of the recovery of the Holy Land.
Experience had proved, he wrote, that the crusaders might be able to defeat
the Byzantine empire, but they could not command the loyalty and the hearts
of its inhabitants—and such a conquest would be meaningless. This had been
proved by the hostility of the native population to the Latin rulers of the
duchy of Athens, Cyprus, Crete, the principality of Achaia, and Nigroponte.
Sanudo said that he had presented these thoughts to several cardinals and
nobles, and particularly to Robert of Naples. Instead of a meaningless occupation of Byzantine territory, which would still leave the inhabitants in schism,
he advocated a union of the churches: "The way by which the church can be
reunited is to have his magnificent person [Andronicus II], and his patriarch,
and other members of his house [join the Roman church]." If this happened,
all Byzantine subjects, as well as the inhabitants of the kingdoms of Serbia,
Bulgaria, and Georgia, and those Orthodox Christians who lived under the
Turks, the Tartars, and the Egyptians, would follow the emperor's example
and return to the true faith.

149. Sanudo, letter 7 in Bongars, p. 299: "et viris Religiosis qui venerant de vestro Imperio,
et praecipue a domino episcopo Caphensi, intellexi de vestra Imperiali sapientia et fide ac
voluntate bona, quam ad unionem Ecclesiarum habetis, de quo cor meum fuit et est non
modicum illaratum: cognoscens quod Ecclesiarum unio est complementum Passagii Terrae
Sanctae." B. Altaner thinks that the "viri Religiosi" refers to Dominicans, and specifically to
Mathaeus of Cortona: B. Altaner, "Die Kentniss des Griechischen in den Missionsorden
während des 13. und 14. Jahrhunderts," *Zeitschrift für Kirchengeschichte*, 53 (1934), 457.

150. Letter 8 in Bongars, pp. 299–300. Bongars dates this letter 1324; Magnocavallo, *Marin
Sanudo*, pp. 109–110, dated it 1323, thinking that the bishop of Caffa died in 1323. Golubovich,
however, has proved that the bishop did not die before the end of 1325, and thus the date 1324
may be restored: Golubovich, *Biblioteca Bio-Bibliografica*, III, 56–57. Both Norden (*Papsttum und
Byzanz*, pp. 684–688), and Dürrholder, (*Johann XXII*, pp. 36–39) claim that union negotiations
began in 1323, but there is no evidence that would support this. Perhaps they were misled by
Magnocavallo's false dating. Dölger adopts the date 1323 (*Regesten*, no. 2492); his sources are
Norden, Dürrholder, and Muratore.

Sanudo promised that if Andronicus II tried to implement church union, he would have the support of Robert of Naples; but since Robert and his family had certain rights in the Byzantine empire, they should receive due compensation. The king of France and the French nobles who were involved in crusading projects would also welcome the union of the churches, especially if Andronicus II promised to help the crusade. The help of Venice would be necessary, and forthcoming.

Several important conclusions may be drawn from these letters, which are the only source for the negotiations of 1324. First of all, it is clear that Sanudo was *not* acting as Andronicus' representative to the French assembly of 1323, as Petit has claimed.[151] Far from having represented Andronicus in 1323, Marino Sanudo was asking the bishop of Caffa to introduce him to the emperor in 1324. If Sanudo had told the French prelates and barons not to attack the Byzantine empire, he had not done so because a frightened Andronicus had commissioned him. He had merely presented his own brand of the crusade, which did indeed oppose wasting the resources of Europe against the Byzantine empire while Egypt was still powerful.

Sanudo's two letters of 1324 also prove that the bishop of Caffa was Andronicus II's emissary to Avignon, and indicate that the aim of this embassy was to discuss the union of the churches. Hieronymus had been sent as a missionary to the Mongols in 1300, and since then he had spent a long time in the East. Becoming bishop of Caffa in 1317, he visited Constantinople and Pera and met Andronicus II. In 1318 and again in 1321 until the spring of 1322 he was at Avignon. Then he returned to the East, and in April 1324 he came to Avignon once more. There he probably discussed Andronicus' proposals. In December 1324 he was in Venice on his way to Constantinople, where he died, in late 1325 or early 1326.[152] According to the information given in Sanudo's letters, Hieronymus' embassy to Avignon in the spring of 1324 was the first contact of Andronicus II and John XXII on the question of church union.

Only one phrase in Sanudo's letter to the bishop of Caffa could be used to support the theory that Andronicus II was forced into union negotiations because he feared a western crusade. Discussing the benefits which would accrue from Andronicus' conversion, Sanudo wrote: "that would be a great benefit for the men of his empire, as much for their souls as for their bodies."[153] Taken out of context, this phrase might seem to hold an implied threat to the Byzantines, if they should remain in schism. In context, however, the phrase means something entirely different: Sanudo was arguing that when the Byzantines, the Serbs, Bulgarians, Georgians, and the Orthodox who lived under Frankish, Tartar, and Egyptian domination had returned to communion with

151. Petit, *Charles de Valois*, p. 201.

152. Golubovich, *Biblioteca Bio-Bibliografica*, III, 38–48, 53–57. Golubovich makes the point that since both Hieronymus and Sanudo were at Avignon in 1322, they may have discussed the question of church union; perhaps, but Sanudo still wrote in 1324 as though he had had no contact with Andronicus with regard to this issue.

153. Sanudo, letter 8 in Bongars, p. 300: "quod quidem esset maximum bonum pro gente sui imperii, tam pro anima quam pro corpore."

Rome, peace would reign, and Andronicus' empire would face no danger from any of these states.[154]

The discussions which began in 1324 continued during the following year. Constantine Physcomallos, who was in Venice in February 1325 to receive Soranzo's confirmation of the Byzantine–Venetian treaty, also carried Andronicus II's letter to Marino Sanudo Torsello. Sanudo answered, through the same emissary, and in 1326 he wrote two letters to Andronicus II and another two letters to Stephen Syropoulos, the chief of the Byzantine foreign office, and a man who had often traveled to the West on imperial business.[155] Although the Byzantine part of the correspondence has been lost its contents can be reconstructed from Sanudo's letters.

To Andronicus II, Sanudo stressed his own efforts to effect the union of the churches and to promote the crusade. He had visited the pope, the king of France, and the king of Naples, at his own expense, in order to present his ideas to them. He pressed Andronicus II to try to implement church union in the immediate future: "this union should not be deferred; for that which is easily achieved at one time . . . may become impossible if it is postponed."[156] He added that the nobles and prelates of Europe would accept joyfully an end to the schism, and he repeated his willingness to serve Andronicus II in this matter. The entire letter was an urgent plea to the emperor to persevere in his efforts for church union. Andronicus II, "if he destroyed the schism, would be worthy of being inscribed in the catalogue of saints."[157]

The three remaining letters, from 1326, form one group.[158] They were written to Stephen Syropoulos and to Andronicus II, in response to Syropoulos' letters. Andronicus II also had written to Sanudo, but his letter had been lost. Sanudo urged Syropoulos to work for the union of the churches, which would be to the benefit of the Byzantine empire, as well as to that of Christianity as a whole. In his letter to Andronicus II, the Venetian said that he was planning to go to Constantinople, to talk to the emperor "of great and secret matters." He had been unable to leave with that year's Venetian convoy, but he was sending as his representative a certain Maio Marioni, whom he recommended to Andronicus. A contemporary letter to Syropoulos explained that the emperor should greatly desire Sanudo's personal arrival at

154. Raynaldus, *Annales Eccl.*, 1324, §39, wrote that in 1324 Andronicus II was motivated by the fact of the Tartar invasion in Thrace, and by the rumor of a western crusade which might be diverted to Constantinople. But Raynaldus' only source for the latter motivation was the two letters of Sanudo.

155. Bongars, letters 9, 12 (to Andronicus II), 10, 13 (to Syropoulos). Internal evidence indicates that letter 9 precedes the other three which were written close together. Cf. Dölger, *Regesten*, nos. 2543, 2544. Sanudo addressed Syropoulos as *Imperatoris Turchimanno*; the word is a corruption of the Greek δραγούμενος itself a corruption of the Arabic word *turgŭman*. Meaning "interpreter," the term δραγούμενος appeared in the Byzantine Empire in the twelfth century: L. Bréhier, *Les Institutions de l'Empire byzantin* (Paris, 1949), p. 303. Syropoulos, of course, was much more than an interpreter. We have seen that, since 1310, he had headed some of the most important Byzantine embassies to Europe.

156. Letter 9 in Bongars, p. 302.

157. Letter 9, p. 301: "bene essetis digni sanctorum adscribi catalogo, si possetis istud schisma destruere."

158. Letters 10, 12, 13 in Bongars.

Constantinople, for Sanudo had important things to relate about the West—both about what was happening at the moment, and about events of the past. The secretive tone of the last two letters is tantalizing. In both letters, Sanudo implied that secret affairs were brewing, "which, as they stand, are fraught with danger, both to your empire and to others."[159] The letter to Syropoulos reveals that Andronicus II had sent another embassy to the pope. The new ambassador, a certain Frater Andreas, of the Dominican order, was at Avignon, "and he is taking care of the affairs of our lord" (*et procurat negotia domini nostri*). Sanudo expressed his conviction that the "negotia" improved constantly, and that they would be happily resolved if Andronicus II should persevere.[160]

So, in 1325 and 1326 Andronicus II was still engaged in union negotiations. Not only did he write to Sanudo, who had become the most active western advocate of church union, but he also sent a Dominican to represent his views to the pope. In the context of Sanudo's interests, which revolved around the crusade and the union of the churches, the "negotia" he mentioned to Syropoulos can only have concerned Andronicus' efforts to unite the churches. This point is significant, for the latest to study the subject, Father T. Käppeli, has written that in 1326 Andronicus II simply intended to conclude a non-aggression treaty with France, and that the westerners misinterpreted his intention as an offer to unite the churches.[161] Andronicus II, well aware of the power alignments in western Europe, could hardly have thought that the French and Angevin royal houses would treat with him independently of the papacy; and he could come to no understanding with John XXII while the Byzantine church remained in schism.

The very secrecy Sanudo employed in his letters is instructive. Union negotiations were a very delicate subject, both in Byzantium and in western Europe. John XXII, so strict against all schismatics, had to be convinced that Andronicus II, "who entitles himself emperor and moderator of the Romans" was sincere in his efforts.[162] And in Byzantium, the issue of church union was explosive indeed. Sanudo must have realized that complete secrecy should be preserved until Andronicus II and John XXII could reach an agreement. But there is no question that negotiations were indeed taking place in 1325 and 1326. Writing to the archbishop of Capua and chancellor of the kingdom of Naples in 1326, Sanudo reiterated his plan to travel to the Romania, and said that the pope and the king of Naples should interest themselves in the issue of church union, "the most important affair in the church." He insisted that it was easy to bring this matter to a happy conclusion.[163] Sanudo was able to say this only because he was convinced that Andronicus II was seriously concerned with the issue.

The embassy of Frater Andreas at Avignon, mentioned by Sanudo in his

---

159. Letter 12 in Bongars: "quae sic stantibus negotiis non parvum periculum secum trahunt, et vestro imperio et aliis."

160. Letter 13 in Bongars. Cf. Altaner, "Kentniss des Griechischen," p. 457.

161. T. Käppeli, "Deux nouveaux ouvrages de Fr. Philippe Incontri de Péra, O.P.," *AFP*. 23 (1953), 172. Käppeli has not used Sanudo in this connection.

162. Raynaldus, *Annales Eccl.*, 1326, §26.

163. Letter XI in Bongars.

letter, initiated the most active period of negotiations between Andronicus II and the West on the matter of church union. On March 31, 1326, John XXII wrote to Charles IV of France, acknowledging the king's letters which had referred to the crusade. The letters had been brought by Benedict of Como, a Dominican who was master of theology at the University of Paris. John sent Benedict back to Paris, with answers to the king's letters. At the same time, the pope announced to Charles IV that something was taking place at the court of Avignon, "which has great bearing on the holy Catholic faith," and for which he needed the help of Benedict of Como and of other masters of theology. He continued, "meanwhile, an embassy from the Romania has arrived, which, we believe, will prove very pleasing to your majesty."[164] This must have referred to Andreas' embassy, and the fact that John XXII required the presence of several theologians at Avignon probably indicates that he was engaged in union negotiations.

In the same year, perhaps concurrently, Andronicus II sent an emissary to Charles IV. Simone D'Oria, a Genoese noble, came to Paris, carrying imperial letters, and he told Charles IV that the Byzantine emperor desired peace and friendship (*pacem et amorem*) with all men, and especially with all Christians, and particularly with the king and royal house of France. On its own, this statement could indeed be interpreted as an effort by Andronicus to reach a simple political understanding with France. But the embassy to France was only part of a double Byzantine probe, which sent a Dominican friar to Avignon and a Genoese layman to Paris. Charles IV's immediate reaction indicates the close link between union negotiations and political arrangements. The king decided that he wanted further information about Andronicus' intentions, and he proposed to send Benedict of Como to Constantinople.[165] It may be safely assumed that such an ambassador would discuss theological rather than simply political matters.

Charles IV did not send his ambassador on a purely personal commission. Benedict was instructed to stop at Avignon before going to Constantinople. At Avignon, John XXII listened to his report, and decided that Benedict should discuss with Andronicus II the question of church union. On August 23, 1326, John XXII gave Benedict special permission to talk with Greek laymen and ecclesiastics, although in general Catholics were not permitted to consort with schismatics; Benedict was allowed to discuss the matter of church union, both in public and in private. On August 20, 1326, the pope had ordered Benedict of Como to see Robert of Naples and Philip of Taranto, both of whom were directly concerned with this affair, and to seek their advice.[166]

Benedict of Como left for the Byzantine empire sometime in the autumn of 1326, carrying two letters of Charles of Valois to Andronicus II. The French

164. Käppeli, "Benedetto di Asinago," document 2, p. 94. Käppeli (p. 86) recognizes that this refers to a Byzantine embassy but does not connect it with Frater Andreas.

165. Raynaldus, *Annales Eccl.*, 1325, §§26–27.

166. Norden, *Papsttum und Byzanz*, document 15, pp. 761–762; Raynaldus, *Annales Eccl.*, 1326, §§26–27; the letter of John XXII to Robert of Sicily gives us much of the information about Benedict's commission. Date corrected by Käppeli, "Benedetto di Asinago," p. 86. Cf. Kunstmann, "Studien," letter 2, p. 765 (1330).

king also sent letters to Theodore Metochites. One of Charles's letters to the emperor consisted of copies of the letters Andronicus had transmitted through Simone D'Oria. The other was an expression of good will, and urged Andronicus II to work toward establishing peace and friendship between the two states. Benedict also brought oral messages both from Charles IV and from John XXII. Replying to Charles IV in May 1327, Andronicus II wrote that he had listened carefully to Benedict, and had given him confidential messages to bring back to Paris. Theodore Metochites wrote a similar letter to the French king.[167]

John XXII did not give any written messages to Benedict to bring to Andronicus II. However, he had already sent letters to the emperor, through Theodore of Montferrat. Since Theodore had arrived at Constantinople in June or July 1325, it must be assumed that Andronicus II's unionist efforts of 1324 had already elicited a response from the pope. In 1327, the emperor wrote a very deferential letter to the pope, whom he addressed as "lord and father of our majesty." He said that he had read diligently John's letters, and had held lengthy discussions with Benedict of Como, whom the pope had entrusted with oral messages. Finding Benedict "an obedient man, who reveres and fears God," Andronicus spoke to him openly, truthfully, and with full confidence, and gave him messages for the pope. The letter to John XXII ended with an expression of Andronicus' respect to the pope.[168]

The embassy of Benedict of Como to Byzantium achieved no results, and by May 1327 Andronicus II had been forced to put an end to the negotiations he had initiated. In a letter to Benedict, the emperor explained why he could not, at the moment, pursue the matter of church union any further:

> When you [Benedict] came to us . . . , and presented to us those things which had been commissioned to you, inviting us to do and perform what would promote peace in the church of God, we answered to you then, and we answer now by these letters that it would be desirable to us to . . . achieve peace in the church of Christ. But we think that it is very difficult to achieve, because of the suspicion it would arouse in all our people.[169]

In his letter to Charles IV, Andronicus wrote:

> Brother Benedict has clearly understood how much difficulty we and our subjects face in bringing about peace in the church. He has understood it from what we have said to him confidentially, and he must relate these things to you.[170]

167. H. Omont, "Projet de réunion des églises grècque et latine sous Charles le Bel en 1327," *BEC.*, 53 (1892), letter 2, pp. 255–256, and letter 3, p. 257.

168. H. Omont, "Lettre d'Andronic II Paléologue au Pape Jean XXII," *BEC* 67 (1906), 587. The letter begins: "Sanctissimo et beatissimo summor pontifici apostolice sedis Veteris Rome, reverentissimo et dignissimo pape domino J[oanni], domino et patri imperii nostri." The closing reads as follows: "quia cum cognoscamus diligenter quantum sit nostrum debitum reverentiam omnimodam offerre semper S[anctitati] V[estre] parati sumus et erimus debitum honorem attribuere semper Vestre Paternitati."

169. Ibid., letter 1, p. 255.

170. Omont, "Projet de réunion," letter 2, p. 256.

Seeing that nothing more could be done in Byzantium, Benedict of Como returned to Paris before September 1327. On September 21, 1327, Pope John XXII wrote to Charles IV that he had spoken with Benedict and read Andronicus' letter. In this he found nothing which would indicate that the negotiations had made any progress. He asked Charles IV to see what other measures could be taken on this matter.[171]

Andronicus II's efforts to achieve church union with Rome ended in failure in 1327. Modern historians have concluded from this either that Andronicus had been simply trying to forestall a western invasion, or that he never contemplated more than a political alliance with France. But contemporary observers explained the failure differently. Two unconnected sources discuss the reasons why Andronicus II abandoned his policy of reconciliation with Rome. One is a passage in a small work by Philip Incontri, a Dominican who lived in Pera. The work, entitled *Libellus qualiter Greci recesserunt ab obediencia Ecclesie Romane*, was written in 1356–1357, but the author had met Benedict of Como in 1326–1327.[172] The other source, which has never been used in this connection, is a letter of Marino Sanudo Torsello to Philip VI of France (1328–1350), written on October 13, 1334.[173]

Philip Incontri gives an interesting account of Andronicus II's motivations throughout the period of union negotiations:

> The Emperor Andronicus, conscious of the evil he had done by dividing the churches, used to say this, as I heard from a certain monk, his secretary: "I reign impiously, for I have divided the church which I found united when I came to the throne." So, in his old age, he sought again to unite the churches.[174]

The embassy of Simone D'Oria was the direct result of Andronicus II's change of heart, and subsequently John XXII sent Benedict of Como to Constantinople to discover the truth about the emperor's intentions. But, says Incontri, when Benedict arrived, he found the old emperor in the midst of grave difficulties: his grandson had left Constantinople, and the third stage of the civil war was beginning.

Andronicus II, afraid that the inhabitants of Constantinople might rebel if they heard of his unionist plans, told Benedict that the westerners had misinterpreted the message he had sent through D'Oria, and that he had never really suggested a church union. While the papal ambassador was staying in Pera, Simone D'Oria providentially arrived, on a Genoese galley. Immediately,

---

171. Norden, *Papsttum und Byzanz*, document 16, p. 762: "nichil prorsus inde collegimus quod ad processum suadeat pro parte nostra negocii memorati. Super quo videat regia providentia alterius quod agendum."

172. Käppeli, "Philippe Incontri," pp. 171, 173.

173. Kunstmann, "Studien," letter 6.

174. Käppeli, "Philippe Incontri," p. 173: "Andronicus autem imperator, conscius tot malorum que fecerat in divisione ecclesie, sepe hoc dicebat, ut audivi a quodam calogero, suo secretario: impius regno, quia cum invenissem ecclesiam unitam, divisi. In sua autem antiquitate quesivit iterum unionem, sed peccatis eius impedientibus non meruit."

Benedict and Simone appeared together before the emperor, who could no longer deny the fact that he had, indeed, initiated union negotiations. Afraid of losing his throne, Andronicus II could say nothing to Benedict, except: "this is not the time for such matters" ("videtis, quod modo non est tempus"). Thus, Philip Incontri ascribed Andronicus' inability to continue the dialogue with the West to the civil war, which had, in fact, entered its final stage by the spring of 1327.

However, the fact that the internal circumstances of his empire forced Andronicus II to wear once again the mantle of Orthodoxy does not necessarily mean that his earlier effort to establish closer relations with western Europe had been a mere ruse designed to forestall a western attack. Marino Sanudo Torsello who, more than any other westerner, was aware of conditions in the empire, realized that Andronicus' excuse in 1327 was a valid one. In 1334 Sanudo was trying to persuade the West, and in particular the pope, Philip VI of France, and Robert of Naples of the need to cooperate with Byzantium against the Turks. He said then that the Byzantines were ready for church union, and that Andronicus III was eager to enter the appropriate discussions. Trying to answer possible objections, he wrote that previous negotiations had failed not because of Greek duplicity, but rather because of difficulties which could not have been resolved:

> If someone should object, that the church has sent there many men for this cause, and especially that our lord the pope . . . and . . . Charles . . . king of France sent there the reverend brother Benedict . . . now bishop of Como, I will answer that at that time there was great dissension between the emperor of the Greeks, Andronicus, who is now dead, and his grandson. Because of this division, neither dared speak openly of the faith, for fear that their people would oppose them.[175]

Andronicus II had seen, in his youth, how strong the opposition of his subjects to church union could be. He, who had buried his father secretly in order not to arouse the fury of the fanatically Orthodox, could not risk a policy which would further isolate him in his already isolated capital. The fact that, knowing his subjects' feelings, he had been at all involved in union negotiations forces the historian to give serious consideration to Andronicus' relations with Europe in the years 1324–1327.

In the last years of his reign, Andronicus II wanted to effect a diplomatic reversal, which would end the hostility of the papacy, the French, and the Angevins to the Byzantine empire. His policy was not a response to an immediate threat from the West; rather, he wanted to free his state of the *constant* western danger which had existed since 1261. He realized that a political settlement could only be achieved if the Byzantine church abandoned its independence, but he was willing to discuss such a possibility. This, of course, is an almost complete reversal of his attitude during the first years of his reign. But why should a young man's policy command more respect than a mature

175. Kunstmann, "Studien," letter 6, p. 804.

emperor's deliberations? Andronicus' earlier policy of disengagement from the West had been intimately connected with his desire to concentrate his resources on Asia Minor. When the failure of his Anatolian plans became evident, when, after 1311, it became clear that Asia Minor was lost, he slowly moved toward reestablishing closer relations with western Europe. In the last years of his reign, not only was the loss of Asia Minor brought home with the fall of Brusa, but his state was threatened internally by his grandson, externally by the Tartars. His search for allies then included western European powers which he had considered inherently hostile.

The factor of age may also have been significant, although not in the way it was presented by Philip Incontri. In the last years of his life, Andronicus II found that most of his policies had failed, and most of his friends had abandoned him. Is it not natural that he should look back on his father's successes with a respect of which he had been incapable in his earlier days? Michael VIII had been able to preserve and extend his empire because of his flexible diplomatic contacts with the West; and he had hoped to use his western allies to recover Asia Minor. When all else had failed, and when he was challenged by a younger man, Andronicus II shed his violent feelings against his father's policies, and tried to emulate them.

His one close friend and close companion, Theodore Metochites, was also involved in the negotiations for church union, and he too must have suffered a similar reversal of emotions and opinions. He was, after all, the son of George Metochites, the close adviser of Michael VIII and an advocate of church union, and his father was still alive—and in prison—until 1328.[176] Philip Incontri admired George Metochites, and it is likely that the "monk, one of Andronicus' secretaries" who had told Philip of the emperor's desire to negotiate with Rome was Theodore Metochites.[177] The emperor and his friend, two old men whose greatest dream—the salvation of Asia Minor—lay shattered, whose policies had been discredited, had returned to the formula devised by their fathers.

176. V. Laurent, "Jean Beccos," pp. 316–319.
177. Käppeli, "Philippe Incontri," p. 173. Theodore became a monk in 1328; Incontri, writing in 1356–1357, could easily have been confused, and thought that Theodore was a monk before 1328, i.e. while he was still Andronicus' "secretary."

Appendices
Bibliography
Index

Appendix I

Some Letters of the Patriarch of Constantinople, Athanasios I

The ten letters of the Patriarch Athanasios published below have been selected because of their particular relevence to the subject of this book. Certain issues, such as the disobedience of the higher clergy and the provisioning of Constantinople, were raised repeatedly in Athanasios' correspondence. However, since the purpose here is to illustrate points made in the text, rather than to publish the patriarch's correspondence, the letters provide only examples of Athanasios' treatment of various controversial subjects.

The patriarch's writings exist in a number of manuscripts, the oldest and most complete of which is the Codex Vaticanus Graecus 2219. This manuscript usually gives the most correct reading, but it does contain some errors which may be corrected by collating it with the two other good manuscripts, the Codex Parisinus Graecus 137 (sixteenth century), and the Codex Parisinus S Graecus 516 (fifteenth century). The Codex Parisinus 1351 A is less complete than the other three. The letters here have been transcribed from the Vatican Codex, with corrections from the Codex Parisinus Graecus 137 wherever appropriate. The heading of the letters is a translation of the description given by the scribe of the Parisian Codex. The letters contain many grammatical, syntactical, and orthographical errors which have been neither corrected nor noted.

In the first two letters, the patriarch exhorts Andronicus II to induce the prelates to leave Constantinople and return to their sees. There are a number of similar letters, one of which has been published by Migne.[1] The first letter castigates the prelates for their greed and fractiousness. In the second, the patriarch appears particularly anxious about the fate of Asia Minor, whose higher clergy prefer to stay at Constantinople instead of tending their flock. Both letters probably belong to the first period of Athanasios' patriarchate (1289–1298), when the troubles of the church were compounded by the presence in the capital of many members of the clergy who had come to participate in the discussions which ensued from Andronicus' break with Rome. The second letter shows Athanasios at the end of his tether; it may have been written during the last year of his first patriarchate. He suggests that he be translated to another see so that he can carry on the proper work of a prelate, while the troublemakers divide Constantinople among themselves.

The third and fourth letters discuss the question of morals, especially those of the rich, and urge the Byzantines to return to a godly life. The imperial officials in particular are reproved for their behavior. In Letter 3, the patriarch presents one of his favorite arguments, that the only salvation for the empire lies in the reform of morals; Asia Minor will be saved by God, and help from the West would be useless, and should not be sought. A similar argument was made in a letter written in May or June 1305, in which Athanasios tried to convince Andronicus II not to send the Despot John to Montferrat to assume the government of that state.[2]

Letters 5 and 6 deal with the particular problems of refugees and the protection of Constantinople. Letters 7–10 refer to the question of food, and the measures which should be taken to end profiteering and to ensure the availability of bread. I have published elsewhere two other letters dealing with the famine of the winter of 1306–

---

1. Migne, *Patrologia Graeca*, CXLII (Paris, 1885), col. 523; cf. col. 504.
2. Laiou, "Theodore Palaeologus," pp. 392–394, 404–410.

Appendix I

1307.[3] These letters clearly belong to the second period of Athanasios' patriarchate (1303–1309). Letter 3 mentions the future marriage of Nicephorus Choumnos' daughter to Andronicus' son, and thus was written in 1303 or early 1304.

1. Cod. Vat. Gr. 2219, fol. 58ro (Cod. Par. Gr. 137, fols. 80 ro-vo). Letter to the emperor, urging that each prelate remain in his see, and on how the clergy become wild over offices and salaries.

Εἰ μέγα τι ἠτησάμεθα τὴν ἐκ Θεοῦ βασιλείαν σου, πῶς τῆς αἰτήσεως ἐπετύχομεν, ὁπότε ἐννόμως καὶ ἐγκανόνως, τῷ τοιούτῳ προσκείμενοι, μέχρι καὶ νῦν, οὐκ εἰσακουόμεθα; Τί γὰρ μὴ ἕκαστος τῶν ἀρχιερέων ὡς τοῖς κανόσι δοκεῖ, τῇ τούτου λαχούσῃ προσκαρτερεῖ; Τὶς δὲ ὁ μὴ κέρδους χάριν αἰσχροῦ καὶ ξενίων, ἢ[4] ἀνέσεως καὶ σπατάλης τούτους ὑπειληφώ; παρεδρεύειν τῇ βασιλίδι, θείων κατορχουμένους θεσμῶν, ἐκ παρεισπράξεων πληθυσμοὺς Τὶ δὲ μὴ καὶ τῶν τοῦ κλήρου ὀλίγων τινῶν ἀφηνιαζόντων τῆς ἐκκλησίας, καὶ ὥσπερ οὐ κατὰ χρέος κατὰ δὲ χάριν εἰσερχομένων ὅτε καὶ βούλονται καὶ ὡς βούλονται, καὶ ἄλλους ἐκδιδασκόντων τὸ αὔθαδες, τὸ μήτε ὑπηρεσίαν ἀποπληροῦν, μήτε στολῇ ἁρμοδίῳ τῇ ἐκκλησίᾳ καθωραΐζεσθαι, ἀλλὰ πρὸς μέμψεις καὶ γογγυσμοὺς τὴν διάνοιαν ἔχοντες, ἕνεκεν ὀφφικίων καὶ ῥόγας ὑπὲρ ὧν οὐ κεκοπιακάσιν, ὡς ἀδικούμενοι τὰ μεγάλα καταστενάζουσι. Πρὸς τίνος δὲ καὶ κριθῆναι ἑτέρου δικαίως ἐπιδραμούμεθα ὡς ἐφορῶντος Θεοῦ, εἰμὴ παρὰ τοῦ τῆς ἐκκλησίας υἱοῦ τῆς ἐκ Θεοῦ βασιλείας σου, ἣν καὶ ἀδικουμένην μὴ δικαιοῦν τὸ κρίμα βαρύ; Ἡ οὐχὶ ἐκ τοῦ μὴ ἐκφέρεσθαι τὰς κρίσεις εὐθεῖς, ἡ βλάβη τῇ οἰκουμένῃ μεγάλη ἐξεγένετο κατὰ γενεὰς ὡς καὶ σήμερον; Ἔνθεν ἐν ὅσῳ καιρὸν ἔχομεν, χεῖρα παρέξομεν καὶ τῇ ἐκκλησίᾳ καὶ ἀδικουμένῳ παντί, ἐν εὐθύτητι. Καὶ γὰρ ἐξανθούσης δικαιοσύνης καὶ ἀληθείας, ἀναμφιβόλως κακία πᾶσα ἐκμαρανθήσεται. Καὶ οὕτω συνάγοντες ὦμεν μετὰ Χριστοῦ.

2. Vat. Gr. 2219, fols. 13vo-14ro (Cod. Par. Gr. 137, fols. 25 ro-vo). Letter to the emperor on the prelates; that each should return to his see, to teach his people.

Εἰ μὲν ἐπέγνως ἅγιε βασιλεῦ, τὴν ἐν τῇ ἀνατολῇ τῶν πόλεων ἐξολόθρευσιν, ὅπερ μὴ ἴδοιμεν, διατὶ μὴ καὶ τοὺς ἐκεῖ ἐνοικοῦντας ἐκέλευσας [14vo] ἐξελθεῖν καὶ τὰ ὧδε καταλαβεῖν, ὡς τὴν πάντων ἀπὸ Θεοῦ φροντίδα ἐγχειρισθείς, ἀλλὰ τοῖς ἀρχιερεῦσι μόνοις τοῦτο κεχάρισαι; Εἰ δὲ διὰ τῆς χάριτος τοῦ μεγάλου Θεοῦ, τῇ ἐνούσῃ σοι ἐκ Θεοῦ φρονήσει καὶ διακρίσει[5] φιλανθρώπως οἶδας, παιδεύειν ἡμᾶς τὸν Θεὸν οὐ πρὸς ὄλεθρον, ἀλλὰ πρὸς ἐπιστροφήν, τί μὴ ἐκέλευσας καὶ τοὺς ποιμένας ἐκείνων, ἐν τοῖς ἑαυτῶν ποιμνίοις εὑρίσκεσθαι, καὶ τοῦτο μὲν δι' εὐχῶν καὶ δεήσεων τῶν πρὸς τὸν Θεόν, τοῦτο δὲ διὰ παραινέσεων ἢ καὶ ἐπιτιμήσεων, πρὸς ἀναμαρτησίαν διατηρεῖν, καὶ οὕτως ἐξιλεοῦσθαι Θεὸν παρενέγκαι τὴν ἀπειλήν; Ἄρα εἰ πρόβατα ἐνεπίστευσας τῶν ποιμένων τινί, εἶτα ἐκεῖνα μὲν ἔγνως μόνα καταλιπόντα, ἐκεῖνον δέ, οἰκείων ὀρέξεων καὶ ἀναπαύσεων φροντίζοντα, πρὸς τῆς ἀληθείας αὐτῆς παρέδραμες ἀτιμώρητον; Εἶτα τῶν μὲν ἀλόγων προβάτων, ὁ μὴ φροντίζων, ἀνεύθυνος οὐδαμῶς. Τῶν δὲ τοῦ Χριστοῦ λογικῶν προβάτων[6], ἐάσωμεν ἀνευθύνους τοὺς ποιμαίνειν ἐπιλιπόντας, νῦν ἑαυτοὺς βόσκειν ἀλλ' οὐ τὰ πρόβατα; Καὶ ποίαν ἐκεῖ τὴν ἀπολογίαν εὑρήσομεν; Εὔχομαι μὴ ὀνειδισθῶμεν, ὅτι πάντες τὰ ἑαυτῶν ζητοῦσιν, οὐ τὰ τοῦ Χριστοῦ Ἰησοῦ καὶ Θεοῦ. Τί δὲ καὶ τὸ ἐκ τούτων ἐνταῦθα γινόμενον ὄφελος, ἐδίδαξεν ὁ τῆς Τραϊανοῦ. Εἰ γὰρ λιταῖς ὀκνοῦσι καὶ ἀγρυπνίαις, καταμωκῶνται δὲ καὶ ἡμῶν σπουδαζόντων τοιούτοις, ἐκ τούτου τὸ πλέον νοεῖν ἀρκετὸν τοῖς νοῦν ἔχουσι. Οὐδὲ γὰρ ἄλλο προτέρημα τούτοις, ἢ τοῦ καταβιβάζειν πατριαρχεύοντας, καὶ δωροδοκεῖσθαι παρὰ τῶν κρινομένων, καὶ ὅσα ἐδίδαξε περὶ τοιούτων ἡμῖν ὁ καιρός. Ἡ οὖν κελευσθήτωσαν ἀποκαταστῆναι τῇ οἰκείᾳ ἕκαστος ποίμνῃ, ἢ μίαν ἡμᾶς παραχωρήσατε ποίμνην, ἀπελθεῖν εἰς αὐτήν. Καὶ δίδομεν ὅρκον, ὡς οὔποτε ἀποστῶμεν ἐκείνης, ἐνταῦθα ἐλθεῖν. Αὐτοὶ καὶ τὴν μεγαλόπολιν μερισάσθωσαν. Καὶ γὰρ ὄντως ἐλεεινὸν ἐν ἄλλῃ μὲν πόλει τὸν ταύτης ποιμένα ὡς δύναμις διοικεῖν, ἐνταῦθα δὲ μόνον ἀντικαθέζεσθαι τὸν βουλόμενον. Ἀλλ' εἴ τι ἐμοὶ πείθοι

3. Laiou, "Provisioning," pp. 108–113.
4. Cod. Par. Gr. 137, καὶ.
5. Cod. Par. Gr. 137, διακριτικότητι.
6. Cod. Par. Gr. 137, omits ὁ μὴ φροντίζων through προβάτων.

βασιλέων ὁ εὐλαβέστατος, θέλε μᾶλλον τούτους λυπῆσαι καὶ μὴ Θεόν. Καὶ γὰρ σήμερον εἰπέρποτε δίκαιον τῇ οἰκείᾳ ποίμνῃ συναποθνήσκειν αὐτούς. Εἰ δὲ τούτοις τηρεῖν τὸ αἰδέσιμον βούλει, ἀλλὰ μὴ τὸ ὀφειλόμενον, ἐγὼ τὸ ὑπὲρ αὐτῶν καταδεξάμενος κρίμα, ἢ ἑκόντας ἢ ἄκοντας ἐξελάσω τῆς πόλεως. Καὶ λόγον ὑφέξω Χριστῷ, τοῦ τοιούτου τολμήματος.

3. Cod. Vat. Gr. 2219, fols. 17ro-vo (Cod. Par. Gr. 137, fols. 29ro-30ro). Letter to the emperor, urging a return to God. And that everyone should take care of public and private affairs. And on that earthquake.

Ἡ τῆς ἀνομίας ἡμῶν καὶ ἀκαθαρσίας κραυγή, πρὸς Θεὸν ἀνέβη, οὐ τοῦ λαοῦ παντὸς μόνου, ἀλλὰ καὶ μᾶλλον μοναζόντων καὶ ἱερέων ἐντεῦθεν τοῦ Θεοῦ τῶν δυνάμεων, ἀγανάκτησις καὶ ὀργὴ ἀνυπόστατος, ἐπὶ κεφαλῆς ἡμῶν κρέμαται. Καὶ οὐ μόνον ἐρχόμεθα εἰς συναίσθησιν ἐν οἷς εὑρισκόμεθα, ἀλλὰ καὶ ὡς τοῦ Θείου θεραπευταὶ ἐκεῖθεν τὰ δοκοῦντα ἡμῖν αἰτοῦμεν αἰτήματα. Καὶ λέγω ἐνώπιον τοῦ Θεοῦ τῶν δυνάμεων εἰ μὴ αἱ θεοπειθεῖς καὶ πολλαὶ πρεσβεῖαι τῆς Θεομήτορος δι᾽ ὀλίγων τινῶν λίαν εὐαριθμήτων δεομένων αὐτῆς, οὔτε αὕτη ἡ πόλις ἐσῴζετο ὡς νῦν ἀπὸ τῆς τῆς ιγ᾽ τοῦ δεκεβρίου, ἡνίκα ὅτε τρυγὼς ἐκεῖνος ἐγένετο κτύπος, οὔτε τὰ τῆς ἀνατολῆς ἀπ᾽ αὐτῆς τῆς Ἀνίας μέχρι τοῦ Σκουταρίου. Καὶ μὴ νομίσῃς ὡς δι᾽ ἐπιβουλῆς στρατευμάτων ἰσχύσομεν τί, λέγω γὰρ καὶ πάλιν ἐνώπιον τοῦ Θεοῦ, ὡς οὐδ᾽ ἂν αὐτὴ ἡ ἑσπέριος εἰ ἦν δυνατὸν ὅλη συνήχθη εἰς τὴν βοήθειαν. Ἀλλὰ τί; Ἐπιστροφὴ καὶ μετάνοια εἰς δύναμιν πρὸς Θεόν. Δι᾽ ἃ καὶ μακροθυμεῖ ἀναμένων. Εἰ οὖν βουλόμεθα καὶ ἑαυτοὺς καὶ τὸν κόσμον κερδῆσαι, ἕκαστος ἐπιγνῶμεν καὶ τὰ οἰκεῖα καὶ τὰ κοινά, οἱ διοικοῦντες τὰ δημόσια ἐξαιρέτως, καὶ τὰ τοῦ κόσμου καὶ τὰ τῶν ἐκκλησιῶν. Καὶ παυσώμεθα τῶν κακῶν. Τοὺς δὲ τοῦτο μὴ βουλομένους, παυέτω ἡ ἐξουσία. Λέγω γὰρ πάλιν ἐνώπιον τοῦ Θεοῦ τῶν δυνάμεων, ὡς εἰ γένηται ὁλόκληρος ἡ ἐπιστροφὴ ὅσον τὸ κατὰ σέ, οὐ μόνον ἐλευθερίαν πάλιν ἡ ῥηθεῖσα γῆ τῆς ἀνατολῆς πλουτήσει, καὶ ἀπολαύσει, ἀλλὰ συντρίψει καὶ τοὺς ἐπαναστάντας ἰσμαηλίτας, καὶ τὰ ὅρια ἐκείνων δεσπόσει. Εἰ δ᾽ ὅπερ ἀπεύχομαι μὴ τελεία γένηται ἡ ἐπιστροφὴ ἀλλ᾽ ἐκ μέρους, ἐσεῖται καὶ ἡ εὐεργεσία ἐκ μέρους. Εἰ δὲ οὐδόλως, οὐδόλως, κἂν μυρίας ἐπιβολὰς στρατευμάτων ἢ καστελλίων ἀνεγέρσεις ἐπινοήσωμεν, ἀλλὰ καὶ ὅπερ ἂν τῶν εἰς ἀσφάλειαν δοκούντων μεταχειρισώμεθα, εἰς τὸ ἐναντίον ἐκβήσεται. Διὰ ταῦτα ἠθέλησα ὁ ἀνάξιος ἐγὼ τοῦ οὐρανοῦ καὶ τῆς γῆς, ἀνοῖξαι τὴν θύραν, καὶ τοὺς ἐρχομένους [17vo] παρακαλεῖν καὶ εἰς δύναμιν νουθετεῖν πρὸς ἐπιστροφὴν καὶ μετάνοιαν. Διὰ ταῦτα καὶ πεμφθῆναι τινὰ εἰ καὶ οὐκ εἰσηκούσθην, ὑπέμνησα πρὸς ἀνατολήν, καὶ πάλιν παρακαλῶ καὶ τὰ ἴχνη κατασπάζομαι τῶν ποδῶν σου. Βλέψωμεν πρὸς ἐπιστροφὴν καὶ μετάνοιαν βλέψωμεν. Μὴ δὲ τὰς ὀρέξεις ζητῶμεν ἡμῶν ὥσπερ ὁ κανικλείου, μὴ ζητῶν καταλλαγῆναι Θεῷ εἰς ὅσα τῇ ἐξουσίᾳ ἐχρήσατο ἀσυμφόρως, ἀλλὰ μόνον γενέσθαι τοὺς γάμους ὡς δυναμένους αὐτὸν τῶν χειρῶν[7] τοῦ Θεοῦ ἐξελεῖν. Ζητήσωμεν τὰ ἀρέσκοντα τῷ Θεῷ. Σπεύσωμεν διορθῶσαι καὶ τὰ οἰκεῖα καὶ τὰ κοινά. Πόθεν γὰρ ἐλπίζομεν ἀντίληψιν ἐκ Θεοῦ τῆς ἀνομίας ἀνερχομένης εἰς οὐρανούς; Ταῦτα ἀναγγεῖλαι σοι ἐκελεύθην ἐνώπιον τοῦ Θεοῦ. Εἰ μὲν οὖν εἰς ἀκουόντων ὦτα ἀνήγγειλα, τῷ Θεῷ μου χάρις καὶ τῇ σῇ ἁγίᾳ ψυχῇ. Εἰ δὲ βαρὺς φαίνομαι ἐνοχλῶν, δέομαι πάλιν καὶ τοῖς σοῖς προσπίπτω ποσίν, ἵνα ἐάσῃς με καὶ μηνύειν καὶ βλέπειν. Οὐδὲ γὰρ ἄξιος ἐγὼ ἐν ἀνομίαις συλληφθεὶς καὶ ταλαίπωρος ὢν καὶ ἀκάθαρτος, ὁρᾶσθαι παρά τινος, καὶ πολλῷ μᾶλλον παρ᾽ ὀρθοδόξου βασιλέως καὶ εὐσεβοῦς.

4. Cod. Vat. Gr. 2219, fols. 39ro-40ro (Cod. Par. Gr. 137, fols. 50vo-51vo). Letter to the emperor, on those who thirst to devour God's people. And on how the patriarch also suffers in the resulting evils, because of friends and relations.

Τοῦ κυρίου μου λέξαντος, εἰ ἐν τῷ μαμωνᾷ τῷ ἀδίκῳ πιστοὶ οὐκ ἐγένεσθε, τὶς ὁ παρέξων ὑμῖν τὸ ἀληθινόν; Καὶ εἰ δοκεῖ τὰ τῆς ἀληθείας εἶναι τοῦ μαμωνᾶ, ἀλλ᾽ οἶμαι τοῦ τῇδε βίου τὸ πᾶν, ὑπὲρ τὸν μαμωνᾶν τελεῖν καὶ τὸ ἄδικον. Διὰ τοῦτο τῆς ἐκ Θεοῦ βασιλείας σου δέομαι, τῶν ἰχνῶν αὐτῆς ἐφαπτόμενος, ὡς ἔχεις ἐν τούτοις καιρὸν τὰ ἀληθῆ καὶ αἰώνια κέρδανον. Αἰσχύνην ἐπέρδυσον[8] τοὺς ἐχθρούς, σὺν τοῖς κόλαξι τῶν ψεύδεσθαι φρονιματευομένων. Ἐντροπῆς τὰ πρόσωπα πλήρωσον. Οἱ διψῶντες τὴν ἀδικίαν καὶ ἁρπαγήν, καὶ κέρδος οἰκεῖον λογιζόμενοι τὴν τοῦ γένους συμφοράν, καὶ ἐν βρώσει ἄρτου ἐπιθυμοῦντες

7. Cod. Par. Gr. 137, αὐτῶν χειρῶν.
8. Cod. Par. Gr. 137, ἐπέρδυσε.

καταφαγεῖν τὸν λαὸν τοῦ Θεοῦ, ἀρίστῃ ψήφῳ δικαιοσύνης, χαίρειν εἰς μάτην ἐξελεγχθή-
τωσαν. Οἱ ἐν μανίᾳ ἀκολασίας καὶ βορβόρῳ ἰλυσσώμενοι σωφροσύνης φαρμάκῳ θερα-
πευέσθωσαν καὶ μὴ θέλοντες. Οἱ κλέπτειν τετολμηκότες, ἢ φόροις ἢ γοητείαις ἢ ἐπιλοίπῳ
προστετηκότες [39νο] ἀρρητουργίᾳ δικαζέσθωσαν δικαιότατα. Τούτων γὰρ ἕνεκεν καὶ
Θεὸς ἐνέδυσε τὴν ἰσχὺν τὴν ἐκ Θεοῦ βασιλείαν σου, εἰς τὸ τοὺς νόμους αὐτοῦ καὶ τὴν
ἐκκλησίαν διεκδικεῖν ἀνδρικώτατα. Ἕνεκεν τούτων καὶ τὴν μάχαιραν ἐνεχείρισεν, ὁ
στρέφειν καὶ τὴν εὐώνυμον κελεύσας τῷ παίοντι. Ἀπείροις σε ἀγαθοῖς ὁ ὑπεράγαθος
καθωράϊσε. Τήρησον τούτου τὰ δικαιώματα. Ἐν τούτοις ἡμᾶς καὶ μὴ θέλοντας ὤθισον.
Εὔφρανον τὸν ποιήσαντα, πλῆσον ἕνεκεν τούτων χαρᾶς καὶ τοὺς ὄντως φιλοῦντάς σε, καὶ
μὴ διά τι τῶν γεηρῶν. Ἵνα δὲ καὶ αὐτὸς ἐν Χριστῷ τι καυχήσωμαι, τῆς φωνῆς μου εἰσάκουε.
Τὸ ἀξίωμά μου εἰσερχέσθω ἐνώπιόν σου. Οὐ γὰρ εὗρές τινά ὡς ἐμὲ τὸν φιλοῦντά σε, καὶ
τὴν σὴν εὐφροσύνην οἰκείαν ποιούμενον τὴν σωτήριον, οὐ δὲ τὸν ἐν τοῖς ἐπερχομένοις
ἀνιαροῖς ὡς ἐμὲ συναλγοῦντά σοι, ἢ τὸν δόξης καὶ σωτηρίας τῆς σῆς κηδόμενον ὡς ἐμέ,
εἰ καὶ πολλοῖς σχηματίζεται τὸ φιλεῖν. Ὡς ἀπόλοιτο ἡ ὑπόκρισις ἢ καὶ σαφῶς ἐξελέγχεται
εἰ τῆς ἐλπίδος ἀποσφαλῶσιν οἱ ταύτῃ προσκείμενοι. Ἕνεκεν τούτων ἀντιβολῶ ζῶσαι
ὥσπερ ἀνὴρ τὴν ὀσφύν σου δυναμούμενος ἐν Χριστῷ. Εἰς Θεοῦ παράταξιν ἀριθμήθητι.
Ἀρίστευσον κατὰ πάντων ὧν ἐχθραίνει Θεός. Περίζωσαι τὴν ῥομφαίαν σου, ὅσα μὴ φίλον
ἐκείνῳ καὶ τοὺς τεκταίνοντας τὰ τοιαῦτα ἀκρατῶς συγκόπτων καὶ ἀφειδῶς τῷ κράτει τοῦ
σωτῆρος θέντος. Τό τε καὶ γὰρ ἐνωτίσαι ἀπὸ Κυρίου ἐν τούτῳ νίκα κατὰ παντός, μὴ ὑπὸ
φίλων καὶ συγγενῶν, μὴ ὑπὸ δυναστείας τῶν ὀφειλόντων ἀνακοπτόμενος. Πάντα γὰρ
δυνατὰ τῷ πιστεύοντι. Ἐπικοπτέτω σοι μέριμνα μὲν ἡδονήν, τὴν λύπην δὲ πάλιν ἡ κρείττω
ἐλπίς. Λέγε τεθαρρηκώς, ἰδοὺ Κύριος Ἰησοῦς, τίς κακώσει με; Εἰπέ, Κύριος ἐμοὶ βοηθός,
καὶ οὐ φοβηθήσομαι τί ποιήσει μοι ἄνθρωπος. Ἔχε θαρροῦντως, ἀγαθὸν πεποιθέναι ἐπὶ
Κύριον, ἢ πεποιθέναι ἐπ' ἄνθρωπον, πίστευσον ἐν αἰσθήσει, ὅτι Κύριός ἐστιν ὃς δια-
σκεδάζει βουλὰς ἐθνῶν, πρὸς δὲ καὶ λαῶν καὶ ἀρχόντων βουλὰς ἀθετεῖ. Μόνη δὲ μένει
δεδοξασμένη εἰς τὸν αἰῶνα ἡ τούτου βουλή. Παρρησιάσθητι πρακτικῶς καὶ μάλιστα νῦν
ἐν ἡμέρᾳ τῶν θλίψεων ἵνα ἴδωμεν ἐπὶ σοὶ τὸ ἐπικάλεσαί με ἐν ἡμέρᾳ θλίψεως σου καὶ
ἐξελοῦμαί σε καὶ δοξάσεις με. Τί μὲ παραλυπεῖς ἀγωνιζόμενον ἐν τοῖς ὑπὲρ σοῦ καὶ γνησίως
σοι συλληπούμενον ὥσπερ ἐκ διαμέτρου, μὴ ποθῶν εἰσακούειν μου; Εἰ γάρ τινος κέρδους
ἢ δόξης ἐμῆς, ἢ φίλων ἢ συγγενῶν ἕνεκεν, ἢ ἀνέσεως καὶ οἰκείων ὀρέξεων, ἃ [40νο] καὶ
πολλάκις ἀποχαρίζῃ τισί, δι' αὐτὸν τὸν Θεὸν μηδαμοῦ μηδόλως ποτὲ εἰσακούσῃ μου,
μηδ' ἔριφόν μοι παρέξεις εὐφρανθῆναι μετὰ τῶν φίλων μου. Εἰ δ' ἕνεκεν τοῦ Θεοῦ καὶ
τῶν τοῦ Θεοῦ καὶ ὧν ὀφείλεις ἀπαραιτήτως Αὐτῷ δόξης τε καὶ μεγαλωσύνης καὶ σωτηρίας
τῆς σῆς, δι' ἃ καὶ παρὰ Κυρίου εἰ πείθου, ἕψεταί σοι καὶ δόξα καὶ σωτηρία καὶ ἀντίληψις
ταχεινὴ καὶ τιμή. Τί μὴ ἐπαγωνίζῃ ἐν ὅσῳ κύριος εἶ καὶ συναγωνιζομένους εὕρηκας καὶ
ἡμᾶς ὑπὲρ τῶν σῶν προθυμότατα; Ἔστι γὰρ ἀναμφίβολον, ὡς ὑπὲρ ὧν ἐξαιτοῦμαι, προθύμως
ἀποπληροῖς τὰ εἰς δύναμιν, ὅτι μὴ δὲ ζητοῦμεν τὰ ὑπὲρ δύναμιν, Θεὸς μυριοπλασίως
εὐφρανεῖ, καὶ μεγαλυνεῖ, στηρίξει τε καὶ σθενώσει τὴν ἐκ Θεοῦ βασιλείαν σου, ἀραρότως
ὑπερασπίζων αὐτῆς καὶ ὧδε καὶ ἐν τῷ μέλλοντι.

5. Cod. Vat. Gr. 2219, fol. 12ro (Cod. Par. Gr. 137, fol. 21vo). To the emperor,
a letter on charity, and asking for a decision on the captives [refugees].

Πολλάκις ἀναφέρω τῇ ἐκ Θεοῦ βασιλείᾳ σου πρᾶγμα ἀποβλέπον εἰς σωτηρίαν ψυχῆς
ἀνέξοδον, μηδενὸς ἄλλου δεόμενον, εἰ μὴ μόνης κελεύσεως, καὶ διὰ τὰς ἐμὰς ὡς ἔοικεν
ἁμαρτίας παρατρέχει ὁ καιρὸς καὶ καταλιμπάνεται ἀθεράπευτον. Διὰ τοῦτο παρακαλῶ
κἂν τὰ μὴ σκέψεως δεόμενα ἢ ἐξόδου ἂς γίνωνται. Εὑρίσκονται δὲ καὶ ἐντὸς τῆς πόλεως
αἰχμάλωτος λαὸς πολύς, καὶ ἔνι δέον νὰ συναντιλήψωνται οἱ δυνάμενοι, ἕκαστος καθὼς
προαιρεῖται. Ζητῶ δὲ βουλὴν περὶ τῶν ἀρχόντων, ὡσὰν ἐὰν φανῇ καλὸν πέμπω εἰς ἕνα
ἕκαστον τῶν τοιούτων ἀρχόντων ἀναφορὰν χάριν τούτου. Ἢ ἐπειδὴ ἔγραψα κοινῶς γράμμα,
ἵνα ἀναγνωσθῇ ἐν τῷ παλατίῳ συνηγμένων πάντων, καὶ ὅσον καὶ οἷον προαιρεθῇ ἕκαστος.
Δύο γὰρ ζητῶ, ἢ ἵνα προσλάβηται ἕκαστος κατὰ δύναμιν, ὅσους προαιρεῖται μέχρι θέρους,
ἢ δώσει ὅσον προαιρεῖται.

6. Cod. Vat. Gr. 2219, fols. 9vo-10vo (Cod. Par. Gr. 137, fols. 16vo-19ro). Letter
to the emperor, telling him that he should make more frequent appearances, especially
at the walls and the gates of the city. And that no one should enter the city armed.

Τὰ παρά τισι μὲν εἰς παράβασιν θείων θεσμῶν πραττόμενα τολμηρῶς, ὑφ' ἡμῶν δέ, πῶς
οὐκ οἶδα, ἀνεκδίκητα καταλιμπανόμενα μικρὰ καὶ μεγάλα, ἐν οἷσπερ σήμερον εὑρισκόμεθα

τὰ ἡμέτερα κατηντήκασι. Διὰ τοῦτο κᾂν, ἀπόγε τοῦ νῦν, διαναστῆναι παρακαλῶ. Καὶ γὰρ καὶ τῷ τῆς Θείας δυνάμεως ῥήματι, τὸ πᾶν κινεῖται καὶ φέρεται, ἀλλὰ βούλεται καὶ ἡμᾶς μὴ ἀργοὺς ὁρᾶσθαι μὴ δὲ ἀπράγμονας, ὅτι μὴ δὲ κατὰ τὸ σωτήριον θέσπισμα ζῶντες ἐσμὲν μόνην τὴν τοῦ Θεοῦ δικαιοσύνην ζητοῦντες καὶ βασιλείαν ἀλλὰ μὴ ἃ ὀρεγόμεθα. Διὰ ταῦτα ἀνιστορῶ, προόδους ποιεῖσθαι τὴν βασιλείαν σου συχνοτέρας, καὶ μᾶλλον περὶ τὰ τείχη καὶ πύλας τῆς πόλεως, καὶ ἐντὸς καὶ ἐκτὸς ὄκνου χωρίς. Καὶ μὴ δὲ προφασιζομένους τὴν ὀλιγότητα μὴ δὲ τὴν οἰκείαν ἀσφάλειαν, ὧν ὑμῖν Θεὸς ἐνεχείρισε τούτῳ ἢ ἐκείνῳ καταπιστεύωμεν. Ὀφθαλμοὶ γὰρ ὠτίων πιστότεροι. Κέλευσον ὃ δίκαιον, τῆς πόλεως εἴσω μηδένα μεθ᾽ ὅπλων εἰσέρχεσθαι, καὶ μάλιστα τῶν Λατίνων. Εἰς γὰρ ἀσφάλειαν μέγα καὶ τοῦτο. Καὶ μὴ δὲ ὀκνῶμεν τὰ εἰς δύναμιν ἥκοντα ὑμετέραν ἀποπεραίνειν καλά, ὡς τὰ μείζω μὴ ἐξισχύοντες, μὴ δὲ παραπέμπωμεν εἰς τὴν αὔριον, τὸ μὴ δῴης εἰς σάλον τὸν πόδα σου, καὶ οὐ μὴ νυστάξῃ ἀκουτισθέντες ὁ φυλάσσων σε ἄγγελος. Γενέσθω φροντὶς εἰσαχθῆναι λαὸν εἰς ἀσφάλειαν, ὅτι μέγα τοῖς ἀντιπάλοις δέος καὶ τοῦτο. Ὁ εὑρισκόμενος ἅπας λαὸς ὁμιλίας ἀπολαβέτω γλυκείας καὶ εὐχαρίστου. Οἱ δὲ τῶν ἐν στρατείᾳ καὶ πλέον, εἰ δυνατὸν καὶ μικρᾶς ἀσχολήσεως ἢ σίτου ὀλίγου. Εἰ δ᾽ οὖν κᾂν, μὴ διενοχλῶνται ἀτίμως, παρὰ τῶν ἐνεργούντων καὶ τὰ οἰκεῖα ἁρπάζωνται. Ἔχουσι δὲ τὴν ὀφείλουσαν ὑποταγὴν καὶ διάθεσιν, μοχθηρῶν ὀλίγων ἐκτός, κᾂν καίτινες τῶν ἀποβλεπόντων μόνον πρὸς τὸ λαβεῖν, ἐκταράττειν ἐπὶ [10νο] χειροῦσι τὴν ἐκ Θεοῦ βασιλείαν σου κατ᾽ αὐτῶν. Ὅτι δὲ ἀπὸ συμπαθείας ὡς ἀπὸ τῆς βασιλείας σου ὁ Δοσίθεος ἤκουσεν ἀναγκάζεσθαι ἀναφέρειν ἐμὲ ὑπὲρ ὧν μοι δοκεῖν ἐκπιέζειν ἀδίκως σιτασσόμενοι ἐνεργεῖν ὡς καὶ ὁ τῆς αὐλῆς πριμμικήριος, ἀλλὰ μὴ ἀκριβῆ κατακαλύψει καὶ ἀληθῆ. Εἴθε καὶ ἦν μοι ψυχὴ ἐλεήμων καὶ συμπαθής, καὶ μάλιστα κᾂν τῷ νῦν δεομένῳ πολλῆς συμπαθείας καιρῷ. Οὐ γὰρ ἠγνόησα εἰ τοῦτο προσῆν μοι, ἀκμὴν μικρὰ αἰσθανόμενος. Τοῦτο γὰρ τῇ ἐκ Θεοῦ βασιλείᾳ σου ἐχαρίσθη τὸ μέγα ἡ συμπάθεια λέγω, ἀλλὰ καὶ κεχρεώστηται. Ἐμοὶ δὲ ἀληθεύω εἰς ταῦτα, καὶ ψυχρὰ ψυχὴ ἐνυπάρχει καὶ σκληρὰ καὶ ἀπόκροτος κατὰ τὸν πρεπόντως ἐκεῖνον στηλιτευόμενον πλούσιον, εἰ μή με ἡ προφανὴς ὠμότης ἐκείνου, καὶ τὸ κατεσθίειν ὡς ἄρτον τοὺς πένητας ἀδεῶς, καὶ τῆς σῆς ἡσθανόμην συμπαθοῦς ψυχῆς, ἐμοί τε τὸ κατεπεῖγον τοῦ χρέους εἰς δέος ὠθοῦν τοῦ οὐαί, ἀπό τε τοῦ παρασιωπᾶν τὴν κακίαν ἀπό τε τοῦ τὸ πικρόν, πικρὸν μὴ λέγειν ἀλλὰ γλυκύ. Πλὴν ἀλλὰ δέομαι, πῶς τοὺς ἐπὶ πολλοῖς ἔτεσι τὰς πύλας φυλάσσοντας, καὶ παρὰ μηδενὸς ὧν ἐγχειρισθέντων τὴν κατ᾽ αὐτῶν ἐξουσίαν καταγνωσθέντας σήμερον, ἢ διδόναι τὸ ἱκανόν, εἰ διώκεσθαι καὶ εἰ παρ᾽ ἄλλου πλέον δοθῇ κατακρίνονται, καὶ μάλιστα ἐν τοιούτῳ καιρῷ, τοὺς μὴ μαρτυρίαν δόντας, φυλακὴν τοιαύτην, διὰ τὸ δοῦναι καταπιστεύεσθαι. Εἰδὲ ὅτι τῆς ἐκ Θεοῦ βασιλείας σου κατενώπιον ἃ συνέρχονται τοῖς τοιούτοις λαλοῦσι, καὶ παρὰ τῶν αὐτοὺς συγκροτούντων εὐυλογοῦνται καὶ θαυμαστῶν, ἀεὶ τοῦ ψεύδους ἐκκεχυμένου, καὶ μάλιστα τοῖς περὶ τὸ λέγειν δεινοῖς ἐκπαιδεύσεως, εἰ μὴ ἐθέλουσιν ἀτενίζειν πρὸς τὸ ἀλάθητον τοῦ κριτοῦ. Δι᾽ ἃ καὶ ταύτης ἀντιβολῶ, πνεύματι μὴ πιστεύειν παντί, προβαίνειν δὲ καὶ συχνότερον καὶ ἀκούειν καὶ βλέπειν, καὶ ὡς δέον διατιθέναι κᾂν τὰ ἐγγύς. Οὐ γὰρ ἐκκόψαι ἡμᾶς τῶν δημοσίων τὴν εἰσφοράν, τὸ ἐκεῖθεν δέος καὶ τὴν ἐπαινουμένην ἀσφάλειαν καὶ ὑποταγήν, συνεργοῦντες ἢ ὀρεγόμενοι ἀναφέρομεν. Μὴ οὕτω μανείημεν οὐδὲ τοῦτον φιλοῦντες κἀκεῖνον ἀπεχθανόμενοι οὐδὲ φιλίας λήμματι χαριζόμενοι, ἀλλ᾽ ὡς ὁ πλάσας ἐπίστασαι συντηρεῖσθαι τὴν δόξαν τῆς βασιλείας ἢ ἐχαρίσθη τῷ γένει Χριστιανῶν μόνιμον καὶ διηνεκῆ καὶ ἐξηρημένην ἐκ τῶν εἰς δύσιν, πίστιν καὶ ἀρέσκειαν ὑφ᾽ ἡμῶν πραττομένων Θεοῦ καὶ ἀναφέρομεν καὶ ζηλοῦμεν καὶ ἐκκαιόμεθα, καὶ εὐχόμεθα. Καὶ ἵνα καὶ τῇ συγκλήτῳ τῇ ἱερᾷ μὴ προσῇ ὅσα ὁ μεγαλοφωνότατος ὀνειδίζει ἀπὸ Θεοῦ τὴν Ἱερουσαλήμ. Οἱ ἄρχοντες [10νο] σου ἀπειθοῦσι φησὶν ἀγαπῶντες δῶρα, διώκοντες ἀνταπόδομα, ὀρφανοῖς οὐ κρίνοντες καὶ κρίσιν χηρῶν οὐ προσέχοντες. Εἰ δὲ καὶ ἀνεξετάστως διακονῶν φιλοτιμίᾳ, ἀναφέρειν τὰ ἁπλῶς ἀκουόμενα νομιζόμεθα, καὶ τοσοῦτον ἢ ἑαυτοὺς ἠγνοήσαμεν ἢ τὸ ὕψος τῆς βασιλείας, ἢ τὴν ἀλήθειαν καὶ τὸ δίκαιον, ὃ ὀφείλεται καὶ τοῖς ὑπηρετοῦσι τῇ βασιλείᾳ καὶ δι᾽ ἃ καὶ ἀντιλαμβάνονται πρὸς Θεοῦ τὰ ἡμέτερα, καὶ μὴ διὰ φόβον Θεοῦ καὶ ἀγάπην καὶ τὸ ἔμισθον χρέος τῆς βασιλείας καὶ τὴν τῷ ὑπηκόῳ πρέπουσαν διεξαγωγήν, καὶ τὸ ἐμοὶ ὀφειλόμενον ἀναφέρω. Στελλέσθω διὰ Θεὸν εὐσυνείδητος ἄνθρωπος καὶ ταύτης πιστός, καὶ μὴ τὴν ἀλήθειαν διαστρέφειν διὰ λῆμμα προσεθισθείς, ἢ καὶ πρόσωπα σὺν ἐμοὶ ἐξετάσων, ἅπερ ἀνέφερον ἢ ἀναφέρω. Καὶ ἢ μὴ ὀλίγα ἐκ τῶν πολλῶν καὶ ἐξεχόμενα ἀληθείας καὶ ζήλου καὶ ἐκδικήσεως ἀλλ᾽ ὀρέξεως ἢ καὶ τάχα ἀκαίρου φιλανθρωπίας καὶ συμπαθείας φανῶσι, καὶ ἐν τοῖς κατ᾽ ἀλήθειαν εἰσακούομαι. Μὴ οὖν ἐῶμεν τὰ πρέποντα καὶ ὀφείλοντα ὅτι σωφρόνων τὸ κρίνειν διὰ Θεὸν ἀνθρώπους μᾶλλον παραλυπεῖν, ἢ δι᾽ ἀνθρώπους Θεόν. Καὶ μὴ δεδιέναι τὴν μοχθηρίαν τινῶν ἀποβλέποντας εἰς Θεόν, ἀγαθὸν εἰδότας, μὴ ἐπ᾽ ἄνθρωπον πεποιθέναι ἀλλ᾽ ἐπὶ Κύριον, καὶ ἀγαθὸν ἐλπίζειν ἐπὶ Θεόν, μετὰ ἐπ᾽ ἄρχοντας. Κατὰ τῶν θείως γὰρ ζώντων, ῥάβδον ἄλλως ἁμαρτωλῶν, Ἰησοῦς ὁ ἡμέτερος οὐκ ἐᾷ, ἀλλ᾽ ὅταν μὴ εἰς Αὐτὸν καὶ ἃ κελεύει ὁρῶμεν, φοβερὸν ἄλλό τι τοῦ θείου φόβου ὑπολαμβάνοντες. Ἐξευμαρίζει γὰρ ὡς Θεὸς καὶ τὰ δυσχερῆ, καὶ σωτηρία σου ταῖς ψυχαῖς ἡμῶν ἐγώ εἰμι λέγει καὶ ἔργοις ἀποπληροῖ. Διατὶ γὰρ κατεστραμμένην ὁρῶμεν⁹ τὴν ἐκκλησίαν καὶ ἀνεχόμεθα; Διατὶ ἀδικία, μοιχεία, πορνεία καὶ ὅσα τοιαῦτα πράττομεν εἰς τὸ φανερόν, οὐκ ἔχεις ἐκδίκησιν; Εἰ γὰρ καὶ ἀρχῆθεν εἰσὶ τὰ κακά, ἀλλὰ λαθραίως πως καὶ κρυφιωδῶς ὑπὸ τῶν νόμων καὶ παιδευόμενα, καὶ ἀναστελλόμενα καὶ καταισχυνόμενα. Ἡνίκα δὲ ῥαθυμίᾳ ἢ ἐμπαθείᾳ ἢ λήμμασιν ἢ προσώποις ἢ καὶ καταφρονήσει ἡ ἀκρίβεια καὶ τὸ δίκαιον ἀπεμποληθῇ παρὰ τοῖς προέχουσιν, ἀδύνατον μὴ ἐπάγεσθαι παιδείαν τὴν ἐξ ὀργῆς. Καὶ ἴδοι τις ἂν τοῦτο ἀρχῆθεν καὶ μέχρι παντός, εἰ θέλει λίαν ὁρᾶν, θαυμάζων δικαίως καὶ μεγαλύνων τῆς προνοίας τὸ ἄφυτον. Ὅπερ ἐπισταμένη ἡ ἐκ Θεοῦ βασιλεία σου εἰς τοῦτο διαναστήτω θερμότερον Θεὸν ἔχων τὸν συναντιληψόμενον καὶ τὴν Θεομήτορα.

7. Cod. Vat. Gr. 2219, fols. 53ro-vo (Cod. Par. Gr. 137, fols. 72vo-74ro). To the emperor, on the famine which has taken place among the people.

Πρῴην διερχομένων ἡμῶν τὰς ὁδούς, ἄλλος ἄλλό τι τῶν πενήτων ἐζήτει ἡμᾶς. Νῦν δὲ ὁμοφώνως ἀποδυρώμενοι ὑπὲρ σίτου, πάντες μικροῦ ἵνα μὴ ἐξέρχηται τῆς μεγαλοπόλεως παρακαλοῦσιν ἐλεεινῶς, καὶ ὅρκοις καταδεσμοῦσι πρὸ αἰτήματος ἄλλου παντός, πρὸς τῆς ἐκ Θεοῦ βασιλείας σου, τὴν ἀναφορὰν ὑπὲρ τοῦ σίτου ποιεῖσθαι με. Τῇ συμφορᾷ δὲ τῇ τούτων καὶ αὐτὸς συνθρηνῶν ἅμα καὶ συναλγῶν καὶ πειθόμενος, στοχαζόμενός τε τὰ ἐκ σιτοδείας δεινὰ συναντήσοντα τοῖς ἐμοῖς ἀδελφοῖς καὶ συμπένησι, καὶ τὸ ἀποβησόμενον πάλιν ἐκ τοῦ τοιοῦδε κακοῦ πάθος, τοῖς ὑπολειφθεῖσιν ἐκ τῆς διὰ τὰς ἐμὰς ἁμαρτίας συμβάσης Χριστιανοῖς ἀπειλῆς, τῆς ἐκ Θεοῦ βασιλείας σου δέομαι ἐνωτίσασθαι ἐν αἰσθήσει, τὰς ἐμὰς ὑπὲρ σίτου κἀκείνων φωνάς, καὶ μὴ παραχωρεῖν τοῖς ξενίοις ἢ νόσῳ πλεονεξίας ἢ καὶ φιλίας ἁπλῶς προτιμῶντας τὸν χρυσὸν τοῦ Χριστοῦ, ὃς διαθρύπτειν πεινῶσι τὸν ἄρτον, ἀλλὰ μὴ προτιμήσει χρυσοῦ, ἀποκτένειν τοὺς τοῦ Χριστοῦ ἐνετείλατο. Τί γὰρ αὐτοὺς ὠφελήσει, ἐὰν κερδήσωσιν ὅλον τὸν κόσμον, ὅπερ ἀδύνατον, ζημιωθῶσι δὲ τὴν οἰκείαν ψυχήν; Κερδῆσαι μὲν γὰρ ὅλον τὸν κόσμον τῶν ἀδυνάτων τινά, ζημιωθῆναι δὲ ἕκαστον τὴν οἰκείαν ψυχὴν εἰ θέλει τῶν δυνατῶν. Ὦ πόσης αἰσχύνης καὶ ψόγου, ὑπὲρ ἀδυνάτου κακοῦ προδοῦναι τινὰ τὸ δυνατὸν ἀγαθόν, τῶν ὀλίγων τὸ ἀγνοεῖν. [53vo] Δέον γὰρ ἔχειν αὐτοὺς κατὰ νοῦν τό, πλοῦτος ἐὰν ῥέῃ μὴ προστίθεσθαι καρδίᾳ, καὶ πλοῦτος ἀδίκως συναγόμενος ἐξεμεθήσεται, καὶ οἱ βουλόμενοι πλουτεῖν, εἰς πειρασμὸν καὶ παγίδα τοῦ διαβόλου ἐμπίπτουσι. Καὶ τὸ ὁ τιμιουλκῶν σῖτον δημοκατάρατος, εὐλογία δὲ εἰς κεφαλὴν τοῦ μεταδιδόντος. Ταῦτα παρὰ τῆς ἐκ Θεοῦ βασιλείας σου δέομαι ἢ διδαχθήτωσαν, ἢ ἐπιτιμηθήτωσαν. Καὶ τὸ μὴ πεποιθέναι ἐπὶ ἀδηλότητι πλούτου, ἀλλ' ἐπὶ τῷ ζῶντι Θεῷ τῷ πλουσίως ἡμῖν εἰς ἀπόλαυσιν ἀγαθὴν πάντα παρέχοντι, ὅτι δεινὸν καὶ πέραν δεινῶν. Ἐμὲ μὲν μετὰ τῶν συμπενήτων μου ἀδελφῶν καὶ πτωχῶν, προσπίπτειν καὶ δέεσθαι βασιλέως μεγάλου εὐσεβάστου ὀρθοδόξου καὶ φιλοχρίστου, ἐλεήμονος ὑπερβολικῶς καὶ τῇ τῆς οἰκείας ψυχῆς συμπαθείᾳ καὶ ἀγαθότητι ἐπικαμπτομένου τῇ θλίψει τοῦ ὑπηκόου καὶ συμφορᾷ. Τοῖς τοσούτοις δὲ ἀγαθοῖς, ὀλίγα κατακαυχᾶσθαι δῶρα καὶ ξένια, καὶ τὸν ποθητὸν ἡμῖν σῖτον ὡς μὴ ὠφελεῖν ἐκκενοῦνται τῆς πόλεως, καὶ ταῦτα μὴ ἀγνοούντων τὴν μέλλουσαν ἐπιπίπτειν ἀνίατον νόσον καὶ συμφορὰν τοῖς πενομένοις ἡμῖν οἱ τὰ πολλὰ ἔχοντες, καὶ τὴν ἁρπαγὴν τοῦ πτωχοῦ ἐν τοῖς οἴκοις, καὶ τὰ ἑαυτῶν ἑκόντες ἀποκλείοντες ὦτα τοῦ μὴ ἀκοῦσαι τὸν ὑπὸ τοῦ Κυρίου στηλιτευόμενον, διὰ τὸ τὰς ἀποθήκας γρηγορεῖν κακῶς καθελεῖν, εἰς μειζόνων ἀνέγερσιν. Πρὸς ταύτην τὴν νόσον, οὐκ ἄρχων, οὐχ ἱερεύς, οὐ λευΐτης ἐπάξει τὴν ἰατρείαν, ἀλλὰ μόνη ἡ ἐκ Θεοῦ βασιλεία σου μετά τινος Σαμαρείτου, ὃς καὶ τὸν ὑπὸ τῶν λῃστῶν πληγέντα, οὐ παρέδραμε βδελυξάμενος. Αὐτὸς γὰρ καὶ τῇ ἐκ Θεοῦ βασιλείᾳ¹⁰ σου δύο δέδωκε τὰ δηνάρια, τὴν εὐσέβειαν καὶ τὴν βασιλείαν. Αὐτὸς καὶ τὸ ἐφόσον ἐποιήσατε ἑνὶ τούτων τῶν ἐλαχίστων ἐμοὶ βοᾷ ἐποιήσατε, καὶ ἐν τῷ ἐπανέρχεσθαι τοῦτον τὴν βασιλείαν παρέξει σοι ἣν ἐπορεύθη λαβεῖν, κἂν οἱ τυχόντες πολῖται δοῦναι Αὐτῷ οὐκ ἠθέλησαν ἣν εἶχε μὲν ὡς Θεός, ἔχει δέ, ὡς Θεάνθρωπος, καὶ βασιλεύων τοῦ οὐρανοῦ καὶ τῆς γῆς, καὶ τοῦ στεναγμοῦ τῶν πενήτων καὶ τῆς ταλαιπωρίας ἐθέσπισεν ἕνεκεν ἀναστήσεσθαι. Αὐτῷ ἡ δόξα εἰς τοὺς αἰῶνας, ἀμήν.

8. Cod. Vat. Gr. 2219, fol. 54vo (Cod. Par. Gr. 137, fols. 74vo-75vo). Letter to the emperor, on the same affair [the famine] and against profiteering.

Εἰ καὶ ἕνεκεν αὐχημάτων πατρῴων κράτιστε βασιλεῦ καὶ ἀδελφῶν ἀδικίας, καὶ σωφροσύνης ὑπερφυοῦς ὥς τι ἀσύγκριτον ἐδόθη καὶ μέγα τῷ Ἰωσὴφ σιτοδοσία πρὸς τοὺς ὁμογενεῖς, ἡμεῖς ἐξόδου καὶ κόπου χωρίς, μὴ ἀποστερηθῶμεν αὐτῆς, μηδὲ διά τι τῶν ἀνθρωπίνων

9. Cod. Par. Gr. 137, omits ὁρῶμεν.
10. Cod. Par. Gr. 137, τῆς ἐκ Θεοῦ βασιλείας σου.

ἀποβαλώμεθα δέομαι ὑπὲρ ἧς ἅπας λόγος τοῖς συνιοῦσι καὶ ἅπαν μυστήριον, τὸ τίμιον ταύτης καὶ ἀναγκαῖον, γνωριζόμενον ἐν τῷ μέλλοντι. Τί γὰρ τοῦ πεινῶσι τινὰ διαθρύπτειν τὸν ἄρτον μακαριώτατον; Στέρξον οὖν τὴν ἀγαθωσύνην ἧς Θεός σοι τὸ κράτος παρέσχετο, καὶ μόνον λόγῳ εἰπέ, καὶ καταισχυνθήσονται μὲν οἱ πλούτισμα καὶ τρυφὴν καὶ ἀδιάδοχον δόξαν λογιζόμενοι τὸ τιμιουλκεῖν χρειώδη πάντα. Ἡσθήσονται δὲ καὶ ἀγαλλιάσονται οἱ πρός τε Θεὸν καὶ μετὰ Θεὸν διακρίνοντες δεξιῶς, καὶ λεῖα βλέποντες καὶ ἐλπίζοντες, καὶ δὴ καταλειφθέντες εἰς χεῖρας τὰς σὰς ἰσχύος ἐξ ἀνθρωπίνης ἀπροστάτευτοι πάμπαν καὶ ἄποροι, καὶ πάντας κατεπτηχότες καὶ μηδὲ γρῦξαι δυνάμενοι, πρὸς ἀμυθήτους μακρηγορίας τῶν σοφῶν πρὸς τὸ ἀδικεῖν, δι' οὓς καὶ τὸ βασιλεύεσθαι ὑπ' ἀνθρώπων ἀνθρώπους Θεὸς ἐδικαίωσε, μήπως καθὰ οἱ ἰχθύες, ὁ μείζων τῶν ἐλαχίστων, αὐθαδῶς ποιῆται κατάποσιν. Ἕνεκεν τούτων ἀντιβολῶ, ἀνθρώπους λυπῶμεν καὶ μὴ Θεόν, πεποιθότας τῷ πλούτῳ ἀλλὰ μὴ πένητας, Θεῷ δοκοῦντας δουλεύειν καὶ μαμωνᾷ δυνατόν. Ἡ οὐκ ἀναντιρρήτως ἅπας ἀλυκτοπέδαις τοῦ μαμωνᾶ πεδηθείς, αὐτόχρημα καθορᾶται εὐαγγελίων μυκτηριστής; Ἐπίστηθι οὖν τοῖς τοιούτοις βασιλικώτερον δέομαι. Ἔλεγξον, ἐπιτίμησον, ἀποστράφηθι, ἔνδυσαι τὴν προσήκουσαν λεοντήν, εἰς δόξης αἰωνιζούσης καταστολήν. Καὶ οὕτω διακειμένων ἡμῶν, ὑπερασπίσαι ἐξεγερθήσεται ὁ παμμέδων ὡς δυνατὸς καὶ κεκραιπαληκὼς ἐξ οἴνου πατάξων εἰς τὰ ὀπίσω σου τοὺς ἐχθρούς, καὶ εἰς αἰώνιον ὄνειδος ταῖς μετέπειτα γενεαῖς ὑποθήσων.

9. Cod. Vat. Gr. 2219, fols. 75ro-vo (Cod. Par. Gr. 137, fols. 99ro-vo). Letter to the emperor, on reconsidering the matter of cereals and bread, that they should be sold at a just price.

Ὥσπερ ἡλίου τὸ φέγγειν καὶ θάλπειν τὸ ἰδιαίτατον, οὕτω καὶ βασιλείῳ περιωπῇ δικαιοσύνη, καὶ εὐνομία τῶν πόλεων, κἀντεῦθεν τῷ δήμῳ ἐκ δικαιοπραγίας καὶ σωφροσύνης κοινῆς, ὁ τοῦ Θεοῦ ἔλεος. Ἐξ ὧν καὶ ἐπίκοινος πλουτισμός, φιμουμένων δικαιοσύνη πλεονεκτῶν ἀεὶ τὰ κοινὰ θησαυρίζειν ἐπισφαλῶς ἰδιοποιουμένων, καὶ τῷ λαῷ τοῦ Θεοῦ προστριβόντων πενίαν, ἐξ ἁρπαγῆς καὶ ὠμότητος. Ἔνθεν εἰ μέχρι καὶ νῦν οὐ προήχθην καταναγκάσαι πρὸς πλήρωσιν αἰτημάτων τὴν ἐκ Θεοῦ βασιλείαν σου, ποιεῖσθαι δὲ μόνην ἀναφορὰν τῆς αὐτῆς διακρίσει ἀνατιθέντα, ἀλλὰ νῦν ὑπὲρ εὐνομίας καὶ εὐθύτητος, ὅπως προσῇ ἀναφαίρετος τῇ βασιλίδι τῶν πόλεων, οὐ μόνον ἀντιβολῶ καὶ βιάζω, ἀλλὰ καὶ βιάζειν οὐ παύσομαι. Κατεξαίρετον, ἀναθεωρῆσθαι τὰ τῶν γεννηματικῶν καὶ τῶν ἄρτων εἰς δικαίαν ἐξώνησιν, καὶ ἡ τούτων ἐπιστασία πρὸς τῶν εὐλαβεστέρων τινός, ὅθεν οὐκ οἶμαι εὑρεῖν εὐλαβέστερον καὶ πιστότερον Δερμοκαΐτου τοῦ Σεβαστοῦ. Διὰ τοῦτο ἵνα καὶ ἔθει βασιλικῷ χρήσωμαι, παρακαλῶ, παρακαλῶ, παρακαλῶ ταχθῆναι αὐτῷ πρὸς τῆς ἐκ Θεοῦ βασιλείας σου εὐεργεσίας [75vo] προμήθειαν, πολλὰ συντελοῦντα πρὸς τὸ τῆς εὐνομίας ἀσυγκρίτως καλὸν μεγάλην τῆς πολιτείας ὑποστάσης ζημίαν ὑπὸ τοῦ λιμοῦ, ὡς μικροῦ τὴν περιουσίαν ῥωμαίων, ἐν ταῖς χερσὶ τῶν Λατίνων χρυσίου καὶ ἀργυρίου εἰσενεχθῆναι. Τὸ δὲ μεῖζον, ἡ τούτων ὀφρύς, ἐπιγελώντων ἡμῖν ἐξ ἀγερωχίας, καὶ τοσοῦτον ὑπερφρονεῖν, ὡς τὰς γυναῖκας τῶν πολιτῶν, ἀντάλλαγμα σίτου λαμβάνειν φρυαττομένους ὅπερ μὴ ἴδοιεν. Ἕνεκεν τούτου ἀντιβολῶ, τῇ τοιαύτῃ σπουδῇ ἐπιμελείᾳ τῆς ἐκ Θεοῦ βασιλείας σου, μὴ ἐπιπλέον κατακαυχήσωνται, ἀλλ' αἰσχύνην ὡς διπλοΐδα, ὁ τὰς βουλὰς τῶν ἐθνῶν περιτρέπων ἐπενδυεῖ αἰωνίως αὐτοῖς.

10. Cod. Vat. Gr. 2219, fols. 53vo-54vo (Cod. Par. Gr. 137, fols. 74ro-vo). Once more on the same affair (the famine), and that no one should sell wheat without the patriarch's knowledge.

Ἥπερ ἀναφορὰν πεποιήμην ὑπὲρ σίτου κράτιστε βασιλεῦ, διὰ Θεὸν μὴ ἐπιληθῶ, ὡσὰν μὴ ἄλλῳ τινὶ τῶν ἀρχόντων τὴν διοί[54το]κησιν τὴν περὶ τοῦ σίτου ἐκχωρηθῇ τοῦ οἰκονομεῖν, ἐκτὸς οὗ ἀνέφερον εὐλαβοῦς. Καὶ δοθῇ καὶ ἡμέτερος μοναχός. Καὶ ἵνα μηδὲ αὐτός, ἐπιτιμίου χωρίς, τοῦ μὴ πρὸς πρόσωπα, μὴ πρὸς χάριν, μὴ πρὸς φιλίαν, μὴ πρὸς δῶρα καὶ ξένια, τὰ καὶ σοφῶν ὀφθαλμοὺς ἐκτυφλοῦντα, ἀλλ' ἕνεκεν οἴκτου καὶ ἀληθείας Θεοῦ καὶ δικαιοσύνης, μήτε μὴν συγχωρεῖν ἐξωνεῖσθαι τὸν σῖτον τοὺς τοῦτον διψῶντας τιμιουλκεῖν, οἵ καὶ ἐπάρατοι ἐπιμίσγοντες ἄχυρα ἢ σῖτον διασαπέντα, ἢ ὅσα αὐτοῖς ὁ σατᾶν ὑποτίθεται, τὰς τοῦ Χριστωνύμου λαοῦ συμφοράς, ὦ ζημίας ἐξωνούμενοι[11] ἐλεεινῶς, εἰδείας τῆς ἐκ Θεοῦ βασιλείας σου, ὡς εἰ καί που περὶ τινων ὄντων ἐν βίᾳ πρὸς αὐτὴν πεποιήμην ἀναφοράν, ἀλλ' οὔ ποτε κατηνάγκασα. Ἐν δέ γε τοῖς νῦν ὡς ὄντος κοινοῦ ναυαγίου, τὸ κοινῆς

11. Cod. Par. Gr. 137, ἐξωνυμένοις.

Appendix I

συμφορᾶς παραμύθιον, οὐχ ἁπλῶς ἀναφέρω, ἀλλ᾽ ἀξιῶ καὶ καταναγκάζω, καὶ εἰ μὴ εἰσακουσθῶ τῇ συνέσει θαρρῶν, καὶ ὀργίζομαι. Βλέψον οὖν εἰς Θεὸν τὸν τὴν χεῖρα ἀνοίγοντα ἐμπιπλᾶν. Βλέψον υἱέσιν ἀπόροις καὶ ἀδυνάτοις, καὶ τὸ μειζόνως συνθρύπτ᾽ ἐμὲ λιμώττουσιν ἄρτου, καὶ φιλοτέκνου πρὸς ὀφειλὴν καὶ δυνατοῦ ἐνδειξάμενος. Βλέψον ψυχῆς βασιλικωτάτης οἷον[12] ὀφείλει βασιλικόν, ἐν τοιούτοις ἐνδείκνυσθαι φρόνημα, καὶ βαθυτέρους τρόπους οἰκονομίας, μὴ ῥαδίους πολλοῖς. Καὶ εἰ μήπου τῶν ἐν τῇ νέᾳ θαυμαστωθέντων πρὸς μέτρον πεφθάκαμεν, τοῦ, ηὐχόμην νεανιεύσασθαι, ὦ ψυχῆς μακαρίας, ἀνάθεμα εἶναι ἀπὸ Χριστοῦ. Ὀλίγων γὰρ τοῦτο τῶν πάνυ καὶ ὀλιγάκις. Ἀλλά γε κἂν, τῶν ἐν τῇ παλαιᾷ μὴ κατόπιν βαδίσωμεν δυσωπῶ. Ἢ οὐδὲ ἐκθεάσαι ἀδυνατοῦμεν Μωσέα; Εἰ μὲν ἀφεὶς τὴν ἁμαρτίαν αὐτοῖς πρὸς Θεὸν δυσωποῦντα, ἄφες. Εἰ δ᾽ οὖν ἀλλ᾽ ἐξάλειψόν γε κἀμοῦ, ἐξ ἧς γεγράφηκα[13] βιβλίου, καὶ ἄλλος μὴ κατισχύσητέ με παρακαλῶ, ἐπὶ τῇ συντριβῇ τῆς θυγατρὸς τοῦ γένους μου, καὶ ἄλλος ἄφετέ με πικρῶς ἀποκλαύσασθαι. Τί δὲ ὁ μέγας Δαβὶδ ἐπὶ τῇ θειλάτῳ ὀργῇ; Οὐχὶ ταύτην ἐκάλει πρὸς ἑαυτόν; Εἰ ἐγὼ ὁ ποιμὴν ἐκακοποίησα φάσκων, τὸ ποίμνιον τί πεποίηκεν; Ἐπ᾽ ἐμὲ γερέσθω ἡ χείρ σου καὶ ἐπὶ τὸν οἶκον τοῦ πατρός μου. Καὶ πλείους εἶχον ἐξαριθμήσασθαι, εἰ μή που πρὸς οἶκον σοφίας καὶ οἴκτου ἐχάραττον, ἔμπλεων καὶ μόνον διψῶντα λαβεῖν ἀφορμήν, μακρὰν τῶν ῥηθέντων γινώσκων ἐμέ, καὶ συστελλόμενος ταῦτα ὑποτιθέναι [54vo] ἢ καὶ πλείω λαλεῖν, τοῦ μήπως ὀφλήσω καὶ γέλωτα. Τούτου γε χάριν εἰσακουσθῆναι ἀντιβολῶ, εἰ καὶ μὴ λέγειν ἀξίως πεπαίδευμαι.

12. Cod. Par. Gr. 137, οἶνον.
13. Cod. Par. Gr. 137, γεγράφηκας.

Appendix II

Two Letters to Charles of Valois and Catherine of Courtenay

The first letter published here survives in two copies, J 510 nr. 25[2] §1, and J 510 nr. 27[7]. Both are fourteenth-century manuscripts, written by two different hands, and the first copy is somewhat more legible than the second. There are a few differences in the text of the two copies; these will be indicated in footnotes. The two copies are designated A and B. The second letter also survives in two copies, without textual variations. The two copies are J 510 nr. 25[3] §2, hereafter designated as C, and J 510 nr. 25[8] §2, hereafter designated as D. They were written, respectively, by the same scribes as A and B.

Various historians have dated the letters variously, from 1306 (Du Cange), to 1308 (Omont, Rubió y Lluch, Burns).[1] Dade's date of 1307 is based on three references. Two are from the first letter: "per gratiam dei . . . et per opus tuum regna sunt pacificata", and "inveniuntur Cathalani qui tenent fortilicias in partibus Galipolis et nominant te dominum." The third reference is Limpidaris' complaint that the cities of Asia Minor "have been under blockade for four years because of his [the emperor's] evil counsel."[2] Dade thinks that "regna sunt pacificata" refers to the end of the French wars in Flanders, particularly to the treaty of Athis-sur-Orge (1305), and that Limpidaris' statement refers to Michael IX's unfortunate expedition of 1302.

But it is unlikely that Monomachos knew about the treaty of Athis-sur-Orge; if he were well-informed enough to know about it, he cannot possibly have thought, in 1307 or 1308, that it brought peace to France. In fact, we know that in 1307 Charles of Valois was forced to postpone his expedition to Constantinople precisely because of troubles in Flanders.[3] Furthermore, the text speaks of "regna," and Flanders was not a kingdom. The first reference should be taken to apply to the peace of Caltabelotta. This is supported by the text, which specifically mentions Charles' intervention ("per opus tuum") and which seems to link this pacification of the kingdoms to the advent of the Catalans.

As for the third point, the reference to the four years during which Asia Minor has been in a state of siege, this could refer either to the failure of Michael IX's expedition in 1302 (making the date of the letter 1306) or to the after-effects of the Catalan campaign in Asia Minor (1304), thus making the date of the letter 1308. There is also the possibility that "four years" is used loosely by the author.

The point on which an accurate dating can be based is the reference to the Catalans "qui tenent fortilicias in partibus Galipolis et nominant te dominum." We have already seen, from other evidence, that the Catalans were not Charles's vassals while at Gallipoli; but they did begin their negotiations with Thibaut de Chepoy before reaching Macedonia. If we may assume that these negotiations were fairly open and widely known, then we must accept that Monomachos' letter was written while the first negotiations were going on, just before the Catalans reached Macedonia. The date, therefore, is the summer of 1307, either July or August. All of the letters, these published here and the three published by Omont and Miklosich and Müller, were written at roughly the same time, since they all refer to the same persons, Matteo Balbo and Philippo Marchiano, who were the emissaries of the Greeks to Charles of Valois. Indeed, the style and the contents of Monomachos' and Limpidaris' letters are so similar as to suggest cooperation between the two men.

1. Rubió y Lluch, "Companyía Catalana," p. 16.
2. Moranvillé, "Projets," letter 2: ὅτι χρόνους τέσαρι ἔναι ἀποκλεισμαῖναι.
3. Above, "Charles of Valois, Venice, and Byzantium," in Chapter VII.

Appendix II

Letter 1. Letter of John Monomachos informing Charles of Valois of the future arrival of two envoys, and of Monomachos' willingness to fight for Charles.

Peramabilis frater fortunatissimi et altissimi Regis Francie sancte mi domine et cum deo Imperator Constantinopolis et totius Imperii Romeorum. Ego Johannes Monomachus audacter notifico tuo sancto Imperio quod per aliquos annos confiderunt et crediderunt in me Philippus Marchianus et Matheus Balbus consilia et verba eorum privata. Et quia ego invenio eos esse consanguineos meos et operari bonum opus pro Christianis recepi[4] libenter verba eorum et feci me cum promptitudine socium cum eis. Consilium hoc est.[5] Postquam fuimus certi quod accepistis Uxorem Neptem domini mei quondam beatissimi Baldouini potentem et sanctam dominam meam hereditariam Imperatricem et jure dominam omnium Romeorum proposuerunt suprascripti venire ad tuum Imperium sanctum notificaturi tibi quomodo facilius est tuum sanctum Imperium hereditarium recuperandum.[6] Et expectavimus semper adventum tuum. Et quia intelligebant quod multa alia tibi[7] ardua incumbebant retardaverunt suprascripti ad te venire. Nunc autem audivimus quod per gratiam dei et misericordiam et sue matris sanctissime et per opus tuum regna sunt pacificata et inveniuntur Cathalani qui tenent fortilicias[8] in partibus Galipolis et nominant te dominum.[9] Et Patria ista devastata est multum a paganis et aliis inimicis propter inhertiam[10] istius innaturalis domini et est in periculo perditionis residuum. Propter que gentes nequentes persecutiones huiusmodi ulterius[11] sustinere, non solum tuum Imperium recipient cum gaudio sapientes tanquam naturalis domini sed etiam cuiuscumque[12] qui eos guereret et defenderet.[13] Nichil aliud scribo nisi quod unum sum cum istis et quid isti dicunt ego dico. Et pro fide adhibenda misi cum eis fratrem meum Constantinum[14] Monomachum. Et quomodo magis[15] greci se tibi reddent absque preliis et effusione sanguinis Christianorum. Hii[16] sunt sufficientes ostendere tibi modum cum desiderium et voluntatem Grecorum cognoscant multis modis. Pro deo miserere Grecorum et accelera adventum tuum quia gentes perduntur et gentibus perditis locus vacuus parvum valet. Ego autem servitudinarie supplico[17] tuo sancto Imperio quatenus in futuro non inveniam a te gravamen, nec me incorrigibilem reputes de eo quod primus scripsi tibi.[18] Sed hec recipe gratanter propter tuam misericordiam. Et sicut ego scribo multi alii scriberent qui sunt de isto consilio maiores nisi timerent ingrati reputari. Sed si Deus posuerit in corde tuo quod significes cum aliis capitulis preceptum tuum Grecis quod[19] ipsi qui ad vos veniunt Grecis publice ostendere possint videlicet percipiendo et publicando quod si quis Grecorum[20] inclinet scribet ut[21] villas reddet seu aliud faciet

4. Du Cange: accepi.
5. No period in B, comma in Du Cange.
6. No period in B.
7. Du Cange: multa tibi alia.
8. Du Cange: fortalitias.
9. No period in B.
10. Du Cange: inertiam.
11. B: ulterius persecutiones huiusmodi.
12. B adds alterius.
13. Du Cange has comma instead of period.
14. Du Cange: Ioannem.
15. B adds voluntaire.
16. Du Cange: ii.
17. Du Cange omits one line, Grecorum to tuo sancto.
18. Du Cange has comma instead of period.
19. Du Cange: quia.
20. B adds se.
21. Du Cange: vel.

gratum imperio tuo a te inveniet gratiam et utilitatem ut fidelis non solum litteras multi et magni et nobiles mittent sed etiam personaliter venient ad inclinandum tuum imperium. Ego autem sum de parte orientis Romanie et custodio fortiliciam[22] attesalonicensem tamquam capitaneus ipsius fortilicie.[23] Sunt multi orientales mecum fugati de partibus suis doloribus afflicti et solum quod ego videam certam imperii tui potentiam.[24] Spero in Deo et in sua matre sanctissima quod magnum servicium pro te perficiam. Deincips ergo remaneat in conscientia et misericordia tui sancti Imperii cuius tamquam servus audacter hec scribo.

Letter 2. Constantine Limpidaris to Catherine of Courtenay, urging the speedy conquest of the Byzantine Empire.

Audax servus potentis et sancti Imperii tui Imperatrix mi sancta, notifico ego Constantinus Dux Lymbidaris[25] quam servitutem habeo ad tuum sanctum Imperium et quomodo divulgatur per me preconium tuum in omnes Grecos et quot alleti[26] ad servitutem tui Imperii, hii[27] qui veniunt ad inclinandum tuo sancto Imperio videlicet Philippus Marchianus et Matheus Balbus notificabunt sicut de aliis et de me. Ego quidam tamquam servus primus tui Imperii sancti supplico quatenus perficiatur cito id quod isti conservi mei tibi dicent et quod notifico domino meo Imperatori quia locus est in periculo et postquam annititur populus remaneat vacans et parvum valet.[28] Maneat in misericordia tui sancti Imperii, cuius parvus servus hec tibi notifico.

22. Du Cange: fortalitiam.
23. Du Cange: fortalitie.
24. Du Cange has comma instead of period.
25. D: Limbidaris.
26. Du Cange: alleci.
27. Du Cange: si.
28. Du Cange has comma instead of period.

Bibliography

An Essay on Sources

It is customary among Byzantine historians to preface a study such as this with a survey of the sources they have used. This is done because much depends on the historian's assessment of the reliability of a relatively small number of major sources. There is also the need to indicate how far the weight of the narrative is carried by western and how far by Greek sources. Since such a long preface is unwieldy, however, it has seemed more appropriate to discuss the sources at the end, rather than at the beginning, of this book.

The most important Byzantine sources consist primarily of narrative histories, and only secondarily of diplomatic materials. Among the narrative historians, George Pachymeres is the best source for the years 1256–1307. His history, a continuation of George Akropolites', covers the two reigns of which he was a personal witness, that of Michael VIII (in six books), and that of Andronicus II (in seven books); it is absolutely essential for the study of that period. Unfortunately, no modern scholar has published an adequate analysis of Pachymeres' work. After Colonna and after Moravcsik we are still left almost solely with the information given by Karl Krumbacher in his *Handbuch der Byzantinischen Litteratur*.[1] António Rubió y Lluch has done some work on Pachymeres, but he was mainly concerned with Pachymeres as a source for the Catalan expedition.[2] For the rest, Pachymeres' difficult language and complicated style have led historians to agree with N. Iorga who dismissed him and a whole period with the words "his work as a writer is worth just as much as the political accomplishments of his imperial master, the deplorable Andronicus II"—a comparison unfair to Pachymeres.[3]

George Pachymeres was born in Nicaea in 1242, and came to Constantinople upon the recovery of the city by the Byzantines in 1261. He was well educated in the classics, and his language abounds in homerisms, archaisms, and references to ancient authors. He was no less learned in ecclesiastical literature, and could follow and expound a theological argument in subtle and complex detail. Pachymeres held high state and

1. Karl Krumbacher, *Handbuch der Byzantinischen Literatur*, 2d ed., in I. Müller, *Handbuch der Altertums-Wissenschaft* (Munich, 1897); Gyula Moravcsik, *Byzantinoturcica. Die byzantinischen Quellen der Geschichte der Türkvölker* (2 vols.; Budapest, 1942), reprinted in 1958; M. E. Colonna, *Gli storici bizantini dal IV al XV secolo. 1. Storici profani* (Naples, 1956). These works are useful for further bibliography. As far as the writers of our period are concerned, Colonna and Moravcsik add little to the information given by Krumbacher, a real revision of whose work would be most useful.

2. A. Rubió y Lluch, *La Espedición y Dominación de los Catalans en Oriente juzgadas por los Griegos* (Barcelona, 1883), Memóries de la Real Academia de Buenos Letras de Barcelona, IV, esp. pp. 47–57; A. Rubió y Lluch, *Paquimeres y Muntaner*. Memóries de la secció històrico-arqueològica del Institut d'Estudis Catalans, I (Barcelona, 1927); A. Rubió y Lluch, *La companyía Catalana, passim*.

3. N. Iorga, "Médaillons d'histoire littéraire byzantine," *Byzantion* 2 (1926), 291–292. On Pachymeres, see also V. A. Mystakides, «Παχυμέρης Γεώργιος, πρωτέκδικος καὶ δικαιοφύλαξ καὶ Μ. Κρούσιος,» Ἐναίσιμα Χρυσοστόμου Παπαδοπούλου, (Athens, 1931), pp. 214–232. The importance and reliability of Pachymeres as a historian has been recognized by V. Laurent, in "Notes de chronographie et d'histoire byzantines," *Échos d'Orient*, 36 (1937), 157–174.

ecclesiastical office.[4] During the reign of Michael VIII he participated in the council that condemned the patriarch Arsenius (1265). Later, he disagreed with Michael's ecclesiastical policy and opposed the union with the church of Rome. He described at length both the persecutions of those who opposed the union, and the restoration of Orthodoxy under Andronicus II. His account of these events is reasoned and he sets out the views of both sides while clearly indicating his own standpoint. His personal involvement in these disputes, as well as the fact that he was close to both Michael VIII and Andronicus II and had access to state documents make his testimony invaluable.

George Pachymeres, like most other Byzantine historians of the time, had an exalted sense of his function as a historian. The Byzantines were keenly aware of their obligations to the historical muse and to posterity; by contrast, western historians of the time, when not writing simple chronicles, were, like Joinville or Muntaner or Froissart, writing the history of a man, or an expedition, or a war, without much interest in developing a philosophy of history to guide them. Pachymeres was very explicit as to what he wanted to do and why. He was writing the history of his times for the benefit of future generations. He was sworn to truth and impartiality: "for truth is . . . the soul of history, . . . and he who prefers lies to the truth is sacrilegious." If there were truths which he could not reveal, he preferred to omit them, rather than lie; for it was better for posterity to be ignorant of something, than to be wrongly informed. At the very beginning of his history, Pachymeres also expounds his method of collecting evidence. He does not rely merely on hearsay; he writes of the things he himself saw, or heard about from participants whose stories have been checked against the evidence of others.[5] For the most part Pachymeres is able to keep his pledge. Compared to Gregoras, the other Byzantine historian who wrote about the same period, Pachymeres is a more accurate historian, with better critical judgment.

In a way, the times made it easier for Pachymeres to keep his promise of impartiality. For he was not singing the praise of a period or of a man. He could not—the period was inglorious and full of disasters, Michael VIII he disagreed with, and Andronicus II was no hero. Thus, Pachymeres' history is no eulogy and it is hardly a polemic— except perhaps in some passages concerned with doctrine. He was painfully aware of the decline of the empire, and of the inadequacy of its leaders. He respected the church and the emperor as institutions; yet he often exposed the mistakes of one or the other. Although almost every page noted the disasters that befell the Byzantine state, he had great faith in and touching love for his compatriots. Writing of the demands of the people of Constantinople that the fleet be rebuilt (1305), at a time when everyone saw disaster at the gates of the city, he insisted that the empire had not lost its strength; the spirit was there, whole and wholesome, and the weakness of the members of the body politic, especially the army, could easily be corrected.[6]

Pachymeres is not an easy historian to read. The very advantages of his work contribute to its weaknesses. Because he is not writing of one set of events, his account tends to be disjointed. He often interrupts his narrative to introduce a wholly new subject, and

---

4. Georgii Pachymeres, *De Michaele et Andronico Palaeologis libri tredecim*, ed. I. Bekker (Bonn, 1835), in two volumes. The few details of his life are given in Pachymeres, I, 11. On Pachymeres' historical work, see also V. Laurent, "Les manuscrits de l'histoire byzantine de Georges Pachymère," *Byzantion*, 5 (1929–1930), 129–205; V. Laurent, "L'histoire byzantine de Georges Pachymère. Un nouveau témoin, "l'Athén. Gennad. 40," *Byzantion*, 6 (1931), 355–367; V. Laurent, "Deux nouveaux manuscrits de "l'histoire byzantine" de Georges Pachymère," *Byzantion*, 11 (1936), 43–47. He held the ecclesiastical office of protekdikos, and the state office of dikaiophylax.

5. Pachymeres, I, 11–13.

6. Ibid., II, 545–546.

then sometimes summarizes developments which took place years before, without warning the reader. At times one year runs into the next without his taking any notice of the fact. His difficult language compounds the problem. The reader often feels lost, especially in matters of chronology, and many historians have been misled. Fortunately, today we have the work of three historians who have tried to correct the chronology of Pachymeres, as it was established by Possinus, the first editor of the history.[7] This work has not yet finished. The traditional dating of several events has been corrected in other parts of this book.

The second part of Pachymeres' work, the seven books on Andronicus II, is more concerned with internal affairs and with developments in Asia Minor and the Balkans than with relations with the West. This is partly the result of the growing isolation of the empire, and partly a reflection of Pachymeres' interests. We gather information nowhere else available about major and minor controversies within the church, about conditions in Asia Minor, about Byzantine relations with the Serbs, the Bulgarians, the states of Epirus and Thessaly, about the state of the Byzantine army and finances. But there is virtually nothing on Byzantine relations with the principality of Achaia. There is but limited information on Andronicus' various matrimonial negotiations and alliances with western Europe. Pachymeres does not even mention the treaties with the Venetians and the Genoese. On the other hand, he does give some information on the Venetian–Byzantine war of 1296–1302, and the details he provides on the attitude and activities of the Genoese in the empire, and on the Byzantine reaction, are very important.

Much of the last two books of Pachymeres' history is concerned with the Catalan expedition. Since we have other sources of information for this enterprise, we can check both Pachymeres' account and his reliability as a historian. On the whole, Pachymeres is well informed about the leaders and the progress of the Catalan campaign. For instance, he gives a fairly detailed and accurate account of the origins and past history of Roger de Flor, as well as of the war between Aragon and the Angevins of Naples—unlike Gregoras, who makes a number of mistakes. He even warns the reader that he is not an expert on European affairs, and if what he reports is inaccurate, the blame is not his, but belongs to the "report" (φήμη) he is following.

Despite the fact that Pachymeres is very clearly anti-Latin, he speaks of Roger de Flor's valor and of his prowess in war. He gives a long account of the Catalan depredations in Asia Minor and Thrace; in this he conflicts with the other major source, the Catalan Muntaner, who depicts his fellow-countrymen as a well-behaved army, until the iniquity of the Greeks forced them to break faith. I have had occasion to discuss in context which of the differing accounts I have followed. I should, however, note here that I believe Pachymeres gives a more complete and satisfactory account of the over-all behavior of the Catalan Company.[8] To Pachymeres also we must look for most of the details of the Catalan campaign in Thrace, which Muntaner treats very summarily,

7. Possinus' chronological notes and other notes have been incorporated in the Bonn edition. His observations on chronology are on pp. 689–766 of vol. 1, and pp. 776–870 of vol. 2. Cf. G. Caro, "Zur Chronologie der drei letzten Bücher des Pachymeres," *BZ* 6 (1897), 114–125; Pia Schmidt, "Zur Chronologie von Pachymeres, Andronikos L. II–VIII," *BZ* 51 (1958), 82–86; R. Verpeaux, "Notes chronologiques sur les livres II et III du De Andronico Palaeologo de Georges Pachymère," *REB.*, 17 (1959), 168–174. Verpeaux' dates are, on the whole, more reliable than Pia Schmidt's.

8. A. Rubió y Lluch, *Espedición*, pp. 50–57, claims that Pachymeres' account is overly biased, and that Muntaner was closer to the truth. He does admit, however, that Roger de Flor is presented as a more varied and real personality in Pachymeres than in Muntaner's glorified description: Rubió y Lluch, *Paquimeres y Muntaner*, p. 15. On several major points, the documents published in Rubió y Lluch's *Diplomatari*, support the evidence of Pachymeres rather than of Muntaner.

and for which we have limited documentary information. It is a great pity that Pachymeres should end his history in the early summer of 1307. Since Muntaner also stops his detailed account of the exploits of the Catalan campaign at approximately the same time, we are reduced to insufficient and very fragmented accounts for the campaigns of Macedonia and Thessaly.

For the purposes of this work, I consider Pachymeres as one of the best sources of the period, certainly the best narrative source. He does make mistakes, either out of ignorance or out of carelessness, and I have noted these wherever I found them. On the whole, however, he is very reliable. I should perhaps, make a note here of the use I have made of reported speeches of various personages. Ever since Thucydides, historians have reported orations which they never heard, but which serve to liven the narrative, to present the issues or to illustrate the character of the orator. I believe that most of the speeches recorded by Pachymeres were probably accurately reported. This is particularly so with Andronicus' speeches, for Pachymeres was close to the emperor, and probably heard himself or heard from many witnesses what Andronicus had to say to the prelates, to the Catalan leaders, to the people or the notables of Constantinople. Equally trustworthy are the reported words of the patriarchs John XII and Athanasios I, as well as those of various persons who spoke in church assemblies.

Apart from his history, Pachymeres has left many other works, some of which have been published. Among his nonhistorical writings, there are works on philosophy, poetry, and astronomy and some unpublished letters. He wrote a study on the quadrivium, arithmetic, music, geometry, and astronomy, thirteen studies on various subjects, and a work on rhetoric.[9] He died sometime after the summer of 1307, and his student, Manuel Philes, wrote a lament on the occasion of his death.

Nicephorus Gregoras is the second major Byzantine historian of the period. Perhaps because his career was more varied than that of Pachymeres, and his life more interesting, his work has been studied by modern historians, especially by R. Guilland.[10] Thus, he is less of an unknown quantity than Pachymeres. There is, however, still the need for a short discussion of his historical work, because most studies of his life have concentrated on the period 1330–1360, when he became involved in religious controversies.

Gregoras was born in Heracleia, a town in Paphlagonia, probably in 1295. He studied first under his uncle, Bishop John of Heracleia. At the end of 1315 Gregoras arrived at Constantinople, where he had the good fortune to study under two of the most learned men of his time, the patriarch John XIII Glykys (1315–1319), who taught him philo-

9. Σύνταγμα τῶν τεσσάρων μαθημάτων, ἀριθμητικῆς, μουσικῆς, γεωμετρίας καὶ ἀστρονομίας, published in J. F. Boissonade, *Anecdota Graeca e codicibus regiis*, V (Paris, 1833), 350ff; J. F. Boissonade, *Pachymeris declamationes XIII* (Paris, 1848). For further bibliography on Pachymeres' works, see Krumbacher, *Handbuch*, pp. 290–291, and Moravcsik, *Byzantinoturcica*, I, 280–282.

10. Rodolphe Guilland, *Essai sur Nicéphore Grégoras; l'homme et l'oeuvre* (Paris, 1926); R. Guilland, *La correspondance de Nicéphore Grégoras* (Paris, 1927). On Gregoras, see also Krumbacher, *Handbuch*, pp. 293–298; Colonna, *Storici bizantini*, pp. 58–60; Moravcsik, *Byzantinoturcica*, I, 450–453; S. G. Mercati, "Sulle poesie di Niceforo Gregora," *Bessarione*, 34 (1918), 90–98; S. G. Mercati, "Nota all' epigramma di Niceforo Gregora in morte del Metochita," *Bessarione*, 34 (1918), 237–238; St. Bezdechi, "Le portrait de Théodore Métochite par Nicéphore Grégoras," *Mélanges d'histoire générale* (Cluj, 1927), pp. 57–67; N. A. Bees, «Κριτικὰ καὶ διορθωτικὰ εἰς Βυζαντιακὰ κείμενα. Εἰς Νικηφόρου Γρηγορᾶ Ῥωμαϊκὴν Ἱστορίαν,» *Viz. Vrem.* 20 (1913), 67; T. Hart, "Nicephorus Gregoras, Historian of the Hesychast Controversy," *Journal of Ecclesiastical History*, 2 (1951), 169–179; A. Rubió y Lluch, "Nicéforo Gregoras y la expedición de los Catalanes á Oriente," *Museo Balear de Historia y Literatura, Ciencias y Artes*, 2d series, II (1885), 401–408, 522–528, 561–574, 601–611 (a short introduction on Gregoras and translation into Spanish of the chapters dealing with the Catalan expedition); Rubió y Lluch, *Espedició*, pp. 57–65.

logy, and Theodore Metochites, who instructed him in philosophy and astronomy. He always retained his connection with Metochites, who left him the monastery of Chora (Khariye-djami), and his library.[11] Gregoras' friends moved in high circles and he was himself presented to Andronicus II in 1322 or thereabouts. Andronicus admired Gregoras, and Gregoras, in return, remained loyal to the emperor even during the civil war with Andronicus III (1321–1322, 1327–1328). His most important activities after Andronicus II's death had to do with religious controversies; he opposed the ideas of Barlaam and, later, of Gregory Palamas. He was forced by the emperor John Cantacuzenus (1347–1354) to immure himself in a monastery, but was released in 1355, when John V Palaeologus had come to power. He died in 1360.

Nicephorus Gregoras was a very well-educated man; indeed, Krumbacher has called him the greatest polymath of the fourteenth century, and later historians have followed Krumbacher's judgment. His writings include works on rhetoric, philosophy, astronomy (he tried to reform the calendar in 1326), grammar and, history.[12] For all his great knowledge, Gregoras is less of a historian than George Pachymeres. His *Roman history*, in thirty-seven books, covers the period 1204–1359. For our purposes, the most important books are the first nine, dealing with the years 1204–1331. The first seven books are based on the accounts of Akropolites and Pachymeres, whom he summarizes as well as completes.[13] Gregoras must also have had access to other, supplementary works, because at times he introduces details which are absent from Pachymeres. In general, his account up to 1307 is of only limited value, for we have the much more detailed and accurate work of Pachymeres. Gregoras becomes indispensable for the years after 1307, when Pachymeres' history stops; the next important historian, John Cantacuzenus, does not deal in any detail with the years before 1321.

Like Pachymeres, Gregoras has an introduction on the nature and importance of history; he also writes about it in later chapters. Like Pachymeres, he pledges himself to impartiality. But, even in the first seven books, he succeeds less well than Pachymeres. For he takes a didactic view of history. History not only teaches us what has happened, but enables us to predict the future and shows us the futility of evil, which in the long-run finds its punishment.[14] This is a dangerous concept of history; it tempts the historian to present such a view of events as will help his case. Gregoras does sometimes succumb to this temptation, as well as to that of oversimplification. When he discusses the events or developments of the years 1204–1320, he often speaks in broad generalizations. These are not the result of reasoned synthesis; they more often are due to carelessness, and to his desire to present a large picture without taking into account the complexities of the subject he is treating. His disrespect for detail often leads him to make mistakes which could have been avoided. On the whole, I have used Gregoras very cautiously, and I have usually found that when there are discrepancies between Gregoras and Pachymeres, Pachymeres is right.

11. Guilland, *Grégoras*, pp. 4–7; V. Grecu, "Das Geburtsjahr des byzantinischen Geschicht-schreibers Nikephoros Gregoras," *Académie Roumaine, Bulletin de la section historique*, 27 (1946), 56–61; Moravcsik, *Byzantinoturcica*, I, 450–451; Krumbacher, *Handbuch*, pp. 293–298.

12. Krumbacher, *Handbuch*, p. 294; Moravcsik, *Byzantinoturcica*, I, 451. The most detailed bibliography of Gregoras' published and unpublished works is to be found in Guilland, *Grégoras*, pp. xxxi–xxxv. Further bibliography in Moravcsik, *Byzantinoturcica*, I, 450–453.

13. N. Iorga, "Médaillons," pp. 293–296, is quite wrong in thinking that Gregoras did not know the work of Pachymeres.

14. Nicephori Gregorae, *Byzantina Historia*, I (Bonn, 1929), 3–6; II (Bonn, 1830), 573–576. On this, see Guilland, *Grégoras*, 228–257. Guilland takes a dim view of Gregoras as a historian, for reasons slightly different from my own. Guilland, however, was mostly looking at Gregoras' discussion of events after 1320. Notice also that Guilland does not see much difference between Gregoras' and Pachymeres' concept of history.

Gregoras' history is not well-organized, but because the period before 1320 is treated so summarily, his narrative is easier to follow than that of Pachymeres. His language is also less tortuous than Pachymeres', and his chronology somewhat easier to determine. It should be added that Gregoras did not have the time to finish or polish his historical work. But his incapacity for original historical thinking, his banality and frequent superficiality of judgment could not have been corrected by any amount of revision.

John Cantacuzenus who, as John VI, was emperor for seven years (1347–1354), wrote the history of his times after his retirement from office.[15] His *Histories* is an elegant piece of work. Cantacuzenus took pride in his classical education, and he consciously emulated the style of Thucydides. Unfortunately, we shall never know whether he imitated the substance as well as the style. His description of the plague of 1348 is heavily indebted to Thucydides' description of the plague which struck Athens in 430–429 B.C. Cantacuzenus' discussion of the evils of the civil war between Andronicus II and Andronicus III (1321–1328) and of the revolution of the Zealots in Thessalonica contains thoughts and phrases reminiscent of Thucydides' description of the revolution at Corcyra (427 B.C.) and its effects. Was Cantacuzenus drawing a valid comparison, or was he merely carried away by his admiration for Thucydides? The same questions arise with regard to the long and learned orations, written in Attic Greek, which Cantacuzenus constantly reports. They may be literary exercises, or they may truly indicate the speaker's thoughts; it is difficult to decide which is the case.

Cantacuzenus' history begins in 1320. It is the best single source for the civil war, despite the fact that he had a strong bias in favor of Andronicus III. As far as foreign policy is concerned, he gives virtually no information. He had little connection with the government of Constantinople until 1328, when his friend, Andronicus III, became sole emperor, so he could have but limited knowledge of Andronicus II's diplomatic maneuvers. Besides, Cantacuzenus' history, especially in the first book (1320–1328), is an apologia for his imperial friend, and for himself. Very little else is allowed to intrude into Cantacuzenus' effort to convince posterity that right was on his side during the civil war. This biased account is balanced by the equally biased account of Gregoras, the supporter of Andronicus II, who wrote the history of the civil war from the viewpoint of Constantinople.

Turning from the work of Byzantine historians to other contemporary literary sources, the obvious starting point is the work of Theodore Metochites. He was one of the main literary and political figures of the early fourteenth century. From an unhappy youth, tainted with the stigma of his father's unionist policy, Metochites rose to the highest state office, becoming secretary of the private purse in 1295–1296, secretary of the treasury in 1305–1306, and megas logothete (the equivalent of the first minister of the state) in 1321. His literary and scientific work (he was one of the best astronomers of his time) is large and varied. Fortunately, we now have the excellent book of Ihor Ševčenko on Metochites and Choumnos, to which I have had frequent occasion to refer.[16] For our

15. Cantacuzenus' historical work has been published in the Bonn series: *Ioannis Cantacuzeni eximperatoris Historiarum Libri IV*, ed. L. Schopen, in 3 vols. (Bonn, 1828, 1831, 1832). On his life and work see V. Parisot, *Cantacuzène, homme d'état et historien* (Paris, 1845). On his life see also Günther Weiss, *Joannes Kantakuzenos—Aristokrat, Staatsmann, Kaiser und Mönch—in der Gesellschaftsentwincklung von Byzanz im 14. Jahrhundert* (Wiesbaden, 1969). D. M. Nicol's *The Byzantine Family of Kantakouzenos (Cantacuzenus) ca. 1100–1460*, Dumbarton Oaks Studies, XI (Washington, 1968) contains an excellent bibliography. For Cantacuzenus' Thucydidian style, see Parisot, *Cantacuzène*, pp. 6–14.

16. See Ševčenko, *Métochite et Choumnos*. On Metochites, see also H.-G. Beck, *Theodoros Metochites, Die Krise des Byzantinischen Weltbildes im 14 Jahrhundert* (Munich, 1952); H. Hunger,

purposes, Metochites' two most important works are his two orations to Andronicus II, which provide unique insights into the condition of Asia Minor, and into Andronicus' Anatolian policy in the late thirteenth century. These are unpublished, save for one excerpt published by K. Sathas. Sathas has also published Metochites' account of his embassy to Serbia in 1298–1299, a valuable source for conditions in Serbia and for developments in Macedonia, so often disregarded by historians who lived in Constantinople.[17] In addition to prose writings, Metochites has left us an autobiographical poem, written in a language and style which imitate Homer.[18]

Metochites became one of Andronicus' main advisers from the time when he was sent to Thessalonica to watch over the behavior of the Empress Irene (1303 or 1304). Unfortunately, he was no politician, nor was he an attractive public figure. He fell with Andronicus II in 1328.

Thomas Magister who, on becoming a monk, took the name of Theodulos, is a particularly important source for our period. Thomas was, first and foremost, a philologist, and moved in the literary circle of Theodore Metochites and Nicephorus Gregoras. He has left us a number of letters, orations and philological works.[19] For the historian, his most important contributions consist of one letter and three orations. Thomas apparently lived in Thessalonica for a long time. For this reason, he was able to give to his friends in Constantinople, to the philosopher Joseph in particular, information about the Catalan attack against Thessalonica, in 1308.[20] It is unfortunate that he was interested in style as much as in content and so his letter is a literary exercise as well as a description. Even so, we glean some information about the state of mind of the inhabitants of Thessalonica, and about the steps they took to defend their city.

To the same period belongs an oration to Andronicus II on behalf of the general Chandrenos, whose success against the Catalans aroused the envy of certain persons in Constantinople who probably accused him of treason. Thomas then wrote this oration in Chandrenos' defense.[21] It must have been written sometime after 1310, because the latest developments it describes took place in that year. It may have been written quite a few years after 1310, because Thomas, referring to Chandrenos' Thessaly campaign of 1309, said "even up to now the Thessaliots sing of this [his exploits]."[22] This would indicate that some time had passed between 1309 and the date the oration was written.

Thomas Magister also wrote two orations on the duties of the emperor and those of his subjects.[23] I have been unable to date these. The frequent references to the

---

"Theodorus Metochites als Vorläufer des Humanismus in Byzanz," *BZ* 45 (1952), 4–19; J. Verpeaux, "Le *cursus honorum* de Théodore Métochite," *REB* 18 (1960), 195–198.

17. The βασιλικὸς α΄ is found in the Cod. Vindobon. Philol. Gr. 95, fols. 81ro–96ro; the βασιλικὸς β΄ in the same codex, fols. 145vo–158ro; Cf. K. Sathas, Μεσαιωνικὴ Βιβλιοθήκη, I (Venice, 1872). Professors Ševčenko and Hunger are planning to publish the imperial orations. The embassy to Serbia is in Μεσαιωνικὴ Βιβλιοθήκη, I, 154–193.

18. Letter A in Max Treu, *Dichtungen des gross-Logotheten Theodorus Metochites*, Programm des Victoria-Gymnasiums zu Potsdam., Ostern, 1895 (Potsdam, 1895).

19. For a bibliography of Thomas' works, see Krumbacher, *Handbuch*, pp. 548–550; Moravcsik, *Byzantinoturcica*, I, 548.

20. Published in Boissonade, *Anecdota Graeca*, II, 212–228.

21. Published in ibid., II, 188–211.

22. Ibid., II, 199. On Chandrenos, see above, "The Catalans in Athens," in Chapter VII.

23. Published in J. P. Migne, *Patrologia Graeca*, 145 (Paris, 1865 and 1904), cols. 447–548. See G. Kyriakides, Θωμᾶς ὁ Μάγιστρος καὶ Ἰσοκράτης, diss., Erlangen, 1893; also, Karl Krumbacher's review in *BZ* 5 (1896), 212.

unreliability of mercenaries may indicate that they were written after the Catalan expedition, which, more than anything else, proved this point. On the other hand, Thomas makes no mention of the civil war which erupted in 1321, as I think he would have done had he been writing after 1321. The orations are written in a style reminiscent of Isocrates, and some of the ideas expressed may also seem at first glance simply to copy the political thinking of ancient Greece. I am referring particularly to Thomas' conviction that the cities of the empire should follow the examples set by Athens and Sparta. However, in the early fourteenth century, some Byzantine cities, especially those of Macedonia and Greece, attained a high degree of independence, which may have recalled classical prototypes to an educated man. On the whole, Thomas was probably giving voice and coherent expression to ideas and practices which were current at his time. The two political orations provide very important information about administrative practices at the time of Andronicus II.

There is a more specialized Byzantine source of information about the Catalan attack on Mount Athos and Thessalonica. That is the biography of St. Savvas the Young, written by the patriarch of Constantinople Philotheus Kokkinos (1353–1354, 1364–1376).[24] The patriarch, who had been abbot of the monastery of Lavra, is a well-known hagiographer, although his biography of St. Savvas has not been noted by Krumbacher or Moravcsik.[25] St. Savvas was a monk in Mt. Athos, and most of his activity falls in the years after 1320. During his youth, he lived through the Catalan attack on Macedonia, and he returned to his native city of Thessalonica for the duration of the Catalan attack on Mt. Athos. His biographer noted this, and we are indebted to him for our meager information on Andronicus' efforts to defend the Holy Mountain.

Another particularly important though rarely used ecclesiastical source is the correspondence of the patriarch of Constantinople Athanasios I (October 1289–October 1293, June 1303–September 1309).[26] His character, as well as the importance of his correspondence, has already been discussed in the text of this book. A biography, probably of the fourteenth century, gives us the details of his life as well as information about conditions in Constantinople during Athanasios' times.[27] Although Guilland and Bănescu have studied Athanasios' work and published their conclusions as well as summaries of some of the letters, most of Athanasios' correspondence has, as yet, remained unpublished.[28]

The poems of Manuel Philes, who was born in Ephesus and lived in Constantinople, ca. 1275–1345, cast some light on the times in which he lived. In his youth he was a

24. Published by A. Papadopoulos-Kerameus: «Τοῦ πατριάρχου Κωνσταντινουπόλεως κυρῦο Φιλοθέου Βίος καὶ πολιτεία τοῦ ὁσίου καὶ θεοφόρου Πατρὸς ἡμῶν Σάβα τοῦ Νέου.» Ἀνάλεκτα Ἱεροσολυμιτικῆς Σταχυολογίας, V (St. Petersburg, 1898).

25. Krumbacher, *Handbuch*, pp. 107–109, 204–205.

26. On Athanasios' life and work, see N. Bănescu, "Le Patriarche Athanase Ier et Andronic II Paléologue: État religieux, politique et social de l'Empire," *Académie Roumaine. Bulletin de la section historique*, 23 (1942), 28–56; R. Guilland, "La correspondance inédite d'Athanase, Patriarche de Constantinople, (1289–1293; 1304–1310)," *Mélanges Charles Diehl* (Paris, 1930), I, 121–140.

27. Published by H. Delehaye, "La vie d'Athanase, Patriarche de Constantinople," *Mélanges d'Archéologie et d'histoire de l'école française de Rome*, 17 (1897), 39–75; see also «Βίος καὶ πολιτεία Ἀθανασίου Α', Οἰκουμενικοῦ Πατριάρχου, συγγραφεὶς ὑπὸ Ἰωσὴφ Καλοθέτου μοναχοῦ,» Θρᾳκικά, 13 (1940), 56–107.

28. A few of his letters have been published in Migne, *PG* 142 (Paris, 1885), cols. 471–528, and in G. Rallis and M. Potlis, Σύνταγμα τῶν θείων καὶ ἱερῶν κανόνων, V (Athens, 1855), 121–126. See also Laiou, "Provisioning," pp. 108–113, and Laiou, "Theodore Palaeologus," pp. 404–410. Mrs. Alice-Mary Talbot is preparing a philological edition and translation.

friend of Pachymeres, and he wrote a poem on the occasion of Pachymeres' death. He traveled extensively in the Orient, in Persia, Arabia, and India. In 1305 he was sent by Andronicus II to the king of Georgia, to request help against the Catalans. Philes' poems, as published by E. Miller and A. E. Martin, have yielded useful information about such matters as communications between Constantinople and Asia Minor, the Byzantine campaign in Bulgaria in 1304, the siege of Adrianople by the Catalans. Unfortunately, however, the details he gives are not always correct, and his account of the siege of Adrianople is most probably taken from Pachymeres' history.[29]

Byzantine diplomatic sources have yielded less material on Andronicus' foreign policy than have the Byzantine narrative sources already discussed and the collections of European documents. The texts of Byzantine treaties with Venice, Genoa, and Aragon, published by F. Miklosich and J. Müller, are valuable. So are a number of chrysobulls granting privileges to the king of Serbia, to the Empress Irene, to the church and commune of Ioannina, all published in the same collection. On the whole, however, most of the surviving Byzantine documents of this period are chiefly important for the internal history of Byzantium, for they are *praktika*, or grants of land to churches, monasteries, and individuals. Thus, although some pertinent information can be drawn from them, they have not been used extensively. Several very important documents have survived only through the narrative sources in which they are mentioned; Franz Dölger's *Regesten der Kaiserurkunden des Oströmischen Reiches* has been an indispensable guide to these, as well as to most other imperial documents, wherever they may be found.[30]

The western sources for the period are many and varied; most of them are too well known to merit a detailed description here. I shall divide them into three groups, according to the use I have made of them in this work.

The first group includes French, Italian, and Spanish annals and chronicles which occasionally yield limited but useful information about relations between Byzantium and the West. The information from the annals is sometimes biased and almost always incomplete. It has to be supplemented from Byzantine sources and from western diplomatic sources, since treaties and their terms are only rarely discussed in the annals. The French chronicles have been used only sparingly, in connection with the plans of Charles of Valois and Philip of Taranto, and in connection with French crusading plans during the reigns of Philip V the Tall (1316–1322) and Charles IV (1322–1328).

The second group consists of narrative sources with a particular subject or interest. Of these, the most important has been Ramon Muntaner's chronicle of the Catalan

29. Above, "Diplomatic Efforts," in Chapter VI; Krumbacher, *Handbuch.* 774–780; Moravcsik, Byzantinoturcica, I, 416–417; E. Miller, *Manuelis Philae Carmina*, in 2 vols. (Paris, 1855–1857); A. E. Martini, "Manuelis Philae Carmina Inedita," *Atti della Reale Academia di Archeologia, Lettere e belle Arti*, 20 (1900), Supplement. Cf. E. Kurtz, "Emendationsvorschläge zu den Gedichten des Manuel Philes," *Byzantinisch-Neugriechische Jahrbücher*, 4 (1923), 51–76; N. Bees, «Κριτικὰ καὶ διορθωτικὰ εἰς Βυζαντιακὰ κείμενα. Εἰς Μανουὴλ Φιλῆν,» *Viz. Vrem*, 20 (1913), 66–67. On his poems concerning the Bulgarian campaign, see Chr. Loparev, *Vizantiiskii poet' Manuil' Fil', k' istorii volgarii XIII–XIV v.* (Petersburg, 1891); K. Jireček, "Die bulgarischen Burgen bei Manuel Philes," *Sitzungsberichte der philosoph.-hist. Klasse der K. Akademie der Wiss.* (Vienna, 1897), pp. 77–85; cf. above, "Toward a Byzantine Defense," Chapter VI.

30. F. Miklosich and J. Müller, *Acta et Diplomata Graeca medii Aevi*, in 6 vols. (Vienna, 1860–1890); F. Dölger, *Regesten der Kaiserurkunden des Oströmischen Reiches*, I (1924), II (1925), III (1932), IV (1960), V (1965), especially vol. IV.

campaign in Byzantium.[31] Muntaner was a Spanish nobleman whose ancestors participated in the Aragonese wars of conquest against the Muslims of Spain. He wrote his account of the Catalan expedition at Valencia in 1325, when he was already a fairly old man. Because over twenty years had passed from the beginning of the expedition, he naturally made mistakes. It is a tribute to Muntaner that his account of facts, if not his interpretation, usually agrees with that of Pachymeres or with the information gleaned from contemporary documents. The interpretation, however, is his own, and it is usually biased. Unlike Pachymeres, Muntaner is writing a *Res Gestae*, a book with a hero, first Roger de Flor and then the infante Ferran of Mallorca. Only once did Roger take the wrong decision—it was fatal to him—and not once did he behave in an unchivalrous way. The Catalan Company also is presented as a body of loyal men—at least until Berengar de Rocafort takes over the leadership—and only rarely appear as the group of fearsome, self-interested mercenaries that they were. The Byzantines, on the other hand, are viewed from the standpoint of traditional western prejudices and charged with cowardice, duplicity, arrogance, lack of loyalty to friend and foe—in short, they are men whom it would be proper for a Christian and a knight to fight. Only Michael IX is admired as a good knight, but then he is so totally defeated by the Catalans that his worth only enhances the valor of the Company.

For all that, Muntaner's chronicle is an indispensable source for the years of the Catalan campaign. It is also more pleasant reading than the Byzantine historians of the same period. Muntaner writes in a simple narrative style with very few interruptions and digressions. He gives an almost strictly chronological account of events, and his unassuming language is refreshing after the learned perorations of Pachymeres.

The great body of literature usually described as crusading propaganda has not been used extensively. For we have been concerned here with political plans and alliances, and the ideas of crusading propagandists have seemed relevant only when they influenced the actions of political leaders. Thus, the theories of Pierre Dubois have been discussed in the text because they appealed to Philip IV of France and to his brother, Charles of Valois. On the other hand, the ideas of Guillaume d'Adam and Fidenzio of Padua have only been mentioned in passing.[32]

Marino Sanudo Torsello the Elder (ca. 1270–ca. 1343) stands out as a particularly important advocate of the crusade. He was a Venetian of good family, who had traveled extensively in both the Greek and the Latin parts of the Byzantine Empire and who, unlike other crusading propagandists, had a thorough knowledge of the empire.[33] Indeed, he rightly considered himself an expert in the affairs of the East. He also had family ties with the Sanudi of Naxos. Marino was, first and foremost, an ardent advocate of the interests of Venice. For this reason, his work is particularly interesting as a mirror of Venetian aims in the Levant. After 1323 he became more friendly toward Byzantium,

31. Lady Goodenough, *The Chronicle of Muntaner*, in 2 vols. (London, 1920, 1921). On Muntaner, see Rubió y Lluch, *Paquimeres y Muntaner*, passim; N. Iorga, "Ramon Muntaner et l'Empire byzantin," *Revue historique du sud-est Européen*, 4 (1927), 325–355, is a somewhat uncritical discussion of Muntaner's account of the Catalan expedition. On Muntaner see also A. de Bofarull y Broca, *Ramon Muntaner, gueriero y cronista* (Barcelona, 1883); E. Aguiló, "Alguna noticia més sobre En Ramon Muntaner, i sa família," *Revista de Bibliografia catalana*, 3 (1903), 26–38; C. Rahola, *En Ramon Muntaner; L'home. La Cronica* (Barcelona, 1922); L. Serra-longa, and J. M. Casacuberta, "Index del noms propis de la Crònica d'En Muntaner," *Estudis Universitaris Catalans*, 8 (1914), 103–147. In Chapters V, VI and VII, above, I have had occasion to evaluate particular passages of Muntaner's Chronicle.

32. Above, "Charles of Valois, Venice, and Byzantium," Chapter VII.

33. On Sanudo, see A. Magnocavallo, *Marin Sanudo il Vecchio e il suo Progetto di Crociata* (Bergamo, 1901).

and advocated friendship and common action instead of war and conquest.[34] His voluminous correspondence is one of the very few sources for the negotiations between Andronicus II and Pope John XXII concerning the union of the Greek and Roman churches (1324–1327). Of his other writings, the *Istoria del Regno di Romania*, whose importance as a source for the history of Frankish Greece was first noticed by Karl Hopf, gives some information on the reign of Andronicus II. His *Fragmentum*, now recognized as a continuation of Villehardouin, is also useful.[35]

Among the minor crusading propagandists is the anonymous friar who wrote, ca. 1308, a description of eastern Europe.[36] The author, probably a Frenchman, had lived in Serbia and Constantinople, and probably traveled in Asia Minor. His book consists of geographical and historical notes on the countries and the people of eastern Europe. It also contains advice to Charles of Valois, on his future conquest of the empire. Thus, although the author is a minor figure as a crusading propagandist, his knowledge of the affairs of eastern Europe makes his work valuable. He has the usual western prejudices which, by the fourteenth century, are probably just *lieux communs*, endlessly repeated: the Greeks are weak, effeminate, and insincere. The others, Serbs, Bulgarians, are barbarians. The East must return to obedience to the Catholic church. In spite of this banality, he does give us some interesting information.

The author has not dated his *Descriptio*. The editor, Dr. Olgierd Górka, suggests the date February–March 1308, chiefly because the author says that the king of Serbia wanted to give his daughter to a son of Charles of Valois.[37] Stephen Uroš II and Charles of Valois concluded a treaty to that effect on March 27, 1308. But I see no reason to suppose, with Górka, that the book was written before, rather than after the treaty. Górka also indicates that the anonymous author refers to the battle of Bapheus in Asia Minor, as having taken place seven years before. Górka adopts the date 1301 for the battle of Bapheus, but since then the correct date has been found to be 1302. Finally, Górka notes as a discrepancy the author's mention of the conquest of Rhodes by the Hospitallers, which Górka places in 1309. Rhodes was taken on August 15, 1308, and there is no discrepancy if we accept late 1308 as the date the book was written.[38]

One unpublished source presents great interest. That is the "Enseignements" of Theodore Palaeologus, marquis of Montferrat, which was written in Italian and has survived in a French translation, in the Cod. Brux. 11042, fols. 1ro-95ro.[39] He returned

---

34. On the connection between Marino Sanudo's attitude toward Byzantium, and official Venetian policy in the 1320's and early 1330's, see my article, "Marino Sanudo Torsello, Byzantium and the Turks: The Background to the Anti-Turkish League of 1332–1334," *Speculum*, XLV (1970), 374–392.

35. The *Istoria* has been published in K. Hopf, *Chroniques Gréco-romanes* (Berlin, 1873), pp. 99–170. The *Fragmentum* was first published by C. DuFresne du Cange, *Histoire de Constantinople sous les Empereurs français* (Paris, 1657), pp. 230ff, and subsequently by J. A. Buchon, *Recherches et matériaux pour servir à une histoire de la domination Française au XIIIe, XIVe, et XVe siècles, dans les provinces démembrées de l'Empire Grec à la suite de la quatrième croisade* (Paris, 1840), II, 9ff, and by Hopf, *Chroniques Gréco-romanes*, pp. 171–174. It has been republished, with an introduction and notes, by R. L. Wolff, "The So-Called 'Fragmentum' of Marino Sanudo Torsello," *Joshua Starr Memorial Volume* (New York, 1956), pp. 149–159. Wolff proves that the 'Fragmentum' is a continuation of Villehardouin.

36. Published by Olgierd Górka, *Anonymi Descriptio Europae Orientalis* (Cracow, 1916). See also, N. Iorga, "Encore un traité de croisade, 1308," *Bulletin de l'Institut pour l'étude de l'Europe sud-orientale* (1921), pp. 59–64.

37. Górka, *Descriptio*, pp. iv–vi.

38. Ibid., pp. vii–viii. Cf. above, Chapter IV, "Asia Minor," and V. Grumel, *La Chronologie. Bibliothèque byzantine* (Paris, 1958), p. 402.

39. On this, see J. Bastin, "Le traité de Théodore Paléologue dans la traduction de Jean de Vignai," *Études romanes dédiées à Mario Roques*, (Paris, 1946), pp. 78–88; C. Knowles, "Les enseignements de Théodore Paléologue," *Byz.* 22 (1952), 389–394.

to Byzantium from Montferrat on at least two occasions, in 1316–1318, and in 1325.[40] He has much to tell us about Byzantium during these years, and some of the information he gives is relevant to Andronicus' foreign policy.

In my discussion of the relations between Byzantium, Serbia, and the Catalans (1307–1313), I have made use of the work of Danilo, abbot of the Serbian monastery of Chilandar, on Mount Athos.[41] Danilo is not very clear about details, and his admiration for the Serbs sometimes leads him to exaggerate grossly their exploits. Since, however, he is one of the few sources we have on the Catalan campaign in Macedonia as well as on Serbian–Byzantine relations in the early fourteenth century, he is quite valuable.

The third group of western sources consists of diplomatic material, much easier of access and better known than the parallel Byzantine sources. It is far more valuable than the western European narrative sources. Diplomatic documents from the Aragonese, Neapolitan, Genoese, Venetian, French, and papal archives have been used extensively. A full bibliography of the diplomatic sources for this work will be found at the end of the book. Of the published sources, particular mention should be made of A. Rubió y Lluch's *Diplomatari de l'Orient Catala, 1302–1409*. Published in 1947, this work includes essential material on the Catalan campaign and on the involvement of the royal houses of Aragon, Sicily, and Mallorca in this enterprise. It contributes new material on the relations between Genoa and Byzantium, and sheds new light on the old information we have from the narrative sources of the Catalan campaign. One can no longer interpret Pachymeres and Muntaner without referring to the documents published in this collection. Furthermore, the old chronology of the Catalan expedition can now be checked and corrected. Rubió y Lluch himself made use of some of these documents while they were still unpublished.

Despite the fact that western diplomatic materials on the whole are very valuable for the period under discussion, a significant lacuna occurs in the Venetian diplomatic sources thus presenting problems to the modern researcher. The most important governmental institution in Venice in the fourteenth century was the Consilium Rogatorum, or Consiglio dei Rogati, later called the senate. The discussions and decisions of the senate are found in three series of documents: the Misti, the Secreti, and the Sindicati, i.e. the decisions of the doge which made mandatory the decisions of the Senate. Of these three series, the Sindicati begin in June 1329, and the Secreti in 1345. The Misti series covers the years 1293–1440, but, unfortunately, most of the texts referring to the period 1293–1332 have been destroyed. We have the full texts of some discussions of the years December 1300–February 1303. For the rest, we have only the captions of the discussions; these do provide a certain amount of information, but have to be used with great caution. The Collegio, also called Signoria and Minor Consiglio, was another important institution of government, and for this period we have some of its deliberations. Finally, the deliberations of the Maggior Consiglio have been published by Cessi, in full where they exist, their captions if only these remain. The greatest loss lies in the destruction of the Misti of the senate, since it was the senate which had jurisdiction over foreign affairs, shipping, trade, and diplomacy.[42]

40. F. Cognasso, "Una crisobolla di Michele IX Paleologo per Theodoro I di Montferrato," *Studi Bizantini*, 2 (1927), 43, 45, and above, Chapter VIII, "The Italian Maritime Cities," in Chapter VIII.

41. Published by Dj. Daničić, *Z̆ivoti kraljeva i archiepiskopa Srpskich, napisao Danilo i Drugi* (Zagreb, 1866); new editions by L. Mirković, *Z̆ivoti kraljeva i archiepiskopa Srpskich* (Belgrade, 1935).

42. The latest, and the best, edition of the Misti of the Senate is by R. Cessi and P. Sambin: *Le deliberazioni del Consiglio dei Rogati (Senato) Serie "mixtorum"*, I (libri I–XIV), Deputazione di

Unpublished Sources

A full bibliography of the diplomatic sources used in this work will be found at the end of the book. I have also used some unpublished material from the French National Archives, especially from the J and JJ series, all concerned with the family affairs of Philip IV of France and of Charles of Valois: Charles's marriage to Catherine of Courtenay, the marriage of Catherine of Valois to Philip of Taranto, Philip IV's support of Charles of Valois' Byzantine ambitions, the crusading plans of Philip IV, Philip V, and Charles IV. Besides giving us valuable information about all these affairs, the French documents illuminate the involvement of French kings in western projects for the reconquest of Constantinople. Philip IV's *vidimus* (reissues of earlier documents) are particularly important by their very nature. Reissued at various times, at the request of the interested parties, they help us to discover the progress of crusading plans at those times.

Storia Patria per le Venezie (Venice, 1960). There is only one series of documents for the deliberations of the Collegio during this period: G. Giomo, *Lettere segrete del Collegio, rectius Minor Consiglio*, in *Miscellanea di storia Veneta*, R. Deputazione di Storia Patria, 3d series, I (1910), 269–403. It covers the years 1308–1310. The deliberations of the Maggior Consiglio have been published by R. Cessi, *Deliberazioni del Maggior Consiglio di Venezia*, in 3 vols. (Bologna, 1931–1950). Summaries of the deliberations of various other instruments of government which have special bearing on Venetian relations with Byzantium and the East are being published by F. Thiriet, *Délibérations des assemblées vénitiennes concernant la Romanie*, I, (1160–1363) (Paris, 1966). His *Régestes des délibérations du Sénat de Venise concernant la Romanie*, I (1329–1399) (Paris, 1958), falls just outside our period.

I. Unpublished Sources

Greek

Athanasios I, Patriarch of Constantinople, letters: Cod. Vat. Gr. 2219, fols. 1ro–274ro, esp. fols. 1ro–89vo; also contained in Cod. Par. Gr. 137, fols. 16ro–111vo, Cod. Par. S Gr. 516, and Cod. Par. 1351 A.

Gregoras, Nicephorus. Eulogies to Andronicus II: Cod. Par. Gr. 3040, fols. 29ro-vo, 22vo–25vo, 61vo–63vo.

————. Monody to the Emperor Andronicus II: Cod. Par. Gr. 2077, fol. 278ro.
Metochites, Theodore. βασιλικὸς α′, βασιλικὸς β′ (Imperial Orations), in Cod. Vindobon. Philol. Gr. 95. Excerpts have been published by K. Sathas, in Μεσαιωνικὴ Βιβλιοθήκη, I (Venice, 1872).

————. Laments. Cod. Par. Gr. 2003, fols. 56ro–58ro.

Philes, Manuel. Στῖχοι μονῳδικοὶ εἰς τὸν Ἀνδρόνικον τὸν Παλαιολόγον τὸν μετωνομασθέντα Ἀντώνιον (Monody to Andronicus II), Cod. Par. Coisl. 192, fols. 98ro–100ro.

French

A.N. J510 nos. 21, 21bis no. 2, 21 ter: Philip IV to Philip of Taranto (April 1313).

A.N. JJ 268 no. 21: Philip V to Philip of Taranto (October 7, 1321).

Payments to Philip of Taranto: A.N. JJ 268 no. 21, fol. 37vo. JJ 64 no. 222, fol. 125vo–126ro.

A.N. J164 A no. 25, May 21, 1312: Philip IV to Charles of Valois.

A.N. J164 A nos. 26, 27: Philip IV to Charles of Valois (August, 1312).

A.N. J509 no. 16; J509 no. 16bis: Philip IV's confirmation of Clement V's letters to Venice and Genoa (January 14, 1306).

A.N. J510 no. 18: Philip IV, *vidimus* (1313) of the treaty between Charles of Valois and Frederick of Sicily, 1302.

A.N. JJ vol. 46, fol. 18: Philip IV's gift to Charles of Valois; confirmed in June 1310.

A.N. J167 no. 4: marriage settlement of Catherine of Courtenay; confirmed by Philip IV, March 1301: A.N. JJ 38, no. 64.

A.N. J164 A no. 11: Charles of Valois to Philip IV (1301).

A.N. J510, nos. 19, 20: Agreement between Hugues of Burgundy and Catherine of Valois (1303).

A.N. J509, no. 15: *Vidimus* of Philip IV of the treaty of Viterbo.

A.N. J509, no. 12; J512, no. 21: *Vidimus* of Philip IV in 1313 of his *vidimus* of 1306 of the pact between Charles of Valois and Charles II of Italy (March 11, 1302).

A.N. J510 no. 19; JJ 49 no. 59; KK 549 fols. 17ro–19ro: Negotiations on the Valois–Taranto marriage (June 1313). JJ 59 nos. 56, 77, 75, 78: Philip IV's confirmation and approval, 1313.

A.N. R^4 799 vol. I fols. 68ro–vo: Philip IV's testament.

B.N. lat. 9783 fol. 115ro: expenses of Philip IV.

A.N. J510 no. 25^2 no. 1, J510 no. 25^7: John Monomachos to Charles of Valois. Published here, Appendix II.

A.N. J510 no. 25^3 2, J510 no. 25^8 2: Constantine Limbidaris to Catherine of Courtenay; published in Appendix II.

Theodore Palaeologus, Marquis of Montferrat, Enseignements, translated from the Italian by Jean de Vignai: Cod. Brux. 11042 fols. 1ro–95ro.

II. Published Documents

Greek

Boissonade, J. F., ed. *Anecdota Graeca e codicibus regiis.* Vol. II, Paris, 1830; vol. V, Paris, 1833.

———, ed. *Anecdota Nova.* Paris, 1844.

Dölger, Franz. *Facsimiles byzantinischer Kaiserurkunden.* Munich, University Press, 1931.

———. *Regesten der Kaiserurkunden des Oströmischen Reiches.* 5 vols. Munich and Berlin, R. Oldenbourg, 1924, 1925, 1932; C. H. Beck, 1960, 1965.

Mai, Angelo, ed. *Scriptorum Veterum Nova Collectio.* Rome, 1827.

———. *Patrum Novae Bibliothecae.* Vol. VIII, Rome, 1871; vol. X, Rome, 1905.

Miklosich, Franz and J. Müller, eds. *Acta et Diplomata Graeca medii aevi.* 6 vols. Vienna, 1860–1890.

Mošin, Vladimir, ed. *Akti iz Svetogorskich archiva, Spomenik der K. Serb. Akademie.* 2d ser., 70, 5. Belgrade, 1939.

———. *Supplementa ad Acta Graeca Chilandarii.* Ljubljana, 1948.

Ralles, G. A. and M. Potles. Σύνταγμα τῶν Θείων καὶ Ἱερῶν Κανόνων. 6 vols. Athens, 1852–1859.

Sathas, K. N. Μεσαιωνικὴ Βιβλιοθήκη. 7 vols. Venice, 1872–1894.

Zepos, J. and P. Zepos. *Jus Graecoromanum.* 8 vols. Athens, 1934.

Published Documents

French, Italian, Spanish and Slavic

Archivio Storico Italiano. 4th ser. Vols. III, IV.

Belgrano, L. T. "Cinque documenti Genovesi-Orientali," *Atti della Società Ligure di storia patria*, 17 (1885), 221–253.

————. "Prima serie di documenti riguardanti la colonia di Pera," *Atti della Società Ligure di storia patria*, 13 (1877–1884), 99–317.

Bertolotto, G. "Nuova serie di documenti sulle relazioni di Genova coll'impero bizantino," *Atti della Società Ligure di storia patria*, 28 (1898), 344–560. Appendix, Rome, 1902.

Böhmer, J. F., ed. *Regesta Imperii: Die Kaiserurkunden Ludwigs des Baiern*. Frankfort, 1838.

Brătianu, G. I. *Actes des notaires génois de Péra et de Caffa de la fin du XIIIe siècle*. Académie Roumaine, Études et Recherches, vol. II. Bucharest, Cvltvra Nationala, 1927.

Buchon, J. A. C., ed. *Chroniques étrangères relatives aux expéditions françaises pendant le XIIIe siècle*. Paris, 1840.

————. *Recherches et matériaux pour servir à une histoire de la domination française en Grèce*. Paris, 1840.

Carini, Isidoro. *Gli archivi e le biblioteche di Spagna in rapporto alla storia d'Italia in generale e di Sicilia in particolare*. Palermo, 1884–1897.

Cessi, Roberto, ed. *Deliberazioni del Maggior Consiglio di Venezia*. 3 vols. Bologna, N. Zanichelli, 1931–1950.

———— and P. Sambin, eds. *Le deliberazioni del Consiglio dei Rogati (Senato)*, serie *"mixtorum."* Vol. I, books 1–14. Deputazione di Storia Patria per le Venezie. Venice, 1960.

Coulon, Auguste, ed. *Lettres secrètes et curiales du Pape Jean XXII,1316–1334, relatives à la France, extraites des registres du Vatican*. 4 vols., 9 fascis. Paris, Fontemoing, 1900–1965.

D'Achéry, Luc, ed. *Spicilegium*. 2d ed. Vol. III. Paris, 1723.

De rebus regni Siciliae, documenti inediti, 1282–1283. Palermo, 1882.

Du Cange, Charles du Fresne. *Histoire de l'Empire de Constantinople sous les empereurs françois*. Paris, 1657. The second part of this work includes the texts of some important documents. The newer edition, by J. A. C. Buchon, in 2 vols., Paris, 1826, does not always reproduce the documents.

Finke, Heinrich. *Acta Aragonensia*. 3 vols. Leipzig and Berlin, W. Rothschild, 1908, 1922.

Gay, Jules, ed. *Les registres de Nicolas III*. Paris, 1898.

Giomo, Giuseppe. "Le Rubriche dei Libri misti del Senato perdutti," *Archivio Veneto*, 18 (1879), 40–338; 19 (1880), 90–117; 20 (1880), 81–95.

————. *Lettere segrete del Collegio, rectius Minor Consiglio*, in *Miscellanea di storia Veneta*, R. Deputazione di storia patria, 3d ser. Vol. I. Venice, 1910.

Grandjean, Charles, ed. *Les registres de Benoit XI*. Paris, Thorin, 1905.

Guiraud, Jean, ed. *Les registres de Grégoire X*. Paris, Fontemoing, 1892–1906.

Historiae Patriae Monumenta; Leges Municipales. Vol. I. Turin, 1838.

Huillard-Bréholles, J. L. A., ed. *Titres de la maison ducale de Bourbon*. 3 vols. Paris, 1867–1874.

Kern, Fritz, ed. *Acta Imperii Angliae et Franciae, 1267–1313.* Tübingen, J. C. B. Mohr, 1911.

Langlois, Charles V. *Collection des textes pour servir à l'étude et l'enseignement de l'histoire.* Paris, 1891.

Langlois, Ernest, ed. *Les registres de Nicholas IV.* Paris, E. Thorin, 1905.

Liber Jurium reipublicae Genuensis, ed. H. Ricottius, in *Monumenta Historiae Patriae.* Vols. I, II. Turin, 1872.

Makušev, V. V., ed. *Monumenta historica slavorum meridionalium vicinorumque populorum e tabulariis et bibliothecis italicis deprompta.* Vol. I. Warsaw, 1874–1882.

———. *The Italian Archives and the Materials They Contain on the History of the Slavs.* Vol. II. St. Petersburg, 1871.

Mansi, J. D., ed. *Sacrorum Conciliorum nova et amplissima collectio.* 31 vols. Florence and Venice, 1759–1798.

Martin-Chabot, E. "Un document relatif à l'expédition de la Compagnie Catalane en Orient, 1304," *Moyen Âge,* 2d ser., 23 (1910), 198–203.

Mas-Latrie, Louis de, ed. *Commerce et expéditions de la France et de Venise au moyen-âge.* Paris, 1880.

Miklosich, Franz, ed. *Monumenta Serbica spectantia historiam Serbiae Bosniae Ragusii.* Vienna, 1858.

Minieri-Riccio, Camillo. *Alcuni fatti riguardanti Carlo I di Angiò dal 6 di Agosto 1252 al 30 di Dicembre 1270.* Naples, 1874.

———. "Il regno di Carlo I d'Angiò dal 2 Gennaio al 31 Dicembre 1283," *Archivio storico Italiano,* 4th ser., 3 (1879), 161–170.

———. *Saggio di codice diplomatico.* Vol. I and supplement I. Naples, 1878, 1882.

Potthast, August. *Regesta Pontificum Romanorum.* Vol. II. Gratz, 1957; original ed., Berlin, 1873–1875.

Promis, Vincenzo, ed. *Magnum Statutum Peyrae,* in *Miscellanea di Storia Italiana.* Vol. XI. Turin, 1870.

Raynaldus, Odoricus. *Annales ecclesiastici denuo excusi ab A. Theiner.* Barri-Ducis, 1870; originally published in Rome, 1646–1727.

Recueil des historiens des croisades, Documents arméniens. 2 vols. Paris, Académie des inscriptions et des belles-lettres, 1869, 1906.

Regestum Clementis Papae V. 7 vols. Rome, Benedictine Order, 1885–1888.

Rubió y Lluch, Antonio. *Diplomatari de l'Orient Català, 1302–1409.* Barcelona, Institut d'Estudis Catalans, 1947.

Tafel, G. L. and G. M. Thomas, eds. *Urkunden zur älteren Handels-und Staatsgeschichte der Republik Venedig mit Besonderer Beziehungen auf Byzanz und die Levante.* 3 vols. Vienna, 1856–1857; anastatic ed., 1964.

Theiner, Augustin, ed. *Vetera Monumenta Historica Hungariam Sacram Illustrantia.* Vol. I. Rome, Paris, Vienna, 1859.

———. *Vetera Monumenta Slavorum Meridionalium.* Vol. I. Rome, Zagreb, 1863.

——— and F. Miklosich, eds. *Monumenta spectantia ad unionem ecclesiarum Graecae et Romanae.* Vienna, 1852.

Thiriet, Freddy. *Délibérations des assemblées vénitiennes concernant la Romanie.* Vol. I: 1160–1363. Paris, Mouton, 1966.

Thomas, Antoine, M. Faucon and C. Digard, eds. *Les registres de Boniface VIII.* Paris, Thorin, 1907.

Thomas, G. M. and R. Predelli, eds. *Diplomatarium Veneto-Levantinum sive acta et diplomata res Venetas Graecas atque Levantis Illustrantia, a. 1300.* Vol. I. Venice, 1880.

Turgenev, Λ. I., ed. *Historica Russica Monumenta.* 2 vols. St. Petersburg, 1842.

Viard, Jules, ed. *Les Journaux du Trésor de Charles IV le Bel.* Paris, 1917.

Wadding, A. R. P. *Annales minorum seu trium ordinum a S. Francisco institutorum.* 2d ed. Vol. VII. Rome, 1733.

Zurita, Geronimo. *Los Anales de la Corona de Aragon.* 6 vols. Saragossa, 1668–1670; republished in Barcelona, 1852.

III. Narrative Sources

Greek

Acropolita, G. *Opera*, ed. A. Heisenberg. 2 vols. Leipzig, B. G. Teubner, 1903.

———. *Historia*, ed. I. Bekker. Bonn, 1837.

Arsenius. *Testament*, in J. P. Migne, ed., *Patrologia Graeca*, CXL, cols. 947–951. Paris, 1865; anastatic ed., 1887.

Athanasios I, Patriarch of Constantinople. *Novella*, ed. G. Ralles and M. Potles, Σύνταγμα τῶν Θείων καὶ Ἱερῶν Κανόνων, V, 121–126. Athens, 1855.

———. *Letters*, in J. P. Migne, ed. *Patrologia Graeca.* Vol. CXLII, cols. 471–528. Paris, 1865; anastatic ed., 1885.

———. Two letters, ed. Γεννάδιος, Μητροπολίτης Ἡλιουπόλεως, «Δύο ἀνέκδοτα γράμματα τοῦ Πατριάρχου Κωνσταντινουπόλεως Ἀθανασίου Α'» Ἐπετηρὶς Ἑταιρείας Βυζαντινῶν Σπουδῶν, 22 (1952), 227–232.

Delehaye, R. P. H., ed. "La vie d'Athanase, Patriarche de Constantinople," *Mélanges d'Archéologie et d'histoire de l'école française de Rome*, 17 (1897), 39–75. This life has also been published by A. Papadopoulos-Kerameus (St. Petersburg, 1905), and by Archimandrites Athanasios Pantocratorinos, «Βίος καὶ πολιτεία Ἀθανασίου Α', οἰκουμενικοῦ Πατριάρχου, συγγραφεὶς ὑπὸ Ἰωσὴφ Καλοθέτου μοναχοῦ,» Θρᾳκικά, 13 (1940), 56–107.

Cantacuzeni, Ioannis Eximperatoris. *Historiarum libri IV.* Vol. I, ed. L. Schopen; vol. II, ed. B. G. Niebuhr; vol. III, ed. B. G. Niebuhr. Bonn, 1828, 1831, 1832.

Charanis, Peter. "An Important Short Chronicle of the 14th Century," *Byzantion*, 13 (1938), 355–362.

Choniates, Nicetas. *Historia*, ed. I. Bekker. Bonn, 1835.

Cinnamus, Johannes. *Epitome rerum ab Ioanne et Alexio Comnenis gestarum*, ed. Augustus Meineke. Bonn, 1836.

Codinus Curopalata. *De officialibus palatii Constantinopolitani et de officiis magnae ecclesiae liber*, ed. I. Bekker. Bonn, 1839.

Georgius, Cyprius. *Vita*, in J. P. Migne, ed. *Patrologia Graeca.* Vol. CXLII, cols. 20–211. Paris, 1865.

Gorjanov, B. T., ed. "Anonymous Byzantine Chronicle of the XIV Century" (in Russian), *Vizantiiskii Vremennik*, n.s., 2 (1949), 276–293.

Gregorae, Nicephori. *Byzantina Historia.* Vol. I, ed. L. Schopen; vol. II, ed. L. Schopen; vol. III, ed. I. Bekker. Bonn, 1829, 1830, 1855.

Guilland, Rodolphe, ed. *La correspondance de Nicéphore Grégoras*. Paris, Les Belles lettres, 1927.

Hyrtakenos, Theodore. *Correspondence*, ed. F. J. G. de la Porte du Theil, in *Notices et extraits des manuscrits de la Bibliothèque nationale*, VI. Paris, 1800.

Lambros, Spyridon. «Ἐνθυμήσεων ἤτοι χρονικῶν σημειωμάτων συλλογὴ πρώτη,» Νέος Ἑλληνομνήμων, 7, (1910), 113–314.

———— and K. I. Amantos. Βραχέα Χρονικά. Athens, Ἀκαδημία Ἀθηνῶν, 1932.

Loenertz, R.-J. "La Chronique brève de 1352, texte, traduction et commentaire," *Orientalia Christiana Periodica*, 29 (1963), 331–356; and pt. 2, *Orientalia Christiana Periodica*, 30 (1964), 39–64.

Martini, A. E., ed. "Manuelis Philae, Carmina inedita," *Atti della Reale Academia di Archeologia, Lettere e belle Arti*, 20 (1900), supplement.

Metochita, Georgius. *De historia dogmatica, sermo III*, A. Mai, ed. in *Patrum Novae Bibliothecae*, X, pt. 1, 319–370. Rome, 1905.

————. Λόγος ἀντιρρητικὸς ἐπὶ τῷ τοῦ Κυπρίου τόμῳ, A. Mai, ed. in *Patrum Novae Bibliothecae*, VIII, pt. 2, 179–227. Rome, 1871.

Metochitae, Theodori. Πρεσβευτικός, ed. K. Sathas, in Μεσαιωνικὴ Βιβλιοθήκη. Vol. I. Venice, 1872.

Miller, Emmanuel, ed. *Manuelis Philae Carmina*. 2 vols. Paris, 1855–1857.

Müller, C. G. and T. Kiessling, eds. *Theodori Metochitae Miscellanea*. Leipzig, 1821.

Pachymeres, Georgii. *De Michaele Palaeologo*, ed. I. Bekker. Bonn, 1835.

————. *De Andronico Palaeologo*, ed. I. Bekker. Bonn, 1835.

Philotheus, Patriarch of Constantinople. Τοῦ Πατριάρχου Κωνσταντινουπόλεως κυροῦ Φιλοθέου Βίος καὶ πολιτεία τοῦ ὁσίου καὶ θεοφόρου πατρὸς ἡμῶν Σάβα τοῦ Νέου, ed. A. Papadopoulos-Kerameus, in Ἀνάλεκτα Ἱεροσολυμιτικῆς Σταχυολογίας, V. St. Petersburg, 1898.

Phrantzes (Sphrantzes), Georgius. *Chronicon*, ed. I. B. Papadopoulos. Leipzig, 1935.

Sathas, K. N., ed. Χρονικὸν ἀνέκδοτον τοῦ Γαλαξειδίου. Athens, 1865; new ed. by G. Valetas, Athens, 1944.

Schmitt, John, ed. *The Chronicle of the Morea*. London, Methuen and Co., 1904. This is the Greek version of the chronicle of the Morea. Later edition by P. Kalonaros. Athens, Οἶκος Δημ. Δημητράκου, 1940. Translated into English by H. E. Lurier, *The Chronicle of the Morea*. New York, Columbia University Press, 1964.

Sphrantzes, Georgios. *Memorii (1401–1477)*. In anexă, Pseudo-Phrantzes: Macarie Melissenos. *Chronica, 1258–1481*, ed. V. Grecu. Bucharest, Editura Academiei, 1966. *See also* Phrantzes.

Strzygowski, J. "Das Epitalamium des Paläologen Andronikos II," *Byzantinische Zeitschrift*, 10 (1901), 546–567.

Thomas Magister (Theodulos Monachos). Πρεσβευτικὸς πρὸς Ἀνδρόνικον Β΄ τὸν Παλαιολόγον, in J. F. Boissonade, ed. *Anecdota Graeca*. Vol. II, 188–212. Paris, 1830.

————. Τῷ ἰσαγγέλῳ πατρί μου καὶ φιλοσόφῳ Ἰωσὴφ περὶ τῶν ἐν τῇ Ἰταλῶν καὶ Περσῶν ἐφόδῳ γεγενημένων, in J. F. Boissonade, ed. *Anecdota Graeca*. Vol. II, 212–228. Paris, 1830.

————. Περὶ βασιλείας, περὶ πολιτείας, in J. P. Migne, ed. *Patrologia Graeca*. Vol. CXLV, cols. 448–548. Paris, 1865; anastatic ed., 1904.

Treu, Max, ed. *Dichtungen des Gross-Logotheten Theodorus Metochites*. Programm des Victoria-Gymnasiums zu Potsdam, Ostern 1895. Potsdam, 1895.

Narrative Sources

————. *Maximi monachi Planudis epistolae.* 5 Programm des Kgl. Friedrich-Gymnasiums zu Breslau, 1886–1890.

Troitskii, I. E., ed. *Imperatoris Michaelis Palaeologi De Vita Sua Opusculum.* St. Petersburg, 1885.

Wassilievsky, B. and V. Jernstedt, eds. *Cecaumeni Strategikon et incerti scriptoris de officii libellus.* St. Petersburg, 1896.

Latin and Vernacular

d'Adam, Guillaume. *De modo Saracenos extirpandi,* ed. Charles Koehler in *Recueil des historiens des croisades, documents arméniens.* Vol. II. Paris, Académie des inscriptions et des belles lettres, 1906.

Annales Placentini Ghibellini, in G. H. Pertz, ed., *Monumenta Germaniae Historica, Scriptores.* Vol. XVIII. Hanover, 1863; reprinted, Stuttgart and New York, Hiersemann-Kraus, 1963.

Annales Veronenses de Romano, ed. Carlo Cipolla, in *Antiche Cronache Veronesi.* Vol. I. Venice, 1890.

Auriae, Jacobi. *Annales,* in G. H. Pertz, ed. *Monumenta Germaniae Historica, Scriptores.* Vol. XVIII. Hanover, 1863; reprinted Stuttgart and New York, Hiersemann-Kraus, 1963.

Ašikpašazade, Dervis Ahmed. *Tevarikh-i al-i Osman,* ed. Ali. Constantinople, 1916.

Bartolomeo of Neocastro. *Historia Sicula,* ed. G. Paladino, in L. A. Muratori, ed. *Rerum Italicarum Scriptores.* New rev. ed. by G. Carducci and V. Fiorini, vol. XIII, pt. 3. Bologna, 1921.

Benvenuto di San Giorgio. *Historia Montis Ferrati,* in L. A. Muratori, ed. *Rerum Italicarum Scriptores.* Vol. XXIII, cols. 307–662. Milan, 1733.

Bratutti, V. *Chronica dell'origine e progressione della casa ottomana* (translation of Sa'deddin), I. Vienna, 1649.

Buchon, J. A. C. *Chroniques étrangères relatives aux expéditions françaises pendant le XIIIe siècle.* Paris, 1841.

Chronicae illorum de Solario, ed. V. Promis in *Miscellanea di Storia Italiana.* Vol. IX (1870), 133–137.

Chronique parisienne anonyme, ed. A. Hellot, in *Mémoires de la Société de l'histoire de Paris.* Vol. XI. Paris, 1884.

Continuator of Girard de Frachet, in *Recueil des historiens des Gaules et de la France.* Vol. XXI, 1–70. Paris, 1855.

Continuator of Jacopo da Varagine, ed. V. Promis, *Continuazione della cronaca di Jacopo da Varagine.* Genoa, 1876.

Continuator of Jacopo da Varagine, in L. A. Muratori, ed., *Rerum Italicarum Scriptores.* Vol. IX. Milan, 1726.

Cronaca di Morea, ed. Karl Hopf in *Chroniques Gréco-romanes.* Berlin, 1873. Italian version of the Chronicle of the Morea.

Danduli, Andreae. *Chronicon,* in L. A. Muratori, ed. *Rerum Italicarum Scriptores.* Vol. XII, cols. 1–524. Milan, 1728.

Daničić, Djuro, ed. *Životi kraljeva i archiepiskopa Srpskich, napisao Danilo i Drugi.* Zagreb, 1866.

Dubois, Pierre. *De recuperatione Terre Sancte; traité de politique générale*, ed. Charles-V. Langlois. Paris, 1891.

———. *The Recovery of the Holy Land*, trans. into English by W. I. Brandt. New York, Columbia University Press, 1956.

———. *Oppinio cuiusdam suadentis regi Franciae ut regnum Jerosolymitanum et Cipri pro altero filio suorum ac de invasione regni Egipti*, ed. Charles-V. Langlois, in *Collection des textes pour servir à l'étude et l'enseignement de l'histoire*. Paris, 1891.

———. *Libellus super abbreviatione guerrarum et huiusmodi provisionibus*, ed. Charles-V. Langlois, *Collection des textes pour servir à l'étude et l'enseignement de l'histoire*. Paris, 1891.

Galeotto del Carretto. *Cronica di Monferrato in Monumenta Historiae Patriae, Scriptorum.* Vol. III. Turin, 1848.

Giustiniani, Agostino. *Annali della Repubblica di Genova*, ed. G. B. Spotorno. Genoa, 1854.

Górka, Olgierd, ed. *Anonymi descriptio Europae orientalis*. Cracow, 1916.

Jacobi de Varagine. *Chronicon Januense*, in L. A. Muratori, ed. *Rerum Italicarum Scriptores*. Vol. IX, cols. 1–56. Milan, 1726.

John of St. Victor. *Memoriale historiarum*, in *Recueil des historiens des Gaules et de la France*. Vol. XXI, 630–676. Paris, 1855.

Longnon, Jean de. *La chronique de Morée: Livre de la conqueste de la princée de l'Amorée.* Paris, Librairie Renouard, H. Laurens, successeur, 1911. French version of the Chronicle of the Morea.

Mirkhović, L., ed. *Životi kraljeva i archiepiskopa Srpskich*. Belgrade, 1935.

Memoriale Potestatum Regiensium, in L. A. Muratori, ed. *Rerum Italicarum Scriptores*. Vol. VIII, cols. 1069–1180. Milan, 1726.

Morel-Fatio, Alfred, ed. *Libro de los Fechos et Conquistas del Principado de la Morea.* Geneva, 1885. Aragonese version of the Chronicle of the Morea.

Muntaner, Ramon. *Cronica Catalana*, ed. Antonio de Bofarull. Barcelona, 1860. Other editions: Karl Lanz, *Chronik des edlen En Ramon Muntaner*. Stuttgart, 1844; L. Nicolau d'Olwer, *Ramon Muntaner. L'expedició dels Catalans a Orient*. Barcelona, 1926; trans. into English by Lady Goodenough, *The Chronicle of Muntaner*. 2 vols. London, Hakluyt Society, 1920, 1921.

Nangis, Guillaume de. *Chronique latine*, ed Hercule Géraud, in *Société de l'histoire de France*. Paris, 1843. Also published in *Recueil des historiens des Gaules et de la France*. Vol. XX, 542–582. Paris, 1840.

Navagero. *Storia Veneziana*, in L. A. Muratori, ed. *Rerum Italicarum Scriptores*. Vol. XXIII, cols. 919–1216. Milan, 1733.

Pegolotti, Francesco Balducci. *La pratica della mercatura*, ed. Allan Evans. Cambridge, Mass., Mediaeval Society of America, 1936.

Robert of Torigny. *Chronica*, in G. H. Pertz, ed. *Monumenta Germaniae Historica. Scriptores*. Vol. VI. Hanover, 1864. Reprinted, Stuttgart-New York, Hiersemann-Kraus, 1963.

Salimbene Parmensis. *Chronicon ab a. 1167–1287*, ed. Oswald Holder-Egger, in *Monumenta Germaniae Historica, Scriptores*. Vol. XXXII. Hanover, Hahn, 1905–1913. New edition by Ferdinando Bernini, 2 vols. Bari, 1942.

Sanudo Torsello, Marino. *Secreta Fidelium Crucis*, in J. Bongars, ed. *Gesta Dei per Francos*. Vol. II. Hanover, 1611.

————. *Istoria del Regno di Romania*, ed. Karl Hopf, in *Chroniques Gréco-romanes*. Berlin, 1873.

————. *Fragmentum*, ed. Karl Hopf, in *Chroniques Gréco-romanes*. Berlin, 1873.

————. *Fragmentum*, ed. R. L. Wolff, "The So-called Fragmentum of Marino Sanudo," *Joshua Starr Memorial Volume*, 149–159. New York, Jewish Social Studies, 1956. (See also, R. L. Wolff.)

————. *Letters*, ed. F. Kunstmann, "Studien über Marino Sanudo Torsello den Aelteren," *Abhandlungen der Bayerischen Akademie der Wissenschaften, historische Klasse*. Vol. VII (Munich, 1853), 695–819. (See also, F. Kunstmann.)

————. *Letters*, ed. C. de la Roncière and L. Dorez, in "Lettres inédites et mémoires de Marino Sanudo l'ancien," *Bibliothèque de l'École des Chartes*, 56 (1895), 21–44.

Sanuto, Marin. *Vitae Ducum Venetorum*, in L. A. Muratori, ed. *Rerum Italicarum Scriptores*. Vol. XXII, cols. 401–1252. Milan, 1733.

Sicard of Cremona. *Cronica*, in *Monumenta Germaniae Historica, Scriptores*. Vol. XXXI. Hanover, 1903. Reprinted, Stuttgart-New York, Hiersemann-Kraus, 1963.

Specialis, Nicolaus. *Historia Sicula*, in L. A. Muratori, ed. *Rerum Italicarum Scriptores*. Vol. X, cols. 917–1092. Milan, 1727.

Stellae, Georgii. *Annales Genuenses*, in L. A. Muratori, ed. *Rerum Italicarum Scriptores*. Vol. XVII. Milan, 1730.

William of Tyre. *A History of Deeds Done Beyond the Sea*, trans. E. A. Babcock and A. C. Krey. New York, Columbia University Press, 1948.

Villani, Giovanni. *Cronica*, ed. F. G. Dragomanni. 4 vols. Florence, 1844–1845.

Villehardouin, Geoffroi de. *La conquête de Constantinople*, ed. Edmond Faral. Paris, Les Belles lettres, 1939.

IV. Secondary Works

Aistermann, Balduinus. *Beiträge zum Konflikt Johanns XXII mit dem deutschen Königtum*. Bonn, Georgi, 1909.

Alexander, P. J. "A Chrysobull of the Emperor Andronicus II Palaeologus in Favor of the See of Kanina in Albania," *Byzantion*, 15 (1940–1941), 167ff.

Alexoudes, Anthimos, Metropolitan of Berat. Σύντομος περιγραφὴ τῆς ἱερᾶς Μητροπόλεως Βελεγράδων. Corfu, 1868.

Allatius, Leo. *De Ecclesiae Occidentalis atque Orientalis perpetua consensione libri tres*. Cologne, 1648.

Amantos, K. I. «Συμβολὴ εἰς τὴν Μεσαιωνικὴν ἱστορίαν τῆς Χίου,» Ἐπετηρὶς Φιλοσοφικῆς Σχολῆς Πανεπιστημίου Ἀθηνῶν, ser. II, 5 (1954–1955), 153–164.

Amari, Michele. *La guerra del Vespro Siciliano*, 9th ed. Milan, 1886.

Andréadès, A. M. "Byzance, paradis du monopole et du privilège," *Byzantion*, 9 (1934), 171–181.

————. "De la monnaie et de la puissance d'achat des métaux précieux dans l'Empire byzantin," *Byzantion*, 1 (1924), 75–115.

————. "Floraison et décadence de la petite propriété dans l'Empire byzantin," *Mélanges offerts à Ernest Mahaim*, 261–266. Paris, Librairie de Recueil Sirey, 1935.

Angelov, D. S. "Prinos Kŭm Pozemlete otnošenija vŭv Vizantija prez XIII vek," *Godišnik na Filosof.-Ist. Fak.* 2 (Sofia, 1952), 1–103.

Argenti, P. P. *Bibliography of Chios from Classical Times to 1936*. Oxford, 1940.

Arnakis, G. G. "Byzantium's Anatolian Provinces During the Reign of Michael Palaeologus," *Actes du XIIe Congrès International d'études byzantines*. Vol. II, 37–44. Belgrade, 1964.

Artonne, André. *Le mouvement de 1314 et les chartes provinciales de 1315*. Paris, Libr. F. Alcan, 1912.

Asal, Josef. *Die Wahl Johanns XXII*. Berlin and Leipzig, Rotschild, 1909.

Athenagoras, Metropolites. «Συμβολαὶ εἰς τὴν ἱστορίαν τοῦ Βυζαντινοῦ οἴκου τῶν Φιλανθρωπηνῶν,» Δελτίον Ἱστορικῆς καὶ Ἐθνολογικῆς Ἑταιρείας τῆς Ἑλλάδος, Vol. I, 4, 61–74. Athens, 1929.

Atiya, A. S. *The Crusade in the Later Middle Ages*. London, Methuen & Co., 1938.

Bakalakis, G. «Τὸ περὶ τὴν Χριστούπολιν τείχισμα,» Ἑλληνικά, 10 (1935), 307–318.

Bănescu, Nicolae. "A propos de Kekaumenos," *Byzantion*, 13 (1938), 129–138.

―――. "Le Patriarche Athanase Ier et Andronic II Paléologue: État religieux, politique et social de l'Empire," *Académie Roumaine. Bulletin de la section historique*, 23 (1942), 28–56.

Bastin, Julia. "Le traité de Théodore Paléologue dans la traduction de Jean de Vignai," *Études romanes dédiées à Mario Roques*. Paris, E. Droz, 1946.

Beck, Hans-Georg. *Theodoros Metochites: Die Krise des byzantinischen Weltbildes im 14 Jahrhundert*. Munich, C. H. Beck, 1952.

Bees, N. A. "Übersicht über die Geschichte des Judentums von Janina," *Byzantinisch-Neugriechischen Jahrbücher*, 2 (1921), 159–177.

―――. «Κριτικὰ καὶ διορθωτικὰ εἰς Βυζαντιακὰ κείμενα,» *Vizantiiskii Vremennik*, 20 (1913), 58–69.

Bertelè, Tommaso. "Autocratori dei Romani, di Constantinopoli e della Macedonia," *Numismatica*, n. s., 2 (1961), 75–82.

Bezdechi, S. "Le portrait de Th. Métochite par Nicéphore Grégoras," *Mélanges d'histoire générale*. Cluj, 1927.

Binon, S. "L'histoire et la légende de deux chrysobulles d'Andronic II en faveur de Monembasie," *Échos d'Orient*, 37 (1938), 274–311.

Bloch, Marc. *La société féodale*. 2 vols. Paris, A. Michel, 1939.

Borsari, Stéphane. "I rapporti tra Pisa e gli stati di Romania nel duecento," *Rivista di storia Italiana*, 67 (1955), 477–492.

Bosch, U. V. *Andronikos II Palaiologos. Versuch einer Darstellung der byzantinischen Geschichte in den Jahren 1321–1341*. Amsterdam, Hakkert, 1965.

Boutaric, Edgard. *La France sous Philippe le Bel; étude sur les institutions politiques et administratives du moyen-âge*. Paris, 1861.

Bozzola, Annibale. "Guiglielmo VII, marchese di Monferrato e Carlo I d'Angiò," *Archivio Storico per le province Napoletane*, 36 (1911), 289–328, 451–74; 37 (1912), 1–28.

―――. "Un capitano di guerra e signore subalpino," *Miscellanea di storia Italiana*, R. Deput. di storia patria per le antiche provincie, 3d ser., vol. 19, 263–439. Turin, 1922.

Brătianu, G. I. "Contributions à l'histoire de Cetatea Alba (Akkerman) aux XIIIe et XIVe siècles," *Bulletin de l'Académie Roumaine, Section historique*, 13 (1927), 25–31.

―――. *Études byzantines d'histoire économique et sociale*. Paris, P. Geuthner, 1938.

Secondary Works

—————. "L'hypérpère byzantin et les monnaies d'or des républiques italiennes au XIIIe siècle," *Mélanges Charles Diehl.* Vol. I, 37–48. Paris, E. Leroux, 1930. Also published in *Études byzantines d'histoire économique et sociale.* Paris, P. Geuthner, 1938.

—————. "Notes sur le projet de mariage entre l'Empereur Michel IX Paléologue et Catherine de Courtenay," *Revue historique du sud-est Européen,* 1 (1924), 59–63.

—————. *Privilèges et franchises municipales dans l'Empire byzantin.* Paris and Bucharest, P. Geuthner, 1936.

—————. *Recherches sur le commerce dans la mer Noire au XIIIe siècle.* Paris, P. Geuthner, 1929.

—————. *Recherches sur Vičina et Cetatea Alba.* Bucharest, Universitatea din Iasi, 1935.

Bréhier, Louis. "Attempts at Reunion of the Greek and Latin Church," *Cambridge Medieval History.* Vol. IV (1923), 594–626.

—————. *Les institutions de l'Empire byzantin.* Paris, Michel, 1929.

—————. *Vie et mort de Byzance.* Paris, Michel, 1948.

Buchon, J. A. C. *Nouvelles recherches historiques sur la principauté française de Morée.* Paris, 1843.

—————. *Recherches historiques sur la principauté française de Morée et ses hautes baronies.* 2 vols. Paris, 1845.

Burmov, A. K. *Istorija na Bulgarija prez vremeto Šišmanovci (1323–1396).* Vol. I. Godišnik na Sofiskija universitet, Istor. Filol. Fakultet, 43, 1946–1947.

Burns, Ignatius, S. J. "The Catalan Company and the European Powers, 1305–1311," *Speculum,* 29 (1954), 751–771.

Byrne, E. H. *Genoese Shipping in the Twelfth and Thirteenth Centuries.* Cambridge, Mass., Mediaeval Academy of America, 1930.

Caggese, Romolo. *Roberto d'Angiò e i suoi tempi.* 2 vols. Florence, R. Bemporad, 1922, 1930.

Cahen, Claude. *Pre-Ottoman Turkey.* London, Sidgwick & Jackson, 1968.

Caldas, Carlos de. *El Tratado de Caltabelotta.* Barcelona, Hormiga de Oro, 1943.

Capmany, Antonio de. *Memórias historicas sobre la Marina, Comercio y artes de la antigua Ciudad de Barcelona.* Vol. II. Madrid, 1779; reprinted, Barcelona, Cámara de Comercio, 1962.

Carabellese, Francesco. *Carlo d'Angiò nei rapporti politici e commerciali con Venezia e l'oriente.* Bari, Vecchi & Co., 1911.

Caro, Georg. "Zur Chronologie der drei letzten Bücher des Pachymeres," *Byzantinische Zeitschrift,* 6 (1897), 114–125.

—————. *Genua und die Mächte am Mittelmeer, 1257–1311.* 2 vols. Halle, 1895, 1899.

Cartellieri, Otto. *Peter von Aragon und die Sizilianische Vesper.* Heidelberg, C. Winter, 1904.

Carucci, Carlo. *La guerra del Vespro Siciliano nella frontiera del principato.* Subiaco, 1934.

Cessi, Roberto. *Politica ed Economia di Venezia nel trecento.* Rome, Edizioni di storia e letteratura, 1952.

—————. *Storia della repubblica di Venezia.* Milan and Messina, Principato, 1944.

Chalandon, Ferdinand. *Essai sur le règne d'Aléxis Ier Comnène.* Paris, A. Picard, 1900.

—————. *Jean II Comnène et Manuel I Comnène.* Paris, A. Picard, 1912.

Chapman, Conrad. *Michel Paléologue, restaurateur de l'Empire byzantin, 1261–1282.* Paris, E. Figuière, 1928.

Charanis, Peter. "An Important Short Chronicle of the 14th Century," *Byzantion*, 13 (1938), 355–362.

———. "The Monastic Properties and the State in the Byzantine Empire," *Dumbarton Oaks Papers.* Vol. IV (1948).

———. "On the Social Structure and Economic Organization of the Byzantine Empire in the 13th century and later," *Byzantinoslavica*, 12 (1951), 94–153.

Cheyette, F. L. "The Sovereign and the Pirates, 1332," *Speculum*, 45 (1970), 40–68.

Cognasso, Francesco. "Partiti politici e lotte dinastiche in Bisanzio," *Mem. R. Acc. Scienze.* Turin, 1912.

———. "Una crisobolla di Michele IX Paleologo per Teodoro I di Monferrato," *Studi Bizantini*, 2 (1927), 39–47.

Colonna, M. E. *Gli storici bizantini dal IV al XV secolo.* Vol. I: *Storici profani.* Naples, Armanni, 1956.

Constantinidi-Bibicou, Hélène. "Yolande de Montferrat, Impératrice de Byzance," *L'Hellénisme Contemporain*, 2d ser., 4 (1950), 425–442.

Cordellas, P. S. "Théodore Métochite," *Actes du VI Congrès international des Études byzantines.* Vol. I. Paris, 1950.

Dade, Erwin. *Versuche zur Wiedererrichtung der lateinischen Herrschaft in Konstantinopel im Rahmen der abendländischen Politik (1261 bis etwa 1310).* Jena, Verlag der Frommann-schen Buchhandlung Walter Biedeman, 1938.

Dalleggio, d'Alessio, Eugenio. "Recherches sur l'histoire de la latinité de Constantinople," *Échos d'Orient*, 25 (1926), 21ff.

———. "Galata et la souveraineté de Byzance," *Revue des études byzantines*, 19 (1961), 315–327.

Danstrup, J. "Indirect Taxation at Byzantium," *Classica et Mediaevalia*, 8 (1946), 139–167.

Dawkins, R. M. "The Catalan Company in the Traditions of Mount Athos," *Homanatge a Antoní Rubió y Lluch.* Vol. I. Barcelona, Biblioteca Balmés, 1936.

De Boislisle. "Projet de croisade du premier duc de Bourbon, 1316–1333," *Annuaire-Bulletin de la société de l'histoire de France* (1872), 230–236, 246–255.

De la Roncière, D. and L. Dorez. "Lettres inédites et mémoires de Marino Sanudo l'Ancien," *Bibliothèque de l'École des Chartes*, 56 (1895), 21–44.

Delaville le Roulx, Joseph. *La France en Orient au XIVe siècle.* 2 vols. Paris, 1886.

Delehaye, R. P. H. "La vie d'Athanase, Patriarche de Constantinople," *Mélanges d'Archéologie et d'histoire de l'école française de Rome*, 17 (1897), 39–75.

Delisle, L. "Notice sur 5 manuscrits de la Bibliothèque Nationale, sur un manuscrit de la Bibliothèque de Bordeaux contenant les recueils épistolaires de Bérard de Naples," *Notices et extraits de la Bibliothèque Nationale*, (1879), 87–167.

De Negri, T. O. *Storia di Genova.* Milan. A. Martello, 1968.

Der Nersessian, Sirarpie. "The Kingdom of Cilician Armenia," in K. M. Setton, R. L. Wolff, and H. W. Hazard, eds. *A History of the Crusades.* Vol. II. Philadelphia, University of Pennsylvania Press, 1962.

Desimoni, Cornelio. "I Genovesi ed i loro quartieri in Constantinopoli nel secolo XII," *Giornale Ligustico di Archeologia*, 3 (1876), 217–274.

Diehl, Charles. *Figures byzantines*. 2 vols. Paris, A. Colin, 1925, 1927.

──────. "Un haut fonctionnaire byzantin, le logothète τῶν σεκρέτων," *Mélanges N. Iorga*. Paris, J. Gamber, 1933.

──────. *Impératrices de Byzance*. Paris, 1959.

Diomedes, A. N. «Τὰ αἴτια τῆς οἰκονομικῆς παρακμῆς τοῦ Βυζαντίου,» Ἐπιθεώρησις Κοινωνικῆς καὶ Δημοσίας Οἰκονομικῆς, 6 (1937), 139–155.

Doehaerd, Renée. *Les relations commerciales entre Gênes, la Belgique et l'Outremont d'après les archives notariales génoises aux XIIIe et XIVe siècles*. 3 vols. Brussels, Institut historique belge de Rome, 1941.

Dölger, Franz. *Beiträge zur Geschichte der byzantinischen Finanzverwaltung besonders des 10 und 11 Jahrhunderts*. Leipzig and Berlin, Teubner, 1927.

──────. "Die byzantinische und mittelalterliche serbische Herrscherkanzlei," *Actes du XIIe Congrès international d'études byzantines*. Vol. I, 83–103. Belgrade, 1963.

──────. "Die dynastische Familienpolitik des Kaisers Michael Palaiologos," *E. Eichmann Festschrift*. Paderborn, Schöningh, 1940.

──────. "Die Kaiserurkunde der Byzantiner als Ausdruck ihrer politischen Auschauungen," *Byzantinische Zeitschrift*, 159 (1938–1939), 229–250.

──────. "Neues zu Alexios Metochites und zu Theodoros Meliteniotes," *Miscellanea Giovanni Mercati*. Vol. III. Vatican City, 1946.

──────. "Die Urkunden des byzantinischen Kaisers Andronikos II für Aragon–Katalonien unter die Regierung König Jakobs II," *Estudis Universitaris Catalans*, 18 (1933), 300–307. Also published in *Byzanz und die Europäische Staatenwelt* (Buch Kunstverlag Ettal, 1953).

Duby, George. *La société aux XIe et XIIe siècles dans la région mâconnaise*. Paris, Colin, 1953.

Dürrholder, Gottfried. *Die Kreuzzugspolitik unter Papst Johann XXII, 1316–1334*. Strassburg, Heitz, 1913.

Du Cange, Charles Du Fresne. *Histoire de l'Empire de Constantinople sous les empereurs françois*. Paris, 1657. Republished, with some changes, by J. A. Buchon, *Collection des Chroniques Nationales françaises; Histoire de l'Empire de Constantinople sous les empereurs français*. 2 vols. Paris, 1826.

Dujčev, Ivan. "Una poesia di Manuele Filè dedicata a Irene Paleologina Asenina," *Mélanges Georges Ostrogorsky*. Vol. II. Belgrade, Naučno delo, 1964.

Dupont-Ferrier, Gustave. *Institutions financières de la France à la fin du moyen-âge*. 2 vols. Paris, Firmin-Didot, 1930–1932.

Ebersolt, Jean. *Les arts somptuaires de Byzance*. Paris, E. Leroux, 1923.

Evert-Kapessowa, Halina. "La société byzantine et l'union de Lyon," *Byzantinoslavica*, 10 (1949), 28ff.

──────. "Une page de l'histoire des relations byzantino-latines," *Byzantinoslavica*, 17 (1956), 1–18.

Ferjančić, Božidar. "Počeci solunske Kraljevnie 1204–1209," *Mélanges Georges Ostrogorsky*. Vol. II. Belgrade, Naučno delo, 1964.

Fisher, Elizabeth, "A Note on Pachymeres' 'De Andronico Palaeologo'," *Byzantion*, 40 (1970), 230–235.

Flemming, Barbara. "Landschaftsgeschichte von Pamphylien, Pisidien und Lykien im Spätmittelalter," in *Abhandlungen für die Kunde des Morgenlandes*. Vol. XXXV, pt. 1. Wiesbaden, 1964.

Francès, E. "La féodalité byzantine et la conquête turque," *Studia et Acta Orientalia*, 4 (1962), 69–90.

――――. "La féodalité et les villes byzantines au XIIIe et au XIVe siècle," *Byzantinoslavica*, 16 (1955), 76–96.

Gabotto, Ferdinando. *Asti e la politica sabauda in Italia al tempo di Guglielmo Ventura*, *Biblioteca della Società Storica Subalpina*. Vol. XVIII (1903).

Gardner, Alice. *The Lascarids of Nicaea: The Story of an Empire in Exile*. London, Methuen & Co., 1912.

Gaudioso, Matteo. *La schiavitù domestica in Sicilia dopo i Normanni*. Catania, Galátola, 1926.

Geanakoplos, D. J. *The Emperor Michael Palaeologus and the West, 1258–1282*. Cambridge, Mass., Harvard University Press, 1959.

――――. "Michael VIII Paleologos and the Union of Lyons," *Harvard Theological Review*, 46 (1953), 79ff.

Gedeon, M. I. Ὁ ῎Αθως. Constantinople, 1885.

Gelzer, Heinrich. "Ungedruckte und wenig bekannte Bistümerverzeichnisse der orientalischen Kirche," *Byzantinische Zeitschrift*, 2 (1893), 22–72.

Georgiades-Arnakes, George. «Ἡ περιήγησις τοῦ ῎Ιμπν Μπαττούτα ἀνὰ τὴν Μικρὰν Ἀσίαν καὶ ἡ κατάστασις τῶν Ἑλληνικῶν καὶ Τουρκικῶν πληθυσμῶν κατὰ τόν ΙΔ´ αἰῶνα,» Ἐπετηρὶς Ἑταιρείας Βυζαντινῶν Σπουδῶν, 22 (1952), 135–149.

――――. Οἱ πρῶτοι ᾽Οθωμανοί. Athens, 1947: *Texte und Forschungen zur Byzantinisch-Neugriechischen Philologie*.

Gerland, Ernst. "Creta als Venezianische Kolonie," *Jahrbuch der Görresgesellschaft*, 20 (1899), 1–24.

Gibbons, H. A. *The Foundations of the Ottoman Empire*. Oxford, Clarendon Press, 1916.

Gill, J. "Emperor Andronicus II and Patriarch Athanasius I," Βυζαντινά, 2 (1970), 13–19.

Giunta, Francesco. *Aragonesi e Catalani nel Mediterraneo, II: La presenza Catalana nel Levante dalle origini a Giacomo II*. Palermo, Manfredi, 1959.

Golubovich, Girolamo. *Biblioteca Bio-Bibliografica della Terra Santa e dell'Oriente Franciscano*. Vol. III. Quaracchi, 1919.

Gorjanov, B. T. "Anonymous Byzantine Chronicle of the XIV Century" (in Russian), *Vizantiiskii Vremennik*, n. s., 2 (1949), 276–293.

――――. *Pozdnevizantiiskii Feodalizm*. Moscow, Akad. nauk., 1962. Reviewed by V. Hrochová, *Byzantinoslavica*, 26 (1965), 140–144.

――――. "Vizantiiskoe Krest'janstvopri Paleologach," *Vizantiiskii Vremennik*, n. s., 3 (1950), 19–50.

Gouillard, Jean. "Après le schisme arsénite; La correspondance inédite du pseudo-Jean Chilas," *Académie Roumaine, Bulletin de la section historique*, 25 (1944), 174–211.

Grecu, V. "Das Geburtsjahr des byzantinischen Geschichtschreibers Nicephoros Gregoras," *Académie Roumaine, Bulletin de la section historique*, 27 (1946), 56–61.

Grumel, V. "Les ambassades pontificales à Byzance après le IIe concile de Lyon," *Échos d'Orient*, 23 (1924), 437–447.

――――. *La chronologie: Bibliothèque byzantine*. Paris, Presses universitaires de France, 1958.

Secondary Works

————. "La date de l'avènement du Patriarche de Constantinople Niphon," *Revue des études byzantines*, 13 (1955), 138–139.

————. "Le mois de Marie des Byzantins," *Échos d'Orient*, 31 (1932), 257–269.

————. "En Orient après le IIe concile de Lyon," *Échos d'Orient*, 24 (1925), 321–325.

Guilland, Rodolphe. "Aléxis Philanthropène," *Revue des Lyonnais*, (1922), 47–59.

————. "La correspondance inédite d'Athanase, Patriarche de Constantinople (1289–1293) (1304–1310)," *Mélanges Charles Diehl*. Vol. I. Paris, E. Leroux, 1930.

————. *Essai sur Nicéphore Grégoras; l'homme et l'oeuvre*. Paris, P. Geuthner, 1926.

————. *Études byzantines*. Paris, Presses universitaires de France, 1959.

————. "Études de titulature et de prosopographie byzantines. Les chefs de la marine byzantine: drongaire de la flotte, grand drongaire de la flotte, mégaduc," *Byzantinische Zeitschrift*, 44 (1951), 221–240.

————. "Études de titulature et prosopographie byzantines. Le Protostrator," *Revue des études byzantines*, 7 (1949), 156–179.

————. "Fonctions et dignités des eunuques," *Études byzantines*, 2 (1944), 185–225; 3 (1945), 179–214.

————. "Les noces plurales à Byzance," in R. Guilland, *Études Byzantines*. Paris, 1959.

————. "Le palais de Théodore Métochite," *Revue des études grècques*, 35 (1922), 82–95.

————. "Les poésies inédites de Théodore Métochite," in R. Guilland, *Études Byzantines*. Paris, 1959.

Halecki, Oskar. *Un Empereur de Byzance à Rome; Vingt ans de travail pour l'union des églises et pour la défence de l'Empire d'Orient, 1355–1375*. Warsaw, Nakl. Tow. Naukowego Warszawskiego, 1930.

Hammer, Joseph von. *Geschichte des Osmanischen Reiches*. 10 vols. Budapest, 1827–1835.

Hart, T. "Nicephorus Gregoras, Historian of the Hesychast Controversy," *Journal of Ecclesiastical History*, 2 (1951), 169–179.

Heers, M.-L. "Les Génois et le commerce de l'alum à la fin du Moyen-Âge," *Revue d'histoire économique et sociale*, 32 (1954), 31–53.

Hefele, C.-J. *Histoire des conciles*. Vol. VI, pt. 2. Paris, Letouzey et Ané, 1915.

Heisenberg, August. *Aus der Geschichte und Literatur der Palaiologenzeit. Abhandlungen der Bayerischen Akademie der Wissenschaften, Philosophisch-Philologische-Historische Klasse*. Munich, 1920.

Hervieu, H. E. *Recherches sur les premiers États Généraux*. Paris, 1879.

Heyd, William. *Histoire du commerce du Levant au moyen-âge*. 2 vols. Leipzig, O. Harrassowitz, 1923.

Hill, Sir George Francis. *A History of Cyprus*. 4 vols. Cambridge, Eng., Cambridge University Press, 1940–1952.

Hopf, Karl. *Chroniques Gréco-romanes*. Berlin, 1873.

Hopf, Karl. *Griechische Geschichte*. Vol. 85 of J. S. Ersch and J. G. Gruber, eds. *Allgemeine Encyklopädie d. Wissen. und Künst*. Leipzig, 1870.

Hunger, Herbert. "Theodorus Metochites als Vorläufer des Humanismus in Byzanz," *Byzantinische Zeitschrift*, 45 (1952), 4ff.

Hvostova, K. V. *Osobennosti agrarnopravovyh otnošenii v pozdnei Vizantii (XIV–XV vv.)*. Moscow, Akademija nauk, 1968.

Iorga, Nicolae. "Encore un traité de croisade, 1308," *Bulletin de l'institut pour l'étude de l'Europe sud-orientale*, (1921), 59–64.

———. *Histoire de la vie byzantine*. 3 vols. Bucharest, author's edition, 1934.

———. "Médaillons d'histoire littéraire byzantine," *Byzantion*, 2 (1926), 237–298.

———. "Ramon Muntaner et l'Empire byzantin," *Revue historique du sud-est Européen*, 4 (1927), 325–355.

Janin, Raymond. *Constantinople byzantine*. Paris, Institut français d'études byzantines, 1950.

Jireček, K. J. *Das Fürstentum Bulgarien*. Prague, 1891.

———. *Geschichte der Bulgaren*. Prague, 1876.

———. *Geschichte der Serben*. Gotha, Perthes, 1911.

———. "Staat und Gesellschaft in Mittelalterliches Servien," *Denkschriften den Kais. Akad. der Wissenschaften*. Vienna, 1914.

Jordan, Édouard. *Les origines de la domination angevine en Italie*. Paris, A. Picard, 1909.

Kaeppeli, R. P. T. "Benedetto di Asinago da Como (†1339)," *Archivum Fratrum Praedicatorum*, 2 (1941), 83–94.

———. "Deux nouveaux ouvrages de fr. Philippe Incontri de Péra," *Archivum Fratrum Praedicatorum*, 23 (1953), 163–183.

Každan, A. P. *Agrarnye otnošenija v Vizantii XIII, XIV vv*. Moscow, 1952.

Knowles, Christine. "Les Enseignements de Théodore Paléologue," *Byzantion*, 22 (1952), 389–394.

Kokylides, K. «Γεωργιανοὶ ἢ Ἴβηρες ἐν τοῖς Ἁγίοις Τόποις,» Νέα Σιών, 15 (1920).

Kolias, G. T. «Ἡ μεταξὺ Καταλάνων καὶ Μεγάλου Δουκὸς τῶν Ἀθηνῶν μάχη,» Ἐπετηρὶς Ἑταιρείας Βυζαντινῶν Σπουδῶν, 26 (1956), 358–379.

Koukoules, Phaidon. «Συμβολὴ εἰς τὸ περὶ γάμου κεφάλαιον παρὰ Βυζαντινοῖς,» Ἐπετηρὶς Ἑταιρείας Βυζαντινῶν Σπουδῶν, 2 (1925), 3–41.

Kretschmayr, Heinrich. *Geschichte von Venedig*. 2 vols. Gotha, F. A. Perthes, 1905, 1920.

Kretschmer, Konrad. *Die italienischen Portolanen des Mittelalters*. Berlin, E. S. Mittler, 1909.

Krumbacher, Karl. *Handbuch der byzantinischen Litteratur*, 2d ed., in I. Müller *Handbuch der Altertums-Wissenschaft* (Munich, 1897).

Kunstmann, F. "Studien über Marino Sanudo Torsello den Aelteren," *Abhandlungen der Bayerischen Akademie der Wissenschaften, historische Klasse*. Vol. VII (Munich, 1853), 695–819.

Laiou, Angeliki. "The Provisioning of Constantinople during the Winter of 1306–1307," *Byzantion*, 37 (1967), 91–113.

———. "A Byzantine Prince Latinized: Theodore Palaeologus, Marquis of Montferrat," *Byzantion*, 38 (1968), 386–410.

———. "Marino Sanudo Torsello, Byzantium and the Turks: The Background to the Anti-Turkish League of 1332–1334," *Speculum*, 45 (1970), 374–392.

La Mantia, G. "Studi sulla rivoluzione siciliana del 1282," *Archivio Storico Siciliano*, 6 (1940).

Lambros, Spyridon. «Τὸ Ἅγιον Ὄρος καὶ οἱ Καταλώνιοι,» Νέος Ἑλληνομνήμων, 6 (1909), 319–321.

———. Λεύκωμα Βυζαντινῶν Αὐτοκρατόρων. Athens, Ἐλευθερουδάκης Α. Ε. 1930.

373

Secondary Works

————. «Μιχαὴλ Λουλλούδης ὁ ᾿Εφέσιος καὶ ἡ ὑπὸ τῶν Τούρκων ἅλωσις τῆς ᾿Εφέσου,» Νέος ῾Ελληνομνήμων, 1 (1904), 209–212.

Lamma, P. "Un discorso per l'incoronazione di Michele IX Paleologo," *Aevum*, 29 (1955), 49–69.

Lane, F. C. *Venice and History*. Baltimore, Johns Hopkins Press, 1966.

Langlois, Charles-V. in E. Lavisse *Histoire générale de la France*. Vol. III, pt. 2. Paris, Librairie Hachette, 1901.

———— and Charles Koehler, "Lettres inédites concernantes les croisades," *Bibliothèque de l'École des Chartes*, 52 (1891), 46–63.

Laskaris, Michael. *Vizantiske Princeze u srednjevekovnoj Srbiji. Prilog istoriji vizantiskosrpskich odnosa odkraja XII do XV veka*. Belgrade, F. Baha, 1926.

Laurent, M.-H. *Le bienheureux Innocent V et son temps*. Vatican, Vatican Library, 1947.

————. "Georges le Métochite ambassadeur de Michel VIII Paléologue auprès du bienheureux Innocent V," *Miscellanea Giovanni Mercati*. Vol. III. Vatican City, 1946.

Laurent, Vitalien. "La chronique anonyme du Cod. Mosq. Gr. 426 et la pénétration turque en Bithynie au debut du XIVe siècle," *Revue des études byzantines*, 7 (1949), 207–211.

————. "La chronologie des patriarches de Constantinople de la première moitié du XIVe siècle, 1294–1350," *Revue des études byzantines*, 7 (1949), 145–155.

————. "Les crises religieuses à Byzance; le schisme antiarsénite du métropolite de Philadelphie Théolepte, †c. 1324," *Revue des études byzantines*, 18 (1960), 44–54.

————. "La croisade et la question d'Orient sous le pontificat de Grégoire X," *Revue historique du sud-est Européen*, 22 (1945), 105–137.

————. "La date de la mort de Jean Beccos," *Échos d'Orient*, 25 (1926), 316–319.

————. "Deux nouveaux manuscrits de l''Histoire byzantine' de Georges Pachymère," *Byzantion*, 11 (1936), 43–47.

————. "Les grandes crises religieuses à Byzance; La fin du schisme arsénite," *Académie Roumaine, Bulletin de la section historique*, 26 (1945), 225–313.

————. "Grégoire X et son projet de ligue anti-turque," *Échos d'Orient*, 37 (1938), 257–273.

————. "L'histoire byzantine de Georges Pachymère. Un nouveau témoin, l'Athén. Gennad. 40," *Byzantion*, 6 (1931), 355–367.

————. "Les manuscrits de l''Histoire byzantine' de Georges Pachymère," *Byzantion*, 5 (1929–1930), 129–205.

————. "Notes de chronographie et d'histoire byzantines," *Échos d'Orient*, 36 (1937), 157–174.

————. "Notes de titulature byzantine," *Échos d'Orient*, 38 (1939), 355–370. Reviewed by F. Dölger, *Byzantinische Zeitschrift*, 40 (1940), 518–520.

————. "Le rapport de Georges le Métochite, apocrisiaire de Michel VIII Paléologue auprès du Pape Grégoire X; 1275–1276," *Revue historique du sud-est Européen*, 23 (1946), 233–247.

————. "Les signataires du 2me synode de Blachernes," *Échos d'Orient*, 26 (1927), 129–149.

————. "Une famille turque au service de Byzance, les Mélikès," *Byzantinische Zeitschrift*, 49 (1956), 349–368.

Lehugueur, P. *Histoire de Philippe le Long*. Vol. I. Paris, 1897.

Lemerle, Paul. *L'Émirat d'Aydin, Byzance et l'Occident*. Paris, Presses universitaires de France, 1957.

———. *Philippes et la Macédoine orientale à l'époque Chrétienne et Byzantine*. Vol. I. Paris, E. de Boccard, 1945.

Loenertz, Raymond. "Le chancelier impérial à Byzance," *Orientalia Christiana Periodica*, 26 (1960), 275–300.

———. "Manuel Paléologue et Démétrius Cydonès," *Échos d'Orient*, 36 (1937), 271–287; 37 (1938), 107–124.

———. *La Société des Frères Pérégrinants*. Vol. I. Institutum Historicum Fratrum Praedicatorum, Romae ad S. Sabinae. Rome, 1937.

———. "Theodore Métochite et son père, *Archivum Fratrum Praedicatorum*, 23 (1953), 184–194.

Longnon, Jean. *L'Empire latin de Constantinople et la principauté de Morée*. Paris, Payot, 1949.

Loparev, Chr. *Vizantiiskii poet' Manuil' Fil', k' istorii volgarii XIII-XIV v*. Petersburg, 1891.

Lopez, R. S. "The Dollar of the Middle Ages," *Journal of Economic History*, 11 (1951), 209–234.

———. *Genova marinara nel duecento: Benedetto Zaccaria ammiraglio e mercante*. Messina and Milan, G. Principato, 1933.

———. *Storia delle colonie Genovesi nel Mediterraneo*. Bologna, N. Zanichelli, 1938.

——— and I. W. Raymond. *Medieval Trade in the Mediterranean World*. New York, Columbia University Press, 1955. Review by F. Dölger, in *Byzantinische Zeitschrift*, 49 (1956), 456–459.

Lot, F. "Projets de croisade sous Charles le Bel et sous Philippe de Valois," *Bibliothèque de l'École des Chartes*, 4th ser., 5 (1859), 503–509.

Luzzatto, Gino. *Storia economica di Venezia dall XI al XVI secolo*. Venice, Centro internazionale delle arti e del costume, 1961.

———. *Studi di storia economica veneziana*. Padua, Cedam, 1954.

Magnocavallo, Arturo. *Marin Sanudo il Vecchio e il suo Progetto di Crociata*. Bergamo, Istituto italiano d'arti grafiche, 1901.

Manfroni, Camillo. "Le relazioni fra Genova, l'impero bizantino e i Turchi," *Atti della Società Ligure di storia patria*, 28, fasc. 3 (1898).

———. *Storia della marina italiana dalle invasione barbariche al trattato di Ninfeo*. Livorno, 1899.

———. *Storia della marina italiana dal trattato di Ninfeo alla caduta di Constantinopoli*. 3 vols. Livorno, R. Accademia Navale, 1902–1903.

Marin, C. A. *Storia civile e politica del commercio de' Veneziani*. Venice, 1800.

Marinesco, C. *La Catalogne et l'Arménie au temps de Jacques II, 1291–1327*. Paris, 1923.

———. "Notes sur les Catalans dans l'Empire byzantin pendant le règne de Jacques II (1291–1327)," *Mélanges d'histoire du Moyen-âge offerts à M. F. Lot*. Paris, E. Champion, 1925.

———. "De nouveau sur Constance de Hohenstaufen," *Byzantion*, 1 (1924), 451–468.

———. "Tentatives de mariage de deux fils d'Andronic II Paléologue avec des princesses latines," *Revue historique du sud-est Européen*, 1 (1924), 139–143.

Secondary Works

Mas-Latrie, Louis de. *Histoire de l'île de Chypre sous le règne des princes de la maison des Lusignan.* 3 vols. Paris, 1852–1861.

Max, Georg. *Geschichte des Fürstentums Grubenhagen.* Vol. I. Hannover, 1862.

Meliarakes, Antonios. Ἱστορία τοῦ Βασιλείου τῆς Νικαίας καὶ τοῦ Δεσποτάτου τῆς Ἠπείρου, 1204-1261. Athens, 1898.

Mercati, S. G. "Nota all'epigramma di Niceforo Gregora in morte del Metochita," *Bessarione,* 34 (1918), 237–238.

Miller, William. *Essays on the Latin Orient.* Cambridge, Eng., Cambridge University Press, 1921.

———. *The Latins in the Levant. A History of Frankish Greece,(1204–1566).* London, J. Murray, 1908.

———. "The Zaccaria of Phocea and Chios, 1275–1329," *Journal of Historical Studies,* 31 (1911), 42–55.

Minieri-Riccio, Camillo. *Della dominazione Angioina nel Reame di Sicilia.* Naples, 1876.

Miret y Sans, Joaquín. "Nuevos documentos de la tres princessas griegas," *Revue hispanique,* 19 (1908), 112–134.

———. "La princessa Griega Lascaris," *Revue hispanique,* 11 (1903), 455–470.

———. "Tres princessas griegas en la corte de Jaime II de Aragón," *Revue hispanique,* 15 (1906), 668–716.

Mollat, Guillaume. *Les papes d'Avignon, 1305–1378.* 10th ed. Paris, Letouzey et Ané, 1964.

Monti, G. M. *Da Carlo I a Roberto di Angiò; Ricerche e documenti.* Trani, Vecchi & Co., 1936.

Moranvillé, H. "Les projets de Charles de Valois sur l'Empire de Constantinople," *Bibliothèque de l'École des Chartes,* 51 (1890), 63–86.

Moravcsik, Gyula. *Byzantinoturcica. Die byzantinischen Quellen der Geschichte der Türkvölker.* 2 vols. Budapest, M. Pázmány, 1942. Reprinted in Berlin, Akademie der Wissenschaften, 1958.

Mosto, Andrea da. *I Dogi di Venezia.* Milan, Martello, 1960.

Müller, J. "Die Legationen unter Papst Gregor X," *Römische Quartalschrift,* 37 (1929,) 57–135.

Muratore, Dino. "Una principessa Sabauda sul trono di Bizanzio: Giovanna di Savoia, imperatrice Anna Paleologina," *Mémoires de l'Académie de Savoie,* 4th ser., 11 (1909), 221–475.

Mystakides, V. A. «Παχυμέρης Γεώργιος, πρωτέκδικος καὶ δικαιοφύλαξ καὶ Μ. Κρούσιος,» Ἐναίσιμα Χρυσοστόμου Παπαδοπούλου, 214-232. Athens, 1931.

Nicol, D. M. "Constantine Akropolites: A Prosopographical Note," *Dumbarton Oaks Papers,* 19 (1965), 249–256.

———. *The Byzantine Family of Kantakouzenos (Cantacuzenus), ca. 1100–1460.* Dumbarton Oaks Studies, Vol. XI. Washington, 1968.

———. "Mixed marriages in Byzantium in the Thirteenth Century," *Studies in Church History,* 1 (1964), 160–172.

Nikov, P. "Tatarobulgarski otnošenija prez srednite vekove," *Godišnik na Sofiskija Universitet, Ist. Fil. Fakultet,* 15–16 (Sofia, 1919–1920), 54–95.

Norden, Walter. *Das Papsttum und Byzanz.* Berlin, B. Behr, 1903; reprinted, New York, B. Franklin, 1958.

Novaković, Stojan. "Le prix normal du blé à Constantinople pendant le moyen-âge et le Code de St. Dushan," *Archiv für slavische Philologie*, 27 (1905), 173–174.

————. *Srbi i Turci XIV i XV veka.* Belgrade, 1893; New Serbian ed., Belgrade, Kultura, 1960. German edition: *Die Serben und Türken im XIV und XV Jahrhundert.* Semlin, 1897.

————. *Strumska oblast u XIV veku i car Stephan Dušan.* Belgrade, 1893.

Ohnsorge, Werner. "Eine Verschollene Urkunde des Kaisers Andronikos III. Palaiologos für Heinrich, dictus de Graecia, Herzog zu Braunschweig (-Grubenhagen), vom 6. Januar 1330," in Werner Ohnsorge, *Abendland und Byzanz.* Darmstadt, Geutner, 1958.

Omont, Henri. "Lettre d'Andronic II Paléologue au pape Jean XXII," *Bibliothèque de l'École des Chartes*, 67 (1906), 587.

————. "Projet de réunion des églises grècque et latine sous Charles le Bel en 1327," *Bibliothèque de l'École des Chartes*, 53 (1892), 254–257.

Ostrogorsky, Georges. "Les grands domaines dans l'Empire byzantin," in *Recueils de la Société Jean Bodin.* Vol. IV: *Le Domaine.* Paris, 1949.

————. *Histoire de l'état byzantin.* Paris, Payot, 1956. English ed. *History of the Byzantine State*, trans. Joan Hussey. Oxford, Blackwell, 1956.

————. "Löhne und Preise in Byzanz," *Byzantinische Zeitschrift*, 30 (1932), 293–333.

————. *Pour l'histoire de la féodalité byzantine.* Corpus Bruxellense Historiae Byzantinae, Subsidia I. Brussels, 1954.

————. *Quelques problèmes de la paysannerie byzantine.* Corpus Bruxellense Historiae Byzantinae, Subsidia II. Brussels, 1956.

Papadatos, S. I. «Ἡ διοικητικὴ ἀνεξαρτησία τοῦ Ἁγίου Ὄρους ἐπὶ Βυζαντινῶν,» Ἐπετηρὶς Ἑταιρείας Βυζαντινῶν Σπουδῶν, 32 (1963), 427–483.

Papademetriou, S. «Ὁ ἐπιθαλάμιος Ἀνδρονίκου Β´ τοῦ Παλαιολόγου,» *Byzantinische Zeitschrift*, 11 (1902), 452–460.

Papadopulos-Kerameus, Athanasios. Ἀνάλεκτα Ἱεροσολυμιτικῆς Σταχυολογίας. Vol. V. St. Petersburg, 1898.

Papadopulos, A. T. *Versuch einer Genealogie der Palaiologen, 1259–1453.* Munich diss. Speyer, Pilger-Druckerei, 1938.

Pappadopulos, J. B. *Théodore II Laskaris, empereur de Nicée.* Paris, A. Picard, 1908.

Parisot, Valentin. *Cantacuzène, homme d'état et historien.* Paris, 1845.

Petit, Ernest. *Histoire des ducs de Bourgogne de la race capétienne.* 9 vols. Dijon, Darantière, 1885–1905.

Petit, Joseph. "Un capitaine du règne de Philippe le Bel, Thibaut de Chepoy," *Moyen Âge*, 2d ser., 2 (1891), 224–239.

Petrov, P. "Bŭlgaro-vizantiĭskite otnošenija prez vtorata polovina na XIIIv, otrazeni v poemata na Manuil Fil 'za poennite podvisi na izvestnija čutoven protostrator'," ("Les relations bulgaro-byzantines au cours de la seconde moitié du XIIIe siècle, reflétées dans le poème de Manuel Philès 'Les exploits du célèbre protostrator',"), *Izvestija na Instituta za Bŭlgarska istorija.* Vol. VI, 545–576. Sofia, 1956.

Picot, Georges. *Documents relatifs aux États généraux et assemblées réunies sous Philippe le Bel.* Paris, Imprimerie nationale, 1901.

Pirenne, Henri. *Histoire de Belgique.* 7 vols. Brussels, Lamertin, 1902–1947.

Plancher, Dom. *Histoire générale et particulière de Bourgogne.* Vol. II. Dijon, 1741.

Romanin, Samuele. *Storia documentata di Venezia*. Vol. II. 2d ed., 10 vols. Venice, 1853–1861. Reprinted, 1925.

Rouillard, Germaine. "Les Taxes maritimes et commerciales d'après des actes de Patmos et de Lavra," *Mélanges Charles Diehl*. Vol. I. Paris, E. Leroux, 1930.

———. *La vie rurale dans l'empire byzantin*. Paris, Librairie d'Amérique et d'Orient, 1953.

Rubió y Lluch, Antonio. *La companyía Catalana sota el Comandament de Teobald de Çepoy, 1307–1310*. Institut d'Estudis Catalans. Barcelona, 1923.

———. "Contribució a la biografía del'infant En Ferràn de Mallorca," *Estudis Universitaris Catalans*. Vol. VII. Barcelona, 1913.

———. *La Espedición y Dominación de los Catalans en Oriente juzgadas pos los Griegos*. Memóries de la Real Academia de Buenos Letras de Barcelona. Vol. IV. Barcelona, 1893.

———. "Mitteilungen zur Geschichte der griechischen Sklaven in Katalonien im XIV Jahrhundert," *Byzantinische Zeitschrift*, 30 (1930), 462–468.

———. "Nicéforo Gregoras y la expedición de los Catalanes á Oriente," *Museo Balear de Historia y Literatura, Ciencias y Artes*, 2d ser., 2 (1885), 401–408, 522–528, 561–574, 601–611.

———. "Notícia geográfica de l'Orient segons En Muntaner," *Butlletí del Centre Excursionista de Catalunya*, 1 (Barcelona, 1891), 139–147, 223–235.

———. *Paquimeres y Muntaner*. Memóries de la secció històrico-arqueològica del Institut d'Estudis Catalans. Vol. I. Barcelona, 1927.

Runciman, Steven. "The Ladies of the Mongols," Εἰς μνήμην Κ. Ἀμάντου, pp. 46–53. Athens, 1960.

———. *The Sicilian Vespers*. Cambridge, Eng., Cambridge University Press, 1958.

———. "Thessalonica and the Montferrat Inheritance," Γρηγόριος ὁ Παλαμᾶς, 42 (1959), 26–35.

Salvatorelli, Luigi. *L'Italia comunale, del secolo XI alla metà del secolo XIV*. Milan, A. Mondadori, 1940.

Samaran, Charles and G. Mollat. *La fiscalité pontificale en France au XIVe siècle*. Paris, A. Fontemoing, 1905.

Sambin, Paolo. "La politica mediterranea di Venezia alla fine della guerra del Vespro," *Istituto Veneto di Scienze, Lettere e Arti, Atti*, 104 (1944–1945).

Sauli, Lodovico. *Storia della colonia dei Genovesi in Galata*. 2 vols. Turin, 1831.

Sboronos, I. N. «Βυζαντιακὰ νομισματικὰ ζητήματα,» *Journal international d'archéologie numismatique*, 2 (1899), 341–402.

Schlumberger, Gustave. *Expédition des "Almugavares" ou routiers Catalans en Orient*. Paris, Plon-Nourrit, 1902.

———. "Le sceau de la Compagnie des routiers Catalans à Gallipoli en 1305," *Comptes rendus de l'Académie des inscriptions et des belles lettres*, (1925), 131–137.

———. "Le tombeau d'une impératrice byzantine à Valence en Espagne," in G. Schlumberger, *Byzance et Croisades*. Paris, 1927.

Schmidt, Pia. *Die Diplomatischen Beziehungen zwischen Konstantinopel und Kairo zu Beginn des 14. Jahrhunderts im Rahmen der Auseinandersetzung Byzanz-Islam*. Munich diss., 1956. (Unavailable to me.)

————. "Zur Chronologie von Pachymeres, Andronikos L. II-VII," *Byzantinische Zeitschrift*, 51 (1958), 82–86.

Schreiner, P. "Zur Geschichte Philadelpheias," *Orientalia Christiana Periodica*, 35 (1969), 375–431.

Setton, K. M. *The Catalan Domination of Athens, 1311–1388*. Cambridge, Mass., Mediaeval Academy of America, 1948.

————, R. L. Wolff and H. W. Hazard, eds. *A History of the Crusades*. Vol. II. Philadelphia, University of Pennsylvania Press, 1962.

Ševčenko, Ihor. *Études sur la polémique entre Théodore Métochite et Nicéphore Choumnos*. Corpus Bruxellense Historiae Byzantinae, Subsidia III. Brussels, 1962.

————. "The Imprisonment of Manuel Moschopoulos," *Speculum*, 27 (1952), 133–157.

————. "Léon Bardales et les juges généraux, ou la corruption des incorruptibles," *Byzantion*, 19 (1949), 247–259.

————. "Nicholas Cabasilas' Anti-Zealot Discourse: A Reinterpretation," *Dumbarton Oaks Papers*. Vol. XI (1957).

Simonsfeld, Henry. "Studien zu Marino Sanudo dem Aelteren," *Neues Archiv für Gesellschaft für Aeltere deutsche Geschichtskunde*, 7 (1882), 45–72.

Singer, Charles. *The Earliest Chemical Industry, An Essay in the Historical Relations of Economics and Technology Illustrated from the Alum Trade*. London, Folio Society, 1948.

Sokolov, I. "Kroupnye i melkie vlasteli v Fessalii," *Vizantiiskii Vremennik*, 24 (1925–1926), 35ff.

Soldevila, Ferran. *Els Almogàvers*. Barcelona, Barcino, 1952.

Soloviev, Alexander. "Fessalijskie arkhonti v XIV v," *Byzantinoslavica*, 4 (1932), 159ff.

Souarn, R. "Tentatives d'union avec Rome; un patriarche grec catholique au XIIIe siècle," *Échos d'Orient*, 3 (1899), 229–237, 351–361.

Stamatiades, E. I. Οἱ Καταλάνοι ἐν τῇ Ἀνατολῇ, οἷς προσετέθη καὶ ἀνέκδοτός τις χρονολογία τῶν Ἀθηνῶν. Athens, 1869.

Stefano, Antonino de. *Federico III d'Aragona, Rè di Sicilia, 1296–1337*. Palermo, F. Ciuni, 1937.

Stein, Ernst. "Untersuchungen zur spätbyzantinischen Verfassungsgeschichte," *Mitteilungen zur osmanischen Geschichte*, 2 (1924), 1–62.

Stephanides, Basileios. Βυζαντινὴ Ἐκκλησιαστικὴ Ἱστορία. Athens, 1948.

Strayer, J. R. and C. H. Taylor. *Studies in Early French Taxation*. Cambridge, Mass., Harvard University Press, 1939.

Strzygowski, J. "Das Epitalamium des Paläologen Andronikos II," *Byzantinische Zeitschrift*, 10 (1901), 546–567.

Sykoutres, Ioannes. «Περὶ τὸ σχῖσμα τῶν Ἀρσενιατῶν,» Ἑλληνικά, 2 (1929), 257ff.

Tabacco, Giovanni. *La casa di Francia nell' azione politica di papa Giovanni XXII*. Rome, Istituto storico Italiano, 1953.

Tafel, G. L. *De Thessalonica eiusque agro, dissertatio geographica*. Berlin, 1839.

———— and G. M. Thomas. *Der Doge Andrea Dandolo und die von ihm angelegten Urkundensammlungen. Abhandlungen der Bayerischen Akademie der Wissenschaften, Historische Klasse*. Munich, 1855.

Tafrali, Oreste. *Thessalonique des origines jusqu'au XIVe siècle*. Paris, E. Leroux, 1917.

Secondary Works

————. *Thessalonique au quatorzième siècle*. Paris, P. Geuthner, 1913.

Taylor, C. H. "French Assemblies and Subsidy in 1321," *Speculum*, 43 (1968), 217–244.

————. "The Composition of Baronial Assemblies in France, 1315–1320," *Speculum*, 29 (1954), 433–459.

Thalloczy, Lajos, ed. *Illyrisch-Albanische Forschungen*. Munich and Leipzig, Duncker and Humblot, 1916.

Theocharides, G. I. "Μιχαὴλ Δούκας Γλαβᾶς Ταρχανειώτης (Προσωπογραφικά)," Ἐπιστημονικὴ Ἐπετηρὶς τῆς Φιλοσοφικῆς Σχολῆς τοῦ Πανεπιστημίου Θεσσαλονίκης, 7 (1957), 183–206.

Theotokis, S. «Ἡ πρώτη συμμαχία τῶν κυριάρχων κρατῶν τοῦ Αἰγαίου κατὰ τῆς καθόδου τῶν Τούρκων,» Ἐπετηρὶς Ἑταιρείας Βυζαντινῶν Σπουδῶν, 7 (1930), 283–298.

Throop, P. *Criticism of the Crusade: A Study of Public Opinion and Crusading Propaganda*. Amsterdam, N. V. Swets & Zeitlinger, 1940.

Tierney, B. *The Crisis of Church and State, 1050–1300*. Englewood Cliffs, N.J., Prentice-Hall, 1964.

Tomaschek, W. *Zur historischen Topographie von Kleinasien im Mittelalter. Abhandlungen der Bayerischen Akademie der Wissenschaften*. Vienna, 1891.

Tramontana, Salvatore, "Per la storia della 'Compagnia Catalana' in Oriente," *Nuova Rivista Storica*, 46 (1962), 58–95.

Treitinger, Otto. *Die Oströmische Kaiser-und Reichsidee nach ihrer Gestaltung im höfischen zeremoniel*. Darmstadt, H. Geutner, 1956.

————. "Vom Oströmischen Staats-und Reichsgedanken," *Leipz. Viertalschr. f. Südost. Eur.*, 4 (1909), 1–26.

Treu, Max. "Athanasios Chatzikes," *Byzantinische Zeitschrift*, 18 (1909), 481–489.

Troitskii, I. E. *Arsenii, Patriarhi Nikeiskii i Konstantiniopoliskii i Arseniti*. St. Petersburg, 1873.

Ubičini, A. *Ougovor o savezou i priateilstvou medjou Karlom od Valoa i poslanitzina Srbskog Kralia Ourocha*. Belgrade, 1870. Reviewed in *Bibliothèque de l'École des Chartes*, (1873), 116–118.

Underwood, P. J. *The Kariye Djami*. 3 vols. New York, Pantheon, 1966.

Usseglio, L. *I Marchesi di Monferrato in Italia ed in Oriente*. Vol. II. *Biblioteca della società Storica subalpina*, n. s., vols. VI, VII. Turin, 1926.

Vacalopoulos, A. E. *A History of Thessaloniki*, trans. T. F. Carney. Thessalonica, Institute for Balkan Studies, 1963.

————. Ἱστορία τοῦ Νέου Ἑλληνισμοῦ, Vol. I. Thessalonica, N. Nikolaides, 1961. Trans. Ian Moles *Origins of the Greek Nation; The Byzantine Period, 1204–1461*. New Brunswick, Rutgers University Press, 1970.

Verlinden, Charles. *L'esclavage dans l'Europe médiévale*, I: *Péninsule Ibérique-France*. Bruges, De Tempel, 1955.

Verpeaux, Jean. "Le cursus honorum de Théodore Métochite," *Revue des Études byzantines*, 18 (1960), 195–198.

————. *Nicéphore Choumnos, homme d'état et humaniste byzantin, 1255–1327*. Paris, Picard, 1959.

————. "Notes chronologiques sur les livres II et III du De Andronico Paleologo de Georges Pachymère," *Revue des Études byzantines*, 17 (1959), 168–174.

Viller, M. "La question de l'union des églises entre Grecs et Latins depuis le concil de Lyon jusqu'à celui de Florence, 1274–1436," *Revue d'histoire ecclésiastique*, 17 (1921), 260–305; 515–532; 18 (1922), 20–60.

Wächter, Albert. *Der Verfall des Griechentums in Kleinasien im XIV. Jahrhundert*. Leipzig, Teubner, 1903.

Weiss, Günther. *Joannes Kantakuzenos—Aristokrat, Staatsmann, Kaiser und Mönch—in der Gesellschaftsentwincklung von Byzanz im 14. Jahrhundert*. Wiesbaden, 1969.

Wieruszowski, Hélène. "Conjuraciones y alianzas politicas del rey Pedro de Aragón contra Carlos de Anjou antes de las Vísperas Sicilianas," *Boletín de la Acad. de Historia*, 107 (1935), 547–602.

———. "La corte di Pietro d'Aragona e i precedenti dell'impresa Siciliana," *Archivio Storico Italiano*, 96 (1938), 141–162; 97 (1939), 200–217.

Winter, D. A. *Die Politik Pisas während der Jahre 1268–1282*. Halle, a.S., 1906.

Wirth, P. "Die Begründung der Kaisermacht Michaels VIII. Palaiologos," *Jahrbuch der österreichischen byzantinischen Gesellschaft*, 10 (1961), 85–91.

Wittek, Paul. *Das Fürstentum Mentesche*. Istanbul, Universum Druckerei, 1934.

Wolff, R. L. "The Fourth Crusade," and "The Latin Empire of Constantinople," in K. M. Setton, R. L. Wolff and H. W. Hazard, eds. *A History of the Crusades*. Vol. II. Philadelphia, University of Pennsylvania Press, 1962.

———. "Mortgage and Redemption of an Emperor's Son: Castile and the Latin Empire of Constantinople," *Speculum*, 29 (1954), 45–84.

———. "A New Document from the Period of the Latin Empire of Constantinople: The Oath of the Venetian Podestà," *Mélanges Henri Grégoire*. Brussels, Sécrétariat des éditions de l'Institut, 1953.

———. "The so-called Fragmentum of Marino Sanudo," *Joshua Starr Memorial Volume*. New York, Jewish Social Studies, 1956.

Wroth, Warwick. *Catalogue of the Imperial Byzantine Coins in the British Museum*. Vol. I. London, British Museum, 1908.

Zakythinos, D. A. *Crise monétaire et crise économique à Byzance du XIIe au XVe siècle*. Athens, L'Hellénisme contemporain, 1948.

———. *Le despotat grec de Morée*. 2 vols. Paris, Les Belles lettres, 1932, 1953.

———. «Ὁ Μαρκήσιος τοῦ Μομφερράτου Θεόδωρος Αʹ ὁ Παλαιολόγος καὶ ὁ βασιλεὺς τῆς Γαλλίας Φίλιππος ΣΤʹ,» Ἐπετηρὶς Ἑταιρείας Βυζαντινῶν Σπουδῶν, 11 (1935), 16–28.

———. «Μελέται περὶ τῆς διοικητικῆς διαιρέσεως καὶ τῆς ἐπαρχικῆς διοικήσεως ἐν τῷ Βυζαντινῷ κράτει,» Ἐπετηρὶς Ἑταιρείας Βυζαντινῶν Σπουδῶν, 21 (1951), 179–217; 22 (1952), 159–182.

Zimmermann, Paul von. *Das Haus Braunschweig-Grubenhagen*. Wolfenbüttel, 1911.

Zotos, A. D. Ἰωάννης ὁ Βέκκος, Πατριάρχης Κωνσταντινουπόλεως, Νέας Ῥώμης, ὁ Λατινόφρων. Munich, 1920.

Index

Harvard Historical Studies

Harvard Historical Studies

84. *Marvin Arthur Breslow.* A Mirror of England: English Puritan Views of Foreign Nations, 1618–1640. 1970.

85. *Patrice L.-R. Higonnet.* Pont-de-Montvert: Social Structure and Politics in a French Village, 1700–1914. 1971.

86. *Paul G. Halpern.* The Mediterranean Naval Situation, 1908–1914. 1971.

87. *Robert E. Ruigh.* The Parliament of 1624: Politics and Foreign Policy. 1971.

88. *Angeliki E. Laiou.* Constantinople and the Latins: The Foreign Policy of Andronicus, 1282–1328. 1972.